ANCHORAGE, DENALI & THE KENAI PENINSULA

DON PITCHER

Contents

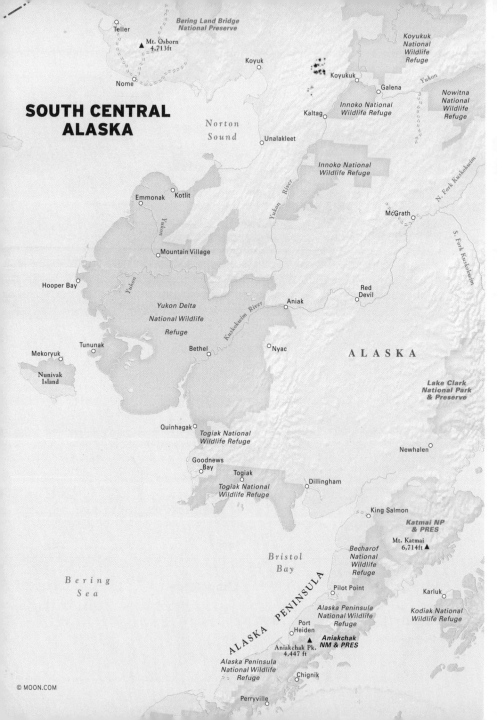

SOUTH CENTRAL
ALASKA

Teller

▲ Mt. Osborn
4,713ft

Nome

Bering Land Bridge
National Preserve

Koyuk

Koyukuk
National
Wildlife
Refuge

Koyukuk

Galena

Yukon

Nowitna
National
Wildlife
Refuge

Kaltag

Innoko National
Wildlife Refuge

Norton
Sound

Unalakleet

Innoko National
Wildlife Refuge

N. Fork Kuskokwim

Emmonak   Kotlit

McGrath

Yukon

Yukon River

S. Fork Kuskokwim

Mountain Village

Hooper Bay

Yukon

Red
Devil

Yukon Delta
National Wildlife
Refuge

Kuskokwim River

Aniak

Mekoryuk

Tununak

Bethel

Nyac

ALASKA

Nunivak
Island

Lake Clark
National Park
& Preserve

Quinhagak

Togiak National
Wildlife Refuge

Newhalen

Goodnews
Bay

Togiak

Dillingham

Togiak National
Wildlife Refuge

King Salmon

Katmai NP
& PRES

Bering
Sea

Bristol
Bay

Becharof
National
Wildlife
Refuge

Mt. Katmai
6,714ft ▲

Pilot Point

Karluk

ALASKA PENINSULA

Alaska Peninsula
National Wildlife
Refuge

Kodiak National
Wildlife Refuge

Port
Heiden

Aniakchak
NM & PRES

Aniakchak Pk.
4,447 ft ▲

Alaska Peninsula
National Wildlife
Refuge

Chignik

© MOON.COM

Perryville

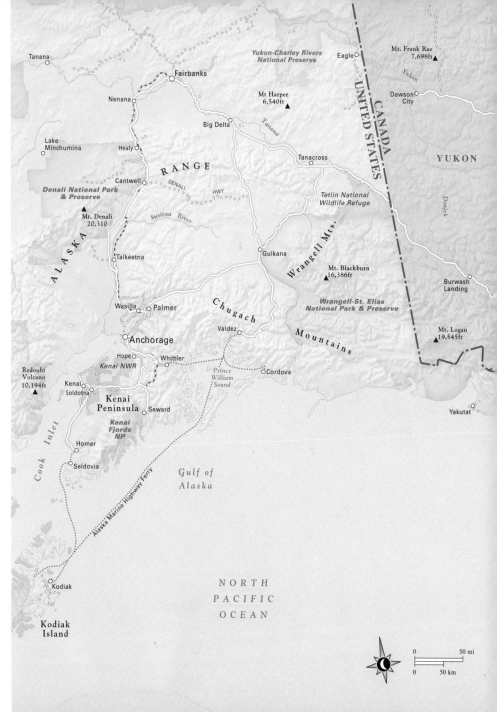

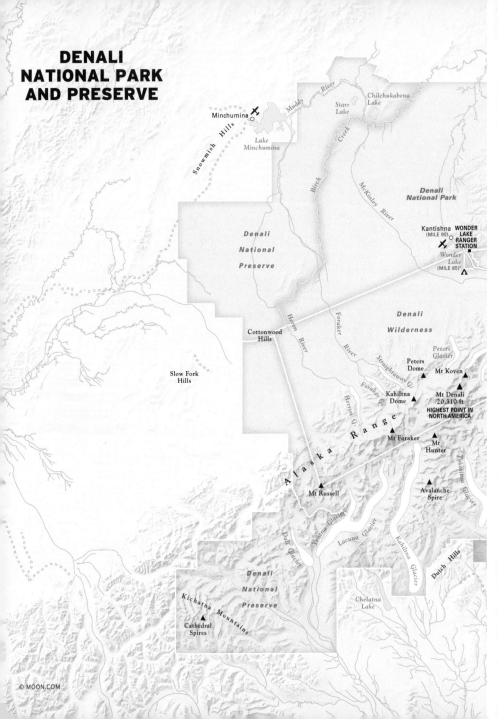

DENALI
NATIONAL PARK
AND PRESERVE

Minchumina

Lake
Minchumina

Snowmish Hills

Muddy River

Starr Lake

Chilchukabena Lake

Birch Creek

McKinley River

Denali
National Park

Kantishna
(MILE 90)

**WONDER
LAKE
RANGER
STATION**

Wonder
Lake
(MILE 85)

Denali

National

Preserve

Cottonwood
Hills

Herm River

Foraker River

Denali

Wilderness

Slow Fork
Hills

Straightaway Gl.

Peters
Glacier

Peters
Dome ▲

▲ Mt Koven

Kahiltna
Dome ▲

Foraker Gl.

Herm Gl.

▲ Mt Denali
20,310 ft
**HIGHEST POINT IN
NORTH AMERICA**

▲ Mt Foraker

▲ Mt
Hunter

A   l   a   s   k   a   R   a   n   g   e

Tokositna Glacier

▲ Mt Russell

▲ Avalanche
Spire

Kahiltna Glacier

Dall Glacier

Yentna Glacier

Lacuna Glacier

Dutch Hills

Denali

National

Preserve

Kichatna Mountains

Chelatna
Lake

▲ Cathedral
Spires

© MOON.COM

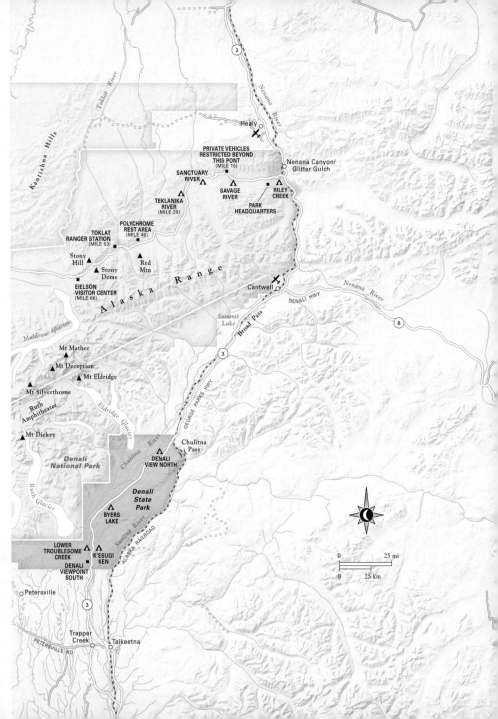

3

Nenana River

Healy

Toklat River

Kantishna Hills

PRIVATE VEHICLES
RESTRICTED BEYOND
THIS POINT
(MILE 15)

Nenana Canyon/
Glitter Gulch

SANCTUARY
RIVER

SAVAGE
RIVER

RILEY
CREEK

TEKLANIKA
RIVER
(MILE 29)

PARK
HEADQUARTERS

POLYCHROME
REST AREA
(MILE 46)

TOKLAT
RANGER
STATION
(MILE 53)

Stony
Hill

Stony
Dome

Red
Mtn

Alaska Range

Nenana River

Cantwell

DENALI HWY

8

EIELSON
VISITOR
CENTER
(MILE 66)

Summit
Lake

Broad Pass

Muldrow Glacier

Mt Mather

Mt Deception

Mt Eldridge

3

Mt Silverthrone

Ruth
Amphitheater

Eldridge Glacier

GEORGE PARKS HWY

Mt Dickey

Chulitna River

Chulitna
Pass

Denali
National Park

DENALI
VIEW NORTH

Denali
State
Park

Ruth Glacier

BYERS
LAKE

Susitna River

ALASKA RAILROAD

LOWER
TROUBLESOME
CREEK

K'ESUGI
KEN

DENALI
VIEWPOINT
SOUTH

Petersville

3

PETERSVILLE RD

Trapper
Creek

Talkeetna

0   25 mi

0   25 Km

DISCOVER

Anchorage, Denali & the Kenai Peninsula

There is something about Alaska that has always stirred the imagination. From the first migrants who crossed the Bering land bridge during the ice ages to today's travelers escaping the madness of city life, Alaska draws people from the world over to see its wonders: dramatic mountains and immense glaciers, rivers thick with salmon, northern lights dancing across a velvety winter sky.

First-time visitors quickly discover how vast the state is, and how difficult it is to see everything in a short period of time. Instead of trying to see it all, many choose to explore south-central Alaska—focusing on Anchorage, Denali, and the Kenai Peninsula. This is Alaska at its most accessible and diverse.

This guide is for those Alaska travelers who are looking for a way to kayak in front of glaciers, fish for halibut on a charter boat, explore remote backcountry areas in Denali, and watch brown bears catching salmon on a remote shore, but who also enjoy a fine Anchorage restaurant, snowboarding at Alyeska Resort, or staying at a luxurious bed-and-breakfast. Spend an evening in Anchorage dining on king crab and sampling French wines, then the next day, take a one-hour

Clockwise from top left: baby moose eating fireweed; cross-country skiers in Homer; sea kayaking trips depart from Homer, Whittier, and Seward; bikers on Curry Ridge Trail in Denali State Park; hiking trail.

floatplane ride to a cabin where the only sounds are singing loons and droning mosquitoes.

Anchorage is the natural focal point. The city's Ted Stevens International Airport has scheduled flights from a dozen U.S. cities, plus direct international flights from Frankfurt, Vancouver, Reykjavik, and even Petropavlovsk-Kamchatsky. Fly into Anchorage and use this city of 300,000 people as a base to explore surrounding areas, most notably Denali National Park to the north and the Kenai Peninsula to the south. All the major rental car companies have operations at the airport, and many people rent a car or RV to explore on their own. Buses serve the major towns, and the Alaska Railroad connects Anchorage with Seward, Talkeetna, Denali, Whittier, and Fairbanks.

Let this book open the doors to this truly unique, amazing, and beautiful part of Alaska. If you haven't visited Alaska before, you're in for a treat. If you have, you will certainly want to return.

Clockwise from top left: kayakers in Prince William Sound; ice skating in front of Grewingk Glacier near Homer; Dall sheep in Denali National Park; Salty Dawg Saloon on the Homer Spit

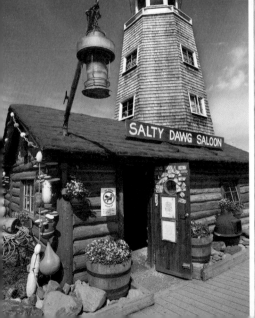

10 TOP
EXPERIENCES

1 Go Flightseeing: Only in Alaska can you land on a glacier beneath the summit of America's tallest mountain (page 137).

2 **View Wildlife in Denali:** Spotting grizzlies, brown bears, caribou, and wolves is a highlight of this unique park (page 157).

3 **Cruise alongside Glaciers:** Boat tours are the best way to see glaciers, whales, puffins, otters, and other crowd-pleasers. Popular trips include **Prince William Sound** (page 105) from Whittier, **Kenai Fjords National Park** (page 230) from Seward, and **Kachemak Bay** (page 287) from Homer.

4 **Explore Homer Spit:** This peninsula extending into Kachemak Bay is packed with fishing boats, restaurants, and galleries. It's also the launching point for wildlife tours (page 262).

5 **Kayak on the Kenai Peninsula:** The towns of **Homer** (page 270) and **Seward** (page 216) are bases for excellent guided sea kayaking trips.

6 **Discover Urban Alaska:** Home to flower-lined streets, fine museums, and memorable restaurants, **Anchorage** (page 42) is Alaska's "Big City."

>>>

7 **Go Fish:** Salmon and halibut draw charter boats from **Homer** (page 272) and **Seward** (page 215), while the **Kenai River** (page 235) is a hotbed of combat fishing.

8 **Take a Scenic Drive:** Alaska's most memorable road trips include the dramatic **Denali Highway** (page 151), the **Seward Highway** along the shore of **Turnagain Arm** (page 90), and winding **Hatcher Pass** (page 124).

9 **Watch Whales:** Boat tours out of Homer, Seward, and Whittier provide photo ops for humpbacks and orcas, while Turnagain Arm is a showcase for belugas (pages 211 and 90).

>>>

10 **Enjoy Quirky Small Towns:** Visit rustic **Talkeetna** (page 133), happening **Homer** (page 260), old-timey **Hope** (page 202), and ski haven **Girdwood** (page 92). Atmospheric towns like these are the heart and soul of Alaska.

Planning Your Trip

Where to Go

Anchorage and Vicinity

Anchorage is home to nearly half the state's population, an international airport, and a multitude of **cultural attractions.** Especially notable are the **Anchorage Museum,** the largest museum in the state, and the **Alaska Native Heritage Center.** A paved trail skirts the city's shoreline, and **great hiking** is a short drive away in massive **Chugach State Park.** Spend Saturday or Sunday at the downtown **Anchorage Market and Festival,** where you'll find hundreds of vendors selling everything from Native artwork to birch syrup.

Head south along **Turnagain Arm,** with its **enormous tides** and **beluga whales,** to **Crow Creek Mine** and **Alyeska Resort** in **Girdwood.** Nearby are the **Alaska Wildlife Conservation Center** and **Portage Glacier.** The Alaska Railroad runs fun daytrips to **Spencer Glacier.**

North of Anchorage is the **Matanuska-Susitna Valley,** home to fast-growing **Wasilla** and **Palmer.** Beyond lies **Hatcher Pass** with its pretty **alpine country** and historic **mine buildings.**

Denali National Park and Vicinity

Alaska's most loved national park, Denali National Park is 175 air miles north of Anchorage. The park's crowning jewel is 20,320-foot **Mount Denali.** A narrow dirt road—open only to tour buses—runs through the heart of Denali, providing opportunities to see **caribou, brown bears, wolves,** and other wildlife, plus amazing **Alaska**

Denali National Park

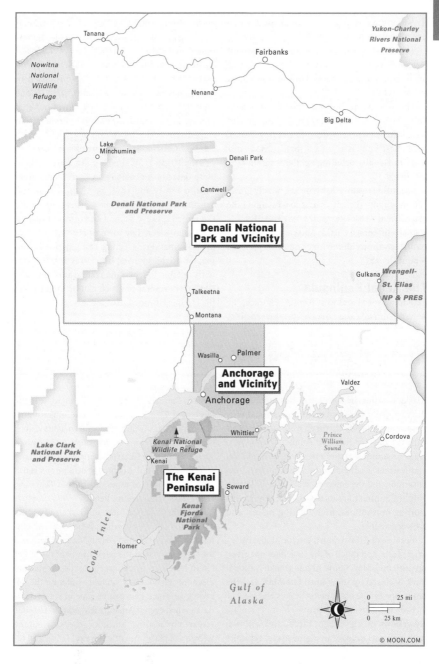

Tanana

Yukon-Charley
Rivers National
Preserve

Fairbanks

Nowitna
National
Wildlife
Refuge

Nenana

Big Delta

Lake
Minchumina

Denali Park

Cantwell

Denali National Park
and Preserve

**Denali National
Park and Vicinity**

Gulkana Wrangell-
St. Elias

NP & PRES

Talkeetna

Montana

Wasilla Palmer

**Anchorage
and Vicinity**

Valdez

Anchorage

Whittier

Prince
William
Sound

Cordova

Lake Clark
National Park
and Preserve

Kenai National
Wildlife Refuge

Kenai

**The Kenai
Peninsula**

Seward

Kenai
Fjords
National
Park

Cook Inlet

Homer

Gulf of
Alaska

0   25 mi

0   25 km

© MOON.COM

Range vistas. Hop on a bus for an all-day ride into the park: It's an eight-hour round-trip to Eielson Visitor Center, famous for its Mount Denali views. Or take the 11-hour round-trip ride to Wonder Lake and the old mining settlement of Kantishna.

The quaint, pedestrian-friendly town of Talkeetna, halfway between Anchorage and Denali, has historic buildings and fun shops, but is best known as a base for flightseeing trips to Denali, including exhilarating glacier landings.

Beautiful Denali Highway is a mostly gravel 126-mile route that slices east to west along the magnificent Alaska Range. Denali State Park is virtually unknown outside Alaska, but its alpine country affords alpine hikes and fine views of Mount Denali.

The Kenai Peninsula

Extending south and west from Anchorage, the Kenai Peninsula is a recreational paradise, with fishing, hiking, rafting, sightseeing, and camping options galore. The peninsula is dominated by Chugach National Forest, Kenai National Wildlife Refuge, and Kenai Fjords National Park. The last of these is based in Seward, where you can join boat tours to look for whales, puffins, and glaciers within Kenai Fjords, take a guided kayak trip in Resurrection Bay, discover diving sea lions at the Alaska SeaLife Center, or hike along Exit Glacier.

Tiny Hope is an almost-ghost town with an abundance of historic log cabins, plus great hiking trails and river rafting. Kenai and Soldotna are bases for sportfishing, including the famed sockeye salmon combat fishing on the Kenai River. The town of Homer is a premier destination for fishing, sea kayaking, hiking, fat-tire biking, and bear-viewing flights, with notable lodges, fine restaurants, and art galleries, several of which can be found along the famous Homer Spit.

Know Before You Go

Alaska is primarily a summer destination, and the vast majority of its two million annual visitors travel mid-May through mid-September, with the peak in July and August. The advantages of summer travel are obvious: long days and warmer weather, not to mention the return of salmon and the emergence of bears and other wildlife. Summer has its drawbacks, though, including mosquitoes, high lodging prices, and crowded venues.

Because of Alaska's northern location, spring arrives late, and much of the state does not green up until mid-May. The road into Denali National Park is closed by snow until late May, and the landscape can be bleak before leaves emerge.

Fall comes early. Autumn colors (primarily yellows on the aspen, birch, and willows, with reds and oranges in alpine areas) typically peak in early September in Denali, and a couple of weeks later in south-central Alaska. Days shorten dramatically by October—en route to the December 21 winter solstice—but longer nights also make Alaska's famous northern lights visible. Winter visitors come to view them, and to watch such events as the Iditarod. Denali can be bitterly cold in winter, but Anchorage and points south are typically milder, especially by mid-February, as the days begin to lengthen.

With the right planning, an Alaskan adventure can be the trip of a lifetime. Book well ahead for shuttle bus trips into Denali National Park and for lodging around the park. Many of the larger chain hotels in Anchorage provide substantial discounts if you reserve in mid-winter for the following summer. Leave some time in your schedule to relax, even if you have just a week. Do your research by reading this guide, checking out the websites of places you might want to visit, and requesting a copy of the *Alaska Vacation Planner* (800/862-5275, www.travelalaska.com).

Affordable Alaska

Alaska is a notoriously expensive place to visit. It's easy to spend $250 a night for an Anchorage or Denali hotel, and when you add in high fuel and food prices, car rental costs, a flightseeing trip, a day of bear-viewing, and a boat tour, you're starting to talk serious money. Fortunately, there *are* ways to explore south-central Alaska without watching your credit card explode in flames.

- **Book flights well in advance and watch for bargain airfares.** Anchorage is the hub of air travel to Alaska, with all the major airlines and international flights. Check Google Flights for the best deals; you can even pull up a monthly calendar of bargain rates. Alaska Travelgram (www.alaskatravelgram.com) has hot tips on fares to and from Alaska.

- **Take buses whenever possible.** Anchorage's People Mover city buses provide inexpensive connections to the airport, and Valley Transit buses continue north into the Mat-Su Valley for just a few dollars. Private buses are a fair bargain, connecting larger towns and cities in the region.

- **Many Anchorage and Denali hotels provide free airport or train shuttles.** Hotels at the entrance to Denali National Park provide inexpensive shuttles from campgrounds and RV parks to shops and restaurants. The park has a free shuttle to mile 15 of the Park Road. The hourly Denali Salmon Bake Shuttle costs just $5 all day.

- **Public campgrounds are found throughout the region, and in Anchorage.** It costs just $24 to camp at Denali's Riley Creek Campground, or you can drop $350 for a hotel room a mile away.

- **Make car rental reservations well ahead, and check Travelocity or Expedia for the best rates.** Many companies offer discounts if you have a Costco, AAA, or AARP card.

- **Hostels offer an inexpensive lodging option.** Bent Prop Inn & Hostel Downtown

hostel near Denali National Park

(Anchorage), Denali Mountain Morning Hostel and Lodge (near the park), Nauti Otter (Seward), and Seaside Farm Hostel (Homer) are all great choices.

- **Save money by cooking your own meals.** Most hotels provide in-room microwaves and small refrigerators, and many also include a decent breakfast. Hostels (and a few hotels) have full kitchens for guests.

- **Book your hotel stay well in advance for the best prices.** Although most mom-and-pop outfits don't lower their prices for advance bookings, the bigger hotels in Anchorage and Denali often offer early-bird discounts of 10 percent or more.

- **Travel in the shoulder season.** Lodging rates are often substantially lower if you're willing to visit Alaska in May or September, and prices drop even more over the winter months.

The Best of Anchorage

The following itineraries offer the best that south-central Alaska has to offer. You'll want to spend 2-4 days in Anchorage; decide whether to explore the city at the beginning or the end (or at both ends) of your trip. Using Anchorage as a travel hub, you can visit Denali National Park or travel along the Kenai Peninsula, spending time in towns like Hope, Seward, Soldotna, and Homer while mixing travel by train, bus, car, boat, and air.

Day 1

Fly into Anchorage, get a rental car, then find your hotel and settle in. **Copper Whale Inn** or **Anchorage Grand Hotel** are attractive and reasonably priced downtown options. Or book a couple of nights at **SpringHill Suites Anchorage University Lake** for in-town lodging with an out-of-town lake and mountain view.

If you're planning on doing some outdoor excursions, check out the gear at **REI**, then grab lunch at **Middle Way Café.** Get oriented by heading to the **Log Cabin Visitors Center** downtown, and the nearby **Alaska Public Lands Information Center.** Enjoy a fine seafood dinner at **Simon & Seaforts,** where you can sip a nighttime cocktail as the sun arcs across the shimmering summer sky over **Cook Inlet.**

Day 2

Drop by **Side Street Espresso** downtown for an espresso and croissant. Spend the day exploring the **Anchorage Museum** and the **Alaska Native Heritage Center.** There's a free shuttle between the two, and you can save money by purchasing an Alaska Culture Pass ticket that covers both attractions. If the weather cooperates, take a stroll along the **Tony Knowles Coastal Trail.** It offers great vistas across Cook Inlet and is readily accessible from downtown.

Alaska Native Heritage Center

Top Day Hikes

With millions of acres of wild country in all directions, it's easy to find great hikes in south-central Alaska. Even Anchorage has challenging trails just a 20-minute drive from downtown.

ANCHORAGE

- **Flattop Mountain Trail** in Chugach State Park near Anchorage

- **Tony Knowles Coastal Trail** in downtown Anchorage

- **Turnagain Arm Trail** in Chugach State Park south of Anchorage

- **Lakeside Trail-Eklutna Glacier Trail** in Chugach State Park north of Anchorage

- **Crow Pass Trail** in Chugach State Park near Girdwood

- **Portage Pass Trail** in Chugach National Forest near Whittier

- **Reed Lake Trail** at Hatcher Pass State Park north of Palmer

DENALI

- **Curry Ridge Loop Trail** in Denali State Park

- **Savage Alpine Trail** in Denali National Park

- **Mount Healy Overlook Trail** in Denali National Park

- **Alpine Trail** near Eielson Visitor Center in Denali National Park

- Tundra country around **Wonder Lake** in Denali National Park (spectacular hiking but not on developed trails)

KENAI PENINSULA

- **Resurrection Pass Trail** in Chugach National Forest between Hope and Cooper Landing

hikers on Grace Ridge Trail in Kachemak Bay State Park

- **Summit Creek Trail** in Chugach National Forest near Summit Lake

- **Lost Lake Trail** in Chugach National Forest north of Seward

- **Skilak Lookout Trail** on Kenai National Wildlife Refuge near Cooper Landing

- **Glacier Spit Trail** in Kachemak Bay State Park near Homer

- **Grace Ridge Trail** in Kachemak Bay State Park near Homer

Helpful hiking guides for south-central Alaska include *50 Hikes in Alaska's Kenai Peninsula* by Taz Tally, *50 Hikes in Alaska's Chugach State Park* by Shane Shepherd, and *Denali National Park: Guide to Hiking, Photography and Camping* by Ike Waits.

Day 3

Take a day hike in **Chugach State Park.** Head to the Glen Alps parking lot for access to **Flattop Mountain Trail**—a steep climb with a big reward at the end—or the easier saunter up the trail to **Powerline Pass.** Flattop Mountain Shuttle provides transportation from downtown if you want to leave the driving to someone else. Alternatively, take a flightseeing trip over glacier-filled Prince William Sound or a longer flight around Mount Denali. A great dinner option is the ever-popular **Moose's Tooth Pub & Pizzeria.**

Day 4

Start your day with brunch at **Snow City Café** and browse downtown Anchorage's shops. If you're in town on a weekend, be certain to take in the huge **Anchorage Market and Festival** at 3rd Avenue and E Street downtown. From Anchorage, drive south along **Turnagain Arm** and watch for beluga whales in the water and Dall sheep along mountain slopes. Stop in Girdwood to pan for gold at **Crow Creek Mine** and ride the Mount Alyeska **aerial tram.** At the top, take in the vistas and hike the alpine paths.

Back in Anchorage, couples will enjoy the ultimate Alaskan dining experience at **Marx Bros. Café,** while families may opt for **Glacier BrewHouse.** If you still have party energy, hit crazy-busy **Chilkoot Charlie's** in Midtown or **Humpy's Great Alaskan Alehouse** downtown.

Onward Travel

From Anchorage, you can travel north to Denali National Park (see page 26). Going south, Portage Glacier and Girdwood are popular day trips from Anchorage, but they can also make good stops en route to the Kenai Peninsula (see page 30).

Destination: Denali

Denali National Park is about 240 miles north of Anchorage, a five-hour trip by car. The best way to travel to Denali, though, is by train, where you can relax and enjoy the scenery. The Alaska Railroad runs trains from Anchorage to Denali, with stops at Wasilla and Talkeetna in between. You can take the eight-hour ride straight to Denali, but stopping for a night in Talkeetna is highly recommended.

Day 1

From Anchorage, go to the **Alaska Railroad** depot and hop on the morning *Denali Star* train headed north, arriving in Talkeetna three hours later. Upgrading to the luxurious double-decker GoldStar railcar costs more, but its upper level provides better views of the grand scenery along the way; the price also includes meals and alcoholic beverages. If The Mountain (Mount Denali, of course) is out, book a flightseeing trip to the park from a charter company like **Talkeetna Air Taxi, K2 Aviation,** or **Sheldon Air Service.**

Flights with a glacier landing are particularly memorable. Head to dinner at **Wildflower Café** on Talkeetna's Main Street, and spend the night at **Denali Overlook Inn,** five miles outside Talkeetna.

Day 2

Get breakfast and a to-go lunch at **Talkeetna Roadhouse.** Next, explore the funky historic buildings in town, starting with **Nagley's Store,** open since the 1920s. Then hop aboard the *Denali Star* once more, where you'll arrive at Denali National Park by late afternoon. From the train depot, find the Dine Denali Shuttle and ride into nearby Healy. Stay at **Earth Song Lodge** and join the pub fun at **49th State Brewery.** Be sure to get a selfie photo in the bus used in the movie *Into the Wild;* it's right out front.

Day 3

This is your day to explore **Denali National Park** by tour bus (private vehicles are prohibited

Understanding the Denali Maze

Denali National Park requires considerable planning. Here are some tips to make your trip go as smoothly as possible.

- **Book your shuttle bus first.** These all-day tour buses fill early, so make reservations (www.reservedenali.com) as soon as you have travel dates for the park.

- **Book train travel on the Alaska Railroad** if you're traveling by train from Anchorage to Denali.

- **Reserve lodging in advance,** especially for the peak of the season in July and August.

- **Plan at least three days and nights** in the Denali area. The park is an all-day drive or train ride from Anchorage (or two days if you stop in Talkeetna). The Park Road itself is an all-day ride if you want to reach Eielson Visitor Center or Wonder Lake. You'll want downtime to explore areas around the park entrance or to camp inside the park.

- **Bring a big lunch, water, light jacket, camera, and binoculars** on the shuttle bus ride.

- **Take a natural history tour to learn more.** Although shuttle bus drivers stop for wildlife, you'll learn much more about the park by joining one of the nature tour buses. They're a bit more expensive, but worth it.

- **Reserve a campsite** at one of Denali National Park's six campgrounds. Riley Creek Campground at the entrance is open to cars and RVs, and some other campgrounds allow limited vehicle access, but three of the campgrounds are only accessible via bus.

- **Backcountry campers need to plan for wilderness conditions.** There are only a handful of trails within Denali; much of the country is relatively open tundra. You'll need a backcountry permit and a reservation for a camper bus to your starting point, and you must attend a safety briefing.

Mount Denali from Talkeetna

- **Carry bear spray on all hikes.** Although brown bear attacks are extremely rare, it's always wise to carry "bear mace" as a precaution. Talk with rangers for safety tips when hiking in bear country.

- **Rent a mountain bike** if you want to really explore the Park Road. They're available just outside the park entrance and can be carried onto camper buses. Reservations are necessary, since only two bikes are allowed per bus.

- **Visit in early September,** when fall colors dominate the landscape and fewer travelers crowd the shuttle buses and campgrounds.

- **Try for the Road Lottery.** As fall comes to Denali, the Park Road is opened to private vehicles for four days in mid-September. A total of 400 cars are allowed, with the winners chosen at random. You'll need to apply by June 30; find details at the park website (http://go.nps.gov/denalilottery).

Alaska Railroad train along Turnagain Arm

beyond mile 15 of the Park Road). **Advance reservations** are absolutely necessary for this all-day adventure, and many people book several months ahead of time to be sure of a space. Most buses turn around at **Eielson Visitor Center** (eight hours round-trip), where you'll get a fine view of Mount Denali if it isn't obscured by clouds. You could also ride to **Wonder Lake** and back (11 long hours) or take a shorter wildlife-focused tour on one of the park's tan buses. You're likely to see grizzlies, moose, caribou, Dall sheep, and the occasional wolf along the way. Return to Earth Song Lodge for a second night, but stop in "Glitter Gulch" for a traditional Serbian dinner at **Moose-Aka's.**

If you'd like to spend more time in Denali and are on a budget, plan ahead by making a reservation at one of the park's six campgrounds, like **Riley Creek Campground** or **Savage River Campground.**

Day 4

If you have decided to spend two full days at Denali, use today to take the free park shuttle to Savage River, where you can climb **Savage Alpine Trail** for a peek at the peak of Denali, or **float the Nenana River** with one of the local rafting companies. If you're planning on returning to Anchorage today, visit the **sled dog demonstrations** or do a short hike in the morning (try the **Horseshoe Lake Trail** for a chance at seeing beavers). Take the noon *Denali Star* train south; you'll arrive back in Anchorage that evening.

Backcountry Travel

Denali is backcountry wilderness: vaster and wilder than anyplace most people have ever visited. If you're planning on venturing into the backcountry during your visit to Denali, you'll want to visit the **Backcountry Information Center** at the park. For more information see page 174.

Bear-Viewing

Bear-viewing is a booming business in Alaska, and visitors never forget their first sighting. Most folks choose a package trip to areas where the bears have become somewhat habituated to the presence of humans—but there are more adventurous opportunities as well.

The most famous places to see and photograph brown bears are **Denali National Park, Katmai National Park,** and **McNeil River.** Some boats and planes also offer bear-viewing day trips to coastal Lake Clark National Park.

World-famous **Brooks Camp** within Katmai National Park (907/246-3305, www.nps.gov/katm) is one of the few places where large numbers of visitors can see wild bears throughout the summer. Bear activity centers on the Brooks River and particularly Brooks Falls, where those legendary bear-with-jumping-salmon photos are taken. Air taxis in Anchorage, Homer, Kenai, and Soldotna all provide floatplane flights to Naknek Lake, just a short hike from the river. (Many people also fly an Alaska Airlines jet from Anchorage to King Salmon and then hop on a floatplane to Brooks Camp.) The Park Service maintains a campground at Brooks Camp; lodging and meals are available at **Brooks Lodge** (907/243-5448 or 877/708-1391, www.katmailand.com).

One of Alaska's best-known places to see bears is **McNeil River State Game Sanctuary** on the Alaska Peninsula approximately 100 air miles west of Homer and adjacent to Katmai National Park. This state sanctuary—made famous in *National Geographic* specials—allows just 10 visitors per day to the viewing area. The application process is highly competitive, with just 10 percent of applicants actually getting permission to visit McNeil. It's managed by the **Alaska Department of Fish and Game** (907/267-2189, www.wildlife.alaska.gov), with complete details on access and the application process at their website.

brown bears

Two other popular places to see brown bears are **Silver Salmon Creek** and **Chinitna Bay** within **Lake Clark National Park** (907/781-2218, www.nps.gov/lacl), on the Alaska Peninsula southwest of Anchorage. Access is by air from Anchorage, Soldotna, or Homer, or check out lodges in the park, including **Silver Salmon Creek Lodge** (907/252-5504 or 888/872-5666, www.silversalmoncreek.com) and **Alaska Bear Camp** (866/411-2327, www.greatalaska.com).

In addition to the official areas, many air-taxi operators fly out of Anchorage, Homer, Kenai, and Soldotna on daylong **bear-viewing trips** in search of brown bears. Most of these head to the outer coast, landing on beaches within Katmai National Park and Preserve. These once-in-a-lifetime day trips typically cost $650-800 pp.

The Best of the Kenai Peninsula

The Kenai Peninsula is the Alaska that most people dream about. Distances here are great, but it's worth traversing them to see highlights like Exit Glacier and the towns of Seward and Homer. This itinerary generally alternates driving days with more active and adventurous days. You can add additional days in any location if you want to pack in more excursions—or if you prefer a more leisurely pace.

En Route to the Kenai Peninsula
DAY 1: PORTAGE GLACIER AND GIRDWOOD

Drive south from Anchorage, stopping at **Potter Marsh** to watch for arctic terns and other birds. Continue along **Turnagain Arm,** famous for its bore tides, beluga whales, and cliff-traipsing Dall sheep.

Get a filling lunch at **The Bake Shop** in Girdwood and drive south to Portage, where you can visit the **Alaska Wildlife Conservation Center** to see brown and black bears, bison, moose, and other critters up close. Take an hour-long boat cruise to **Portage Glacier** and visit the **Begich, Boggs Visitor Center** to learn more about glaciers and Alaska's rapidly warming climate. Alternatively, ride the Alaska Railroad from Portage to **Spencer Glacier** for hiking, kayaking, and river rafting.

Backtrack a few miles to Girdwood and overnight at **Hotel Alyeska.** Take the **Alyeska Resort tram** to a gourmet dinner at **Seven Glaciers Restaurant,** high above Turnagain Arm.

DAY 2: DAY CRUISE FROM WHITTIER

Drive south to Portage and through the 2.5-mile tunnel to the little town of **Whittier,** a popular

kayaking in Prince Williiam Sound near Whittier

rafting on the Kenai River near Cooper Landing

port for cruise ships and day tours. **Phillips Tours and Cruises** has all-day boat tours to the spectacular glaciers of western Prince William Sound. You can also opt for a leisurely five-hour **glacier tour** to **Blackstone Bay.** Seals lounge on the icebergs, and several active glaciers are visible at once.

Drive back through the tunnel and head south, stopping for a pleasant dinner at **Summit Lake Lodge,** and overnight at **Inn at Tern Lake** near Moose Pass.

The Kenai Peninsula
DAY 3: SEWARD AND EXIT GLACIER

Drive the 36 miles from Inn at Tern Lake to the town of Seward. Get a latte and check out the artwork at **Resurrect Art Coffeehouse Gallery,** then make the 12-mile drive north to **Exit Glacier.** In an hour or two you can explore the country around this fast-retreating glacier, or opt for an all-day hike to massive Harding Icefield. **Exit Glacier Guides** leads ice-climbing trips onto the glacier if you're feeling adventurous.

Reward yourself with a farm-to-table dinner at **The Cookery** and spend the night at **Alaska Paddle Inn,** just south of town on Lowell Point. (A less expensive alternative is **Nauti Otter** yurts.)

DAY 4: DAY CRUISE FROM SEWARD

Take a half-day wildlife boat tour around **Resurrection Bay** or an all-day trip to Northwestern Fjord or Aialik Bay within **Kenai Fjords National Park.**

In the late afternoon, visit Seward's **Alaska SeaLife Center,** where enormous tanks house puffins, seals, and playful sea lions. Enjoy a "bucket of butt" halibut dinner at **Thorn's Showcase** or a burger and brew from **Seward Brewing Company.** Spend a second night in Seward.

DAY 5: COOPER LANDING

Drive north to the tiny settlement of **Cooper Landing** along the Kenai River. Take the day to relax with a float trip on the Kenai River from **Alaska River Adventures,** or go for an

Day Cruises

One of the most enjoyable and fun ways to see south-central Alaska's wild places is by boat. On-the-water tours—from half-hour water-taxi rides to 11-hour national park tours—are available in the following places:

- **Resurrection Bay day tours** from Seward
- **Kenai Fjords National Park tours** from Seward
- **Prince William Sound tours** from Whittier
- **Portage Glacier tours** from Portage
- **Kachemak Bay tours** from Homer
- **Seldovia tours** from Homer
- **Halibut Cove tours** from Homer
- **Susitna River trips** from Talkeetna
- **Water-taxi rides** of any length from Seward, Whittier, or Homer
- **Fishing float trips** on the Kenai River from Cooper Landing
- **White-water rafting** from Hope, Spencer Glacier, Talkeetna, Cooper Landing, Matanuska Glacier, or Denali National Park

tour boat at Kenai Fjords National Park

hour-long trail ride with **Alaska Horsemen Trail Adventures.**

Kingfisher Roadhouse has delicious meals with a rustic setting and an enclosed deck facing Kenai Lake. Settle in for an angelic night at **Alaska Heavenly Lodge.**

DAY 6: SOLDOTNA AND KENAI

Drop by **Gwin's Lodge** for a filling down-home breakfast. Head west along the Sterling Highway, stopping at Mile 55 to ride the self-propelled **Russian River Ferry** across the river where salmon anglers stand shoulder to shoulder for "combat fishing" during the peak of the sockeye run.

Take the scenic route from here by turning onto **Skilak Lake Loop Road.** This pretty 16-mile dirt road crosses the heart of Kenai National Wildlife Refuge, with campgrounds and hiking trails. If you have the time, take one of these hikes: the **Bear Mountain Trail** is a short one with impressive views.

Back on the Sterling Highway, continue west to **Soldotna,** where you can stock up on groceries at the big Fred Meyer store or a lunchtime soup and sandwich at **Odie's Deli** and let the kids run wild at **Soldotna Creek Park.** Once they're corralled back in the car, continue to the Kenai Spur Highway junction, and turn north through the small city of **Kenai** (home to the Peninsula's only Walmart), and then another 15 miles to tiny Nikiski. Stop by **Kassik's Brewery** for a growler of Moose Point Porter and order fish tacos at **Playa-Azul Mexican Restaurant.** Overnight in a cozy lakeside cabin at **Daniels Lake Lodge B&B,** where you can listen to the calls of loons echoing across the lake.

DAY 7: KENAI, NINILCHIK, AND ON TO HOMER

In the morning, head to the **Kenai Visitors and Cultural Center** for local information, then visit **Veronica's Café** for breakfast blintzes and espresso. Wander a bit farther west to sand dunes along Cook Inlet at the mouth of the Kenai River. In July you'll see hundreds of **dipnetters** catching salmon from the riverbanks.

Drive south from Kenai via Kalifornsky Beach Road, turning south on the Sterling Highway at Kasilof. As you're driving, look across the inlet for views of snowy mountains and active volcanoes.

Around 25 miles later, you'll find yourself in **Ninilchik,** home to the **Transfiguration of Our Lord Russian Orthodox Church,** located on a

dramatic hilltop facing the volcanic summit of Mount Iliamna. Pause at **The Buzz Café** for a caffeine boost if needed.

It's another 45 miles south to the small city of **Homer,** where the Sterling Highway ends. Stop at the big hilltop overlook just before you reach Homer for an all-encompassing vista across Kachemak Bay, and spend the night at **Driftwood Inn** or **Kenai Peninsula Suites.** For an Italy-meets-Alaska dinner, head to **Fat Olives.**

DAY 8: HOMER

After an enticing breakfast at **Two Sisters Bakery,** head down the street to **Bishops Beach** for a Kachemak Bay stroll, then to **Islands and Ocean Visitor Center** and the **Pratt Museum** for excellent introductions to the area.

Homer's most-loved destination is the four-mile-long **Homer Spit.** This natural peninsula of land extends into Kachemak Bay, with a busy boat harbor and a cluster of shops, galleries, restaurants, campgrounds, and lodging at the end. Two excellent Spit dinner options are **Finn's**

Skilak Lake from Bear Mountain Trail

Pizza and **Little Mermaid Café**. Save room for a treat from **Carmen's Gelato**.

DAY 9: DAY TRIPS FROM HOMER

This is a day that could go in three completely different directions. If you have the cash ($700 pp or so), hop on one of the all-day bear-viewing flights from Homer to **Katmai National Park.** Sea kayaking is a less expensive option: **True North Adventures** has all-day kayak trips at Yukon Island and stand-up paddleboarding on Grewingk Glacier Lake. The third option is to join an early morning halibut and salmon fishing charter; find one through **Central Charters & Tours.** You're almost certain of getting your limit, and **Coal Point Seafood** will process, freeze, and ship your catch.

For dinner, check out **Wasabi's** for Asian fusion cuisine or **Café Cups** for creative seafood.

DAY 10: RETURN TO ANCHORAGE VIA HOPE

It's a five-hour, 225-mile drive back to Anchorage, but if you get going early enough, you can still have fun along the way. This will be a long day, so start with a best-in-Alaska cappuccino at **K-Bay Caffé** or a best-in-Alaska bagel at **The Bagel Shop** before leaving town. It's an hour and a half to Soldotna, where you can pick up a hoagie from **Jersey Subs.** Then drive another 93 miles (via the Sterling Highway, Seward Highway, and Hope Highway) to the historic town of **Hope,** with its quaint log buildings and great hiking trails. An easy day hike follows the shore of Turnagain Arm to **Gull Rock,** or for something more challenging, the 38-mile **Resurrection Pass Trail** begins a few miles from Hope. Get dinner at **Creekbend Café,** and after your detour to Hope, return to the Seward Highway for the drive to Anchorage. A fine lodging choice is **Dimond Center Hotel.**

Anchorage and Vicinity

Home to nearly 300,000 people, Anchorage is an eminently enjoyable *and* affordable place to hang out.

It certainly has one of the most flower-filled downtowns of any American city; visitors are always impressed with the summertime bounty of blooms. You can easily fill a whole day touring downtown, or just lying around a park for the one day in four that the sun shines. Explore Anchorage's far-flung corners, such as the resort town of Girdwood, south of the city (popular for winter skiing and summer hiking); rapidly growing Matanuska-Susitna Valley (home to the towns of Palmer and Wasilla); grand mountain country at Hatcher Pass; and calving glaciers in Prince William Sound.

Of course, you can simply breeze into town, make your connection,

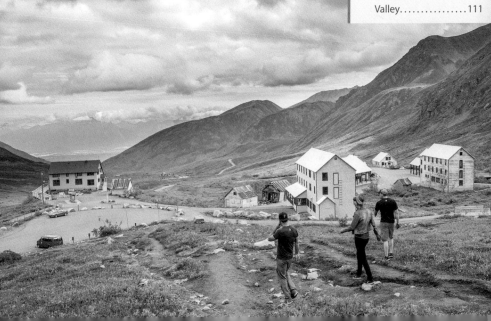

Highlights

Look for ★ to find recommended sights, activities, dining, and lodging.

★ **Anchorage Museum:** Alaska's largest and finest museum has fascinating exhibits, the kid-friendly Imaginarium, and a planetarium with music and light shows (page 43).

★ **Alaska Native Heritage Center:** Learn about the state's Native peoples through exhibits, demonstrations, and cultural presentations (page 48).

★ **Anchorage Market and Festival:** This downtown gathering is packed with Alaskan arts and crafts, great food, and live music every weekend (page 54).

★ **Chugach State Park:** Who would imagine that you could get into the wilderness so quickly from Anchorage? Lots of wonderful hiking trails are here, especially the climb up Flattop Mountain (page 88).

★ **Turnagain Arm:** South of Anchorage, this long inlet is a great place to watch for beluga whales and bore tides or see Dall sheep on the cliffs (page 90).

★ **Crow Creek Mine:** Just a few miles from Alyeska Ski Resort in Girdwood are picture-perfect log cabins from this authentic old mine, where you might find gold in the creek (page 94).

★ **Portage Glacier:** This is one of the state's most visited glaciers. A boat tour across Portage Lake leaves hourly from the visitors center (page 101).

★ **Spencer Glacier:** Access to this beautiful glacier is only by Alaska Railroad day trips. Activities include hiking, river rafting, and kayaking among the icebergs (page 103).

★ **Prince William Sound Tours:** Two companies offer all-day glacier tours out of Whittier, providing a front-seat view of calving glaciers, lounging seals, and dramatic peaks (page 105).

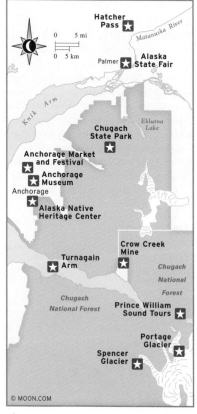

© MOON.COM

★ **Alaska State Fair:** Where else can you find a demolition derby, supersize turkey legs, enormous peonies, and 100-pound cabbages (page 113)?

★ **Hatcher Pass:** This beautiful area is perfect for hiking in the summer or cross-country skiing when the snow flies. Take time to explore the weathered old buildings of Independence Mine State Historical Park (page 124).

and quickly "get back to Alaska." But if you want a fully rounded experience of the 49th state, get to know Anchorage, *urban* Alaska, and come to your own conclusions.

HISTORY

In June 1778, Captain James Cook sailed up what's now Turnagain Arm in Cook Inlet, reaching another dead end on his amazing search for the Northwest Passage. But he did dispatch William Bligh (of HMS *Bounty* fame) to explore, and he saw some Tanaina people in rich otter skins. George Vancouver, who'd also been on Cook's ship, returned in 1794 and noted Russian settlers in the area. A century later, prospectors began landing in the area and heading north to south-central Alaska's gold country, and in 1902 Alfred Brooks began mapping the Cook Inlet for the U.S. Geological Survey. In 1913, five settlers occupied Ship Creek, the point on the inlet where Anchorage now stands.

A year later, Congress passed the Alaska Railroad Act, and in April 1915 the route for the federally financed railroad from Seward to Fairbanks was made official: It would pass through Ship Creek, where a major staging area for workers and supplies would be located. This news traveled fast, and within a month a ramshackle tent city of nearly 2,000 railroad job seekers had sprung up. Things developed so quickly that in July the U.S. Land Office auctioned off 650 parcels at the new town site. The settlement, renamed Anchorage, grew quickly, with water, telephone and power lines, sidewalks, and schools in place within a year.

Slumps and Spurts

Railroad laborers, earning 37 cents per hour (low for Alaska), went on strike in 1916, after which the minimum wage was raised to 45 cents per hour. The population continued to boom, topping out at around 7,000 in 1917. With World War I and completion of the southern portion of the railroad, the number of people dropped below 2,000 in 1920, when the town incorporated, electing its first mayor and city council. Through the 1930s, Anchorage held steady at 3,000 to 4,000 people, but World War II changed that in a hurry. The town's strategic location led to a huge influx of military personnel when the U.S. Army's Fort Richardson and the Army Air Corps' Elmendorf Field were constructed outside of town. By 1950, Anchorage was a prosperous small city of over 11,000. In the following decade Anchorage also experienced the postwar boom, with the attendant shortages of housing and modern conveniences, which created the city's own construction mini-boom. In 1957, when Richfield Oil discovered black gold on the Kenai Peninsula, the oil companies started opening office buildings in the city, and the economy stabilized.

Since Statehood

Much of Anchorage collapsed in the incredible Good Friday Earthquake of March 27, 1964, which lasted an interminable five minutes, registering magnitude 9.2. The north side of 4th Avenue wound up 8-10 feet lower than the south side of the street. A very rich residential section on the bluff overlooking Knik Arm was destroyed. Nine people were killed and upward of $300 million in damages were recorded ($2.5 billion in today's dollars). Anchorage was rebuilt, and because only a few large buildings survived the quake, nearly everything in the city today was built after 1964.

Now more than 100 years old—it celebrated its centennial in 2015—Anchorage is the economic and population center of Alaska. Though the pipeline doesn't come within 300 miles, oil money towers over the city in the form of tall office buildings scattered around town. The military still plays an important role in the local economy, with Elmendorf Air Force Base and Fort Richardson on the margins of town, and

Anchorage and Vicinity

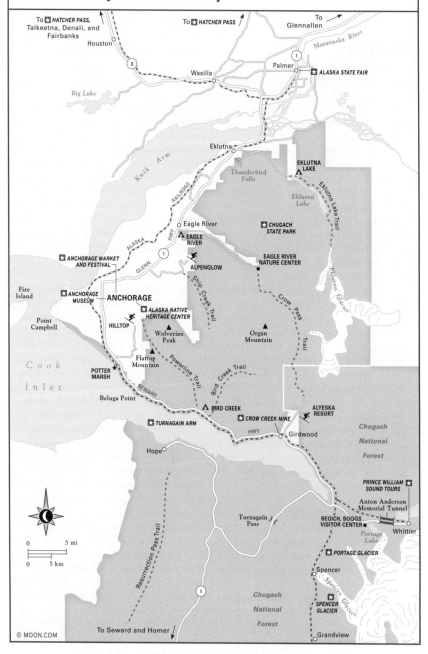

To ✪ HATCHER PASS, Talkeetna, Denali, and Fairbanks
Houston

To ✪ HATCHER PASS

To Glennallen

Matanuska River

Palmer

✪ ALASKA STATE FAIR

Wasilla

Big Lake

Knik Arm

Eklutna

EKLUTNA LAKE

Thunderbird Falls

Eklutna Lake

Eklutna Lake Trail

RAILROAD

Eagle River

✪ CHUGACH STATE PARK

EAGLE RIVER

ALPENGLOW

EAGLE RIVER NATURE CENTER

Eklutna Glacier

✪ ANCHORAGE MARKET AND FESTIVAL

ALASKA HWY

GLENN

Crow Pass Trail

Fire Island

✪ ANCHORAGE MUSEUM

ANCHORAGE

Ship Creek Trail

Point Campbell

✪ ALASKA NATIVE HERITAGE CENTER

HILLTOP

Wolverine Peak

Organ Mountain

Flattop Mountain

Cook Inlet

POTTER MARSH

Powerline Trail

Bird Creek Trail

SEWARD

Beluga Point

BIRD CREEK

ALYESKA RESORT

✪ CROW CREEK MINE

Chugach National Forest

✪ TURNAGAIN ARM

HWY

Girdwood

Hope

PRINCE WILLIAM SOUND TOURS ✪

Anton Anderson Memorial Tunnel

Turnagain Pass

BEGICH, BOGGS VISITOR CENTER

Portage Lake

Whittier

Resurrection Pass Trail

0   5 mi
0   5 km

✪ PORTAGE GLACIER

Spencer

Spencer Glacier

✪ SPENCER GLACIER

1

Chugach National Forest

© MOON.COM

To Seward and Homer

Grandview

military jets and surveillance planes a common presence in the sky. Tourism also affects Anchorage enormously, especially in the summer months when the city is a waypoint for many travelers. Anchorage fancies itself quite the cosmopolitan city, boasting dozens of arts organizations, a modern performing arts center, a 16-theater cinema with stadium seating, plus many fancy hotels, restaurants, cafés, and bars catering to the thousands of suits who fill the skyscrapers that gleam in the light of the midnight sun. Indeed, if Juneau is bureaucratic Alaska, and Fairbanks is rank-and-file Alaska, then Anchorage is corporate and commercial Alaska.

CLIMATE

Two of the deciding factors in choosing Anchorage as a main construction camp for the Alaska Railroad were mild winters and comparatively low precipitation. The towering Alaska Range shelters Cook Inlet Basin from the frigid winter breath of the arctic northerlies; the Kenai and Chugach Mountains cast a rain shadow over the basin, allowing only 15-20 percent of the annual precipitation that communities on the windward side of the ranges get. Anchorage receives around 20 inches of annual precipitation (10-12 inches of rain, 60-70 inches of snow), while Whittier, 40 miles away on the Gulf side of the Chugach, gets 175 inches. Anchorage's winter temperatures rarely drop much below 0°F, with only an occasional cold streak, compared with Fairbanks's frequent -40°F; its summer temperatures rarely rise above 65°F, compared with Fairbanks's 80s and 90s.

PLANNING YOUR TIME

Anchorage is an outstanding base for travelers to south-central Alaska's heartland, with Denali National Park, the Kenai Peninsula, and a multitude of other attractions within a day's drive. The state's largest airport provides flights to all regions of the globe, and the Alaska Railroad has daily trains north to Denali and Fairbanks or south to Seward and Whittier. Anchorage has long served as a hub for travelers, but it also offers many attractions not available elsewhere, and one could easily spend two or three days here.

The city's highlights include its outstanding **Anchorage Museum** (the state's largest), the **Alaska Native Heritage Center,** the **Alaska Heritage Museum,** and an abundance of good restaurants, hip coffeehouses, hopping bars, the **H2Oasis Indoor Waterpark,** and two minor-league baseball teams. Don't forget the **Anchorage Market and Festival** every summer weekend, with locally made crafts, tasty finger food, live music, and even a bit of fresh produce from the farmers.

There are also attractions you would only find in an Alaskan city: a wonderful coastal trail that starts right downtown; great hiking in nearby **Chugach State Park;** fascinating **Turnagain Arm** with its enormous tides and beluga whales; and places to outfit yourself for any adventure in the Alaskan outdoors. Anchorage is within striking distance of some of the most exciting and extensive hiking, climbing, fishing, kayaking, river rafting, flightseeing, and wilderness areas.

To the south, the town of Girdwood is home to Alyeska Resort—Alaska's only significant ski area—and funky **Crow Creek Mine,** where you still might find a gold nugget in your pan. A bit farther south is the much-photographed **Portage Glacier,** accessed by a tour boat from the U.S. Forest Service visitors center. Hop on the Alaska Railroad to spend a day kayaking in front of **Spencer Glacier.** Accessed through a long tunnel, the town of **Whittier** serves as a launching point for glacier sightseeing tours and sea kayaking adventures.

North of Anchorage, the Glenn Highway passes a tiny Tanaina Native Alaskan village where **Eklutna Historical Park** houses a picturesque graveyard filled with spirit houses before emerging in the Matanuska-Susitna Valley (Mat-Su, for short), where the pastures and farms of the past are giving way to homes and strip-malls for folks fleeing Anchorage's housing prices and crowding.

Anchorage

© MOON.COM

0
0
2 km
2 mi

★ TURNAGAIN ARM

Turnagain Arm

Jewel Lake

Campbell Lake

DIMOND BLVD

DIMOND CENTER MALL

ALASKA RAILROAD

(1)

NEW SEWARD HWY

★ H2OASIS INDOOR WATERPARK

★ POTTER MARSH

DEARMOUN RD

HUFFMAN RD

ANCHORAGE GOLF COURSE

ALASKA ZOO ★

ABBOT RD

RABBIT CREEK RD

POTTER SECTION HOUSE

To Girdwood, Seward, and Flower

Turnagain Arm "Trail"

ALASKAN SUNDANCE RETREAT B&B

O'MALLEY RD

Hillside Park

HILLSIDE DR

ALASKAN FRONTIER GARDENS B&B

GLEN ALPS TRAILHEAD

PROSPECT HEIGHTS TRAILHEAD

HILLTOP SKI AREA

McHUGH CREEK TRAILHEAD

CHUGACH STATE PARK

Flattop Mtn ▲

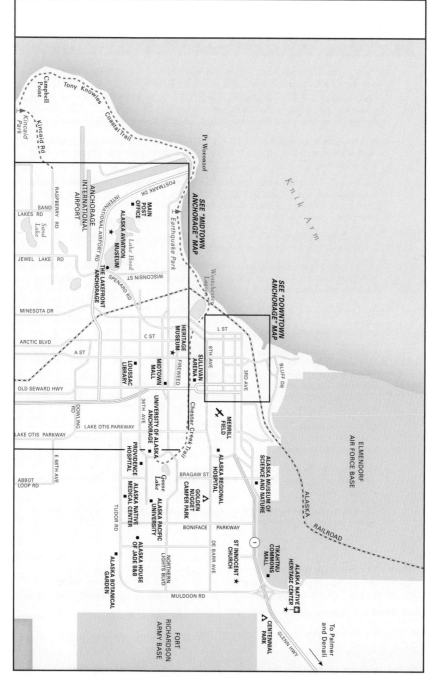

Campbell Point
Kincaid Park
Kincaid Rd
Tony Knowles Coastal Trail
Pt Woronzof
Knik Arm

SAND LAKES RD
RASPBERRY RD
Sand Lake
JEWEL LAKE RD
MINESOTA DR
ARCTIC BLVD
A ST
OLD SEWARD HWY
DOWLING RD
LAKE OTIS PARKWAY
E 68TH AVE
ABBOT LOOP RD

ANCHORAGE INTERNATIONAL AIRPORT
INTERNATIONAL AIRPORT RD
MAIN POST OFFICE
ALASKA AVIATION MUSEUM
Lake Hood
THE LAKEFRONT ANCHORAGE
SPENARD RD
WISCONSIN ST
POSTMARK DR
Earthquake Park
Westchester Lagoon

SEE "MIDTOWN ANCHORAGE" MAP
SEE "DOWNTOWN ANCHORAGE" MAP

HERITAGE MUSEUM
C ST
L ST
8TH AVE
3RD AVE
BLUFF DR
MIDTOWN MALL
FIREWEED
LOUSSAC LIBRARY
SULLIVAN ARENA
UNIVERSITY OF ALASKA ANCHORAGE
36TH AVE
Chester Creek Trail
MERRILL FIELD
PROVIDENCE HOSPITAL
Goose Lake
BRAGAW ST
ALASKA REGIONAL HOSPITAL
ALASKA MUSEUM OF SCIENCE AND NATURE
ELMENDORF AIR FORCE BASE
ALASKA NATIVE MEDICAL CENTER
ALASKA PACIFIC UNIVERSITY
GOLDEN NUGGET CAMPER PARK
ALASKA RAILROAD
BONIFACE PARKWAY
DE BARR AVE
ST INNOCENT CHURCH
TIKAHTNU COMMONS MALL
ALASKA HOUSE OF JADE B&B
NORTHERN LIGHTS BLVD
ALASKA NATIVE HERITAGE CENTER
TUDOR RD
MULDOON RD
ALASKA BOTANICAL GARDEN
CENTENNIAL PARK
GLENN HWY
To Palmer and Denali
FORT RICHARDSON ARMY BASE

One Day in Anchorage

For many visitors, Anchorage is a place to spend a night and then head out to Alaska's wild places. If you only have a day to explore Anchorage, here are a few highlights:

- Spend some time in the heart of Anchorage at **Town Square** (5th Ave. and E St.), with its flowerbeds and hanging baskets. The **Performing Arts Center** is that colorful building with the Olympic-like rings. Step inside to watch one of the hourly northern lights shows.

- Walk down 4th Avenue to the **Log Cabin Visitors Center,** with its sod roof and Crossroads of the World sign. Step around the back for a plethora of travel brochures at the Visit Anchorage office.

- Head inside the **Alaska Public Lands Information Center** (APLIC) for an introduction to national parks and the wildlife of Alaska. But be sure to bring your ID; this is still a federal courthouse that requires security screening. Step outside the APLIC for a juicy reindeer sausage with grilled onions from the food cart with the perpetual queue of hungry people.

- The **Anchorage Museum** has an amazing Native Alaskan collection, plus art, hands-on science toys at the Discovery Center, a planetarium, and historical exhibits.

- For just $32 you can purchase a pass to both the Anchorage Museum and the **Alaska Native Heritage Center,** a great place to learn about Alaska's first peoples. The heritage center is on the northeast side of town, but a free shuttle takes you directly there from the museum.

- The **Tony Knowles Coastal Trail** starts downtown at the west end of 5th Avenue and curves along the shore of Turnagain Arm all the way to Kincaid Park, 11 miles away. On a sunny day you can take in the summits of Mount Denali, Sleeping Lady, and several volcanoes.

- Anchorage has an abundance of dining places in the heart of town. For breakfast, visit **Snow City Café** (1034 W. 4th Ave.). Grab a coffee and take a gander at today's artwork at **Side Street Espresso** (412 G St.), or an upscale lunch a block away at **Crush Wine Bistro** (328 G St.). Alaska's best pastries await at **Fire Island Rustic Bakery** (1343 G St.). Plenty of dinner choices are downtown too, including **Glacier BrewHouse** (737 W. 5th Ave.) for a hip setting and wood-fired pizzas, or old-timey **Club Paris** (417 W. 5th Ave.) for Alaska's finest steaks.

- On summer weekends, the **Anchorage Market and Festival** should not be missed. It takes place in the parking lot at 3rd Avenue and E Street, and features over 300 vendors with arts, crafts, produce, and tasty finger food.

- For a break from the city, head up to **Flattop Mountain,** where you can hike onto the summit for a fine city panorama. Flattop Mountain Shuttle provides transport from downtown if you don't have a car.

- Take a flightseeing trip from one of the floatplane companies based on **Lake Hood.** The best ones include a glacier lake landing.

The valley's two main towns are booming Wasilla and semirural Palmer, home to a fun Musk Ox Farm and the **Alaska State Fair,** a 12-day blast starting in late August. North of the valley, the Talkeetna Mountains rise abruptly, bisected by a road over Hatcher Pass, where **Independence Mine State Historical Park** provides a base for day hikes or wintertime skiing.

Sights

It doesn't take long to get the hang of **downtown Anchorage**. The blocks are square, with the lettered streets (A through L) going north-south and the numbered avenues (starting at 2nd Avenue, just up the hill from the tracks) running east-west. Once you get east of the lettered streets, they start over again using alphabetized names (Barrow, Cordova, Denali, Eagle, Fairbanks).

Beyond downtown, the city of Anchorage sprawls across the Anchorage Bowl, with **Hillside** homes peering down on the masses below. A number of neighborhoods are scattered around Anchorage, but most travelers are likely to spend their time in downtown and **Midtown,** a collection of malls, shopping centers, supermarkets, fast-food joints, bars, movie theaters, discount stores, gas stations, and other businesses just a 20-minute walk or a 10-minute bus ride south of downtown. Midtown encompasses the area within Northern Lights and Benson Boulevards between Minnesota Drive and Old Seward Highway. It isn't exactly a tourist attraction, but this, along with shopping malls on the south and east end of town, is where locals—and others looking to save money—spend their cash. Another large shopping district is along Dimond Boulevard in South Anchorage, where all the stalwarts are: Best Buy, Walmart, Costco, and more.

DOWNTOWN

Start your visit to Anchorage by dropping by the **Log Cabin Visitors Center** (4th Ave. and F St., 907/276-4118, www.anchorage.net, 8am-7pm daily mid-May-mid-Sept. and 9am-4pm daily mid-Sept.-mid-May). The cabin itself is worth a photo, and the benches out front are a nice place to take in the action. Head out the back door to find the **Anchorage Visitors Center.**

Town Square (5th Ave. and E St.), on the spacious front lawn of the Performing Arts Center, is a fine flower-filled field of fecundity. It's a wonderful place to meet up with friends or just relax on a sunny summer day.

Alaska Public Lands Information Center

Kitty-corner from Visit Anchorage's log cabin is the old Federal Building, which now houses the **Alaska Public Lands Information Center** (APLIC, 605 W. 4th Ave., 907/644-3678 or 866/869-6887, www.alaskacenters.gov, 9am-5pm daily late May-early Sept., 10am-5pm Tues.-Fri. early Sept.-late May, free). This is a great place to learn about federal lands in Alaska. There's always a National Park Service ranger on staff, and the center also hosts agencies that oversee national forests, wildlife refuges, and the Bureau of Land Management areas. Displays introduce you to Alaska's wildlife and wild places, the touchscreen kiosk features interactive maps, daily historical walks are offered throughout the summer, the bookstore has a selection of Alaskan titles, and there's even free Wi-Fi. You can also book Kenai Fjords National Park cabins here, and the auditorium opens for daily nature talks, downtown walking tours, and high-definition nature videos all summer. Take a look around this old building to find classic Depression-era paintings of Alaska. The only problem with APLIC is access: Because it's also a courthouse, all visitors will need to go through a security screening at the entrance. It's a minor hassle, but generally not a long delay.

★ Anchorage Museum

A massive $106 million expansion in 2009 transformed the **Anchorage Museum** (625 C St., 907/929-9200, www.anchoragemuseum.org, 9am-6pm daily May-Sept., 10am-6pm Tues.-Sat., noon-6pm Sun. Oct.-Apr., $18 adults, $12 seniors, students, and military, $9 ages 3-12, free under age 3) into the state's largest—170,000 square feet—and finest

Downtown Anchorage

Knik Arm

0
0
0.25 km
0.25 mi

Tony Knowles Coastal Trail

RESOLUTION PARK

COPPER WHALE INN

OSCAR GILL HOUSE B&B

PARKSIDE GUEST HOUSE

O ST

N ST

OSCAR ANDERSON HOUSE

M ST

L ST

SUSTINA PLACE B&B

CLARION SUITES DOWNTOWN

W 5TH AVE

CAPTAIN COOK HOTEL

I ST

BENT PROP INN & HOSTEL

H ST

BUS TRANSIT CENTER

G ST

F ST

Delaney Park

DENA'INA CIVIC & CONVENTION CENTER

PERFORMING ARTS CENTER

EGAN CENTER

W 9TH AVE

W 8TH AVE

E ST

D ST

ANCHORAGE MUSEUM

C ST

FEDERAL BUILDING

B ST

A ST

Town Square

5TH AVE MALL

LOG CABIN VISITOR CENTER

ALASKA PUBLIC LANDS INFO CENTER

MARX BROS CAFE

W 2ND AVE

ANCHORAGE GRAND HOTEL

ANCHORAGE HOTEL

POST OFFICE

ALASKA STATE TROOPER'S MUSEUM

ALASKA RAILROAD DEPOT

ANCHORAGE MARKET AND FESTIVAL

W 3RD AVE

OCEAN DOCK RD

COMFORT INN

SALMON VIEWING PLATFORM

Ship Creek

Alaska Railroad

LOOP RD

BARROW ST

CORDOVA ST

DENALI ST

EAGLE ST

1ST AVE

Alaska Railroad

ANCHORAGE UPTOWN SUITES

ARCTIC FOX INN

E 10TH AVE

FAIRBANKS ST

GAMBELL ST

E 9TH AVE

E 8TH AVE

E 7TH AVE

E 6TH AVE

E 5TH AVE

E 4TH AVE

E 3RD AVE

ANCHORAGE SHIP CREEK RV PARK

INGRA ST

JUNEAU ST

INGRA HOUSE HOTEL

1

1

1

1

© MOON.COM

Wilderness in the City

In Anchorage, it's surprisingly easy to get away from busy city streets to the wilderness at the city's borders. Here are a few city getaways:

- Walk or bike the **Tony Knowles Coastal Trail.**
- Climb **Flattop Mountain** within massive Chugach State Park.
- Drive along **Turnagain Arm** to watch for beluga whales, Dall sheep, and bore tides. Stop to hike trails that lead to dramatic vistas.
- Go mountain biking in **Kincaid Park.**
- Check out the **Alaska Zoo.**
- Ride the **aerial tramway** to the top of Mount Alyeska for great hikes and fine dining.
- Visit the **Alaska Botanical Garden.**
- Catch a king, silver, or pink salmon in **Ship Creek,** right in the heart of Anchorage.
- Visit the **Alaska Wildlife Conservation Center** near Portage to see brown bears, moose, and other wildlife up close.

museum. One very popular feature is the kid-friendly **Discovery Center,** with 80 hands-on science exhibits, including the chance to encase yourself in bubbles, a magic-planet globe that displays today's weather patterns (and much more), live marine touch tanks (with sea stars, crabs, and anemones), an air cannon, and pulley chairs. Exhibits focus on Alaskan science, especially earthquakes and volcanoes.

Also on the first level is the **Thomas Planetarium.** This isn't one of those ordinary point-out-the-stars shows, but a fun 3-D trip beyond the solar system. Especially fun is Pink Floyd's *Dark Side of the Moon* music and light show ($10). Other highlights include a gallery of Alaskan art that features Sydney Laurence's 6-by-10-foot oil painting of Mount Denali. The upper levels contain galleries with contemporary Native Alaskan art, Alaskan history, and rotating shows that change every few months. Don't miss the second-floor **Living Our Cultures** collection of some 600 archaeological pieces on long-term loan from the Smithsonian Museum—they're the high point of the museum. Also impressive are the permanent collections displayed in

the bright **Art of the North** galleries and the **Alaska Exhibition.** Upper levels are devoted to changing exhibitions, with fine mountain and city vistas from the 4th floor.

In addition to exhibits, the Anchorage Museum has a gift shop and historical photos in the resource center. Enjoy an upscale lunch at trendy **Muse Restaurant** (907/929-9210, www.muse.anchoragemuseum.org), or look over the works by local artists in the atrium during June-July. Free hour-long **museum tours** (11am, noon, and 1pm daily summer) are offered. Outside is a two-acre commons, perfect for summer afternoon picnics or letting the kids run around.

The Anchorage Museum and Alaska Native Heritage Center have teamed up to offer the **Alaska Culture Pass** (www.alaskaculturpass.org, $32), providing entrance to both of these facilities plus a free shuttle; get tickets at either facility.

Museums and Historic Buildings

Anchorage is pretty short on historic buildings, since much of the city was severely damaged in the 1964 quake, and most of the city's

Midtown Anchorage

0   0.5 km
0   0.5 mi

SAND LAKE RD

TED STEVENS
ANCHORAGE
INTERNATIONAL AIRPORT

POSTMARK DR

Lake
Hood

Earthquake
Park

★ ALASKAN AVIATION
MUSEUM

AERO AVE

W NORTHERN LIGHTS BLVD

MILKY WAY DR

Lake
Spenard

SPENARD HOSTEL
INTERNATIONAL ●

WISCONSIN ST

COAST
INTERNATIONAL INN ●

W 42ND
AVE

SPENARD RD

LAKE HOOD
INN ●

LAKESHORE
INN & SUITES ●

COMFORT
SUITES ●

NORTHWOOD DR

CARRS ■

BASE CAMP
ANCHORAGE ●

SAND LAKE RD
JEWEL LAKE RD
STRAWBERRY RD
RASPBERRY RD

Sand
Lake

Delong
Lake

Connors
Lake

JEWEL LAKE RD

W INTERNATIONAL AIRPORT RD

MICROTEL INN
AND SUITES ●

MINNESOTA DR

SPENARD RD

ALASKA
HERITAGE
MUSEUM ★

SOCKEYE
INN ●

FIREWEED LN

NORTHWOOD DR

MINNESOTA DR

HILTON
GARDEN INN ●

ARTIC BLVD

W BENSON BLVD

BENT PROP
INN & HOSTEL ●

ARTIC BLVD

POTTER DR

HOMEWOOD SUITES ●

C ST

HAMPTON
INN ●

E BENSON BLVD

WALMART ■

A ST

MIDTOWN
MALL/REI ■

EMBASSY
SUITES ■

E NORTHERN LIGHTS BLVD

COSTCO ■

E DIMOND BLVD

E DOWLING RD

E INTERNATIONAL AIRPORT RD

MOTEL 6 ●

HILTON
GARDEN INN ●

LOUSSAC
LIBRARY ■

OLD SEWARD HWY

FRED
MEYER ■

DIMOND
CENTER
HOTEL ●

DIMOND
CENTER
MALL ■

To Seward
and Homer

LORE RD

E 68TH AVE

OLD SEWARD HWY

SEWARD HWY

E INTERNATIONAL AIRPORT RD

①

E TUDOR RD

E 36TH AVE

E NORTHERN LIGHTS BLVD

LAKE OTIS PKWY

© MOON.COM

development and growth has taken place since the 1970s. The neighborhood around 2nd Avenue and F Street includes several of the original town-site homes constructed in the early 1900s, and historical panels describe the city's early days.

A few other structures survive from quieter times, including the **Oscar Anderson House Museum** (420 M St., 907/274-2336, www.aahp-online.net, noon-4pm Wed.-Sat. June-Aug., $10 adults, $5 under age 13), open for 45-minute guided tours. This refurbished little bungalow—built in 1915 by Anchorage's first butcher—is the oldest frame residence in this young city. Outside the summer months, it reopens during the first two weekends of December, when it is festooned with traditional Swedish Christmas decorations. The Tony Knowles Coastal Trail passes right in front of the Oscar Anderson House, and adjacent is tiny **Elderberry Park,** a pleasant place to relax on a sunny afternoon, with picnic and playground facilities.

Across the street from the old Federal Building is the **4th Avenue Theater** (630 W. 4th Ave.), built in 1947 and one of the few structures to survive the 1964 earthquake. Unfortunately, it is no longer open to the public. Up the street and right next to the log cabin is **Historic City Hall** (524 4th Ave., 907/276-4118, 8am-5pm Mon.-Fri., free), housing the offices of Visit Anchorage. Step inside the lobby for a few exhibits and historical photos from early Anchorage.

The **Alaska Law Enforcement Museum** (245 W. 5th Ave., 907/279-5050, www.alaskatroopermuseum.com, 10am-4pm Mon.-Fri., noon-4pm Sat., free) is worth visiting to check out the gleaming black 1952 Hudson Hornet patrol car.

Immediately north of downtown is the **Alaska Railroad Depot** (411 W. 1st Ave., 907/265-2494 or 800/544-0552, www.alaskarailroad.com), where you can book train travel or check out the 1907 train engine out front.

Delaney Park

Known locally as the **Park Strip,** enjoyable **Delaney Park** (bounded by 9th Ave., 10th Ave., L St., and Barrow St.) marked the boundary where the town stopped and the wilderness started. In 1923 the strip where the park is today was cleared as a firebreak. Since then it has served as a golf course and an airstrip and now hosts half a dozen softball games every night of summer, tennis and basketball courts, and large grassy sections for Frisbee, hacky sack, tai chi, sunbathing, or people-watching. Right next to the park is a cage housing **Star, the pet reindeer** (10th Ave. and I St.). The owners have had a succession of reindeer here since 1960; this is number seven.

Resolution Park

Tiny **Resolution Park** (west end of 3rd Ave. at L St.) consists of a viewing platform and a statue of Captain James Cook, who encountered what is now called Cook Inlet in 1778. The park is named for his ship, the *Resolution.* On clear days you'll delight in the mountainscape vistas. Mount Denali rises 125 miles to the north, and the low mountain just northwest across Cook Inlet is aptly named Sleeping Lady (the maps call it Mount Susitna). Behind it, and just a bit south, stands a chain of active volcanoes that dump ash on Anchorage every few years, including Mount Spurr and Mount Redoubt. If you have eagle eyes and crystalline weather, you might pick out a third volcano, Mount Iliamna, far to the southwest. Out of sight is yet a fourth volcano, Mount Augustine, which last spewed ash in 2006.

Tony Knowles Coastal Trail

This is one of Anchorage's highlights, a wonderful 11-mile asphalt track that wends its way along the shore from downtown past the airport to Kincaid Park at Point Campbell, where the Knik and Turnagain Arms meet. From downtown, the trail is accessible from the west ends of 2nd, 5th, and 9th Avenues, with additional access at Westchester Lagoon, Earthquake Park, Point Woronzof, and Kincaid. Stroll the trail a ways, at least through the tunnel, beyond which you leave downtown behind and emerge into a new world: the grand sweep of the Arm, tidal flats, railroad tracks, and a residential neighborhood. On warm summer evenings this trail is more like a freeway, with people on every kind of wheels imaginable: bike riders, inline skaters, skateboarders, and babies in carriages. In winter they trade the wheels for skis. The Coastal Trail gets especially crowded around duck-filled **Westchester Lagoon,** a mile south of downtown, which is also the city's favorite wintertime ice skating rink.

A second paved path intersects the Coastal Trail at Westchester Lagoon, the **Chester Creek Trail,** which creates another greenbelt across Anchorage. This one heads east along the creek, continuing for five miles to the University of Alaska Anchorage campus.

BEYOND DOWNTOWN

Earthquake Park, out on West Northern Lights Boulevard near the airport, has interpretive signs about the Big One on Good Friday 1964, and a view of the skyline and the Chugach Mountains. But the views are even more dramatic from **Point Woronzof,** another mile or so out. Tony Knowles Coastal Trail parallels the coast along Earthquake Park and Point Woronzof; it continues from downtown all the way south to **Kincaid Park.** And speaking of Kincaid, the trails here are a destination for hikers and mountain bikers all summer, and cross-country skiers when the snow flies.

Covering 11 acres of cultivated gardens, the **Alaska Botanical Garden** (4601 Campbell Airstrip Rd., 907/770-3692, www.alaskabg.org, daylight hours daily year-round, donation) is home to more than 1,100 varieties of plants. An information kiosk is at the entrance, and a pleasant one-mile nature trail leads through the perennial, rock, wildflower, and herb gardens. Join a guided tour of the garden (1pm daily June-Aug.). The Botanical Garden is on the southeast end of Anchorage off East Tudor Road.

★ Alaska Native Heritage Center

Located on a 26-acre site facing the Chugach Mountains, the **Alaska Native Heritage Center** (8800 Heritage Center Dr., Glenn Hwy. and Muldoon Rd., 907/330-8000 or 800/315-6608, www.alaskanative.net, 9am-5pm daily mid-May-mid Sept., $25 adults, $21 seniors and military, $17 ages 7-16, free under age 7) provides an excellent introduction to Native Alaskan culture in the state. The Welcome House has exhibits and artifacts from the five primary Native cultures in Alaska, along with a gift shop featuring quality Native art, a theater where you can watch cultural movies, a café, and a central space for concerts, dances, crafts, and Native games demonstrations. Outside, five traditional village structures have been recreated around a small pond, and Native Alaskan guides explain Alaska's various cultures. Free tours of the grounds are given four times daily.

The Heritage Center is east of downtown near the intersection of the Glenn Highway and Muldoon Road; follow the signs. A free shuttle runs from the downtown Log Cabin Visitors Center and the Anchorage Museum six times daily in summer, with the last run departing downtown at 2pm. Save money by purchasing an **Alaska Culture Pass** (www.alaskaculturpass.org, $32), which provides entrance to both facilities plus a free shuttle; tickets are at either facility.

Alaska Heritage Museum

Housed in the lobby of the Wells Fargo bank in Midtown, the **Alaska Heritage Museum** (301 Northern Lights Blvd., 907/265-2834, www.wellsfargohistory.com, noon-4pm Mon.-Fri., free) has one of the state's largest privately owned collections of Alaskan artifacts and books. It will keep you spellbound for hours, if you have the time. Be sure to check out the 3.2-pound (!) gold nugget found in 1963

near Ruby, Alaska. Other highlights include many Native Alaskan baskets, parkas made from bird skins and walrus intestines, Sydney Laurence's paintings, Nome and Fairbanks newspapers from the early 1900s, and bookcases filled with rare books and maps. This little gem of a museum is not to be missed.

Alaska Museum of Science and Nature

Located off Mountain View Drive on the northeast end of town, the **Alaska Museum of Science and Nature** (201 N. Bragaw St., 907/274-2400, www.alaskamuseum.org, 10am-4pm Thurs.-Sat., $8 adults, $7 seniors and military, $6 ages 3-18, free under age 3) houses kid-friendly exhibits on polar dinosaurs, the ice age, birds, and geology.

Alaska Aviation Museum

The **Alaska Museum** (4721 Aircraft Dr., 907/248-5325, www.alaskaairmuseum. org, 9am-5pm daily, $15 adults, $12 seniors and military, $8 ages 5-17, free under age 5, $40 family) is off the Lake Hood exit from International Airport Road. This unusual museum displays 30 vintage aircraft in three connected hangars—from a 1928 Stearman up to an old Alaska Airlines 737—as well as Japanese artifacts from the World War II

Aleutian Island battles and historical photos. The theaters show videos on early Alaskan aviation, and the museum fronts **Lake Hood,** the world's largest seaplane base, where floatplanes take off and land almost constantly in the summer.

Alaska Zoo

Located two miles east of New Seward Highway, the **Alaska Zoo** (4731 O'Malley Rd., 907/346-2133, www.alaskazoo.org, 9am-9pm daily June-Aug., 9am-6pm daily May and Sept., 10am-5pm daily Mar.-Apr. and Oct., 10am-4pm daily Nov.-Feb., $15 adults, $10 seniors and military, $7 ages 3-17, free under age 3) is connected by a free summer-only shuttle bus from the Transit Center. The zoo has wooded grounds, enjoyable shady paths, and all the Alaskan animals (bears, caribou, wolves, foxes, seals, otters, and more), plus a number of more exotic critters. If you have kids, they'll enjoy it, especially the star attraction: Lyutyik the polar bear. You can watch his underwater antics through the glass of the swimming pool, or check out the polar bear cam on the zoo's website. Other Alaskan animals sure to please are the brown bears and wolves; less expected are two rare Amur tigers. The zoo has daily keeper talks and a variety of other programs.

Entertainment and Events

NIGHTLIFE

The best sources for Anchortown action are the Thursday edition of *Anchorage Daily News* (www.adn.com) and the *Anchorage Press* (www.anchoragepress.com), a free weekly newspaper available in racks all over town.

Anchorage has joined many other American cities by banning smoking in bars and virtually all other indoor places. Bars in Anchorage are typically open until 2am.

Bars and Clubs

Anchorage is a *Cheers*-type town, with lots of corner bars and local pubs tucked away. Downtown, a popular place is **F Street Station** (4th Ave. and F St., 907/272-5196, 9am-11pm daily), which also serves good-value lunches and dinners. And did I mention the cheese? You'll just have to see it for yourself.

Darwin's Theory (426 G St., 907/277-5322, 10am-2am daily) attracts a fun after-work crowd in a tiny dive-bar setting. There is free hot pepper schnapps—if you can stomach it—when the bartender rings the bell (quite often some evenings). You'll also appreciate the golden-oldies jukebox and free popcorn.

Popular Anchorage sports bars include **Peanut Farm** (5227 Old Seward Hwy., 907/563-3283, www.wemustbenuts.com, 6am-2:30am Sun.-Thurs., 6am-3am Fri.-Sat.), **Crossroads Lounge** (1402 Gambell St., 907/276-9014, 10am-2:30am Sun.-Thurs., 10am-3am Fri.-Sat.), and **Eddie's Sports Bar** (6300 Old Seward Hwy., 907/563-3970).

Anchorage's favorite downtown bar is **Humpy's Great Alaskan Alehouse** (610 W. 6th Ave., 907/276-2337, www.humpysalaska. com, 11am-2am Mon.-Thurs., 11am-2:30am Fri., 10am-2:30am Sat., 10am-2am Sun.). Drop by on any night of the week to rub shoulders (and arms, legs, and other body parts—it gets mighty crowded) with a hip, raucous, and youthful crowd. The bar has more than 60 craft beers on tap, the kitchen cranks out excellent pub fare, bands play Thursday-Sunday nights, and there's never a cover charge. Humpy's is a must-see place if you're staying downtown, especially if you're single.

Chilkoot Charlie's (2435 Spenard Rd., 907/272-1010, www.koots.com, 11:45am-2:30am Mon.-Thurs., 10:30am-3pm Fri.-Sat., 10:30am-2:30pm Sun.) is a ramshackle building where you can do some serious jumping up and down to real rock and roll and generally have a night of good raunchy fun. There are three separate dance floors and nine bars inside; there's even a Russian Bar with Soviet-era memorabilia. It's big enough to get lost in. The main stage has loud and very live rock, while the other dance floors are filled with folks dancing to DJ Top 40 or whatever else is hot. 'Koots is a love-it-or-hate-it sort of place; if you aren't into the cruising and pickup scene, try elsewhere. But you should at least go here to say you didn't miss the most famous place in town. 'Koots gets extremely crowded on weekend nights (cover charge), so you may have to wait quite a while to get in if you come after 10pm. You can't miss Chilkoot Charlie's: just look for the tall lighted windmill.

McGinley's Irish Pub (645 G St., 907/279-1782, www.mcginleyspub.com, 11am-10am Mon.-Thurs., 11am-late Fri.-Sat., noon-9pm Sun.) has Guinness on tap, Irish music, weekend bands, and no cover.

Several Anchorage bars provide a quiet and romantic atmosphere. If you luck into a clear evening, have packed something a little dressy, and don't mind blowing two days' budget on a beer, head up to the **Crow's Nest** (939 W. 5th Ave., 907/276-6000, www.captaincook. com, 5pm-10:30pm Mon.-Sat.) atop Hotel Captain Cook—the view is worth the effort. The **Fancy Moose Lounge** (4800 Spenard Rd., 907/266-2249, www.millenniumhotels. com, 11am-midnight daily) at The Lakefront Anchorage has an upscale bar with outdoor seating overlooking the floatplane action on Lake Hood.

Breweries and Distilleries

Anchorage has an ever-growing craft beer scene, with new breweries cropping up every year. These include: **Anchorage Brewing Co.** (148 W. 91st St., 907/677-2739, www.anchoragebrewingcompany. com, 2pm-8pm Tues.-Sun.), **Broken Tooth Brewing** (2021 Spar Ave., 907/222-1560, www.brokentoothbrewing.net), **49th State Brewing Co.** (717 W. 3rd Ave., 907/277-7727, www.49thstatebrewing.com, 10:30am-1am daily mid-May-Sept., 11am-midnight daily Oct.-mid-May), **Glacier BrewHouse** (737 W. 5th Ave., 907/274-2739, www. glacierbrewhouse.com, 11am-9:30pm Sun.-Mon., 11am-10pm Tues.-Thurs., 11am-11pm Fri.-Sat.), **King Street Brewing Company** (9050 King St., 907/336-5464, www. kingstreetbrewing.com, 2pm-8pm Mon.-Thurs., noon-8pm, Fri.-Sun.), and **Midnight Sun Brewing Co.** (8111 Dimond Hook Dr., 907/344-1179, www.midnightsunbrewing. com, 11am-8pm Mon.-Fri., 10am-8pm Sat.-Sun.).

Two other Anchorage businesses craft spirits and offer tours. **Anchorage Distillery** (6310 A St., 907/561-2100, www. anchoragedistillery.com, 2pm-8pm Tues.-Sat.) is for vodka and gin lovers. **Double Shovel**

Cider Co. (502 W. 58th Ave., 907/562-1100, www.doubleshovelcider.co, 4pm-8pm Mon.-Thurs., 2pm-8pm Fri., noon-9pm Sat., 11am-7pm Sun.) makes hard cider from Alaskan apples, pears, and berries.

Many breweries provide tours and tastings at their facilities and most serve food or have adjacent food trucks. Big Swig Tours (907/268-0872, www.bigswigtours.com, $109 pp) offers very popular four-hour tours to three local breweries. You'll get lots of background information and the chance to learn from brewmasters. Other options include bike-and-brew tours ($209) and all-day train tours to Talkeetna-area breweries ($289).

Brewers Guild of Alaska (www.brewersguildofalaska.org) details the two dozen small breweries across Alaska.

Gay and Lesbian Nightlife

Mad Myrna's (530 E. 5th Ave., 907/276-9762, 4pm-2:30am Sun.-Thurs., 4pm-3am Fri.-Sat.) has drag shows on Friday, karaoke on Thursday, and DJ tunes on Friday and Saturday. It's a crazy place with a high-energy setting and free pool on Tuesday nights.

The Raven (708 E. 4th Ave., 907/276-9672) is a mellower gay bar with pool tables, dart boards, an outdoor deck, and reasonably priced drinks.

Cannabis

Alaska's legalization of marijuana in 2014 led to a plethora of retailers around Anchorage. Head (pun intended) to cannabis websites such as PotGuide (www.potguide.com) or Weed Maps (www.weedmaps.com) to find more than 20 local shops, with creative names like Cannabaska, AlaskaBuds, AK Joint, Hollyweed 907, AK Fuzzy Budz, and Arctic Herbery (the first licensed shop in Alaska).

PERFORMING ARTS

Anchorage's active cultural scene centers on the downtown Alaska Center for the Performing Arts (621 W. 6th Ave., 907/263-2900, www.myalaskacenter.com, free), better known as "the PAC," short for Performing Arts Center. It's an unusual brick-and-glass building with colorful Olympic-like rings of light around the top. Inside are three auditoriums with wonderful acoustics and an array of events. The Sydney Laurence Theatre here has hourly showings of northern lights images by photographer Dave Parkhurst (www.thealaskacollection.com, 9am-9pm daily late May-Aug., $12 adults, $9 seniors and military, $7 under age 19).

Check the PAC's calendar for events throughout the year, including modern dance, ballet, Broadway musicals, comedy troupes, opera, and concerts by nationally known artists, along with winter performances by the Anchorage Concert Association (907/272-1471, www.anchorageconcerts.org), Anchorage Symphony Orchestra (907/274-8668, www.anchoragesymphony.org), the Anchorage Concert Chorus (907/274-7464, www.anchorageconcertchorus.org), and the Anchorage Opera (907/279-2557, www.anchorageopera.org).

Call 907/566-2787 for a recording of upcoming events at the PAC and elsewhere. Tickets are available at the PAC box office or through CentertTix (907/263-2787, www.centertix.net). Friday's Anchorage Daily News (www.adn.com) also lists upcoming events.

Anchorage is a city that showers appreciation on traveling musicians who come out of their way to visit the city, particularly those with a folk-rock bent. Many of Anchorage's best performances arrive courtesy of Whistling Swan Productions (www.whistlingswan.net); visit the website for upcoming shows.

For plays, check out productions by Cyrano's Theatre Company (3800 Debarr Rd., 907/274-2599, www.cyranos.org), Out North Contemporary Art House (333 W. 4th Ave., www.outnorth.org), and Anchorage Community Theatre (1133 E. 70th Ave., 907/344-4713, www.actalaska.org).

MOVIES

The downtown Alaska Center for the Performing Arts (5th Ave. and G St.) has hourly showings of northern lights images by photographer Dave Parkhurst (www.thealaskacollection.com, 9am-9pm daily late May-Aug., $12 adults, $9 seniors and military, $7 under age 19).

Bear Tooth Theatrepub (1230 W. 27th Ave., 907/276-4200, www.beartooththeatre.net, movies $4) has a winning combination: inexpensive second-run and art-house movies, tasty light meals (including tacos, nachos, salads, burritos, and pizzas), plus brewery-fresh draft beer. It's a great place with a family atmosphere, and is run by the same geniuses that created Moose's Tooth Pub & Pizzeria. You can eat downstairs and drink while watching the movie; upstairs is reserved for underage kids. The adjacent Bear Tooth Grill serves sit-down meals. Bear Tooth is a victim of its success, and parking can be a real challenge, especially on weekends. Parking spots are available just down the street, but whatever you do, don't park across the street from the theater, where a tow truck driver takes pleasure in hauling cars away.

See what's showing at local theaters by visiting www.anchoragemovies.com. Anchorage's main theater is the Century 16 (36th Ave. and A St., 907/929-3456), where all 16 theaters have stadium seating and reclining chairs. Located in the Muldoon area of northeast Anchorage, Regal Tikahtnu Stadium 16 (1102 N. Muldoon Rd., 907/338-6252) is the newest place in town, with an IMAX theater that shows special-effects movies. Other Anchorage multiplexes include Regal Cinemas Totem 8 (3131 Muldoon Rd., 907/566-3329) and Regal Dimond Center 9 (Dimond Mall, Dimond Blvd. and Old Seward Hwy., 907/566-3327).

FESTIVALS AND EVENTS

Winter is the time for Anchorage's best-known events, the Iditarod and Fur Rendezvous, but the city is certainly full of life in the summer. Check the Visit Anchorage website (www.anchorage.net) for a complete listing of events.

Summer

At noon every Wednesday and Sunday, head downtown for free Music in the Park (4th Ave. and E St., 907/279-5650, www.anchoragedowntown.org), next to the visitors center. Other events take place here most other weekday afternoons all summer.

Several times each summer, the big parking lot at Moose's Tooth Pub & Pizzeria (3300 Old Seward Hwy., 907/258-2537, www.beartooththeatre.net) becomes a stage for acclaimed bands such as Jane's Addiction, Wilco, Incubus, Modest Mouse, Portugal The Man, Cake, and Michael Franti. Check their Facebook page for upcoming events, and be sure to get tickets well in advance.

The Arctic Thunder Air Show (907/552-7469, www.arcticthunderopenhouse.com, June) at Joint Base Elmendorf-Richardson features a stunning performance by the Air Force's Thunderbirds. Shows occur in even-numbered years—2020, 2022, etc.

Three Barons Renaissance Faire (3400 E. Tudor Rd., 907/868-8012, www.3barons.org, early June) takes place at Hilltop Ski Area, and the crowd gets into the act by pelting rotten acting with rotten tomatoes.

Alaska's biggest running event is the Anchorage Mayor's Marathon & Half Marathon (www.mayorsmarathon.com, late June), which attracts a serious cadre of runners on the summer solstice. It's a qualifying race for the Boston Marathon. Visit the Anchorage Running Club's website (www.anchoragerunfest.org) for details on other Anchorage races.

On Independence Day, there's a Fourth of July parade (9th Ave. and K St., www.anchoragejuly4thcelebration.com) downtown in the morning, but when the fireworks show starts at midnight, the sky still isn't very dark!

Also in early July, the Bear Paw Festival (907/694-4702, www.bearpawfestival.org) comes to nearby Eagle River, with a classic car show, races, a chili cook-off, carnival rides, and the state's biggest parade.

Winter

In recent years, tourism to Alaska has increased in the winter months as visitors discover what Alaskans already know: that winter opens up a panoply of outdoor options. Several companies specialize in winter tours and activities; stop by the visitors center for brochures.

The **Anchorage Folk Festival** (www.anchoragefolkfestival.org, late Jan.) is a major winter diversion, with free concerts that fill two consecutive weekends at the University of Alaska Anchorage campus.

Fur Rendezvous (907/274-1177, www.furrondy.net, last weekend in Feb. and 1st weekend in Mar.) is one of the city's biggest annual events. Expect all sorts of fun activities during the 10-day-long festival, affectionately called "Fur Rondy." A carnival packs a downtown lot, and there are fireworks, snow sculpture and ice carving contests, dress balls, concerts, dog-pulling contests, the world championship sled dog race, and a very popular run-with-the-reindeer event (slightly)

modeled after the running of the bulls in Pamplona.

The one Alaskan event that always attracts national attention is the **Iditarod Trail Sled Dog Race** (starts in downtown Anchorage, 907/376-5155, www.iditarod.com, early Mar.) from Anchorage to Nome.

The **Nordic Skiing Association of Anchorage** (907/276-7609, www.anchoragenordicski.com) keeps dozens of miles of local trails groomed, and puts on such events as the 50k **Tour of Anchorage** (www.tourofanchorage.com, early Mar.). The **Alaska Ski for Women** (www.alaskaskiforwomen.org, early Feb.) on Super Bowl Sunday is the largest North American ski event for women, attracting more than 1,500 participants.

Spring Carnival and Slush Cup (Girdwood, www.alyeskaresort.com, mid-Apr.) is a wet and wild event for skiers and boarders as they try to cross a slushy pond at Alyeska Resort.

Shopping

Although big-city folks sometimes complain that Anchorage doesn't have the fancy boutiques they're accustomed to finding, it *does* have just about every other sort of place—from Costco to Nordstrom and H&M. The city is a car haven, so many of these stores are scattered in the various shopping malls that help give Anchorage its urban sprawl. Anchorage has a strict **plastic bag ban;** paper bags cost $0.10 each. Reusable cloth bags are sold in all stores.

★ ANCHORAGE MARKET AND FESTIVAL

Anchorage's finest and freshest produce can be found at the **Anchorage Market and Festival** (3rd Ave. and E St., 907/272-5634, www.anchoragemarkets.com, 10am-6pm Sat., 10am-5pm Sun. mid-May-mid-Sept.), held at

the downtown parking lot on weekends. More than 300 vendors offer local arts and crafts, a diverse mix of finger food—everything from salmon quesadillas to sweet funnel cakes—and, of course, produce. Live music and entertainment add to the allure.

There is also a smaller **Wednesday Market** (Northway Mall, 3101 Penland Blvd., 907/272-5634, 9am-4pm Wed. July-early Oct.).

MALLS

Downtown Anchorage's **5th Avenue Mall** (320 W. 5th Ave., 907/258-5535) includes two big stores—JCPenney and Nordstrom—along with Alaska's only official Apple store and several dozen storefronts on four levels.

The city's largest mall is **Dimond Center** (www.dimondcenter.com), on the south end of town at the corner of Dimond Boulevard and Old Seward Highway. It's a two-level place popular with teens, featuring H&M, Best Buy, Aerie, Forever 21, Old Navy, and many other stores, plus an indoor ice rink with skate rentals.

Tikahtnu Commons (www. tikahtnucommons.com) covers 95 acres near the junction of North Muldoon Road and the Glenn Highway. Anchor stores include Target, Best Buy, Kohl's, Lowe's, Sports Authority, and the Regal Tikahtnu Stadium Theater.

Anchorage has all the national megastores, including Walmart, Target, Fred Meyer, Costco, Lowe's, Home Depot, and Barnes & Noble.

GIFTS AND NATIVE ART

Much of downtown is given over to shops selling tourist doodads, particularly along 3rd and 4th Avenues, where you'll find everything from $2 made-in-China trinkets to $20,000 sculptures.

One of the finest places to buy Native Alaskan crafts is the out-of-the-way **Alaska Native Medical Center Craft Shop** (4315 Diplomacy Dr., 907/729-1122, www.anmc.org, 10am-2pm Mon.-Fri.). Excellent grass baskets, dolls, masks, yo-yos, and more are sold on consignment. The downtown **Anchorage Museum** (625 C St., 907/929-9200, www.anchoragemuseum.org, 9am-6pm daily May-Sept.; noon-6pm Sun., 10am-6pm Tues.-Sat., Oct.-Apr.) has a fine gift shop with quality Native arts, as does the **Alaska Native Heritage Center** (8800 Heritage Center Dr., Glenn Hwy. and Muldoon Rd., 907/330-8000 or 800/315-6608, www.alaskanative.net, 9am-5pm daily mid-May-mid-Sept.).

An unusual (and very expensive) purchase to consider is *qiviut*: caps, scarves, shawls, sweaters, or baby booties, hand-knitted by Native Alaskans from the wool of domestic musk oxen (the Musk Ox Farm is outside Palmer). Many times warmer and lighter than wool, these fine knits can be seen and salivated over at **Oomingmak Co-op** (604 H St.,

907/272-9225 or 888/360-9665, www.qiviut.com, 10am-6pm Mon.-Sat.).

The Ulu Factory (211 W. Ship Creek Ave., 907/276-3119 or 800/488-5592, www.theulufactory.com, 9am-6pm Mon.-Fri., 10am-6pm Sat.-Sun.) crafts unique Native ulu knives. The shop is very touristy, but has an interesting video on how the curved blades have been used for centuries in the Arctic. There's a free trolley from downtown to the factory.

Alaska Wild Berry Products (5225 Juneau St., 907/562-8858 or 800/280-2927, www.alaskawildberryproducts.com, 10am-9pm daily June-early Sept., 10am-8pm daily early Sept.-June) has a large chocolate factory in Midtown. This is a fun place for chocoholics; there's even a 20-foot melted-chocolate falls. Fifteen-minute tours are available, and the gift shop offers all the standard tourist souvenirs (and then some).

GALLERIES

On the **First Friday** of each month, Anchorage's art scene comes alive with openings, hors d'oeuvres, and the chance to meet regional artists at a dozen or so galleries. Check the weekly *Anchorage Press* for details.

Anchorage's premier gallery is the **International Gallery of Contemporary Art** (427 D St., 907/279-1116, www.igcaalaska.org, noon-4pm Tues.-Sun.), with something new each month from top regional artists. Also of note are **Georgia Blue Gallery** (3555 Arctic Blvd., 907/563-2787, www.georgiabluegallery.com, 11am-6pm Tues.-Sat., 11am-5pm Sat.), **2 Friends Gallery** (341 E. Benson Blvd., 907/277-0404, www.2friendsgallery.com, 11am-6pm Tues.-Fri., 10am-5pm Sat., noon-5pm Sun.), **Katie Sevigny Studio** (608 W. 4th Ave., 907/258-2787, www.katiesevignystudio.com, 10am-9pm Mon.-Sat., 11am-7pm Sun.), **Stephan Fine Arts** (939 W. 5th Ave., 907/274-5009, www.stephanfinearts.com, 10am-10pm daily) inside Hotel Captain Cook, and the jam-packed **Aurora Fine Art** (737 W. 5th Ave.,

907/274-0234, www.aurorafineart-alaska.com, 11am-6pm Mon.-Sat.).

OUTDOOR OUTFITTERS

Anchorage is a good place to stock up on outdoor gear before heading into Alaska's bush. The biggest place to shop—and one of the finest—is REI (600 E. Northern Lights Blvd., 907/272-4565, www.rei.com, 10am-8pm Mon.-Fri., 10am-6pm Sat.-Sun.), with a sparkling location in the Midtown Mall. This cooperative has knowledgeable staff that offers free clinics and talks throughout the year. You can also rent canoes, kayaks, stand-up paddleboards, tents, backpacks, sleeping bags, stoves, bear-proof containers, skis, snowshoes, and other outdoor equipment from REI.

An excellent outdoor store with a technically adept staff is Alaska Mountaineering & Hiking (2633 Spenard Rd., 907/272-1811, www.alaskamountaineering.com, 9am-7pm Mon.-Fri., 9am-6pm Sat., noon-5pm Sun.)—better known as AMH. Though much smaller than REI, AMH often has equipment that is unavailable elsewhere. This is where the hardcore climbers and backcountry skiers go.

Check the bulletin boards at AMH and REI for used gear. Across the street from AMH, Play It Again Sports (2636 Spenard Rd., 907/278-7529, www.playitagainsports.com, 10am-8pm Mon.-Fri., 10am-7pm Sat., 11am-6pm Sun.) sells used equipment of all sorts, from backpacks and tents to baseball gloves and fishing poles. They also buy used gear if you need a little cash on your way out of town.

Just up the street is Hoarding Marmot (1231 W. Northern Lights Blvd., 907/334-3333, www.hoardingmarmot.com, 10am-7pm Mon.-Sat., 10am-6pm Sun.), the best place to find gently used sleeping bags, boots, jackets, packs, rafting, bikes, and more. It's well worth a look for serious outdoors freaks. This consignment shop also provides a drop-off service for repairs of clothing, backpacks, zippers, straps, and more through The Fixed Line (907/631-1449, www.thefixedline.com).

Famous among hunters and anglers, Cabela's (155 W. 104th Ave., 907/341-3400, www.cabelas.com, 9am-9pm Mon.-Sat., 9am-7pm Sun.) is in South Anchorage. Dozens of big game heads decorate the walls, and it's the only store anywhere with a floatplane hanging from the rafters.

Downtown shoppers head to Big Ray's (320 W. 4th Ave., 907/279-2401, www.bigrays.com, 8am-8pm Mon.-Fri., 9am-6pm Sat.-Sun.) for more traditional Alaskan outdoor clothing and boots. B&J Sporting Goods (113 W. Northern Lights Blvd., 907/274-6113, www.bnjsg.com, 10am-6pm Mon.-Sat.) has two levels packed with sport and commercial fishing supplies. This is where you'll find heavy-duty clothing and equipment at fair prices.

Stewart's Photo Shop (531 W. 4th Ave., 907/272-8581, www.stewartsphoto.com, 10am-6pm Mon.-Sat., 11am-5pm Sun.) has the most complete selection of photographic equipment in the state. They also rent Canon, Nikon, Sony, and Fuji cameras and lenses, plus tripods and other equipment. It's located downtown across from the Visit Anchorage log cabin. Camera Service Center (1231 W. Northern Lights, 907/274-0055, www.camerasalaska.com, 10am-5:30pm Mon.-Fri.) is the only camera repair shop in south-central Alaska. It's also a good place for used gear if you're in the market.

BOOKS AND MUSIC

Alaska's largest independent bookstore is Title Wave Books (1360 W. Northern Lights Blvd., 907/278-9283, www.wavebooks.com, 10am-8pm Mon.-Sat., 11am-7pm Sun.). Offering a fine choice of new and used titles, this is a great hangout spot, with a literate crowd and an adjacent Kaladi Brothers shop to sip coffee and surf the web.

In Midtown, Barnes & Noble (200 E. Northern Lights Blvd., 907/279-7323, www.barnesandnoble.com, 9am-10pm Sun.-Thurs., 9am-11pm Fri.-Sat.) has a wide array of books, magazines, and CDs, plus a Starbucks.

1: Fur Rondy mushing in downtown Anchorage;
2: Anchorage farmers markets take place every summer weekend

The bright orange building that houses **Writer's Block Bookstore & Café** (3656 Spenard Rd., 907/929-2665, www. writersblockak.com, 8am-10pm Tues.-Wed., 8am-11pm Thurs.-Sat., 8am-10pm Sun.) was for many years a seedy porn shop. After lots of cleaning (and the burning of sage to assuage the past) the shop was transformed into a women-owned haven for food, coffee, live music, books, poetry, beer, and just hanging out in a chill setting.

Recreation

SUMMER
Hiking

One of the most popular hiking trails in Alaska is the 1.5-mile path to the summit of **Flattop Mountain** in Chugach State Park. The trailhead is on the southeastern edge of Anchorage, so you'll need a car to get here.

If you're apprehensive about heading out on your own, book a guided hike through **Chugach Guides Alaska** (907/744-7078, www.anchoragehikes.com). Owner-guides Ryan and Sudevi pick guests up at their hotels and head into Chugach State Park for a few hours—or all day. The trips are geared to ability: short hikes (around two hours on the ground) are $70 pp, and all-day hikes cost $150 pp. Sudevi speaks German.

The **Mountaineering Club of Alaska** (www.mtnclubak.org, membership $20) promotes safe climbing in Alaska through educational climbs, mountaineering classes, and other activities. Meetings take place at 6:30pm on the first Wednesday of each month at BP Energy Center (1014 Energy Court), and nonmembers are welcome. Members can go along on any of their frequent outings. The club maintains seven remote mountain huts (free, but basic) near glaciers in the Chugach and Talkeetna Mountains.

Biking

Anchorage has 200 miles of urban cycling and jogging trails. The city of Anchorage produces a helpful free **Anchorage Bike Map**, available at the Visit Anchorage log cabin or online (www.muni.org). It shows bike-friendly street routes and pathways. City buses all have front bike racks.

A delightfully easy ride—it's all paved—goes 11 miles from the west end of 2nd Avenue along the **Tony Knowles Coastal Trail,** past Westchester Lagoon, Earthquake Park, and Point Woronzof, and then all the way to Kincaid Park at Point Campbell, out on the western tip of the city. The **Chester Creek Trail** meets the Coastal Trail at Westchester Lagoon and takes you almost five miles to Goose Lake, where you can take a dip if you're hot. Or just bomb around to wherever the wind blows you. Note, however, that the major Anchorage arteries are not especially bike-friendly, so you may want to stick to the side streets to avoid contending with exhaust fumes and speeding pickup trucks. Biking and hiking trails abound within **Kincaid Park, Hillside Park,** and **Far North Bicentennial Park,** or you can head up **Powerline Pass Trail** inside Chugach State Park or to **Eklutna Lake** (bike rentals available on-site).

One of the newest innovations is the advent of fat-tire bikes, with outsize balloon tires for riding on snow and other soft surfaces. They're sold in local bike shops and are becoming increasingly common on winter trails throughout Alaska. Based in Anchorage, the **Arctic Bicycle Club** (907/566-0177, www. arcticbike.org) organizes races and tours and has a very helpful website.

For mountain bike rentals, head to **Downtown Bicycle Rental** (333 W. 4th Ave., 907/279-3334, www.alaska-bike-rentals.com, 10am-7pm daily May-Sept.), or two shops across from each other on L

Street: **Anchorage Bike Rentals** (440 L St., 907/746-4644, www.lifetimeadventures. net, 10am-7pm daily May-Sept.) and **Pablo's Bicycle Rentals** (415 L St., 907/277-2453, www.pablobicyclerentals.com, 10am-7pm daily May-Sept.). All three are near the Coastal Trail and rent a variety of bikes. Rentals cost $16-20 for 3 hours or $32-50 for 24 hours.

Looking for guided rides? **Alaska Trail Guides** (907/317-5707, www. alaskatrailguides.com) operates bike tours in Anchorage and Girdwood. All gear is provided and trips range from easy coastal trail rides to single-track mountain biking.

Glacier Tours

Two companies have all-day glacier and wildlife boat tours from Anchorage to glaciers in Prince William Sound (via Whittier) or Resurrection Bay (via Seward). **Phillips Tours and Cruises** (907/276-8023, www. phillipscruises.com) goes to Prince William Sound, and **Kenai Fjords Tours** (907/224-8068 or 888/478-3346, www.alaskacollection. com) and **Major Marine Tours** (907/274-7300 or 800/764-7300, www.majormarine. com) head into Resurrection Bay and Kenai Fjords National Park. Rates vary depending upon the tour destination and length; prices for all-day cruises with lunch vary, but usually run $150-200. All companies can arrange bus transport to the starting points in Seward or Whittier, or you can ride the Alaska Railroad. Also popular are the day trips from Anchorage to Portage Glacier operated by **Gray Line of Alaska** (907/264-7950 or 888/425-1737, www. graylinealaska.com, $90).

Flightseeing

The best way to get a bird's-eye view of the Anchorage area is from a bird's-eye vantage point: in an airplane. Anchorage has a large number of companies offering flightseeing. Visit the flightseeing links on www. anchorage.net for a complete listing or peruse their brochures at the downtown Log Cabin Visitors Center.

Three respected Lake Hood operations have been around for decades: **Rust's Flying Service** (907/243-1595 or 800/544-2299, www.flyrusts.com), **Regal Air** (907/243-8535, www.regal-air.com), and **Ellison Air** (907/243-1959, www.ellisonair.com). Rust's is easily the largest, with a fleet of 10 planes in Anchorage, plus another dozen in Talkeetna under their K2 Aviation subsidiary. Several smaller one-person companies are also based at Lake Hood, including **Skydance Aviation** (907/301-6118, www.skydanceaviation.com), **Wings Aero Tours** (907/441-5736, www. wingsaerotours.com), and **Trail Ridge Air** (907/248-0838, www.trailridgeair.com).

Three companies operate out of Merrill Field on the east side of Anchorage: **Spernak Airways** (907/272-9475, www.spernakair. com), **Sound Aviation** (907/229-2462, www. soundaviation.com), and **Alaska Air Service** (907/694-8687, www.flyakair.com).

Typical flights include a short half-hour flight over the Chugach Mountains ($110 pp); a 90-minute flight over the Chugach Mountains and Knik Glacier ($260 pp or $310 pp with a lake landing); a three-hour flight over Prince William Sound and Columbia Glacier ($400 pp, includes a remote water landing); a three-hour flight over Mount Denali ($425 pp); a bear-viewing flight to Redoubt Bay in Lake Clark National Park ($700 pp for a six-hour trip); plus a trip to watch the bears at Brooks Camp within Katmai National Park ($900 pp for a 10-12-hour trip).

The air taxis also feature fly-in fishing, primarily to the Susitna River area, where Rust's has rental cabins available. Charter service may be the way to go if you have a group of four or more people and a specific destination, such as a public cabin in Chugach National Forest.

Rock Climbing

Alaska Rock Gym (4840 Fairbanks St., 907/562-7265, www.alaskarockgym.com) has climbing walls, classes, a pro shop, locker rooms, and a weight room. For the real thing, most folks head south to Turnagain

Arm, which is also popular with ice climbers in the winter. Talk to folks at **Alaska Mountaineering & Hiking** (AMH, 2633 Spenard Rd., 907/272-1811, www.alaskamountaineering.com, 9am-7pm Mon.-Fri., 9am-6pm Sat., noon-5pm Sun.) or **REI** (600 E. Northern Lights Blvd., 907/272-4565, www.rei.com, 10am-8pm Mon.-Fri., 10am-6pm Sat.-Sun.) for details on other climbing options.

Paragliding

Operated by Scott Amy—a commercial pilot and former U.S. National Champion paraglider—**Skydance Paragliding** (16348 Noble Point Dr., 907/301-6118, www.skydanceparagliding.com) has tandem paragliding instruction. A three-hour adventure (30 minutes in the air) costs $200; prior experience is not required. Departure locations depend upon weather conditions, but Hatcher Pass is the most common spot. Plan to hike uphill for the takeoff. Call a week in advance to reserve.

Fishing

Although Anchorage sits along Cook Inlet, wild tides and strong winds create notoriously treacherous conditions. As a result, there are no charter-boat fishing operations out of Anchorage. A popular salmon-fishing stream, **Ship Creek,** flows right through downtown and has good runs of king salmon (late May-July) and silver salmon (Aug.-mid-Sept.). It's probably the only place where you can catch kings within sight of office highrises. But watch out for the quicksand-like mud at the mouth of the creek; it can trap unwary anglers. You can also rub shoulders with fellow anglers in midsummer at **Bird Creek,** 25 miles south of town on the Seward Highway. Rent fishing poles, waders, landing nets, and tackle boxes at **The Bait Shack** (212 W. Whitney Rd., 907/522-3474, www.thebaitshackak.com, 10am-8pm Mon.-Sat., 10am-6pm Sun.), downtown along Ship Creek. Guided fishing is also available.

To figure out where the fish are running, or what the local regulations are, contact **Alaska Fish and Game** (recorded message 907/267-2510, www.adfg.alaska.gov) or visit the downtown **Public Lands Information Center** (605 W. 4th Ave., 907/644-3678 or 866/869-6887, www.alaskacenters.gov, 9am-5pm daily late May-early Sept., 10am-5pm Tues.-Fri. early Sept.-late May) for a copy of the fishing regulations. All local air-taxi services offer guided or unguided trips to nearby rivers and lakes for world-class salmon fishing.

Rafting and Paddleboarding

Two companies lead white-water trips down wild Sixmile Creek near Hope: **Chugach Outdoor Center** (907/277-7238 or 866/277-7238, www.chugachoutdoorcenter.com) and **Nova Riverrunners** (907/745-5753 or 800/746-5753, www.novalaska.com). **Alaska Paddle Board** (907/250-4685, www.alaskapaddleboard.com) offers stand-up paddleboard lessons and tours for families and groups. Owner Karl "with a K" Mittelstadt is one of the most experienced boarders in Alaska (he was one of the first snowboarders in the state), and emphasizes safety and fun. He operates from a large van, traveling to lakes and ponds around Anchorage and along Turnagain Arm. Karl also leads more experienced stand-up paddleboarders on trips down the Portage River and riding the currents of Turnagain Arm. Rates depend upon the number of participants, but start at $70 for a two-hour semiprivate session.

Swimming

The city of Anchorage has two lakes with municipal public beaches if you're lucky enough to be in town during a hot spell. **Jewel Lake** (W. 88th Ave. at Gloralee St., off Jewel Lake Rd., www.muni.org) is on the south end of town. **Goose Lake** (3220 E. Northern Lights Blvd. at UAA Dr.) is near the University of Alaska Anchorage. Both lakes have

1: ice climbers along Turnagain Arm south of Anchorage; 2: cross-country skiing on the Tony Knowles Coastal Trail; 3: boat tour of Surprise Glacier in Prince William Sound

swimming beaches, restrooms, picnic shelters, playground equipment, bike trail access, and lifeguards on duty (noon-9pm daily late May-mid-Aug.). Unfortunately, both lakes are prone to a skin rash called swimmer's itch later in the summer (it's easily treatable with over-the-counter hydrocortisone 1 percent creams).

Anchorage is a good place to experience Alaska's love affair with Olympic-size indoor pools. There are seven to choose from, including five at the various high schools (check www.muni.org for locations and hours). Other pools are at the University of Alaska Anchorage (UAA, 907/786-1800, www.uaa. alaska.edu, $8). With its high ceiling, taut diving boards, and hard-bodied swimmers, the UAA pool is easily the finest in Alaska, and your entrance fee also provides access to the other facilities at the Wells Fargo Sports Complex, including a fine ice rink, a weight room, saunas, racquetball courts, and a gym.

Golf

There are four Anchorage-area public golf courses: Anchorage Golf Course (3651 O'Malley Rd., 907/522-3363, www. anchoragegolfcourse.com, 18 holes), on lower hillside in South Anchorage; Russian Jack Springs Course (5200 DeBarr Rd., 907/343-6992, www.muni.org, 9 holes); Tanglewood Lakes Golf Club (11801 Brayton Dr., 907/345-4600, 9 holes); and Moose Run Golf Course (27000 Arctic Valley Rd., 907/428-0056, www.mooserungolfcourse.com, 36 holes).

Spectator Sports

Anchorage has not one but two semipro baseball teams: the Anchorage Bucs (907/561-2827, www.anchoragebucs.com) and the Anchorage Glacier Pilots (907/274-3627, www.glacierpilots.com). That means there's usually a game worth watching June-early August. Past players have included such pro stars as Reggie Jackson, Dave Winfield, Mark McGwire, and Randy Johnson. Games take place at Mulcahy Stadium, near the corner of East Northern Lights Boulevard and Cordova Street.

WINTER

Contrary to popular belief, Alaska—and Anchorage in particular—does not go into hibernation for the long months of winter. Instead, many locals look forward to the cold and snow because of the wonderful outdoor activities they bring. Anchorage is a national center for cross-country skiing, dogsledding, skijoring (skiing behind a dog), hockey, and all sorts of other winter fun.

Visitors soon discover what the residents already know—the city is blessed with excellent facilities for all these activities. There are dogsled racetracks, dozens of miles of free groomed ski trails, several excellent ice rinks, and three downhill ski areas, including the state's best resort, Alyeska. Add in such events as the Iditarod, Fur Rendezvous, and the college hockey games, and it's easy to see why more and more visitors are coming to Anchorage in the winter.

Downhill Skiing and Sledding

Alpine skiers and snowboarders head 37 miles south of Anchorage to Alyeska Resort (Girdwood, 907/754-1111 or 800/880-3880, www.alyeskaresort.com) for the finest skiing to be found, and some of the deepest snow at any American resort (if global warming doesn't melt it all).

Hilltop Ski Area (Abbott Rd. near Hillside Dr., 907/346-1446, ski hotline 907/346-2167, www.hilltopskiarea.org, 3pm-8pm Mon.-Thurs., 3pm-9pm Fri., 9am-9pm Sat., 9am-5pm Sun. late Nov.-early Apr., $34 adults, $32 ages 8-18, free under age 8 with an adult) is right on the eastern edge of Anchorage and consists of a small chairlift and a rope tow. It has lights for night skiing, plus a lodge with rentals and a snack bar. Hilltop is a favorite place to learn skiing and boarding or to play around without the 45-minute drive to Alyeska. The Hillside Nordic Ski Trails are adjacent.

A bit farther afield is the nonprofit Arctic

Family Fun in Anchorage

Anchorage has plenty of family-friendly options to keep the kids entertained.

The **Anchorage Museum's Discovery Center** (page 43) is filled with a myriad of hands-on exhibits. Kids will also love the **Alaska Museum of Science and Nature** (page 50), the **Alaska Zoo** (page 50), and the **Alaska Rock Gym** (page 59). Head to **Delaney Park** (page 47) on the downtown Park Strip to visit with Star, the pet reindeer.

H2Oasis Indoor Waterpark (11030 Chelea St., 907/522-4420, www.h2oasiswaterpark. com, 10am-9pm daily late May-early Sept.; 3pm-7pm Mon., Wed., and Fri., 10am-7pm Sat.-Sun. mid-Sept.-early May, $25 ages 13 and older, $20 ages 3-12, younger children free with adult) is a cavernous indoor water park near the intersection of O'Malley Road and New Seward Highway on the south end of Anchorage. It's a fun break—especially on a dark winter day—with a wave pool, pirate ship, lazy river, body slide, and several water rides, including the roller coasterlike Master Blaster. Hot tubs are reserved for the over-16 set. Towel and swimsuit rentals are available and the food court sells snacks. There have been complaints that the rides don't always work, so ask to look around before plunking down your cash.

If your kids have a bad case of the wiggles, take them to **Get Air Anchorage** (11051 O'Malley Centre Dr., 907/891-7026, www.getairanchorage.com, noon-10pm Mon.-Fri., noon-midnight Fri.-Sat., 10am-8pm Sun., $14 for one hour) or **Shockwave Trampoline Park** (Northway Mall, 3101 Penland Parkway, 907/339-9283, www.shockwave.com, noon-9pm Mon., 2pm-9pm Tues.-Thurs., 2pm-11pm Fri., 10am-11pm Sat., 11am-8pm Sun., $15 for one hour). Both have a variety of bouncy surfaces, swings, dodgeballs, basketball dunking, climbing walls, and ball pits.

Valley (907/428-1208, www.arcticvalley.org, weekends and holidays early Nov.-mid-Apr., $40 adults, $30 ages 8-18, $20 ages 7-12, free over age 70 and under age 7). There are two chairlifts and a T-bar providing access to a wide range of slopes and conditions, and the tube park ($15) is a fun alternative. Arctic Valley is entirely run by volunteers. From Anchorage, take the Glenn Highway north to Arctic Valley Exit and continue seven miles to the ski area.

Downhill skis and snowboards can be rented from several places in Anchorage, including REI and the ski areas.

Sledders of all ages play on the steep powerline slope that cuts along the road up to **Arctic Valley,** with parents taking kids back uphill in their cars. Another great sledding hill, with a 600-foot run, is in **Centennial Park.** Popular short sledding hills are at **Kincaid Park** and **Service High School.**

Cross-Country Skiing

Any Anchorageite over the age of four seems to be involved in cross-country skiing in one form or another. The city is laced with trails that serve as summertime cycling and jogging paths and wintertime ski routes. Most of these are groomed, with set tracks for traditional cross-country skiers and a wider surface for the skate-skiing crowd. Skijorers are also often seen on the Coastal Trail in this dog-happy town (dogs aren't allowed on most ski trails).

The **Nordic Skiing Association of Anchorage** (907/276-7609, www. anchoragenordicski.com) is Alaska's largest cross-country association, and its website has all sorts of information on the sport. Pick up *The Alaska Nordic Skier* (Oct.-Apr.) at local ski shops and newsstands.

The best-known cross-country area is **Kincaid Park** (9401 Raspberry Rd.), where a convoluted maze of lighted paths covers the rolling terrain, offering fun for all ability levels. One of the top three competitive ski venues in the United States, Kincaid often hosts national meets. You can warm up inside the Kincaid chalet and enjoy the vistas of Sleeping Lady and Mount Denali.

Russian Jack Springs Park (near DeBarr Rd. and Boniface Pkwy.) has many more groomed ski trails, as well as a small rope tow and a warming house. Several more miles of lighted groomed trails await at Hillside Park (off Abbott Rd.) next to Hilltop Ski Area; watch out for the moose here. All these trails are groomed for both traditional cross-country and the faster skate skis. Rent cross-country skis from REI (600 E. Northern Lights Blvd., 907/272-4565, www.rei.com) or AMH (2633 Spenard Rd., 907/272-1811, www.alaskamountaineering.com, 9am-7pm Mon.-Fri., 9am-6pm Sat., noon-5pm Sun.).

Backcountry Skiing

If you're more ambitious—and have the wheels to get there—you'll find incredible backcountry skiing all around Anchorage. The Chugach Mountains offer an endless choice of skiing options that last from mid-October all the way into late June in some places. Note, however, that these areas are *not* for novices, so don't head out without knowing about and being prepared for such dangers as avalanches and hypothermia. Quite a number of skiers (and more snowmobilers) have died in mountain avalanches near Anchorage. Even such favorites as the nearby summit of Flattop Mountain have taken a high human toll over the years.

The best-known backcountry areas are in Chugach State Park and at Turnagain Pass and Hatcher Pass. Pick up a winter routes map for Chugach State Park (park headquarters, Mile 115, Seward Hwy., 907/345-5014, www.alaskastateparks.org) from the state park office near Potters Marsh. Turnagain Pass is 60 miles southwest of Anchorage on the way to Seward. The west side of the road is open to snowmobilers, but tele-skiers avoid them by heading to the east side. There's a big parking lot, and from here you can continue into the open meadows or high into the mountains for deep untracked powder.

Located 70 miles northeast of Anchorage, Hatcher Pass (907/745-2827) is a favorite backcountry area and serves as a training area for the U.S. National Cross-Country Ski Team. The road can sometimes be a bit treacherous if you don't have studded tires, so be sure to call the park for road conditions. Just downhill from Hatcher Pass, Government Peak Recreation Area (907/746-8757, www.matsutrails.org) has outstanding trails groomed for skate and classic skiers.

Ice Skating and Hockey

Anchorage is wild about ice skating and hockey. The UAA Seawolves (907/786-1293, www.uaa.alaska.edu) attract crowds all season. Four indoor rinks are open year-round and offer skate rentals as well as instruction: Ben Boeke Ice Arena (334 E. 16th Ave., 907/274-5715, www.benboeke.com) in the Sullivan Arena, which features an Olympic-size hockey rink; Dempsey Anderson Ice Arena (1741 W. Northern Lights Blvd., 907/277-7571, www.sullivanarena.com); UAA Sports Center (2801 Providence Dr., 907/786-1233); and Dimond Ice Chalet (800 E. Dimond Blvd., 907/344-1212, www.dimondicechalet.com) in the Dimond Mall.

Ice Climbing

When winter arrives, local waterfalls freeze over, creating perfect conditions for ice climbing. Anchorage has an active community of climbers, with the primary focus along Turnagain Arm between Anchorage and Girdwood. Dozens of icefalls here attract locals; visit Alaska Ice Climbing (www.alaskaiceclimbing.com) for details, or stop by REI (600 E. Northern Lights Blvd., 907/272-4565, www.rei.com, 10am-8pm Mon.-Fri., 10am-6pm Sat.-Sun.) or AMH (2633 Spenard Rd., 907/272-1811, www.alaskamountaineering.com, 9am-7pm Mon.-Fri., 9am-6pm Sat., noon-5pm Sun.). If you've never climbed before, take an ice climbing class from Girdwood-based The Ascending Path (907/783-0505, www.theascendingpath.com). In the summer, these take place on Spencer Glacier, with access by train, van, kayak, and foot!

Food

Anchorage's size and diverse population are mirrored in a wide range of places to eat, from grab-a-bite fast-food joints to high-class (and high-priced) gourmet restaurants. To reach many of the best places, you'll need a vehicle or knowledge of bus schedules, but there are several fine restaurants right downtown. Pick up the free *Local Flavor: Restaurant & Entertainment Guide* from racks around town. All Alaska restaurants and bars are smoke-free.

BREAKFAST

Looking for a great downtown breakfast? Join the throngs at the spacious ★ Snow City Café (1034 W. 4th Ave., 907/272-2489, www.snowcitycafe.com, 7am-3pm Mon.-Fri., 7am-4pm Sat.-Sun., $11-17), where meals are ample, reasonably priced, and dependably good. Breakfast and lunch items are available all day. Try the Kodiak benedict, the crabby omelet, or one of the day's breakfast specials, including plenty of healthy choices. Get here early on weekends to avoid a lengthy wait (up to an hour some mornings), or make reservations on the website. Lunchtime sandwiches—including a tasty chicken salad BLT—bring in the legal staff from nearby offices along "lawyer row." The café also has free Wi-Fi.

If you're in Midtown, head to ★ Middle Way Café (1200 W. Northern Lights Blvd., 907/272-6433, www.middlewaycafe.com, 7am-6pm Mon.-Fri., 8am-6pm Sat.-Sun., $7-13) for yummy French toast, huevos rancheros, breakfast burritos, omelets, and vegan specials in a bright and colorful setting. The café is also extremely popular for its great lattes, smoothies, and lunches (sandwiches, burgers, and salads) too, not to mention the free Wi-Fi. Order at the counter and take a number while you wait for the server to deliver your food. Big art decorates the wall at this trendy and spacious café next to Title Wave Books.

A little hole-in-the-wall brunch spot with a cluttered interior of Iditarod memorabilia, Granny B's Café (1201 W. Tudor Rd., 907/563-0476, 7am-3pm Tues.-Sat., 8am-3pm Sun., $8-12) serves heaping helpings of comfort food for breakfast and lunch. Homemade biscuits with sausage and gravy are popular, along with omelets, wonderful blueberry pancakes (weekends only), and lunchtime burgers. Granny B's is in Midtown. Prices are reasonable. This is a cash-only place, but an ATM is next door.

An old-time favorite, Gwennie's Old Alaska Restaurant (4333 Spenard Rd., 907/243-2090, www.gwenniesrestaurant.com, 6am-10pm Mon.-Sat., 8am-9pm Sun., breakfast $8-15) specializes in traditional American breakfasts (available all day), especially sourdough pancakes and reindeer sausage. Meals are Alaska-size, so those with small appetites may want to split an order. Memorabilia crowds the walls on this sprawling two-story greasy spoon, and the big tables fill with families.

BAKERIES AND SWEETS

Tucked into a quiet neighborhood between downtown and Midtown, ★ Fire Island Rustic Bakery (1343 G St., 907/569-0001, www.fireislandbread.com, 7am-6pm Wed.-Sun., $5-11) is Anchorage's finest bakery. It's all fantastic: the breakfast focaccia, baguette sandwiches, sweet and savory croissants, macaroons, scones, tarts, cakes, cinnamon rolls, poppy seed rolls, and unforgettable chocolate chip cookies. And yes, the breads are equally yummy, from French baguettes and whole-wheat sourdough to the Friday-only challah. Be prepared for a queue most days. Seating is limited. The success of the original Fire Island has spawned two sequels: one in East Anchorage (2530 E. 16th Ave., 907/274-0022) near UAA and another in South Anchorage (160 W. 91st Ave., 907/519-2290) in an industrial part of town. Anchorage Brewing Company is cross the parking lot, and provides spent grain for use in Fire Island breads.

Located within the 5th Avenue Mall, **Alaska Cake Studio** (320 W. 5th Ave., 907/272-3995, www.akcake.com, 9am-9pm Mon.-Sat., 11am-6pm Sun., $6-12) has sinfully decadent cakes, chocolates, ice cream, and baked goods right in the center of the downtown action. It's a dessert-lovers paradise, with picture-perfect fruit tarts, strawberry champagne cupcakes, bacon cheesecake, chocolate truffles, and tiramisu filling the cases. Daily soups, quiche, scones, coffee, and tea are also available.

COFFEE AND TEA

Anchorageites love strong coffee, and the town is packed with espresso stands and cafés—including the commonplace Starbucks versions. A personal favorite is the local chain of 11 **Kaladi Brothers** espresso shops, which includes branches inside New Sagaya (3700 Old Seward Hwy. and 900 W. 13th Ave.) grocery stores and adjacent to Title Wave Books. All have free Wi-Fi. Many other Alaskan coffee shops buy their espresso beans from Kaladi Brothers, and they even have a shop in Seattle—the heart of enemy (Starbucks) territory.

The other big roaster in Anchorage is **SteamDot Coffee Roasters** (10950 O'Malley Centre Dr., 907/344-4422, www.steamdot.com, 6am-7pm Mon.-Fri., 7am-6pm Sat.-Sun., $4-8), with a second shop in the Midtown Mall (600 E. Northern Lights Blvd.). The company features single-origin and micro-lot coffees, and the cafés are chic and spare. Baristas are skilled in creating all sorts of cappuccino-capping foam designs.

There are literally dozens of coffee shops in Anchorage, but tiny **Side Street Espresso** (412 G St., 907/258-9055, 7am-3pm Mon.-Sat., $4-8) has its own unique atmosphere. Friendly and frumpy, with a mishmash of tables and chairs, the café is decorated with the often political daily drawings of co-owner George Gee.

You'll find occasional music and monthly art shows, but no Wi-Fi, and it's cash only.

LUNCH AND QUICK MEALS

Anchorage's proliferation of fast-food eateries are scattered across town, particularly in the Midtown area. Downtown's **5th Avenue Mall** (320 W. 5th Ave., 907/258-4003, www.simon.com, 10am-9pm Mon.-Sat., 11am-6pm Sun.) is home to dozens of shops of all types. Take the elevator to the 4th floor for the food court, where fast-food eateries of all persuasions—from Thai to frozen yogurt—await. The Nordstrom store on the 2nd level has a popular café ($12-15) with lunchtime soups, salads, and paninis.

Urban Greens (304 G St., 907/276-0333, www.urbangreensak.com, 9am-3pm Mon.-Fri., $10-12) is arguably Anchorage's best sandwich shop, where the subs are made with hoagies from French Oven Bakery. Try the bootlegger club with turkey, pastrami, mortadella, and Swiss cheese. Fresh soups and a good variety of salads are also served.

Don't miss perpetually crowded **L'Aroma Bakery and Deli** (Midtown: 3700 Old Seward Hwy.; near downtown: 900 W. 13th Ave., www.newsagaya.com, $5-9) at both New Sagaya's stores, for panini sandwiches, small pizzas baked in wood-fired ovens, fresh sushi, spring rolls, salads, Chinese specials, and American "comfort food" (mac and cheese, meatloaf, and lasagna), along with freshly baked breads and sweets. You're guaranteed to find something that appeals. Eat here or get it to go.

One of Anchorage's go-to brunch spots, ★ **Middle Way Café** (1200 W. Northern Lights Blvd., 907/272-6433, www.middlewaycafe.com, 7am-6pm Mon.-Fri., 8am-6pm Sat.-Sun., $7-13) seems perpetually crowded. Look for today's specials on the board, then stand in line, order at the counter,

1: Jens' is a favorite fine dining Anchorage restaurant; 2: Middleway Café; 3: crowds at Moose's Tooth Pub and Pizzeria

take a number, and wait to be called. The big menu includes huevos rancheros, blueberry French toast, vegetarian and meat sandwiches and wraps, burgers, noodle bowls, salads, fruit smoothies, and daily specials. The barista will craft a mocha while you wait or serve a big slice of carrot cake. The café has free Wi-Fi.

Just up the street from REI in Midtown, Spenard Roadhouse (1049 W. Northern Lights Blvd., 907/770-7623, www. spenardroadhouse.com, 11am-11pm Mon.-Fri., 9am-11pm Sat.-Sun., $10-26) is a hectic, noisy lunch and late-night place. The menu somehow blends hipster cuisine with American comfort food. Carnivores gravitate to the bacon jam burger (with cambozola cheese and grilled apple), or order rockfish and chips, spicy Thai chicken curry, or a prosciutto fig pizza. Super tots appetizers—tater tots topped with cheddar, bacon, green onions, and sour cream—are always fun, and the Roadhouse stays open late for an after-the-movie bite. Brunch (only available on weekends) includes stuffed French toast, veggie benedict, and sweet-potato crepes. The bar features house-infused vodkas and the largest whiskey selection in Alaska. There are no reservations, so you may end up waiting awhile for a table. Spenard Roadhouse is owned by the same folks who bring you Crush Bistro and Snow City Café, two of Anchorage's most-loved restaurants.

On weekends in the summer, your best downtown bet is the weekend Anchorage Market and Festival (3rd Ave. and E St., 907/272-5634, www.anchoragemarkets.com, 10am-6pm Sat.-Sun. mid-May-mid-Sept.).

Anchorage's two top burger-and-fries joints are Arctic Roadrunner (5300 Old Seward Hwy., 907/561-1245, 10:30am-9pm Mon.-Sat., under $10, cash only) and Tommy's Burger Stop (1106 W. 29th Place, 907/561-5696, www.tommysburgerstop.com, 10:30am-8pm Mon.-Fri., 11am-8pm Sat., noon-4pm Sun., $8-13). Be sure to order the homemade onion rings at either place.

Fat Ptarmigan (441 W. 5th Ave., 907/777-7710, www.fatptarmigan.com, 11am-9pm Mon.-Thurs., 11am-10pm Fri., noon-10pm Sat., noon-9pm Sun., $12-19) is a trendy downtown restaurant across from the Performing Arts Center. Wood-fired pizzas are the main attraction—notably the steak and stilton pizza—but the house-made meatball sandwiches get plenty of praise.

ETHIOPIAN

Alaska's only African restaurant, Queen of Sheba Ethiopian Restaurant (2813 Dawson St., 907/222-1010, www.queenofshebaalaska. com, 11am-7pm Wed.-Sun., $14-20) takes some getting used to if you've never eaten Ethiopian food. Meals are served on a platter-sized piece of *injera,* a wonderfully spongy flatbread that you dip into bowls of complicated spicy dishes. Forget about silverware; this is finger food. The bare bones decor and a strip-mall location is forgettable, but the food certainly isn't. There are plenty of choices to please carnivores—notably *yebeg tibs* lamb sautéed with onions and garlic—as well as vegetarians. Try the veggie combo to sample them all. Service can be slow; no desserts or alcohol are available.

MEDITERRANEAN AND PIZZA

Anchorage has all the national pizza chains and dozens of mom-and-pop pizza joints. Pizza Olympia (2809 Spenard Rd., 907/561-5264, www.pizzaolympia.us, 11am-11pm Mon.-Fri., 3pm-11pm Sat., $15-28) is a personal favorite. Four generations of the Maroudas family run this place with authentic affection, rolling out such unique offerings as garlic and feta cheese pizzas and all the standard Greek specialties, including moussaka, shish kebabs, and *kalamarakia.*

Three excellent pizza options are Moose's Tooth Pub & Pizzeria (3300 Old Seward Hwy., 907/258-2537, www.moosestooth. net, 10:30am-11pm Mon.-Thurs., 10:30am-midnight Fri., 11am-midnight Sat., 11am-11pm Sun., $8-20), L'Aroma Bakery & Deli (Midtown: 3700 Old Seward Hwy., downtown: 900 W. 13th Ave., www.newsagaya.com,

6am-6pm daily) inside New Sagaya's grocery stores, and Fat Ptarmigan (441 W. 5th Ave., 907/777-7710, www.fatptarmigan.com, 11am-9pm Sun.-Thurs., 11am-10pm Fri.-Sat., $20) in downtown Anchorage.

Other good pizza places include Sorrento's (610 E. Fireweed Lane, 907/278-3439, www.sorrentosak.com, 3:30pm-10pm Mon.-Thurs., 3:30pm-10:30pm Fri., 2pm-10:30pm Sat., 2pm-9:30pm Sun., $18-25), with the best southern Italian food in Anchorage, and Fletcher's (Hotel Captain Cook, 5th Ave. and K St., 907/276-6000, www.captaincook.com, 11:30am-1am daily, $12-32) with small, crunchy pizzas.

A delightful Italian café and deli, Originale (400 D St., 907/868-7900, www.originaleak.com, 10am-4pm Mon.-Sat., $7-18) has a convenient downtown location that's perfect for lunch. Originale serves some of the best paninis you'll ever taste, including the Il Diavolo: salami, *coppa*, fresh mozzarella, spicy pepper sauce, and hot olive oil. Sandwiches are served with a side of homemade potato salad topped with spices and a drizzle of olive oil. The shop also features imported Italian foods and wonderful off-season-only cannoli (the café is too busy in summer to handle demand).

For delicious northern Italian dinners with an Alaskan twist, visit the small CampoBello Bistro (601 W. 36th Ave., 907/563-2040, www.campobellobistro.com, 11am-2pm and 5pm-9pm Tues.-Fri., 5pm-9pm Sat., $18-39). Located rather incongruously in a Midtown strip-mall, this authentic Italian restaurant is a relaxing and romantic spot for lunch or dinner; try the duck à l'orange or seafood crepes. Save room for the lemon-zest ice cream.

For creative Tuscany-meets-Alaska fare in the heart of town, head to Orso (737 W. 5th Ave., 907/222-3232, www.orsoalaska.com, 5pm-10pm Sun.-Thurs., 5pm-11pm Fri.-Sat., $20-38). This popular restaurant exudes energy, and the menu encompasses crispy ravioli, lamb shank, king crab corn dogs, and a calamari appetizer, along with a surprising selection of gluten-free and vegetarian dishes.

The dessert selection stars a wonderful chocolate torte with ice cream and distinctive white cheddar cheesecake. The bar serves ales from nearby Glacier BrewHouse (same owners), plus a fine choice of wines by the glass or bottle. Dinner reservations are recommended.

If you're downtown looking for a slice of pizza, stop by Flattop Pizza + Pool (600 W. 6th Ave., 907/677-7665, www.flattopbar.com, 11am-12:30am Sun.-Wed., 11am-2am Thurs.-Sat., $16-22), with the same management as ever-popular Humpy's Alehouse next door. Flattop serves Chicago-style deep dish, pizza by the slice, stone-baked subs, and pastas, and has the best pool tables in town.

THAI AND VIETNAMESE

Anchorage has a multitude of Thai restaurants—30 at last count. None of these measures up to what you'd find in Thailand, but several are well worth a visit. A longtime favorite is Thai Kitchen (3405 E. Tudor Rd., 907/561-0082, www.thaikitchenak.com, 11am-3pm and 5pm-9pm Mon.-Sat., 5pm-8pm Sun., $12-15), tucked away in a strip-mall on Tudor Road near Bragaw Street. With 100 choices on the menu, you're sure to find something to your taste, but favorites include Panang curry, Bangkok noodles, or eggplant tofu. Get there early, since it closes at 9pm, even on weekends. Service is not the strong suit, so don't expect to be pampered. The Monday-Friday lunch combo is a great deal if you're in a hurry; $11 gets you three items and rice from the big buffet.

Thai Orchid Restaurant (5905 Lake Otis Pkwy., 907/868-5226, www.thaiorchidalaska.com, 11am-3pm and 4:30pm-9pm Mon.-Fri., 5pm-9pm Sat., $11-16) has the best pad Thai and fresh spring rolls in town. The diverse menu includes many vegetarian choices.

If you've been to Thailand, think of So Thai (2602 Spenard Rd., 907/277-8424, 11am-7:30pm Wed.-Mon., $11-12) as the no-frills street version of Thai cooking. Sandwiched between a Swedish massage studio and the Enlighten cannabis shop, this hole-in-the-wall has zero pretense, but the food is authentic, cheap, spicy, and filling. Order at the counter and find a seat. There's sometimes only one person running the place, so you may have to wait.

Step inside **Pho Lena** (3311 Spenard Rd., 907/277-9777, www.pholena.com, 11am-10pm Mon.-Fri., noon-10pm Sat., 3pm-10pm Sun., $9-14) to discover a delightful family-run place serving spicy Lao, Thai, and Vietnamese dishes. The lunch specials (entrée, soup, and eggroll for $10) attract local workers. The big bowls of curry, *pho* soups, and sidewalk noodles are all good, but the peanut curry noodle soup and the papaya salad are favorites.

Anchorage's best Vietnamese restaurant is **Ray's Place** (2412 Spenard Rd., 907/279-2932, www.raysplaceak.com, 10am-3pm and 5pm-9pm Mon.-Fri., $10-17). *Pho* chicken soup, pork cold noodle salad, seafood sauté noodles, and sautéed lamb curry with vegetables are a few favorites from Ray's extensive menu. Don't come here on a weekend; Ray's is closed Saturday-Sunday.

CHINESE

Many of Anchorage's Chinese restaurants are actually run by Korean Americans, who are a large community in the city.

Charlie's Bakery (2729 C St., at Northern Lights Blvd., 907/677-7777, 11am-8:30pm Mon.-Sat., $7-19) does have breads, éclairs, and other baked goods, but they aren't the main attraction at this plain-Jane shop tucked into a Midtown strip-mall. The menu (with pictures) covers plenty of Chinese options and daily specials—from spicy Szechuan wonton soup to barbecue eel with rice—but it's the dim sum that attracts aficionados looking for a fix of crystal dumplings or barbecue pork steamed buns. Service can be slow, and there's often a wait on Saturday.

In business for more than 40 years, **Twin Dragon Mongolian Bar-B-Que** (612 E. 15th Ave., 907/276-7535, 11am-10pm daily, lunch $15, dinner $17) is a fun place to watch the chef do his thing on the giant barbecue grill. In addition to the meat and veggie stir-fry, meals include an all-you-can-eat buffet of Chinese specialties. Kids pay $1.40 per year of age; the older they are, the more they pay.

In the heart of Midtown, **Panda Chinese Restaurant** (605 E. Northern Lights Blvd., 907/272-3308, www.akpandarestaurant.com, 11am-midnight Mon.-Sat., noon-10pm Sun., $10-14) has a big Chinese menu and equally impressive fish tank. Service is fast, portions are ample, and they're open late, making this a great place for takeout. Be sure to check the board for the specials of the day; they're usually your best bargain.

Just outside Elmendorf Air Base in the Government Hill neighborhood north of downtown, **China Town** (836 E. Loop Rd., 907/274-3322 www.chinatownalaska.com, 11am-10pm Mon.-Sat., $10-15) has a popular lunch buffet ($11) that includes sushi and crab Rangoon. It's one of the few truly Chinese restaurants in town; ask for the Chinese menu for the most authentic meals. (This is where Chinese President Xi Jinping dined during his visit in 2017.)

Alaska's only Tibetan restaurant, **Yak & Yeti Himalayan Restaurant** (3301 Spenard Rd., 907/743-8078, www.yakandyetialaska.com, 5pm-9pm Wed.-Sat., $9-14) is a relaxing Midtown spot with a mix of vegetarian and meaty dishes. Kids appreciate the Lhasa *momos* (Tibetan beef dumplings), and grown-ups rave about the spicy goat curry and pork vindaloo. Yak & Yeti has a second café (1360 W. Northern Lights Blvd.), next to Tidal Wave Books.

JAPANESE AND FUSION

Don't be put off by the strip-mall setting for **Sushi & Sushi Restaurant** (3337 Fairbanks St., 907/333-9999, www.sushiandsushiak.com, 11am-10pm Mon.-Thurs., 11am-11pm Fri., noon-11pm Sat., noon-10pm Sun., $16-44). Inside, it's surprisingly upscale, with a sushi and sake bar and a big menu. House favorites include ultra-fresh sashimi, halibut tempura, and the large bento boxes. Be sure to try the tempura Oreos for dessert.

Trendy pan-Asian **Ginger** (425 W. 5th Ave., 907/929-3680, www.gingeralaska.com,

5pm-10pm Mon.-Fri., 11am-2:30pm and 5pm-10pm Sat.-Sun., $20-40) has hardwood floors, stylish black tables, and big art on the walls. The menu encompasses everything from Panang beef curry to seared duck breast; be sure to sample the spicy ahi tuna tower appetizer. Weekend brunches include breakfast tacos, baked scallops, and hoisin barbecue short-rib sandwiches. The restaurant gets quite noisy at times.

Down-home **Naruto Japanese Restaurant** (3600 Minnesota Dr., 907/278-3050, 11:30am-3:30pm and 5pm-10pm Tues.-Fri., 12:30pm-10pm Sat., 12:30pm-8:30pm Sun., $11-13) is Anchorage's best place for Japanese comfort food, especially the *tonkatsu* miso ramen, Naruto *udon,* and chicken *katsu.* Prices are very reasonable, and the service is fast and friendly.

INDIAN AND MIDDLE EASTERN

Bombay Deluxe (555 W. Northern Lights Blvd., 907/277-1200, www.bombaydeluxe.com, 11am-9pm Mon.-Fri., noon-9pm Sat.-Sun., $17-24) has an ample weekday lunch buffet ($13-16 adults, $8 children) with all the Indian standards. Try the lamb tikka masala with garlic naan.

Turkish Delight (2210 E. Northern Lights Blvd., 907/258-3434, Tues.-Fri. 11am-3pm, 4:30pm-9pm, Sat. noon-9pm, $13-28) is a colorful and atmospheric Midtown restaurant serving the only authentic Middle Eastern meals in Alaska. The menu includes flavorful vegetarian appetizers such as spinach-stuffed spanakopita and baba ghanoush with pita, along with meaty entrées, including spicy chicken kebab, shepard's stew, and lamb pirzola. Top it off with fragrant rose tea or thick Turkish coffee and pieces of honey-sweet baklava.

MEXICAN

In existence for more than 65 years, **La Cabaña** (312 E. 4th Ave., 907/272-0135, www.alaskalacabana.com, 11am-9:30pm Mon.-Thurs., 11am-10:30pm Fri., noon-10:30pm Sat., 11am-9pm Sun., $14-20) is Alaska's oldest Mexican restaurant. Fast service, good food (tacos, enchiladas, burritos, and flautas), and icy margaritas keep bringing folks back for lunch and dinner. Try the halibut fajita tacos.

Mexico in Alaska (7305 Old Seward Hwy., 907/349-1528, www.mexicoinalaska.com, 11am-9pm Tues.-Fri., noon-9pm Sat., $16-20) has been here since 1972. This is one of the more authentic south-of-the-border spots, but it's a long way out if you don't have a car. There are quite a few vegetarian offerings for non-carnivores.

When I'm looking for a fast and inexpensive meal, ★ **Taco King** (113 W. Northern Lights Blvd., 907/771-6054, www.tacokingak.com, 10am-11pm Mon.-Sat., 10am-10pm Sun., $7-10) never fails to hit the spot. This authentic Mexican taqueria serves fat burritos, tacos, tostadas, and enchiladas. A big plate of carne asada, beans, and rice is just $12. Order at the counter and then slather it up with your choice of salsas and sour cream. You'll never want to go Taco Bell after this! They deliver too. There are eight Taco King locations around Anchorage, but the original—and best—is in Midtown at the corner of Northern Lights and C Street.

On the east side of Anchorage, **El Rodeo** (385 Muldoon Rd., 907/338-5393, www.elrodeoak.com, 11am-10pm Mon.-Fri., noon-10pm Sat., noon-9pm Sun., $14-20) isn't much to look at on the outside, but inside, the Mexican food is filling and the service is friendly. Choose from house specials such as Mexican scampi, asada tacos, or steak ranchero.

ORGANIC AND VEGETARIAN

Almost all Anchorage restaurants have extensive organic and vegetarian menu choices, including Glacier BrewHouse, Middle Way Café, and most Thai restaurants.

Located at the corner of C Street and 36th Avenue in Midtown, **Natural Pantry** (3680 Barrow St., 907/770-1444, www.natural-pantry.com, 9am-9pm Mon.-Sat., $7-13) is easily Alaska's largest and most attractive natural foods grocer. In addition to overpriced groceries, supplements, and organic produce, the store houses a bakery, a salad bar, and a deli. The store is a pleasant place to hang out, with plenty of windows and a fireplace.

In the heart of Spenard, **Organic Oasis** (2610 Spenard Rd., 907/277-7882, www.organicoasis.com, 11am-7pm Mon.-Wed. and Fri.-Sat., 11am-8:30pm Thurs., noon-5pm Sun., $10-17) serves organic wraps and sandwiches, fresh-squeezed juices, smoothies, and other lunch and dinner fare. Freshly baked breads, house-made chai teas, and vegan specialties are here, but you'll also find grilled chicken salads, bacon bleu cheese burgers, and pizzas. There's a baby grand piano and live music until 8:30pm Thursday evening.

SEAFOOD

It seems that almost every Anchorage restaurant serves some type of Alaskan seafood, whether it's king crab or a simple order of fish-and-chips. Some of the best is served at fine-dining establishments.

Located on pilings over Ship Creek, **Bridge Seafood** (221 W. Ship Ave., 907/644-8300, www.bridgeseafood.com, 4pm-10pm daily May-early Sept., $30-68) has the most unusual setting of any local restaurant. It's a bright and open place where you can watch anglers catching salmon in the urban creek below. Entrées cover the spectrum from rockfish Olympia to king crab, with a few non-piscatorial items (steaks, chicken breast, and mac and cheese) and an excellent all-you-can-eat "starter bar" of unique salads, sourdough rolls, and smoked salmon spread. The restaurant is only open in the summer months, and reservations are recommended. It is owned by celebrity chef Al Levinsohn, winner of many national awards and a frequent guest on the Food Network.

Popular seafood-focused restaurant **Kinley's Restaurant & Bar** (3230 Old Seward Hwy., 907/644-8953, www.kinleysrestaurant.com, 5pm-9pm Mon., 11:30am-9pm Tues.-Thurs., 11:30am-10pm Fri., 5pm-10pm Sat., $20-36) provides an upscale dining experience. Kinley's is next door to the incredibly popular Moose's Tooth Pub & Pizzeria, providing a good dining alternative if the queue at the Tooth is too long. Start with the bacon-wrapped dates or lobster ravioli appetizers (reduced prices 4pm-6pm) before moving on to a main course of almond halibut, seared duck breast, sesame-crusted rockfish, or filet mignon. For lunch, sandwiches (including a popular halibut BLT), ahi tuna tacos, and caprese salads are featured. Choose from more than 100 beers and a wide choice of wines by the glass, but don't miss the excellent desserts, including an espresso-soaked mocha bourbon pecan torte. Reservations are recommended, especially on Friday and Saturday night.

STEAK

Anchorage's old-time steak house, ★ **Club Paris** (417 W. 5th Ave., 907/277-6332, www.clubparisrestaurant.com, 11:30am-2:30pm and 5pm-10pm Mon.-Sat., 5pm-10pm Sun., $23-43) has been an unstylish fixture on the downtown scene since 1957. The atmosphere is dark—the building once housed a mortuary—and one wall is lined with photos of the famous and infamous visitors who've eaten here over the decades. Super-tender filet mignon is the house specialty ($43 for the 14-ounce version, and worth it), but other items are somewhat cheaper, including Alaskan seafood, freshly ground burgers, sandwiches, and salads. The resident butcher cuts all meat on the premises, slicing 500 steaks every week. This is one of the few union-shop restaurants in Anchorage, and many of the staff have worked here for 15 or more years. Reservations are recommended.

BREWPUBS AND WINE BARS

Anchorage's food-and-booze scene is thriving, with a variety of options from which to choose. Right downtown, ★ **Glacier BrewHouse** (737 W. 5th Ave., 907/274-2739, www.glacierbrewhouse.com, 11am-9:30pm Sun.-Mon., 11am-10pm Tues.-Thurs.,

11am-11pm Fri.-Sat., $19-37) is a lively and noisy place that overflows most evenings; reservations are strongly recommended if you want to avoid the two-hour weekend wait. The central fireplace and open ceilings provide a relaxing but noisy setting, and you can watch hard-working chefs in the open kitchen. House dinner favorites include smoked salmon dip, herb-crusted halibut, king crab legs, seafood chowder, BrewHouse blue salads, brick-oven pizzas, and lots of gluten-free and vegetarian options. Save room for the famous chocolate peanut butter pie. The bar pours a dozen or so specialty ales made in the behind-the-glass brewery. Lunch specialties include sandwiches, salads, rotisserie chicken, baby back ribs, pizzas, and delicious bread pudding. The weekend brunch features a Bloody Mary bar, eggs benedict, biscuits and gravy, and Alaskan seafood scramble. There's free Wi-Fi too.

A few blocks away is **49th State Brewing Co.** (717 W. 3rd Ave., 907/277-7727, www.49thstatebrewing.com, 10:30am-1am daily mid-May-Sept., 11am-midnight daily Oct.-mid-May, $14-25), owned by the same folks who seem to run half the businesses around Denali National Park. The gleaming brewery sits behind big glass windows on the main level, but the best views are from the fantastic patio and rooftop deck overlooking Cook Inlet; that white triangle in the distance is Mount Denali. Featured menu choices include halibut burgers, stone-fired pizzas, yak burgers, king crab grilled cheese, seafood artichoke dip, and handmade Bavarian pretzels. The beer selection features 49th State brews such as Baked Blond Ale, White Peach Wheat, and Solstice IPA, and a multitude of Alaskan craft beers. Can't choose? Get a flight of beer samples. The brewery has a reduced late-night menu from 10pm till closing.

★ **Moose's Tooth Pub & Pizzeria** (3300 Old Seward Hwy., 907/258-2537, www. moosestooth.net, 10:30am-11pm Mon.-Thurs., 10:30am-midnight Fri., 11am-midnight Sat., 11am-11pm Sun., medium pizzas $14-25) is *the* Anchorage place for pizza and beer,

hands down. The huge parking lot fills with cars most evenings, and you're likely to endure a wait for a table—up to two hours in the summer—since they don't take reservations. (Get a slice to go if you're in a hurry, but these are only available 10:30am-2pm Mon.-Fri.) Distinctive pizzas are all made from scratch and baked in a stone oven. Crowd favorites include chipotle steak, meatball parmesan, and amazing apricot (blackened chicken, cream cheese, apricot sauce, and red peppers—it's much better than it sounds). Caesar salads and the homemade Hungarian mushroom soup are also popular. The 15 or so prize-winning beers from their Broken Tooth Brewery make the perfect accompaniment. Moose's Tooth hosts nationally known bands in the parking lot a couple of times each summer.

The same folks own the equally popular **Bear Tooth Grill** (1230 W. 27th Ave., 907/276-4200, www.beartoothgrill.net, 11am-10:30pm Mon.-Wed., 11am-11pm Thurs.-Fri., 9:30am-11pm Sat., 9:30am-10:30pm Sun., $13-20), with great food in the heart of Midtown. The brunch and dinner menu features fish tacos, burgers, Mexican platters, pasta, seafood, and salads. Alaska cod fish-and-chips ($14) are always a good choice. Locals say Bear Tooth Grill has the best margaritas in Anchorage. Give them a taste! Since reservations are not available, you may face a lengthy wait on weekends. Next door is **Bear Tooth Theatrepub & Café** (907/276-4200, www. beartooththeatre.net, 11am-10pm Sun.-Thurs., 11am-11pm Fri.-Sat., $14-24), where you can take in a $5 movie while munching on pizza and sipping a beer. Parking for both Bear Tooth venues can be a problem, but they have a parking lot a block down the street. Whatever you do, don't park across the street from the theater, where a tow truck driver takes pleasure in hauling cars away.

You'll never go wrong with a meal at tiny ★ **F Street Station** (325 F St., 907/272-5196, 9am-11pm daily, $12-21), offering reasonably priced ultra-fresh daily seafood specials, fast service, Guinness on tap, and a convivial white-collar atmosphere. Try the perfectly cooked beer-batter halibut or the New York steak and fries. Be sure to ask the bartender the story behind the huge hunk of Tillamook sharp cheddar that's always on the counter. And despite the sign, you can cut the cheese (so to speak). If I had to choose one Anchorage restaurant, this would be the place. F Street's only problem is its popularity. You'll probably end up waiting for a bit—sometimes quite a while—and sharing your table. Also, this is a bar, so it's not for kids, and big families or groups should head elsewhere. The blackboard always has some pithy statement. Last time I visited, it had this quote from Andy Rooney: "Life is like a roll of toilet paper. The closer it gets to the end, the faster it goes."

They don't make their own beer, but **Humpy's Great Alaskan Alehouse** (610 W. 6th Ave., 907/276-2337, www.humpysalaska. com, 11am-2am Mon.-Thurs., 11am-2:30am Fri., 10am-2:30am Sat., 10am-2am Sun., kitchen till midnight, $10-28) has one of Alaska's largest assortment of brews. The beers change all the time, but you'll find at least 60 on tap. Humpy's attracts a 20-something crowd with a pub menu of halibut tacos, reindeer burgers, crab legs, fish-and-chips, nachos, and other crunchy fare. Live bands play Thursday-Sunday nights in this perpetually packed, no-cover-charge hangout. There's a patio out back (with tents and heaters) for those long summer days. It's located downtown across the street from the Performing Arts Center.

The industrial setting for **Midnight Sun Brewing Co.** (8111 Dimond Hook Dr., 907/344-1179, www.midnightsunbrewing. com, 11am-8pm Mon.-Fri., 10am-8pm Sat.-Sun., $9-20) is reflected in 16 or so unusual craft beers, including the award-winning Arctic Devil Barleywine Ale. The brewery's upstairs loft serves an eclectic mix of sandwiches and salads, along with daily hot dishes such as taco Tuesdays and posole (a hearty Mexican stew) Thursdays. Midnight Sun is out of the way on the south end of Anchorage near New Seward Highway and East Dimond

Boulevard. There are free brew house tours (6pm Thurs.).

Anchorage's trendiest wine bar, **Crush Wine Bistro and Cellar** (328 G St., 907/865-9198, www.crushak.com, 11am-10pm Mon.-Thurs., 11am-midnight Fri.-Sat., $14-35) is popular with 20-somethings and has been voted one of the top 100 wine restaurants in America by *Wine Enthusiast Magazine*. It's crowded, urbane, and stylish, with a menu that includes small entrées of prosciutto-wrapped dates and a surprisingly good baked mac and cheese. More substantial dishes are also available, such as lamb tagine, filet mignon, and salmon with stir-fried veggies. Sample a flight of choice wines (3 for $15) or head to the adjacent Crush Bottle Shop for bottles to go. Dinner reservations are recommended.

FINE DINING

Anchorage's several fine-dining establishments include Italian **Orso** (737 W. 5th Ave., 907/222-3232, www.orsoalaska.com, 5pm-10pm Sun.-Thurs., 5pm-11pm Fri.-Sat., $20-38) and steak house **Club Paris** (417 W. 5th Ave., 907/277-6332, www.clubparisrestaurant. com, 11:30am-2:30pm and 5pm-10pm Mon.-Sat., 5pm-10pm Sun., $23-43). Reservations are strongly advised or required for all of the following restaurants.

In a downtown office building, **Simon & Seaforts** (420 L St., 907/274-3502, www. simonandseaforts.com, 11:30am-2:30pm and 5pm-9pm Mon.-Fri., 10am-2:30pm and 4:30pm-10pm Sat.-Sun., $20-69) has an eclectic menu, efficient service, inviting setting, and splendid Turnagain Arm vistas. Simon's serves daily fresh fish specials, Alaskan king crab, and rock salt-roasted prime rib; wonderful cracked wheat sourdough bread comes with each meal. Lunch (try the Cajun chicken fettuccine) is considerably less expensive than dinner. If you don't have reservations, head to the more relaxed bar, where the menu ($13-19) is more limited but still diverse enough to satisfy. Once in the bar, check out the collection of single-malt scotch whiskeys, said to be one of the largest in the nation. Return on a weekend for brunch; try the bourbon-pecan praline French toast or crispy cod tacos. Be sure to request a window seat when making reservations.

A far smaller and quieter place than Simon's, elegant ★ **Marx Bros. Café** (627 W. 3rd Ave., 907/278-2133, www.marxcafe. com, 5:30pm-10pm Tues.-Sat. May-Sept., 6pm-9:30pm Tues.-Thurs., 5:30pm-10pm Fri.-Sat. Oct.-Apr., $40-50) is everybody's favorite Alaskan fine-dining restaurant. There are only 14 tables, so reservations are essential; book weeks ahead of your visit to be assured of a table. Marx Bros. has been here since 1979, but the ever-changing menu remains fresh and innovative. The caesar salad—made at your table—is especially memorable, and the big wine list and good dessert selection complement the meal. A meal for two with wine, salads, and dessert will cost upward of $200.

One of Anchorage's most unique restaurants nestles in a Turnagain neighborhood. **Rustic Goat** (2800 Turnagain St., 907/334-8100, www.rusticgoatak.com, 6am-10pm Mon.-Thurs., 6am-11pm Fri., 7am-11pm Sat., 7am-10pm Sun., $15-32) is in a playful, industrial-chic, two-level building with views of the mountains from the upper-level deck seats. Downstairs, patrons grab stools along a long table where half the fun is the busy open kitchen. Rustic Goat is noisy and fun, with wood-block tables and a modern comfort food menu that includes something for everyone—from Cholula chicken pizzas and bison sliders to coffee-crusted rib-eye steaks and Rustic Goat hot pot. Appetizers include pulled-pork empanadas and halibut corn fritters. Brunch is a bit less crowded, with sourdough pancakes, shrimp and grits, and chicken-fried steak on a biscuit. Parking is very limited, so you may need to wait for a spot. Avoid the crowds by eating late; the restaurant stays open until 11pm on weekends.

In the heart of downtown, across from the Performing Arts Center, **Pangea Restaurant & Lounge** (508 W. 6th Ave., 907/222-3949, www.pangearestaurantandlounge.com, 11am-10pm Mon.-Fri., 10:30am-11pm Sat.-Sun., $24-33) serves a cultural mélange of dishes befitting the name. Pangea's small-plates menu is fine if you're not too hungry; try the surf and turf or roasted Brussels sprouts. Popular dinner entrées include roasted Peking duck, Filipino chicken adobo, and Moroccan goat tagine. Return for an unusual weekend brunch (10:30am-4pm Sat.-Sun.) of falafel benedict, chicken and waffles, or chorizo frittata. The setting is open, colorful, and inviting.

Crow's Nest (939 W. 5th Ave., 907/343-2217, www.captaincook.com, 5pm-9:30pm Mon.-Sat., last seating at 9:15pm, $36-68) sits atop the Hotel Captain Cook, 20 floors above the masses, with fine dining and prices (and a view) to match. Order off the sky-high menu and ask the sommelier for assistance in choosing a matched wine from the restaurant's 10,000-bottle wine cellar. This is one of the only places in Alaska where you can't eat in Carhartt work clothes; not only would you stand out from the rest of the crowd, but there's actually a "business casual" dress code. Reservations are strongly recommended; when booking, request a window seat. The lounge is in the center (away from the windows), with more limited views, and serves meals a bit later on Friday and Saturday nights. Crow's Nest is a bit too stodgy and old-school for my taste, but perfect for an anniversary or milestone birthday celebration.

Don't let the strip-mall setting for ★ **Jens' Restaurant** (701 W. 36th Ave., 907/561-5367, www.jensrestaurant.com, 11:30am-2pm Mon., 11:30am-11pm Tues.-Fri., 4pm-11pm Sat. Feb.-Dec., $22-50) throw you off—this is a delightful European-style bistro with an Alaskan twist. The atmosphere is art-filled, and the food is equally beautiful, from the Kodiak scallops and calamari *la piccata* to the filet mignon à la wellington. Attentive service, a nice wine list, and delectable desserts (especially the crème brûlée) complete the picture. Reservations are recommended. It's easy to spend well over $150 for two people, but you'll leave satiated and happy. You can also hang out at the raucous wine bar, which serves appetizers until 11pm. The Danish roots of Jens' show through on weekday lunches with such specialties as *frikadeller med rødkål* (pan-fried veal and port meatballs with red cabbage).

It's pretty far off the main tourist trails, but **Kincaid Grill** (6700 Jewel Lake Rd., 907/243-0507, www.kincaidgrill.com, 5pm-10pm Tues.-Sat., $34-44) is worth the detour. Telegenic owner-chef Al Levinsohn—whom you might recognize from his Food Network appearances—has created a playful setting with a wine bar and an ever-changing menu. King crab cake appetizers are a great way to start your meal, and Alaskan seafood is always available, along with cioppino, spicy lamb chops, house gumbo, and the finest toasted marshmallow s'mores you'll ever taste. The location in a corner strip-mall just down from Tastee Freeze leaves something to be desired, but the food is sumptuous. No reservations? Join the teens at Tastee Freeze for a vastly different dining experience; there are great shakes too.

GROCERIES

Carrs Safeway (www.carrsqc.com, open 24 hours daily) has nine stores scattered around Anchorage, including the Carrs Safeway in Midtown (1650 W. Northern Lights Blvd.) and a brand new flagship store in the Midtown Mall (New Seward Hwy. and Benson). Grocery prices are sometimes a bit lower at the four big **Fred Meyer** (www.fredmeyer.com, 7am-11pm daily) stores, including one at Northern Lights Boulevard and New Seward Highway. Most Carrs Safeway and Fred Meyer stores have delis, fresh sushi, salad bars, ATMs, and in-store Starbucks outlets. **Costco** (www.costco.com) has two mega-mart Anchorage stores (330 W. Dimond Blvd. and 4125 Debarr Rd.) with groceries and fast food—along with lawn furniture, TVs, and down coats. Anchorage also has two **Walmarts** (www.walmart.com, 6am-midnight daily) with full grocery sections in Midtown (3101 A St.) and South Anchorage (8900 Old Seward Hwy.).

A distinctive gourmet grocer is **New Sagaya's** (3700 Old Seward Hwy. and 900 W. 13th Ave., www.newsagaya.com, 6am-10pm Mon.-Sat., 6am-10pm Sun.), where the featured attractions include exotic produce and Asian foods, outstanding delis, L'Aroma Bakeries, Kaladi Coffee, live crab and oysters, and fresh-from-the-sea seafood.

A good place to find fresh fish, clams, crab, and other Alaskan specialties is **10th & M Seafoods** (1020 M St., 907/272-3474 or 800/770-2722, www.10thandmseafoods.com, 9am-6pm Mon.-Sat.). If you've caught your own fish, 10th & M will store your catch in their freezers for a fee. For smoked salmon, drop by **Alaska Sausage & Seafood** (2914 Arctic Blvd., 907/562-3636 or 800/798-3636, www.alaskasausage.com, 8am-6pm Mon.-Fri., 9am-3pm Sat.).

Accommodations

As might be expected in a city of nearly 300,000 people, Anchorage has a wide range of lodging options. Unfortunately, most of these also have Alaska-size prices. A good one-stop place to begin your search for local lodging is the **Visit Anchorage** website (www.anchorage.net).

Anchorage is a spread-out city, and much of the lodging recommended in this guide is in Midtown rather than downtown, making a rental car a wise investment. Parking may or may not be available at downtown locations, so ask ahead to be sure. Add a **12 percent lodging tax** to the rates listed in this guide. Most Alaskan hotels and B&Bs do not have air-conditioning. This is not usually a problem, but hotel rooms can get warm on a mid-summer day.

Be sure to make Anchorage lodging reservations far ahead for July-August. Find hundreds of Anchorage vacation rentals online at **VRBO** (www.vrbo.com), **Airbnb** (www.airbnb.com), and similar sites.

HOSTELS

Anchorage has a plethora of hostel-type accommodations that are perfect for young independent travelers or oldsters who don't mind sleeping in a bunk bed with snoring strangers.

Bent Prop Inn & Hostel Downtown (700 H St., 907/276-3635, www.bentpropinn. com/downtown, dorm $32 pp, private room $79 d, private room with bath $119 d) is *the* downtown place for budget travelers. The owners are friendly and keep a clean, well-run operation. It has the perfect location: just a few steps from the Transit Center, and downtown's many restaurants, bars, and attractions are within walking distance. The hostel houses 22 dorm rooms with 4-8 bunks in each. Several private rooms with double beds are also available, and one room has a queen bed and private bath. The hostel contains a large central kitchen, showers, laundry, TV room, sitting room, free computers, and luggage storage. Lockers are provided in each room, so bring a padlock. There is no curfew and no alcohol or drugs, but quiet time is enforced after 10pm. Note: This is a hostel, so don't expect a lot of privacy, since the walls are thin. Upgrading to a private room here makes for a better night's sleep. Parking on the street requires feeding the meters, but there are pay-to-park lots nearby. Call at least four months ahead for midsummer reservations to be sure of a space at this very popular hostel. Some folks book up to a year in advance.

Bent Prop Inn & Hostel Midtown (3104 Eide St., 907/222-5220, www.bentpropinn. com/midtown, dorm $32 pp, semi-private bunk rooms $35 pp, private apartments $144) occupies a quiet apartment building two blocks from Walmart and many other Midtown businesses. Like its downtown sister, the Midtown Bent Prop Inn has clean rooms and ultra-friendly managers who go out of their way to help guests. Each dorm-style room includes three pairs of bunk beds and access to a common kitchen, TV room, and laundry, with lockers and free computers. Alcohol and drugs are not allowed in the dorms, and quiet is enforced after 10pm. Semiprivate bunk rooms have two bunk beds in each and are a much better deal. These are actually separate apartment units, each with its own kitchen, bath, living room, and TV. More expensive—but perfect for families— are the private one-bedroom apartments, each with a queen bed and two bunks, bath, kitchen (stocked with breakfast ingredients), living room, and TV. There's plenty of free parking. Call at least four months ahead for summer reservations to be sure of a space.

Centrally located in Midtown and close to Chilkoot Charlie's, **Base Camp Anchorage** (1037 W. 26th Ave., 907/274-1252, www. basecampanchorage.com, May-Sept., dorm beds $34 pp, private room $82 d) is a good option for outdoor enthusiasts on a budget. The single private room goes fast (make reservations well in advance), but six coed or single-sex dorms each have two bunk beds. Base Camp Anchorage is clean, with an energetic vibe and all sorts of amenities: a full kitchen, three baths, bike rentals ($15 per day), laundry, guest computer, a backyard tepee, and a locked storage room where you can leave items while you travel around the state. There's even a saltwater float tank for relaxation (not recommended if you're claustrophobic). Children under 13 are not allowed.

A reasonable option is **Spenard Hostel International** (2845 W. 42nd Place, 907/248-5036, www.alaskahostel.org, dorm $37 pp, private rooms $60 d, tents $22 s or $37 d), with five dorm rooms and eight private rooms (some of these are for long-term guests only). The hostel has a kitchen (very limited fridge space), four baths, and laundry facilities. They rent mountain bikes ($15 per day) and have space for tents in the backyard. Sheets and blankets are provided. Call for reservations 2-4 weeks ahead of your visit if arriving on a midsummer weekend. There is no curfew; alcohol is allowed.

UNDER $100

Anchorage is an expensive place, and if you don't want a hostel experience, your options are limited.

In the heart of Midtown at Fireweed and C Street, **Sockeye Inn** (303 W. Fireweed Lane, 907/771-7300, www.sockeyeinn.com, rooms $79-89 d, suites $119 d) contains simple rooms with a mix of bed types (from units with double beds to those with king and twin combos), full fridges, and small TVs. Each of the three floors has 20 rooms with six baths; guests can use the communal kitchen and laundry. There are also two suites, each with a king bed, a private bath, and a full kitchen. Call several weeks ahead for midsummer reservations since the hotel fills quickly. The windows lack screens and street noise can be a problem with open windows; ask for a room away from the street.

You'll find the same owners and a similar setup at **Ingra House Hotel** (641 Ingra St., 907/278-9656, www.ingrahouse.com, $72 s or $83 d) in downtown Anchorage. Think of the Ingra as a half-step between a hostel and a hotel. This clean, three-story hotel's 40 rooms share six baths (two on each floor), and each unit contains a double bed, a full-size fridge, a TV, and a microwave. Full kitchens are on each floor, and the hotel has heated floors, laundry facilities, and free parking. Rooms are small, so this well-run budget hotel really only works for individuals or couples. The downtown neighborhood is okay, but get a room on the upper floors for security when the windows are open.

$100-200

Centrally located **Creekwood Inn** (2150 Gambell St., 907/258-6006 or 800/478-6008, www.creekwoodinn-alaska.com, $123-143 d) is a Midtown motel with a variety of reasonably priced but basic rooms. Choose from standard rooms with one queen bed, up to one-bedroom suites with kitchens that sleep four people.

If you're looking for plenty of space, the 19-unit **Anchorage Uptown Suites** (234 E. 2nd Ave., 907/279-4232, www.anchorageuptownsuites.com, $139-159 d) has one-bedroom apartments with full kitchens and big baths. German is spoken, and some units have fireplaces or whirlpool tubs. The downsides are train noise at night and the lack of an elevator (a challenge if you're dragging luggage up three flights of stairs).

Close to the airport, **Lakeshore Inn & Suites** (3009 Lakeshore Dr., 907/248-3485 or 800/770-3000, www.lakeshoremotorinn.com, $155-225 d) has affordable rates and clean rooms. Choose from standard rooms with two double beds, units with one queen, kitchenette units, and suites. Amenities include a free airport shuttle, continental breakfast, and mini fridges. Airport noise can be a problem at times.

Right in the heart of town near the railway depot, the 31-room **Anchorage Grand Hotel** (505 W. 2nd Ave., 907/929-8888 or 888/800-0640, www.anchoragegrand.com, $189-239 d) is a cozy all-suites place with friendly service, full kitchens, free parking, and a business center. A continental breakfast and newspaper are left at your door each morning. Passing trains sometimes make for noisy nights.

Close to the airport, **Microtel Inn & Suites** (5205 Northwood Dr., 907/245-5002 or 888/293-6978, www.wyndhamhotels.com, $190 d) is one of the better moderately priced options, especially if you're arriving late at night. Continental breakfast and an airport shuttle are included with the large guest rooms.

Best Western Golden Lion (1000 E. 36th Ave., 907/561-1522 or 844/791-9215, www.bestwestern.com, $190 d) is a moderately priced Midtown hotel with in-room fridges, microwaves, and larger, nicely appointed rooms. Don't expect a fancy exterior or amenities, but the location is convenient to popular restaurants (including Moose's Tooth), Barnes & Noble, and Fred Meyer. Off-season rates are often some of the most reasonable in Anchorage.

OVER $200

Inlet Tower Suites (1200 L St., 907/276-0110 or 800/544-0786, www.inlettower.com, $226-235 d, suites $280 d) is a 14-story tower atop a hill halfway between downtown and Midtown. The hotel began life as an apartment building in 1953 and was one of the few large buildings to come through the 1964 earthquake in good shape. Guest rooms are large, with great views of the mountains or Cook Inlet from higher levels. There are rooms with one or two queen beds, microwaves, and fridges, as well as king suites with a separate living room. Inlet Tower's elevators are notoriously slow, the Wi-Fi is spotty, and rooms are in need of a makeover, but this is a decent bargain for the location. Free airport or railroad transportation is included (saving a $15 taxi ride), along with an exercise facility. PubHouse Restaurant is on the premises, and it's just a block to the New Sagaya's gourmet market and deli.

It's hard to beat the location for **Copper Whale Inn** (440 L St., 907/258-7999 or 866/258-7999, www.copperwhale.com, $199 d shared bath, $229-249 d private bath, $289 suite), right on the edge of downtown with a flower-packed back patio overlooking Cook Inlet. Next door is Simon & Seaforts, one of the city's finest restaurants, and a seasonal kiosk rents bikes out front. This attractively appointed inn has two guest rooms that share a bath, while the other 13 small guest rooms have private baths. Request a room with a private balcony. A continental-style buffet breakfast is included. Pay for hotel parking ($24 per day) or take your chance with the parking meters.

A decent moderately priced hotel, **Coast International Inn** (3450 Aviation Ave., 907/243-2233 or 800/716-6199, www.coasthotels.com, rooms $199 d, suites $299-329 d) is close to Lake Hood and the airport. Hotel amenities include spacious rooms, queen or king beds, a 24-hour airport shuttle, and a walk-in freezer for fish storage. There's no elevator, so you'll need to schlep your bags up if you have a room on the second floor.

Piper's Restaurant is on the premises and the lounge is a good place to watch a game.

One of my favorite Anchorage hotels, ★ **Dimond Center Hotel** (700 E. Dimond Blvd., 907/770-5000 or 866/770-5002, www.dimondcenterhotel.com, $260 d), has a less-than-appealing location next to Walmart and the Dimond Mall on the south side of town. But inside you'll find a gorgeous lobby, custom-designed furnishings, and luxurious rooms with plush beds, large flat-screen TVs, microwaves, and fridges. Even the baths are special, with big soaking tubs and windows that swing open into the main room. A great hot breakfast is included, and the hotel has a business center and guest passes to a nearby athletic club, plus free airport shuttle.

Historic Anchorage Hotel (330 E St., 907/272-4553, www.historicanchoragehotel.com, $270 d, suites $285 d) is a classy, 26-room boutique hotel built in 1916 and now on the National Register of Historic Places. There are standard guest rooms—small in size—and spacious two-room suites. The hotel has a concierge, continental breakfast, an exercise facility, large-screen TVs, and a multilingual staff that speaks Spanish and Japanese. Parking is $10 per day.

Hotel Captain Cook (939 W. 5th Ave., 907/276-6000 or 800/843-1950, www.captaincook.com, rooms from $255 d, suites $355-725 d) occupies an entire block, with three towers and three restaurants. The hotel is owned by the family of late governor Wally Hickel, who also served as President Nixon's secretary of the interior in the 1970s. The hotel's 550 rooms follow a nautical theme (befitting the name), and the building has an old-money feeling with dark woods and lots of suits and power ties. Amenities include concierge service and a full athletic club with a hot tub, a sauna, and an indoor pool. Rooms range from standard guest rooms to junior suites up to the 19th-floor Crow's Nest suite atop tower 3. Needless to say, this is where President Obama stayed when he visited Alaska in 2015.

Anchorage's all-suites hotels are geared to

business travelers and families looking for more space who don't mind the big-box hotel atmosphere. These places typically have one room with two queen beds and a separate sitting room with a pullout sofa, plus a microwave and a fridge. All also include indoor pools, hot tubs, exercise facilities, a breakfast buffet, and shuttles to the airport and train station.

Close to the UAA campus, ★ **SpringHill Suites Anchorage University Lake** (4050 University Lake Dr., 907/751-6300 or 888/287-9400, www.marriott.com, $275 d) is an excellent option if you have a rental car. The hotel fronts on University Lake, with a big patio providing a fine view of the Chugach Mountains, and a hiking trail that skirts the shore. It's the most natural setting for any Anchorage hotel; you might even spot a beaver paddling around the lake. Rooms are modern, large, and stylish, with separate sleeping and working areas, plus fridges and microwaves. Hotel amenities include a hot breakfast, a business center, an indoor pool and whirlpool, and a fitness center. Rates are fairly reasonable—especially considering the setting and amenities—for studios with one king or two queen beds and for larger studio units. The hotel has a shuttle to the airport and downtown visitor center, but you'll need a vehicle to go anywhere else.

One of the nicest Anchorage lodging choices, **Embassy Suites** (600 E. Benson Blvd., 907/332-7000 or 800/445-8667, www.embassysuitesanchorage.com, $320 d) gets kudos for spacious upscale suites with a separate bedroom and kitchenette, friendly staff, and such amenities as a fitness center, indoor pool and hot tub, hot breakfasts, free transport, valet service, and more. It's in Midtown with a phalanx of malls in all directions.

Centrally located in Midtown and modern, **Homewood Suites** (101 W. 48th Ave., 907/762-7000 or 800/225-5466, www.hamptoninn.com, $245 d) features immaculately maintained suites with full kitchens, a hot breakfast buffet, an indoor pool and exercise facility, a free shuttle to the airport and

around town, a complimentary light dinner Monday-Thursday evenings (with wine), and laundry.

Quite a few recently built Midtown and downtown places have similar facilities and prices, including spacious modern rooms, hot breakfast buffets, indoor swimming pools, hot tubs, fridges, microwaves, exercise facilities, business centers, laundries, and a complimentary airport shuttle. All of the following offer variations on these themes with peak-season prices around $300 d: **Comfort Suites International Airport** (2919 W. International Airport Rd., 907/243-8080 or 877/424-6423, www.choicehotels.com), **Clarion Suites Downtown** (1110 W. 8th Ave., 907/222-5005 or 800/424-6423, www.choicehotels.com), **Hilton Garden Inn** (4555 Union Square Dr., 907/562-7000 or 877/214-6725, www.hilton.com), and **Hampton Inn** (4301 Credit Union Dr., 907/550-7000 or 877/214-6725, www.hamptoninn.com).

BED-AND-BREAKFASTS

Anchorage has dozens of B&Bs, including luxurious hillside homes with spectacular vistas, snug downtown places, and rent-out-the-spare-room suburban houses. An excellent starting point when looking for a local B&B is the **Anchorage Alaska B&B Association** (907/272-5909, www.anchorage-bnb.com). The website has links to 20 or so B&Bs, with location and price details. See the *Official Guide to Anchorage* (available from the visitors information center downtown or online at www.anchorage.net) for a fairly complete listing of local B&Bs, or take a look at the blizzard of B&B brochures filling visitors center racks. Online standbys such as **Airbnb** (www.airbnb.com) or **VRBO** (www.vrbo.com) are worth checking out too.

Downtown

Built in 1913, **Oscar Gill House B&B** (1355 W. 10th Ave., 907/279-1344, www.oscargill.com, $120-150 d) is a historic home facing the downtown Park Strip. Two attractive guest rooms share a bath, while the largest has its own. Guests appreciate the central location, full hot breakfasts, friendly owners, and grandma's-house atmosphere. Call well ahead, since Gill House fills fast.

Close to downtown in one of the nicer sections of Anchorage, ★ **Wildflower Inn** (1239 I St., 907/274-1239 or 877/693-1239, www.alaska-wildflower-inn.com, $159-179 d, add $20 pp for extra guests) is a charming two-story home built in the 1940s. Rooms are elegantly appointed, flowers decorate the exterior, and a delicious full breakfast is included. The Wild Iris room has a queen bed and a private bath with jetted tub, and two suites contain queen or king beds, private baths, and sitting rooms with double futons. New Sagaya's is across the street, and it's a short walk to Anchorage's finest bakery, Fire Island.

An elegant home furnished in the arts and crafts style, **Parkside Guest House** (1302 W. 10th Ave., 907/683-2290, www.parksideanchorage.com, June-mid-Sept., $260 d) has a convenient downtown location. Three guest rooms are beautifully appointed, with a continental breakfast (fresh-baked scones) and laundry. Relax in the spacious living room, where large windows face the Park Strip. The family who owns Parkside also owns famed Camp Denali and North Face Lodge within Denali National Park.

The primary attraction for **Susitna Place B&B** (727 N St., 907/274-3344, www.susitnaplace.com, $125 d shared bath, $155d private bath, $195-215 d suites, add $20 pp for extra guests) is its location on the west edge of downtown with a sweeping view of Sleeping Lady, Cook Inlet, and Mount Denali. Seven reasonably priced guest rooms are available, and two suites include private baths with jetted tubs, fireplaces, and private decks. A generous continental breakfast is provided. The B&B has a big communal area and covered parking spaces.

Arctic Fox Inn (327 E. 2nd Court, 907/274-1239 or 877/693-1239, www.arcticfoxinn.com, rooms $125-169 d, studio apartments $169 d, 1-bedroom apartments $189 d, 2-bedroom apartments $249-299 for 4 guests, additional guests $20 pp) has six guest rooms with private or shared baths, along with four remodeled apartments containing full kitchens, living rooms, and private baths. Families or couples traveling together can rent two-bedroom apartments. The tri-level building has Wi-Fi, and mornings begin with a big buffet breakfast served on the middle floor and a large deck.

Beyond Downtown

Located on a lush three-acre Hillside spread, **Alaskan Frontier Gardens B&B** (7440 Alatna Ave., 907/345-6556, www.alaskafrontiergardens.com, $125 d, suites $175-225 d) is known for its spectacular gardens, Alaskan artifacts, accommodating host, big breakfasts, and friendly dogs. Amenities include private baths, TVs, and fridges. Two guest rooms are available, along with two suites with gas fireplaces. The 700-square-foot Ivory suite is larger than some apartments, and also has a jetted tub and sauna.

A beautiful tri-level on the east side of town, ★ **Alaska House of Jade B&B** (3800 Delwood Place, 907/337-3400, www.alaskahouseofjade.com, mid-May-mid-Sept., $165-189 d, add $20 pp for extra guests) contains five large and nicely appointed suites with private baths and offers gourmet Alaskan breakfasts. Hosts Krista and Zack Walker make visitors feel at home, and they have a good knowledge of local attractions.

Alaska Sundance Retreat B&B (12351 Audubon Dr., 907/522-5596, www.aksundanceretreat.com, $99 d shared bath, $129-189 d private bath, additional guests $30 pp) is located on Hillside in South Anchorage, a 20-minute drive from downtown. Eagles and moose are often seen in the yard, and the B&B has perennial and vegetable gardens, a gorgeous mountain view from the outdoor hot tub, private baths, and gourmet breakfasts. Rooms are lavishly furnished, and the executive apartment has a king bed, a queen foldout, a steam shower, private laundry, and a mini kitchen.

CAMPING

For a city this size, the camping options are limited and not all that great. The city-run **Centennial Campground** (8300 Glenn Hwy., 907/343-6986, www.muni.org, late May-early Sept., $25) has 100 spaces for tents and RVs, but no hookups. Showers leave much to be desired, and some of the people wandering around may make you uncomfortable, but the park is in the trees and has limited Wi-Fi. Take Muldoon Road south from the Glenn Highway, follow the first left onto Boundary Avenue, then take the next left onto the highway frontage road for 0.5 miles to the campground. It's a 15-minute drive from downtown Anchorage. Other than this, the closest public campgrounds are Eagle River Campground, 13 miles northeast of Anchorage, or Bird Creek Campground, 25 miles south.

Anchorage Ship Creek RV Park (150 N. Ingra St., 907/277-0877 or 800/323-5757, www.bestofalaskatravel.com, May-Sept., tents $29, RVs $29-59) is close to downtown, with well-maintained facilities, including laundry, showers, and a gift shop. Sites are jammed together, and the homeless shelter and railroad tracks are nearby, so expect noise when the train rolls past. The park is close to downtown shops and weekend markets.

Golden Nugget RV Park (4100 DeBarr Rd., 907/333-2012 or 800/449-2012, www.goldennuggetcamperpark.com, year-round, RVs $40-50, no tents) has an East Anchorage location with 215 sites, clean restrooms, showers, laundry, and Wi-Fi. Request a space on the west side of the park; the east side is primarily long-term tenants and not as well maintained. Golden Nugget is directly across the street from Costco.

Creekwood Inn (2150 Gambell St., 907/258-6006 or 800/478-6008, www.creekwoodinn-alaska.com, May-Oct., RVs $50, no tents) has a Midtown location fairly close to stores and restaurants, and offers showers, laundry, cable TV, and a freezer for your fish.

Many travelers also park RVs for free (boondocking) in the **Fred Meyer** parking lots, but check with store managers for any restrictions.

Information and Services

VISITOR INFORMATION

Start your tour of downtown at **Visit Anchorage** (4th Ave. and F St., 907/276-4118, www.anchorage.net, 8am-7pm daily mid-May-mid-Sept., 9am-4pm daily mid-Sept.-mid-May), a sod-roofed log cabin that's commonly referred to as the **Log Cabin Visitors Center.** The cabin isn't actually the main place for information; go out the back door to a more spacious visitors center, where you'll find a plethora of brochures from around the state and helpful staff. Be sure to pick up a copy of the *Official Guide to Anchorage,* which includes a downtown walking tour and an Anchorage-area driving tour, plus details on sights, attractions, activities, lodging, restaurants, and more. Free Wi-Fi is available, along with 25 or so menus from local restaurants.

For a quick one-hour introduction to the city, hop on one of the red **Anchorage City Trolley Tours** (4th Ave. and F St., 907/276-5603 or 888/917-8687, www.alaskatrolley.com, departures on the hour 9am-8pm daily May-late Sept., $20 adults, $10 ages 4-12, free under age 4). Tours begin in front of the Log Cabin Visitors Center.

Visit Anchorage also maintains two 24-hours-a-day **Airport Visitors Centers:** one near the baggage area in the **domestic terminal** and the other in the **international terminal.** They are not staffed but contain a plethora of regional brochures.

The **Department of Natural Resources Public Information Center** (550 W.

7th Ave., 12th Fl., 907/269-8700, www.alaskastateparks.org, 10am-5pm Mon.-Fri.) has helpful staff and details on state parks, public-use cabins, where to pan for gold, state land sales, and much more.

CONVENTION CENTERS

Near the Performing Arts Center are **Egan Civic and Convention Center** (555 W. 5th Ave., 907/263-2800, www.anchorageconventioncenters.com) and the beautiful **Dena'ina Civic and Convention Center** (600 W. 7th Ave., 907/263-2850, www.anchorageconventioncenters.com).

LIBRARIES

The **Z. J. Loussac Library** (3600 Denali St., 907/343-2975, www.anchoragelibrary.org, 10am-8pm Mon.-Thurs., 10am-6pm Fri.-Sat., 1pm-5pm Sun.) is a spacious facility out in Midtown. You could easily lose an afternoon just wandering among the stacks, enjoying the cozy sitting room on level 3, studying the huge relief map of the state, browsing among the paintings hanging on the walls, or just hanging out on a rainy afternoon. The library has computers with free Internet access and a café with espresso and treats.

BANKING AND POST OFFICES

As might be expected, **ATMs** can be found practically anywhere, including many grocery stores, hotels, and bars. Downtown's 5th Avenue Mall houses an ATM that provides international currency (including euros) if you're headed elsewhere, but there are no currency exchanges in the city.

The downtown **post office** (344 W. 3rd Ave., 907/279-9188, www.usps.com, 10am-5:30pm Mon.-Fri.) is near the Hilton Hotel.

MEDICAL SERVICES

Alaska's three largest hospitals are in Anchorage. Of the first two, **Alaska Regional Hospital** (2801 DeBarr Rd., 907/276-1131, www.alaskaregional.com) and **Providence Alaska Medical Center** (3200 Providence Dr., 907/562-2211, www.providence.org), Providence has a better reputation and is a nonprofit. The modern **Alaska Native Medical Center** (4315 Diplomacy Dr., 907/257-1150, www.anmc.org) is perhaps the finest facility in Alaska, but is only for Native Alaskans.

Several "doc-in-a-box" offices are scattered around Anchorage, but you're likely to see a physician's assistant rather than a doctor. Try **Urgent Care** (3410 Minnesota Dr., 907/677-9200) or **Primary Care Associates** (12350 Industry Way., 907/677-2007, www.primarycareak.com).

Getting There and Around

GETTING THERE
Air

Almost everybody who flies into Alaska from the Lower 48 lands at **Ted Stevens Anchorage International Airport** (ANC, 907/266-2525, www.anchorageairport.com), even if just to connect to other carriers to travel around the state. The airport is six miles southwest of downtown, named in honor of the U.S. senator who for decades brought home federal funds for Alaskan projects, including the airport. All this money is evident, with big windows facing the mountains and a classy design. There is free Wi-Fi here too.

If you have time to kill while waiting for a flight, head upstairs to the **observation deck** for a quiet space decorated with Native art; look for the stairs next to Starbucks. It's a great place to catch a few Z's, watch the planes come and go, or surf the web.

Visit Anchorage maintains two 24-hours-daily **Airport Visitors Centers:** one near the baggage area in the **domestic terminal** and the other in the **international terminal.** They are not staffed, but contain a plethora of regional brochures.

You can store luggage and even coolers of frozen fish at a space operated by **Huntleigh** (907/301-2007, www.huntleighusa.com).

The **People Mover bus 40** (907/343-6543, www.peoplemover.org, 7am-11pm Mon.-Fri., 9am-9pm Sat., 11am-7pm Sun., $2 adults, $1 ages 5-18 and seniors) runs from the lower level into downtown Anchorage. There's always a line of cabs ($20-25 to downtown) waiting out front as you exit the baggage claim area.

The Alaska Railroad has a terminal at the airport that is used by cruise ship companies, with passengers flying into Anchorage and riding the train to Whittier or Seward, where they disembark for their cruise to southeast Alaska (or vice versa). In addition to passengers, the airport serves as a vital link for air cargo companies. Both Federal Express and UPS have major international terminals, and hundreds of cargo flights land and refuel each week.

DOMESTIC

Many of the big domestic carriers fly into and out of Anchorage from the Lower 48, including **Alaska Airlines** (800/426-0333, www.alaskaair.com), **American** (800/433-7300, www.aa.com), **Delta** (800/221-1212, www.delta.com), **JetBlue** (800/538-2583, www.jetblue.com), **Sun Country Airlines** (800/752-1218, www.suncountry.com), and **United** (800/241-6522, www.united.com). Most of these flights arrive via Seattle, but Alaska Air also has year-round nonstop flights to Chicago, Hawaii (Honolulu, Kona, and Maui), Los Angeles, Phoenix, and Portland, with connecting service via Seattle or Portland to most Western cities and cities across the United States, plus to Costa Rica and a number of Canadian and Mexican cities. Delta flies nonstop year-round to Salt Lake

City, and United flies to San Francisco and Denver. Summer-only nonstop Anchorage flights arrive from Atlanta (Delta), Chicago (United), Dallas (American), Los Angeles (American), Houston (United), Minneapolis (Delta and Sun Country), Newark (United), Portland (JetBlue), and Seattle (JetBlue).

INTERNATIONAL

Several companies offer nonstop international service to Anchorage: **Air Canada** (888/247-2262, www.aircanada.com) from Vancouver, **Condor** (800/524-6975, www.condor.com) from Frankfurt, **Iceland Air** (800/223-5500, www.icelandair.us) from Reykjavik, and **Yakutia Airlines** (www.yakutia.aero) from Petropavlovsk-Kamchatsky in Russia. **Alaska Air** flies to destinations across Mexico (with a stop in Los Angeles or San Diego), and even as far as Costa Rica.

REGIONAL AIRLINES

Alaska's largest regional airline is **Ravn Alaska** (907/266-8394 or 800/866-8394, www.flyravn.com), with direct flights connecting Anchorage with Aniak, Bethel, Cordova, Dillingham, Fairbanks, Homer, Kenai, King Salmon, Kodiak, Kotzebue, Prudhoe Bay, St. Marys, Unalakleet, and Valdez. From these hubs, flights continue to dozens of smaller villages across the state.

Grant Aviation (907/290-3383 or 888/359-4726, www.flygrant.com) provides daily flights connecting Anchorage with Kenai.

PenAir (907/771-2500 or 800/448-4226, www.penair.com) flies from Anchorage to Cold Bay, Dillingham, King Salmon, McGrath, Pribilof Islands, and Sand Point.

Alaska Railroad

Anchorage is a major stop for the Alaska Railroad, with service north all the way to Fairbanks and south to Seward and Whittier. The **Alaska Railroad train depot** (411 W. 1st Ave., 907/265-2494 or 800/544-0552, www.alaskarailroad.com) is just down the hill from the center of Anchorage. Its daily express to Fairbanks has prices comparable to those of the tour buses but is a much more comfortable, historical, enjoyable, and leisurely ride. The *Denali Star* train (departs Anchorage 8:15am daily mid-May-mid-Sept., $171 adults, $86 children one-way to Denali, $244 adults, $122 children one-way to Fairbanks) runs from Anchorage to Denali (arriving 4pm) and Fairbanks (arriving 8pm). The train also stops in Wasilla and Talkeetna (arrives Talkeetna 11:05am, $104 adults, $52 children), where you can hop off, but you're not allowed to check any luggage to these destinations—only what you can carry on.

Take the *Coastal Classic* train (daily mid-May-mid-Sept., $108 adults, $54 children one-way) south to Seward for a fantastic over-the-top voyage across the Kenai Peninsula. The route diverges from the highway near Portage and then winds steeply into the Kenai Mountains past several glaciers. Trains depart Anchorage at 6:45am, arriving in Seward at 11:05am, and then return at 6pm, reaching Anchorage at 10:15pm. These trains also stop in Girdwood ($82 adults, $41 kids one-way), but only hand-carried baggage is allowed from there.

The Alaska Railroad also offers a luxurious way to travel: **GoldStar** double-decker train cars with glass dome ceilings that ensure incredible views along the way. Ride a premium GoldStar car from Anchorage to Denali ($314 adults, $174 children one-way), Seward ($212 adults, $124 children one-way), and Fairbanks ($441 adults, $252 children one-way). The fare for GoldStar service includes full meals from a menu, along with two alcoholic beverages per trip. For Anchorage to Denali, breakfast and lunch are included, and for Anchorage to Fairbanks, passengers are served breakfast, lunch, and dinner in the GoldStar cars.

The Anchorage-to-Whittier *Glacier Discovery* train (late May-mid-Sept., $100 adults, $50 children round-trip) departs Anchorage at 9:45am, arriving in Whittier at 12:05pm. It departs for Anchorage at 4:40pm, arriving at 9:15pm. The schedule is timed for glacier tours out of Whittier, and you can book trips through the Alaska Railroad that

include round-trip service to Whittier and a five-hour cruise to Blackstone Glacier or other destinations.

The *Glacier Discovery* train also stops at Portage, Spencer Glacier, and Grandview on these day trips from Anchorage ($125 adults, $63 children to Spencer Glacier round-trip). This is an extremely popular trip, with guided hikes and adventure activities at Spencer Glacier, plus the chance to visit the Alaska Wildlife Conservation Center at Portage.

The railroad added a special **Diesel Motor Unit (DMU)** car to *Glacier Discovery* trains. This self-propelled double-decker car is typically attached to other trains, but can also operate independently. If you're looking for the best views, be sure to reserve seats on the DMU (no extra charge) when you book your rail ticket. Contact the Alaska Railroad for details on all these options.

In the off-season, the railroad operates the **Aurora Winter Train,** which connects Anchorage with Talkeetna, Healy, Nenana, and Fairbanks. Trains operate on winter weekends in both directions, with occasional midweek service.

Buses and Vans

A number of bus companies head out from Anchorage to other parts of the state, and most will carry bikes for an extra charge. Try a Valley Transit city bus for a cheaper option ($7) if you're just heading to Palmer or Wasilla from Anchorage.

Alaska/Yukon Trails (907/888-5659, www.alaskashuttle.com, daily Apr.-Sept.) operates 7-passenger and 16-passenger vans between Anchorage and Fairbanks. From Anchorage, one-way rates are $62 to Talkeetna, $75 to Denali, or $99 to Fairbanks. Vans can stop anywhere along the highway (with advance reservations), including Wasilla, Willow/Big Lake, Trapper Creek, Byers Lake, Coal Creek Trailhead, Cantwell, and Healy. Travelers can get off the van and reboard at a later date for a $10 fee.

Park Connection (907/245-0200 or 800/266-8625, www.alaskacoach.com, daily mid-May-mid-Sept.) operates large and modern buses between Seward and Denali, but these only stop at the main towns and Princess lodges en route. From Anchorage, the one-way rates are $65 to Talkeetna, $90 to Denali, and $65 to Seward or Whittier. Children under age 11 ride for half price.

Interior Alaska Bus Line (907/883-0207 or 800/770-6652, www.interioralaskabusline.com) provides year-round service three times a week from Anchorage to Tok, continuing north to Fairbanks ($160). It does not connect Anchorage with Denali, Talkeetna, or Seward.

The Stage Line (907/868-3914, www.stagelineinhomer.com) runs year-round vans between Anchorage and Cooper Landing ($75 one-way), Soldotna ($75), and Homer ($100). Drivers can stop almost anywhere along the route to pick up or drop off passengers, but call 24 hours ahead to set this up.

Seward Bus Lines (907/563-0800 or 888/420-7788, www.sewardbuslines.net) provides year-round bus service to Seward. The 9:30am departure to Seward ($65) includes a sightseeing tour, but the 2pm departure ($50) doesn't stop en route. In Anchorage, buses stop at 1130 West International Airport Way, and can take you directly to your hotel for an extra $5. Summer-only service is also offered to Whittier ($50).

GETTING AROUND
City Buses
People Mover (907/343-6543, www.peoplemover.org, 6am-10pm Mon.-Fri., 9am-8pm Sat., 10am-6pm Sun., $2 adults, $1 ages 5-18 and seniors, $5 day pass), Anchorage's public bus system, covers the entire Anchorage Basin. Weekday service is extensive, with all routes operating. On Saturday, most lines run, but Sunday service is only offered on certain routes. Visit the **Transit Center** (6th Ave. and G St., 7am-6pm Mon.-Fri.) or get their mobile ticketing app for your phone. Exact fare is required, and transfers are valid only on a different bus traveling in the same direction within two hours of the time of receipt. All buses have front bike racks. A

day pass ($5)—good for unlimited rides—is sold on all buses.

All People Mover buses can transport wheelchairs, or call the **Anchor Rides** program (907/343-6543, www.muni.org) for special transportation needs. You'll need to contact them at least a day in advance.

Valley Transit (907/864-5000, www.valleytransitak.org, $7) has inexpensive commuter runs connecting Anchorage with Wasilla.

Taxis and Shuttles
There's always a line of waiting cabs outside the airport if you are just arriving and need a way into Anchorage; the fare is around $20-25 to downtown. **Alaska Yellow Cab** (907/222-2222, www.alaskayellowdispatch.com) and **Anchorage Checker Cab** (907/644-4444, www.akcheckercab.com) are the two primary companies. Both **Uber** (www.uber.com) and **Lyft** (www.lyft.com) operate in Anchorage.

Both **Shuttleman Transportation** (907/677-8537, www.shuttleman.net) and **Alaska Shuttle** (907/338-8888 www.alaskashuttle.net) provide airport van service along with door-to-door transport to other destinations throughout south-central Alaska.

Turnagain Arm Shuttle (907/764-2067, www.turnagainshuttle.com, 8am-8pm daily mid-May-mid-Sept., $69 pp) provides transportation along Turnagain Arm between downtown Anchorage and Portage Valley—a distance of 50 miles—with stops at Beluga Point, Indian Valley, Girdwood, the Alaska Wildlife Conservation Center, and Portage. Buses run hourly in the summer, departing from the downtown visitors center. You can hop on or off at any time, making this a great way to check out the sights without a car.

Car Rentals
Anchorage is car-happy, so rental cars can be very hard to come by. Make car reservations as much as two months ahead to be sure of a car in the peak season.

The airport's **Rental Car Center** (www.

dot.state.ak.us/anc) is located across from the South Terminal. A free airport shuttle bus travels between the South Terminal, North Terminal, and the Rental Car Center every 15 minutes, 24 hours a day. It's also accessible on foot via a pedestrian tunnel from the South Terminal. Most of the major companies (Alamo, Avis, Budget, Dollar, Enterprise, Hertz, National, Thrifty, and Alaska 4x4) have counters here. Note, however, that renting a car here adds an extra 29 percent tax to the rate, versus 18 percent in town. Especially for long rentals, it's usually best *not* to get a rental car from the airport.

Two local companies have off-airport car rentals with free shuttles and lower rates: **ABC Motorhome & Car Rentals** (907/279-2000 or 800/421-7456, www.abcmotorhome.com) and **GoNorth Car and RV Rentals** (907/479-7272 or 866/236-7272, www.gonorth-alaska.com).

The best at-the-airport rates are generally through **Alamo** (907/243-3255 or 888/826-6893, www.alamo.com), **National** (907/243-3255 or 877/222-9058, www.nationalcar.com), **Budget** (907/243-6492 or 800/248-0150, www.budgetalaskaonline.com), **Dollar** (907/248-5338 or 800/800-4000, www.dollar.com), and **Thrifty** (907/276-2855 or 800/334-1705, www.thrifty.com). **Alaska 4x4 Rentals** (907/290-0173, www.alaska4x4rentals.com) rents trucks, vans, SUVs, and Jeeps at the airport.

Alaska 4x4, ABC, and GoNorth let users drive on the McCarthy Road, Petersville Road, Denali Highway, and other rough gravel roads, but most other car rental operations prohibit this. Even those that allow use on these roads may tell you it's "at your own risk." In the past the requirement was often violated, but today the companies sometimes have GPS transponders in their vehicles, so they know when you've been naughty and charge a substantial penalty.

When making a reservation, be sure to mention if you have an AAA or Costco card; you can often save substantially on the rates. Don't even think of renting a car in Anchorage

and leaving it elsewhere in Alaska; the charges are sky-high for this luxury.

Winter travelers should ask for a car with studded tires, which are—surprisingly—not on many Anchorage rental cars. Your best bets are through Thrifty or Alaska Car & Van Rental. There are occasional reports of rental cars without spare tires or jacks. You don't want to discover this in the middle of nowhere, so it's always a good idea to take a check first before leaving the car rental office.

RV Rentals

Quite a few places let you rent Alaska-size RV land yachts. Recreational vehicles may be useful for larger groups, but consider their potentially disastrous environmental impact before renting them for fewer than six people—most RVs average just four miles to the gallon. The following Anchorage companies rent RVs: **Great Alaskan Holidays** (907/248-7777 or 888/225-2752, www.greatalaskanholidays.com), **Clippership Motorhome Rentals** (907/562-7051 or 800/421-3456, www.clippershiprv.com), **ABC Motorhome & Car Rentals** (907/279-2000 or 800/421-7456, www.abcmotorhome.com), **Alaska Travel Adventures** (907/789-0052 or 800/323-5757, www.alaskatraveladventures.com), and **GoNorth Car and RV Rentals** (907/479-7272 or 866/236-7272, www.gonorth-alaska.com).

Tour Buses

At least a half-dozen tour companies are happy to sell you bus tours of Anchorage and the surrounding area; get their brochures from the visitors center. The largest companies also offer a wide range of other package trips on land, sea, or air throughout Alaska: **Gray Line of Alaska** (907/277-5581 or 888/452-1737, www.graylinealaska.com) and **Princess Tours** (206/336-6000 or 800/426-0500, www.princess.com).

Boat

There are no boat tours out of Anchorage, but the city is a departure point for trips from Whittier through **Phillips Tours and Cruises** (907/276-8023, www.phillipscruises.com) and from Seward through **Kenai Fjords Tours** (907/224-8068 or 888/478-3346, www.alaskacollection.com) and **Major Marine Tours** (907/274-7300 or 800/764-7300, www.

majormarine.com). The companies offer bus or train transport options from Anchorage.

The **Alaska Marine Highway** (907/465-3941 or 800/642-0066, www.ferryalaska.com) ferry does not reach Anchorage, but you can connect up with the system in Whittier via the Alaska Railroad or in Homer by bus.

Vicinity of Anchorage

★ CHUGACH STATE PARK

Alaska's second-largest chunk of state-owned land, **Chugach State Park** (park headquarters, Mile 115, Seward Hwy., 907/345-5014, www.alaskastateparks.org) encompasses nearly half a million acres—half the size of Delaware. The park covers the entire Chugach Range from Eagle River, 25 miles north of Anchorage, to Girdwood, 35 miles south. It could take a committed hiker years to explore all of its trails, ridges, peaks, and passes. From the short but steep 1.5-mile trail up Flattop Mountain in Anchorage to the 25-mile trek from the Eagle River Nature Center over Crow Pass down to Girdwood, there are a wide range of trails to choose from, each varying in length, elevation, difficulty, access, and congestion.

Pick up hiking brochures at the Alaska Public Lands Information Center in Anchorage, decide on a trail, and then dress for rain. The clouds often sit down on these city-surrounding mountaintops, and when it's sunny and hot in Anchorage, it could be hailing only a few minutes away on the trails. But don't let that stop you. This whole park is within a few miles of where half of Alaska's population huddles, but up in these mountains it's easy to pretend you're a hundred years behind the crowds, and all the hustle and bustle on the inlet flats is far in the future.

Hillside Trails

Two trailheads on the city's southeastern outskirts give access to a network of crisscrossing and connecting trails in the section of the range that hems in Anchorage Bowl. They're all off Hillside Drive, which skirts a suburb of sparkling glass houses and gorgeous views of the skyline, inlet, and Mount Susitna to the west. City buses do not reach the park in this area, so you'll really need a vehicle (day-use parking $5) to get to the Hillside trailheads.

For the **Glen Alps Trailhead,** drive south on New Seward Highway and turn east toward the mountains on O'Malley Road. Follow it to Hillside Drive, where you turn right, then left on Upper Huffman Road. In 0.5 miles, go right again onto aptly named Toilsome Hill Drive. Toil steeply uphill for 2.5 miles to reach the Glen Alps parking lot (day-use $5). On warm summer weekends, every space in the lot fills with cars, so get here early or take the **Flattop Mountain Shuttle** (907/279-3334, www.hike-anchorage-alaska.com, daily mid-May-mid-Oct., $23 round-trip). The shuttle leaves downtown at 1pm and stays in the park for three hours before heading back for a 4:30pm return. It stops at the Alaska Zoo on the way back, where you can step off and later catch a free zoo shuttle back downtown.

Take a look from the nearby overlook, and then head up the **Flattop Mountain Trail** for even better views. This extremely popular 1.5-mile trail gains 1,500 feet and is very steep near the top as you scramble through the boulders. Look for blueberries on the lower slopes of Flattop in late summer.

Also from the Glen Alps Trailhead are several moderate and very scenic hikes: **Little O'Malley Peak,** 7.5 miles round-trip; the

Ramp and Wedge, 11 miles round-trip; and **Williwaw Lakes,** 13 miles round-trip. A great mountain bike route is the 11-mile (one-way) **Powerline Trail** that also takes off from the Glen Alps Trailhead and goes over 3,550-foot Powerline Pass all the way to the Indian Creek Trailhead on Turnagain Arm.

Continue north on Hillside Drive past Upper Huffman Road and take a right on Upper O'Malley Road. The second left leads to **Prospect Heights Trailhead,** where the **Wolverine Peak Trail** leads to the top of this 4,455-foot mountain (11 miles round-trip). You'll discover great views of the Alaska Range and Anchorage, but go in late summer when the snow has melted.

Naturalist guides from **The Ascending Path** (907/783-0505, www.theascendingpath.com) lead an array of day hikes in the Anchorage area, primarily from the Glen Alps Trailhead. A half-day hike ($129) includes round-trip van transportation from your hotel.

Eagle River Area

Take the Eagle River exit 13 miles north of Anchorage on the Glenn Highway, then your first right onto Eagle River Road, a dazzling, paved 11-mile ride right into the heart of Chugach State Park. Rafters and kayakers on the Class II Eagle River can put in at two access points (Miles 7.5 and 9) along this road. The road ends at the **Eagle River Nature Center** (907/694-2108, www.ernc.org, 10am-5pm Wed.-Sun. May-Sept., 10am-5pm Fri.-Sun. Oct.-Apr., parking $5), which features a "close-up corner" with furs and a track book, as well as an aurora display and a gift shop. Park rangers lead hikes (1pm daily June-Aug.). The **Rodak Nature Trail** (0.75 miles round-trip) is a wide gravel route with informative signs on snow, glaciers, salmon, the forest, and the seasons. It's 30 minutes well spent. For a longer walk, take the three-mile **Albert Loop Trail** along the Eagle River.

Eklutna Lake

Twenty-six miles north of Anchorage on the Glenn Highway is the exit for **Eklutna Lake,** a favorite weekend destination. Narrow and winding Eklutna Road follows the Eklutna River 10 miles to the lake, where you'll find day-use parking ($5), a picnic area, and a pleasant small **campground** ($15) with potable water and outhouses.

The 14-mile **Lakeside Trail-Eklutna Glacier Trail** starts nearby, skirting the west side of Eklutna Lake for eight nearly level miles, and then climbing to this very scenic glacier. Three side trails lead off the main route to Twin Peaks, Bold Ridge, and the East Fork of Eklutna River. This is an outstanding mountain biking area in summer, and a popular wintertime skiing and snowmobiling trail. Most of the route is also open to ATVs (Sun.-Wed.), so you may not have peace and quiet. Experienced skiers may want to continue beyond Eklutna Glacier via a multi-glacier traverse that leads 31 miles to Crow Pass. The **Mountaineering Club of Alaska** (www.mtnclubak.org) has three huts along the way.

Kayak and bike rentals are available near the Eklutna Campground from **Lifetime Adventures** (907/746-4644, www.lifetimeadventures.net), along with a popular paddle-and-pedal option: kayak across the lake and return along the trail by mountain bike ($90 pp). Two public-use cabins (www.dnr.alaska.gov/parks, $80-100) are next to the day-use area, with a third cabin on the south side of the lake (only accessible by kayak or canoe).

Also from the Eklutna exit, you can follow the access road a mile south to scenic **Thunderbird Falls** (if you're heading north from Anchorage, there's a marked Thunderbird Falls exit before you reach the Eklutna exit). The trail takes you on an easy one-mile hike up Thunderbird Creek. Follow your ears to the falls.

Crow Pass

For one of the longest and most scenic hikes in the park, head out on the 25-mile **Crow Pass Trail.** This trail (also known as the Historic Iditarod Trail) provided a turn-of-the-20th-century overland route from Seward through the Chugach to the interior gold mining town of Iditarod. The gradual climb to Crow Pass fords several streams, including the Eagle River midway along the trail. It might be wise to camp overnight and cross the river in the morning, when the glacial runoff is lower. Raven Glacier and Crystal Lake are scenic highlights near Crow Pass, where you leave Chugach State Park and continue in immense Chugach National Forest. The Forest Service's popular **Crow Pass Cabin** (518/885-3639 or 877/444-6777, www.recreation.gov, $75 plus $10 reservation fee) is an A-frame structure on the summit. From the cabin it's four miles down to the trailhead on rough Crow Creek Road, then another five miles to the Alyeska Ski Resort access road. Experienced skiers sometimes use the Iditarod and Crow Pass Trails for a winter traverse of the mountains, but be aware that avalanche danger can be very high.

Camping and Cabins

Developed state park campgrounds are found at **Eklutna Lake** ($15) and **Eagle River** (907/746-4644, www.lifetimeadventures.net, $20) north of Anchorage, and at **Bird Creek** ($20) to the south. All three have outhouses and water, and are generally open May-September. Located just off the Hiland Road exit, 12 miles north of Anchorage, is the often full Eagle River Campground; make reservations in advance.

The delightful **Yuditnu cabin** (www.dnr.alaska.gov/parks, $80) is on the shore of Eklutna Lake, and three **yurts** and an **eight-person cabin** (907/694-2108, www.ernc.org, $75) are near the Eagle River Nature Center.

NORTH OF ANCHORAGE

Chugach State Park includes several popular destinations north of Anchorage around Eklutna Lake and the Eagle River.

Arctic Valley

Six miles north of Anchorage along the Glenn Highway is the exit to Arctic Valley Road, which climbs seven steep miles to the parking lot at the Arctic Valley ski area. A trailhead about a mile before road's end leads to long **Ship Creek Trail,** which, with a little cross-country hiking, hooks up with Bird Creek and Indian Creek Trails via the passes of the same names. It's 22 miles from Arctic Valley to Indian Creek Trailhead. Plan on 2-3 days to do this traverse. From the Arctic Valley parking lot, a two-mile trail goes up to **Rendezvous Peak,** an easy hike with great views of the city, the inlet, and even Mount Denali if you're lucky.

Eklutna Historical Park

Eklutna Historical Park (907/688-6026, www.eklutnahistoricalpark.org, 10am-5pm Mon.-Sat. mid-May-mid-Sept., $5 adults, $2.50 seniors and children) is one of those surprising discoveries just off the Glenn Highway. Take the Eklutna Road exit (26 miles northeast of Anchorage) and cross back over the highway to Eklutna Village. Russian Orthodoxy is strongly overlaid on Native Alaskan culture from this point, at the site of the first Tanaina (a branch of the Athabascans) settlement on the inlet, down through the western Kenai Peninsula, Kodiak, and the Aleutians. The ancestors of most of these indigenous people were converted by Russian missionaries, and **St. Nicholas Russian Orthodox Church**—a miniature log chapel that dates from the 1830s and was reconstructed in the 1970s—is the oldest building in the Anchorage area. Nearby is a newer and larger church. Both are set against a backdrop of 80 or so colorful **spirit houses** that sit atop Native Alaskan graves. Tours may be available, or you can stroll the grounds at other times. A small gift shop sells Native Alaskan crafts and souvenirs.

TOP EXPERIENCE

★ TURNAGAIN ARM

Cook Inlet bends east from Anchorage, becoming Turnagain Arm. The inlet was named by Captain James Cook's master, William

Bligh, who later captained the ill-fated HMS *Bounty*. The Seward Highway curves around Turnagain Arm, past the town of Girdwood and the turnoff to Portage Glacier and Whittier, and finally south over the Kenai Mountains to Seward, 127 miles away. The Turnagain Arm stretch is exceptionally scenic, but traffic is often heavy, so drive carefully and keep your headlights on at all times. Many people have lost their lives in traffic accidents on this narrow highway jammed against the cliffs, so always use extreme caution. Travelers will find places to watch birds, beluga whales, Dall sheep, and rock climbers, and you can stop for hikes or to fish along the way.

Turnagain Arm Shuttle (907/764-2067, www.turnagainshuttle.com, 8am-8pm daily mid-May-mid-Sept., $69 pp) provides transportation along Turnagain Arm between downtown Anchorage and Portage, with stops at Beluga Point, Indian Valley Mine, Turnagain Art Gallery, Girdwood, the Alaska Wildlife Conservation Center, and Portage Valley. Buses run hourly in the summer, departing from the downtown Anchorage visitors center.

Potter Marsh Area

On the south end of Anchorage, wedged between the Seward Highway and hillside homes, Potter Marsh is a great spot to look for migrating and nesting birds, moose, and spawning salmon. A boardwalk extends into the marsh, providing views of Canada geese, trumpeter swans, and even the flyin'-fool arctic terns. Bring binoculars and a light jacket for the often breezy conditions. This marsh was created when the railroad builders installed an embankment to protect the track from Turnagain Arm's giant tides, which dammed the freshwater drainage from the mountains.

A mile south on the other side of the highway is the **Potter Section House** (115 Seward Hwy., 907/345-5014, 8am-4:30pm Mon.-Fri. year-round, free), a small railroad museum of interpretive displays and signs

outside and inside the restored original "section" house. This is also headquarters for Chugach State Park; get brochures on local trails here. Check out the nine-foot rotary snowplow once used to clear avalanches. A little gift shop sells railroad memorabilia and books.

Turnagain Arm Trail

Across the highway from Potter Section House is the parking lot for **Potter Creek Trailhead,** the first access to the Turnagain Arm Trail, which parallels the highway for over nine miles, with good opportunities to see Dall sheep, moose, and spruce grouse. The trail began as a turn-of-the-20th-century wagon road built to transport railroad workers and supplies. This is a very popular early summer path since its south-facing slopes lose the snow early. In three miles is **McHugh Creek,** an always-crowded day-use area and trailhead for the seven-mile hike up to **Rabbit Lake.** You can continue south along the Turnagain Arm Trail past three more trailheads all the way to **Windy Corner Trailhead,** nine miles from your starting point and not far from Beluga Point.

Beluga Point

Twenty miles south of Anchorage is Beluga Point, a good place to see the small white **beluga whales** cavorting in Turnagain Arm in late May and late August; they follow salmon into these shallow waters. Unfortunately, overhunting by Native Alaskans caused the population of belugas to plummet in the 1990s, and they still have not recovered.

Look behind you for the **Dall sheep** that often wander close to the highway in this area. Or just have a picnic and wait for the Cook Inlet's famous bore tides. The tides here, at 30 feet, are among the world's highest, and the lead breaker can be up to 6 feet high, a half mile across, and can move at over 10 miles per hour. This is the only bore tide in the United States, created when a large body of water (Cook Inlet) is forced by strong tidal action into a narrow shallow one (Turnagain Arm). Look for a series of small swells (2-3 feet high, larger depending on the wind) that crash against the rocks and send up a mighty spray. Bore tides peak when tides are largest, during the new or full moon phases. The bore tide passes Beluga Point roughly two hours after low tide in Anchorage—check the tide tables online or pick up a tide chart from local outdoor stores. One warning: **Never go out on the Turnagain Arm mudflats at any time.** The mixture of glacial silt and mud creates quicksand; people have drowned after getting their feet stuck in the mud and being inundated by the incoming tide. Don't take a chance!

When the wind is cranking, you'll see a number of kiteboarders riding the waters of Turnagain Arm near Beluga Point. To give it a try, contact Tom Fredericks of **Alaska Kite Adventures** (907/947-4775, www.alaskakiteadventures.com). Three-day lessons (12 hours total for $650, including dry suit and board) include a day on land learning the skills followed by time on the waters around Anchorage. When winter descends, Tom offers snow-kite lessons on the coastal flats and other areas around Anchorage. Check out **Kiting Alaska** (www.kitingalaska.com) for more on the sport.

Indian

Twenty-five miles south of Anchorage, and right before Turnagain House Restaurant in Indian, take a left on the gravel road and head 1.5 miles to the **Indian Valley Trailhead.** This trail, which follows Indian Creek over Indian Pass (especially rewarding during Indian summer), is five miles of easy walking on a well-maintained path. You can then continue for several miles of undeveloped hiking until you hook up with the Ship Creek Trail, which runs 22 miles to Arctic Valley north of Anchorage. The Powerline Pass Trail goes 11 miles from the Glen Alps Trailhead to Indian Creek Trail; look for the signed turnoff 100 yards up the Indian Valley Trail.

Historic **Indian Valley Mine** (Mile 104, Seward Hwy., 907/444-6898, www.indianvalleymine.com, 9am-9pm daily mid-May-mid-Sept., $1 pp) has summertime gold panning ($20 and up), historic buildings, a little museum, a gift shop, and lodging at the modern **Turnagain View Lodge** (907/444-6898, www.turnagainviewlodge.com, $189-289 d).

Bird Creek

Two miles down the highway from Indian is the Bird Creek area, where dozens of cars line the roadside on July-August afternoons. They're all here trying to hook a silver salmon in this very productive creek. A half mile north of the creek is a parking area for **Bird Ridge Trail,** which climbs straight up this 3,500-foot promontory in less than two miles.

Also nearby is the **Bird Creek Campground** (Mile 101, Seward Hwy., $20), a surprisingly pretty place just off the busy Seward Highway. Campsites are just a few feet from Cook Inlet. This thickly forested campground is often full of anglers working Bird Creek. The **Bird to Gird Bike Trail** runs right through the middle of the campground, continuing north for three miles to Indian and south three miles to Girdwood along the old highway.

TOP EXPERIENCE

GIRDWOOD

The town of Girdwood is officially part of the hectic Anchorage municipality but feels a world away. Located 37 miles south via the Seward Highway, the original town was leveled by the 1964 earthquake. A cluster of businesses stands along the highway, providing a rest stop for travelers, but Girdwood and the Alyeska Resort sit at the end of a three-mile access road (Alyeska Hwy.). The primary focus is Alyeska Resort, with a small town center (of sorts) a mile away. For many years, it

1: bore tide along Turnagain Arm south of Anchorage; 2: the annual end-of-winter Slush Cup at Alyeska Resort; 3: spirit houses at Eklutna Historical Park; 4: Crow Creek Mine in Girdwood

was a draw as a winter resort; today Girdwood is equally popular as a summer destination, with great hiking and biking trails, a fascinating mine, spectacular tram rides into the alpine, fine restaurants, and glacier landings. A free shuttle bus makes it easy to get around.

Sights

Adjacent to The Bake Shop, **Girdwood Center for Visual Arts** (194 Olympic Mountain Loop, 907/783-3209, www.gcvaonline.org, 10am-6pm daily May-Sept., 10am-5pm Thurs.-Mon. winter) is a co-op gallery with pottery, paintings, photography, glasswork, jewelry, and other locally crafted pieces. Also worth a visit is **Slack Tide Gallery** (153 Alyeska Hwy., 907/783-1860, www.alaskanrafting.com), featuring the works of regional artists.

★ CROW CREEK MINE

The gravel Crow Creek Road leads from Girdwood three miles to **Crow Creek Mine** (Crow Creek Rd., 907/229-3105, www.crowcreekmine.com, 9am-6pm daily mid-May-mid-Sept., $12 adults, $5 ages 4-12, free under age 4), one of the earliest gold strikes in Alaska (1896) and south-central Alaska's richest mine. The area was actively mined until World War II, producing over 45,000 ounces of gold. There's still a lot of gold to be found, and the creek attracts both casual panners looking for a flake of gold and those who come with metal detectors and large suction dredges. Eight of the original mine buildings have been lovingly restored by the Toohey family and are filled with all sorts of flotsam and jetsam from the past, including a classic Model A Ford truck.

Crow Creek is a great place to learn how to pan for gold ($24 adults, $20 seniors and military, $15 under age 12). You'll get a gold pan, a shovel, a bucket, a panning demonstration, and a pay dirt packet with a few flakes of gold. Crow Creek has a gift shop, sluice box rental (if you want to get serious), and overnight campsites ($10, no hookups or reservations). It's a gorgeous place with a rich history, and a

must-stop in the Girdwood area. On Monday nights in July-August, the mine puts on a delicious salmon bake with live music ($24 adults, $16 children); BYOB.

Four miles down Crow Creek Road beyond Crow Creek Mine is the **Crow Pass Trailhead.** It's an invigorating and beautiful 3.5 miles to the pass, with a 2,000-foot elevation gain. The trail is in the alpine area for much of the route and passes old mining ruins and the **Crow Pass Cabin** (518/885-3639 or 877/444-6777, www.recreation.gov, $75 plus $10 reservation fee). A half mile beyond the pass is Raven Glacier, where you enter Chugach State Park.

Entertainment and Events

NIGHTLIFE

Alyeska's après-ski party haven, **Sitzmark Bar & Grill** (Alyeska Resort, 907/754-2256, www.thesitzmark.com, noon-midnight Fri., noon-2am Sat., noon-9pm Sun. mid-May-late Sept., 11am-midnight Sun.-Thurs., 11am-2am Fri.-Sat. late Nov.-mid-Apr.) is packed and loud on winter weekends. Summers are a bit tamer, but the pub menu remains the same: burgers, dogs, fish tacos, burritos, nachos, pretzel sticks, wings, and fries. Order a pitcher of Alaskan Amber to help it go down. The bar has live music and dancing Saturday in the summer and both Friday and Saturday nights all winter.

FESTIVALS

The big summertime event is **Girdwood Forest Fair** (www.girdwoodforestfair.com, early July), an annual event for more than 40 years. Hundreds of folks show up to buy arts and crafts, graze through the food booths, and listen to bands cranking out the tunes from two separate stages. It's a three-day party that seems to attract every free-spirited hippie left in Alaska. No dogs, politicians, or religious orders are allowed.

Skiing and snowboarding events fill the winter calendar at Alyeska Resort; the most fun for spectators is the **Spring Carnival and Slush Cup** (Alyeska Hwy., 907/754-1111, www.alyeskaresort.com, late Apr.), when costumed skiers and boarders blast downhill and attempt to make it across a slushy pond. There are lots of cold, wet folks at this one.

Recreation
SUMMER

First, check out **Alyeska Resort** (Alyeska Hwy., 907/754-1111, www.alyeskaresort.com) and the impressive lobby of the enormous Hotel Alyeska. Next, catch a ride 2,300 feet up Mount Alyeska on the **aerial tramway** (907/754-2275 or 800/880-3880, www. alyeskaresort.com, $30 adults, $22 ages 13-18 and seniors, $15 ages 6-12, free under age 6). On top are two restaurants and a stupendous vista over Turnagain Arm and the surrounding mountains. The two 60-passenger tram cars are entirely wheelchair accessible. Follow the well-marked trail to the alpine overlook of Alyeska Glacier, a hanging glacier. If you have reservations to dine at Seven Glaciers Restaurant, the tram ride is free. There's also a popular tram-and-lunch special to **Bore Tide Deli** ($39, with a $20 food credit).

Roundhouse Museum (10am-7pm daily summer, 11am-3pm daily winter, free) is an elevated octagonal structure built in 1960. Located at the top of the original chairlift, it served as a warming hut for the newly opened Alyeska Ski Area. Today, the aerial tram terminates next to the Roundhouse, now operated as a small museum and gift shop with panoramic views from the windows.

The resort's **Downhill Bike Park** utilizes three chairlifts to access a maze of fast and fun bike trails. A day pass is available for the chairlifts ($45), and full-suspension bike rentals ($100 per day) are available at the day lodge. A paved path parallels the road to the Hotel Alyeska, and Crow Creek Road provides an easy dirt road for mountain bikers. The paved 13-mile **Bird to Gird Bike Trail** follows the shore of Turnagain Arm north from Girdwood.

Naturalist guides from **The Ascending Path** (907/783-0505, www.theascendingpath. com) lead an array of summertime day hikes

from their yurt office next to the base of the tram. Nature hikes are an easy introduction to the forests around Girdwood. A three-hour hike runs through the rainforest along **Winner Creek Trail** ($69 pp). The **alpine hike** ($109 pp) is more adventurous, with a tram ride up the mountain followed by a two-hour hike to small Alyeska Glacier. The seven-hour hike to **Crow Pass** ($147 pp) climbs high up this very scenic trail to Raven Glacier; it's best in late summer. One of their most popular hikes includes a ride on the Alaska Railroad to Spencer Glacier. From there, access is via a van ride and kayak across the glacial lake. Once at the glacier's edge, you learn about travel on the ice, strap on crampons and a helmet, and head out for two hours of exploration of the crevasses, ice caves, and other glacial features. The trip to **Spencer Glacier** includes guided ice climbing ($499 pp), with a similar trip without time on the ice ($389 pp). The Ascending Path also offers a number of other trips, including Anchorage-area hikes, private rock climbing trips, and even helicopter-based ice climbing adventures.

Chugach Adventures (153 Alyeska Hwy., 907/783-1860, www.alaskanrafting.com, from Anchorage $244 adults, $128 children, from Portage $200 adults, $106 children) guides a dozen different day trips and heli-adventures in the area. Their most popular is the Iceberg and Placer River Float. This trip begins with a train ride from Anchorage (or Portage) to Spencer Glacier, where you're transported by van to Spencer Lake. From there, a guided raft trip takes you through floating icebergs and seven miles down the Placer River for the train ride back to Anchorage.

Operating out of Alyeska Hotel, **Alaska Backcountry Access** (907/783-3600, www. alaskabackcountryaccess.com) leads a plethora of outdoor adventures. One of their most popular trips is a three-hour canyoneering expedition ($150 adults, $140 ages 8-12) to cliffs created by historic placer mining at Crow Creek Mine. Participants get to hike into this fascinating area and rappel next to a 50-foot waterfall. Another favorite is a sit-on-top kayaking tour that includes a jet-boat ride to Twentymile Glacier Lake (5 hours, $219 adults, $169 children) where you can paddle this remote wilderness lake. A third option is a three-hour white-water rafting trip ($135 adults, $125 children) down the Class II-III waters of Glacier Creek near Girdwood. In addition to these summer activities, Alaska Backcountry Access has a number of winter trips—from dogsled tours and snowmobiling to glacier trekking and snowshoeing—that are dependent on snow conditions.

Based at the Girdwood airstrip, **Alpine Air** (907/783-2360, www.alpineairalaska.com) has helicopter flightseeing, tours of Prince William Sound, and a very popular two-hour dog-mushing adventure ($529 adults, $499 children) that includes a landing on Punchbowl Glacier and the chance to drive a team of sled dogs. The camp is managed by the Seavey family, seven-time winners of the Iditarod. Take a quick 30-minute flight above the glaciers and mountains surrounding Girdwood ($279 pp).

WINTER

Alaska's primary center for downhill skiing and boarding, **Alyeska Resort** (Alyeska Hwy., 907/754-1111 or 800/880-3880, www.alyeskaresort.com, 10:30am-5:30pm Sun.-Wed., 10:30am-9:30pm Thurs.-Sat. winter, reduced hours early and late in the season) encompasses the ski and snowboard area, a large hotel, and several restaurants. The resort covers 1,600 skiable acres and has 76 trails, a 60-passenger tram, two high-speed detachable quad lifts, two fixed quad lifts, and two magic carpets for beginners. Most of the ski runs are at the intermediate or advanced level. In addition to abundant natural snowfall in a typical year (depths generally exceed 10 feet and the top averages 669 inches of snow annually), there is snowmaking capability on the lower slopes.

Unlike most ski areas, Alyeska's base is just a few feet above sea level and it's susceptible to a warming climate. In the past decade, rising temperatures have often brought more rain than snow at the lower levels. Fortunately, colder temperatures at higher elevations often mean that it can be drizzling at the base when it's snowing at the top of the tram 2,300 feet above. Many folks ride the tram up and stay on the upper mountain all day to avoid these warmer conditions below.

Alyeska Resort generally opens for skiing and snowboarding around Thanksgiving and closes at the end of April. Full-day weekend lift tickets cost $85 adults, $68 ages 13-18 and seniors, $43 ages 6-12, and $16 over age 70. Weekday prices are $10-20 lower, and the weekend half-day rate is $75 adults, $60 ages 13-18, and $38 ages 6-12. On Thursday-Saturday there's night skiing for no extra charge. If you just want to ride the tram to the top and don't have a lift pass, the round-trip cost is $30 adults, $22 ages 13-18 and seniors, $15 ages 6-12, free under age 6. The resort has discounted rates for multiple days, especially if you're staying at Alyeska Hotel. Skiing and snowboarding classes at all levels are available, and you can rent downhill skis and snowboards, cross-country skis, and snowshoes in the day lodge and at the hotel. The hotel also rents ice skates for the pond out back when conditions permit.

The day lodge houses a basic cafeteria, along with Java Haus for espresso and brunch. Sitzmark Bar & Grill—at the base of the mountain—is a very popular meeting place for lunch or après-ski beers, and atop the tram are Bore Tide Deli and the upscale Seven Glaciers Restaurant.

Traffic between Anchorage and Girdwood can back up on winter weekends, so head out early if you're driving. Call 907/754-7669 or visit www.alyeskaresort.com for the latest snow conditions. Hot tip: Costco stores in Anchorage often have discounted Alyeska ski and lodging passes; they're a good deal for families.

Based in Girdwood, **Chugach Powder Guides** (907/783-4354, www.chugachpowderguides.com) leads ultimate heli-skiing adventures into some of the wildest mountain country anywhere. The company also provides snowcat skiing at Alyeska Resort, accessing areas away from the groomed runs.

Cross-country skiers will find five kilometers of groomed trails in the flats around Hotel Alyeska. Get details from the **Girdwood Nordic Ski Club** (www.skigirdwood.org).

Glacier City Snowmobile Tours (907/783-5566 or 877/783-5566, www.snowtours.net, $250 pp) guides half-day trips to Spencer Glacier if the snow is deep enough. These trips include 3.5 hours of time on the machines and a chance to ride among towering icebergs. Shorter trips ($200 pp) are offered early in the winter to the Crow Creek Mine area. These trips are snow-dependent, and Alaska's rapidly warming climate means they may not be available at all some years.

Food
BREAKFAST AND LUNCH
At the intersection of the Girdwood Spur Road and Seward Highway is a little strip-mall with a variety of services, including a gas station-convenience store, a coin laundry, a video store, and a restaurant. Travelers heading south to Seward or north to Anchorage stop here before pushing back out on the highway. **Alpine Café & Bakery** (Alyeska Hwy. at Seward Hwy., 907/783-2550, www.alpinecafeandbakery.com, 7am-10pm daily mid-May-Sept., 8am-7pm daily Oct.-mid-May, $3-9) serves meals, but it is best known for the display cases filled with pastries, including gargantuan 10-inch ham and cheese "croissants."

At the Alyeska Resort is **The Bake Shop** (194 Olympic Mountain Loop, 907/783-2831, www.thebakeshop.com, 7am-6pm daily, $7-12), a fine spot for breakfast, lunch, or an after-ski warm-up. Homemade sourdough bread (with century-old starter), hearty soups, sandwiches, omelets, pancakes, hefty sweet rolls ($4 and worth every penny), ice cream, espresso, and pizza fill out the menu. The tables all have containers of real maple syrup to top off your french toast and pancakes. The

front yard is packed with flowers in summer, including some enormous peonies.

In town, **The Grind** (236 Hightower Rd., 907/783-2020, www.girdwoodgrind.com, 7am-7pm daily, $4-8) is an old-school hipster espresso shop. Owner John O'Leary roasts organic coffee beans for the house brews.

PIZZA AND AMERICAN
Across from the post office on Hightower Road, **Chair 5 Restaurant** (171 Lindblad Ave., 907/783-2500, www.chairfive.com, 11am-11pm daily, $15-35) is a townie spot for very good pizzas, halibut and chips, rib-eye steaks, and daily specials. You can easily spend almost $35 for a rib-eye steak, or fill up on a tasty $17 blackened halibut burger with fries. Pizzas start at $21 for a large pepperoni. The bar (open till 1am) has a great choice of single-malt scotches, along with some 60 microbrews on tap. The atmosphere is loud, crowded, and high-energy. There are no reservations, and the place gets busy on weekends, so grab a beer and enjoy a game of pool or sports on the TVs while you wait.

Silvertip Grill (165 Hightower Rd., 907/783-2584, www.silvertipgrill.com, 9am-midnight Wed.-Mon., $12-20) has the tastiest burgers in town, with live music on weekends and a rough-around-the-edges dive-bar setting. Breakfast is served all day and features chicken-fried steak with house-made reindeer sausage gravy. The outdoor tables are great for a summer afternoon.

Girdwood Brewing Company (2700 Alyeska Hwy., 907/783-2739, www.girdwoodbrewing.com, noon-8pm daily) crafts a wide variety of beers, including No Woman No Cryo (tropical flavors) and Hippy Speedball (oatmeal coffee stout). Get four-ounce tastings ($2 each) or call ahead for an hour-long tour ($20) with a flight of samples in the taproom. There's always a food truck parked outside so you can enjoy tasty bites with your beer.

The local grocery store, **Crow Creek Mercantile/Safeway** (150 Hightower St., 907/783-3900, 7am-midnight Mon.-Fri.,

8am-midnight Sat.-Sun.), has all the basics, plus deli sandwiches, liquor, firewood, and propane. This cramped little place is easily the smallest Safeway store in the nation.

ALYESKA RESTAURANTS

Looking for coffee? Head to Alyeska Daylodge, where **Java Haus** (907/783-2827, www.girdwoodjava.com, 7am-5pm daily mid-Nov.-mid-Apr., $5-10) has K-Bay espresso plus tasty wraps, breakfast burritos, bagels, sandwiches, soups, and smoothies. It's the best place to go for a fast and reasonably priced lunch if you're hitting the ski slopes.

Several options are available if you're staying at Alyeska Resort, including **Sakura** (5pm-10pm Fri.-Mon. June-mid-Sept. and Dec.-mid-Apr., no reservations, $20-42), with creative sushi, meats, fresh seafood, tempura, and bento box dinners. Also inside the hotel is **Pond Café** (907/754-2237, 7am-11am daily mid-May-Sept. and late Nov.-mid-Apr.), with a generous breakfast buffet of waffles, eggs, bacon, muffins, and more ($20 adults, $9 ages 6-12, free under age 6).

On top of the mountain and accessible only by tram, **Seven Glaciers Restaurant** (907/754-2237, www.alyeskaresort.com, 5pm-10pm daily mid-May-late Sept., noon-3pm and 4pm-9:30pm daily late Nov.-mid-Apr., entrées $42-59) offers excellent food with one of the finest views you're ever likely to get while dining. Sitting on a crag at 2,303 feet above sea level, you can see the valley below, across to the Crow Pass area, and up the waters of Turnagain Arm. Main courses include salmon, Alaskan king crab, and Wagyu beef New York steak. It's *très élégant*, but not at all stuffy or pretentious. The seven-minute tram ride gives you the chance to survey the area, and if you have lunch or dinner reservations (required), the tram ride is free. Lunch is available in the winter ski season.

FINE DINING

Seven Glaciers Restaurant isn't the only upscale restaurant in the resort town of Girdwood. Just a short distance downhill from Alyeska is ★ **Jack Sprat Restaurant** (165 Olympic Mountain Loop, 907/783-5225, www.jacksprat.net, 4:30pm-10pm Mon.-Fri., 10am-10pm Sat.-Sun., entrées $21-50), with tall windows and a lively setting just a short walk from the ski slopes. Dinners include everything from Alaskan bouillabaisse to vegetable curry and *dol sot bibimbap*, with a decadent crème brûlée for dessert. There are lots of options for both meatheads and vegans. Brunches are available on weekends, featuring gluten-free crepes, red flannel hash, yam fries, reindeer sausage omelet, and eggs benedict. Service is slow, and the cramped restaurant gets very noisy, so don't come here expecting a quiet dinner.

In business since 1962, famous **Double Musky Inn** (3 Crow Creek Rd., 907/783-2822, www.doublemuskyinn.com, 5pm-10pm Tues.-Thurs., 4:30pm-10pm Fri.-Sun. early Dec.-late Oct., $30-50) is 0.25 miles up Crow Creek Road on the left. It's crowded and loud, with long waits, high prices, a tacky New Orleans-meets-Alaska decor, and brief visits from your server. They don't take reservations either. Despite these drawbacks, the food is dependably good, if not stellar. Featured attractions are shrimp étouffée, rack of lamb, and the house specialty, French pepper steak. Save space for the ultra-rich Double Musky chocolate pie.

Accommodations

Because of its resort status, Girdwood has a large number of lodging options, from basic hostel rooms to high-end suites. Add a **12 percent tax** to all rates quoted.

The luxurious 307-room **Hotel Alyeska** (1000 Arlberg Ave., 907/754-1111 or 800/880-3880, www.alyeskaresort.com, rooms $359-399 d, suites $429) is an eight-story, 304-room hotel where nicely appointed rooms include heated towel racks, fridges, and safes. Other in-hotel amenities include an ostentatious lobby, three restaurants, a first-rate fitness center, a large saltwater indoor swimming pool, and a hot tub. The tram to the top of Mount Alyeska is right out the back door.

Lodging rates vary, with the lowest prices for small rooms on level 3, and the most expensive suites on the top level facing the mountain. It's expensive, but be sure to check out the royal suite on the hotel website. This 1,275-square-foot two-level suite has amazing panoramic views, a master bedroom with marble bath, and cherrywood accents. All this can be yours for just $750. Alyeska institutes a $10 resort fee for access to the pool and fitness facility. Be sure to ask about discounted rates and packages, including ski-and-stay winter packages; your savings can be substantial. During the summer, the resort is a popular wedding destination.

Heading toward the resort on the access road, go right on Timberline, pass gorgeous ski chalets, and then turn right again on Alpina. Around a couple of curves is **Alyeska Hostel** (227 Alta Dr., 907/783-2222, www.alyeskahostel.com, dorm $25 pp, private rooms $80 d, studio $125 d, cabin $100 d, additional guests $25 pp). The hostel has a six-bed coed dorm, a private room, a cabin, and a studio unit that sleeps five, plus a full kitchen and two baths. It gets noisy at times and walls are thin, but it's clean and well maintained. Families and couples should book the cabin or studio if possible. Reservations are recommended in summer and mid-winter, especially for the private room and cabin. There is no lockout and no curfew, but no alcohol either.

Ski Inn (189 Hightower Rd., 907/783-0002, www.akskiinn.com, $100 d shared bath, $125-150 d private bath) is a budget choice in the heart of "downtown" Girdwood. Four of the eight rooms include private baths, while the others share baths. Ski Inn also has one room with four bunks ($40 per bed or $120 for the room). Rooms are cramped and noise can be an issue if there's a live band at the bar next door, but everything is clean. Rates include a continental breakfast in the common area. The hotel has the same owner as Alyeska Hostel.

One of the finest B&Bs in Alaska, ★ **Hidden Creek B&B** (739 Vail Dr., 907/783-5557, www.hiddencreekbb.com, $185-225 d) is a modern craftsman home with three gorgeous rooms, some with Stickley furniture. There's a hot tub out back, and a gas fireplace and wet bar in the common area. Enjoy a gourmet Alaskan breakfast in the morning. Friendly innkeepers Ron and Michelle Tenny are knowledgeable about Alaska, but have also traveled extensively around the globe. Kids under age five are not allowed.

Carriage House Accommodations (388 Crow Creek Rd., 907/783-9464, www.thecarriagehousebandb.com, rooms $150-170 d, cottage $175-225 d, additional guests $25 pp, two-night minimum in summer) is an excellent bed-and-breakfast, with a full guest kitchen, king or queen beds, an outdoor hot tub and gazebo, private baths, and delicious gourmet breakfasts served on a hand-carved table. The B&B sits directly across the street from Double Musky and has four guest rooms and a luxurious cottage.

Just two blocks from the ski lifts, **Bud and Carol's B&B** (211 Brighton Rd., 907/783-3182, www.budandcarolsbandb.com, $145 d) has two guest rooms, each with a queen bed and a private bath with a jetted tub. The rooms share a full kitchen with all the ingredients for a hearty self-serve breakfast.

Alyeska Accommodations (907/783-2000 or 888/783-2001, www.alyeskaaccommodations.com) is the best source for condo, chalet, and home rentals around Girdwood. **Alyeska-Girdwood Accommodations** (907/222-4858, www.alyeskagirdwoodaccommodations.net) provides descriptions and links to local B&Bs and guesthouses.

Information and Services

Girdwood lacks a visitors center, but you'll find information online at www.girdwoodchamber.com. Girdwood's cozy **Gerrish Library** (250 Egloff Dr., 907/343-4044, 10am-6pm Tues. and Thurs.-Sat., 1pm-8pm Wed.) has Internet access. The **post office** (118 Lindblad Ave., 907/783-2922, 9am-5pm Mon.-Fri., 10am-noon Sat.) is across from Chair 5 Restaurant. Wash clothes or take showers at **Girdwood Laundry** (158 Holmgren Place, 907/317-0512).

The Forest Service's **Glacier Ranger District office** (907/783-3242, www.fs.usda.gov/chugach, 8am-5pm Mon.-Fri.) is on the left as you drive into town from the Seward Highway. It can provide details and maps for hikers, anglers, sea kayakers, and other recreation enthusiasts heading into Chugach National Forest.

Getting There and Around

The **Alaska Railroad** (907/265-2494 or 800/544-0552, www.alaskarailroad.com) has two trains connecting Girdwood with Anchorage daily in summer. The trains stop at a small shelter out near the Seward Highway, and only carry-on luggage is allowed. When heading north, you'll need to make advance reservations for a Girdwood pickup. *Glacier Discovery* trains (one-way $67 adults, $34 children, round-trip $105 adults, $53 children) depart Anchorage at 9:45am, arriving in Girdwood at 10:55am before continuing to Whittier. They then return north from Girdwood at 7:45pm, arriving in Anchorage at 9:15pm. *Coastal Classic* trains (one-way $82 adults, $41 children, round-trip $127 adults,

$64 children) leave Anchorage at 6:45am, arriving in Girdwood at 8am, and continuing to Seward. On the way north, they stop in Girdwood at 8:55pm, reaching Anchorage at 10:15pm.

Glacier Valley Transit (907/382-9909, www.glaciervalleytransit.com) provides daily free bus transportation throughout Girdwood, from the Seward Highway to Alyeska, and most other points around the valley, including Crow Creek Mine. Buses have bike racks for summer and wintertime ski and snowboard racks.

The Stage Line (907/868-3914, www.stagelineinhomer.com) stops in Girdwood on the way to Anchorage, Homer, or Seward, but call ahead for a pickup at the Tesoro station along the highway.

PORTAGE AREA

Fifty miles south of Anchorage on the Seward Highway is the turnoff to Portage Glacier and Whittier. The old town of Portage was located here, along the Placer River where it flows into Turnagain Arm. The massive 1964 earthquake dropped the land 6-10 feet, flooding Portage with saltwater, but you can still see ruins of the old Portage Garage, along with a "ghost forest" of dead spruce trees. The salt

Portage area at the head of Turnagain Arm

Portage and Whittier Area

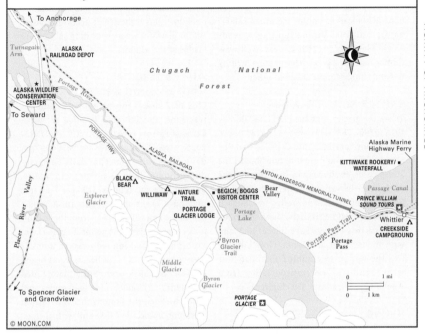

To Anchorage

Turnagain Arm

ALASKA RAILROAD DEPOT

Chugach National Forest

★ ALASKA WILDLIFE CONSERVATION CENTER

Portage River

To Seward

PORTAGE HWY

ALASKA RAILROAD

Valley

Placer River Valley

Explorer Glacier

BLACK BEAR

WILLIWAW

NATURE TRAIL

BEGICH, BOGGS VISITOR CENTER

PORTAGE GLACIER LODGE

Bear Valley

ANTON ANDERSON MEMORIAL TUNNEL

Portage Lake

Byron Glacier Trail

Byron Glacier

Middle Glacier

To Spencer Glacier and Grandview

PORTAGE GLACIER

Alaska Marine Highway Ferry

KITTIWAKE ROOKERY/ WATERFALL

Passage Canal

PRINCE WILLIAM SOUND TOURS

Whittier

CREEKSIDE CAMPGROUND

Portage Pass Trail

Portage Pass

0   1 mi
0   1 km

© MOON.COM

acted as a preservative, and many trees are still standing more than 50 years later.

Today, Portage has an Alaska Railroad station on the east side of the highway and the Alaska Wildlife Conservation Center on the west side. Portage Highway heads east from here to Portage Glacier before passing through a long tunnel and ending at the town of Whittier.

★ Portage Glacier

Portage Highway is a six-mile access road through scenic Portage Valley to Portage Glacier.

VISITORS CENTER

The Forest Service's **Begich, Boggs Visitor Center** (907/783-2326, www.fs.usda.gov/chugach, 9am-5pm daily late May-mid-Sept., $5 adults, free under age 16) is named after Nicholas Begich, U.S. representative from Alaska and father of former U.S. Senator Mark

Begich, and Hale Boggs, majority leader of the U.S. Senate and father of journalist Cokie Roberts, whose plane disappeared in the area in 1972. They were never found. A large picture window overlooks the narrow outlet of Portage Lake. When the visitors center first opened in 1986, the glacier was readily visible, but it is now out of sight around a corner, and in recent years the number of icebergs entering the lake has decreased greatly as it continues to shrink as the climate warms.

The visitors center boasts an array of displays, including an ice cave, a small iceberg hauled in from the lake, an engrossing relief map of local icefields, and everything you ever wanted to know about glaciers, including displays on glacial motion and crevasses. Don't miss the vial of tiny ice worms, which inhabit the surfaces of glaciers, feeding on pollen grains and red algae and surviving within a delicate, near-freezing temperature range. A 20-minute film, *Retreat and Renewal,* describes the changing world of Portage Glacier.

During the summer, U.S. Forest Service naturalists lead 0.5-mile "ice worm safari" nature walks (assuming funding is available). The **fish platform** near Williwaw Campground is a good place to see spawning red and chum salmon in late summer.

EXPLORING THE GLACIER

To see the glacier, take the **Portage Glacier Cruise** (907/783-3117 or 888/425-1737, www.alaska.com, mid-May-mid-Sept., $39 adults, $19 children). You'll need to hop aboard the 200-passenger *Ptarmigan* tour boat at the dock near the visitors center. Operated by Gray Line of Alaska and staffed by Chugach National Forest naturalists, these one-hour cruises across Portage Lake start at 10:30am, with the last tour at 4:30pm. Gray Line offers the option to combine the boat tour with round-trip bus transportation from Anchorage ($90 adults, $50 children).

HIKING

Two hikes are within walking distance of the visitors center. The **Moraine Loop Trail,** accessible from the path to the lodge, is a five-minute stroll through typical moraine vegetation; Portage Glacier occupied this ground only 100 years ago. Follow the access road past the visitors center (south) just under a mile. At the back of the parking lot starts the **Byron Glacier Trail,** an easy 0.75-mile walk along the runoff stream to below this hanging glacier.

At Williwaw Campground, the 1.25-mile **Williwaw Nature Trail** provides an easy introduction to the area, and **Trail of the Blue Ice** continues to the Begich, Boggs Visitor Center.

CAMPING

Two seasonal U.S. Forest Service campgrounds near Portage contain woodsy sites. **Black Bear Campground** ($14) has 13 sites for tent camping and is not recommended for RVs. The larger **Williwaw Campground**

(518/885-3639 or 877/444-6777, www.recreation.gov, $18 tents, $28 RVs, plus $10 reservation fee) has 60 tent and RV sites (no hookups), plus a wheelchair-accessible observation platform where spawning salmon are visible in the summer.

Alaska Wildlife Conservation Center

One of Alaska's most popular visitor attractions, the 140-acre **Alaska Wildlife Conservation Center** (AWCC, 907/783-2025, www.alaskawildlife.org, 8:30am-7pm daily May-Aug., 9am-6pm daily Sept., reduced hours daily Oct.-Apr., $15 adults, $12 military and seniors, $10 ages 7-17, free under age 7) sits along Turnagain Arm just across the Seward Highway from the turnoff to Portage Glacier. This nonprofit game farm for orphaned and injured Alaskan animals houses brown and black bears, wood bison, moose, elk, musk oxen, Sitka black-tailed deer, lynx, caribou, coyotes, bald eagles, and even Snickers, the famous (on YouTube, at least) porcupine. AWCC is a hit with all ages, providing an up-close look at animals you normally see from a distance—if at all. The 18-acre bear facility (the largest in the United States) is particularly impressive, with an elevated walkway to separate people from the brown and black bears.

Visit in early summer for the chance to watch those ever-cute musk ox babies. For a more informative visit, join one of the free daily programs that include caribou walks, lynx feeding, small animal programs, and brown bear feeding. Free shuttle bus tours are offered four times a day June-August, and a fun children's playground is across from the gift shop.

Use extreme caution when turning into AWCC off the busy Seward Highway; multiple fatalities have occurred at this intersection. The Alaska Railroad's Portage train station is directly across the road, and Chugach Adventures offer a special tour ($205 pp from Anchorage) that includes a 1.5-hour visit to AWCC and a train ride to the scenic Grandview and Spencer Glacier region.

★ Spencer Glacier

The **Alaska Railroad** (907/265-2494 or 800/544-0552, www.alaskarailroad.com, daily late May-mid-Sept.) has very popular scenic trips into the Kenai Mountains south of Portage, stopping at Spencer Glacier and Grandview. The *Glacier Discovery* **train** (June-mid-Sept.) departs Anchorage at 9:45am, with stops in Whittier and Portage before reaching Spencer Glacier at 1:45pm. At Spencer, people can debark the train for an afternoon of adventure, while others stay on board as the train continues into the mountains. The *Glacier Discovery* turns around at Grandview (3:30pm) for the trip back to Spencer (4:30pm) and Portage (5:15pm), where you board a free bus for the return to Anchorage, arriving at 6:30pm. (If you stay on the train, it makes yet another side trip to Whittier, finally reaching Anchorage 2.5 hours later at 9:15pm.) Because of the train schedule, people who get off at Spencer have almost three hours to explore the area. If you want to just hike on your own around the Spencer Glacier area, the round-trip train ride from Anchorage is $125 adults, $63 children. For Grandview (you can't get off the train here) the cost is $135 adults, $68 children.

Because *Glacier Discovery* trains stop at Portage, many people start their Spencer Glacier trip there instead of Anchorage. The cost is substantially lower ($44 less for adults), but you'll need a rental car to drive the 50 miles each direction to Portage and back.

EXPLORING THE GLACIER

The Spencer Glacier train stop has shelters, interpretive kiosks, restrooms, and an impressive 280-foot-long pedestrian bridge over the Placer River. A U.S. Forest Service naturalist meets the trains, leading free 2.5-mile hikes to the glacier. Two private companies provide glacier hikes, ice climbing, and float trips—all timed so you're back on board when the train returns to Anchorage.

Guides from **The Ascending Path** (907/783-0505, www.theascendingpath.com) meet guests at the train and transport them by van to the lake. Here, they paddle a short distance by kayak and then strap on crampons for two hours of exploration of the crevasses, ice caves, and other glacial features. The cost is $389 pp, including the train from Anchorage, a guide, a kayak, gear, and lunch. The same trip plus guided ice climbing costs $499 pp.

Chugach Adventures (907/783-1860, www.alaskanrafting.com) has a popular float trip ($244 adults, $128 children) that departs from the Spencer train stop. A van takes guests to Spencer Lake, where they hop in rafts and paddle among the icebergs before floating seven miles down the Placer River to the train at Portage. Rates include the train from Anchorage, a guide, the raft, and a snack; add $70 for a 1.5-hour visit to the Alaska Wildlife Conservation Center in Portage.

Another unique option is a Chugach Adventures train-and-kayak tour ($337 pp) to Spencer Glacier. These include an Alaska Railroad train from Anchorage, three hours of kayaking in front of the glacier, lunch, and a return train and bus to Anchorage. Morning trips are recommended for calmer water conditions.

To really see this fantastic area, plan an overnight or two near Spencer Glacier. Once the last train leaves at 4:40pm, you'll have things pretty much to yourself, and free **campsites** are available along the lakeshore if you want to rough it.

The U.S. Forest Service's six-person **Spencer Bench Cabin** (518/885-3639 or 877/444-6777, www.recreation.gov, $85 plus $10 reservation fee) has a jaw-dropping view of Spencer Glacier and Placer River Valley. The cabin fills well in advance, so reserve months ahead for a summer stay. Spencer Bench Cabin is a five-mile hike from Spencer Glacier train stop, and you'll gain 1,600 feet in elevation along the way.

WHITTIER

Named for poet John Greenleaf Whittier, this town of 300 friendly people has a picturesque mountains-and-bay setting. Unfortunately, the town itself is anything but poetic. Thousands of tourists pass through this settlement every week, but very few choose to spend much time in this strange place, where the entire population lives in concrete high-rises and the wind never seems to stop. In the peak of tourist season, Whittier becomes a giant parking lot with a handful of businesses scattered along the harbor.

Whittier *does* have a gorgeous setting and lots of great outdoorsy things to do on nearby Prince William Sound. So come here for the surrounding land, but don't expect to fall in love with the town, no matter how poetic the name.

All the businesses in Whittier are clustered around the harbor within a short walk from each other, so addresses are relatively meaningless (and thus have not been provided).

History

The construction of the railway to Whittier was one of the great engineering feats of World War II. Two tunnels—1 mile and 2.5 miles long—were carved through the Chugach Mountains to link the military bases in Anchorage and Fairbanks to a secret saltwater port. Seward, the main ice-free port in south-central Alaska at that time, was considered too vulnerable to Japanese attack, so in 1941-1943 the Army blasted through the mountains and laid the tracks that would ensure the flow of supplies for the defense of Alaska. After the defeat of Japan, the military pulled out of Whittier, but a year later they were back as the Cold War began with the Soviet Union. Whittier became a permanent base, and the large concrete buildings were built at that time. The 14-story Begich Towers (completed in 1954), an unlikely skyscraper in this small village, is near another anomaly, the "City under One Roof," which once housed 1,000 personnel and was the largest building in Alaska. Why did they build high-rises? To lessen the need for snow removal in a place where the snow sometimes tops 14 feet.

The base was deactivated in 1960, and the buildings were heavily damaged in the 1964 earthquake. One of them (the Buckner Building) is still vacant, but Begich Towers has been restored and converted into condos; 85 percent of residents live here. A third high-rise, Whittier Manor, was privately built in the 1950s and later turned into more condos. The military presence today is limited to an oil pipeline that supplies military installations in Anchorage. Ships from Princess Cruises and Carnival Cruise Line stop in Whittier, but most of their passengers quickly depart the town.

For nearly half a century, the town of Whittier was connected to the road system only via the Alaska Railroad. This changed in 2000, when an $80 million project made it possible for cars to drive in directly from the Seward Highway through two tunnels, one of which is shared with the railroad.

Sights

Most travelers never get farther than the tourist action on the waterfront, where boats of all sizes bob in the picturesque harbor.

Follow the signs for Whittier down past the dry dock, then go left across the tracks onto Whittier Street. Take a right on Glacier Avenue to the **Begich Towers.** In its 198 condos live most of the town's population; the rest reside in the 70 condos at **Whittier Manor.** Many are owned by Anchorageites who use them for weekend and summer getaways, boosting Whittier's summer population to nearly 1,000.

Continue 0.25 miles out on Eastern Avenue to quiet and scenic **Smitty's Cove,** where one of Whittier's few freestanding residences sits. You'll get a view across Passage Canal of waterfalls, a kittiwake rookery, and Billing's Glacier.

Stop by the Anchor Inn building to visit the surprisingly interesting **Prince William Sound Museum** (100 Whittier St., 907/472-2354, www.pwsmuseum.org, 10am-8pm daily late May-early Sept., $5), which focuses on Whittier's military past, including several detailed ship models. Exhibits begin with the exploration of Prince William Sound by the Spanish navy in 1790, through the construction of the tunnel in World War II and the military presence during the Cold War.

The **Fourth of July celebration** features a parade, a picnic, games for kids, and fireworks.

Shopping

With an exterior in all sorts of Alaskan memorabilia, **Log Cabin Gifts** (907/472-2501, May-Sept.) features arts and crafts items, ivory, and watercolors by the owner, Wilma Buethe Wilcox. Check out **Sound Ideas** (907/472-2535, www.whittierfudge.com, daily May-mid-Sept.) for gifts and homemade fudge.

Recreation

TOP EXPERIENCE

★ PRINCE WILLIAM SOUND TOURS

From mid-May to early October, Whittier is a popular departure point for day trips to the glaciers of Prince William Sound. **Phillips Tours and Cruises** (907/276-8023 or 800/544-0529, www.26glaciers.com) operates the five-hour 26-Glacier Cruise ($159 adults, $99 ages 2-11). The trip aboard its 340-passenger *Klondike Express*—a high-speed three-deck catamaran—covers a lot of water but still allows plenty of time to linger at the faces of several actively calving glaciers. A hot lunch (salmon chowder or chili) is included, there's a bar on board (glacier ice margaritas!), and the lounges provide plenty of room inside should the weather be less than perfect. Phillips also offers a shorter and more relaxed four-hour Glacier Quest Cruise ($109 adults, $69 children) to the glaciers and waterfalls of Blackstone Bay. The schedule for both trips is timed so that you can ride the train from Anchorage and back (an additional $100 adults, $50 children) or take a bus (add $60 adults, $30 children). The boats include

USB ports to charge your phone, and binoculars are available to rent. A Chugach National Forest ranger is on board all Phillips cruises.

A number of locals also have small-boat trips into Prince William Sound. The prices may be a bit higher, but you get a far more personal journey at your own pace. Expect to pay around $200 pp (four-person minimum) for a five-hour Blackstone Glacier tour. Recommended for sightseeing, fishing, water taxis, and kayak drop-offs are **Lazy Otter Charters** (907/694-6887 or 800/587-6887, www.lazyotter.com) and **Epic Charters** (907/242-4339 or 888/472-3742, www.epicchartersalaska.com).

HIKING

The most popular Whittier trail is up to **Portage Pass.** In the early days when gold was discovered around Hope on the Kenai Peninsula, Hope-bound hopefuls would boat to this harbor, portage their supplies over the glacier pass, and float down Turnagain Arm to their destination. This highly recommended day hike from Whittier affords splendid views of Passage Canal, Portage Glacier, and the Chugach Mountains. On a clear day, the views of the glacier from the Portage Pass area are far superior to those from the Portage visitors center.

This trail starts near the oil tanks and tunnel entrance at the foot of Maynard Mountain. Cross the tracks on the dirt road to the left. Take the road to the right and climb southwest along the flank of the mountain up a wide, easy track. If you walk briskly, you can be at Portage Pass (700 feet) in less than an hour. There are places to camp or picnic beside Divide Lake, but beware of strong winds at the pass. From the lake, veer left and follow the stream down toward the glacier, then find a way via a tributary on the right up onto one of the bluffs for a view of Portage Lake. Deep crevasses in the blue glacial ice are clearly visible from here. Portage Glacier has receded far enough that the gold-rush route is no longer traversable because of the lake; you must go back the way you came. Allow a minimum of three hours round-trip. There is no clear trail beyond Divide Lake, so you must find your own way. Never attempt to walk on the glacier itself, as the crevasses can be deadly.

KAYAKING AND PADDLEBOARDING

Although it is possible to paddle from Whittier to the heart of Prince William Sound, most people prefer to get a boat ride out so that they can spend more time near the glaciers and wild country that make this such a special place. Local water taxis provide these services, transporting sea kayaks, paddlers, and their gear, then picking them up several days later.

The following Whittier companies have kayak rentals and guided day trips: **Sound Paddler** (907/472-2452, www.pwskayakcenter.com), **Alaska Sea Kayakers** (907/472-2534 or 877/472-2534, www.alaskaseakayakers.com), **Epic Charters** (907/242-4339 or 888/472-3742, www.epicchartersalaska.com), **Lazy Otter Charters** (907/694-6887 or 800/587-6887, www.lazyotter.com), and **Tundra Adventure Charters** (907/301-9532, www.tundraadventurecharters.com). Sound Paddler (a.k.a. Prince William Sound Kayak Center) and Alaska Sea Kayakers are the largest and most experienced operators. Take an easy three-hour paddle to the kittiwake rookery ($89 pp) or an all-day Blackstone Glacier trip ($345 pp, four-person minimum). Multiple-night trips are available, and Sound Paddler also has stand-up paddleboard rentals and lessons.

FISHING

A number of charter fishing boats operate out of Whittier harbor, and a full day of halibut or salmon fishing costs around $270 pp. The companies include **PWS Eco-Charters** (907/244-0234, www.pwseco.com), **Saltwater Excursions** (907/360-7975, www.saltwaterexcursions.com), **Bread N Butter Charters** (907/887-9464, www.mjsbreadnbuttercharters.com), and **Whittier Marine Charters** (907/440-9510,

www.fishwhittier.com). Looking for a do-it-yourself alternative? **Whittier Boat Rentals** (907/232-2783, www.alaska-boat-rentals.com) has enclosed cabin boats for rent, along with bait, tackle, and ice. They're right next to the fuel dock.

Food

With windows facing the harbor, **Lazy Otter Café** (907/694-6887, www.lazyotter.com, 6:30am-6pm Mon.-Thurs., 6:30am-7pm Fri.-Sun. May-Sept., $5-15) serves espresso, breakfast sandwiches, seafood chowder, sandwiches, baked goods, and soft-serve ice cream. If you're heading out on the water, ask for a box lunch ($15).

Swiftwater Seafood Café (907/472-2550, www.swiftwaterseafoodcafe.com, 11:30am-9pm daily early May-early Sept., $14-21) is popular for fish-and-chips, halibut burgers, fried zucchini, calamari, and seafood chowder. The same owners at **Varley's Ice Cream and Pizza Parlor** (907/472-2547, www.swiftwaterseafoodcafe.com, 11:30am-9pm daily early May-early Sept., $6-20), serve ice cream cones, shakes, malts, strawberry-rhubarb sundaes, toasted subs, and pizza by the slice or pie. It gets crowded on those rare sunny days.

Inn at Whittier (907/472-3200, www.innatwhittier.com, 7am-10pm daily May-Sept., entrées $24-35) has a fantastic location, with tall windows fronting on the boat harbor, and friendly staff. Dinner entrées include filet mignon, stuffed pork tenderloin, seafood fettuccine, and more.

Directly in front of the Inn at Whittier, **Wild Catch Café** (907/472-2354, 6am-8pm daily May-Sept., $9-23) serves breakfast burritos, great grass-fed beef burgers, halibut fish-and-chips, sandwiches, and more. There's a covered front porch with a big wraparound deck fronting the harbor. Wild Catch is a good place to order a box lunch for your fishing charter. Free Wi-Fi is available too.

1: Log Cabin Gifts in Whittier; **2:** kayaks on the shore in Prince William Sound

China Sea Restaurant (907/472-3663, www.chinasearestaurant.com, 11am-11pm daily May-Sept., $13-23 entrées, $14 buffet) has an all-you-can-eat lunch buffet on Wednesday and Saturday with soup and a salad bar, plus all the standards, from hot and sour soup to shrimp chow mein. There are good harbor views too.

Accommodations

June's Whittier Condo Suites (907/472-6001, www.juneswhittiercondosuites.com, $100-195 1-bedroom, $250 2-bedroom, $200-375 3-bedroom) consists of seven condo suites on the 14th and 15th floors of Begich Towers, ranging from one-bedroom apartments to three-bedroom units that sleep eight. All have picture-postcard vistas of nearby mountains and glaciers, and include full kitchens (with dishes) and private baths.

It's hard to miss the Inn at Whittier (Harbor Rd., 907/472-3200, www.innatwhittier.com, $189-219 d, suites $239-299, mid-Apr.-Sept.), an elaborate three-story New England-style building right on the harbor. Owned by Hooper Bay Native Corporation, the hotel has 23 standard rooms and a pair of two-story townhouse suites with king and queen beds, two fireplaces, and a hot tub. A popular restaurant and tavern occupy the center of the building, with a fine harbor vista. Wi-Fi can be spotty when those giant cruise ships pull in nearby.

Camping

Whittier's Creekside Campground (100 Kenai St., 907/472-2670, www.whittierparking.com, late May-early Oct., $10 tents, $20 RVs) behind Begich Towers has secluded spots and a shelter for cooking and socializing in the rain. There are no hookups or running water, but you can use baths on the 1st floor of Begich Towers, and showers are available at the harbormaster's office. The RV dump station is in front of the city shops. A walking trail leads uphill from the campground to a high point over Whittier.

Practicalities

Get local information from the Whittier Chamber of Commerce website (www.whittieralaskachamber.org).

Anchor Inn (100 Whittier St., 907/474-2354 or 877/870-8787, www.anchorinnwhittier.com) has a small grocery store, but don't miss the Harbor Store (Harbor View Rd., 907/244-1996), a combination grocery, dry goods, clothing, sporting goods, laundry, hardware, bait-and-tackle, snacks, liquor, department store, and car rental place—all in an ancient ATCO trailer. Be sure to ask about the elusive pink mamba "snake" that haunts the store.

The post office is on the 1st floor of Begich Towers, and the library is in the fire hall. Get showered at the Harbor Office, next to Hobo Bay. Find free Wi-Fi at Anchor Inn and the Inn at Whittier, along with ATMs at Anchor Inn and Harbor Store.

Getting There

Whittier is accessible by boat, ferry, train, or car. Drivers get here by turning from Seward Highway at Mile 79 (50 miles south of Anchorage) onto Portage Glacier Highway. The road to Whittier splits off near the Begich, Boggs Visitor Center and heads through a 400-foot tunnel before emerging into Bear Valley. Here you'll find a staging area for access to the 2.5-mile Anton Anderson Memorial Tunnel (907/472-2584 or 877/611-2586, www.tunnel.alaska.gov, eastbound toll $13 autos, $38 RVs, westbound is free) that is shared by both trains and cars. It's the longest auto tunnel in North America, and one of the only tunnels in the world where the same roadbed is used by both rail and auto traffic. The tunnel is open to one-way travel throughout the day, but only for 15 minutes out of each hour in each direction (and not at all when trains are transiting the tunnel). The tunnel generally opens from 30 minutes after the hour to 45 minutes past (e.g., 1:30pm-1:45pm) heading to Whittier and the first 15 minutes of the hour (e.g., 1pm-1:15pm) departing Whittier. Ferry travelers and anyone else on a tight schedule should check the tunnel times in advance to make sure they don't miss their connections.

The tunnel is not recommended for anyone with claustrophobia, and you will be driving on an odd roadbed over the railroad tracks. There are pullouts for emergency use, and enormous fans to clean the air after trains pass through. Whittier has four cops, and one of them always seems to be waiting to catch folks speeding to make the tunnel before it closes. You have been warned!

GETTING AROUND

Once you reach Whittier, a few two-hour parking spots are available in the "downtown" triangle area, but most folks will need to pay to park. The privately run **Whittier Parking** (907/472-2670, www.whittierparking.com) charges $10 per day; they're right across the railroad tracks from the glacier cruises.

Avis (907/440-2847, www.avisalaska.com, mid-May-mid-Sept.) has one-way car rentals available if you want to put your car on the ferry to Valdez and end back in Anchorage. Find them at the Harbor Store.

Whittier Shuttle (907/227-8174, www.bearvalleyroadrunner.com) is the local taxi service and can transport you to or from Anchorage ($75 pp, two-person minimum).

TRAIN AND BUS

The **Alaska Railroad** (907/265-2494 or 800/544-0552, www.alaskarailroad.com, June-mid-Sept., $100 adults, $50 children round-trip) connects Whittier with Anchorage, departing Anchorage at 9:45am and arriving in Whittier at 12:05pm. The northbound train leaves Whittier at 6:05pm and arrives in Anchorage at 9:15pm. This makes an excellent day trip from the city, and is timed for boat tours out of Whittier. A trivia note: The railroad route to Whittier was used in the 1986 film *Runaway Train.*

Seward Bus Lines (907/563-0800 or 888/420-7788, www.sewardbuslines.net, $50 one-way) provides summer transport between Anchorage and Whittier. You'll need to call ahead for reservations, and there's a two-person minimum.

Park Connection (907/245-0200 or 800/266-8625, www.alaskacoach.com, daily mid-May-mid-Sept.) operates large buses connecting Whittier with Anchorage ($65 one-way), Talkeetna ($130), and Denali ($155). It's primarily used by cruise ship passengers.

FERRY

The **Alaska Marine Highway** (907/465-3941 or 800/642-0066, www.ferryalaska.com) has daily ferry service connecting Whittier with Valdez and Cordova on both the high-speed *Fairweather* and the older (and much slower) *Aurora,* with a U.S. Forest Service naturalist on board. In addition, the *Kennicott* has a once-a-month summer sailing across the Gulf of Alaska from Whittier to Yakutat, continuing south to Juneau, and then all the way to Prince Rupert, British Columbia, and Bellingham, Washington.

Matanuska-Susitna Valley

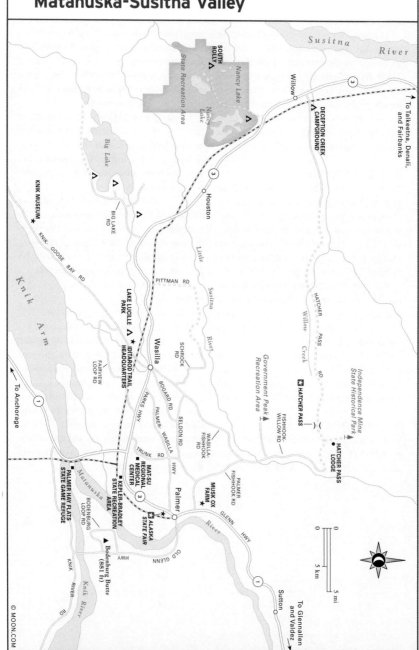

Susitna River

SOUTH ROLLY
State Recreation Area
Nancy Lake
Nancy Lake

Willow

DECEPTION CREEK CAMPGROUND

3

To Talkeetna, Denali, and Fairbanks

Big Lake

KNIK MUSEUM

BIG LAKE RD

3

Houston

KNIK GOOSE BAY RD

Little Susitna River

PITTMAN RD

Knik Arm

HATCHER PASS RD

Willow Creek

Independence Mine State Historical Park

LAKE LUCILLE PARK

IDITAROD TRAIL HEADQUARTERS

Wasilla

SCHROCK RD

Government Peak Recreation Area

HATCHER PASS

FAIRVIEW LOOP RD

To Anchorage

1

PARKS HWY

BOGARD RD

SELDON RD

PALMER-WASILLA HWY

WASILLA-FISHHOOK RD

FISHHOOK-WILLOW RD

PALMER FISHHOOK RD

HATCHER PASS LODGE

TRUNK RD

MAT-SU REGIONAL MEDICAL CENTER 3

KEPLER-BRADLEY STATE RECREATION AREA

Palmer

MUSK OX FARM

Matanuska

PALMER HAY FLATS STATE GAME REFUGE

BODENBURG LOOP RD

ALASKA STATE FAIR

GLENN HWY

River

OLD GLENN HWY

Bodenburg Butte (881 ft.)

KNIK

KNIK RIVER RD

Knik River

1

To Glennallen and Valdez

Sutton

0   5 km
0   5 mi

© MOON.COM

Matanuska-Susitna Valley

The Parks Highway heads north from Anchorage to Denali and Fairbanks, but before you're even close to either of these, the road takes you through the heart of the Matanuska-Susitna Valley, named for the two rivers that drain this part of Alaska. Originally established as an agricultural center, the Mat-Su is now primarily a bedroom community for Anchorage, with reasonably priced homes and fast-spreading semiurban sprawl. Two towns dominate the valley: The old farming settlement of Palmer is along the Glenn Highway, 42 miles from Anchorage, while Wasilla is 40 miles north of Anchorage along the Parks Highway.

PALMER

For its first 20 years, Palmer (pop. 6,000) was little more than a railway depot for Alaska Railroad's Matanuska branch. Then in May 1935, during the height of both the Depression and a severe drought in the Midwest, the Federal Emergency Relief Administration of President Franklin D. Roosevelt's New Deal selected 200 farming families from the relief rolls of northern Michigan, Minnesota, and Wisconsin and shipped them here to colonize the Matanuska Valley. Starting out in tent cabins, the colonists cleared the dense virgin forest, built houses and barns, and planted crops pioneered at the University of Alaska's Agricultural Experimental Station. These hardy transplanted farmers endured the inevitable first-year hardships, including disease, homesickness, mismanagement, floods, and just plain bad luck. But by the fall of 1936 the misfits had been weeded out, 120 babies had been born in the colony, and fertile fields and long summer days were filling barns with crops. The colonists celebrated with a three-day harvest festival, the forerunner of the big state fair. After a few more years, Palmer had become not only a flourishing town but also the center of a bucolic and

beautiful agricultural valley that was and still remains unique in Alaska.

Driving into Palmer from Wasilla along the Palmer-Wasilla Highway is a lot like driving into Wasilla from the bush on the Parks Highway—a time warp. The contrast between Palmer, an old farming community, and Wasilla, with its helter-skelter development, is startling. Suffice it to say that Palmer is more conducive to sightseeing.

Today, downtown Palmer is a blend of the old and new, with Klondike Mike's Saloon just up the street from a fine Tuscany-inspired bistro. Palmer is also home to the Alaska campus of the **National Outdoor Leadership School** (907/745-4047, www.nols.edu). From this base, NOLS offers a range of courses that involve backpacking, sea kayaking, and mountaineering in remote parts of Alaska.

Sights

Start your visit at the **Palmer Museum and Visitor Center** (723 S. Valley Way, 907/746-7668, www.palmermuseum.org, 9am-6pm daily May-Sept., 10am-5pm Wed.-Fri., 10am-2pm Sat. Oct.-Apr., free). Inside, load up with brochures and take a gander at historical items, old photos, and a video from the time when colonists first settled in the valley. Outside, the immaculate garden features elephantine produce and abundant flowers by late summer.

Colony House Museum (316 E. Elmwood Ave., 907/745-1935, www.palmerhistoricalsociety.org, 10am-4pm Tues.-Sat. summer only, $2 adults, $1 children) is just up the block. Built by the Beylund family, who moved here in 1935 from Wisconsin, it has been restored and filled with period furnishings to provide a window into the life of the Matanuska colonists.

Continue another block east on East Elmwood to visit the appropriately named **Church of a Thousand Logs** (713 S. Denali

Palmer

St., 907/745-3822, www.palmerlogchurch.com), built by the colonists in 1936-1937 and still in use.

MUSK OX FARM

While in Palmer, take the opportunity to visit the world's only domestic **Musk Ox Farm** (12850 E. Archie Rd., 907/745-4151, www.muskoxfarm.org, 10am-6pm daily early May-mid-Sept., $11 adults, $9 seniors, $5 ages 6-17, free under age 6) and see 80 or so of these fascinating prehistoric arctic creatures up close.

During the 45-minute tour you'll learn that these exotic animals were hunted nearly to extinction in the 1860s, but have been reestablished in northwestern and arctic Alaska. The farm is just east of Palmer near Mile 50 of the Glenn Highway.

The musk ox wool (*quviut*) is collected here, shipped back east to be spun, then woven into *qiviut* wool products. *Qiviut* is eight times warmer than sheep's wool and much softer and finer even than cashmere. Scarves, stoles, and caps are sold in the showroom; don't miss the display of little squares of *qiviut*, cashmere, alpaca, and wool from sheep, camels, and llamas to compare the softness.

The farm opens on Mother's Day in May (a great time to see the calves) and remains open all summer. Get there by taking the Glenn Highway north of town to Mile 50 and following the signs to this nonprofit facility. A summer Music with Musk Oxen series ($15) brings live bands to the grounds; bring your own beer. Winter tours are by reservation only.

FAIRGROUNDS AND FARMS

Heading north through downtown, take a right on Arctic Avenue, which turns into the Old Glenn Highway. About a mile south of town on the Glenn Highway is the **Alaska State Fairgrounds.** At the fairgrounds is **Colony Village** (2075 Glenn Hwy., 907/745-4827, 10am-4pm Mon.-Sat., free), which preserves some of Palmer's early buildings, including houses (one built in 1917 in Anchorage), several barns, a church, and a post office.

Alaska Farm Tours (907/519-7067, www.alaskafarmtours.com, mid-June-mid-Sept., $95 adults, $80 seniors, $50 children) leads educational farm-and-brewery tours, farm-to-picnic foodie tours, and historical walking tours.

Five miles south of Palmer on the Old Glenn Highway, **Bodenburg Loop Road** is a five-mile drive through some of the most gorgeous valley farmland, with 6,400-foot **Pioneer Peak** towering behind. To see some of the original colony farms, head three miles north along the Glenn Highway to **Farm Loop Road.** The valley's best-known crop isn't mentioned in any of the tourism brochures: marijuana. The local version (Matanuska Thunder-F—) has a reputation as big as Alaska and is some of the most potent in the nation. It was formerly grown outside, but today nearly all grow operations are indoors under lights.

Knik River Road splits off the Old Glenn Highway at Mile 9. Turn here and drive four

miles to the trailhead for the **Pioneer Ridge-Knik River Trail,** which climbs a staggering 5,100 feet in less than six miles. Beyond this alpine ridge, only experienced rock climbers should consider heading to the twin summits of Pioneer Peak.

Seven miles south of Palmer on the Old Glenn Highway is the **Reindeer Farm** (5561 S. Bodenburg Loop Rd., 907/745-4000, www.reindeerfarm.com, 10am-6pm daily May-early Sept., $11 adults, $9 seniors and ages 3-11, free under age 3), where tours are offered daily. The farm has 150 or so reindeer, along with elk, horses, and Dolly the bison. Children especially love the chance to pet a baby reindeer. One-hour horseback trail rides cost $60 pp.

Knowledgeable guides and gentle horses make **Alaska Horse Adventures** (18810 E. Walling Rd., 907/229-4445, www.alaskahorseadventures.com) a great way to explore the countryside along the Knik River. A 1.5-hour trail ride is $99 pp, and three-hour rides are $199 pp. These are an excellent family trip. Wintertime sleigh rides are $49 adults, $35 children for a 45-minute ride.

Entertainment and Events
★ ALASKA STATE FAIR

Don't miss Alaska's biggest summertime event, a 12-day party to bring down the curtain on summer that draws 300,000 visitors annually. The **Alaska State Fair** (2075 Glenn Hwy., 907/745-4827 or 800/850-3247, www.alaskastatefair.org, $15 adults, $10 seniors and youths, free under age 6, parking $5) cranks up the next-to-last Thursday in August and continues through Labor Day in early September. On a weekend it may seem as though half of Anchorage has driven up to the fair. Long lines of cars wait to turn into the open field parking lots around the grounds, and crowds throng the 4-H displays, livestock auctions, horse shows, and carnival rides. There's live music daily, a rodeo, a demolition derby, three nights of fireworks, and lots of food and craft booths. Favorites always include the roasted corn on the cob, sickly

sweet elephant ears, supersize turkey legs, and finger-lickin' halibut tacos. One big attraction is the gargantuan vegetables, including 125-pound pumpkins, 10-pound onions, and 2-pound radishes. The cabbage weigh-off makes front-page news in Alaska each year; a world record was set in 2012 when a Palmer man grew a 138-pound cabbage. The state pumpkin record was set in 2018 by a 1,469-pound monstrosity.

The **Alaska Railroad** (907/265-2494 or 800/544-0552, www.alaskarailroad.com) has direct—and inexpensive—train service from Anchorage to the fairgrounds during the state fair ($16 adults, $12 under age 12, free for younger children); it's a great way to avoid the traffic jams and parking hassles. These sell out fast on weekends, so book ahead.

EVENTS

The **Palmer Friday Fling** (across from the downtown visitors center, 907/745-4577, www.fridayfling.net, 10am-5pm Fri. mid-May-mid-Aug.) features local produce, food, crafts, and musical entertainment.

Colony Days (downtown Palmer, 907/745-2880, www.palmerchamber.org/colony-days, 2nd weekend in June) includes a downtown parade, arts and crafts booths, bed races, foot races, and games. The main wintertime event is the **Colony Christmas** (downtown Palmer, 907/745-2880, www.palmerchamber.org/colony-christmas), with a lighted parade held on the second Friday and Saturday of December, along with reindeer sled rides, caroling, arts and crafts, visits with Santa, and fireworks.

NIGHTLIFE

Klondike Mike's (820 S. Colony Way, 907/745-2676) has DJ tunes and karaoke in a rustic Alaskan setting. Also check the lineup at **Vagabond Blues** (642 S. Alaska St., 907/745-2233), which comes alive on

weekends when singer-songwriter musicians pack the coffeehouse.

Recreation

Two excellent hikes are accessible off the Old Glenn Highway east of Palmer. Heading north from downtown, go right on Arctic Avenue, which becomes the Old Glenn Highway. Just beyond the bridge across the Matanuska River, go left onto Clark-Wolverine Road, then continue about a mile until the next junction. Take a right on Huntley Road, go about a mile, bear right at the fork, and then drive 0.25 miles to the trailhead for **Lazy Mountain.** It's a two-mile hike to the summit of this 3,270-foot mountain with views of the Matanuska Valley.

A better view and a shorter hike are to the top of **Bodenburg Butte** (881 feet). Keep going south on the Old Glenn Highway, pass the first right onto Bodenburg Loop Road, and take the second right. A parking lot ($4) is 0.25 miles up the road, and a 45-minute trek (504 stairs!) rewards you with a 360-degree view of the farm-filled valley, Chugach, the Talkeetnas, Knik Glacier, and some of the uncleared forest, which graphically illustrates what the colonists confronted in "clearing the land."

Palmer Hay Flats State Game Refuge (907/357-8711, www.palmerhayflats.org) covers 45 square miles of wetlands, tidal sloughs, forests, and lakes. The area is vital habitat for many birds and other animals, and is popular for hiking, fishing, and duck hunting. A two-story viewing tower at Reflections Lake provides a bird's-eye view of the flats. Get there by taking the Knik River Access exit at Mile 31 of the Glenn Highway. Follow the trail to the right for 0.3 miles to the tower.

Swimming is available at the **Palmer High School pool** (1170 W. Arctic Ave., 907/861-7676, www.matsugov.us). The **Palmer Golf Course** (1000 Lepak Ave., 907/745-4653, www.palmergolfcourse.com) is an 18-hole course along the Matanuska River.

The **Mat-Su Miners** (2075 Glenn Hwy., 907/745-6401, www.matsuminers.org) play

1: Palmer water tower; 2: productive garden outside Palmer Museum and Visitor Center; 3: Musk Ox Farm in Palmer

Side Trip to Matanuska Glacier

One of Alaska's most accessible glaciers, Matanuska Glacier is 60 miles east of Palmer on the Glenn Highway, and a two-hour drive from Anchorage. It's a very scenic road, and the trip provides the perfect opportunity to get up close and personal with a glacier. Along the way you'll pass the **Alpine Historical Park** (www.alpinehistoricalpark.org) in Sutton, with its open-air museum and dramatic pyramidal-shaped **King Mountain**.

Located at Mile 102 of the Glenn Highway, Matanuska Glacier is 27 miles long and 4 miles wide; 18,000 years ago it reached all the way to Palmer. The glacier continues to slowly retreat, moving back 100 yards in the last 30 years.

Much of the land in front of the Matanuska Glacier was owned by Jack Kimball, who home-steaded here in 1964 and spent decades developing a road and bridges to a bluff overlooking the ice. Access to privately owned **Matanuska Glacier Park** (907/745-2534 or 888/253-4480, www.matanuskaglacieradventures.us, $30 pp) is via a three-mile dirt road. A gate and small gift shop are located a mile down this road. Stop here to check in, pay your entrance fees, and sign waivers. Continue another two miles to a parking area just a 10-minute walk from the toe of the glacier. Despite occasional signs to the contrary (there's a longstanding battle between local landowners who periodically put up "Danger: Road Unsafe" signs) the road is passable for all vehicles, including RVs.

You can hike on the easier sections of the glacier with tennis shoes, but will need a guide and crampons for the steeper parts of the glacier. Glacier Park also leads two-hour walking hikes onto the glacier for $100 pp, including the access fee; three other companies provide more adventur-ous tours.

Based just up the road, **MICA Guides** (Mile 103, Glenn Hwy., 907/351-7587, www.micaguides.com, mid-May-early Sept.) leads four-hour icefall treks ($89 adults, $69 ages 8-12), four-hour ice cave adventures ($119 adults, $99 ages 8-11), all-day ice climbing adventures ($179 over age 12), and helicopter glacier hikes (from $299 pp); the $30 pp entrance fee to Glacier Park is not included in these prices.

For an adrenaline-pumping experience, MICA has set up two not-for-the-faint-of-heart **Extreme Zip Adventure** ($79 adults, $59 children over age 6). The Nitro zip line launches from a three-story tower and covers 1,500 feet of cable at speeds of 30-40 miles per hour. The G2 has dual zip lines so you can race a friend as you careen along at up to 60 miles per hour for 2,200 feet—almost half a mile.

Nova Glacier Guides (907/746-5753 or 800/746-5753, www.alaskaglacierguides.com, mid-May-early Sept.) leads 3.5-hour glacier hikes ($90), 4.5-hour adventure treks ($159), and five-hour ice climbing classes ($179); the $30 entrance to Glacier Park is extra. Nova is best known as a river rafting company. A fun half-day float trip ($89) starts at Matanuska Glacier and heads down the Matanuska River through Class II white water.

Out along the highway is **Matanuska Glacier State Recreation Site** (Mile 102, Glenn Hwy., www.dnr.alaska.gov, $15 campsites), on a hillside overlooking the ice giant. The six camp-sites have a water pump, picnic tables, fire pits, and outhouses. The campground is maintained by nearby **Long Rifle Lodge** (Mile 102, Glenn Hwy., 907/745-5151, www.longriflelodge.co), with homemade meals ("best chili in Alaska"), a lounge stuffed with stuffed dead animal heads, and motel rooms ($75 shared bath, $85 d private bath). However, the real reason to stop here is the view from the dining room of the nearby glacier and valleys—it's hard to keep your eyes on your plate with this mountain panorama in front of you.

semiprofessional baseball on the Alaska State Fairgrounds throughout the summer. They're part of the Alaska Baseball League.

Food

Vagabond Blues (642 S. Alaska St., 907/745-2233, 6am-8pm Mon.-Sat., 7am-7pm Sun., $5-13) is a longtime favorite, serving house-made pastries, espresso, and tasty lunches—including paninis, salads, quiche, breakfast burritos, BLTs, and wraps. You won't go wrong ordering today's soup, served in hand-painted pottery and served with a hunk of freshly baked bread. Wi-Fi is free too.

★ **Turkey Red** (550 S. Alaska St., 907/746-5544, www.turkeyredak.com, 7am-9pm Mon.-Sat., $15-21) is Palmer's standout restaurant, with a relaxed, colorful setting and an emphasis on fresh, local, and organic ingredients. Owner-chef Alex Papasavas hails from Tuscany, crafting a Mediterranean-Alaskan menu that includes beefsteak salad, *scaloppini ai funghi* (chicken in a creamy Portobello mushroom sauce), 12-inch pizzas, distinctive lunchtime sandwiches, breakfast omelets, and daily seafood specials. The wine selection is first-rate.

Humdinger's Gourmet Pizza (173 S. Valley Way, 907/745-7499, www.humdingerspizza.com, 11am-8pm Tues.-Thurs., 11am-9pm Fri.-Sat., noon-8pm Sun., medium pizza $14-20) serves some of the best pizzas in the Mat-Su Valley, including a south-of-the-border version, gluten-free options, and the cherry bomb dessert pizza. Don't come here in a hurry; you may need to wait quite a while for your pizza.

Palmer has a **Carrs grocery store** (Glenn Hwy. and Palmer-Wasilla Hwy., 907/761-1400, www.carrsqc.com, 5am-1am daily) and a **Fred Meyer** (545 W. Evergreen St., 907/707-0400, www.fredmeyer.com, 7am-11pm daily) just up the street.

Brewpubs

Located in a historic creamery, **Palmer City Alehouse** (320 E. Dahlia St., 907/746-2537, www.alaskaalehouse.com, 11am-9pm Mon.-Wed., 11am-10pm Thurs.-Fri., 9am-9pm Sun., $15-32) is one of three brewpubs owned by the same folks; the others are Eagle River Alehouse and Anchorage Alehouse. The building itself is half the draw, with a covered back deck and beer garden for the open-air concerts on summer weekends. A sprawling pub menu pleases most tastes—from prime rib dip sandwiches and ahi tuna tacos to Thai chicken pizzas. The bar has 44 taps with local microbrews, featuring those made by Matanuska Brewing Company (which owns the Alehouse).

Arkose Brewery (650 E. Steel Loop, 907/746-2337, www.arkosebrewery.com, 1pm-7pm daily) crafts four flagship beers along with seasonal brews. Take a brewery tour ($5) and sample a pint or two of brewmaster Stephen Gerteisen's German-inspired beers; they're available in growlers to go. The brewery is located directly behind the Alaska State Fairgrounds.

Accommodations

Lodging is reasonable in Palmer—at least by Alaska standards. Visit the **Mat-Su Bed & Breakfast Association's** website (www.alaskabnbhosts.com) for links to local places.

Built in 1935 as a teachers' dormitory for the Matanuska Valley Colony, **Colony Inn** (325 E. Elmwood Ave., 907/745-3330 or 800/478-7666, www.akcolonyinn.com, $100-120 d) is one of the oldest buildings in Mat-Su Valley. Today this historic structure has been transformed into a 12-room hotel with a central sitting room with a fireplace and wing-back chairs. The spacious rooms contain antiques, quilts, microwaves, fridges, flat-screen TVs, Wi-Fi, a queen or two twin beds, and jetted tubs. It's managed by the Valley Hotel (five blocks away at 606 S. Alaska St.), which is where you register.

In the heart of town, **Pioneer Motel** (124 W. Arctic, 907/745-3425, www.thepioneermotel.com, rooms $125-140 d, cabins $150-160) has large attractive rooms with kitchenettes. Eight small cabins with kitchens and private baths are also available.

Set on 15 acres with a spectacular Pioneer Peak backdrop, ★ **Alaska's Harvest B&B** (2252 N. Love Dr., 907/745-4263, www.alaskasharvest.com, rooms $149 d, suite $169 d, cabin $300 for 4 people, additional guests $20 pp) is an exquisite place to relax. Five guest rooms have private baths and kitchenettes, and the 900-square-foot suite includes a king bed, a day bed, a kitchenette, and a private bath. A cozy three-bedroom log cabin with a full kitchen and all the amenities is also available. All guest rooms are stocked with breakfast ingredients. Shetland sheep graze the pasture out front.

Dramatic mountain and glacier vistas are at the modern and immaculately maintained **Alaska Garden Gate B&B** (950 S. Trunk Rd., 907/746-2333, www.gardengatebnb.com). The B&B has an array of options, all with private baths, private entrances, TVs, and a big buffet served each morning in the breakfast hall. Budget-priced rooms ($143 d) are perfect for families, with queen bunk beds and space for five. Other choices include studio apartments ($170 d), luxury one-bedroom cottages ($180 d), and a two-bedroom two-bath apartment ($233 d). The apartments and cottages all have fireplaces, and some units contain jetted tubs. Add $20 each for additional guests.

Camping

Palmer has one of the most luxurious city campgrounds in Alaska and it's just 0.5 miles east of town. **Matanuska River Park** (925 E. Arctic Ave., 907/746-8612, www.matsugov.us/parks, late May-early Oct., tents $17, RVs $27 with hookups) occupies a lush site full of big old cottonwoods and wild roses. There's lots of space among the 86 campsites, which are usually not crowded except at state fair time. Surrounding the campground is a day-use area, complete with picnic tables, softball and volleyball, horseshoe pits, and a nature trail around the ponds. The park also has potable water, flush toilets, coin-operated showers, firewood, trails, river access, and an observation deck.

A popular area for fishing, hiking, canoeing, and biking, **Matanuska Lakes State Recreation Area** (Mile 36, Glenn Hwy., www.dnr.alaska.gov, $25) comprises three large lakes and eight smaller ones. It's just west of Palmer, with six campsites, toilets, potable water, and canoe rentals.

Kepler Park Campground (1.5 miles east of the Parks Hwy.-Glenn Hwy. interchange, 907/745-3053, May-mid-Sept., camping $22, day-use $15) is adjacent to Kepler and Bradley Lakes. The lakes are stocked with rainbow trout, and the family-friendly campground has rowboats or ones with electric motors ($12 per hour). Campsites are simple, with picnic tables, barbecue grills, and outhouses. There are no RV hookups.

Fox Run RV Campground (4466 S. Glenn Hwy., 907/745-6120, www.foxrunak.com, $24 tents, $45 RVs) is just east of the Parks and Glenn Highways intersection, so expect traffic noise. The RV park sits on the shore of pretty Matanuska Lake, with rowboat and canoe rentals, showers, laundry, Wi-Fi, and even a good little restaurant with three meals a day. The RV park stays open all year, with cabins, rooms, and lakefront efficiencies ($70-140 d) available.

Three miles south of Palmer off the Old Glenn Highway, **Mountain View RV Park** (1405 N. Smith Rd., 907/745-5747, www.mtviewrvpark.com, $40 RVs) has a large no-frills location with showers, laundry, and limited Wi-Fi.

Services

Palmer Public Library (655 S. Valley Way, 907/745-4690, www.pplak.org, 10am-8pm Mon. and Wed., 10am-6pm Tues. and Thurs., 10am-2pm Fri.-Sat.) has public-use computers with Internet access. Take showers in downtown Palmer at **Wash Day Too** (127 S. Alaska St., 907/746-4141).

Mat-Su Regional Medical Center (2500 S. Woodworth Loop, 907/861-6620, www.matsuregional.com) occupies the hilltop just off the Parks Highway at Trunk Road. It's the only hospital in the valley.

Getting There and Around

Valley Transit (907/864-5000, www. valleytransitak.org, $7) has weekday service throughout the valley and commuter runs to Anchorage.

KNIK GLACIER

Knik Glacier is a one-hour drive from Anchorage via the Glenn Highway, South Old Glenn Highway, and Knik River Road. Visible approximately seven miles up Knik River Road, this massive glacier is primarily accessible by airboat. (An eight-mile hiking trail leads to the glacier but has two water crossings, one of which requires a pack raft.) Knik Glacier—like almost all glaciers—is retreating rapidly; in the last decade it has receded almost 1.5 miles. The lake is now six miles long in front of the glacier, with massive icebergs.

In 2012, a National Guard helicopter was flying over Knik Glacier when the crew noticed something strange on the ice below. Investigators later discovered the remains of a C-124A Globemaster cargo plane that crashed in 1952, killing all 52 people on board. The wreckage had been buried by heavy snow shortly after the crash, and it wasn't until its rediscovery 60 years later that some of the remains could be removed.

Knik Glacier Tours (Mile 82, Knik Glacier Rd., 907/745-1577, www.knikglacier. com, mid-May-mid-Sept., $125 adults, $65 children), runs three-hour jet-boat trips to the glacier. Tours begin with a four-mile monster-truck safari ride (good for viewing moose and spawning salmon), followed by a fast jet-boat trip upriver to the glacier. Guests spend an hour at a Weatherport camp next to the glacier's terminal moraine. There, they can hike and explore the area before returning. A longer adventure tour provides four hours at the glacier and the chance to use the kayaks, paddleboards, and pack rafts to paddle around the icebergs; call for details. Campsites are available next to the tour office on Knik Glacier Road if you're taking a tour.

Knik River Lodge (907/745-5002 or 877/745-4575, www.knikriverlodge.com,

May-Sept., $299 d, additional guests $30 pp) has 22 cabins 11 miles out on Knik River Road. All include private baths, decks, microwaves, fridges, and a full hot breakfast, but no Wi-Fi or TV. On-site is Raven's Perch Restaurant, with a changing menu that emphasizes locally grown produce, meats, and seafood. **Anchorage Helicopter Tours** (907/272-7777, www.anchoragehelicoptertours.com) provides a number of flights from the lodge, including heli-hiking, glacier landings, and a popular glacier dogsled tour ($549 pp, one hour on the glacier) to Troublesome Glacier.

WASILLA

In 2008 the town of Wasilla vaulted into the big time as the home of Alaska's then-governor and U.S. vice presidential candidate Sarah Palin. Her meteoric rise to fame brought international attention to Wasilla—not all of it positive. Wasilla is also home to the gorgeous mountains at nearby Hatcher Pass. You may not be able to see Russia from here, but you can see Alaska from Wasilla.

In 1977, Wasilla consisted of a landing strip and a grocery store that advertised the convenience of flying in from the bush, buying Matanuska Valley produce, and flying out again—without the hassles of Anchorage. Then, when the capital looked like it might be moved to Willow, 25 miles up the highway, Anchorageites began to discover Wasilla's quiet, beauty, and affordable land, and contractors took advantage of the town's lax restrictions on development. And develop it did, with a vengeance. During 1980-1982, the town's population of 1,200 doubled, then doubled again in 1982-1984. Stores, malls, and fast-food chains popped up. Teeland's General Store was jacked up, moved from the corner it had sat on for over 60 years, and unceremoniously dumped in a parking lot around the block to make way for a 7-Eleven. The original airstrip, which had kept Wasilla on the map for so long, was moved out from the middle of all the hustle and bustle of town.

The unbridled growth continues today, as relatively low real estate prices and good roads make the area a favorite of Anchorage commuters wanting a piece of the suburban lifestyle. In the 1990s, Wasilla's Walmart proved so popular that after just a few years Walmart built a new and much larger version across the highway. It's been followed by Target and Walgreens stores, plus dozens of strip-type buildings crowding the highway. Driving south into and through Wasilla on the Parks Highway is like passing through any Southern California suburb, with auto dealers, chain restaurants, mega stores, and (minor) traffic jams. In other words, Wasilla is everything travelers want to escape when they visit Alaska.

Sights

Make sure to visit **Wasilla Museum** (391 N. Main St., 907/373-9071, www.cityofwasilla. com/museum, 9am-5pm Tues.-Fri., $3 adults, free under age 13) on Main Street, just off the Parks Highway. The museum houses historical photos and artifacts from early settlers and the Iditarod, plus interesting downstairs exhibits of the mining era, including a diorama of Independence Mine. The adjacent **Old Wasilla Townsite** contains a schoolhouse, a bunkhouse, a smokehouse, a steam bath, a blacksmith shop, and a cache. Just up the street is **Teeland's Store** (405 E. Herning Ave.), built in 1917, one of the oldest buildings in Alaska. Today the beautifully restored structure houses a sandwich shop.

About four miles north of town at Mile 47, take a left at the sign and head 0.75 miles down to the **Museum of Alaska Transportation and Industry** (3800 W. Museum Dr., 907/376-1211, www.museumofalaska.org, 10am-5pm daily mid-May-early Sept., $8 adults, $5 seniors and ages 3-17, free under age 3, $18 families). This museum contains an extensive collection of antiques relating to Alaskan aviation, railroading, fishing, mining, and road transportation. Take a gander at the "Chitina auto railer," an old car built to run on rail tracks. Outside are wooden boats, farm machinery (much of it still running), ancient snowmobiles, and several railcars.

OUT KNIK ROAD

Wasilla is the headquarters for the 1,049-mile Iditarod Trail Sled Dog Race from Anchorage to Nome. The **Iditarod headquarters** (2100 S. Knik-Goose Bay Rd., 907/376-5155, www.iditarod.com, 8am-7pm daily mid-May-mid-Sept., 8am-5pm Mon.-Fri. winter, free) includes a log museum containing race memorabilia, Native Alaskan artifacts, videos, and dog-mushing equipment. Also here is Togo, the stuffed sled dog who led Leonhard Seppala's team during the 1925 serum delivery to Nome. Find Togo and friends two miles out on Knik Road. Want to try your hand at mushing? Take a summer ride on a wheeled dogsled ($10).

Knik Museum (907/376-7755, www. wkhsociety.org, 1pm-6pm Wed.-Sun. May-Sept., $3 adults, $2 seniors, free under age 18, $5 families) is 14 miles west of Wasilla on Knik Road. Built in 1910 as the Fulton and Hirshey Pool and Billiard Hall, the building exhibits fascinating photos and memorabilia from the Knik gold rush of 1897-1917 and the Iditarod Trail, with an upstairs Musher Hall of Fame. At its peak, Knik was home to 1,500 people, but only a handful call it home today.

Shopping

The **Wasilla Farmers Market** (907/357-1464, 10am-6pm Wed. June-mid-Sept.) takes place weekly in summer at the old Wasilla town site (Nelson St. and Weber St.).

Recreation

Lakeshore Park at Wasilla Lake right off the highway has swimming (not too cold), picnic tables, and a view of the craggy Chugach Mountains—a great place to set up your tripod. A less crowded day-use lake area is at **Matanuska Lakes State Recreation Site** (Glenn Hwy.) just beyond the junction of the Parks and Glenn Highways, heading toward Palmer.

Wasilla's big **Brett Memorial Ice Arena** (9746 E. Bogard Rd., 907/376-9260, www. matsugov.us) has year-round skating and hockey. For the unfrozen version, swim at the

The Last Great Race

The most Alaskan of all Alaskan events is the Iditarod Trail Sled Dog Race from Anchorage to Nome. The "Last Great Race" is run each March, attracting 60 or more of the world's best mushers, each with a team of up to 20 dogs. With a top prize of $75,000 and a $500,000 purse for the top 20 teams, the race has become an event with an international following.

Today's Iditarod Trail Sled Dog Race is run on the historic Iditarod Trail, a path that had its origins in the 1908 discovery of gold along a river the Ingalik people called *hidedhod,* meaning "distant place." Thousands of miners flooded into the region following the find, and trails were cut from Seward to the new boomtown of Iditarod so that mail and supplies could be brought in and gold shipped out. After a few years, once the gold ran out, the miners gradually gave up and left, and the old town began a long slow return to quietude. But other events would eventually bring Iditarod back to life in a new form.

During the winter of 1925, a diphtheria epidemic broke out in Nome, and the territorial governor hurriedly dispatched a 20-pound package of life-saving antitoxin serum to halt the disease's spread. Regular boat mail would take 25 days, and the only two airplanes in Alaska were open-cockpit biplanes. With temperatures far below zero and only a few hours of light each day (it was mid-January), that option was impossible. Instead, the package was sent by train from Seward to Nenana, where mushers and their dogs waited to carry the antitoxin on to Nome. What happened next is hard to believe: A Herculean relay effort by 20 different mushers and their dogs brought the vaccine to Nome in just six days. They somehow managed to cover the 674 miles in conditions that included whiteout blizzards, 80 mph winds, and temperatures down to -64°F. The incident gained national attention, and President Coolidge thanked the mushers, presenting each with a medal and $0.50 for each mile traveled.

Long after this heroic effort, two more people entered the picture: Dorothy Page ("Mother of the Iditarod") and Joe Redington Sr. ("Father of the Iditarod"). In 1967 the two organized a commemorative Iditarod race over a small portion of the trail. Six years later they set up a full-blown dogsled race from Anchorage to Nome, a distance that is officially called 1,049 miles. It took winner Dick Wilmarth 20 days, 49 minutes, and 41 seconds to make it under the Nome archway. At the finish line, Wilmarth lost his lead dog, Hot Foot. Fourteen days later, the dog wandered into his master's home in Red Devil—500 miles from Nome.

Over the years the race has become much more professional and far faster. The record run of 9 days, 58 minutes, and 6 seconds was set by Doug Swingley in 2000. And this was even with two mandatory layovers of 10 hours along the way. The Iditarod is certainly one of the most strenuous events in the world. With below-zero temperatures, fierce winds, and all the hazards that go with crossing the most remote parts of Alaska in winter, the race is certainly not for everyone. Despite this, the Iditarod has gained a measure of fame as one in which both women and men are winners. Between 1985 and 1993, five of the nine winners were women, and the late Susan Butcher won four of these races. After Butcher won the race three consecutive years, T-shirts began appearing in local stores saying "Alaska: where men are men, and women win the Iditarod." In the last decade, the Seavey family has dominated races, with Mitch Seavey or his son Dallas Seavey winning eight times between 2004 and 2017.

The Iditarod has not one but two actual starts. The official start is from 4th Avenue in downtown Anchorage, where several thousand onlookers cheer each team that leaves the starting line. The mushers and dogs race as far as Eagle River (25 miles), where they're loaded into trucks and driven to the "restart" in Willow. (This is to avoid having to sled over the thin snow conditions around Palmer and open water on the Knik River.) At the restart, the fastest teams into Eagle River leave first, creating chaotic conditions when several 20-dog teams are pulling to the start at once. From here on, it's 1,000 miles of wilderness. In recent years, as the climate warms, low snow has been a serious problem, and there are many photos of dog teams heading across bare tundra with no snow. The race has even been moved to Fairbanks twice to provide adequate snow.

The Iditarod Trail Committee (Knik Rd., 907/376-5155 or 800/545-6874, www.iditarod.com) has its headquarters in Wasilla, where they have a museum of race memorabilia and offer wheeled dogsled rides in summer.

Wasilla High School pool (701 W. Bogard Rd., 907/376-4222).

On the shore of Wasilla Lake, **Alaska Kayak Academy** (2201 E. Palmer-Wasilla Hwy., 907/746-6600 or 977/215-6600, www.kayakcenterak.com) rents kayaks and pack rafts ($40 per day) and has stand-up paddleboards ($15 per hour), plus other gear. They teach classes for all levels of ability.

Food

Perhaps because of all the early-morning commuters to Anchorage, Wasilla seems to have an espresso stand on almost every corner—along with an equal number of gun shops. So holster your gun and cruise over to **Espresso Café** (1265 S. Seward Meridian Pkwy., 907/376-5282, www.espressocafe.biz, 5am-7pm Mon.-Fri., 6am-7pm Sat., 6am-6pm Sun.) for coffee, comfy chairs, and free Wi-Fi. It's across from Walmart, of course.

Wasilla's most historic structure, the Teeland Building (405 E. Herning Ave.) now hosts **Krazy Moose Subs** (907/357-8774, 10:30am-5pm Tues.-Fri., 10:30am-4pm Sat., $8-13). Get a hot or cold sub on a freshly baked roll; chicken bacon ranch is a favorite. The building's interior is beautifully preserved, with a big upstairs section. Krazy Moose is just down the street from the Wasilla Museum and Old Wasilla Townsite.

INTERNATIONAL

Chepo's Fiesta (731 W. Parks Hwy., 907/373-5656, www.cheposfiesta.com, 11am-10pm Sun.-Thurs., 11am-11pm Fri.-Sat., $14-22) serves tasty Mexican food—including vegetarian choices—and good margaritas in a fun setting. It's on the north end of Wasilla in yet another strip-mall.

Marcello's Restaurant (551 W. Parks Hwy., 907/357-4303, www.marcellosak.com, 11am-10pm daily, $13-30) has the expected faux-Mediterranean decor you'd expect in a strip-mall Greek-Italian restaurant in Wasilla, but the food is actually very good. Favorites include the moussaka, halibut *calabrese*

(stuffed with crab, shrimp, and scallops), and thin-crust pizzas.

Mekong Thai Cuisine (473 W. Parks Hwy., 907/373-7690, www.mekongthaicuisine.com, 11am-3pm Mon.-Fri., noon-2pm Sat., $13-19) has excellent Thai meals, notably the curries and noodle dishes. It's on the south side of Wasilla near Value Village.

Find the valley's best sushi at **Zushi** (1731 E. Palmer-Wasilla Hwy., 907/373-0101, www.thezushiak.com, daily 11:30am-9pm, $10-22), near the big Fred Meyer store. It's a stylish spot with industrial-chic seating. Favorites include the dancing dragon roll, spider roll, and even a steak and fry roll (steak, cream cheese, jalapeño, avocado, crab, and shrimp). Service can be a bit slow since everything is made fresh, but it's worth the wait. Zushi is good for to-go orders too.

FINE DINING

Occupying a little yellow house bounded by a white picket fence in "old town," ★ **The Grape Tap** (322 N. Boundary St., 907/376-8466, www.thegrapetap.com, 3pm-9pm Tues.-Sat. mid-May-early Sept., 5pm-9pm Tues.-Sat. early Sept.-mid-May, $20-45) is Wasilla's fine-dining establishment. Not far from the strip-malls that make up the heart of Wasilla, this restaurant has an unexpected ambience. A romantic downstairs lounge has 40 different boutique wines by the glass ($13-19 for a flight of three wines), along with champagne cocktails. The dinner menu (available downstairs as well) includes filet mignon, tenderloin au poivre, and prawns peppernada, but be sure to also order an appetizer of Not so Cheap Dates stuffed with chèvre cheese and wrapped in bacon. Everything is handmade from scratch; no canned sauces here. For lunch, try the clam chowder or salmon *niçoise* salad. When summer rolls in, The Grape Tap opens a big back patio and lawn to relaxing outdoor dining with a light menu available before 5pm. Reservations are advised.

Adjacent to Settlers Bay Golf Course, eight miles out Knik-Goose Bay Road, **Settlers Bay Lodge** (5801 S. Knik-Goose Bay Rd.,

907/357-5678, www.settlersbaylodge.com, 4pm-10pm daily, $17-45) is a destination spot for locals who appreciate the towering windows, deck-with-a-vista dining, and menu of rather predictable steaks, seafood, and pasta along with daily specials.

Accommodations

MOTELS

Alaska's Select Inn (3451 Palmdale Dr., 907/357-4768 or 888/357-4768, www.alaskaselectinn.com, rooms $139 d, suites $159 d) has large economical guest rooms and suites, all with full kitchens and flat-screen TVs.

Best Western Lake Lucille Inn (1300 W. Lake Lucille Dr., 907/373-1776 or 800/780-7234, www.bestwestern.com/lakelucilleinn, $170-200 d, suites $260 d) has 54 roomy guest rooms and suites, many with private balconies overlooking the lake. Guests will also appreciate the fitness center, in-room fridges, business center, and free hot breakfast.

In a quiet residential area, **Agate Inn** (4725 Begich Circle, 907/373-2290, www.agateinn.com) is three miles from Wasilla on the Palmer-Wasilla Highway. A variety of lodging options are scattered across four buildings on 20 wooded acres: motel-type rooms with king beds ($159 d), apartment suites with full kitchens ($195-275 for 4-6 people), a two-bedroom cottage ($225 for 4), and a three-bedroom guesthouse ($375 for up to 6). All units are stocked with continental breakfast ingredients, and two units are wheelchair-accessible. The owners' seven **pet reindeer** are a favorite of guests; join them for feedings at 10am and 6pm daily.

BED-AND-BREAKFASTS

Visit the website for **Mat-Su Bed & Breakfast Association** (www.alaskabnbhosts.com) for links to local B&Bs.

★ **Lake Lucille B&B** (235 W. Lakeview Ave., 907/357-0352, www.alaskaslakelucillebnb.com, $134-149) is a gracious home right on the shore of Lake Lucille, just a short distance from Wasilla. There are

four reasonably priced guest rooms with private or shared baths; you can combine two rooms into a family suite ($169 for 4 people). A hot and hearty breakfast starts each day.

For something more uniquely Alaskan, stay at **Pioneer Ridge B&B Inn** (2221 Yukon Circle, 907/376-7472 or 800/478-7472, www.pioneerridge.com, $139-199 d, cabin $99 d). This unusual former dairy barn sits on a hill in the country south of Wasilla. Six guest rooms with private or shared baths are available, along with a rustic cabin (the bath is in the main house). A buffet breakfast is served in the common room, where you can also play a game of pool or foosball, watch a video, listen to the player piano, surf the web, or simply relax in the sauna. There's a big deck, and atop the house is a unique (and rather bizarre) glass-enclosed Aurora Room with a fireplace and 360-degree views.

Abby's Place B&B (405 N. Old Trunk Rd., 907/745-1005, www.abbysplace.com, $139 d, additional guests $15 pp) has a quiet woodsy 12-acre location, halfway—nine miles in either direction—between Wasilla and Palmer. The modern home has four large guest rooms for couples or families (no extra charge for kids). Each room has a private bath, cable TV, and Wi-Fi access. The friendly owners, and the filling hot breakfast, receive accolades.

CAMPING

City-run **Lake Lucille Park** (Mile 2, Knik-Goose Bay Rd., 907/373-9010, www.cityofwasilla.com, late May-early Sept., tents $10, RVs $20 with electricity) is an 80-acre natural area with trails and campsites two miles south of Wasilla off Knik-Goose Bay Road.

There's a public campground at **Finger Lake State Recreation Site** (Bogard Rd., 907/240-9797, $25-35), six miles east of Wasilla.

Open year-round, **Big Bear RV Park** (2010 S. Church St., 907/745-7445, www.bigbearrv.net, $30 tents, $40-55 RVs, $65-75 cabins) has RV and tent sites, plus a laundry, simple cabins, and Wi-Fi. Showers are $5 if you aren't camping here.

Many RVers park for free in local shopping mall lots, including the Fred Meyer store in Palmer.

Information and Services

The **Wasilla Chamber of Commerce** (415 E. Railroad Ave., 907/376-1299, www.visitwasilla.org, 9am-4:30pm Mon. and Wed.-Thurs., 9am-3pm Fri.) is housed in the historic train depot. Built in 1911, the quaint building has railroad memorabilia and brochures from local businesses. Drop in to have your photo taken with a cardboard cutout of Sarah Palin, but this is probably as close as you'll get. She spends most of her time in Arizona now, like a true Alaskan.

Adjacent to the museum, the **Wasilla Public Library** (391 N. Main St., 907/376-5913, www.cityofwasilla.com/library, 2pm-6pm Mon., 10:30am-7pm Tues. and Thurs., 10:30am-6pm Wed. and Fri., 1pm-5pm Sat.) is a good place to stop and check your email or use the Internet.

Getting There and Around

Valley Transit (907/864-5000, www.valleytransitak.org, $3 per zone, $7 to Anchorage) has weekday service throughout the valley and commuter runs to Anchorage.

Alaska/Yukon Trails (907/888-5659, www.alaskashuttle.com, Apr.-Sept.) has daily van service along the Parks Highway from Anchorage to Fairbanks. Vans stop at Wasilla with advance notice, and one-way rates from Wasilla are $55 to Talkeetna, $75 to Denali, $90 to Fairbanks, and $34 to Anchorage.

TOP EXPERIENCE

★ HATCHER PASS

This is one of the most beautiful parts of the Mat-Su Valley region and a wonderful side trip from either the Parks Highway north of Wasilla or the Glenn Highway at Palmer. It's a 49-mile drive, starting in Palmer and ending at Mile 71 of the Parks Highway (30 miles north of Wasilla).

Most folks get to Hatcher Pass from the Palmer end. Hatcher Pass Road (also called Willow-Fishhook Rd.) begins in rolling forest-and-farm country and then climbs along the beautiful Little Susitna River, which is popular with experienced kayakers who enjoy Class V white water. After passing Motherlode Lodge, the road climbs steeply uphill to Independence Mine State Historical Park at Mile 17, where the pavement ends, before topping out at 3,886-foot Hatcher Pass and Summit Lake in an area of vast vistas, high tundra, excellent hiking, and backcountry camping. Then it's downhill through pretty forests along Willow Creek all the way to the Parks Highway; this route was originally a wagon road built to serve the gold mines. The road is paved from Palmer all the way to Independence Mine, and for 10 miles from the Willow side; the rest is gravel. A bike path follows the road along the Little Susitna River section, and free campsites can be found at Deception Creek, two miles from the Parks Highway.

Independence Mine State Historical Park

It's hard to imagine a park that better combines the elements of the Alaska experience: scenery, history and lore, and that noble yellow metal, gold. This mine is very different from the panning, sluicing, deep-placer, and dredging operations seen in interior Alaska. This was "hard-rock" mining, with an intricate 21-mile network of tunnels under Granite Mountain. The miners drilled into the rock, inserted explosives (which they set off at the end of shifts to give the fumes time to dissipate before the next crew went in), then "mucked" the debris out by hand to be sorted, crushed, amalgamated, and assayed.

Hard-rock, or "lode," mining is often preceded by panning and placer mining. Prospectors who first took gold from

1: skiers at Independence Mine State Park; 2: Hatcher Pass Lodge

Grubstake Gulch, a tributary of Willow Creek, in 1897 noticed the gold's rough unweathered nature, which indicated a possible lode of unexposed gold nearby. In 1906, Robert Lee Hatcher staked the first lode claim, and his Alaska Free Gold Mine operated until 1924. In 1908 the Independence Mine opened on the mountain's east slope, and over the next 25 years it produced several million dollars' worth of gold. In 1937 the two mines merged into the Alaska Pacific Consolidated Mining Company, which operated Independence Mine at peak production through 1942, when World War II shut it down. A series of private sales and public deals with the Alaska Division of Parks culminated in 1980, leaving the state with 271 acres, including the whole mining camp, and deeding 1,000 acres to the Coronado Mining Corporation, which has active operations in the area.

A couple of dozen camp buildings are in various stages of ruin and refurbishing. Start at the **Independence Mine Visitor Center** (Mile 17, Hatcher Pass Rd., 907/745-2827, www.alaskastateparks.org, 11am-6pm daily mid-June-early Sept., parking $5) in the rehabilitated house of the camp manager. Take some time to enjoy the excellent displays: historic charts, an overview of gold mining, a "touch tunnel" complete with sound effects, and wage summaries for workers and management. Park personnel lead guided tours (1pm and 3pm daily, $6 adults, $3 children). At other times, just wander the site on your own; interpretive signs describe the various buildings. Independence Mine State Historical Park is a must-see on any Alaskan itinerary.

Hikers will appreciate several excellent trails at Hatcher Pass. **Reed Lake Trail** follows Reed Creek to its headwater along a 4.5-mile path. The route is entirely in the alpine, with a number of campsites along the way. It starts from a parking area at Mile 2.5 of Archangel Road. The turnoff to Archangel Road is near Mile 15 of Hatcher Pass Road. Archangel Road is a five-mile dirt road with a gentle incline; it's perfect for an easy bike ride.

Just downhill from Hatcher Pass, **Government Peak Recreation Area** (907/746-8757, www.matsugov.us) has eight miles of hiking and mountain biking trails.

Winter Recreation

Just downhill from Hatcher Pass, **Government Peak Recreation Area** (www.matsugov.us) is a Nordic skiing area with four miles of trails groomed for skate and classic skiers. Access is off the Palmer-Fishhook Road and Edgerton Parks Road. Additional Nordic ski trails are maintained next to Independence Mine.

Hatcher Pass Road isn't plowed beyond Independence Mine State Historical Park in winter, but you can park here to play; it's a special favorite of snowmobilers, snowboarders, and skiers. Snowboarders and skiers often catch a ride up the hill to a point below the mine site and then head downhill on ungroomed trails. On a winter weekend you'll see dozens of kids boarding down, with parents and friends waiting at the bottom to drive them back up for another run. The road typically reopens to cars in early June.

Food and Accommodations

A number of lodging options are scattered along the southern section of Hatcher Pass Road north of Palmer. **Hatcher Pass B&B** (9000 N. Palmer Fishhook Rd., 907/745-6788, www.hatcherpassbb.com) has delightful log cabins with kitchenettes, private baths, and TVs. There are small "sourdough" cabins ($129 d) and large two-bedroom "Alaska Grande" cabins ($189 d). All cabins are fully stocked for cook-your-own breakfasts. A two-night minimum is required in summer.

Just downhill from Independence Mine is **Hatcher Pass Lodge** (907/745-5897, www.hatcherpasslodge.com, 8am-8pm daily late May-early Sept., 8am-8pm Sat., noon-6pm Fri. and Sun. early Sept.-late May, meals $18-30, cabins $150). This A-frame lodge is a good spot for sandwiches (try the salmon melt), soups, burgers, and halibut, with a sunset view to die for. Be sure to try the house specialty, fondue made with Swiss gruyère and emmentaler cheeses, *kirschwasser,* and french bread ($30). There are nine cozy cabins for up to four people each and three minuscule upstairs guest rooms; breakfast is available for guests. There are no showers or running water; the cabins have chemical toilets (there's a regular toilet in the main lodge). The creek-side sauna is a fine place to relax late in the day. The lodge is open daily year-round, with a coal stove cranking all winter. Speaking from personal experience, this is the perfect place for a summer wedding. Hatcher Pass Lodge also maintains six miles of groomed ski trails in the winter for both classical and skate skiing; more adventurous backcountry skiers and snowboarders head up the steep (and avalanche-prone) slopes that rise on three sides.

NORTH TO DENALI

It's a long 195-mile drive from Wasilla to Denali National Park (237 miles from Anchorage) on the Parks Highway. After the first few miles, the developments peter out and roadside attractions shift from fast food, gun shops, and video stores to the real Alaska of forests and mountains. The land is a seemingly endless birch and spruce forest, with a smattering of half-finished plywood homesteads covered in blue tarps, their yards piled high with firewood. The road follows a gradual climb toward the magnificent Alaska Range that seems to grow in magnitude the farther north you get. Mile after mile of pink fireweed flowers brighten the roadside in midsummer.

Big Lake

The Big Lake area (907/892-6109, www.biglakechamber.org) is a popular recreation destination, especially on summer weekends when many Anchorageites head to summer homes here. Access is via nine-mile-long Big Lake Road, which splits off the Parks Highway at Mile 52 (10 miles north of Wasilla). Don't expect quiet along this large and scenic lake. In summer, Big Lake is Jet Ski central 24 hours a day, and when winter arrives the

snowmobile crowd comes out for more motorized mayhem.

Big Lake hosts the start of the **Iron Dog Snowmobile Race** (www.irondog.org) in late February. This 2,000-mile race has a halfway stop in Nome before finishing in Fairbanks. It's the world's longest snowmobile race and a big deal for motor heads. The fastest machines often cover the course in less than 40 hours.

Three state park campgrounds (907/317-9094, www.dnr.alaska.gov, $20-30) are in the area: **Rocky Lake State Recreation Site, Big Lake North State Recreation Site,** and **Big Lake South State Recreation Site.**

Operated by four-time Iditarod champion Martin Buser, **Happy Trails Kennel** (Mile 5, W. Lakes Blvd., 907/892-7899, www.buserdog.com, late May-early Sept., $40 adults, $20 children) has 1.5-hour kennel tours and demonstrations all summer.

A luxurious lakeside resort, **Alaska Sunset View Resort** (5322 S. Big Lake Rd., 907/892-8885, www.alaskasunsetviewresort.com, $235-395 d) is popular for weddings and retreats. Ten immaculate guest rooms are available, with such perks as a continental breakfast, whirlpool tubs, a pool table, a gourmet kitchen, laundry, and an exercise facility. The owners also have **Creekside Lodge** ($850), a large and very private six-bedroom log home on 10 acres of land; it is a favorite of honeymooners with cash to spend.

If you're camping in the area, **Doc Rockers Laundromat** (3462 S. Big Lake Rd., 907/892-1800) has showers.

Houston

This gathering of 1,800 or so souls 58 miles from Anchorage includes the usual lineup of suspects: gas, groceries, cafés, lodging, an RV park, a coin laundry, and air-taxi operators, but it is best known for its fireworks stands. Several of these behemoths—it's especially hard to miss **Gorilla Fireworks** (800/770-6555, www.gorillafireworks.com)—sit on the edges of town, pulling families from Anchorage looking for fun on the Fourth of

July. Amazingly, they're all owned by the same family. It's illegal to shoot off fireworks almost anywhere in Alaska. Of course, this is one of those legal niceties that is widely ignored. Due to fire danger, the shops don't sell rockets of any type in the summer; you'll need to wait for winter until they're available.

Little Susitna River Campground (Mile 57, Parks Hwy., 907/892-6812, $15) is an Alaska Department of Fish and Game facility on the south side of Houston.

Nancy Lake State Recreation Area

Access to Nancy Lake is from Mile 67 of the Parks Highway, just south of Willow and 25 miles north of Wasilla. This flat, heavily forested terrain is dotted with over 100 lakes, some interconnected by creeks. As you might imagine, the popular activities here are fishing, boating, and canoeing, plus a comfortable campground and a couple of hiking trails. As you might also suspect, the skeeters here are thick in early summer.

Follow Nancy Lake Road a little more than a mile to **Nancy Lake State Recreation Site Campground** ($20). A half mile past the kiosk is the trailhead to several **public-use cabins** (907/745-3975, www.alaskastateparks. org, $55-100). Reserve months ahead to be sure of getting one of these exceptionally popular cabins. Just under a mile beyond this trailhead is the **Tulik Nature Trail,** an easy walk that takes about an hour. Keep an eye out for loons, beavers, and terns, and watch for that prickly devil's club. **South Rolly Lake Campground** (Mile 7, Nancy Lake Rd., $20), at South Rolly Lake, has 98 campsites and 12 picnic sites, as well as a small boat launch.

The **Tanaina Lake Canoe Route** begins at Mile 5 on Nancy Lakes Road. This leisurely 12-mile, two-day trip hits 14 lakes, between most of which are well-marked portages, some upgraded with boardwalks over the muskeg. Hunker down for the night at any one of 10 primitive campsites (campfires allowed in fireplaces only). Another possibility, though it requires a long portage, is to put in to the

Little Susitna River at Mile 57 of the Parks Highway and portage to Skeetna Lake, where you connect to the southern leg of the loop trail.

Willow

At Mile 69 is Willow (pop. 2,000), a roadside town that you'll miss if you sneeze. It has gas, groceries, hardware, a café, and air service. Back in 1980, Alaskans voted to move the state capital here. A multibillion-dollar city was planned and real estate speculation went wild. When a second vote was held in 1982 to decide whether to actually spend the billions, however, the plan was soundly defeated.

Willow's big event comes in early March, as the **Iditarod Trail Sled Dog Race** slides through town. The race officially begins in Anchorage, but after a 25-mile run to Eagle River, the dogs are trucked north for the "restart" at Willow Lake. Just west of here, the teams move completely away from the road system and are in wilderness all the way to Nome. Because of good snow conditions, a number of well-known dog mushers are based in Willow.

Operated by Iditarod veteran Vern Halter, **Dream a Dream Dog Kennels** (Mile 65, Parks Hwy., 907/495-1197, www. dreamadreamsleddog.com, $109-139 pp) has summertime kennel tours and demonstrations in Willow. Kennel and dog lot tours include a cart ride pulled by the dogs and the chance to hold the pups. The Halters also rent out two apartment suites ($139 d) with full kitchens, private baths, TVs, and Wi-Fi.

Willow Air Service (907/495-6370 or 800/478-6370, www.willowair.com) offer air-taxi service and scenic flights over Knik Glacier, Hatcher Pass, and Mount Denali from Willow.

Right along the creek, **Willow Creek Resort** (Mile 72, Parks Hwy., 907/495-6343, www.willowcreekresortalaska.com, May-Sept., tents $28, RVs $40-50) has spaces for RVs and tents, plus a laundry, showers, Wi-Fi, and raft rentals ($250 per day). The basic cabin comes with a kitchenette but no bath.

North to Talkeetna

Turn west off the Parks Highway at Mile 71 for **Willow Creek State Recreational Area** (day-use $5, campsites $15), four miles down the Susitna River access road. There are 140 campsites, but don't expect a quiet night's repose in the wilderness here if the salmon are running, which they do for most of the summer. The boat launch attracts fishing parties at all hours of the day and night, as well as lots of RVs with their inevitable generator noise. Still, it's a pretty and handy place to spend the night if it's getting late and you plan to travel over the exceptionally scenic Hatcher Pass to Independence Mine State Historical Park.

Hatcher Pass Road (aka Willow-Fishhook Rd.) turns east at Mile 71 of the Parks Highway, continuing for 49 beautiful miles to the Independence Mine State Historical Park at Hatcher Pass. It's paved for the first 10 miles, and then gravel (watch for potholes) the rest of the way. Find good fishing and free campsites at **Deception Creek**, two miles up Hatcher Pass Road.

Perched alongside the Parks Highway at Mile 88, **Sheep Creek Lodge** (907/495-6227, www.sheepcreeklodgeak.com, 8am-9pm Sun.-Thurs., 8am-10pm Fri.-Sat. late May-mid-Sept., 8am-9pm Sun.-Mon. and Wed.-Thurs., 8am-10pm Fri.-Sat. mid-Sept.-late May) is a large log building with all sorts of action. There's home-style cooking at the restaurant ($12-28), and burgers, reubens, pizzas, steaks, and breakfast are served all day. The RV park-campground ($15) has no-hookup sites and outhouses. Nine cozy and pet-friendly cabins ($90) include a variety of beds, along with microwaves, fridges, and stoves, but no water. Cabin guests can use outhouses or baths and showers in the lodge. The largest cabin can sleep eight people for the same price. In addition, two lodge rooms ($145 d) have private baths, TVs, and queen beds. Wi-Fi works in the lodge, but not the cabins or campground. The bar—decorated with stuffed heads and dead critters—features live music most Saturday nights, rambling from old-school rock to blues and even the occasional jazz band. The deck is a good spot for a summer afternoon brew, and all five species of salmon head up the adjacent Sheep Creek.

Mat-Su RV Park (Mile 91, Parks Hwy., 907/495-6300, www.matsurvpark.com, May-Sept., tents $17, RVs $30-40) has a convenience store, laundry, showers, restrooms, and Wi-Fi.

The privately run **Montana Creek Campground** (Mile 97, Parks Hwy., 907/733-5267 or 877/475-2267, tents $20-33, RVs $40-45) provides wooded sites on both sides of this very popular salmon-fishing creek. It's just a mile south of the turnoff to Talkeetna.

Denali National Park

Spectacular Denali National Park is near the center of Alaska, 235 miles north of Anchorage. The park covers nearly six million acres of land on both sides of the Alaska Range, part of a vast terrain of boreal forests, tundra, and towering mountains.

The Parks Highway connecting Anchorage with Denali and Fairbanks is the only paved route through this country. Other roads are more limited: a dirt road extends 92 miles through Denali National Park, and the gravel Denali Highway turns east from Cantwell, paralleling the Alaska Range to Paxson, but the rest of the land has few roads.

One of the wonderful aspects of Alaska's interior is its vastness. Although Talkeetna and the entrance to Denali National Park are

Highlights

Look for ★ to find recommended sights, activities, dining, and lodging.

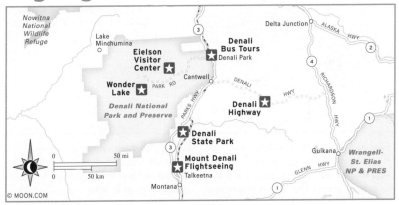

★ **Mount Denali Flightseeing:** Talkeetna is the base for several air charter operators with flights over Denali that include a bush plane landing on Ruth Glacier (page 137).

★ **Denali State Park:** This 325,000-acre park affords breathtaking views of Mount Denali from backcountry trails and roadside pullouts (page 149).

★ **Denali Highway:** This 134-mile mostly gravel road provides dramatic views of the Alaska Range and access to vast stretches of wild country (page 151).

★ **Denali Bus Tours:** This is the only way to reach the heart of Alaska's most famous park. Grizzlies, moose, wolves, and Dall sheep are commonly seen, and you may even see Mount Denali in all its glory (page 165).

★ **Eielson Visitor Center:** This modern eco-friendly visitors center provides spectacular views of Denali when the mountain is out (page 170).

★ **Wonder Lake:** Near the end of the Park Road, Wonder Lake is famous for picture-perfect views of the mountain (page 171).

Denali National Park and Vicinity

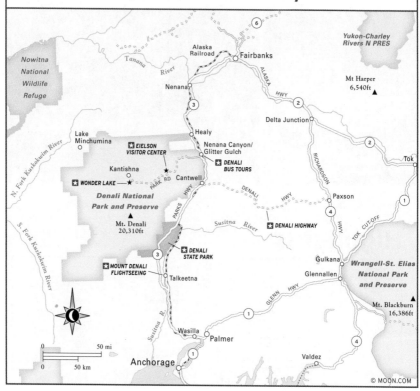

© MOON.COM

both packed with travelers all summer long, it's amazingly easy to escape the crowds and find yourself in a land that seems unchanged from time immemorial. Take the time to pull off the highway and fish on one of the creeks or climb a hill for the view. You won't regret it!

PLANNING YOUR TIME

It's a very scenic five-hour drive (eight re-laxing hours by train) from Anchorage to the entrance to **Denali National Park.** The big draws are 20,310-foot Mount Denali (often obscured by clouds), a grand land-scape of open tundra and boreal forests, and the chance to watch grizzly bears, moose,

wolves, Dall sheep, and caribou. Private cars are not allowed on the 92-mile Park Road, but **shuttle and tour buses** provide a wonderful way to see the park or to access remote areas for hiking and camping. Be sure to book your bus well in advance of your trip since the seats often fill up.

It's 8 hours round-trip to **Eielson Visitor Center,** where most buses turn around, or a challenging 11 hours round-trip to **Wonder Lake,** deep inside the park. Plan to take at least two days—more if at all possible—to explore the park; one day for a ride into the park, and the second for a half-day ranger-led Discovery Hike or other trek. Add another

Previous: Parks Highway bridge over the Nenana River south of Healy; floatplane at Fish Lake near Talkeetna; caribou in Denali National Park

day for a float down the Nenana River just outside the park entrance and to take in the sled dog demonstrations and other activities.

Talkeetna is a delightful destination, with outstanding vistas across to Mount Denali and a quaint historic downtown filled with mountaineers and outdoor enthusiasts. Several air-taxi operators offer Mount Denali flightseeing trips that often include a glacier landing. Farther north is the **Denali Highway,** a partly paved, mostly gravel 134-mile route that cuts east to west along the magnificent Alaska Range. One could easily spend several days hiking backcountry routes, camping beneath the midnight sun, and fishing the lakes and streams along the Denali Highway.

Talkeetna

The outdoorsy and youthful town of Talkeetna (pop. 900) lies at the end of a 14-mile side road that splits away from the Parks Highway, 98 miles north of Anchorage. Two closely related phenomena dominate this small bush community: The Mountain, and flying to and climbing on The Mountain. On a clear day, from the overlook a mile out on the Spur Road, Mount Denali and the accompanying Alaska Range scrape the sky like a jagged white wall.

All summer, local flightseeing and air-taxi companies take off in a continuous parade to circle Mount Denali, buzz up long glaciers or even land on them, then return to Talkeetna's busy airport to drop off passengers whose wide eyes, broad smiles, and shaky knees attest to the excitement of this once-in-a-lifetime thrill. In late April-early July, these same special "wheel-and-ski" planes might be delivering an American, European, Japanese, or Korean climbing expedition to the Kahiltna Glacier (elevation 7,000 feet), from which—if they're lucky—they inch their way up the popular West Buttress route 13,000 feet to the peak. On a clear day, if you're anywhere within striking distance, make a beeline for Talkeetna and be whisked away to some of the most stunning and alien scenery you'll ever see.

If you visit Talkeetna early in the summer, you'll find a peculiar mix of people: the earthy locals with their beards and rusty pickups, the mountaineers—mostly male—decked in color-coordinated Gore-Tex, and the busloads of cruise-ship passengers who unload on the south side of town and wander through in wide-eyed wonder.

Talkeetna ("where the rivers meet"), nesting at the confluence of the Talkeetna, Chulitna, and Susitna Rivers, was originally settled by trappers and prospectors who paddled up the Susitna River to gain access to rich silver, coal, and fur country around the Talkeetna Mountains. The settlement got a boost when the railroad was pushed through in the early 1920s, and it still remains a popular stop on the route. In 1965 the Spur Road from the Parks Highway to Talkeetna was completed, providing further access to the town.

This is one of the few Alaskan villages that still looks the way people imagine Alaskan towns should look, with rustic log buildings lining Main Street and a local population that embraces both grizzled miners and back-to-the-earth tree huggers. Talkeetna men easily win the prize for the highest number of beards per capita anywhere in Alaska! Local bumper stickers proclaim "Talkeetna, where the road ends and life begins." If you ever saw the old *Northern Exposure* on TV, this is the place it's rumored to have been modeled on. In the last decade or so, Talkeetna has really caught on, and summer brings a flood of tourists. The town is still rough, dusty, and rustic around

Talkeetna

TALKEETNA RV

FRONT ST

TALKEETNA'S EASY ST

F ST

G ST

H ST

I ST

ALASKAN RAILROAD

RIVER PARK

HOUSE OF TREES   FAIRVIEW INN

TALKEETNA RANGER STATION

N MAIN ST

NAGLEY'S

TALKEETNA ROADHOUSE

SHELDON COMMUNITY ARTS HANGAR

TALKEETNA HOSTEL INTERNATIONAL

1ST ST

B ST

TALKEETNA HISTORICAL MUSEUM

VILLAGE AIRSTRIP

2ND ST

2ND ST

NORTHERN GUEST HOUSE

MOUNT DENALI FLIGHTSEEING   TALKEETNA AIR TAXI

K2 AVIATION

C ST

3RD ST

3RD ST

ALASKA MOUNTAINEERING SCHOOL

TALKEETNA AIRPORT

SHELDON AIR

D ST

POST OFFICE

TALKEETNA SPUR RD

S TERMINAL AVE

VETERAN'S WAY

ELEMENTARY SCHOOL

Susitna River

LATITUDE 62 MOTEL

TALKEETNA CAMPER PARK

0   200 yds

0   200 m

RAILROAD DEPOT

TALKEETNA LIBRARY

SUSITNA RIVER LODGING

To Denali Viewpoint, Talkeetna Alaskan Lodge, Denali National Park and Preserve, and Anchorage

© MOON.COM

the edges, but locals complain that it's starting to feel a bit like a theme park.

SIGHTS

At Mile 13 of the Talkeetna Spur Road (one mile south of town), a turnout provides a good view of **Mount Denali and the Alaska Range.** Across the road is the driveway for Talkeetna Alaskan Lodge, where the spacious back deck provides even more striking vistas of The Mountain.

Talkeetna is a walk-around town, with most of the action within a couple of blocks of Nagley's Store and the Fairview Inn. On a summer afternoon, the town is packed with tourists; stick around in the evening after the cruise ship folks depart to see the real

Talkeetna, when locals emerge to mingle with travelers in bars and restaurants.

Start your tour of town with a selfie photo at the "Welcome to Beautiful Downtown Talkeetna" sign as you enter town; it's next to a wheelbarrow overflowing with flowers. Across the street is **Nagley's Store** (13650 E. Main St., 907/733-3663, www.nagleysstore. com, 7:30am-9pm daily), a red log building that first opened in the 1920s and moved to the present site in 1945. The crowded interior has a few groceries, ice cream, espresso, beer, and a genuine old-time atmosphere. Head up the stairs for outdoor supplies and to check out the old photos, furs, traps, and snowshoes.

The town's other icon—**Fairview Inn** (101 Main St., 907/733-2423, www.denali-fairview. com, noon-1am Sun.-Thurs., noon-2am

Fri.-Sat.)—sits kitty-corner across the road. Locals rest on the benches out front most afternoons, and music spills out when evening comes. Built in 1923, it's a great place to soak up the old-time atmosphere. But it *is* a bar, so kids don't belong. President Warren Harding ate lunch at the Fairview during his Alaska visit in 1923; it was one of the last meals he had before falling ill and dying.

For a graphic and detailed look at the history of the town and its connection to The Mountain, check out the excellent **Talkeetna Historical Museum** (907/733-2487, www.talkeetnahistoricalsociety.org, 10am-6pm daily May-late Sept., 11am-4pm Sat.-Sun. winter, $5 adults, $4 seniors, free under age 12). Take a left after Nagley's Store; the museum is a half block down the side street on the right in a white schoolhouse built in 1936. Inside are all sorts of local artifacts—including a horsehide coat from the 1890s—but more interesting is the old railroad section house out back, which now houses an enormous relief map of Denali surrounded by photos and the stories of climbers, including several famous adventurers who lost their lives on this treacherous peak. Other exhibits show the gear climbers use, such as the required "clean mountain cans" for transporting human waste. Return at 1pm (Mon.-Fri.) for an informative talk on climbing Mount Denali.

The nonprofit **Susitna Salmon Center** (13512 E. 1st St., 907/315-4632, 10am-6pm daily mid-May-mid-Sept.) has a small visitors center with fish tanks, artwork, and videos about the importance of salmon in Alaska. In summer, naturalists lead informative hour-long walking tours to the river (reservations required, $25 adults, $5 ages 13-17, $3 under age 13); this is a good way to learn about the lives of these fascinating and vital fish.

ENTERTAINMENT AND EVENTS

Stop by **Denali Brewing Company** (Mile 2, Talkeetna Spur Rd., 907/733-2536, www.denalibrewing.com, 11am-8pm daily mid-May-Sept., noon-10pm daily Oct.-mid-May) for a sampling of their beers, or to get a growler or six-pack to go. The brewery typically has 20 beers, hard ciders, and meads on tap. Daily 45-minute tours (noon and 5pm, $10) include the chance to sample four beers. Tours can be booked online in advance. Denali Brewing also owns Denali Brewpub in Talkeetna.

Fairview Inn (101 Main St., 907/733-2423, www.denali-fairview.com, noon-1am Sun.-Thurs., noon-2am Fri.-Sat.) hosts live bands five nights a week in the summer and on Saturday in winter.

The **Sheldon Community Arts Hangar** (downtown behind Nagley's, 907/733-2321) hosts plays and other events in the summer. Legendary bush pilot Don Sheldon used this building as his airplane hangar.

Talkeetna loves to party, especially on the **Fourth of July** with a parade and other events, including a fun Cardboard Boat Regatta at Christiansen Lake. All summer long you can find music in the downtown park during **Live at 5** (Fri.) performances.

Winter arrives with a vengeance this far north, and **Talkeetna Winterfest** (Dec.) brightens spirits, especially those of the many local bachelors. The main events are a Wilderness Woman Contest that includes all sorts of wacky activities, followed later that evening by a Bachelor Society Ball, during which local bachelors are bid on by single women, many of whom drive up from Anchorage for the chance. It has all the sexual energy of a male-stripper night, except that some of the men are considerably less fit and keep their clothes on (at least during the bidding). This is one of Alaska's most authentic winter events, representing the skewed ratio of men to women and the oddball nature of small-town Alaska.

SHOPPING

Talkeetna's **Artisans Open Air Market** (907/733-7829, www.denaliartscouncil.org, 10am-6pm Sat.-Mon. mid-May-mid-Sept.) has booths selling jewelry, clothing, and local

Best Places to See Denali

Mount Denali and Ruth Glacier

Seeing the massive 20,310-foot summit of Mount Denali is a highlight for both newcomers to Alaska and locals. The mountain has notoriously fickle weather, and the summit is often obscured by clouds, but when it emerges, you have no doubt that it's the tallest mountain in North America. The peak is visible from many places in south-central Alaska; here are a few of the best.

- **Earthquake Park** in Anchorage. This city park is out West Northern Lights Boulevard near the airport.

- **Resolution Park** in downtown Anchorage.

- The rooftop bar at **49th State Brewing Co.** in downtown Anchorage.

- Just outside **Talkeetna.** A turnout at Mile 13 of the Talkeetna Spur Road (one mile from Talkeetna) provides an excellent view of The Mountain. Across the way is the turnoff to Talkeetna Alaskan Lodge, with even more impressive Alaska Range vistas from the back deck.

- **Petersville Road.** This long gravel road turns west off the Parks Highway at Trapper Creek (Mile 115), with amazing views of Denali at several points along the way. If you continue out this road, it leads to access points for Denali State Park, where a hike leads to dramatic south-side vistas.

- **Denali Viewpoint South** (Mile 135, Parks Hwy.). Within Denali State Park, this very popular highway stop has signs describing the Alaska Range and telescopes for a closer look. This is probably the best drive-up location to see the mountain.

- **K'esugi Ken** (Mile 135, Parks Hwy.). A paved road leads uphill to this new area within Denali State Park. Stop at the interpretive pavilion, where an easy 0.75-mile loop trail leads to amazing views across the Susitna Valley to Mount Denali.

- **Denali Viewpoint North** (Mile 163, Parks Hwy.). Another large turnout with views of Mount Denali when it's out.

- **Eielson Visitor Center** in Denali National Park. You can't see Denali from the park entrance, but a pullout at Mile 9 of the Park Road has a limited view of the peak. It's an eight-hour round-trip bus ride into the park to reach the beautifully located visitors center at Eielson with panoramic views looking south to Mount Denali. Just before the bus drops down to Eielson, it stops at Stony Hill for a higher perspective.

- **Wonder Lake and Reflection Pond.** Famous Wonder Lake is 85 miles out the Park Road (11 hours round-trip on the shuttle bus), where the mountain is up close and personal. Nearby Reflection Pond is the perfect spot for photos of the mountain and its reflection.

crafts. It's in front of the Sheldon Community Arts Hangar behind Nagley's.

The Dancing Leaf Gallery (Main St., near Nagley's, 907/733-5323, 10am-8pm daily May-mid-Sept.), has a fine selection of local and Alaskan art in a modern timber-frame building.

Kahiltna Birchworks (Mile 1, Talkeetna Spur Rd., 907/733-1409 or 800/380-7457, www.alaskabirchsyrup.com, 10am-6pm daily mid-May-mid-Sept.) is a unique local business where owners Michael and Dulce East produce distinctively tart-sweet birch syrup and other products. They tap more than 13,000 birch trees each spring, using a sophisticated maze of tubing to produce 125,000 gallons of sap that is processed into 1,300 gallons of golden syrup. This is the world's largest producer of birch syrup; okay, there isn't a lot of competition out there. Watch a short video on birch syrup production, then taste a sample or buy a bottle of syrup at their facility, where you can check out the Alaskan-made gifts or get scoops of birch-flavored Alaska Supreme ice cream with berry toppings. Visit in early May to watch them in full production mode.

RECREATION

TOP EXPERIENCE

★ Mount Denali Flightseeing

Talkeetna is famous as a launching point for flights over Mount Denali, and on a clear summer day a constant parade of planes takes off from the airport on the edge of town. The flight services offer a bewildering array of possibilities, including short scenic flights, glacier landings, drop-off hiking or fishing, wildlife-viewing, overnight trips, and flights to, around, or over the top of The Mountain. Rates vary according to the type of airplane, length of the flight, and how many people there are in your group. Most outfits will try to match you up with other folks to maximize your flightseeing dollar. Be flexible in your plans, since weather is infinitely variable and

is always the most important consideration when it comes to flying you safely.

There are one-hour flights ($220 pp, $320 pp with a 30-minute glacier landing), but the most popular tours are 1.25 hours long ($285 pp, $385 pp with a 30-minute glacier landing) and 1.5-hour flights ($335 pp, $435 pp with a 30-minute glacier landing). For a panoramic view of the 500-mile-long Alaska Range, take a tour to the summit of Mount Denali ($335 pp, $475 pp with a 30-minute glacier landing). During this flight you may see mountain climbers as the plane climbs to 20,000 feet, but because of the altitude, oxygen masks are needed, so children under 12 can't participate. Given the choice, I'd always pay a bit more for the glacier landing on any of these trips. It turns a spectacular flight into a once-in-a-lifetime adventure.

Reservations are recommended, but not always necessary, so stop by the airport for details and current weather conditions around The Mountain. Note that the climbing season on Mount Denali runs from early spring until mid- or late June, and the flight services are busiest then. As always with bush flying, risks are involved, and fatalities have taken the lives of some of the best local pilots and climbers over the years. Your odds (not to mention the views) are probably better if you wait until a clear day to fly.

A number of charter companies provide service to Mount Denali from the Talkeetna Airport. **K2 Aviation** (907/733-2291 or 800/764-2291, www.flyk2.com) and **Talkeetna Air Taxi** (907/733-2218 or 800/533-2219, www.talkeetnaair.com) are the largest operators. Talkeetna Air is a favorite of climbers, and provides translations for Korean and Japanese travelers. K2 provides printed material translated in multiple languages to help identify features during the flight. K2 offers a unique fly-in trip ($495 pp) that includes a floatplane trip from Fish Lake near Talkeetna to remote Moraine Lake inside Denali, where you meet a guide for an easy backcountry hike. These four-hour trips are

DENALI NATIONAL PARK
TALKEETNA

only offered after the ice melts from the lake in mid-June.

Owned by Holly Sheldon Lee—daughter of famed pilot Don Sheldon—**Sheldon Air Service** (907/733-2321, www.sheldonairservice.com) is an excellent small family operation offering a personal touch.

Based at Fish Lake, **Alaska Bush Floatplane Service** (Mile 9, Talkeetna Spur Rd., 907/733-1693, www.alaskafloatplane.com, May-Sept.) offers Denali flightseeing, but is better known for fly-in hiking, bear-viewing, and fishing at remote lakes. A one-hour flight over the Talkeetna Range is $220 pp. If you haven't flown on a floatplane before, this is a great opportunity from a very picturesque location.

River Trips

Denali View Raft Adventures (907/757-1391, www.denaliviewraft.com) has 3-hour Susitna River trips ($105 adults, $65 under age 13), 2-hour Talkeetna River floats ($75 adults, $49 children), and a unique 4.5-hour trip that starts with a train ride upriver to Chase, followed by a float and lunch on the Susitna River ($179 adults, $120 children).

Talkeetna River Guides (907/733-2677 or 800/353-2677, www.talkeetnariverguides.com, mid-May-mid-Sept.) leads two-hour Talkeetna River natural history floats ($79 adults, $59 under age 11) and four-hour Chulitna River trips ($139 adults, $119 children). They primarily book customers from the large hotels.

Mahay's Jet Boat Adventures (907/733-2223, www.mahaysjetboat.com) has an exceptionally popular two-hour jet-boat tour up the Susitna River ($75 adults, $57 under age 13). Longer trips are also offered, including a five-hour run into Devil's Canyon ($175 adults, $132 children). Their most unusual offering is a river rail-and-trail tour that starts with a ride aboard the *Hurricane Turn Train* to Curry, followed by a historical tour of the town site, and a jet-boat adventure back to Talkeetna ($165 adults, $124 children). This is a fun family outing.

Fishing in Talkeetna is excellent all summer long; rainbow trout, grayling, Dolly Varden, and all five species of Pacific salmon are there for the catching. Local riverboat services can supply you with a fishing guide or drop you off along the river for the day or overnight. Local fishing guides include **Phantom Tri-River Charters** (907/733-2400, www.phantomsalmoncharters.com), **Talkeetna Wilderness River Fishing Guides** (907/733-4111, www.talkeetnafishing.com), and **Talkeetna Fishing Guides** (907/733-3355 or 800/318-2534, www.talkeetnafishingguides.com).

Zip-Lining

Talkeetna's newest adventure is **Denali Zipline Tours** (13572 E. Main St., 907/733-3988, www.denaliziplinetours.com, $149 adults, $119 ages 10-14, no children under age 10, June-Sept.), located in a birch, spruce, and cottonwood forest three miles from town. The course consists of nine zip lines and three sky bridges, with panoramic views of Denali and the Alaska Range along the way. The highest platform is 60 feet up a tree, and the final zip line—700 feet long—takes you over a small lake. You'll also have an opportunity to rappel from one of the platforms. Three-hour tours take place several times a day all summer, with a maximum of eight guests for two guides. This is a great rainy-day alternative when flights to Denali are cancelled.

Biking, Hiking, and Canoeing

A paved **bike path** parallels the Spur Road all the way to Talkeetna. Turn onto gravel roads at Miles 3 and 12 for out-of-the-way lakes and camping spots. At Mile 13 is the big turnout with an interpretive sign on the Alaska Range and heart-stopping views, if the clouds are cooperating. Talkeetna Alaskan Lodge is on the opposite side of the road; stop in for the Mount Denali view from its back deck even if you aren't overnighting here.

1: Talkeetna Historical Museum; **2:** Nagley's Store; **3:** Talkeetna welcome sign; **4:** air taxi at Talkeetna Airport

North Shore Cyclery (14008 E. 2nd St., 907/733-9999, www.northshorecyclery.bike, 10am-6pm daily, $65 for half-day) rents mountain bikes and fat-tire bikes. It's located next to the airport and is open year-round, with cross-country ski and snowshoe rentals in winter.

It's hard to miss the fluorescent green bikes from **Talkeetna Bike Rentals** (22911 S. Talkeetna Spur Rd., 907/354-1222, www.talkeetnabikerentals.com, 8am-6pm daily May-Sept., $25 per day), located at the big parking lot just before you enter town. These three-speed cruisers are primarily for the cruise ship crowd.

Two miles south of town, **Talkeetna Lakes Park** (off Comsat Rd., www.matsugov.us) covers more than 1,000 acres of forested land around X, Y, and Z Lakes. There is no camping, but the parks have a maze of excellent hiking and biking trails that become cross-country ski trails in winter. Several canoes are stashed at the park; rent one from **Talkeetna Adventure Company** (907/733-3355 or 800/318-2534, www.talkeetnacampandcanoe.com, canoes $35 per day).

Alaska Nature Guides (907/733-1237, www.alaskanatureguides.com, late May-mid-Sept., $64 adults, $44 under age 13) provides excellent three-hour nature walks within Talkeetna Lakes Park. For something unique, try heli-hiking ($443 pp), a 3.5-hour adventure that begins with a helicopter flight into the Talkeetna Mountains, followed by a tundra hike and return flight. Alaska Nature Guides also offers a hike-and-raft trip ($299 pp) that begins in Talkeetna and includes a van ride, a six-mile hike up K'esugi Ridge, lunch at Mary's McKinley View Lodge, and a raft trip back to Talkeetna. All hikes are led by naturalists with years of Alaska experience. The company also offers custom birding, photography, and winter snowshoeing trips.

If your children are bored, take them to the big **Talkeetna Playground** on the south end of town.

Dog Mushing

Tour the kennels of Iditarod musher Jerry Sousa and take a cart ride behind a team of 12 sled dogs at **Sundog Racing Kennel** (Main St., 907/733-3355 or 800/318-2534, www.sundogkennel.com). There are two-hour kennel tours and rides ($75 pp), or for the real deal, join a 10-mile wintertime dog-mushing trip.

Winner of the 2012, 2014, 2015, and 2016 Iditarods, **Dallas Seavey** (www.dallasseavey.com) operates kennels at Mile 7 of the Spur Road. When Dallas won in 2012, he was the youngest person to ever win the race, at 25 years old. Dallas's father, Mitch Seavey, won the Iditarod in 2004, 2013, and 2017, making this the most successful family in dog mushing. **Salmon Berry Tours** (907/278-3572, www.salmonberrytours.com) leads all-day winter tours to Dallas's kennel from Anchorage ($399 pp, including round-trip transportation, a 2.5-hour tour with a guide, and lunch). Tours are led by dog handlers (not Dallas Seavey) and include the chance to drive your own team. Fall drive-a-team dog tours ($299 pp) use a unique four-wheel cart crafted with bicycle wheels.

FOOD

Talkeetna has turned into quite the spot for good food, making it a rarity on the Alaska road system. Most places are downtown, so you can just walk a block or so to see what appeals to you.

Cafés

At ★ **Talkeetna Roadhouse** (Main St. and C St., 907/733-1351, www.talkeetnaroadhouse.com, 6am-8pm daily mid-May-mid-Sept., daily 8am-8pm daily mid-Sept.-mid-May, $10-22), long tables make for fun family-style dining with crowds of locals. Breakfast variations—available till 3pm—include Paul Bunyan-size cinnamon rolls, chocolate potato cake, biscuits and gravy, and gargantuan sourdough hotcakes, from a starter that's been in use since 1902! Lunch options feature reindeer chili, square bun barbecue pulled pork sandwiches, quiche, lasagna, homemade pasties, mac and cheese, sandwiches, salads, and daily soups. Fresh loaves of bread adorn the bakery cases in the afternoon. This is one of the only tip-free restaurants in Alaska; prices are a bit higher so that the staff receive a living wage.

★ **Flying Squirrel** (Mile 11, Talkeetna Spur Rd., 907/733-6887, www.flyingsquirrelcafe.com, 8am-5pm Sun.-Tues., 8am-9pm Wed.-Thurs., 8am-10pm Fri.-Sat. late May-late Oct., 7:30am-6pm Wed.-Sat., 8am-5pm Sun. late Oct.-late May, most items under $14, pizzas $11-26) hides in a birch forest four miles from town. Owner Anita Colton's bakery café is definitely worth the drive. Get a big mug of organic espresso while perusing the cases to see what looks interesting. Daily specials include quiche, soups, hot sandwiches, salads, wraps, desserts, and breads. Delicious pizzas emerge from the brick oven (Wed.-Sat. evening summer, Fri.-Sat. evening winter), there's live music Wednesday evenings, and the café has plenty of vegan and gluten-free options as well as free Wi-Fi.

For an in-town buzz, visit funky and mindful **Conscious Coffee** (Main St., 907/733-7473, 8am-4pm daily, under $10), adjacent to Talkeetna River Guides. The snug cabin has a covered side deck and a selection of crepes, bagel sandwiches, fresh-squeezed juices, smoothies, shakes, yogurt, and espresso.

Quick Bites

Several street vendors serve fast and tasty casual food in Talkeetna. On the left side of the road as you enter town, **Shirley's Burger Barn** (907/315-8838, 9:30am-8pm daily mid-May-mid-Sept., $8-16) serves the best fast food in town. There's a pair of picnic tables out front and plenty of fattening food for the money. Choose from 10 varieties of huge and juicy burgers—from a simple hobo burger to the monstrous double meat, double cheese Denali burger. Shirley's also has hand-cut fries, hot dogs, and Alaska fireweed ice cream.

Occupying a bright silver Airstream trailer next to the K2 shop, **Spinach Bread** (Main St., 907/671-3287, 9am-5pm daily mid-May-mid-Sept., $6-10) is best known for its namesake spent-grain bread topped with spinach, cheese, and garlic (think pizza without tomato sauce), as well as daily specials, breakfast burritos, and limeade and blueberry rhubarb crisp. Eat on the go or at the picnic tables out front.

Out of town at Mile 1 of the Talkeetna Spur Highway, **Payo's Thai Kitchen** (907/733-5503, www.payosthaikitchenandcabins.com, 11am-8pm daily May-Sept., $12-18) serves delicious curries, stir-fries, soups, and other Thai favorites, including *gang phanang* curry, *tom yum gai,* and shrimp with ginger. Payo's operates out of a little trailer, with two covered tables on the deck.

Dinner

Denali BrewPub (13605 E. Main St., 907/733-2537, www.denalibrewing.com, 11am-10pm daily mid-May-mid-Sept., 1pm-9pm Mon.-Wed., noon-9pm Thurs.-Sun. mid-Sept.-mid-May, $14-28) has a crowded front deck in the heart of town. The combined lunch-dinner menu ranges from reindeer meatloaf and halibut fish-and-chips to handmade veggie burgers and Thai coconut shrimp curry. A kids menu ($7) is also available. There's a good selection of appetizers (try the smoked provolone wedges), along with excellent beers and spirits from Denali Brewing (same owners). Wi-Fi is free too.

West Rib Pub and Grill (directly behind Nagley's Store, 907/733-3354, www.westribpub.info, 11am-9pm daily, most entrées $10-26) attracts climbers and locals with a tasty pub-grub menu. Don't let the West Rib name fool you; it's a famous climbing route on Denali, not the house specialty. Ribs are on the menu, but most folks come for burgers, sandwiches, salads, fish-and-chips, halibut tacos, and nightly specials. Portions are ample, and everyone raves about the Northern Lights burger (with a caribou patty and Fatass sauce), but the halibut sandwich and crab legs ($44) are equally popular. Looking for a real artery clogger? The Seward's Folly ($56) plops two pounds of caribou meat, a half-pound of smoked ham, and 12 strips of bacon on a bun, along with Swiss and American cheese and a pound of fries. (Do you wonder why obesity is such a problem in the United States?) The bar serves Alaskan brews and Guinness. There's not much space inside, but the side deck opens on summer evenings.

Housed in a log building in the heart of town, ★ Wildflower Café (Main St., 907/733-2695, www.talkeetnasuites.com, noon-9pm Mon.-Thurs., noon-9:30pm Fri.-Sun. mid-May-mid-Sept., $25-38) serves an Alaskan all-day pub menu of halibut sandwiches, seafood chowder, burgers, soups, salads, pizzas, and fish-and-chips, plus dinner specials such as crab-stuffed halibut, grilled sesame salmon, New York sirloin champignon, and fettuccini alfredo. The front deck is perfect on warm summer afternoons, or head to the outdoor bar next to Wildflower, where you can work your way through 40 or more beers on tap. Make dinner reservations to avoid a long wait. An 18 percent gratuity is automatically added to the bill; it's listed in fine print on the bottom of the menu.

Pizza

Mountain High Pizza Pie (907/733-1234, www.pizzapietalkeetna.com, 11am-10pm Sun.-Thurs., 11am-11pm Fri.-Sat. May-Sept., noon-8pm Tues.-Sat. Oct.-Apr.), in the purple log cabin on Main Street, is a busy spot for pizza by the slice, calzones, flatbreads, salads, and subs. They have standard 15-inch pizzas ($15-25), personal 10-inch pizzas ($12-16), and $5 slices to go. The Mountain High version ($35) is piled with "everything but the mosquitoes." In summer, the side deck is a great spot to enjoy your pizza with a beer (there are a dozen Alaskan brews on tap); it erupts with live music six nights a week all summer.

Markets

Nagley's Store (13650 E. Main St., 907/733-3663, www.nagleysstore.com, 7:30am-9pm daily) opened in the 1920s and is still the main place for (limited) groceries in town, but it has also added such staples of 21st-century life as an ATM, ice cream, and lattes.

Cubby's Marketplace IGA (14 miles south of town at the junction with Parks Hwy., 907/733-5050, www.cubbysmarketplace.iga. com, 8am-8pm Mon.-Sat., 9am-10pm Sun.) is the primary grocery store for the region, with a deli, a liquor store, and an ATM.

ACCOMMODATIONS

There is a 5 percent lodging tax in Talkeetna; add this tax to the base price of your lodging choice. Check Airbnb (www.airbnb.com), VRBO (www.vrbo.com), and online booking sites for other options in the Talkeetna area.

Hostels

Right in the center of Main Street, **House of 7 Trees** (Main St., 907/733-7733, late Apr.-early Sept.) is a quaint, spotlessly clean hostel that attracts travelers of all ages and nationalities. Built in 1936, this charming frame home has lots of history. The back cabin houses six coed hostel bunks ($30 pp), and four private rooms ($85-105 d) are upstairs in the main house. Three of the private rooms have one queen or two twin beds, and the fourth room contains a queen and a twin—all topped with handmade quilts. Guests can access the common room with its baby grand piano, plus the impressive commercial kitchen, two baths (one wheelchair-accessible), and the shady yard. Wi-Fi is available. Make reservations a few weeks ahead, especially for summer weekends.

A few blocks east of downtown near the airport, **Talkeetna Hostel International** (22159 S. I St., 907/733-4678, www.talkeetnahostel. com, mid-Apr.-Sept., dorm $30 pp, private rooms $15 d, tents $80 pp) is quiet and shady, and each of the two dorm rooms (coed or single sex) has four beds. There are also private rooms and a backyard for tents. The hostel has three baths, a kitchen, laundry, and Wi-Fi. It's a well-run, easygoing place where alcohol is allowed and there is no curfew.

Hotels

For a taste of the past, stay at **Talkeetna Roadhouse** (Main St. and C St., 907/733-1351, www.talkeetnaroadhouse.com), a delightful old Alaskan lodge, constructed in 1917 and in business since 1944. It's best known for its home-cooked meals, but also has lodging options. Guests have access to a relaxing central space with books and magazines. Budget travelers and mountaineers appreciate the Roadhouse's four-bed coed hostel ($23 pp) with a bath down the hall. Five simple but clean guest rooms ($50-73 s, $60-85 d) have period antiques and shared baths. Out back is a little two-person cabin ($105 d) with a fridge, a microwave, a TV, and a gas fireplace; it uses baths in the main building. Three blocks away is Trapper John's cabin ($135 d), with two double beds, a fridge, a microwave, running water, and a private bath. Also available is an apartment ($147 d, private bath), located over the historic red schoolhouse at the Talkeetna Historical Museum.

Latitude 62 Motel (next to the airport and railroad depot, 907/733-2262, www.acsalaska.net/~latitude62, $80 s, $90 d, suite $120 d, off-site cabin $160 d) is a two-story log building on the south end of town with 11 small budget rooms and a suite. The furnishings are old, and there are no phones or TVs, but Latitude does have Wi-Fi, plus a full-service restaurant and bar. An off-site log cabin includes a private bath with a jetted tub and a full kitchen.

Downtown over Wildflower Café, **Main St. Suites** (Main St., 907/733-2695, www.talkeetnasuites.com, May-Sept., 1-bedroom suite $147 d, 2-bedroom $165 d, extra guests $20 pp) consists of a one-bedroom suite and a two-bedroom suite, both with private baths and kitchenettes.

Talkeetna Alaskan Lodge (23601 Talkeetna Spur Rd., 907/733-9500 or 877/777-4067, www.talkeetnalodge.com, mid-May-mid-Sept., $329-349 d, $439 d with views of Mount Denali, suites $509-599 d) sits atop a hill one mile south of Talkeetna, with large and modern rooms. There are also luxury suites, most with gas fireplaces and jetted tubs. The grand lobby includes an enormous stone fireplace and towering windows framing The Mountain, and the multilevel back deck is a wonderful place to take in the grandeur while enjoying a meal or drink. There's a free shuttle to town and the train depot. This attractive Native Alaskan-owned lodge serves up million-dollar views from its 212-rooms, and the hotel is packed with cruise ship passengers all summer. Two restaurants provide a big breakfast buffet ($22) along with full lunch and dinner offerings.

Cabins

Paradise Lodge & Cabins (S. Birch Creek Blvd., 907/733-1471 or 888/205-3553, www.paradiselodge.net, mid-May-mid-Sept., $149-179 d) is aptly named, with a peaceful and secluded location along Fish Lake five miles south of Talkeetna. Four rustic log cabins (with double beds and kitchenettes but no running water) share a nearby bathhouse, or you can stay in the main lodge where two rooms share a bath. Also available is a spacious three-bedroom, four-bath home ($750 for up to 8 guests). It has no Wi-Fi, and this off-the-grid place—power comes from a generator—is open only in summer.

Right in town behind Mountain High Pizza, **Talkeetna Cabins** (22137 C St., 907/733-2227 or 888/733-9933, www.talkeetnacabins.org) consists of four duplex log cabins ($205 d, extra guests $20 pp) and a large three-bedroom house ($410 for 4 people, extra guests $20 pp, maximum 12 people). All have full kitchens, private baths, laundry, a grill, Wi-Fi, and plenty of room to relax.

Susitna River Lodging (23094 S. Talkeetna Rd., 907/733-0505, www.susitnariverlodge.com, cabins $249 d, lodge rooms $199 d, extra guests $15 pp) has four lovely cedar cabins and four suites (one is wheelchair-accessible) 0.5 miles south of Talkeetna. All guest rooms and cabins include private baths, kitchenettes, electric fireplaces, barbecue grills, continental breakfast, and Wi-Fi, but no TVs. They're right along the river, and the main lodge has a big porch facing the water.

Three miles from town, ★ **Talkeetna Chalet** (Mile 11, Talkeetna Spur Rd.,

907/733-4734, www.talkeetnachalet.net, late May-mid-Sept., guest suites $225 d, cabins $219-269 d, extra guests $15 pp) is a fine hilltop place with stunning Alaska Range views. Two suites have private baths, while three modern cabins contain kitchenettes and private baths. Guests can use the first two floors of the home. Amenities include freshly baked banana bread, a common room with a large-screen TV, and Wi-Fi.

Looking for a totally unique wilderness experience? ★ **Caribou Lodge** (907/733-2163 or 877/700-2875, www.cariboulodgealaska.com, Jan.-Mar. and June-early Oct., $355 pp d) has a striking location on an alpine lake near the southeast edge of Denali National Park. It's a 15-minute flight from Talkeetna ($370 pp round-trip), but a world away. Owners Joe and Bonnie Bramante provide three simple but nicely set-up cabins for guests. Lodging, meals, canoeing, and guided day hikes—with sightings of abundant wildlife—are included in the rates. There's a two-night minimum stay, and multinight packages are available. Winter guests come for snowshoeing, cross-country skiing, and dramatic northern lights above the summit of Mount Denali. This is a wonderful introduction to a place where TVs, phones, and the hi-tech world don't intrude. There is no indoor plumbing!

Talkeetna Lakeside Cabins (35320 S. St. John Dr., 907/733-2349, www.talkeetnalakesidecabins.com, $190-200 d, extra guests $20 pp) consists of three immaculate cabins along a private lake a mile off Talkeetna Spur Road. All contain private baths and Wi-Fi. Two cabins have full kitchens, and the smaller one contains a microwave and a fridge. There are no TVs, but you can make your own entertainment by rowing around the lake.

Guesthouses

On a hill facing the Alaska Range, and away from the noises of town, **Out of the Wild**

1: deck dining at Denali Brewpub; 2: Spinach Bread food trailer; 3: Mountain High Pizza Pie; 4: bikes outside West Rib Pub

(22198 S. Freedom Dr., 907/733-2701, www.talkeetnapro.com) has a cluster of architecturally unique guesthouses. Co-owner Brian McCullough—an internationally known mountaineer and guide—built them all by hand, filling each with distinctive furnishings. All three places contain private baths and full kitchens stocked with breakfast supplies, Wi-Fi, and TVs. Spacious Mountain House has three upstairs bedrooms and two baths. Kahiltna Chalet ($160 d) is an elegant cottage perfect for romantic getaways, and Stone Hut ($280 for 4 guests) features artistic stonework, three bedrooms, and a spiral staircase. The hilltop location is perfect for winter northern lights viewing. Equally unique is a luxurious, three-bedroom stone-and-log home ($300) home, 0.5 miles away, that sleeps up to eight; it's perfect for families and events.

Just two blocks from Main Street, **Northern Guest House** (13712 2nd St., 907/715-4868, www.northernguesthouse.com, $60 s, $80 d, extra guests $20 pp) has hard-to-beat rates and a generous owner. The three guest rooms each contain a private bath and two beds, and guests can use the full kitchen, dining room, and living room, plus the rec room with table tennis and a piano. Borrow a bike to explore town, or kick back around the enclosed backyard fire pit. Pets are welcome, and Wi-Fi is available. The spiral staircase may be a challenge for people with mobility issues.

Bed-and-Breakfasts

There are more than 30 B&Bs in the Talkeetna area, including several places with dramatic Denali vistas.

Five miles from Talkeetna, ★ **Denali Overlook Inn** (29198 S. Talkeetna Spur Rd., 907/733-3555 or 855/733-3555, www.denalioverlookinn.com, $249-349 d) is a memorable home where the view exceeds your expectations; on a clear day it's impossible to miss Mount Denali and the rest of the Alaska Range. Six bedrooms—the largest features wall-to-wall windows facing The Mountain—have private baths, and a full menu breakfast is included, along with a guest computer and Wi-Fi. Honeymooners will appreciate privacy at the adjacent two-level cabin ($319 d) with a kitchenette and a private bath.

Five miles east of town, **Traleika Mountaintop Cabins** (22216 S. Freedom Dr., 907/733-2711, www.traleika.com, $185-215 d, additional guests $20 pp) has a dramatic location facing Denali. There is a two-bedroom guesthouse and two smaller cabins. All three places include full baths, living rooms, decks, kitchens, and Wi-Fi; the largest sleeps up to eight.

Not far away—with an equally fine vista—is reasonably priced **Freedom Hills B&B** (22046 S. Freedom Dr., 907/733-2455 or 888/703-2455, www.gbfreedomhillsbb.com, May-Sept., $135 d shared bath, $155-190 d private bath), where six immaculate guest rooms are in two adjacent homes. There's an enormous deck on the main house to take in the Denali views, plus continental breakfast and Wi-Fi.

Talkeetna Denali View Lodge & Cabins (15669 E. Coffey Lane, 907/733-4111, www.talkeetnadenaliviewlodge.com, year-round, rooms $145-165 d, suites $195-215 d, cabins $175 d) is 10 miles from town, just off Talkeetna Spur Road. The lodge overlooks two small ponds (favorites of moose and loons) with a good view of Mount Denali from the flower-draped deck. Guests choose from two rooms and two suites in the main lodge or duplex cabins; all have private baths, Wi-Fi, and access to the hot tub and sauna (robes provided). A hot and filling breakfast is served in the dining area each morning. This is an adults-only place; no kids under age 14 are allowed. The owners also run Wilderness River Fishing Guides, with jet-boat fishing trips on local rivers.

Camping

Find camping spots, but no running water, at shady **River Park Campground** (end of Main St., June-Sept., $17). A bit farther from town is **Talkeetna RV** (21889 S. F St., 907/733-2604, www.talkeetna-rv.com, May-Oct., tents and RVs $25), with in-the-trees tent and RV sites. There are no hookups, but some sites are right along the Talkeetna River, and there's a boat launch, good salmon fishing, and Wi-Fi. The campground is on the east side of the railroad tracks from town.

On the right just before you enter town, **Talkeetna Camper Park** (22763 S. Talkeetna Spur Rd., 907/733-2693, www.talkeetnacamper.com, May-mid-Sept., RVs $43-48) has 35 wooded RV sites. It's well maintained, with birch trees, plus showers, laundry, and a dump station.

INFORMATION AND SERVICES

The **Talkeetna Chamber of Commerce** (www.talkeetnachamber.org) has a useful website and brochures. The Park Service's **Walter Harper Talkeetna Ranger Station** (B St., 907/733-2231, www.nps.gov/dena, 8am-5:30pm daily mid-Apr.-early Sept., 8am-4:30pm Mon.-Fri. early Sept.-mid-Apr.) is a pleasant log structure where you can watch a climbing video, talk with a ranger about Denali National Park, or look over the mountaineering books.

Keep in touch with the outside world via the Internet at the cute **Talkeetna Public Library** (24645 S. Talkeetna Spur Rd., 907/861-7645, www.matsugov.us, 11am-6pm Mon.-Sat.), on the south side of town.

Sunshine Community Health Center (Mile 4, Talkeetna Spur Rd., 907/733-2273, www.sunshineclinic.org, 9am-5pm Mon.-Sat.) is the local medical clinic.

Washing machines and showers are downtown at **Talkeetna Roadhouse** (Main St., 907/733-1351, www.talkeetnaroadhouse.com), with more showers at **Talkeetna RV** (907/733-2604, www.talkeetna-rv.com).

GETTING THERE AND AROUND

The turnoff to Talkeetna is 100 miles north of Anchorage on the George Parks Highway, and the town is another 14 miles out on Talkeetna Spur Road.

Buses and Taxis

Two companies connect Talkeetna with destinations along the Parks Highway. **Alaska/Yukon Trails** (907/888-5659, www.alaskashuttle.com, daily Apr.-Sept.) operates 7-passenger or 16-passenger vans with lower one-way rates from Talkeetna: $65 to Denali, $62 to Anchorage, and $92 to Fairbanks. Vans can stop anywhere along the highway (with advance reservations), including Wasilla, Willow-Big Lake, Trapper Creek, Byers Lake, Coal Creek Trailhead, Cantwell, and Healy. You can get off the van and reboard at a later date for a $10 fee.

Park Connection (907/245-0200 or 800/266-8625, www.alaskacoach.com, daily mid-May-mid-Sept.) operates large and very comfortable buses between Seward and Denali, but they only stop at the main towns and Princess lodges en route. From Talkeetna, the one-way rates are $65 to Denali or Anchorage, $13 to Seward or Whittier. Rate for children under age 11 are half-price.

Sunshine Transit (907/733-9279, www.sunshinetransit.com, 8:30am-5pm Mon.-Fri., $3 one-way) is a local not-for-profit van service that operates along the Talkeetna Spur Road, stopping at points along the way, including the Sunshine Community Health Center and Cubby's Market. They also go to Wasilla (Mon.-Fri., $20 round-trip); call 24 hours ahead to reserve. It's a cheap way to get supplies at Fred Meyer or Walmart if you don't have a rental car.

Talkeetna Taxi (907/355-8294, www.talkeetnataxi.com) charges $4 around town or $3 per mile (plus $2 pp) for farther destinations.

Trains

The **Alaska Railroad** (907/265-2494 or 800/544-0552, www.alaskarailroad.com, one-way $104 adults, $52 children) runs the *Denali Star* from Anchorage to Talkeetna. The train leaves Anchorage every morning at 8:15am and arrives in Talkeetna at 11:05am before continuing north to Denali National Park and Fairbanks. A southbound train leaves Fairbanks at 8:15am, stopping in Denali, before reaching Talkeetna at 4:40pm. This train continues south to Anchorage, arriving at 8pm. For the deluxe version, **GoldStar** double-decker cars ($226 adults, $122 children one-way) include second-level window seats with a full breakfast and beer or wine.

In the off-season, the railroad operates the **Aurora Winter** train, which connects Anchorage with Talkeetna, Healy, Nenana, and Fairbanks. Trains operate on winter weekends in both directions, with occasional midweek service.

A local flag-stop train (it stops on an as-needed basis), the *Hurricane Turn* train (Thurs.-Mon. mid-May-mid-Sept., round-trip $106 adults, $53 children), runs the 50 miles from Talkeetna north to Hurricane and back. It's a fun way to see the countryside with locals. Winter travelers can get on or off the flag-stop train at points south of Talkeetna as well.

North from Talkeetna

TRAPPER CREEK

The minuscule settlement of Trapper Creek (pop. 350) is at Mile 115 of the Parks Highway, 16 miles north of the junction with Talkeetna Spur Road. Petersville Road splits off at Trapper Creek, providing access to the western end of Denali State Park and offering some of the finest views of Mount Denali.

It's hard to miss Wal*Mike's (Mile 115, Parks Hwy., 907/733-2637) in Trapper Creek, with a huge roadside collection of flotsam and jetsam. Stop to look over the offbeat collection of junk (or are they treasures?), from glass floats and bear skulls to license plates and totem poles.

Accommodations

Trapper Creek Inn & RV Park (Mile 115, Parks Hwy., 907/733-2302, www.trappercreek. biz, rooms $95-125 d, tents $20, RVs $30-40) has guest rooms, nicely wooded campsites, groceries, free Wi-Fi, a deli, and a coin laundry with coin-op showers. The deli serves burgers, all-day breakfast items, espresso, and more.

McKinley View B&B (Mile 114, Parks Hwy., 907/733-1758, www. mckinleyviewlodging.com, $135 d) is all about the view. Take a seat on the back deck for vistas of the Alaska Range and Mount Denali (when the weather cooperates). Four guest rooms are available, with full breakfasts, private baths and entrances, gracious owners, and Wi-Fi.

Alaska's Northland Inn (Mile 1, Petersville Rd., 907/733-7377, www. alaskasnorthlandinn.com, $120 d, additional adults $30 pp) has a pair of two-level apartments with private baths, full kitchens, two queen beds, continental breakfast (summer only), and Wi-Fi. Relax in the great room with a pool table and satellite TV. In winter, the owners provide groomed cross-country ski trails.

Transportation

Alaska/Yukon Trails (907/888-5659, www. alaskashuttle.com, Apr.-Sept.) has daily van service along the Parks Highway from Anchorage to Fairbanks. Vans will stop at Trapper Creek with advance notice; one-way fares are $55 to Denali, $85 to Fairbanks, and $62 to Anchorage.

PETERSVILLE ROAD

A number of rural subdivisions and homesteads are found along Petersville Road, and this is a popular winter destination for dog mushers and hordes of snowmobilers. The road continues all the way to old mining developments in the Petersville mining camp, 30 miles in, although the last section may not be passable without a high-clearance vehicle. Petersville Road is paved for 10 miles, then gravel the next 9 miles to Forks Roadhouse. The historic Forks Roadhouse, a log structure built in the 1930s, was destroyed in a 2012 fire. It has since been rebuilt, but seems to open on whim. Beyond this point, the road deteriorates. It's decent until around Mile 35, but expect several miles of rocks, potholes, and slow going beyond. The road is generally passable for two-wheel-drive cars (especially in July-August), but most car rental companies prohibit driving on Petersville Road; don't even think of trying this in an RV. Plan on 2.5 hours to drive the 39 miles to Cache Creek.

The Petersville Recreational Mining Area at Mile 32 is popular for camping (no facilities) and recreational gold panning. There's always someone here looking for nuggets, and yes, gold is still present in Peters Creek.

Lifelong Alaskan Richard Humphrey leads Denali Gold Tours (907/733-7660, www. denaligoldtours.com, $125), a four-hour tour that includes a scenic 19-mile van ride to the Cache Creek Mining District, where gold was first discovered in 1905. You'll learn the techniques of gold panning and the history of the area. You probably won't come up with any gold nuggets, but will return with a vial of gold dust.

Accommodations

Set along two ponds, **Gate Creek Cabins** (Mile 11, Petersville Rd., 907/733-1393, www. gatecreekcabins.com, $160 d, additional guests $60 pp) has eight modern log cabins—the largest contains four bedrooms—with kitchens, private baths, TVs, barbecue grills, and Wi-Fi. They're really more like furnished vacation homes, with all the creature comforts in a peaceful and picturesque setting. Guests can borrow a canoe or paddleboat to cruise the ponds or try a bit of trout fishing (mosquitoes can be voracious). The cabins provide an extremely popular winter base for snowmobilers.

If you want remote, check out **Cache Creek Cabins** (907/252-1940, www. cachecreekcabins.com, mid-June-Sept.) located 39 rugged miles out Petersville Road. Road conditions vary greatly with the weather and road maintenance; call ahead for the current situation before heading out. Six rustic little cabins ($55) share a common bathhouse. A nicer two-story cabin ($75 d, or $150 for up to 8 people) sleeps eight and has a private bath. The friendly owners provide gold panning lessons ($25 per day) and a home-cooked breakfast buffet ($15 pp). It's a pretty setting with views of Denali on the drive in. Be sure to ask about the infamous Cache Creek murders of 1939, when four miners were slain in a never-solved murder. There are still rumors of hidden stashes of gold.

★ DENALI STATE PARK

This 325,240-acre state park (907/735-5121, www.alaskastateparks.org, day-use $5) lies just southeast of Denali National Park and Preserve and is bisected by the Parks Highway from Mile 132 to Mile 169. Situated between the Talkeetna Mountains to the east and the Alaska Range to the west, the landscape of Denali State Park varies from wide glaciated valleys to alpine tundra. The Chulitna

and Tokositna Rivers flow through western sections of the park, while the eastern half is dominated by Curry Ridge and K'esugi Ridge, a 35-mile-long section of alpine country.

Denali State Park provides an excellent alternative wilderness experience to the crowds and hassles of its federal next-door neighbor. The Mountain is visible from all over the park, bears are abundant, and you won't need to stand in line for a permit to hike or camp while you wait for Mount Denali's mighty south face to show itself. Several trails offer a variety of hiking experiences and spectacular views.

The spruce bark beetle infestation that has impacted the Kenai Peninsula and other parts of Alaska has now moved into the Mat-Su Valley. Since 2016, beetles have killed virtually every large spruce tree from Talkeetna north thorough Denali State Park.

Sights

Denali State Park is best known for its breathtaking **views of Mount Denali** and the Alaska Range from pullouts along the Parks Highway. If The Mountain or even "just" some of the lower peaks of the Alaska Range are out, you won't need to read the next sentence to know what or where the sights are. The best viewpoint along the highway in Denali State Park, and the most popular, is at Mile 135 of the Parks Highway, where on a clear day you will find an interpretive signboard and crowds of fellow travelers. Set up your tripod and click away. Don't miss the K'esugi Ken area, where a short trail provides an even more impressive vista. Other unforgettable viewpoints are at Miles 147, 158, and 162.

Hurricane Gulch is a deep and steep canyon carved by Hurricane Creek. A 254-foot-high bridge arches over the creek at Mile 174 Parks Highway. Stop at the pullout near the south end of the bridge to check out this impressive canyon.

The western section of Denali State Park lies within the remote **Peters Hills,** an area known for its pristine Mount Denali vistas and open country. This section is accessed via the Petersville Road.

K'ESUGI KEN

Opened in 2017, **K'esugi Ken** (day-use $5) is a highlight for visitors to Denali State Park, with hiking trails, a ranger station, public-use cabins, a campground, and an interpretive pavilion. Access is from Mile 135 of the Parks Highway (just north of the Denali View South overlook), where a wide paved road winds uphill to the K'esugi Ken complex. Stop at the covered interpretive pavilion, where the easy ADA-accessible 0.75-mile **Moose Flats Loop Interpretive Trail** leads to a dramatic vista of Mount Denali—it's probably the finest easily accessible view of The Mountain.

The road to K'esugi Ken is plowed in winter, and the state maintains five kilometers of groomed cross-country ski trails. Three public-use cabins provide an easily accessible yet remote winter destination for viewing northern lights and other winter fun.

BYERS LAKE

The Byers Lake area (day-use $5 per vehicle) is located near Mile 147 of the Parks Highway. Stop here to visit the **Alaska Veterans Memorial,** consisting of five monumental concrete blocks with stars carved out of them. Turn your back to the monument, and if you're lucky, there's blue-white Denali, perfectly framed by tall spruce trees.

Recreation

Across the road from the K'esugi Ken pavilion is the trailhead for the **Curry Ridge Loop Trail** (3 miles one-way). The wide path crosses a series of switchbacks before reaching open tundra and a rocky knob overlooking an alpine lake. You'll gain 1,100 feet en route, but because the trailhead starts at 900 feet elevation (thanks to the road up from Parks Highway), it's a quick way into the high country.

The easy five-mile **Byers Lake Loop Trail** circles the pretty namesake lake. **Cascade Trail** heads uphill from the northeast tip of Byers Lake, climbing two miles into the alpine. There it meets the **K'esugi Ridge Trail** heading north, and **Troublesome Creek Trail,** which continues south. K'esugi Ridge Trail provides unparalleled views of Mount Denali and the Alaska Range when the weather cooperates. It continues north along this alpine ridge before dropping down to the Little Coal Creek Trailhead at Mile 164 of the Parks Highway. K'esugi Ridge is a difficult four-day, 29-mile hike for experienced backpackers who appreciate this spectacular but rugged country. Weather can change quickly in the alpine, and bears are sometimes a problem.

Little Coal Creek (Mile 164, Parks Hwy.) starts five miles south of the park's northern boundary. This trail is the park's gentlest climb to the alpine tundra—five miles east up Little Coal Creek, then southwest along K'esugi Ridge, with amazing views of the range and glaciers; flags and cairns delineate the trail. Watch for bears! The trail goes 27 miles until it hooks up with Troublesome Creek Trail, just up from Byers Lake Campground. About halfway there, **Ermine Lake Trail** cuts back down to the highway, an escape route in case of foul weather.

Guides

Alaska Nature Guides (907/733-1237, www.alaskanatureguides.com, late May-mid-Sept.) leads easy 2.5-hour nature walks ($69 adults, $44 under age 13) from Byers Lake daily in the summer, and also provides custom hiking, birding, and photography trips. Trips are led by expert Alaska naturalists with years of local experience.

Denali Southside River Guides (907/733-7238, www.denaliriverguides.com) has a summer office at the Byers Lake Campground, with rentals of canoes, stand-up paddleboards, and sit-on-top kayaks. The company also leads three-hour kayak tours of Byers Lake ($99 adults, $69 children), half-day Chulitna River floats ($119 adults, $99 children), plus full-day excursions ($199 adults,

$179 children) that combine kayaking on the lake, lunch, and river rafting.

Alaska Nature Guides and Denali Southside River Guides jointly offer a South Denali hike and raft trip ($299 pp). This begins in Talkeetna and includes a van ride, a six-mile hike up K'esugi Ridge, lunch at Mary's McKinley View Lodge, and raft trip back to Talkeetna. This is a wonderful all-in-one adventure.

D&S Alaskan Trail Rides (Mile 133, Parks Hwy., 907/733-2207, www.alaskantrailrides.com, mid-May-late Sept.) has guided two-hour horseback rides ($130 pp) from their location next to Mt. McKinley Princess Wilderness Lodge. Another option is a two-hour wagon ride with gold panning ($90 pp). The latter is primarily for cruise-ship passengers staying at Mt. McKinley Princess Wilderness Lodge.

Accommodations

Turn off the Parks Highway at Mile 133 for a one-mile side road into **Mt. McKinley Princess Wilderness Lodge** (907/733-2900 or 800/426-0500, www.princesslodges.com, mid-May-mid-Sept., $189-199 d). This stylish 460-room retreat is famous for its riverside location and picture-perfect vistas of the Alaska Range and Mount Denali. Most rooms are filled with Princess cruise passengers, but anyone can stay or eat here. The lodge itself centers around a "great room" with a stone fireplace and enormous windows fronting the mountain. Lodging is in smaller buildings scattered around the grounds; ask for one of the new rooms with a king bed. There's also a small fitness center, two outdoor hot tubs, a restaurant, and a café. Wi-Fi is available only in the main lodge.

Located at the southern edge of Denali State Park, **Mary's McKinley View Lodge** (Mile 134, Parks Hwy., 907/733-1555, www.mckinleyviewlodge.com, May-late Sept., $100-120 d) has a down-home restaurant (with pies and giant cinnamon rolls), great views of The Mountain from the deck and picture windows, and five clean but older guest rooms with private baths; there's no Wi-Fi. The gift shop sells autographed copies of books authored by owner Jean Carey Richardson and her late mother, Mary Carey.

Camping

K'esugi Ken Campground ($20 tents, $30 RVs with electricity) has more than 40 nicely situated campsites, including eight walk-in tent spaces and several pull-throughs for big rigs. Park rangers offer interpretive walks and evening programs in summer. Three modern **Public-Use Cabins** (Hunter Cabin, Tokosha Cabin, and Denali Cabin, $90-100) are available year-round. Make campground and cabin reservations online at www.reserveamerica.com ($10 reservation fee).

Byers Lake has three **Public-Use Cabins** (www.reserveamerica.com, $80 plus $10 reservation fee). **Byers Lake Campground** ($20) has 70 large sites, water, outhouses, interpretive signs, and beautiful Byers Lake a stone's throw down the road. Just under two miles along the Loop Trail from the campground (or across the lake by boat) is **Lakeshore Campground,** with six primitive sites, outhouses, and no running water, but unimpeded views of The Mountain and Alaska Range from your tent flap. Across the road and 0.25 miles south, **Lower Troublesome Creek Campground** ($15) has 20 sites and all the amenities of Byers Lake.

Transportation

Alaska/Yukon Trails (907/888-5659, www.alaskashuttle.com, Apr.-Sept.) has daily van service along the Parks Highway from Anchorage to Fairbanks. They will stop at Byers Lake or the Coal Creek Trailhead with advance notice. One-way fares from Byers Lake are $34 to Talkeetna, $55 to Denali, $84 to Fairbanks, and $65 to Anchorage.

TOP EXPERIENCE

★ DENALI HIGHWAY

The Denali Highway, which stretches 136 miles east-west across the waist of mainland

Denali Highway

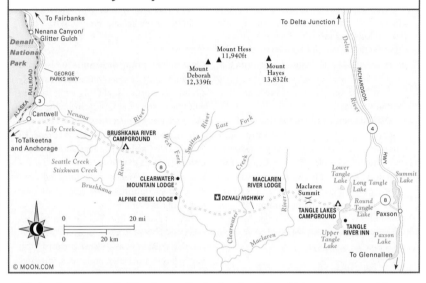

To Fairbanks
Nenana Canyon/
Glitter Gulch
Denali
National
Park
GEORGE
PARKS HWY
Cantwell
ToTalkeetna
and Anchorage
Lily Creek
Seattle Creek
Stixwan Creek
Nenana
Brushkana
BRUSHKANA RIVER
CAMPGROUND
CLEARWATER
MOUNTAIN LODGE
ALPINE CREEK LODGE
Mount Hess
11,940ft
Mount
Deborah
12,339ft
Mount
Hayes
13,832ft
East Fork
Susitna River
West Fork
MACLAREN
RIVER LODGE
DENALI HIGHWAY
To Delta Junction
RICHARDSON River
Lower
Tangle
Lake
Maclaren
Summit
TANGLE LAKES
CAMPGROUND
Round
Tangle
Lake
Long Tangle
Lake
Summit
Lake
Paxson
TANGLE
RIVER INN
Upper
Tangle
Lake
Paxson
Lake
Maclaren River
Clearwater
To Glennallen
0   20 mi
0   20 km

© MOON.COM

Alaska, from Cantwell (30 miles south of Denali National Park) to Paxson (Mile 122, Richardson Hwy.), may be the best-kept secret in Alaska. Originally the Denali Highway was the only road into Denali National Park, and this beautiful side trip has been largely ignored by visitors since the opening of the George Parks Highway in 1971.

Denali Highway is paved for 21 miles on the east end of the road (from Paxson to Tangle Lakes) and for three miles on the western end, but the rest is well-maintained gravel. The road isn't particularly bad, but it's easy to go too fast and hit a pothole or sharp rock, and rollovers occasionally occur—usually from folks hoping to set world land-speed records on their Alaska vacation.

Travelers should be prepared for emergencies. Always carry a spare tire and tire-changing tools, water, some snacks, and warm clothing. Towing is available from Paxson and Cantwell, but it ain't cheap, so take your time and be safe. Clearwater Mountain Lodge (Mile 82) and Maclaren River Lodge (Mile 42) provide tire repair along the highway, but you may need to limp in on one of those useless doughnut tires. Make sure your rental car has both a spare tire and a jack before heading down the highway.

The Denali Highway offers a varied selection of outstanding scenery and wildlife-viewing opportunities. Much of the route punches through the foothills of the magnificent Alaska Range. This area is part of the home range of the huge 30,000-strong Nelchina caribou herd. In the fall they begin to group in the greatest numbers—sightings of several hundred caribou are not unusual.

The Denali Highway is closed October-mid-May. In the winter it becomes a popular trail for snowmobilers, dog mushers, and cross-country skiers. Die-hard Alaskans also use this trail in the winter for access to unparalleled ice fishing and caribou and ptarmigan hunting.

Most rental car companies prohibit drivers from taking their vehicles on the Denali Highway, and many companies monitor usage through a GPS system. Violate the rules and you're likely to face a stiff penalty. **Alaska 4x4 Rentals** (907/290-0173, www.alaska4x4rentals.com), **ABC**

Motorhome & Car Rentals (907/279-2000 or 800/421-7456, www.abcmotorhome.com), and GoNorth Car and RV Rentals (907/479-7272 or 866/236-7272, www.gonorth-alaska.com) in Anchorage allow their cars to be driven on the Denali Highway, but be sure to read the fine print. If you're already in the Denali area, Alaska Auto Rental (907/457-7368, www.alaskaautorental.com, May-Sept., $979 for 24 hours or $1,400 for 3 days) rents Denali Highway SUVs with puncture-resistant tires, two spares, and a CB radio.

Another option is to join an expensive tour through Denali Highway Jeep Excursion (907/683-5337, www.denalijeep.com, $169 adults, $99 children). These five-hour tours depart their Glitter Gulch-Nenana Canyon office and include narration via CB radio and several stops along the way. Tours typically travel 50 miles out the road, as far as the Susitna River. Let's see: If they charge $169 pp, and the vehicle holds four, that's $676 for a half-day Jeep ride!

History

The Denali Highway began as a "cat" track in the early 1950s when a man named Earl Butcher first established a hunting camp at Tangle Lakes. Known for years as Butcher's Camp, it's now the site of Tangle Lakes Lodge. About the same time, Chalmer Johnson established a camp at Round Tangle Lake. Now known as the Tangle River Inn, this lodge is still operated by the Johnson family.

Cantwell

A minuscule settlement (pop. 160) at the junction of the Parks and Denali Highways, Cantwell began as a railroad town, and a cluster of decrepit buildings are strewn along the tracks two miles west of the highway. Cantwell is less than 30 miles south of Denali National Park, and a couple of businesses provide the staples: fuel, food, lodging, coffee, and booze. Most folks stop to fill up on gas, grab a soda, and tool on up the highway. There aren't a lot of reasons to stay in Cantwell itself, though the surrounding country is grand.

Fifty miles south of Cantwell, at Mile 189 of the Parks Highway, you'll pass one of Alaska's stranger sights: an enormous round building with a slight resemblance to an igloo. Leon Smith started the building in 1972, with a dream of turning it into a hotel he would call Igloo Lodge. After building a dome-shaped plywood structure, he covered it with white urethane insulation, but never finished the interior. An adjacent gas station closed more than a decade ago, but the dilapidated igloo still stands, miles from any other business.

FOOD

JP's Coffee House (907/683-2002, www.jpcoffeehouse.com, 8am-6pm daily, $5-8) is the only dining option in Cantwell. Coffee may be in the name and on the menu, but the real attractions are freshly baked scones, potato bread cinnamon rolls, and most surprisingly, homemade meat pies. These are made to be held in your hand and eaten like a sandwich, and are served hot and fresh. There are lots of tasty options to choose from, including cheesesteak, gumbo, chorizo scramble, and barbecue pork.

ACCOMMODATIONS

BluesBerry Inn (Mile 210, Parks Hwy., 916/765-2219, www.bluesberryinn.com, May-Nov.) provides reasonably priced—but very rustic—accommodations. There are dry cabins (a double and a twin bed, electricity, and heat, but no water) with a shared bathhouse ($80 s, $90 d), guest rooms with a double bed and private bath ($110 s, $120 d), and larger rooms ($140 s, $150 d). Most units have TVs (but poor reception) and Wi-Fi.

Backwoods Lodge (0.2 miles up Denali Hwy., 907/987-0960, www.backwoodslodge.com) has clean, simple motel rooms ($170 d) with fridges, microwaves, TVs, and Wi-Fi. A private cabin ($250 for up to 4 people) is also offered, along with a dry cabin ($135 d) with showers in the lodge.

On a 50-acre spread five miles north of Cantwell and 21 miles from Denali, Adventure Denali (Mile 215, Parks Hwy.,

907/768-2620, www.adventuredenali.com, May-Oct., $135 d) is very popular with fishing enthusiasts. Two solar-powered comfortably Alaskan lakeside cabins are available, each with a full kitchen, a private bath, a TV, Wi-Fi, and a floating sauna on the dock. Borrow a rowboat or head out on one of the hiking trails. The big draw is fishing for monster rainbow trout and grayling in three private artificial lakes. Owner Kirk Martakis created this fishery and maintains it as a unique catch-and-release operation. It's the only pay-to-fish place in Alaska, attracting dedicated anglers willing to spend $175 for a half-day of guided fishing. But where else could you land (and release) a trophy 30-inch rainbow?

Cantwell RV Park (907/888-6850, www.cantwellrvpark.com, mid-May-mid-Sept., tents $24, RVs $35) is a basic parking lot 0.2 miles up Denali Highway. Services include Wi-Fi, showers, laundry, and a dump station.

Transportation
Alaska/Yukon Trails (907/888-5659, www.alaskashuttle.com, Apr.-Sept.) has daily van service along the Parks Highway from Anchorage to Fairbanks. Vans will stop at Cantwell with advance notice. One-way fares are $60 to Talkeetna, $30 to Denali, $70 to Fairbanks, and $75 to Anchorage.

EAST ON THE DENALI HIGHWAY
About three miles east of the Denali Highway-Parks Highway junction is a turnout with a view of Cantwell and Mount Denali, if it's out. There's another potential view of the mountain at Mile 13, then in another five miles the highway runs parallel to the Nenana River. The headwaters of the Nenana emanate from a western digit of the icefields atop the Alaska Range trio of peaks: **Mount Deborah** on the left at 12,339 feet, **Mount Hess** in the middle

at 11,940 feet, and **Mount Hayes** on the right at 13,832 feet.

Over the next 10 miles the road crosses Lily Creek, Seattle Creek, and Stixkwan Creek; throw in a line and pull up some grayling or Dolly Varden. At Mile 31 you come to the **Brushkana River,** where the Bureau of Land Management (BLM) has a good free campground right on the river, and over the next 10 miles you get some great views of the three prominent peaks, along with the West Fork Glacier. The southern glaciers off Deborah, Hess, and Hayes feed the Susitna River, which flows west to the Parks Highway, and then south to empty into Cook Inlet, across from Anchorage.

Clearwater and Beyond
Fifty-four miles east of the junction of the Parks and Denali Highways is **Clearwater Mountain Lodge** (Mile 82, Denali Hwy., 907/203-1057, www.clearwatermountainlodge.com, Feb.-Sept.), a friendly place with lodging, meals, and a bar, along with tire repairs and gas. The lodge's Sluice Box Bar serves meals, including burgers, homemade calzones, hot dogs, and even espresso. Get a to-go lunch or sit down for a family style dinner ($25 adults, $15 children). Lodging choices include rooms in the main lodge ($100 s, $120 d) or cabin-style suites and rooms ($140 s, $180 d); all include full breakfast and private baths. Simple rooms with single beds ($85 s, $100 d) don't include breakfast or private baths, but it's a short walk to the shower house. Campers can park RVs ($20) or pitch a tent ($10 pp); both sites include a bathhouse with showers. Phone service into the lodge is via satellite phone, so make reservations via text or through the email on their website. The lodge does provide free Wi-Fi. Clearwater Mountain Lodge has been here since 1957; it was formerly known as Gracious House.

Five miles farther, you cross the single-lane 1,000-foot-long Susitna River bridge. Farther south, the Susitna is a popular river to float, but passage between here and there

1: driving the Denali Highway; **2:** Parks Highway and Mount Denali; **3:** igloo building south of Cantwell; **4:** hikers with an obscured view of Mt. Denali at K'esugi Ken in Denali National Park

is considered impossible because of the impassable Devil's Canyon, just downriver from the bridge.

★ **Alpine Creek Lodge** (Mile 68, Denali Hwy., 907/398-9673, www.alpinecreeklodge.com, year-round) has a beautiful setting for wilderness accommodations. Owners Claude and Jennifer Bondy operate this reasonably priced place with lots of activities. There are 10 lodge rooms ($85 pp) with bunk beds and a shared bath, as well as two suites ($199 d) with private baths. Nearby are five small cabins ($75 pp) with woodstoves; guests can use the bath in the lodge. The largest cabin sleeps up to six. Lodging rates include three meals daily, making this an exceptional deal in backcountry Alaska. If you aren't staying here, **Chrissy's Café** at the lodge serves family style all-you-can-eat breakfasts ($15 pp) and dinners ($20 pp); lunch is by menu. Summer Jeep tours are available, along with fishing, gold panning, hiking, and berry picking. In winter, the lodge is only accessible by snowmobile, and the northern lights are the big attraction. Surprisingly, the lodge has Wi-Fi.

At Mile 79, the highway crosses Clearwater Creek; there are pit toilets at a rest stop and a camping area here. In six miles is a turnout with a view of numerous lakes and ponds that provide a staging area for waterfowl; look for ducks, cranes, geese, trumpeter swans, and migrating shorebirds.

Maclaren

At Mile 93 out of Cantwell, the road crosses the Maclaren River, a tributary of the Susitna, flowing from the southern icefields of mighty Mount Hayes. From here to the other end of the Denali Highway, you get occasional views of the three Alaska Range peaks. A mile west of the bridge is Maclaren River Road, which leads 12 miles north to Maclaren Glacier.

Just before the bridge crossing is **Maclaren River Lodge** (Mile 42, Denali Hwy., 907/388-6361, www.maclarenlodge.com, Feb.-Sept.), catering to hikers, hunters, anglers, cyclists, and sightseers in the summer, and wintertime snowmobilers, cross-country skiers, and fat-tire cyclists. The lodge has a dozen brand cabins ($150 for up to 4 guests), each with two queen beds and private baths, along with two simple dry cabins ($100 d, extra guests $25 pp). There's a central area with satellite TV and limited Wi-Fi. The small bar serves beer and wine, and a full-service **restaurant** (7am-9pm daily, dinner $20-30) serves burgers, steaks, salmon, and great pies. Tire repair and gas ($5 per gallon at last check) are available.

For a trip you won't forget, the lodge has a jet boat that hauls canoes several miles up the **Maclaren River.** Once there, you can paddle back to the lodge. The cost is $150 for two people, including canoe rental; add $65 for additional people. More fun is their remote camp with wall tents, cots, tables, a cooking tent, and an outhouse. It's located 10 miles up the river and a five-mile hike from beautiful Maclaren Glacier. The lodge transports folks to their camp, where you can overnight, hike to the glacier, and then paddle your canoe downriver to the lodge the next day. The cost is $85 pp; canoes are provided, but bring your own sleeping bags and food.

In another seven miles is **Maclaren Summit,** at 4,080 feet the second-highest road pass in Alaska. It provides breathtaking views of Mount Hayes and the Maclaren Glacier. Peer through binoculars at the plains below to spot wildlife. Up at the summit you might see rock ptarmigan.

East End

The BLM's **Tangle Lakes Campground** (Mile 113, 907/822-3217, www.blm.gov/ak, free) has water pumps, pit toilets, blueberries in season, and a boat launch for extended canoe trips into the "tangle" (or maze) of lakes and ponds and creeks in the neighborhood.

One mile east of Tangle Lakes Campground is **Tangle River Inn** (Mile 114, Denali Hwy., 907/822-3970 summer, 907/892-4022 winter, www.tangleriverinn.com, mid-May-late Sept.). Jack and Naidine Johnson have owned this classic Alaskan lodge since 1970; there's even a mountain named for Naidine nearby!

The Johnsons sell gas, liquor, and gifts, and they offer three good home-cooked meals a day (7:30am-9pm daily, burgers $15), a lively bar with pool, foosball tables, and karaoke, along with simple lodging ($105 d shared bath, $135-180 d private bath, bunkhouse $48 pp), canoe rentals, and fishing gear. Tangle River also does tire repairs, a popular service.

The **Tangle Lakes Archaeological District** begins at Mile 119 and extends back to Crazy Notch at Mile 90. A short hike from the highway to any given promontory along this 30-mile stretch could have you standing at an ancient Athabascan hunting camp, where no human footprints have been made for hundreds of years.

At Mile 122, there's a viewpoint from the summit that looks south over a great tundra plain. The three most prominent peaks of the Wrangell Mountains are visible from here: Mount Sanford on the left, Mount Drum on the right, and Mount Wrangell in the middle.

At Mile 125 is a paved turnout with a view of **Ten Mile Lake.** A short trail leads down to the lake, where you can catch grayling and

trout. A turnout at Mile 129 affords a spectacular view of the Alaska Range to the north. The Gulkana and Gakona Glaciers can be seen from this point. The Denali Highway joins the Richardson Highway at Paxson.

Paxson

This tiny settlement occupies the junction at Mile 186 of the Richardson Highway and Mile 136 (from Cantwell) of the Denali Highway. Located just north of the highway junction, **Paxson Alpine Tours** (907/822-5972, www.denalihwy.com) guides Denali Highway van tours, Land Cruiser tours, birding hikes, and river tours. Owners Dr. Audie Bakewell and Jenny Rodina also operate **Denali Highway Cabins** ($250-295 d), where peaceful riverside cabins contain private baths and access to a communal kitchen. Interested in glamping? Stay in one of the deluxe tent cabins on riverside platforms ($195 d). Guests are served a filling breakfast in the great room each morning. Amenities include a grand piano, games, Wi-Fi, and mountain bikes for use on nearby trails. Dinners may also be available.

Denali National Park and Preserve

Alaska's most famous tourist attraction, **Denali National Park** (907/683-2294, www.nps.gov/dena) draws over 530,000 visitors during its brief summer season. Most travelers come to see Mount Denali, the highest peak in North America (20,310 feet), which towers above the surrounding lowlands and 14,000- to 17,000-foot peaks. Although it's visible only one day in three, and often shrouded for a week or more at a time, those who get lucky and see the mountain experience a thrill equivalent to its majesty and grandeur. Those who don't are usually consoled by lower snow-capped mountains and attending glaciers, high passes and adrenaline-pumping drops off the road, tundra vistas and "drunken forests," and an incredible abundance of

wildlife, including caribou, moose, sheep, and bears. But even if the mountain is socked in, the grizzlies are hiding, and the shuttle-bus windows are fogged up, you're still smack in the middle of some of the most spectacular and accessible wilderness in the world. It was the call of the wild that brought you out here in the first place; all you have to do is step outside and answer.

THE LANDSCAPE

The Alaska Range is a U-shaped chain that extends roughly 600 miles from the top of the Alaska Peninsula (at the head of the Aleutians) up through the park and down below Tok. It's only a small part, however, of the coastal mountains that include California's Sierra Nevada, the Northwest's Cascades, the Coast

Denali National Park and Preserve

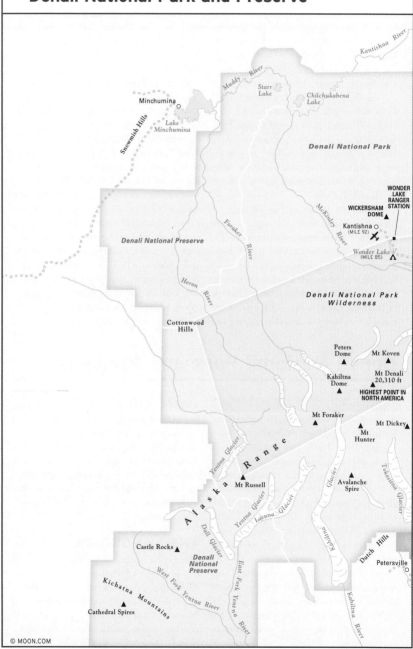

Kantishna River

Muddy River

Minchumina

Starr Lake

Chilchukabena Lake

Denali National Park

Snowmish Hills

Lake Minchumina

McKinley River

WONDER LAKE RANGER STATION

WICKERSHAM DOME

Denali National Preserve

Foraker River

Kantishna
(MILE 92)

Wonder Lake
(MILE 85)

Heron River

Denali National Park Wilderness

Cottonwood Hills

Peters Dome

Mt Koven

Kahiltna Dome

Mt Denali
20,310 ft
HIGHEST POINT IN NORTH AMERICA

Mt Foraker

Mt Dickey

Mt Hunter

Yentna Glacier

A l a s k a   R a n g e

Glacier

Avalanche Spire

Takositna Glacier

Mt Russell

Kahiltna

Dutch Hills

Dall Glacier

Yentna Glacier

Lacuna Glacier

East Fork Yentna River

Petersville

Castle Rocks

Denali National Preserve

West Fork Yentna River

East Fork Yentna River

Kahilina River

K i c h a t n a   M o u n t a i n s

Cathedral Spires

© MOON.COM

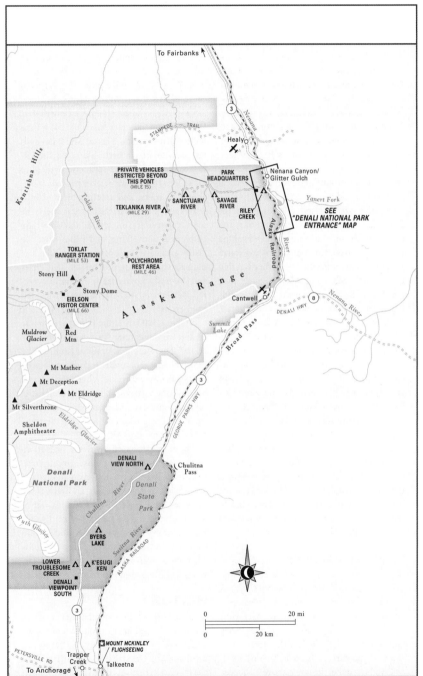

To Fairbanks

STAMPEDE TRAIL

Healy

PRIVATE VEHICLES
RESTRICTED BEYOND
THIS PONT
(MILE 15)

PARK
HEADQUARTERS

Nenana Canyon/
Glitter Gulch

TEKLANIKA RIVER
(MILE 29)

SANCTUARY
RIVER

SAVAGE
RIVER

Yanert Fork

Kantishna Hills

Toklat River

RILEY
CREEK

*SEE
"DENALI NATIONAL PARK
ENTRANCE" MAP*

TOKLAT
RANGER STATION
(MILE 53)

POLYCHROME
REST AREA
(MILE 46)

Stony Hill

Stony Dome

A l a s k a   R a n g e

Cantwell

Alaska Railroad

Nenana River

EIELSON
VISITOR CENTER
(MILE 66)

Summit
Lake

DENALI HWY

8

Muldrow
Glacier

Red
Mtn

Broad Pass

Mt Mather

Mt Deception

Mt Eldridge

GEORGE PARKS HWY

Mt Silverthrone

Eldridge Glacier

Sheldon
Amphitheater

*Denali
National Park*

DENALI
VIEW NORTH

Chulitna
Pass

*Denali
State
Park*

Ruth Glacier

Chulitna River

Susitna River

BYERS
LAKE

Alaska Railroad

LOWER
TROUBLESOME
CREEK

K'ESUGI
KEN

DENALI
VIEWPOINT
SOUTH

0   20 mi

0   20 km

PETERSVILLE RD

MOUNT McKINLEY
FLIGHSEEING

Trapper
Creek

Talkeetna

To Anchorage

Mountains of British Columbia, Yukon's St. Elias Range, and eastern Alaska's Wrangell Range. The Park Road starts out a bit north of the Alaska Range and follows the U for 90 miles southwest toward its heart—Mount Denali. One thing that makes the mountain so spectacular is that the surrounding lowlands are so low: The entrance is at 1,700 feet elevation, and the highest point on the road, Thoroughfare Pass, is just under 4,000 feet. The base of Mount Denali is at 2,000 feet, and the north face rises at a 60-degree angle straight up to 20,000 feet—the highest vertical rise in the world.

Weather patterns here differ between the south side of the range (wetter and cooler) and the north. During the summer, the prevailing winds come from the south, carrying warm moisture from the Pacific. When they run into the icy rock wall of the Alaska Range, they climb, the moisture condenses, and, depending on the amount of moisture and altitude, it either rains or snows—a lot. On top of that whole system sits mighty Mount Denali, high, cold, and alone; it's so alone that the mountain has its own relationship to the weather. The combination of wind, wet, cold, and height creates extremely localized—and often violent—weather around Mount Denali. Storms can blow in within an hour and last a week or more, dumping 10 feet of snow. Winds scream in at up to 80 mph. The mercury drops below zero in mid-July. Some of the worst weather in the world swirls around up there. But when the mountain emerges bright white against bright blue, and you're craning your neck to see the top, it's an unforgettable sight worth waiting around for—even in the rain.

Plants and Animals

From sea level to around 2,300 feet is the habitat for the **boreal forest,** in which the black spruce, with its somber foliage and clusters of tawny cones, is the climax tree. Younger white spruce, along with deciduous aspen, birch, and cottonwood, grow near the streams and the road and in recently burned areas.

Climbing out of the forest above 2,300 feet,

you enter the **taiga,** a Russian word meaning "land of twigs." This transition zone (between the forest below and tundra above) accommodates no deciduous trees; the spruce are thinned out and runty (though they can be over 60 years old), and a green shag carpet of bush, mostly dwarf willow, layers the floor. Sitka spruce is the state tree because of its size, grandeur, and commercial value, but it's the willow that vegetates Alaska. And it has endless uses: Before synthetics like nylon, the willow bark was stripped, split, and braided to make into rope, bows, wicker baskets, snowshoes, fishnets, and small game and bird snares and traps. The inner bark is sweet; the sap is very sweet. Young buds and shoots are edible and nourishing, and willows are the nearly exclusive staple of the moose diet. The taiga also hosts a variety of berries: blueberries and low-bush cranberries by the ton, crowberries, bearberries, soap and salmon berries, and raspberries.

Above 2,500 feet is the **tundra,** its name a Lapp word meaning "vast, rolling, treeless plain." There are two types of tundra: The moist, or Alaskan, tundra is characterized by the taiga's dwarf shrubbery, high grasses, and berries, but no trees; the alpine tundra, the highest zone, has grasses, moss, lichens, and small hardy wildflowers, including the stunning forget-me-not, Alaska's state flower.

The animal life varies with the vegetation. In the forest, look for moose, porcupines, snowshoe hares, martens, lynx, two kinds of weasels, red or tree squirrels, and several varieties of small rodents. On the taiga—or in both the forest and the tundra—you might see coyotes, wolves, foxes, grizzlies, and ground squirrels. In the tundra, keep an eye out for caribou, wolverines, Dall sheep, marmots, voles, lemmings, and shrews.

HISTORY

In 1896 a prospector named Bill Dickey was tramping around interior Alaska looking for gold. Like everyone who sees it, Dickey was captivated by the size and magnificence of the mountain that was then variously known as Tenada, Denali, Densmore's Mountain, Traleika, and Bulshaia. Dickey was from Ohio, William McKinley's home state, and a Princeton graduate in economics. When he came out of the bush and heard that McKinley had been nominated for president, he promptly renamed the mountain "McKinley," wrote numerous articles for stateside magazines, and lobbied in Washington DC in support of adoption of the name, which finally caught on after President McKinley was assassinated in 1901. The name was something of a sore point with Alaskans for more than a century, since McKinley had absolutely nothing to do with the mountain, and the more lyrical Native Alaskan names were completely ignored. Many in Alaska supported renaming the peak Denali ("the high one"), a term used by Native Alaskans of the lower Yukon and Kuskokwim Rivers. For decades, any move to eliminate "McKinley" from maps was inevitably met by howls of protest from Ohio's congressional delegation. Finally, in 2015, President Obama changed the mountain's name to Mount Denali.

Creating a Park

Harry Karstens reached the Klondike in 1898 when he was 19, bored by Chicago and attracted by adventure and gold. Within a year he'd crossed over into U.S. territory and wound up at Seventymile, 20 miles south of Eagle. When the local mail carrier lost everything one night in a card game and committed suicide, Karstens took his place. He became proficient at dog mushing and trailblazing, and within a few years was delivering mail on a primitive trail between Eagle and Valdez, a 900-mile round-trip every month (the Richardson Highway follows the same route). Later he moved on to Fairbanks and began delivering mail to Kantishna, the mining town on what is now the west end of the park, growing very fond of and familiar with the north side of the Alaska Range. So when a naturalist from the East Coast, Charles Sheldon, arrived in 1906 to study Dall sheep in the area, Karstens guided him around Mount Denali's

northern foothills, delineating the habitat of the sheep. Karstens was also the co-leader of the four-man expedition that was the first party to successfully climb the true peak of Mount Denali, the south summit, in 1913.

Meanwhile, Charles Sheldon was back in Washington, lobbying for national-park status for the Dall sheep habitat, and when Mount McKinley National Park was created in 1917, Karstens was the obvious choice to become the first park superintendent. He held that post in 1921-1928, patrolling the park boundaries by dogsled.

Woodrow Wilson signed the bill that created Mount McKinley National Park, Alaska's first, in 1917. The Park Road, begun five years later, was completed to Kantishna in 1940. In 1980, with the passage of the Alaska National Interest Lands Conservation Act, McKinley Park was renamed Denali National Park and Preserve and expanded to nearly six million acres, roughly the size of Vermont.

Pioneer Climbs

Many pioneers and prospectors had seen the mountain and approached it, but Alfred Brooks, a member of the first U.S. Geological Survey expedition in Alaska in 1902, was the first to set foot on it. He approached it from the south and reached an elevation of 7,500 feet before running out of time. He published an article in the January 1903 issue of *National Geographic* in which he recommended approaching the mountain from the north. Following that suggestion, the next attempt was from the north, led by James Wickersham, U.S. district judge for Alaska. Judge Wickersham was sent from Seattle to bring law and order to Eagle in 1900; he moved to Fairbanks in 1903. That summer, he had a spare couple of months and set out to climb the mountain, traveling more than 100 miles overland and reaching the 7,000-foot level of the north face, later named Wickersham Wall in honor of His Honor.

That same summer, Dr. Frederick Cook, who'd been with Peary's first party to attempt to reach the North Pole in 1891 and

Amundsen's Antarctic expedition of 1897, also attempted to climb the mountain from the north and reached 11,300 feet. In 1906, Cook returned to attempt Mount Denali from the south, but he failed to get near it. His party broke up and went their separate directions, and a month later, Cook sent a telegram to New York claiming he'd reached the peak. This was immediately doubted by the members of his party, who challenged his photographic and cartographic "evidence." But through public lectures and articles, Cook's reputation as the first man to reach the peak grew. Two years later, he claimed to have reached the North Pole several months ahead of another Peary expedition, and Cook began to enjoy a cult status in the public consciousness. Simultaneously, however, his credibility among fellow explorers rapidly declined, and Cook vanished from sight. This further fueled the controversy and led to the Sourdough Expedition of 1910.

Four sourdoughs in Fairbanks simply decided to climb the mountain to validate or eviscerate Cook's published description of his route. They left town in December and climbed to the north peak in early April. The three members who'd actually reached the peak stayed in Kantishna to take care of business, while the fourth member, Tom Lloyd, who hadn't reached the peak, returned to Fairbanks and lied that he had. By the time the other three returned to town in June, Lloyd's story had already been published and widely discredited. So nobody believed the other three—*especially* when they claimed they'd climbed up to the north peak and down to their base camp at 11,000 feet in 18 hours, with a thermos of hot chocolate, four doughnuts, and dragging a 14-foot spruce log that they planted up top and claimed was still there. Finally, in 1913, the Hudson Stuck-Harry Karstens expedition reached the true summit, the south peak, and could prove that they'd done so beyond a shadow of a doubt.

Only then was the Sourdough Expedition vindicated: All four members of the Stuck party saw the spruce pole still standing on the north peak!

Today more than 1,000 mountaineers attempt the summit of Mount Denali each year, and approximately half of them actually reach the top. The youngest climbers ever to summit were an 11-year-old boy and a 12-year-old girl; the oldest man was 78, and the oldest woman 70.

PARK ENTRANCE

The entrance to Denali National Park turns off at Mile 237 of the Parks Highway, and Denali Park Road heads west from there for 92 miles through the park. The Denali Visitor Center, Denali Bus Depot, Alaska Railroad depot, Riley Creek Campground, park administrative offices, and other facilities cluster along Denali Park Road within a few miles of the entrance. There are no places to buy anything (other than books) once you get past the entrance area, so be sure to bring what you need for the day on any park bus tour.

Most hotels, restaurants, and other businesses are in a chaotic area two miles north of the park entrance at Mile 239 Parks Highway. This unincorporated settlement goes by a multitude of unofficial names: Nenana Canyon, Glitter Gulch, The Canyon, Denali Park, The Gulch, or simply Denali. I use the name Nenana Canyon in this book, but Glitter Gulch would probably be the most appropriate for this hodgepodge of commercialism just outside Denali.

Planning Your Time

Denali National Park is open year-round, though most facilities only operate mid-May to mid-September. Plowing of the Park Road generally starts in early May, but only the first 30 miles are open before late May, when the shuttle buses begin running. Those who arrive before this date will not be able to reach the best vantage points for Mount Denali.

The wildflowers peak around summer solstice—as do the mosquitoes. The berries,

1: ranger talk at Wonder Lake in Denali National Park; **2:** red fox in Denali National Park

Denali National Park Entrance

To Healy and Fairbanks
Bike Path
Nenana Canyon/ Glitter Gulch
Nenana River
MT HEALY OVERLOOK
0   0.5 mi
0   0.5 km
Horseshoe Lake
Horseshoe Lake Trail
SHUTTLE BUS STOP
SHUTTLE BUS STOP
DENALI BUS DEPOT
Mt. Healy Overlook Tr.
Taiga Trail
MERCANTILE/ POST OFFICE
MURIE SCIENCE AND LEARNING CENTER
SHUTTLE BUS STOP
RILEY CREEK
SHUTTLE BUS STOP
McKinley Station Trail
DENALI VISITOR CENTER/ BACKCOUNTRY INFO CENTER
RAIL DEPOT
Rock Creek Trail
Meadow View Trail
Riley Creek
PARK RD
SUSPENSION BRIDGE
Alaska Railroad
3
Rock Creek
Roadside Trail
Hines Creek
PARK HEADQUARTERS/ RANGER STATION
SLED DOG KENNELS
To Cantwell, Talkeetna, and Anchorage
© MUON.COM

rose hips, and mushrooms are best in mid-August—as are the no-see-ums. The fall colors on the tundra are gorgeous around Labor Day weekend, when the crowds start to thin out and the northern lights start to appear, but it can get very cold. A skeleton winter Park Service crew patrols the park by dogsled. After the first heavy snowfall, the Park Road is plowed only to headquarters. One piece of planning advice: **plan at least three days** for the Denali area, with one of those days set aside for the long bus trip to the heart of Denali.

Visitors Centers

The **Denali Visitor Center** (Mile 1.5, Park Rd., www.nps.gov/dena, 907/683-2294, 8am-6pm daily mid-May-mid-Sept.) is just uphill from the railroad depot. Step inside to explore the interactive exhibits, get oriented from the enormous relief map of the park, talk with the rangers, and view an extraordinary 20-minute film, *Heartbeats of Denali.* Pick up a copy of the park map and official *Summer Guide,* and check the bulletin board for a schedule of the day's guided walks, talks, and kids' programs. Adjacent are an **Alaska Natural History Association Gift Shop** and **Morino Grill** (8am-6pm daily summer, $10-14), serving sandwiches, fish-and-chips, burgers, chili, and soups. Also here is a **baggage claim** where you can leave luggage for a few hours or several days.

Pay the park admission ($10 pp) or buy a **National Park Annual Pass** ($80 per year)—good for all national parks. A **Senior Pass** for all national parks is available to anyone over age 62 for a one-time fee of $80, and people with disabilities can get a free Access Pass that covers all the parks.

On the other side of the traffic circle, the **Murie Science and Learning Center** (907/683-6432, 9am-4:30pm daily) promotes scientific research and education through youth camps, field seminars, and courses in the summer. (The center may be closed in summer due to budget issues.) In the off-season—when other park facilities are closed—the Murie building becomes the **winter park visitors center** (9:30am-5pm daily winter). Check out the dinosaur track here that was found in the park.

Get park shuttle bus tickets and campground information at the **Denali Bus Depot** (http://go.nps.gov/denaliwac, 5am-7pm daily mid-May-mid-Sept.), located 0.5 miles up the Park Road. The reservations desk opens at 5am to handle existing reservations and 7am for booking new tickets. While here, you could also watch a free 18-minute park film called *Across Time and Tundra*. This facility is run by the park concessionaire, Aramark, and also has a little gift shop with snacks, a coffee cart, books, cards, and an ATM.

Sled Dog Demonstrations

One of the highlights of the park is the half-hour **sled dog demonstrations** (10am, 2pm, and 4pm daily in peak season, free) at the kennels behind headquarters. The dogs are beautiful and accessible (the ones not behind fences are chosen for friendliness and patience with people), and the anxious collective howl they orchestrate when the lucky six dogs are selected to run is something to hear. Naturalists talk about the current and historical uses of dogs in the park, their breeding and training, different commands for controlling them, and the challenge of maintaining a working kennel in a national park. Then dogs are hitched up to a wheel sled and run quickly around a gravel track. The enthusiasm of the dogs to get off the chain and into the harness is an eyebrow-raising glimpse into the consciousness of Alaskan sled dogs—they live to run. Don't miss this one!

Parking is extremely limited at the dog kennels, but a free **Sled Dog**

Demonstration shuttle bus (http://go.nps.gov/denalicourtesy) leaves the Denali Visitor Center bus stop 40 minutes before the demonstrations.

GETTING AROUND DENALI

In 1971, before the George Parks Highway connected McKinley National Park to Fairbanks (125 miles) and Anchorage (245 miles), you had to take the train, or from Fairbanks you had to drive down to Delta Junction, take the Richardson Highway to Paxson, the Denali Highway to Cantwell, then the Parks Highway up to the park entrance, for a grand total of 340 miles. From Anchorage you had to drive to Glennallen, then up the Richardson to Paxson, over to Cantwell and beyond, for 440 miles. That year, nearly 45,000 visitors passed through the park. In 1972, when the George Parks Highway radically reduced driving times from both main urban centers, almost 90,000 visitors came. In anticipation of the huge jump in tourism, the Park Service initiated the shuttle system of buses running a regularly scheduled service along the Park Road. Today, the park sees well over 500,000 visitors annually.

Cell phone coverage exists only in the first three miles of the Denali Park Road, but you may have intermittent coverage for a few miles farther. Bus drivers have radio communication, but you'll have to survive without cell service or Wi-Fi.

★ Denali Bus Tours

One unique characteristic of Denali National Park is its limited access. The park is bisected by a 92-mile gravel road, but only the first 15 miles are open to private vehicles. Public access is only by buses that will take you back to your grade-school days: high seats, barebones decor, slide-down windows (perfect for photos), and a noisy interior. It's utilitarian Alaska at its best.

There's no question that the bus system is highly beneficial to the park experience: The road is tricky and dangerous, crowds are

much more easily controlled, there's much less impact on the wildlife (which take the buses for granted), and it's much easier to see wildlife when 40 passengers have eyeballs, phones, binoculars, and telephotos trained on the tundra.

Several types of buses travel the Park Road all summer: **transit buses** (no narration), **camper buses** (backcountry access), **tour buses** (trained naturalists on board), and **private tour buses.** You can tell these buses at a distance; **transit buses** and **camper buses** are **green**, while **tour buses** are **tan** in color. All buses (except camper buses) depart from the Denali Bus Depot near the park entrance.

Bus schedules are readily available on the park website (www.nps.gov/denali), at visitors centers, and in hotels. Bring everything with you on a bus tour; there's nothing (except books and postcards) for sale once you enter the park.

Reserve bus tickets in advance (907/272-7275 or 800/622-7275, www.reservedenali.com) over the phone starting in mid-February or online from December 1 up to the day before you travel. Sixty-five percent of the available tickets for advance purchase are on December 1; the other 35 percent are made available within two days ahead of the travel date. If you wait till the last minute (definitely not advised), purchase tickets at the Denali Bus Depot.

Transit Buses

Up to 30 green transit buses operate daily during Denali's peak summer season. These buses are designed to move folks around the park, getting them from point A to point B. The driver makes regular stops for wildlife viewing and restroom breaks, but doesn't provide narration. The transit bus is best if you're interested in a day hike or just want to enjoy the sights on your own instead of in a group.

It's recommended that you get on an early-morning bus into the park: There is a better chance to see wildlife and the mountain in the cool of the morning, and more time to get off the bus and play in the backcountry.

Green transit buses depart from the **Denali Bus Depot,** with some continuing all the way to Kantishna, an exhausting 92-mile, 13-hour round-trip ride. Most visitors don't go that far (or certainly not in one day), turning around instead at Polychrome Pass, Eielson, Wonder Lake, or other places along the way. Buses for Eielson begin departing from the Denali Bus Depot at 5am and continue roughly every 30 minutes through 3:30pm. Other buses depart during the day for Polychrome-Toklat River and Wonder Lake.

Fares are $32 to **Toklat River** (6 hours round-trip, mid-May-mid-Sept.), $40 to **Eielson Visitor Center** (8 hours round-trip, June-mid-Sept.), $55 to **Wonder Lake** (11 hours round-trip, early June-mid-Sept.), and $60 to **Kantishna** (13 hours round-trip, early June-mid-Sept.). Children under age 16 ride free on all buses. Fares do not include the $10 pp park entrance fee. Approximately half the buses are wheelchair-accessible, and most buses have bike racks (maximum of two bikes). Reservations are required for bicycles on buses heading into the park, but not for those heading eastbound.

You can get off the bus and flag it down to get back on (if there's room; the buses leave with a few seats empty to pick up day hikers in the park) anywhere along the road. Many riders never get off the bus at all, staying on it for the entire exhausting round-trip.

Camper Buses

Specially configured green **camper buses** ($40 round-trip, free under age 16) are only for campers and backcountry travelers. They have fewer seats in order to offer extra space to carry backpacks, camping gear, and bicycles. They're used to transport visitors to campgrounds (Sanctuary River, Teklanika River, Igloo Creek, and Wonder Lake) and for access to backcountry units within the park. Camper buses are infrequent before peak season (twice

1: Denali Visitor Center; **2:** bus on Denali Road; **3:** campers at Wonder Lake; **4:** sled dog demonstration

a day in early June), then run up to six times daily in July and August.

Buses carry a maximum of two bicycles; reserve a space if you're bike camping. Reservations are required for bicycles on buses heading into the park, but not for those heading eastbound out of the park.

Buses depart from the Riley Creek Campground bus shelter (long-term parking available), but also pick up campers from the Denali Bus Depot (no overnight parking) and Denali Visitor Center. Backcountry travelers should make camper bus reservations after obtaining a backcountry permit. If staying in one of the park campgrounds, reserve space on the camper bus in advance from the park concessionaire (Aramark, 907/272-7275 or 800/622-7275, www.reservedenali.com).

Tour Buses

The park's tan **tour buses** (907/272-7275 or 800/622-7275, www.reservedenali.com) leave from the Denali Bus Depot throughout the day. These tours are extremely popular and fill up fast; make reservations as far in advance as possible. Note also that some tours are not available early or late in the season. Bring food and water for these tours.

For a good introduction, take a five-hour **Denali Natural History Tour** (mid-May-mid-Sept., $80 adults, $40 under age 16) to Primrose Ridge (17 miles each way), or for a better look, join the seven-hour **Tundra Wilderness Tour** (mid-May-mid-Sept., $136 adults, $68 under age 16, snack and water provided) to Stony Hill Overlook, a distance of 62 miles each way. A shorter **Tundra Wilderness Tour** ($116 adults, $58 kids) to Mile 53 is offered in May when snow prevents access farther out the Park Road.

Kantishna Experience ($208 adults, $104 under age 16, includes a box lunch) is a 12-hour tour that focuses both on wildlife and the history of this old gold mining town in the heart of Denali.

Private Tour Buses

Kantishna Wilderness Trails (907/374-3041 or 800/230-7275, www.denaliwildlifetour.com, early June-mid-Sept., $190 pp, includes lunch and snacks) has private all-day bus tours that leave Nenana Canyon hotels at 6:30am. Tours take you to Kantishna Roadhouse near the end of the road for lunch, gold panning, and a sled dog demonstration before heading back out, arriving at the hotels by 8pm. No children under age six are allowed. For a faster version (return at 3pm, $480 pp), you can ride the bus to Kantishna and return on a Kantishna Air flight.

Denali Backcountry Adventure (907/376-1900 or 800/808-8068, www.alaskacollection.com, early June-mid-Sept., $189 pp) provides all-day bus tours to Denali Backcountry Lodge in Kantishna. These 13-hour (6am-7:30pm) trips include a lunch buffet, gold panning, and a free shuttle to Wonder Lake for hiking and photography.

Local Shuttles

The Park Service (http://go.nps.gov/denalicourtesy) provides several free shuttles in the entrance area.

The free **Riley Creek Shuttle** (5am-7pm daily mid-May-mid-Sept.) connects the Riley Creek Campground, Denali Bus Depot, and train depot every half hour. In addition, a free bus connects the Denali Visitor Center with Park Headquarters, timed to meet the three-times-daily **sled dog demonstrations.**

The free **Savage River Shuttle Bus** (mid-May-late Sept.) heads out as far as Savage River Bridge at Mile 15, stopping at Riley Creek Campground, Denali Bus Depot, Horseshoe Lake Trailhead, Denali Visitor Center, Mountain Vista, and Savage River Campground. Buses run several time a day in each direction, and bikes can be transported, providing an easy ride-and-cycle option.

Dine Denali Shuttle (907/683-2733, www.dinedenali.com, hourly 8am-1am midsummer mid-May-mid-Sept., $5 day pass) stops at the Denali Visitor Center, Nenana Canyon hotels and restaurants, Denali Park Village, Grizzly Bear Resort, and Healy businesses. The shuttle also heads to Riley Creek

Campground and other destinations on request; call for a pickup.

The larger hotels around the park all operate their own private shuttle buses for guests. These include Denali Bluffs Hotel, Grande Denali Lodge, Denali Park Village, McKinley Chalet Resort, and Denali Princess Wilderness Lodge.

Driving

For most of the summer, only the first 15 miles (to Savage River) of the Park Road are open to private vehicles. This portion is paved and makes for an excellent day trip. From early May, when the road is plowed, to late May, when the shuttle buses start running, it is possible to drive as far as the Teklanika River rest area at Mile 30. The road beyond this doesn't open to buses until late May, so early park arrivals will not be able to see many of the sights for which the park is famous.

At the end of summer, the Park Road is opened to auto traffic for four days in mid-September for the annual **Road Lottery.** Only 400 vehicles are allowed per day, and passes are selected by a lottery. In a typical year, you may be competing with 11,000 other entries for these passes! You'll need to apply during the month of May; contact the National Park Service (907/683-2294, http:// go.nps.gov/denalilottery) for details.

A handful of professional photographers are allowed vehicular access to the park during the summer, but these slots are highly sought after and may require the sacrifice of your eldest child to appease the Park Service gods.

HEADING OUT ON THE PARK ROAD

A few miles beyond headquarters, the road climbs out of the boreal forest, levels off, and travels due west through a good example of taiga. The ridgeline to the north (right) of the road is known as the **Outer Range,** with the foothills of the massive Alaska Range to the south (left). The Outer Range is much older, of different geological origins, and much more rounded and eroded than the jagged Alaska Range. The first view of the mountain comes up at Mile 9; look southwest. The day has to be nearly perfectly clear to see Mount Denali from here: You're at around 2,400 feet, and the mountain is at 20,000 feet, which leaves nearly an 18-grand spread over 70-odd miles of potential cloud cover. That's a lot of potential.

Next you pass the Savage River Campground, then wind down to the river valley and cross the bridge that marks the end-of-road access for those in private vehicles. The "Checkpoint Charlie" kiosk at Mile 15 has a park employee to turn back private vehicles; they're prohibited beyond this point. From the bridge, look upriver (left) and notice the broad, U-shaped, glacial valley with large gravel deposits forming braids or channels, then look right to compare the V-shaped valley obviously cut by running water. The Savage Glacier petered out right where the bridge is now around 15,000 years ago, during the last ice age. Here you also kiss the pavement good-bye, then start climbing Primrose Ridge, which offers excellent hiking, especially in June-early July when the wildflowers are in full bloom. Turn around and look back at the Savage Bridge; the stark rock outcropping just up from it has a distinct resemblance to an Indian's facial bone structure, which is how the Savage got its politically incorrect name. Just up the road is a pullout—if the mountain's out, the driver should stop for the clear shot.

Savage River to Igloo Canyon

Mount Denali disappears behind jagged lower peaks as the road descends into the broad, glacial **Sanctuary River** valley at Mile 23. Watch for moose, caribou, foxes, lynx, waterfowl, and eagles along here. Right on the other side of the Sanctuary is a good view down at a "drunken forest," one effect that permafrost has on the vegetation. Notice how many of the trees are leaning at bizarre and precarious angles, with some of them down entirely. As an adaptation to the permafrost, these spruce trees have evolved a root system that spreads horizontally across the surface soil; there's no taproot to speak of. So the taller a tree grows around here, the less support it maintains, and the more susceptible it is to falling over. When the surface soil becomes saturated (because of lack of absorption over the permafrost), it sometimes shifts, either spontaneously or because of slight tremors (a major fault runs through here), taking the trees with it.

Next, you descend into the broad **Teklanika River** valley, with a good view across the river of the three vegetation zones on the mountain slopes: forest, taiga, and tundra. You pass a number of small ponds in this area, known as "kettles," usually formed when a retreating glacier drops off a large block of ice, which melts, leaves a depression, and fills with rainwater. The stagnant water is rich in nutrients and provides excellent hatching grounds for Alaska's famous mosquitoes, and as such the ponds are good feeding spots for ducks and shorebirds. Look for mergansers, goldeneyes, sandpipers, buffleheads, and phalaropes in these ponds.

Cross the river and enter **Igloo Canyon,** where you turn almost due south. The mountain on the right is Igloo (4,800 feet); the one on the left is Cathedral (4,905 feet). Igloo is in the Outer Range, Cathedral in the Alaska Range. At the closest distance between the two ranges, the canyon is right on the migration route of the Dall sheep and a great place to view them as white dots on the slopes; or climb either mountain to get closer.

Sable Pass (3,900 feet) is next at Mile 38, the second-highest point on the road. This area is closed to hiking and photography because of the large grizzly population. Keep your eyes peeled. The next good views of the mountain are from these highlands.

Over Polychrome Pass to Eielson

Once you cross the **East Fork River** at Mile 44 (there is great hiking out onto the flats from here), you begin your ascent of Polychrome Pass, one of the most spectacular and fear-inducing sections of the road. If you're scared of

heights or become frightened at the 1,000-foot drop-offs, just do what the driver does—close your eyes. These rocks have a high iron content; the rate of oxidation and the combination of the iron with other minerals determine the different shades of rust, orange, red, and purple. Look and listen for hoary marmots in the nearby rocks, and, from here almost the rest of the way to Eielson Visitor Center, watch for caribou and wolves; these are the Murie flats, where wildlife biologist Adolph Murie studied the lifestyle of *Canis lupus.*

Descend to the **Toklat River** at Mile 53, the last and largest you cross before Eielson. This is the terminus of the wildlife tour, but the shuttle buses continue on to Eielson and Wonder Lake. The Toklat's source is the Sunrise Glacier, just around the bend upriver (left). You can see from the size of the river how big the glacier was 20,000 years ago. Buses pull in at **Toklat Rest Stop** (9am-7pm daily late May-late Sept.) for a restroom break, and a small bookshop sells natural history titles. There is great hiking up into the Alaska Range from here. Next you climb up **Stony Hill** and, if the weather is cooperating, when you crest the ridge you're in for the thrill of a lifetime: Denali, The Great One, in all its immense majestic glory. It's hard to believe that the mountain is still 40 miles away! But wait, you get another five miles closer, crossing **Thorofare Pass** (3,950 feet), the highest elevation on the road, at Mile 62.

★ Eielson Visitor Center

Eielson Visitor Center (daily 9am-7pm June-late Sept., http://go.nps.gov/denalievc) is four hours and 66 miles from the park entrance. The view from here—weather cooperating—is unforgettable. Even if you can only see the bottom 12,000-14,000 feet, have a naturalist or your driver point to where the top of Mount Denali is, and visualize it in your mind's eye. Also, things change fast around here, so keep an eye out for the peak popping out of the clouds as a surprise just for you.

The modern, earth-friendly visitors center at Eielson features exhibits, tall windows facing Denali, short-term lockers, an outdoor deck, 24-hour restrooms, and space to enjoy your lunch or relax. Check out the inter-locked moose antlers out front; the two bulls died while sparring, and their antlers became locked together.

Naturalists lead 45-minute walks daily at 1pm. The excellent backpacking zones in this area are usually the first to fill up. There's nothing for sale at Eielson, so be sure to bring food and any needed maps or books.

★ Wonder Lake

Beyond Eielson, the road comes to within 25 miles of the mountain, passing **Muldrow Glacier,** which is covered by a thick black layer of glacial till and vegetation. From Wonder Lake, the **Wickersham Wall** rises magnificently above the intervening plains, with the whole Alaska Range stretching out on each side. In addition, the reflection from the lake doubles your pleasure and doubles your fun, from which even the mosquitoes here, some of the most savage, bloodthirsty, insatiable beasts of the realm, cannot detract.

There's a popular campground at Wonder Lake (Mile 85), and a nearby pond is where those postcard-perfect moose-in-the-lake-with-Mount-Denali photos are taken. Many buses turn around at Wonder Lake, but a few continue to Kantishna.

Kantishna

The town of Kantishna, 92 *long* miles from the park entrance at the western end of the Park Road, has five roadhouses. The area was first settled in 1905, when several thousand min-ers rushed to the foothills just north of Mount Denali to mine gold, silver, lead, zinc, and an-timony. After 1980 and the Alaska National Interest Lands Conservation Act, which ex-panded Denali National Park's boundaries, Kantishna found itself inside the park, and in 1985 mining was halted by court order. The road ends at the last lodge, where buses turn around to return to the park entrance. An air taxi is based here, and most Kantishna lodges have their own shuttle buses and tours.

Ranger-led walks are available daily all summer at both the Denali Visitor Center and Eielson Visitor Center. These typically take place at 10am and 1pm. More ambitious are the half-day **Discovery Hikes** (early June-mid-Sept.) led by rangers to more remote areas. These include several hours on the bus en route to your starting point; reserve a day or two in advance at the Denali Visitor Center. The hikes are free, but there's a $40 pp charge for the "disco hike" bus ride.

Note: Guns are now legally permitted within Denali National Park, but they aren't allowed on most shuttle and tour buses and in some park facilities. Research indicates that hikers carrying guns are more likely to be in-jured in bear attacks than those who carry pepper-based bear sprays such as Counter Assault. There has only been one fatal bear attack in the park (in 2012), but bears certainly are a potential hazard. Be sure to carry bear spray, and have it accessible.

Entrance Area Hikes

Several paths take off from the Denali Visitor Center, including two easy ones: the **Spruce Forest Trail** (15 minutes) and the slightly lon-ger **Murie Science and Learning Center Trail** (20 minutes). **Horseshoe Lake Trail** (three miles round-trip) starts at the shuttle bus stop and then descends to the lake, where you might see waterfowl and beavers.

The 1.6-mile **McKinley Station Trail** connects the visitors center with Riley Creek Campground via a wide gravel path that passes beneath the towering Alaska Railroad trestle. Take a side trip on Triple Lakes Trail; just a short distance up is a fun suspension bridge over Riley Creek.

The 2.3-mile **Rock Creek Trail** begins near the post office and climbs to park head-quarters, gaining 400 feet along the way. You can then loop back along the road via the aptly named 1.8-mile **Roadside Trail.** The **Taiga Trail** is an easy 1.3-mile loop that also begins near the post office.

Hiking the five-mile round-trip **Mount**

Coexisting with Bears

grizzly in Denali National Park

Bears seem to bring out conflicting emotions in people. The first is an almost gut reaction of fear and trepidation: What if the bear attacks me? But then comes that other urge: What will my friends say when they see these *incredible* bear photos? Both of these reactions can lead to problems in bear country. "Bearanoia" is a justifiable fear, but it can easily be taken to such an extreme that one avoids going outdoors at all for fear of running into a bear. The "I want to get close-up shots of that bear and her cubs" attitude can lead to a bear attack. The middle ground incorporates a knowledge of and respect for bears with a sense of caution that keeps you alert for danger without letting fear rule your wilderness travels. Nothing is ever completely safe in this world, but with care you can avoid most of the common pitfalls that lead to bear encounters.

Both brown (grizzly) and black bears occur throughout South-Central Alaska. Old-timers joke that bears are easy to differentiate: A black bear climbs up the tree after you, while a grizzly snaps the tree off at the base. Both grizzlies and black bears pose potential threats to backcountry travelers.

Enter bear country with respect but not fear. Bears rarely attack humans; you're a thousand times more likely to be injured in a highway accident than by a bear. In fact, more people in Alaska are hurt each year by moose or dogs than by bears. Contrary to the stories you often hear, bears have good eyesight, but they depend more upon their excellent senses of smell and hearing. A bear can tell who has walked through an area, and how recently, with just a quick sniff of the air. Most bears hear or smell you long before you realize their presence, and they hightail it away.

Bears are beautiful, eminently fascinating, and surprisingly intelligent animals. They can be funny, playful and inquisitive, vicious or protective, and unpredictable. The more you watch bears in the wild, the more complex their lives seem, and the more they become individual animals, not simply the big and bad.

Healy Overlook Trail is a great way to get the lay of the land, see the mountain if it's out, quickly leave the crowds behind, and get your heart pumping. Once at the overlook (one mile in), keep climbing the ridges for another several hours to get to the peak of Mount Healy (5,200 feet). The trailhead is off the Taiga Trail, not far from the Denali Visitor Center.

A very rewarding but steep hike, **Bison**

Gulch Trail ascends Mount Healy from the other side. The route begins at a small parking area near Mile 244 of the Parks Highway, just north of Nenana Canyon-Glitter Gulch. The challenging seven-mile round-trip hike gains almost 4,000 feet en route, with no shade or protection from the wind. Ambitious hikers can continue downhill from the summit along Mount Healy Overlook Trail.

A straight-up-the-mountain hike climbs 4,674-foot **Sugar Loaf Mountain.** This narrow, unofficial trail begins from the parking lot of Denali Grande Hotel. (The "trailhead" is behind the Dumpsters.) Because the hotel overlooks the valley below, your starting point is already at 1,957 feet elevation, so you're halfway to the top. The trail is very steep in places, but takes you quickly into the alpine. It's a bit over two miles each way; be sure to bring water and sunscreen.

Savage River Hikes

Savage River is the farthest you can drive a private vehicle into the park, and it's a great spot for day hiking. Fifteen miles from the park entrance, the wide, paved road ends at a ranger checkpoint with parking lots along the Savage River. Beyond, the road is only open to park buses. The free Savage River Shuttle provides access from the park entrance, but you'll need to make sure you get back in time for the last bus. The easiest trail, **Savage River Loop Trail** heads upstream along the river for almost a mile before crossing a bridge and returning on the other side.

The **Savage Alpine Trail** connects the Savage River area with Savage River Campground. It's my favorite day hike in Denali, with easy access to the alpine and a big reward from the top. This moderately strenuous trail switchbacks uphill, gaining 1,500 feet to a rocky ridgeline with views of the Alaska Range and Mount Denali. Be on the lookout for ground squirrels (obviously fed by other hikers) along the way. You can return the same way, or continue onward in a downhill loop to the road at the other end, a total distance of four miles. If you hike the entire trail, catch the Savage River Shuttle back to your starting point. It's a two-mile walk on the park road if you miss the shuttle.

Eielson Hikes

The Eielson Visitor Center at Mile 66 is located in open tundra, with Mount Denali and other Alaska Range peaks dominating southern vistas. Just downhill from Eielson is the 0.8-mile **Tundra Loop Trail,** a good place to stretch your legs after the four-hour bus ride from the park entrance. Look for wildflowers and arctic ground squirrels along the way. A spur leads to a knoll overlooking the valley, and across the road from Eielson is an even shorter loop path for a quick jaunt before settling back into your bus.

The **Alpine Trail** is considerably more strenuous, climbing steeply up Thorofare Ridge, which looms above Eielson Visitor Center. It's 2.2 miles each way, with a gain of 1,000 feet in elevation as you hike a series of switchbacks and rock steps. Stop along the way to take in the view. The summit (almost 5,000 feet in elevation) is wide and flat with views in all directions. Grizzly bears and caribou are often spotted along the way. Return the same way, and plan on two hours round-trip. This hike is one of the popular ranger-led Discovery Hikes offered daily at noon in the summer. Make reservations at Eielson (9am-7pm daily June-late Sept., http://go.nps.gov/denalievc), but get here early to reserve your place for this memorable hike (maximum of 11 people).

Wonder Lake Hikes

The open country around Wonder Lake Campground provides relatively easy hiking, or walk up the road to Reflection Pond and the outlet to Wonder Lake. The only trail in the area is the **McKinley Bar Trail,** an easy five-mile round-trip hike from the campground. The trail passes through open country with small ponds, bogs, and creeks before cutting through spruce forests to the McKinley River. The braided river changes channels constantly, with easy hiking opportunities on the open, mile-wide river bar and Denali providing a magnificent backdrop. Do not attempt to cross this large glacier-fed river with its deep, fast-flowing water. The area is plagued by mosquitos much of the summer, so bring a head net and bug dope.

Guided Hikes

Denali Backcountry Guides (830/266-9255, www.walkdenali.com, mid-May-mid-Sept.) offers several unique ways to explore the backcountry inside and outside the park. Especially popular are heli-hikes ($575 pp), with a helicopter flight to the high country followed by a 3.5-hour guided hike. Less-expensive options include three-hour natural history walks ($110 pp) and five-hour wilderness hikes ($140 pp); these are primarily for cruise-ship folks. All trips include round-trip transport from Nenana Canyon hotels. The company also offers multiday wilderness trips.

Alaska Alpine Adventures (907/351-4193 or 877/525-2577, www.alaskaalpineadventures.com) guides an array of backpacking trips in Denali. Trips start with four-day base camp hikes ($2,000 pp) and go all the way up to a 10-day venture that includes eight days in the Denali backcountry ($3,550 pp). Access is via floatplane from Anchorage (included in the cost).

Traverse Alaska (907/903-0979, www.traversealaska.com, May-Sept., $199 pp) guides six-hour hikes around Denali and creates customized private treks for all levels of ability. These are perfect for folks who are interested in Denali backcountry adventures, but are unfamiliar with wilderness travel. Trips might include a "test hike," where guides show clients how to use camp stoves, select a campsite, or stay safe in bear country.

BACKCOUNTRY TRIPS

For details on backcountry hikes and camping, head to the **Backcountry Information Center** (907/683-9590, http://go.nps.gov/denalibackcountry, 8am-5pm daily mid-May-mid-Sept.) inside the Denali Visitor Center. The park ranger can provide details on the various areas within Denali, along with helpful safety information.

Popular backpacking areas include up the Savage River toward Fang Mountain; down the far side of Cathedral Mountain toward Calico Creek (get off the bus just before the Sable Pass closure); up Tatler Creek a little past Igloo Mountain; anywhere on the East Fork flats below Polychrome toward the Alaska Range; anywhere around Stony Hill; and the circumnavigation of Mount Eielson (get off 5-6 miles past the visitors center, cross the 100 or so braids of the Thorofare River, and walk around the mountain, coming back up to the visitors center). There are backcountry description guides at the backcountry desk, or you can find the same info online, with photos.

On all these hikes, you can get off the outbound camper bus, explore to your heart's content, and then get back on an inbound bus, if space is available. Consult with the driver and study the bus schedule closely; the camper buses may have space coming back.

Large as it is, it's hard to get lost in Denali—you're either north or south of the road. And since the road travels mostly through open alpine tundra, there aren't any artificial trails to follow—just pick a direction and go. Usually you'll want to make for higher ground to get out of the knee- to hip-high dwarf shrubbery of the moist tundra and onto the easy hiking of the alpine area, to get to where the breeze will keep the skeeters at bay, and to see more. Or walk along the river gravel bars into the mountains, although depending on the size of the gravel, it can be ankle-twisting. Hiking boots are a must, and you should carry food, water, a compass, binoculars, maps, rain gear, and a bear-proof food canister. Keep your eyes and ears wide open for wildlife that you don't want to get close to, sneak up on, or be surprised by.

1: hikers on the Savage Alpine Trail; **2:** Mt. Denali and Wonder Lake

1

2

Protecting Yourself During a Bear Encounter

If you happen to encounter a bear, stay calm and don't make any sudden moves. Do not run: Bears can exceed 40 miles per hour for short distances. Don't climb a tree, as it may actually incite an attack. Instead, make yourself visible by moving into the open so the bear will identify you as a human and not something to eat. Never stare directly at a bear. Dropping an item such as a hat or jacket may distract the bear, and talking calmly also seems to have some value in convincing bears that you're a human. If the bear sniffs the air or stands on its hind legs, it is probably trying to identify you. When it does, it will usually run away. If a bear woofs and postures, don't imitate—this is a challenge. Keep retreating. Most bear charges are also bluffs; the bear will often stop short and amble off.

If a grizzly bear attacks, freeze. It may well be a bluff charge, with the bear halting at the last second. If the bear does not stop its attack, use bear spray immediately. If the bear is going to make contact, curl up face down on the ground in a fetal position with your hands wrapped behind your neck and your elbows tucked over your face. Your backpack may help protect you. Remain still even if you are attacked, because sudden movements may incite further attacks. Often a bear will only sniff or nip you and leave. The injury you might sustain would be far less than if you tried to resist. After the attack, prevent further attacks by staying down on the ground until the grizzly has left the area. Do not play dead if the bear is at a distance or is leaving the area.

Bear authorities recommend against dropping to the ground if you are attacked by a black bear, because they tend to be more aggressive in such situations and are more likely to prey on humans. If a black bear attacks, use bear spray immediately. If you don't have the spray, fight back with whatever weapons are at hand; large rocks and branches can be effective deterrents, as can yelling and shouting. Aim for sensitive areas such as the bear's eyes or nose. Have a park ranger explain the difference between brown and black bears before you head into the backcountry.

Nighttime bear attacks could happen to even the most seasoned adventurer. In the rare event of a night attack in your tent, defend yourself very aggressively. Never play dead under such circumstances. Before going to bed, try to plan escape routes, and be sure to have a flashlight and pepper spray handy. Keeping your sleeping bag partly unzipped also allows the chance to escape should a bear attempt to drag you away. There are advantages to having multiple tents in case one person is attacked, and if someone is attacked in a tent near you, yelling and throwing rocks or sticks may drive the bear away.

A number of companies sell portable electric fences for safe travel in bear country. These lightweight fences surround a campsite, providing protection from nighttime attacks; a backpacker unit ($300) runs on two D-cell batteries and weighs less than four pounds. Several companies manufacture portable electric fences, including Electro Bear Guard (www.electrobearguard.com), Margo Supplies (www.margosupplies.com), and UDAP Industries (www.udap.com). Alaska Bear Fence Rentals (www.alaskabearfence.com) rents bear fences for $55 per week and delivers to the Anchorage Airport.

Cayenne pepper sprays ($40) such as Counter Assault (800/695-3394, www.counterassault.com) can be useful in fending off bear attacks, and experts recommend that hikers in bear country carry a can. They're sold in most Alaskan camping supply stores.

These sprays are effective only at close range (10-30 feet), particularly in tundra areas, where winds quickly disperse the spray. When you carry pepper spray, make sure it is readily available by carrying it in a holster on your belt or across your chest. Be sure to test-fire it to make sure you are comfortable using it. If you use the spray to drive a bear away, immediately leave the area, since the bear may return. When carrying the spray, be sure the safety clip remains in place so it doesn't accidentally discharge.

Detailed bear safety brochures are available at the Alaska Public Lands Information Center (www.alaskacenters.gov) in Anchorage, or on the Alaska Department of Fish and Game's website (www.adfg.state.ak.us). Two good bear safety books are *Bear Attacks: Their Causes and Avoidance* by Stephen Herrero and *Bear Aware: Hiking and Camping in Bear Country* by Bill Schneider.

Backcountry Permits

You need a free permit to spend the night in the backcountry. Permits are issued up to 24 hours in advance from the Backcountry Information Center. Reservations are not accepted. Plan at least an hour to get your permit. The center closes at 5pm, so don't arrive after 4pm if you intend to head out the same day. Check the big maps and look over descriptions of the 43 units, where a limited number of backpackers are allowed.

Once you have a destination, check the board to find the vacancies in the units. The most popular areas (units 12, 13, and 18) are often full, some are always closed, and others periodically close because of overcrowding or bears. Watch the 30-minute backcountry video that describes bear safety, river crossings, minimum-impact camping, emergencies, and other topics; listen to a 10-minute safety talk; and finally, get a permit from the ranger. You might have to wait a few days for openings in your chosen area, or have a plan B or C in mind. The park loans out free bear-proof food storage containers; be sure to get these for your hike. Bring your own bear spray or purchase a can at the Riley Creek store. Finally, reserve a seat on one of the camper buses ($40 round-trip, free under age 16) to get you and your gear into the park. To plan your trip prior to arriving at Denali, head to www.nps.gov/dena.

RECREATION
Mountain Biking

Mountain bikes provide an excellent way to explore Denali at your own pace. Bikes are allowed on the Park Road and can be transported aboard the green shuttle buses, but be sure to mention the bike when you make a bus reservation. Reservations are only available in the westbound direction (heading into the park), with a first-come, first-served basis in the other direction. Not all buses have bike racks, and those that do only carry two bikes at a time, so it's possible to get far out on the Park Road and then need to wait for several buses before finding one with space. Be sure

to pick up a "rules of the road" handout at the visitors center before heading out. Detailed bike info is also available on the park website (www.nps.gov/dena), including a link to the current shuttle bus schedule showing which buses accept bikes.

Denali Outdoor Center (907/683-1925 or 888/303-1925, www.denalioutdoorcenter. com) has mountain bike rentals at $25 per half day or $40 for 24 hours. They have an office right in the heart of Nenana Canyon-Glitter Gulch, where you can rent bikes and book trips. DOC's main office is eight miles north of Nenana Canyon and two miles south of Healy, with a free shuttle provided. At Otto Lake you can rent bikes or join one of their two-hour bike tours of the area ($57 adults, $47 children, four-person minimum).

Bike Denali Rental Center (Mile 238, Parks Hwy., 907/378-2107, June-mid-Sept.) operates from a cabin on the north end of the bridge over Nenana Canyon. In addition to mountain bike and cruiser rentals, the shop also has bike trailers and kid's bicycles ($9 per hour or $28 per day).

Rafting

Three raft companies run the Nenana River along the eastern margin of the park: **Denali Outdoor Center** (907/683-1925 or 888/303-1925, www.denalioutdoorcenter.com), **Denali Raft Adventures** (907/683-2234 or 888/683-2234, www.denaliraft.com), and **Raft Denali** (907/683-7238 or 800/789-7238, www.raftdenali.com).

Three types of river trips are offered: easy two-hour Class I-III float trips ($95 adults, $65 children), two-hour Class II-IV white-water trips ($95 adults, $75 children), and four-hour trips that combine both segments ($135 adults, $115 children). The last of these is the most interesting, providing a good compromise of both scenic and white-water rafting. Float trips are okay for children over age five, but only adults and kids over age 10 can do the white-water and combination runs. All three companies have offices in Nenana Canyon and provide rain gear, boots, and life jackets, plus transportation to and from local hotels.

Other Denali Raft Adventures options include a four-hour scenic float ($150 adults, $130 children) and an all-day trip that includes floating and rapids ($192 pp). All three companies do a good job, but Denali Outdoor Center would be my first choice, and they also provide inflatable kayak tours for those who want to paddle on their own.

Flightseeing

If the mountain is out and there's room on the plane, this is the time to pull out the credit card. These one-hour flights around Mount Denali will leave you flying high for days.

Denali Air (Mile 229, Parks Hwy., 907/683-2261, www.denaliair.com) operates from a private airstrip eight miles south of the park entrance. Take their one-hour "Peak Experience" flight over the mountain in a twin-engine plane for $399 pp (2-passenger minimum).

Based at Healy Airport—12 miles north of the park entrance—**Fly Denali** (907/683-2899 or 877/770-2359, www.flydenali.com) charges $549 pp for two-hour flight that includes a landing on Ruth Glacier inside Denali.

Located in Kantishna, at the center of the park, **Kantishna Air Taxi** (907/644-8222, www.katair.com) provides charter air service to end-of-the-road Kantishna lodges and flightseeing trips within the park. Quite a few other flightseeing companies operate out of Talkeetna and Anchorage with trips to Denali.

You can go for a helicopter ride on **Temsco Helicopters** (907/683-0683, www.temscoair.com, mid-May-mid-Sept.), based along the river in Nenana Canyon. Tour options include a 35-minute flight over the park ($411 pp), a very popular two-hour trip that includes a 20-minute landing on Yanert Glacier ($536 pp), and a heli-hiking adventure that includes a 10-minute flight plus three hours of hiking with a guide ($599 pp). The least expensive option ($249 pp) includes a short flight and a 15-minute landing high in the tundra. These helicopter flights do not land within Denali National Park.

Mountaineering

Mount Denali—the tallest peak in North America—is a major destination for mountaineers from around the globe. Over 1,100 climbers attempt to summit Mount Denali each year, with three-quarters of these attempts via the West Buttress. The primary climbing season is May-July. From the south side of Mount Denali, the usual approach is by ski plane from Talkeetna to the Southeast Fork of the Kahiltna Glacier or to the Ruth Glacier in the Don Sheldon Amphitheater. From the north, the approach for Denali and other peaks is by foot, ski, or dogsled. Specific route information can be obtained from the Walter Harper Talkeetna Ranger Station. Climbers on Mount Denali and Mount Foraker are charged a special-use fee ($370 pp). Call the ranger in Talkeetna (907/733-2231), or visit the Park Service website (www.nps.gov/dena) for additional mountaineering information.

Six companies are authorized to lead guided mountaineering climbs of Mount Denali and other peaks in the Alaska Range; contact the Park Service for specifics. One of the finest is Talkeetna-based **Alaska Mountaineering School** (907/733-1016, www.climbalaska.org). The company guides 22-day climbs of the West Buttress with nine climbers and three guides; the cost is $8,900 per climber. These depart every week (or more often) in the peak season. The school also teaches intensive mountaineering courses, skills workshops, wilderness first responder classes, glacier treks, and wilderness backpacking. Another recommended climbing program is **NOLS** (907/745-4047, www.nols.edu), based in Palmer.

Dog Mushing

Visitors whose appetite is whetted by the daily

1: cyclists in Denali National Park; **2:** river rafters on Nenana River

1

2

sled dog demonstrations at park headquarters may want to return when the snow flies for the real thing. **Earth Song Lodge** (907/683-2863, www.earthsonglodge.com) offers wintertime dogsled adventure tours into Denali National Park; these range from an easy overnight trip to those lasting seven days.

Four-time Iditarod winner Jeff King lives with his family at Goose Lake near Denali, and his staff offers summertime tours of his state-of-the-art **Husky Homestead** (907/683-2904, www.huskyhomestead.com, 2.5-hour tours $59 adults, $39 under age 13) kennels and training area. Tours and demonstrations depart from local hotels and are a favorite of the cruise-ship crowd. It's by far the most tourist-oriented dog tour you'll ever see, handling almost 100 people at a time on busy summer days.

Tours

Denali Park Adventures (Mile 238, Parks Hwy., 907/683-4288, www.experiencedenali.com) has a small office on the Nenana Canyon-Glitter Gulch boardwalk. This is the parent company for three very popular tours: **Denali Park Zipline** (907/683-2947, www.denalizipline.com), **Denali ATV** (907/683-4288, www.denaliatv.com), and **Denali Highway Jeep Excursion** (907/683-5337, www.denalijeep.com).

ENTERTAINMENT AND EVENTS

The large Nenana Canyon hotels all have lounges, but if you want to hang out with the young working crowd (including lots of college kids from Eastern Europe), head to **Denali Salmon Bake** (Mile 238, Parks Hwy., 907/683-2733, www.denaliparksalmonbake.com, 7am-11pm daily mid-May-late Sept.). If you're looking for a view with your drink, don't overlook **The Overlook** (Mile 238, Parks Hwy., 907/683-3463, www.denalicrowsnestcabins.com, 5pm-11pm daily late May-Sept.) at Denali Crow's Nest Cabins or **Alpenglow Restaurant** (Mile 238, Parks Hwy., 907/683-5100 or 855/683-8600, www.

denalialaska.com, 5am-10pm daily mid-May-mid-Sept.) at Grande Denali Lodge.

Enjoy lighthearted frivolity at **Alaska Cabin Nite Dinner Theater** (McKinley Chalet Resort, 907/276-7234 or 800/276-7234, www.denaliparkvillage.com, 7pm-9pm daily, $75 adults, $38 children) or the **Music of Denali Dinner Theater** (Denali Princess Wilderness Lodge, 907/683-2282 or 800/426-0500, www.princesslodges.com, $70 adults, $35 children). Both productions last approximately two hours, with live entertainment and an all-you-can-eat dinner spread.

Tonglen Lake Lodge (907/683-2570, www.tonglenlake.com) hosts a wide range of summertime events. The amphitheater is a fine place for American roots concerts, classical music, and even Shakespeare plays. The lodge buildings are used for everything from improv workshops and yoga classes to contra dancing and watercolor workshops. There's a big grassy lawn for bocce ball, croquet, and badminton. The restaurant, **Artisan Café,** is open for brunch. Access is a bit tricky for this off-the-beaten-path place, so call ahead or visit the website for directions.

Nature Talks

Park Service rangers give talks, walks, and kids programs. For specifics, check the bulletin boards at the Denali Visitor Center or the park's free *Summer Guide.*

Located on a 10-acre campus south of the park entrance, the nonprofit **Denali Education Center** (Mile 231, Parks Hwy., 907/683-2597, www.denali.org) partners with the National Park Service to provide education and multiday youth field trips, along with a variety of other activities, including a toddler and preschool programs ($5) on Monday and yoga sessions ($10) several days a week in summer.

SHOPPING

Nenana Canyon is filled with gift shops, most of which are completely forgettable—unless you appreciate run-of-the-mill clothing and cheesy trinkets. Find *real* Alaskan art on the boardwalk at **Three Bears Gallery** (907/683-3343) and **Kantishna Gallery** (907/250-3999, www.kantishnagallery.com).

Get quality outdoor gear, freeze-dried food, and clothing from **Denali Mountain Works** (907/683-1542, www.denalimountainworks.com, 9am-9pm daily mid-May-late Sept.). You'll also find rental backpacks, sleeping pads, daypacks, camp cook stoves, hiking poles, bear canisters, and binoculars. It's a good place for that last-minute item you forgot, including bear spray. There are no sleeping bag rentals, but tent rentals may be available.

Denali's Cannabis Cache (907/683-2633, www.denaliscache.com) is the only marijuana shop for more than 100 miles in either direction along the Parks Highway. It's next to Prospectors Pizza, perfect for those munchies.

FOOD

A number of places offer pricey summertime eats just north of the park entrance at the packed settlement of businesses called, alternatively, Nenana Canyon, Glitter Gulch, Denali Park, The Canyon, Denali, or The Gulch; almost all are shuttered when the tourists flee south after mid-September.

Brunch

Begin your day at **Black Bear Coffee House** (907/683-1656, www.blackbeardenali.com, 6am-8pm daily mid-May-Sept., $5-15 breakfast, $11-22 dinner) with eggy breakfast "bearitos," sourdough flapjacks, burgers (beef or vegan), soups, espresso, teas, sandwiches, and sweets. The café has Wi-Fi. Expect a wait for brunch at this popular eatery. Dinner specials start at 5pm and include avocado toast, crispy cauliflower, coconut curry, salmon burgers, barbecue pork sandwiches, and more.

One of the better restaurants in the Denali area is 11 miles south of the park entrance: **McKinley Creekside Café** (Mile 224, Parks Hwy., 907/683-2277, www.mckinleycabins.com, 6am-10pm daily mid-May-mid-Sept., breakfast and lunch $10-16, dinner $14-23). You'll find a diverse menu of tasty breakfasts (including strawberry-rhubarb coffeecake and gigantic half-pound cinnamon rolls), homemade soups, burgers, halibut tacos, and gyros for lunch, plus meatloaf, halibut and chips, and turkey pot pie in the evening, along with Friday night prime rib ($35) and filling box lunches ($14). The little deck is perfect for midsummer dining. The Wi-Fi is free.

Although best known for dinners and drinks, **The Overlook** (907/683-3463, www.denalicrowsnestcabins.com, 6am-10:30am and 5pm-11pm daily late May-Sept., buffet $22 adults, $17 children) has a wonderful breakfast buffet with quiche, scones, French toast, fruit, eggs, bacon, sausage, and more. The restaurant occupies a cozy hillside location and has a deck and big windows.

Denali's most secretive eatery is also one of its finest: ★ **Artisan Café** (Mile 230, Parks Hwy., 907/683-2570, www.tonglenlake.com, 7am-noon daily mid-May-mid-Sept., under $12). Housed within beautiful Tonglen Lake Lodge, this sunlit downstairs café has big windows and a deck fronting swings, a grassy lawn, and an amphitheater where events take place all summer. Tonglen Lake sits on one side, with mountains and forest stretching in all directions. Drop by in the morning for a relaxing brunch of scones (the best you'll ever taste), muffins, quiche, turkey wraps, and espresso. Wi-Fi is free too. You won't need a secret handshake to reach Artisan Café, but it is certainly off the main tourist trail on a narrow dirt road not recommended for RVs. At Mile 230 of the Parks Highway (eight miles south of Denali), turn east onto Old Parks Highway. Go a few hundred feet and turn right at the obvious rocks. Stay right as you travel 0.75 miles uphill to the lodge.

Quick Eats

Looking for cheap, fast eats? **Denali Doghouse** (Mile 238, Parks Hwy., 907/683-3647, www.denalidoghouse.com, 7am-9pm daily mid-May-early Sept., $10-12) has a good variety of hot dogs (including Alaskan reindeer dogs) and burgers on fresh sourdough buns, along with breakfast sandwiches and pancakes for the early morning. It's on the south end of the Nenana Canyon-Glitter Gulch strip.

Thai and Chinese Food 2 Go (Mile 238, Parks Hwy., 907/306-3545, 11am-11pm daily, mid-May-mid-Sept., $12) occupies a small shop on the north end of the Nenana Canyon-Glitter Gulch boardwalk. As the name suggests, it's primarily to go, but does have two enclosed picnic tables. Portions are generous, but service can be slow. Credit cards are not accepted.

Denali Glacier Scoops (Mile 238, Parks Hwy., 907/683-6002, 7am-10pm daily mid-May-mid-Sept.) serves a double scoop of ice cream at Alaskan prices ($8 in a waffle cone). Also available are shakes, sundaes, soft serve, and banana splits.

For something different, head to friendly **Miller's Gourmet Popcorn** (Mile 238, Parks Hwy., 907/229-2107, www.millersgourmetpopcorn.weebly.com, 11am-8pm Mon.-Sat. mid-May-mid-Sept., $6-10), with buttery fudge, roasted nuts, peanut brittle, taffy, slushies, and more than a dozen types of flavored popcorn, from cheese and caramel to caramel chocolate. They give out free samples too.

Bar and Grill

In business for almost three decades, **Denali Salmon Bake** (Mile 238, Parks Hwy., 907/306-0355, www.denaliparksalmonbake.com, 7am-11pm daily mid-May-early Sept., $13-26) is extremely popular for lunch and dinner. When you step into this rustic old building, the severely slanting floors are immediate evidence of melting permafrost beneath the structure; the slope increases by an inch or two every year! The Bake's diverse menu stars king crab grilled-cheese sandwiches and elk burgers for lunch, plus halibut and chips, Mount Denali burgers, Alaskan king crab legs, or king salmon for dinner. The restaurant has free Wi-Fi and offers a shuttle bus ($5 day pass) to local hotels, campgrounds, and the Denali Visitor Center. A sprawling upstairs bar (no smoking) comes alive with bluegrass and folk bands four nights a week and has 21 beers on tap, along with an enormous frozen blue concoction called the McKinley Margarita. Join the Bulgarian, Serbian, and Slavic seasonal workers for crowded Wednesday-night "J-1" dance parties. (See www.thebakerocks.com for upcoming events.) Hungry late? Tacos are available till the bar closes at 3am. The Salmon Bake's owners seem to have half the local businesses, with nine different places at last count, including Denali Salmon Bake Cabins, Prospectors Pizza, 49th State Brewing Co., Denali Crow's Nest Cabins, The Overlook, and Miners Market & Deli.

Pizza

On the north end of the Nenana Canyon-Glitter Gulch action, **Prospectors Pizzeria & Alehouse** (Mile 238, Parks Hwy., 907/683-7437, www.prospectorspizza.com, 11am-11:30pm daily mid-May-late Sept., until 2am some nights, $18-31) gets packed with travelers on summer evenings, so be ready for a 45-minute wait. In addition to wood-fired brick oven stone pizzas, the menu includes salads, pastas, hot sandwiches, and a locally famous baked tomato soup. Lots of pizza choices include gluten-free crusts and even one topped with Alaskan king crab ($60 for the 16-inch version). There's limited outside seating and 49 or so cold beers on tap—including some not available anywhere else in the nation. Prospectors consistently wins national awards as one of the top beer bars in America, and the servers all pass a rigorous test on properly serving beer. Families appreciate the fast service, funky decor, handcrafted root beer, Wi-Fi, and shuttle bus ($5 day pass).

Panorama Pizza Pub (Mile 224, Parks Hwy., 907/683-2623, food until 10pm daily early May-mid-Sept., $14-33) sits along Carlo Creek 14 miles south of Nenana Canyon-Glitter Gulch. The atmosphere is relaxed, with a foosball table, wraparound deck, and fire pit, plus live music several nights a week. Their Denali pizza is topped with pepperoni, sausage, olives, mushrooms, and peppers. Slices only are available after 10pm, but the bar stays open till 3am. The pub provides a free shuttle from hotels in Nenana Canyon.

Fine Dining

At ★ **229 Parks Restaurant** (Mile 229, Parks Hwy., 907/683-2567, www.229parks. com, 5pm-10pm Tues.-Sun., last seating 9:30pm June-Sept., 9am-5pm Fri.-Sat., 9:30am-12:30pm Sun. Nov.-Apr., $18-32), the name is also the location: Mile 229 on the Parks Highway. Housed within a bright timber-frame building nine miles south of the Denali National Park entrance, the restaurant serves a bistro-style menu that changes daily and highlights Alaskan ingredients. Organic, locally grown vegetables and free-range meats are used whenever possible, and everything is made from scratch. Dinner entrées might encompass everything from reindeer *ragù* to Alaskan king crab, with plenty of vegetarian offerings. Lighter, less-expensive choices might include Caesar salads, crispy parsnip chips, or spicy spot prawn. Memorable desserts include a divine rustic fruit tart. The restaurant will also make a gourmet box lunch ($17) if you call a day in advance. Don't come to 229 Parks in a hurry; service can be slow because everything is made fresh. Reservations are strongly recommended since the restaurant fills most nights; call at least a week ahead. If you want to take your chances, the bar has nine seats available on a first-come basis. The restaurant doesn't provide a shuttle, so you'll need your own wheels or a spendy taxi ride from Nenana Canyon. Owner-chef Laura Cole has gained a justifiable national reputation, including being twice nominated for a prestigious James Beard Award. In winter, the restaurant is more relaxed and adds a Sunday brunch ($17).

The biggest surprise on the Nenana Canyon strip is Alaska's only Serbian restaurant, ★ **Moose-AKa's** (907/687-0003, www. moose-akas.com, 5pm-10pm Mon., 11am-10pm Tues.-Sun., $10-22). Co-owner Maja Waring grew up in Serbia and came to Denali as a seasonal worker. After marrying her American husband, Michael-Jared Waring, they opened this cozy, atmospheric little restaurant. The interior is dark and romantic—the opposite of every other local restaurant. Moose-AKa's is best known for Eastern European sweet or savory fried crepes, thick Turkish coffee, moussaka, schnitzel, stuffed red pepper with rice pilaf, and a locally famous sangria. There's also a big selection of Serbian beers and wines. Moose-AKa's attracts crowds all summer, and there's often a long queue for dinner; reservations are recommended.

The Overlook (907/683-3463, www. denalicrowsnestcabins.com, 6am-10:30am and 5pm-midnight daily late May-Sept., $19-58) occupies a cozy hillside location above the frenzy at Nenana Canyon-Glitter Gulch. Big windows and a deck face into the park, and the menu specializes in "farm-to-table and port-to-plate" offerings. This is a wonderful spot for an intimate dinner of king salmon or Alaskan pork chop followed by The Overlook's famous baked Alaska. The small-plates menu is less expensive, but no less adventurous; try the ahi poke nachos or teriyaki beef tips. Choose from a big selection of wines by the glass or draft beers. The restaurant's big breakfast buffet ($22 adults, $12 children) is the best anywhere around.

High atop the bluff behind Nenana Canyon, **Alpenglow Restaurant** (Grande Denali Lodge, Mile 238 Parks Hwy., 907/683-8500 or 855/683-8600, www.denalialaska. com, 5am-10pm daily mid-May-mid-Sept., $32-50) has the most extraordinary vistas in the area. Wraparound windows face Denali National Park, and the high ceilings are accented by a timber-frame design. In addition to steak and seafood selections, there's a lighter small-plates bar menu (under $20) with burgers, salads, and pork verde at the lounge. Call to reserve a window or outside deck table for dinner. Breakfast buffets ($25 adults, $12 children) are a good stuff-yourself deal.

Markets

Canyon Market and Cafe (Mile 238, Parks Hwy., 907/683-7467, 6am-1:30am daily) makes deli sandwiches and pastries and has a decent selection of groceries and produce. There is free Wi-Fi here too.

In the heart of the action, **Lynx Creek Store/The Park Mart** (Mile 238, Parks Hwy., 907/683-2548, 6:30am-11pm daily summer) is a quickie-mart with some of the most expensive gas on the road system (but no diesel), along with such essentials as liquor, soda, sweets, and limited food items. Find a far bigger selection—and lower prices—at the Three Bears Alaska store in Healy, 11 miles north of Nenana Canyon-Glitter Gulch.

ACCOMMODATIONS

Most of the local lodging action centers around busy Nenana Canyon-Glitter Gulch, though other lodges and B&Bs are a few miles south of the park entrance, or 10 miles north in the town of Healy. Denali-area lodging options are expensive, so those on a tight budget will either need to camp or head to the hostel 13 miles south at Carlo Creek.

Nenana Canyon

If you've been driving the Parks Highway north from Anchorage, soaking up the wild Alaskan wilderness, you're in for a rude awakening. Just a mile north of the Denali National Park turnoff, it's impossible to miss the hodgepodge of giant hotels, restaurants, RV parks, rafting companies, and gift shops crammed between the highway and the Nenana River Canyon to the west, and climbing the steep hillside to the east. The area is packed with tour buses, tottering tourists, and rumbling RVs. The unincorporated settlement gets called—take your pick—**Nenana Canyon, Glitter Gulch, Denali Park, The Canyon, The Gulch,** or **Denali.** You may hear any of these names used, and to add to the confusion, Denali Park Village is actually seven miles south of the place some folks call Denali Park. I use the term Nenana Canyon-Glitter Gulch.

Most lodging choices start well over

$200, but one place offers a less-expensive option: **Denali Salmon Bake Cabins** (Mile 238, Parks Hwy., 907/683-2733, www.denalinationalparklodging.net, early May-late Sept.). For the full-on Alaskan experience, stay in an economy cabin ($79 d) consisting of insulated tent-like structures with two double beds but no water. These seven tent-cabin units share three baths. There are also four standard cabins ($149 d) with two full beds, private baths, cable TV, fridges, and air-conditioning. The Bake isn't for everyone, but it's right in the thick of the Nenana Canyon action, with free Wi-Fi. The units all book up, so call at least a month ahead for midsummer lodging.

Denali Crow's Nest Cabins (Mile 238, Parks Hwy., 907/683-2723, www.denalicrowsnestcabins.com, $259-299 d) are perched on five levels of a very steep hill. These nicely appointed log cabins include queen or king beds, private baths, and Wi-Fi, plus impressive views across the canyon. The sauna and outdoor hot tub are relaxing after a day of exploring, and there's a free shuttle to the railroad depot and park visitors center. Also here is The Overlook Restaurant, serving a great breakfast buffet (free for Denali Crow's Nest guests) and upscale dinners.

On the east side of the highway, **Denali Rainbow Village** (Mile 238, Parks Hwy., 907/683-7777, www.denalirv.com, mid-May-mid-Sept.) has a handful of 2nd-floor motel rooms ($195-235 d), each with a queen bed, a private bath, and Wi-Fi. Some units include full kitchens, and a two-bedroom suite sleeps up to eight for $380.

Denali Bluffs Hotel (Mile 238, Parks Hwy., 907/683-7000 or 855/683-8600, www.denalialaska.com, mid-May-mid-Sept., $299-399 d) is a pleasant hillside place where 112 standard rooms all contain two doubles or one king bed. Far nicer are the premium rooms with private verandas overlooking the river and a modern decor.

High atop the bluff sits **Grande Denali Lodge** (Mile 238, Parks Hwy., 907/683-5100 or 855/683-8600, www.denalialaska.com, mid-May-mid-Sept., guest rooms $389-439 d, cabins $499 for up to 4 people), a 166-unit hotel accessed by a very steep switchbacking road marked by amusing road signs. Guests stay in spacious rooms (ask for one with a view) or family-style cabins with private decks and kitchenettes, but the primary attraction is the dramatic hilltop view. The cabins are downhill, and the staff provides golf-cart access if you don't want to walk. There is a free shuttle to the park visitors center or train depot. Both Denali Bluffs and Grande Denali are owned by Old Harbor Native Corporation, based on Kodiak Island.

Two mega-hotels owned by Holland America face the Nenana River on the west side of the Parks Highway at Mile 238. Sprawling **Denali Princess Wilderness Lodge** (907/683-2282 or 800/426-0500, www.princesslodges.com) has 656 rooms and so many buildings that you'll need a map to find your way around. I'm still trying to figure out how this is a "wilderness" lodge! Next door is the 354-room **McKinley Chalet Resort** (907/683-6450 or 800/544-0970, www. westmarkhotels.com). Not surprisingly, both places are crowded with cruise-ship passengers, and dozens of tour buses line up out front. Both have all the amenities you'd expect: spacious and modern rooms, fitness centers, riverside hot tubs, upscale restaurants, cafés, gift shops, and bars. Each even has its own dinner theater. During the peak of summer, rooms at either place go for around $350-400 d, but you'll get far more bang for your dollars elsewhere.

South of Denali

Most of the large Denali-area hotels and lodges are in the Nenana Park area at Mile 238 of the Parks Highway, but a number of smaller family-run places provide excellent lodging choices. Several of these are 14 miles south of the park entrance in the Carlo Creek area at Mile 224.

Denali Mountain Morning Hostel and Lodge (Mile 224, Parks Hwy., 907/683-7503, www.denalihostel.com, early May-late Sept.)

is inexpensive, friendly, and nicely maintained. It's easily the best budget option in the Denali area. The hostel sits on the north side of Carlo Creek, with a variety of earthy accommodations. Hostel beds are in single-sex or coed bunk cabins ($34 pp) that sleep up to six. All hostel rentals include linen and towels, so no need to bring a sleeping bag. A private room ($99 d) is available in the main lodge, and there are six cabins of varying configurations and sizes. The smallest cabin starts at $85 d; the largest cabin sleeps five for $170. Particularly nice is the Iceworm duplex log cabin ($99 d) with a second bed in the loft, and the two-story Razor Back cabin ($114 d). For a bit of old-time Alaska, stay in a wall tent for $34 s or $59 d. Some cabins and wall tents line the babbling creek, while others nestle in the trees. There's a two-night minimum stay for several cabins, but not for hostel bunks. All guests use a central toilet and shower facility, and the main lodge has a full kitchen, laundry, free Wi-Fi, and couches. Rent binoculars and borrow a can of bear spray if you're heading into the park. Two good restaurants—Panorama Pizza and McKinley Creekside Café—are directly across the highway. The hostel provides a free four-times-daily shuttle to the Denali Visitor Center and rail station.

Nearby is **Carlo Creek Lodge** (Mile 224, Parks Hwy., 907/683-2576, www.denaliparklodging.com, late May-early Sept., $75-94 d shared bath, $124-154 d private bath, motel rooms $159-169 d, additional guests $15 pp), which has 10 attractive cabins near the creek. Five of these include private baths, two beds, and kitchenettes, and the others are great for travelers on a budget—if they don't mind walking a short distance to the bath and log shower house. In addition to cabins, there are a dozen motel rooms with queen beds and private baths. All units include microwaves, fridges, and Wi-Fi.

Best known for its popular café, **McKinley Creekside Cabins & Café** (Mile 224, Parks Hwy., 907/683-2277, www.mckinleycabins. com, mid-May-mid-Sept., cabins $239-299 d, lodge rooms $239 d, chalet rooms $329 d, family cabins $369 d) has a wide range of clean and well-maintained rooms and cabins, all with private baths and Wi-Fi. The spacious chalet rooms each come with a private deck, a microwave, and a fridge.

A modern home 10 miles south of the park entrance, **Deneki Lakes B&B** (Mile 227, Parks Hwy., 907/638-4188, www.denekilakesbedandbreakfast.com, $305 d) is a peaceful and spotless place with views of the Alaska Range. The two second-floor guest rooms have private baths, and the hospitable owners serve a delicious hot breakfast each morning.

★ **Tonglen Lake Lodge** (Mile 230, Parks Hwy., 907/683-2570, www.tonglenlake.com, mid-May-mid-Sept., $425 d) is well away from the Nenana Canyon craziness, with a picturesque setting along a small mountain lake. Guests stay in 10 modern cabins, each with a king bed and queen futon, and enjoy a filling breakfast at Artisan Café. All sorts of artistic events also take place at the lodge, from photography workshops to Shakespeare productions. See the lodge website for directions to this out-of-the-way lodge.

Denali Grizzly Bear Resort (Mile 231, Parks Hwy., 907/683-2696 or 866/583-2696, www.denaligrizzlybear.com, mid-May-mid-Sept.) has a range of hillside lodging choices. These include Spartan little cabins with a central coin-op shower house ($88-115 d), cabins with a toilet and a sink ($132-142 d), and ones with full baths, TVs, and private decks ($269-359 d). Hotel rooms ($269 d) each have a deck overlooking the Nenana River, private baths, and TVs. Wi-Fi exists throughout the resort but costs $20 per day. Traffic noise can be an annoyance, and the resort has a mediocre reputation for maintenance, but this is one of the least expensive lodging choices in the area. If you lack a vehicle, you'll need to catch the Dine Denali Shuttle ($5) to the park or Nenana Canyon restaurants. No meals are available at the resort, but Denali Park Village is across the road with several dining choices.

Kantishna Lodges

This private inholding is deep within Denali, 92 miles out the Park Road. Originally a gold mining settlement, it now has several lodges and an air-taxi operator. These upscale lodges are definitely not for budget travelers, and it's a long bus ride to Kantishna, so most guests stay at least three nights in this very scenic area. All five of the lodges are open only early June-mid-September. Private buses transport

Tonglen Lake Lodge

visitors to the lodges at Kantishna, or you can fly out on **Kantishna Air Taxi** (907/644-8222, www.katair.com, $180 pp, 2-person minimum). There is **no cell phone service** in the Kantishna area.

At **Kantishna Roadhouse** (907/683-8003 or 800/942-7420, www.kantishnaroadhouse. com, June-mid-Sept., $1,080-1,280 d), the all-inclusive rate includes lodging in duplex- or fourplex-style cabins, all meals, bus transportation from the park entrance, dogsled demonstrations, mountain bikes, gold panning, fly-fishing, guided hikes, and interpretive programs. There's a bar and restaurant on the premises. A two-night minimum stay is required, and you'll want at least that much time (and probably more) due to the long ride in and out.

Two very special Kantishna area lodges— **Camp Denali** and **North Face Lodge**—are under the same management. At each all-inclusive lodge, the emphasis is on the natural world, with guided hikes, mountain biking, canoeing, fishing, evening programs, and delicious meals. In addition to naturalist-guided hikes and other outdoor activity, the lodges are famous for a special-emphasis series of renowned guest speakers, including ecologists, bird biologists, mountaineers, writers, artists, and aurora experts. Neither lodge has cell phone service or Wi-Fi.

Established in 1952, acclaimed ★ **Camp Denali** (907/683-2290, www.campdenali. com, early June-mid-Sept., 3 nights $1,920 adults, $1,440 under age 12, 4 nights $2,560 adults, $1,920 children, round-trip bus transport included) is operated as a low-key wilderness retreat for a maximum of 40 guests. Lodging is in 18 cozy and immaculate cabins with woodstoves, propane lights and a hot plate, potable water, a private outhouse, and a modern shower building just up the hill. (If you can't handle an outhouse and shared showers, stay at nearby North Face Lodge instead.) The dining hall serves gourmet meals and opens for evening lectures. The lodge has remarkable views of Mount Denali.

One mile from Camp Denali (and 500 feet lower in elevation), ★ **North Face Lodge**, (907/683-2290, www.campdenali.com, early June-mid-Sept., 3 nights $1,920 adults, $1,440 under age 12, 4 nights $2,560 adults, $1,920 children, round-trip bus transport included) operates more like a country inn. The area was homesteaded in 1957 by Grant Pearson, a former park superintendent, and later acquired by the Cole family (who established nearby Camp Denali) to prevent unchecked development. Inside is a comfortable sitting room with a crackling fireplace and a library of natural history books. The spacious outdoor patio provides views of the Alaska Range. The Mountain isn't visible from here, but a 1.5-mile walk takes you to Wonder Lake, famous for its unique Denali vistas. North Face Lodge's 15 comfortable (but small) guest rooms all contain private baths. The lodge is less rustic than Camp Denali, and is perfect for folks who want to stay in the heart of Denali in style.

Denali Backcountry Lodge (907/376-1992 or 800/808-8068, www.alaskacollection. com, early June-mid-Sept., $545 d per day) has cabins and a main lodge at the end of the road. The cabins—all with private baths and one or two beds—range from simple units with no view to nicer ones with decks along the creek. All-inclusive rates include round-trip transport by bus into the park, meals, bikes, fishing, and naturalist presentations. There are no TVs, Wi-Fi, or cell phone coverage. It's a long ride, so some guests opt to ride the bus in and fly back out on Kantishna Air ($180 pp).

Operated by the owners of Kantishna Air Taxi, **Skyline Lodge** (Mile 92, Park Rd., 907/644-8222, www.katair.com, June-Sept.) provides the least expensive accommodations in Kantishna: $375 for one person or $450 for two people, including lodging and meals. Fly-in-bus back options are also available. This solar-powered lodge can accommodate up to 10 guests in five rooms, each with a queen bed downstairs plus a sleeping loft with a double bed. Baths and showers are in the main lodge, and there's no cell phone service, but Wi-Fi is available. Borrow a mountain bike for the beautiful ride to Wonder Lake, take a flight-seeing tour with the pilots who stay here, or just kick back and take in the splendor at this memorable place. There's no minimum stay, but you should plan on at least two nights.

Sheldon Chalet and Mountain House

Deep within Denali is the **Sheldon Mountain House** (907/854-7007, www.sheldonchalet.com, mid-Feb.-June, $500 for up to 4 people), a remote hexagonal cabin constructed on a five-acre outcrop of rock and ice overlooking Ruth Glacier. One of the most famous Alaskan bush pilots, Don Sheldon gained title to the land in the 1950s and built this backcountry getaway in 1966. Today, guests must haul their gear 0.3 mile up the Ruth Glacier, either in a backpack or on a sled. Winter visits provide stunning opportunities to see the northern lights beneath the summit of Denali. Mountain House can book far in advance; call for reservations.

Also owned by the Sheldon family is the sumptuous, 2,000-square-foot ★ **Sheldon Chalet** (907/854-7007, www.sheldonchalet.com, $2,300 pp), a two-story octagonal structure with breathtaking vistas in all directions. This is easily Alaska's most unique lodge—it's the ultimate in remote luxury. Access is by helicopter from Talkeetna, and the chalet has its own helipad. Rates include gourmet meals, round-trip helicopter flights, and guided adventures.

Camping

Inside Denali National Park are six campgrounds, four of which have evening nature programs throughout summer. Riley Creek, Savage River, Teklanika River, and Wonder Lake Campgrounds can be reserved in advance through **Doyan/Aramark** (907/272-7275 or 800/622-7275, www.reservedenali.com) starting in mid-February. You can also reserve campsites at the Denali Bus Depot or Riley Creek Mercantile if they aren't already full, but this is definitely *not* a wise move if you want any choice of where you stay.

You can drive to Riley Creek, Savage River, and Teklanika River Campgrounds, so they fill up fast. Otherwise, campground access is via the **camper buses** ($40 adults round-trip, free under age 16).

If you need to store luggage for a few hours—or days—while hiking or camping, the National Park Service provides a free **baggage claim** building next to the Denali Visitor Center.

RILEY CREEK CAMPGROUND

The largest and most accessible campground in the park, **Riley Creek Campground** ($24-30 pull-in sites, $15 walk-in tent sites, $46 group site, free in winter) has 147 sites just 0.25 miles off the Parks Highway. It's open year-round, with bear-proof food lockers, running water, and flush toilets, but limited facilities and no water September-May. This campground is very popular with RVers and car campers, but suffers somewhat from highway noise. Park rangers provide evening nature programs.

The adjacent **Riley Creek Mercantile** (7am-10pm daily mid-May-late Sept.) has firewood ($10), a handful of outrageously priced groceries, binocular rentals, a dump station with potable water, coin laundry, showers (bring a towel, $5), and free Wi-Fi.

SAVAGE RIVER CAMPGROUND

Near the end of the paved public-accessible portion of the Park Road, **Savage River Campground** (Mile 13, Park Rd., late May-mid-Sept., $24 standard sites, $24-30 pull-through sites, $46 group sites) has 32 wooded sites for vehicles and tents, with bear-proof lockers and flush and vault toilets. Three group sites (tents only) are available. You'll need to bring firewood for campfires; it's available at Riley Creek Mercantile. The **Savage River Shuttle** bus provides free transportation to the campground (assuming space is available for your camping gear),

---

1: Denali Bluffs Hotel; 2: Sheldon Chalet; 3: Denali Visitor Center

but most folks bring their own vehicles. Park rangers put on evening campground programs.

SANCTUARY RIVER CAMPGROUND

Remote and tranquil, **Sanctuary River Campground** (Mile 23, Park Rd., late May-mid-Sept., $15) contains seven heavily forested tent sites. The campground has vault toilets and bear-proof lockers, but no potable water. You'll need to bring water or filter it from the silty river. Campfires aren't allowed. Unlike most Denali campgrounds, reservations aren't taken for Sanctuary River; check at the Denali Bus Depot or Riley Creek Mercantile to see if sites are available. Vehicles are not allowed, so access is only via the **camper bus** ($40 adults round-trip, free under age 16).

TEKLANIKA RIVER CAMPGROUND

Teklanika River Campground (Mile 29, Park Rd., late May-mid-Sept., $25) provides 53 forested sites for tents and vehicles. The braided Teklanika River provides an easy gravel surface for day hikes from the campground, and this is the farthest point RVs can drive into the park. Vault toilets and running water are provided, along with bear-proof food storage, but bring firewood (available at Riley Creek Mercantile) if you want a campfire. Park rangers provide evening campground programs.

When car camping at Teklanika, purchase **"Tek Pass"** ($40) for each member of your party. This allows you to use the park shuttle buses throughout your stay at Teklanika River Campground for the price of just one trip; it's only available for travel farther into the park, not back to the park entrance.

There's a three-night minimum stay for car campers; vehicles must stay at the campsite for the duration of your stay and can only leave when driving back out of the park. There is no minimum stay requirement for campers arriving on the **camper bus** ($40 adults round-trip, free under age 16). Tent campers without a vehicle can use the camper bus pass to travel deeper into Denali at no additional

charge (you don't need to purchase a separate Tek Pass).

IGLOO CREEK CAMPGROUND

Hemmed in by the mountains, little **Igloo Creek Campground** (Mile 35, Park Rd., late May-mid-Sept., $15) features seven wooded tent-only sites. The campground has pit vault toilets, but you'll need to bring plenty of water or a filter. Fires are not permitted and vehicles aren't allowed, so you'll need to arrive via the **camper bus** ($40 adults round-trip, free under age 16). Reservations aren't taken for Igloo Creek Campground, so stop by the Denali Bus Depot or Riley Creek Mercantile to see if sites are available. There's great hiking around Igloo Creek, with relatively easy access to the high country.

WONDER LAKE CAMPGROUND

Wonder Lake Campground (Mile 85, Park Rd., early June-mid-Sept., $16 plus $6 reservation fee) has 28 tent-only sites in one of the most dramatic settings anywhere on the planet. The country is rolling tundra, with a few trees and the potential to see Mount Denali in all its glory (if the weather cooperates). The lake—2.7 miles long by 0.5 miles wide—is a short walk away. Wonder Lake Campground has running water, flush toilets, cooking shelters, and bear-proof storage lockers. Because of its location, Wonder Lake doesn't open until early June. Make reservations well ahead for campsites here, especially when fall colors peak in late August and early September. Park rangers provide evening campground programs.

RV Parks

Denali Rainbow Village (Mile 238, Parks Hwy., 907/683-7777, www.denalirv.com, mid-May-mid-Sept., RVs $53-58) is in the heart of the Nenana Canyon action, with a big gravel parking lot behind the row of buildings on the east side of the road. It has a water, electric, and sewer hookups, plus laundry, Wi-Fi (spotty coverage), picnic tables, a dump station, and cable TV. No tents are allowed.

Eight miles south of the park entrance is **Denali Grizzly Bear Resort** (Mile 231, Parks Hwy., 907/683-2696 or 866/583-2696, www.denaligrizzlybear.com, tents $28, RVs $45, tent cabins $39-45). A central cooking shelter, coin-op showers, laundry, and Wi-Fi ($20 per day) are available. A restaurant and bar are across the road at Denali Park Village.

Fourteen miles south of the park is **Denali Mountain Morning Hostel and Lodge** (Mile 224, Parks Hwy., 907/683-7503, www.denalihostel.com, early May-late Sept., wall tents $34 s, $59 d). Guests stay in wall tents, with sleeping bags, cots, a bathhouse, a central kitchen, a computer, laundry, Wi-Fi, and a free park shuttle. Two of the wall tents are right along Carlo Creek.

Additional RV parks are in Healy, 11 miles north of the park entrance.

INFORMATION AND SERVICES

The large Nenana Canyon hotels all have **ATMs,** as does the nearby **Lynx Creek Store** (907/683-2548, 6:30am-11pm daily summer) and the park's Denali Bus Depot. A small **post office** is adjacent to the Riley Creek Campground inside the park.

For medical help, head to **Canyon Clinic at Denali** (Mile 238, Parks Hwy., 907/683-4433, www.canyonclinicdenali.com, 9am-6pm daily summer, with after-hours emergency service) near Denali Princess Wilderness Lodge. The clinic has a physician assistant and nurse on duty, but the nearest hospital and pharmacy are in Fairbanks—92 miles north.

GETTING THERE

The **Alaska Railroad's** *Denali Star* (907/265-2494 or 800/544-0552, www.alaskarailroad.com, mid-May-mid-Sept.) leaves Anchorage at 8:15am, arriving at Denali at 3:40pm ($171 adults, $86 ages 2-11 one-way); it departs Fairbanks at 8:15am and arrives at the Denali depot at 12:10pm ($171 adults, $86 ages 2-11 one-way). The Anchorage-to-Denali **GoldStar** ($314 adults, $174 children one-way) service is the premium way to travel: bi-level train cars with glass dome ceilings ensure incredible views along the way. The northbound fare includes a full breakfast, lunch, and wine or beer.

Two companies provide van or bus transportation connecting Denali with destinations along the Parks Highway. **Alaska/Yukon Trails** (907/888-5659, www.alaskashuttle.com, daily Apr.-Sept.) operates 7-passenger or 16-passenger vans with lower one-way rates from the park: $65 to Talkeetna, $75 to Anchorage, and $60 to Fairbanks. Vans can stop anywhere along the highway (with advance reservations), including Wasilla, Willow-Big Lake, Trapper Creek, Byers Lake, Coal Creek Trailhead, Cantwell, and Healy. You can get off the van and reboard at a later date for a $10 fee.

Park Connection (907/245-0200 or 800/266-8625, www.alaskacoach.com, daily mid-May-mid-Sept.) operates large and very comfortable buses between Seward and Denali, but they only stop at the main towns and Princess lodges en route. From Denali, the one-way rates are $65 to Talkeetna, $90 to Anchorage, and $155 to Seward or Whittier. Tickets for children under age 11 are half-price.

Local air taxis include **Denali Air** (Mile 229, Parks Hwy., 907/683-2261, www.denaliair.com), operating from an airstrip eight miles south of the park entrance; **Fly Denali** (907/683-2899 or 877/770-2359, www.flydenali.com) from Healy Airport; and **Kantishna Air Taxi** (907/644-8222, www.katair.com) from Kantishna, deep inside Denali National Park. **Temsco Helicopters** (907/683-0683) is based next to the river in Nenana Canyon.

GETTING AROUND

Call **Denali Transportation** (844/907-4387, www.denalitaxishuttle.com) for 24-hour taxi and shuttle service in the Denali National Park area.

Every half hour, the National Park Service's free **Riley Creek Shuttle** (http://go.nps.gov/denalicourtesy, 5am-7pm mid-May-mid-Sept.) provides service connecting the Riley Creek Campground, Denali Bus Depot, Horseshoe Lake Trailhead, Murie Science and Learning Center, Park Headquarters (with sled dog demonstrations), Denali Visitor Center and Train Depot, and Riley Creek Mercantile.

Operated by Denali National Park, the free **Savage River Shuttle** (http://go.nps.gov/denalicourtesy, 6am-8pm daily mid-May-early Sept.) stops at Riley Creek Campground, Denali Bus Depot, Horseshoe Lake Trailhead, Denali Visitor Center and Train Depot, Park Headquarters, and Mountain Vista, and continues all the way to Savage River Bridge at Mile 15.

Private shuttle buses are provided by many local hotels. **Dine Denali Shuttle** (907/683-2733, www.dinedenali.com, mid-May-mid-Sept., hourly 8am-1am daily midsummer, $5 day pass) stops at the Denali Visitor Center, Nenana Canyon hotels and restaurants, Denali Park Village, Grizzly Bear Resort, and Healy businesses. The shuttle also heads to Riley Creek Campground and other destinations upon request; call for a pickup.

HEALY AND VICINITY

Located 11 miles north of the turnoff to Denali National Park at Mile 249 of the Parks Highway, the town of Healy (pop. 1,000) has most of the necessities of life, including gas stations (considerably cheaper than at Nenana Canyon), convenience stores, restaurants, a coin laundry, and a medical clinic.

Healy has grown up around the coal mining that has operated here since the 1930s. **Usibelli Coal Mine** (907/683-2226, www.usibelli.com) is Alaska's only commercial coal mine. Most of its coal was shipped to South Korea and Chile, but a worldwide glut dried up these markets, and Usibelli stopped shipping internationally in 2015. The mine still provides coal for six power plants across interior Alaska, including one in Healy. Coal burning is a significant factor in global warming; there's bitter irony that the burning of Alaskan coal contributes to drastic environmental changes across Alaska. Healy also benefits greatly from tourism to nearby Denali National Park.

Recreation

Two miles south of town, play a round of golf at the nine-hole **Black Diamond Golf Course** (1 mile out Otto Lake Rd., 907/683-4653, www.blackdiamondtourco.com, $30 for 9 holes). The Usibelli family owners have a restaurant on the premises and offer three-hour covered wagon rides ($90 adults, $40 children, including a meal) and three-hour ATV adventures ($120 adults, $50 children). Free bus transport is provided from Nenana Canyon hotels.

Denali Park Zipline (907/683-2947, www.denalizipline.com, mid-May-mid-Sept., $139 adults, $99 ages 8-12) is located north of Healy. Unlike most other Alaskan zip lines, this one operates from pole-supported platforms rather than trees; the spruces and birches are too small in this part of the state. Tours depart from the Denali Park Adventures kiosk in Nenana Canyon and last a total of three hours. Access includes a 15-minute ride up the mountain on a 4WD vehicle. The highest platform is 60 feet off the ground, and there are two suspension bridges, an unusual bridge tower with four connected bridges, and seven zip lines. The last of these is actually two lines, so you can race a friend or family member. The minimum age is eight.

The same folks own **Denali ATV** (907/683-4288, www.denaliatv.com, mid-May-mid-Sept.), offering a variety of popular ATV tours on private roads and trails in the Healy area around Otto Lake. The company has all sorts of vehicles, from one-rider ATVs to four-person units. A 2.5-hour guided tour ($115 for 1 person, $175 for 2) is on a side-by-side ATV. Kids must be 16 to drive, but all ages can ride, even infants in car seats. Transportation is provided from the Denali Park Adventures office in Nenana Canyon-Glitter Gulch.

Food

Healy's main dining attraction is **49th State**

Into the Wild Photo Op

replica of the bus from the film *Into the Wild* in front of 49th State Brewery

A few miles north of Healy is the turnoff for the Stampede Road, made infamous in the book and movie *Into the Wild*. Access to the old bus where Chris McCandless died is very difficult. Here's what the locals tell folks trying to get there: "This is where you turn off the highway; this is where you park the car; this is where you get eaten to death by mosquitoes; this is where you might drown; this is where the bear mauls you; and this is where you starve to death and die." At least one person has died attempting to reach the bus, so don't take the chance. An identical replica of the Magic Bus—it was used in the movie—sits out front of 49th State Brewery in Healy. Take your photo there instead of risking your life!

Brewery (Mile 248, Parks Hwy., 907/683-2739, www.49statebrewing.com, 11am-1:30am daily May-Sept., $15-37), a cavernous industrial-style building with a pub menu of burgers, sandwiches, pizzas, and munchies served all day, plus such dinner entrées as alderwood-smoked barbecue ribs, grilled shrimp tacos, and rib-eye steak. There's an all-you-can-eat pig roast every Friday ($25). The brewery produces a dozen or so beers, including the popular Baked Blonde Ale, and also has a good choice of cocktails, wine, and more than 130 whiskeys. Food is served till 1:30am, with a limited menu after 11pm. The pub provides a shuttle van ($5 all day) to Nenana Canyon-Glitter Gulch and has live music on the patio most summer weekends. The brewery puts on two very popular festivals during the

summer: the Solstice Brewfest (late June) and an authentically Bavarian Augtoberfest (early Aug.). Parked out front is the old Fairbanks city bus featured in the film *Into the Wild*; it's almost identical to the real one a few miles away.

Try the bacon cheeseburgers and home-cooked food at friendly **Rose's Café** (Mile 250, Parks Hwy., 907/683-7673, www.rosescafealaska.com, 7am-7pm daily summer, 7am-2pm daily winter, $8-18). Everything is made from scratch and portions are enormous.

Henry's Coffeehouse at Earth Song Lodge (Mile 4, Stampede Rd., 907/683-2863, www.earthsonglodge.com, breakfast and dinner daily summer) serves bagels, baked goods, soups, sandwiches, salads, pizzas, and espresso. There's free Wi-Fi too.

Black Diamond Grill (Otto Lake Rd., 907/683-4653, www.blackdiamondgolf.com, 7am-10pm daily mid-May-mid-Sept., $16-36) has a dinner menu of crab, pasta, salads, steaks, and halibut. The restaurant provides a free shuttle bus if you're staying in Healy or Nenana Canyon hotels. Black Diamond Grill serves as the clubhouse for Black Diamond Golf Course, with a variety of tours available, including wagon rides and ATV adventures. The various businesses are owned by the Usibelli family, which also operates the coal mine in Healy and Usibelli Vineyards in Napa Valley, California.

Three Bears Alaska (907/683-1300, www. threebearsalaska.com, 7am-10pm Mon.-Sat., 8am-10pm Sun.) is a warehouse-style store with a complete selection of groceries, produce, beer, and wine. The gas station has the cheapest fuel in the area.

Accommodations

Add a 7 percent tax to all Healy lodging rates described below.

★ **Earth Song Lodge** (907/683-2863, www.earthsonglodge.com, small cabins $185 d, family-size cabins $235 d, 2-bedroom cabins $285 d, extra adult guests $10 pp) rents 12 very clean and well-maintained cabins, all with private baths. Earth Song is four miles down Stampede Road off the Parks Highway at Mile 251. The lodge stays open all year, with a nightly slide show at the coffeehouse, Wi-Fi in the lodge, but no TVs (befitting the location), and guided winter dogsledding or cross-country skiing into Denali National Park. Co-owner Jon Nierenberg is a former Denali National Park ranger, and his wife, Karin, is an accomplished author.

For a budget option, head three miles south of Healy to **Denali RV Park and Motel** (Mile 245, Parks Hwy., 907/683-1500 or 800/478-1501, www.denalirvpark.com, mid-May-mid-Sept., rooms $98-103 d, family units $169), with tiny motel rooms and four-person family units containing full kitchens. Units have cable TV and a barbecue area.

White Moose Lodge (Mile 248, Parks Hwy., 907/683-1233 or 800/481-1232, www. whitemooselodge.com, early May-late Sept., $125 d) has 15 reasonably priced and clean no-frills motel rooms with two queen beds and TVs.

Denali Park Hotel (Mile 247, Parks Hwy., 907/683-1800 or 866/683-1800, www. denaliparkhotel.com, early May-late Sept., $159-179 d, 2 extra guests $10) is something of a misnomer. The motel consists of four single-level buildings, each with 12 units. The buildings were originally constructed in 1973 as the two-story McKinley Park Hotel, and were located inside the park before being moved to Healy in 2001. (The National Park Service no longer allows lodging inside Denali.) There's parking right outside your door, and spacious older rooms with queen or king beds, fridges, microwaves, and satellite TVs. The motel lobby is a World War II-era Alaska Railroad railcar, so fittingly enough a complimentary shuttle is provided for visitors arriving by train.

Park's Edge Log Cabin Accommodations (Hilltop Lane, 907/683-4343, www.parks-edge.com, late May-early Sept., $100-125 d, additional guests $10 pp) has modern economical cabins and a larger cabin that sleeps six. The cabins are adjacent to Black Diamond Golf Course and include private baths, fridges, and microwaves.

Open all year, **Aurora Denali Lodge** (Mile 250, Parks Hwy., 907/683-4500 or 800/683-4501, www.auroradenalilodge.com, one queen bed $189 d, two queen beds $199, with kitchenettes $219) has nicely appointed rooms, a full breakfast (summer only), and a guest computer. Request a room in the quieter annex building if possible. Rose's Café is next door.

It's hard to miss the geodesic-shaped **Denali Dome Home B&B** (Healy Spur Rd., 907/683-1239 or 800/683-1239, www. denalidomehome.com, $235 d), where lodging is available in a unique 7,000-square-foot house with rock fireplaces and eight guest rooms, all with king or queen beds and private baths. Two rooms contain jetted tubs, and guests appreciate the sauna, 10 acres of park-like grounds and flower gardens, the extensive art collection, and traditional cook-to-order breakfasts.

Touch of Wilderness B&B (Mile 2.9, Stampede Rd., 907/683-2459 or 800/683-2459, www.touchofwildernessbb.com, rooms $220-275 d, family unit $360) is a luxurious 7,000-square-foot home five miles north of Healy along Stampede Road and 16 miles north of the park entrance. The nine guest rooms—one wheelchair-accessible—have a variety of configurations and beds, plus private baths and comfortable common areas with fireplaces and TVs. Groups appreciate the six-person family unit with a kitchenette. A filling hot breakfast is provided in the huge dining room, and guests can use the kitchen to prepare their own dinners.

Denali Lakeview Inn (Otto Lake Rd., 907/683-4035, www.denalilakeviewinn.com, $179-229 d) is a large place right on Otto Lake with 21 bright guest rooms and suites, plus in-room continental breakfast, microwaves, and fridges. The main attraction here is the spectacular lake-and-mountains view from the decks.

★ **Denali Primrose B&B** (1 Stoney Creek Dr., 907/683-1234, www.denaliprimrose.com, one-bedroom suite $184 d, three-bedroom suite $209 d, extra guests $20 pp) is an immaculate modern home in a quiet neighborhood. Lodging options include a downstairs one-bedroom suite and a three-bedroom upstairs suite with a whirlpool tub. Amenities include private baths, TVs, continental breakfast, and a gracious owner.

Aspen Haus B&B (907/683-2004, www.aspenhaus.com, late May-early Sept., cabins $149 d, suites $179 d, extra guests $15 pp, house $199) has a quiet in-the-trees setting and four spacious cabins, the largest with room for six people, plus two upstairs suites. Each unit includes private baths, queen beds, and a fridge and microwave. A modern

three-bedroom house contains a full kitchen, bath, and laundry, along with plenty of space; it has a two-night minimum.

Operated by the Denali Outdoor Center, **Otto Lake Cabins & Camping** (Otto Lake Rd., 907/683-1925 or 888/303-1925, www.denalioutdoorcenter.com, mid-May-Sept., $106 d, extra guests $10 pp, up to 4) has three economy cabins on the shore of this lake just two miles south of Healy. The cabins share a shower house, laundry, and communal kitchen. The cabins fill early, so book ahead for mid-summer stays.

Totem Inn (Mile 249, Parks Hwy., 907/683-6500, year-round, www.thetoteminn.com, $175 d) is a well-kept and unpretentious log-sided motel with clean rooms, fridges, microwaves, a small fitness center, and filling hot breakfasts. Totem Inn Café is on-site.

Camping

Three miles south of Healy, **Denali RV Park and Motel** (Mile 245, Parks Hwy., 907/683-1500 or 800/478-1501, www.denalirvpark.com, mid-May-mid-Sept., RVs $52-58) has cramped RV spaces and some road noise, but clean showers, Wi-Fi, and cable TV.

Two miles south of Healy, **Otto Lake Cabins & Camping** (Otto Lake Rd., 907/683-1925 or 888/303-1925, www.denalioutdoorcenter.com, mid-May-mid-Sept., $12 pp) has simple lakeside campsites, but no RV hookups. Potable water is provided, and outhouses are available, along with showers, a laundry, canoe rentals ($8 pp per hour), and mountain bike rentals ($40 per day, $25 half-day). The campground is operated by Denali Outdoor Center, known for their Nenana River rafting trips. Showers for non-campers cost $5.

Midnight Sun RV and Campground (Mile 249, Parks Hwy., 907/683-2379, www.midnightsunrv.com, May-Sept., tents $20, RVs $28-43) occupies a quiet and somewhat wooded area just off the highway in Healy. It has a laundry, showers, Wi-Fi, and a shuttle to the park ($5 all day). The campground is adjacent to both 49th State Brewing Co. and the

24-hour Tri-Valley Gas, with fresh produce, good sandwiches, gas, an ATM, espresso, laundry, public showers, and a liquor store.

Information and Services

Healy lacks a visitors center, but the **Denali Chamber of Commerce** (907/683-4636, www.denalichamber.com) will mail brochures. For medical care, head to **Healy Clinic** (Usibelli Spur Rd., 907/683-2211, www.interiorhealthalaska.com, 9am-5pm Mon.-Fri.), where a physician assistant and nurse are on call.

Getting There

Alaska/Yukon Trails (907/888-5659, www.alaskashuttle.com, Apr.-Sept.) provides daily van service from Healy, but you'll need to call ahead for a pickup. One-way rates from Healy are $5 to Denali, $70 to Talkeetna, $55 to Fairbanks, and $80 to Anchorage. Vans will stop anywhere along the highway (with advance notice), and you can get off the van and reboard at a later date ($10 fee).

Getting Around

The **Dine Denali Shuttle** (907/683-2733, www.dinedenali.com, mid-May-mid-Sept., hourly 8am-1am daily midsummer, $5 day pass) stops at 49th State Brewing Co., Tri-Valley Gas, and Healy Base Camp in Healy, plus the Denali Visitor Center, Nenana Canyon hotels and restaurants, Denali Park Village, and Grizzly Bear Resort. The shuttle will also stop at Riley Creek Campground and other destinations on request; call for a pickup.

In the off-season, the **Alaska Railroad** (907/265-2494 or 800/544-0552, www.alaskarailroad.com) operates the **Aurora Winter** train, which connects Anchorage with Talkeetna, Healy, Nenana, and Fairbanks. Trains operate on winter weekends in both directions, with occasional midweek service.

Call **Denali Transportation** (844/907-4387, www.denalitaxishuttle.com) for 24-hour taxi and shuttle service in the Healy and Denali National Park area.

The owners of Denali Dome Home B&B provide rental cars, SUVs, and vans through **Keys to Denali Car Rental** (907/683-5397 or 800/683-1239, www.denalidomehome.com, May-mid-Sept., $120 per day), with free pickups and drop-offs anywhere in the area, including the Denali National Park train depot. This is a good way to explore the area without having to drive all the way from Anchorage.

The Kenai Peninsula

The Kenai Peninsula is like a mini-Alaska, com-
pressing all of the state's features into an area roughly 3 percent the
size of the state. You'll find mountains, icefields and glaciers, fjords
and offshore islands, large fish-filled rivers and lakes, swampy plains,
and a smattering of interesting towns.

   This outdoor playground is possibly the most popular destination
for Alaska residents. The recreational opportunities are practically
inexhaustible—from charter fishing and kiteboarding to river rafting
and dogsledding. Nearly 300,000 Anchorageites live just up the road,
so you probably won't be the only one on that fishing stream. But don't
let the possibility of crowds deter you. The resources are abundant, well

Highlights

Look for ★ to find recommended sights, activities, dining, and lodging.

★ **Hope:** This once-booming mining town is the place that time forgot. Several fine hikes head out from here (page 202).

★ **Alaska SeaLife Center:** The touch tanks and fascinating exhibits are great, but seals and sea lions steal the show at this popular marine science center (page 211).

★ **Resurrection Bay and Kenai Fjords:** Several Seward companies offer wildlife and glacier tours by boat. Half-day excursions tour the bay; all-day versions make it into Kenai Fjords National Park (page 211).

★ **Exit Glacier:** This glacier is part of Kenai Fjords National Park and has camping, hiking trails, and glacier tours (page 230).

★ **Combat Fishing:** The Kenai and Russian Rivers are major destinations for anglers in search of red salmon. It's an elbow-to-elbow frenzy at the midsummer peak (page 235).

★ **Homer Spit:** Jutting four miles into Kachemak Bay, this narrow sandy peninsula provides a great base for halibut charters, sea kayaking, bird-watching, cycling, dining, and shopping (page 262).

★ **Islands and Ocean Visitor Center:** This modern center has exhibits on the Alaska Maritime National Wildlife Refuge (page 262).

★ **Pratt Museum:** One of the finest small museums in Alaska, the Pratt always has something interesting, including a touch tank with tide-pool animals (page 263).

★ **Kachemak Bay and Gull Island:**

Glimpse thousands of nesting seabirds on Gull Island (page 287).

developed, and often isolated. And besides, what's wrong with a little company along the trail or under sail?

At 16,056 square miles, Kenai Peninsula is a little smaller than Vermont and New Hampshire combined. The Kenai Mountains form the peninsula's backbone, with massive Harding Icefield dominating the lower lumbar. The east side, facing Prince William Sound, hosts a spur of the Kenai Mountains, with the glimmering Sargent Icefields; the west side, facing Cook Inlet, is outwash plain, sparkling with low-lying swamp, lakes, and rivers. The icefields, glaciers, and plains are all a result of ice sculpting over the million-year course of the Pleistocene era, with its five major glacial periods. During the last, the Wisconsin Period, Portage Glacier filled the entire Turnagain Arm, 50 miles long and 0.5 miles high. Ten thousand years ago, Portage stopped just short of carving a fjord between Prince William Sound and Turnagain Arm; otherwise, Kenai Peninsula would've been Kenai Island. Still, this peninsula has more than 1,000 miles of coastline. The land is almost completely controlled by the federal government: Chugach National Forest, Kenai National Wildlife Refuge, and Kenai Fjords National Park account for nearly 85 percent of the peninsula.

HISTORY

You begin to feel the Russian influence strongly in this neck of the woods. Alexander Baranov's first shipyard was somewhere along Resurrection Bay, down from present-day Seward. Russians built a stockade near Kasilof in 1786 and a fort at Kenai in 1791. Other than these brief incursions, the land belonged to the Kenai Native Alaskans: The Athabascan people inhabited the north half of the peninsula, while the Alutiiqs (Aleuts) occupied the southern half.

During the gold rush, color was uncovered around Hope and Sunrise on Turnagain Arm,

and at Moose Creek, halfway to Seward. At first, trails ran between the mining communities, then wagon roads, and finally the railroad pushed from Seward through Anchorage to Fairbanks in the early 1920s. The Seward and Sterling Highways were completed in 1952, opening the Kenai's western frontier. When Atlantic Richfield tapped into oil (1957) and gas (1962) off the west coast, the peninsula's economic star began to twinkle. Oil and gas production has dropped steadily since the peak in the 1970s as the reserves are depleted, but new gas deposits have been discovered in recent years and exploration continues. Today, the Kenai Peninsula Borough's 55,000 residents are occupied with fishing, oil and gas, tourism, and services.

PLANNING YOUR TIME

The Kenai Peninsula is readily accessible by car, bus, plane, or train from Anchorage, making it perfect if you have a few days, but adventurers could easily spend considerably longer exploring backcountry areas or playing in the scenic towns.

Driving distances between (relatively) larger towns like Seward and Homer tend to be significant. You can feasibly cover 200-plus miles in a day, but if you have the time to slow down and stop in the smaller villages along the way, you'll get more out of your visit to Kenai Peninsula. Plan on stopping frequently as you drive, for the picturesque views and wildlife sightings are best appreciated outside of the car. This will affect your travel time, so plan your overnights accordingly.

If you're flying, airports in Homer and Kenai have daily flights from Anchorage.

Orientation

Two roads provide the primary access to the Kenai. The 127-mile **Seward Highway** connects Anchorage with Seward on the southwest end of the peninsula, and the 143-mile **Sterling Highway** cuts across the Kenai,

---

Previous: Outside Beach near Seldovia; old boots transformed into planters in Seldovia; Woody's Thai Kitchen in Seward

Kenai Peninsula

To Palmer

Wasilla
3

Knik Arm

1

Eagle River

Anchorage

Cook Inlet

ALYESKA SKI RESORT

Girdwood

Turnagain Arm

Portage Glacier

Whittier

Captain Cook State Recreation Area

HOPE

1

SPENCER GLACIER

Kenai National Wildlife Refuge

ALASKA RAILROAD

Kenai

Sterling

COMBAT FISHING

Cooper Landing

Moose Pass

Chugach

Kalgin Island

Soldotna

1

Kenai Lake

National

Kasilof

Skilak Lake

Russian River

9

Forest

Clam Gulch

Chugach State Park

EXIT GLACIER

RESURRECTION BAY TOURS

Mountains

STERLING HWY

Tustemena Lake

ALASKA SEALIFE CENTER

Seward

Seward Ice Field

Ninilchik

Kenai

Harding Ice Field

1

Resurrection Bay

Anchor Point

ISLANDS AND OCEAN CENTER

Kenai Fjords National Park

PRATT MUSEUM

THE HOMER SPIT

Homer

Halibut Cove

KACHEMAK BAY AND GULL ISLAND

Seldovia

Gulf of Alaska

Kachemak Bay State Park

Kachemak Bay State Wilderness Park

0   10 mi

0   10 km

© MOON.COM

leading west and south from Tern Lake, where it meets the Seward Highway, to Soldotna and Homer.

Alaskans never refer to state highways by their numbers; there are only a handful of main arteries, and the numbering system is confusing. Officially, the Seward Highway is Highway 9 between Seward and Tern Lake, where it becomes Highway 1 (even though it is still the Seward Highway). The Sterling Highway is also part of Highway 1, a route that continues from Homer to Anchorage, and then east all the way to the Canadian border at Tok.

The off-the-beaten-path settlement of Hope has a picture-perfect collection of gold rush-era buildings along Turnagain Arm. A very scenic three-hour drive south from Anchorage, the town of Seward is home to the Alaska SeaLife Center (great for kids), along with Kenai Fjords National Park, where visitors can take guided hikes across Exit Glacier, join Resurrection Bay boat tours, or take longer day (or multiple-night) trips into the park.

Kenai National Wildlife Refuge is home to the Kenai and Russian Rivers, the scene of river rafting and combat fishing, where hundreds of anglers crowd the banks when the salmon are running.

The Homer Spit, a sandy strip of land extending four miles into the bay, is the primary visitor attraction in Homer, with charter halibut fishing, sea kayaking, Kachemak Bay tours to Gull Island or the remote villages of Halibut Cove and Seldovia, and some of the finest restaurants and lodging in Alaska.

Every Kenai Peninsula town of any size has its own chamber of commerce and website; they're listed under the individual towns. A good overall information source is the Kenai Peninsula Tourism Marketing Council (907/262-5229 or 800/535-3624, www. kenaipeninsula.org), which produces a detailed annual travel publication called *Alaska's Playground*.

Eastern Kenai Peninsula

THE SEWARD HIGHWAY

The 127-mile Seward Highway—a National Scenic Byway—connects Anchorage with Seward on the Kenai Peninsula. Mileposts are numbered from the Seward end; subtract these numbers from 127 for the distance to Anchorage. The Seward Highway has passing lanes, wide shoulders, and a 65 mph speed limit much of the way, but take the time to enjoy the scenery. Keep your headlights on at all times, and watch for moose.

Near Portage at Mile 48, the Seward Highway banks sharply to the west along Turnagain Arm before turning again southward as it climbs into the Kenai Mountains. At Turnagain Pass (Mile 69, elevation 988 feet), the west side of the road has a big pullout with outhouses. Stop and stretch in this pretty area—the only road-accessible alpine country on the Kenai—where the snow sometimes lingers until late June. In the winter the snow can top 10 feet (or at least it was before global warming began taking a toll). The west side is popular with snowmobilers, while the east side is reserved for those on skis or snowshoes. Turnagain Pass can be deadly at certain times of the winter, and a number of snowmobilers have died in avalanches while riding on the dangerous upper slopes.

At Mile 64 is the northern trailhead for the Johnson Pass Trail, which goes 23 miles over relatively level terrain (with some short, steep sections) and emerges at Mile 33 of the Seward Highway. Two in-the-trees U.S. Forest Service campgrounds are nearby: Bertha Creek Campground (Mile 65, Seward Hwy., free) and Granite Creek Campground (Mile 63, Seward Hwy., 518/885-3639 or 877/444-6777, www.recreation.gov, $14 plus $10 reservation fee). The paved Sixmile Bike Trail parallels the highway from the Johnson Pass Trailhead south to the junction with the Hope Highway.

Sixmile Creek

At Mile 59 the highway crosses a staging area along Granite Creek for rafters and kayakers down Granite Creek and on to Sixmile Creek. This is one of Alaska's premier white-water areas. Check out the action from the footbridge that crosses Sixmile Creek, accessible via a short path from the parking area just east of the Canyon Creek bridge. Two companies lead white-water trips here: **Chugach Outdoor Center** (907/277-7238 or 866/277-7238, www.chugachoutdoorcenter.com) and **Nova Riverrunners** (907/746-5753 or 800/746-5753, www.novalaska.com). Three-hour trips ($109-120) are on Class IV water, while the five-hour trips ($159-165) include some intense Class V sections of the narrowly constricted lower canyon. Nova is the original company on the river, but Chugach Outdoor is more established, with a permanent office at Mile 7.5 of the Hope Highway; rafters appreciate the hot tub to warm up after the adventure. Children must be age 12 to run the canyon, or age 15 for the Class V section. Chugach also offers family-friendly three-hour Turnagain Pass float trips ($85) on the scenic East Fork of Sixmile Creek; this one is fine for kids age six and older. Check out the rafting action from a dramatic high **footbridge** over the canyon that accesses Gulch Creek Trail. Access is from a pullout at Mile 58 of the Seward Highway, two miles north of the Hope junction.

TOP EXPERIENCE

★ HOPE

Now almost a ghost town, Hope is a charming step into the past, with winding dirt roads, weathered log buildings with piles of firewood on the side, a little museum, a couple of eateries and lodging places, quiet waterside campsites, and great hiking. Bring your bike to ride the back roads of this town that time forgot.

The Hope Highway begins at Mile 56 of the Seward Highway, just west of the towering bridge over Canyon Creek. This sparsely trafficked road follows Sixmile Creek north back up to Turnagain Arm; pan for gold along the first five miles of the creek. The entire 17 miles to Hope is paved.

Gold was discovered on Resurrection Creek in 1888, and by 1896 there were 3,000 people inhabiting this boom neighborhood between Hope and Sunrise on Sixmile Creek. Many came by way of the Passage Canal, where Whittier now squats, portaging their watercraft over the Chugach glacial pass to Turnagain Arm, which is how Portage Glacier got its name. Large-scale mining prospered into the 1940s, but then Sunrise was abandoned and left to the ghosts. Hope hangs on today primarily as a place where recreation and tourism support the town's 190 people.

Sights

Downtown Hope is marked by a cluster of old buildings, some over a century old. Stop here to walk the dirt street past photogenic **Social Hall**—the original Alaska Commercial Co. store from 1902—and down to the tidal flats (caused by the earth sinking seven feet in the 1964 quake). They're dangerous; don't walk on them! Go back and turn left for new Hope, with its post office, red schoolhouse, and beautiful new and old log cabins.

Hope and Sunrise Historical and Mining Museum (907/782-3740, noon-4pm daily late May-early Sept., free) is a collection of log buildings housing historical photos and artifacts from the Turnagain Arm gold rush of 1894-1899. The grounds contain the original Canyon Creek Mining buildings, including the town's original school (1904), a blacksmith shop, a historic barn, and a classic 1947 Dodge Power Wagon.

Worth a stop is **Scott Sherritt Fine Art Gallery** (907/782-3602, www.scottsheritt. com), in a quaint cabin just before you get to "downtown" Hope. The owner lives next door and opens the gallery for visitors.

Recreation

HIKING

Gull Rock Trail begins from Porcupine Campground and parallels the shoreline of Turnagain Arm. It's a fairly easy stroll out to Gull Rock (5 miles), making this a popular family hike or overnight camping trip.

Hope Point Trail starts at the Porcupine Campground and climbs steeply into the alpine for 2.5 miles, passing a microwave tower before reaching the peak. From here you can hike forever along the ridgeline. It's a wonderful day hike, but you're starting at sea level and ending at 3,630-foot Hope Point, so be prepared for a real workout. The trail isn't well maintained but affords a good chance to see mountain goats, bears, and moose.

The **Resurrection Pass Trail** covers 38 miles between the towns of Hope and Cooper Landing. To reach the trailhead, drive 0.5 miles east of Hope on the Hope Highway to the junction with Resurrection Pass Road. Follow it 0.75 miles to a junction and turn left on Palmer Creek Road. It's five miles farther to the **Coeur D'Alene Campground,** with free walk-in campsites containing fire rings and bear boxes, but no water. The road continues another six winding and rough miles (not for RVs). From the end of the road, a trail leads into the alpine past the remains of century-old mines and a pretty waterfall.

KAYAKING AND BIKING

Turnagain Kayak & Coffeehouse (19796 Hope Hwy., 907/715-9365, www. turnagainkayak.com, 7am-3pm daily mid-May-mid-Sept., 7am-3pm Sat.-Sun. mid-Sept.-mid-May) offers classes at all levels for sea kayaks, river kayaks, pack rafts, and stand-up paddleboards. These range from a few hours to several days. They don't rent kayaks or stand-up paddleboards, but they do rent fat-tire bikes ($65 per day, $45 per half-day). Ride nearby roads, along the beach (near Mile 13), or the popular Resurrection Pass Trail.

Food

Built in 1896, picturesque **Seaview Café** (end of Main St., 907/782-3300, www. seaviewcafealaska.com, noon-9pm Sun.-Wed., noon-11pm Thurs.-Sat. mid-May-mid-Sept., $12-18) serves giant burgers, seafood chowder, reubens, and the house specialty—halibut fish-and-chips. There's live music of the roots-Americana type Friday-Saturday evenings in the adjacent bar, or on the deck when the weather cooperates, plus a choice of Alaskan beers on tap.

Creekbend Café (19842 Hope Hwy., 907/782-3274, www.creekbendco.com, 8am-4pm daily mid-May-mid-Sept., 3pm-9pm Mon., Thurs., and Sun., 9am-9pm Fri.-Sat. mid-Sept.-mid-May, $10-17) serves breakfast all day, featuring biscuits and gravy, avocado toast, breakfast burritos, waffles, and more. Lunchtime sandwiches are popular and include a salmon BLT, Tito's turkey apple sandwich, and a bacon cheeseburger. Behind the café is **The Acres at Creekbend,** with a grand lawn for live concerts, from folk to reggae, throughout the summer. See Creekbend's website for upcoming concerts.

For brunch, **Turnagain Kayak & Coffeehouse** (19796 Hope Hwy., 907/715-9365, www.turnagainkayak.com, 7am-3pm daily mid-May-mid-Sept., 7am-3pm Sat.-Sun. mid-Sept.-mid-May, under $12) serves Kaladi espresso, croissant breakfast sandwiches, grilled turkey-bacon sandwiches, and other light fare.

Accommodations

Clustered around a tiny pond, **Hope's Bear Creek Lodge** (Mile 16, Hope Hwy., 907/782-3141, www.bowmansbearcreeklodge.com, May-Sept., $195 d) has a peaceful setting. Six log cabins contain woodstoves and share a bathhouse. Also available are two cottages with separate bedrooms, a full kitchen, and a private bath. Several units are wheelchair-accessible. Guests appreciate the cozy cedar sauna and wood-fired hot tub, plus access to a paddleboat and canoe. The on-site restaurant, **Nini's Kitchen,** serves three meals daily.

The adjacent **Alaskan Byways** (19608 Hope Hwy., 907/748-1111, www.

Resurrection Pass Trail

The Resurrection Pass Trail covers 38 miles between the towns of Hope and Cooper Landing, with two side routes leading off to trailheads along the Seward Highway. You'll gain and lose 2,000 feet in elevation along the way. A series of U.S. Forest Service cabins make this one of the most popular hiking destinations in south-central Alaska. The trail winds through spruce forests and tops out in tundra, affording opportunities to see a variety of habitats. Wildlife, wildflowers, and wild fish in the lakes and streams add to the trail's appeal.

The trail begins four rough miles from Hope up Resurrection Pass Road, where a trailhead has parking, an information signboard, and a fun bridge across the creek. Eight cabins (reservations at www.recreation.gov, $75 plus $10 reservation fee) along the trail, one of which can only be reached via a floatplane, provide a welcome respite from the often inclement weather. The cabins are basic, each consisting of wooden bunks, a table and benches, a countertop for cooking, an outhouse, and a heating stove for warmth, but without running water, cooking utensils, or bedding. The farther in advance you can make plans for these very popular cabins, the more likely you are to secure a reservation.

If you can't secure a cabin, there are plenty of spots to camp for the night. Be very careful with campfires, or better yet, use a camp stove for cooking. Also filter or boil all drinking water.

Local wildlife includes moose, black and brown bears, wolves, mountain goats, Dall sheep, and even a local caribou herd. The caribou are scattered and often hard to spot in the summer, but if you look up high in the Resurrection Pass and Devil's Pass areas, maybe you'll get lucky. They often like to bed down in snow patches during the heat of the day, so look for dark spots in the snow near ridgelines.

Loop trips are possible, and you can do the Devil's Pass Trailhead-Devil's Pass cabin-Cooper Landing trip (27 miles) in three or four days, though hard-core mountain bikers often do it in one day. Hitchhiking to pick up your car is possible, but the Hope trailhead is well off the beaten path for most car traffic.

The high point of the main trail is Resurrection Pass at 2,600 feet. However, even at this comparatively low elevation, the snows of winter can linger well into June. Postholing through thigh-deep snow can dampen the enthusiasm of even the jolliest of hikers. If you're thinking of an early-season hike, check with the U.S. Forest Service office in Anchorage (907/271-2500, www.fs.fed.us/r10/chugach) or the Seward Ranger District (907/224-3374) for trail conditions.

At the southern end of the Resurrection Pass Trail at Cooper Landing, you can continue south on the 16-mile Russian Lakes Trail, which connects with the 16-mile Resurrection River Trail all the way to Exit Glacier near Seward. Together, these three trails make it possible to hike 74 miles, a 12-day trek that covers the Kenai Peninsula from head to toe.

Wildman's (907/595-1456, www.wildmans.org) has a shuttle service for hikers and bikers using the trail.

alaskanbyways.com, $75-95 d basic cabins, $150-195 d cabins) has a variety of cabins. Two cozy "backpacker" cabins ($75-95 d) lack running water; they have outhouses, or guests can use the nearby bathhouse. Three larger cabins and a restored Alaska Railroad train car ($150 d) all include private baths. Built in 1905, the historic Hirshey cabin ($195 for up to 4 people) is a gorgeous two-story place with three bedrooms, a spiral staircase, and a full kitchen with ingredients for breakfast. Most units lack Wi-Fi.

Set on a bluff overlooking Bear Creek and close to the Hope schoolhouse, Discovery Cabins (19170 Discovery Dr., 907/301-0399, www.discoverycabins.com, mid-May-Sept., $95 d, extra guests $15 pp, up to 4) has five modern cabins, each with two double beds or a double and two twins. Cabins share the bathhouse, kitchen, and laundry facilities in the main lodge.

Alaska Dacha (19842 Hope Hwy., 907/782-3223, www.alaskadacha.com, motel rooms $120-135 d, cabin $175) has second-floor motel rooms, each with a private bath, a fridge, a microwave, TV, and Wi-Fi. One unit includes a whirlpool tub. A separate cabin sleeps up to five and contains a kitchen and bath.

Adjacent to Alaska Dacha, **Hope's Hideaway Lodge** (19796 Hope Hwy., 907/764-1910, www.hopeshideaway.com, $175 d plus $40 cleaning fee, extra guests $20 pp) is a duplex cabin where each side has a full kitchen, a private bath, and two bedrooms. A door connects the two units for large groups. The owners also run the adjacent Turnagain Kayak & Coffeehouse.

Three miles from Hope along secluded Middle Creek, ★ **Black Bear B&B** (63640 Resurrection Creek Rd., 907/223-9835, www.alaskablackbearbnb.com, May-Sept., $145 d) is a delightful cabin with a comfortable log bed, a private bath, a wood-burning stove, a screened-in back porch, and a barbecue grill. Breakfast ingredients are stocked in the kitchenette. Owner Maggie Holeman is a gracious host with a lifetime of knowledge about the area.

Travelers on a budget should check out the rustic **Hope Retreat Center** (907/333-5050, www.alaskaumc.org, $75 for up to 5 people), a former church owned by the United Methodist Conference. This pretty log building has a big upstairs sleeping area and a large room (the old sanctuary), kitchen, and bath below. It's comfortable, but not at all fancy. Bring sleeping bags for the cots and bunks, and towels for the bath. You'll need to clean up before leaving.

Seaview Cabins (end of Main St., 907/782-3300, www.seaviewcafealaska.com, $60) has historic miner cabins with woodstoves, electricity, and outhouses; showers are at Alaska Dacha. The cabins sleep up to four.

Camping

At the end of Hope Highway is the U.S. Forest Service's delightful **Porcupine Campground** (Mile 18, Hope Hwy., www.recreation.gov, $18 plus $10 reservation fee), featuring fine views across Turnagain Arm, plenty of shade, and red raspberries as hors d'oeuvres in late summer. The 34-site campground makes an excellent base to explore the area, just a short distance from town and with tall trees and fine hiking opportunities.

Park RVs or pitch a tent in town at **Seaview RV Park** (end of Main St., 907/782-3300, www.seaviewcafealaska.com, tents $6, RVs $20 with electricity, basic cabins $60 d). Sites are along the creek, which is a popular spot to catch pink salmon (humpies) or to pan for gold. There are also several rustic cabins with outhouses available. Get water from adjacent Seaview Café. **Alaska Dacha** (19842 Hope Hwy., 907/782-3223, www.alaskadacha.com, tents $25, RVs $25-40) has full RV hookups at their location along the highway before you get to town.

Showers are available at **Alaska Dacha** (19842 Hope Hwy., 907/782-3223, www.alaskadacha.com).

Information and Services

Alaska Dacha (19842 Hope Hwy., 907/782-3223, www.alaskadacha.com, 9am-9pm daily) has a year-round convenience store, laundry, and showers.

Stop by the **Hope Library** (2nd St. and A St., 907/782-3121, noon-3pm daily), with Wi-Fi, computers, and an adjacent gift shop. Built in 1938, the building served as Hope's schoolhouse until 1986. Across the parking lot is a seasonal espresso stand, **Grounds for Hope.** The **Hope Alaska Chamber of Commerce** is online at www.hopealaska.us.

SOUTH TO SEWARD

Beyond the Hope Highway junction, at Mile 46 the Seward Highway climbs to scenic Summit Lake, 80 miles south of Anchorage. Surrounded by high mountains, the lake makes a great place for summertime photos. Signs warn against stopping in winter, when avalanches have been known to slide across the highway.

Recreation

Just after Mile 40, one mile before the Seward-Sterling junction, is **Devil's Creek**

Trailhead; this trail leads 10 miles to the pass, then another mile to where it joins the Resurrection Pass Trail. The Devil's Pass cabin (518/885-3639 or 877/444-6777, www. recreation.gov, $75 plus $10 reservation fee) sits on the pass. A great overnight hike takes Summit Creek Trail to Resurrection Pass Trail, then back down via Devil's Creek Trail to the highway.

The Carter Lake Trail leaves the highway at Mile 33, climbs nearly 1,000 feet in just over two miles to Carter Lake, and continues another mile around Carter Lake to Crescent Lake. This route gets you into the alpine fast and can be used to loop back to the highway on the Crescent Lake and Crescent Creek Trails. The Forest Service's Crescent Lake cabin (518/885-3639 or 877/444-6777, www. recreation.gov, $75 plus $10 reservation fee) sits on the south shore of the lake.

A half mile beyond the Carter Lake Trailhead is the southern trailhead to Johnson Pass Trail (whose northern trailhead is at Mile 64). Just beyond that is Trail Lakes Fish Hatchery (907/288-3688, www. ciaanet.org, 8am-4:30pm daily, free), which has a fascinating display about spawning and stocking salmon. The facility produces millions of sockeye and coho salmon fry and smolts for lakes across the Kenai Peninsula.

Food and Accommodations

Cozy and well-placed Summit Lake Lodge (Mile 46, Seward Hwy., 907/244-2031, www. summitlakelodge.com, May-mid-Sept., motel rooms $149 d, cabins $235-285 d, additional guests $30 pp) overlooks the lake. The original lodge was built in 1953, but the big fireplace and chimney are the only parts of the building that survived the 1964 quake. The restaurant (11am-8pm Mon.-Thurs., 11am-9pm Fri.-Sun., $22-32) serves walnut-crusted halibut, a popular Denali rib eye with garlic mashed potatoes, and other Alaskan fare, along with a memorable Fruit of the Forest

pie à la mode. A separate ice cream shop scoops 16 flavors, along with espresso and homemade pizza by the slice or pie. Walk out the door for a lovely picnic along the lake. There's also a small motel (no TVs) and 16 spacious waterside or in-the-woods cabins with private baths and TVs; the largest has a king bed and spa with a private deck on the lake. A two-night minimum is required for the larger cabins. Cell phones generally work at Summit Lake, and Wi-Fi is available in the main lodge. All overnight guests are served a made-to-order breakfast.

Just 0.5 mile down the highway from the lodge is the turnoff to Tenderfoot Creek Campground (Mile 46, Seward Hwy., 518/885-3639 or 877/444-6777, www.recreation. gov, $18 plus $10 reservation fee), a beautiful area with 36 campsites on the shores of this alpine lake. Sites can be reserved in advance.

Perfect for a late-summer day hike or an extended backcountry trip, Summit Creek Trail is a hidden gem that gets you into the alpine area in less than an hour. The trailhead isn't signposted, so look for the small parking area on the west side near Mile 44; it is just above the avalanche gates. The trail gains 2,600 feet in elevation over eight beautiful miles to a junction with the Resurrection Pass Trail.

MOOSE PASS

Nestled on the shore of Trail Lake, tiny Moose Pass (pop. 200, www.moosepassalaska.com) is 30 miles north of Seward. Here since 1928, the classic Estes Brothers Grocery (907/288-3151, 8am-7pm Mon.-Sat., 10am-6pm Sun. summer, 8am-7pm Mon. and Wed.-Sat., 10am-6pm Sun. winter) has a limited selection of groceries, along with sandwiches and espresso. Don't miss the 10-foot-high Estes waterwheel just up from the store. The original Pelton waterwheel was built here in 1928, providing hydroelectric power for the store until 1996. Pull out your pocketknife to give it an edge on the grindstone; the sign proclaims, "Moose Pass is a peaceful little town. If you have an axe to grind, do it here."

1: snow on Turnagain Pass; 2: Hope and Sunrise Historical and Mining Museum; 3: rafting Sixmile Creek; 4: Seaview Café in Hope

The main event comes on the **Summer Solstice Festival** (late June), when Moose Pass springs to life with music, food, and games.

Scenic Mountain Air (907/288-3646, www.scenicmountainair.com, May-early Sept.) has floatplanes based at Trail Lake. Options include a quick half-hour flight ($149 pp with 2 passengers, $99 pp with 3) and popular one-hour flights ($298 pp with 2, $199 pp with 3). On a clear day, the views are stunning as you fly over glaciers and mountains and along the coast. The company can also provide wilderness fishing trips and drop-offs at Forest Service cabins.

Accommodations

A large and exquisite B&B, ★ **Inn at Tern Lake** (Mile 36, Seward Hwy., 907/288-3667, www.ternlakeinn.com, $200-225 d) has a mountain-rimmed setting that encompasses muskeg ponds, forests, a putting green, tennis courts, and even a private airstrip. The inn is six miles north of Moose Pass and just south of pretty Tern Lake. Guests stay in four luxuriously appointed suites with private baths, fireplaces, TV, Wi-Fi, and balconies. The inn also has a high-ceilinged great room, a hot tub, and a sauna. Co-owner Rose Hetrick cooks a delicious breakfast each morning, and you can prepare your own dinner in the large kitchen. Tern Lake is a fantastic spot for summer weddings but isn't really set up for young children.

Right in the heart of town, **Trail Lake Lodge** (Mile 30, Seward Hwy., 907/288-3101, www.traillakelodge.com, motel rooms $119 d, lodge units $136 d) is the least expensive place to stay at Moose Pass, with basic motel rooms and larger lodge units, all with TVs and Wi-Fi. There is also a restaurant and a lounge.

★ **Renfro's Lakeside Retreat** (Mile 27, Seward Hwy., 907/288-5059, www.renfroslakesideretreat.com, May-Sept., lakeside cabins $205, woods cabins $165-175, RV hookups $25-45) is eight miles south of Moose Pass—and 20 miles north of Seward—along the shore of Kenai Lake. Here you'll find eight cabins, all with private baths and kitchenettes. Five are right on the beautiful lake and three are back in the woods; all of these sleep four or five people. Full RV hookups are also available, along with Wi-Fi, paddleboats, and a playground. There are no TVs or phones.

South from Moose Pass

Six miles south of Moose Pass is the turnoff for **Trail River Campground** (Trail River Rd., 518/885-3639 or 877/444-6777, www.recreation.gov, $18 plus $10 reservation fee), a quiet wooded campground just over a mile off Seward Highway, with some choice sites on the lakeshore loop. Next up on the left is **Ptarmigan Creek Campground** (Mile 23, Seward Hwy., 518/885-3639 or 877/444-6777, www.recreation.gov, $14 plus $10 reservation fee). **Ptarmigan Creek Trail** climbs from the campground for 3.5 miles along the creek to Ptarmigan Lake, where there's good fishing for grayling. The trail continues another four miles to the east end of the lake.

Magnificent **Kenai Lake** comes into view just south of here: huge, beautiful, blue green, with snowcapped peaks all around. Three-mile **Victor Creek Trail** starts at Mile 20. Three miles south on the Seward Highway is the turnoff to little **Primrose Campground** (Mile 17, Seward Hwy., $14). It's right on the shore of Kenai Lake, a mile up the road.

Eight-mile-long **Primrose Trail** takes off from Primrose Campground, climbing 1,500 feet to Lost Lake, where you can hook up to **Lost Lake Trail** and come out at Mile 5 near Seward. This 15-mile hike is one of the most popular loop trails in the area. If you planned far enough ahead and made a reservation, you can stay at the **Dale Clemens cabin** (Lost Lake Trail, 518/885-3639 or 877/444-6777, www.recreation.gov, $75 plus $10 reservation fee). On clear days, you get a magnificent view of Resurrection Bay and beyond, out to the Gulf of Alaska.

Beautiful **Porcupine Creek Falls** is three miles in on the Primrose Trail and is a favorite day-hike destination. Above the lake are dramatic alpine views and the chance to explore this high and mighty landscape.

Seward

Seward (pop. 3,000) is a pocket-size port town on a sparkling bay surrounded by snowcapped peaks, and is the only large settlement on the east side of the Kenai Peninsula. It's connected by bus, ferry, and plane and has a maritime climate and a seafood industry—just like a half-dozen other places you've visited so far, but with a difference: Seward is right on the doorstep of Kenai Fjords National Park. This park contains some of the most inhospitable country in the state. Boat tours into the park are a major attraction, with a wide variety of day-tour options. Harding Icefield—a prehistoric frozen giant with three dozen frigid fingers—rivals Glacier Bay for scenery and wildlife but is decidedly less expensive to visit. Combine this with Seward's Alaska SeaLife Center, convenient camping, good food, and excellent access by public transportation, and you've got all the elements for a great time in this old town.

Today, Seward has a diverse economy supported by tourism, commercial fishing and sportfishing, fish processing, and other activities. The Alaska SeaLife Center is the main focal point for travelers and has excellent exhibits. The **Alaska Vocational Technical Center** (AVTEC, www.avtec.edu) trains 1,600 students each year in such fields as welding, diesel repair, and marine sciences, and a maximum-security prison on the east side of Resurrection Bay houses another 450 folks in less academic conditions.

A towering coal-shipping facility dominates the harbor. A worldwide glut of coal caused the export facility to close in 2015, though it may open again in the future. Some cruise ships also dock in Seward, but most companies have shifted their ships to Whittier. It's too bad for them, since they miss one of the most enjoyable towns in south-central Alaska.

The **Seward Shuttle** (free) runs from downtown to the harbor, the cruise ship terminal, the train station, and other locations. Buses run the circuit every half hour daily through summer.

HISTORY

In 1791, Alexander Baranov, on a return voyage to Kodiak from around his Alaskan domain, waited out a storm in this bay on the Sunday of Resurrection, a Russian holiday. The sheltered waters of Resurrection Bay prompted Baranov to install a small shipyard. In 1903, surveyors for the Alaska Central Railroad laid out the town site for their port. This private enterprise, financed by Seattle businessmen, established Seward, laid 50 miles of track, and went broke. In 1911, Alaska Northern Railroad extended the track almost to present-day Girdwood. In 1912, the U.S. government began financing the completion of this line, which reached Fairbanks, 470 miles north, in 1923. From then, Seward's history parallels Valdez's as one of the two year-round ice-free ports with shipping access to interior Alaska—Seward's is by rail, Valdez's is by road. And like Valdez, Seward was almost completely destroyed by 1964's Good Friday earthquake.

SIGHTS

There's a bust of **William H. Seward** (Adams St.) next to the Van Gilder Hotel, and murals grace the sides of many Seward buildings. Pick up a brochure showing the locations at the visitors center, or check out www.sewardmuralsociety.com.

Lowell Point Road extends 2.5 miles south of Seward, hugging the shoreline of Resurrection Bay. Just south of the SeaLife Center is a much-photographed **waterfall** on Lowell Creek. The road ends in a cluster of homes, campgrounds, and businesses at **Lowell Point.** Park at Lowell Point State Recreation Site, where a trail leads to the beach. Time your visit with the tides to

Seward

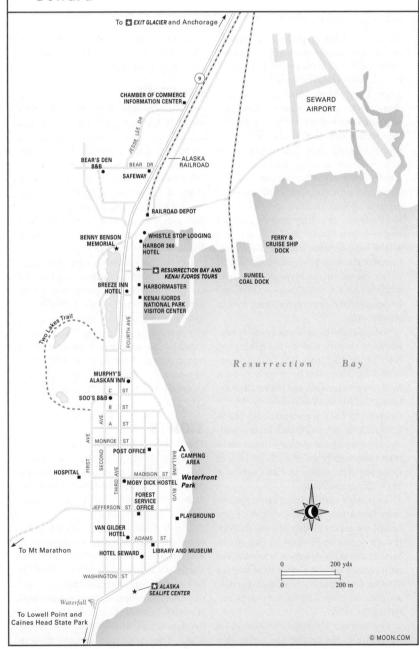

To ★ EXIT GLACIER and Anchorage

SEWARD AIRPORT

⑨

CHAMBER OF COMMERCE INFORMATION CENTER ■

JESSE LEE DR

BEAR'S DEN B&B ●

BEAR DR

ALASKA RAILROAD

SAFEWAY

RAILROAD DEPOT ■

BENNY BENSON MEMORIAL ★

WHISTLE STOP LODGING ●

HARBOR 360 HOTEL

FERRY & CRUISE SHIP DOCK

★ ★ RESURRECTION BAY AND KENAI FJORDS TOURS

SUNEEL COAL DOCK

BREEZE INN HOTEL ●

■ HARBORMASTER

■ KENAI FJORDS NATIONAL PARK VISITOR CENTER

Two Lakes Trail

FOURTH AVE

Resurrection Bay

MURPHY'S ALASKAN INN ●

SOO'S B&B ●

C ST

B ST

A ST

AVE

MONROE ST

FIRST AVE

SECOND AVE

THIRD AVE

POST OFFICE ■

BALLAINE BLVD

Λ CAMPING AREA

HOSPITAL ■

MADISON ST

Waterfront Park

● MOBY DICK HOSTEL

FOREST SERVICE OFFICE ■

JEFFERSON ST

● PLAYGROUND

VAN GILDER HOTEL ●

ADAMS ST

To Mt Marathon

HOTEL SEWARD ●

■ LIBRARY AND MUSEUM

WASHINGTON ST

0   200 yds

0   200 m

Waterfall

★ ★ ALASKA SEALIFE CENTER

To Lowell Point and Caines Head State Park

© MOON.COM

explore nearby tide pools for sea stars, sea anemones, and other creatures. The 4.5-mile Coastal Trail leads to Caines Head.

Seven miles north on the Seward Highway, turn onto Bear Lake Road and continue 0.5 miles to **Bear Creek weir.** The weir is used to count fish returning to Bear Lake, with upward of 20,000 sockeye and coho salmon swimming up this creek to spawn. See the spawning sockeye in June and July, followed by coho late July into September. While here, keep your eyes open for dippers, unusual birds with the ability to walk underwater.

★ Alaska SeaLife Center

Seward's most enjoyable attraction, the **Alaska SeaLife Center** (301 Railway Ave., 907/224-6300 or 888/378-2525, www.alaskasealife.org, 9am-9pm daily mid-May-late Aug., 10am-5pm daily mid-Aug.-Sept., 10am-5pm daily winter, $25 over age 12, $22 seniors and military, $13 ages 4-12, free under age 4) sits on the south edge of town facing Resurrection Bay. This impressive facility provides visitors with a wonderful way to learn about marine wildlife up close. There are informative exhibits about commercial fishing and the impacts of ocean acidification; aquariums filled with crabs, sea jellies, and octopuses; tide-pool touch tanks; and a big gift shop, but the main attractions are three gigantic tanks, each with two-story windows where visitors can take in the undersea world.

The seabird tank houses puffins and other birds whose ability to fly underwater delights all, and the harbor seals' playful personality shows through in their amusing interactions with people. Most extraordinary of all are the amazingly agile Steller sea lions that circle their tanks, coming up to check out children next to their windows. For visitors, the SeaLife Center is a place to learn about the marine environment, but this is also an important center for marine research and the rehabilitation of wildlife, including pigeon guillemots and Steller sea lions.

Behind-the-scenes tours (maximum 12 people per tour, minimum age 12, $15 pp)

provide an excellent hour-long look at the center's facilities, research programs, and wildlife rehabilitation efforts. For a hands-on experience with puffins, harbor seals, a sea otter, and a giant Pacific octopus, take a personalized one-hour **encounter tour** (maximum 5 people, $75). Shorter half-hour versions of the sea otter and octopus tours (maximum 14 people, $25 adults, $20 children) are also available. Reservations are required, so call in advance.

TOP EXPERIENCE

★ Resurrection Bay and Kenai Fjords

Seward's setting at the head of Resurrection Bay and its proximity to Kenai Fjords National Park make it the perfect departure point for boat tours into a stunning array of tidewater glaciers, towering mountains, abundant wildlife, and pristine waters. This is *the* cruise for seeing marine wildlife. On a good day, you could see **humpbacks** and **orcas,** plus porpoises, seals, sea otters, sea lions, hundreds of puffins, kittiwakes, auklets, and the occasional bald eagle and oystercatcher. These trips are guaranteed to be a highlight of your Alaskan visit.

Tour boats operate daily throughout the season, with gray whale trips mid-March-mid-May, and a multitude of other tour options mid-May-early October. Visit early or late in the season and you're likely to find lower prices and fewer people. Half-day trips lead around nearby **Resurrection Bay** and out as far as Rugged Island, while all-day voyages continue into **Kenai Fjords National Park** and the Alaska Maritime National Wildlife Refuge, including Aialik Bay and Holgate Arm (with calving icebergs), the Chiswell Islands (with a Steller sea lion rookery and nesting seabirds—most notably puffins), and remote Northwestern Fjord (seals, whales, and glaciers). These longer trips are far more interesting, but the waters are often rough, so take seasickness pills (Bonine is good to avoid the drowsiness of some brands,

SEWARD

THE KENAI PENINSULA

but your best bet is a prescription for scopolamine, used as a patch behind the ear).

Binoculars and telephoto lenses are handy, and a light jacket is wise. Some Seward B&Bs and hostels offer **10 percent discounts** on Resurrection Bay tours; ask your lodging place if these are available before booking a tour. If you're heading out for the day, boat tour companies provide free lots with shuttle buses back to the harbor; ask for details when you make reservations. Do not try parking along the harbor—except in a paid lot—unless you don't mind a hefty parking ticket.

TOURS

Seward's largest tour company, **Kenai Fjords Tours** (907/224-8068 or 888/478-3346, www. alaskacollection.com) operates 10 surprisingly large 95-foot vessels, each of which holds up to 150 people. They offer a wide variety of cruises, starting with a too-quick 3.5-hour buffet dinner trip to Fox Island ($91 adults, $46 ages 2-11). Better options are a 4.5-hour Resurrection Bay tour ($109 adults, $55 children) that includes a buffet lunch stop on Fox Island; a six-hour trip with time in Kenai Fjords National Park plus lunch ($162 adults, $81 children); or an excellent nine-hour sail to Northwestern Fjord ($199 pp) that includes breakfast and lunch. Their most popular voyage—and my favorite—is an 8.5-hour trip ($199 adults, $100 children) to Aialik Bay that includes lunch plus an hour-long stop on Fox Island where you're served a big salmon and prime rib buffet dinner at Kenai Fjords Wilderness Lodge. Spring trips (late Mar.-mid-May) follow the gray whale migration ($89 adults, $45 children); these last four hours and include lunch.

Major Marine Tours (907/224-8030 or 800/764-7300, www.majormarine.com) offers 3.5-hour cruises to Resurrection Bay ($84 adults, $42 ages 2-11), 6-hour trips to Holgate Glacier ($159 adults, $80 children), and 7.5-hour trips to Holgate or Aialik Glacier in Aialik Bay ($179 adults, $90 children). Add on a filling Copper River salmon and prime rib buffet ($24 adults, $12 children). Boats

heading to Aialik Bay are speedy and stable catamarans, helpful when seas are rough. These are very large vessels, holding up to 250 passengers. For a more personalized trip (perfect for birders), the company has small-boat trips to Northwestern Fjord ($224 pp, with a light breakfast and lunch). This 8.5-hour cruise is not recommended for children. Early in the year (Apr.-mid-May), Major Marine has four-hour gray whale watching trips ($89 adults, $45 children). A National Park Service ranger provides expert narration and commentary on most Major Marine tours; this is the only local company providing this service.

For a more personalized adventure, **Alaska Saltwater Lodge** (907/224-5271, www.alaskasaltwaterlodge.com) has customized small-group trips ($269 adults, $135 children) into the park, with a maximum of 15 passengers (the larger operators sometimes have upward of 250 people on board). Two other good companies with small boats and personalized trips are **Northern Latitude Adventures** (907/422-0432, www.northernlatitudeadventures.com) and **Alaska Fjord Charters** (907/491-1075, www.alaskafjordcharters.com).

If you want a private tour, it's possible to book a water taxi into Kenai Fjords National Park, but these small vessels lack the creature comforts or stability of larger boats. They're primarily used as transport for kayakers and other adventurers.

Seward Museum

The library building houses the **Seward Museum** (239 6th Ave., 907/224-3902, www.cityofseward.us, 10am-5pm Tues.-Sat. mid-May-mid-Sept., noon-5pm Fri.-Sat. mid-Sept.-mid-May, $4). The museum's collection includes Native Alaskan baskets and carved ivory, equipment from the original Brown & Hawkins store, a cross-section of a 350-year-old Sitka spruce, and photographs from the 1964 earthquake that dropped parts of this

---

1: the touch tank at Alaska SeaLife Center; 2: sailboat on Resurrection Bay in front of Bear Glacier

country by six feet. The museum shows fascinating videos (2pm) on the 1964 earthquake and the Iditarod Trail. Also here is Alaska's original flag, designed by a 13-year-old orphan—**Benny Benson**—in 1927. Find a small memorial to Benny Benson on the north side of town along the lagoon.

ENTERTAINMENT AND EVENTS

Downtown Seward has several popular drinking establishments with pool tables and occasional live music. The year kicks off in Seward with the **Polar Bear Jump-Off** (3rd weekend in Jan.), a leap of faith into the frigid 39°F water of Resurrection Bay. All sorts of goofy-costumed jumpers join the fray. It's all for a good cause, however, since jumpers collect pledges for contributions to the American Cancer Society.

The **Mount Marathon Race** (www.mmr.seward.com, July 4) attracts 900 runners, who race up and back down the steep slopes of this 3,022-foot summit that rises behind Seward. The race has been run annually since 1915, and is a major Alaskan institution, filling the bars and campgrounds with runners and 40,000 or so spectators. The race is brutal, with lots of bruises, bloody knees, and even concussions, along with the mysterious disappearance of a 65-year-old runner in 2012; his body was never found. Mount Marathon always attracts the state's top runners, along with a few elite international racers. A few slots are held open to the highest bidder, and folks have been known to bid $1,000 for the privilege to race! Many runners do it in under an hour, and in 2015 Killian Jornet from Spain covered the 3.5-mile course in an incredible 41 minutes and 48 seconds. The fastest woman, Emelie Forsberg from Sweden, ran the race in 47 minutes and 48 seconds that same year. In addition to the Mount Marathon Race, other Fourth of July events include a parade, food and crafts booths, live music, and midnight fireworks. Make lodging or camping reservations far ahead.

At the **Silver Salmon Derby** (www.seward.com, $10 per day, Aug.), the heaviest fish brings in $10,000. It's one of Alaska's richest fishing derbies, and one of the oldest, first established in 1956.

The **Seward Music and Fine Arts Festival** (www.sewardfestival.com, early Oct.) features three days of live music and food.

SHOPPING

Seward has a number of interesting studios scattered around town, including the **Resurrect Art Coffeehouse Gallery** (320 3rd Ave., 907/224-7161, www.resurrectart.com). Also worth a look is **Ranting Raven Gallery** (238 4th Ave., 907/224-2228, mid-May-mid-Sept.), with art and gifts, pastries, and light lunches. **Cover to Cover Bookstore** (215 4th Ave., 907/224-2525, 11am-6pm Tues.-Sun. summer) sells new and used books. Several local galleries stay open late on First Fridays in the summer, with special art openings.

Downtown's **Brown & Hawkins Store** (204 4th Ave., 907/224-3011, www.brownandhawkins.com, May-early Sept.) is Alaska's oldest family-owned business. It's been here since 1900 and still houses the old bank vault and cash register. The store has a good selection of outerwear, but the main draw is Sweet Darlings Candies, with homemade gelato, fudge, and other treats.

Downtown's **Grazing Moose Summer Market and Artists' Co-op** (312 5th Ave., 907/491-1076, 10am-4pm Thurs.-Sun. late May-Sept.) displays pieces by 25 or so local artists. Stop by the little red cottage on Thursday for locally grown organic produce and freshly baked bread.

RECREATION

If you have kids along, give everyone a break at **Seward Community Playground** (just south of the campground at Ballaine Blvd. and Adams St.).

Seward's **Sports and Rec Gym** (519 4th Ave., 907/224-4054, www.cityofseward.us, 9:30am-9pm Tues.-Thurs., $5 adults, $3 kids) has fitness equipment, a rock climbing wall, a sauna, racquetball, and basketball courts.

State Parks

Two popular state parks (907/262-5581, www.alaskastateparks.org) are close to Seward on the shores of Resurrection Bay: Caines Head State Recreation Area and Thumb Cove State Marine Park.

Caines Head State Recreation Area (accessible via the Coastal Trail) was the site of a World War II military base, Fort McGilvray, and the old command post still stands atop a massive 650-foot headland. There are dramatic views of Resurrection Bay and the surrounding country. The 4.5-mile Coastal Trail leads to the old fort from **Lowell Point State Recreation Site** (Mile 2, Lowell Point Rd., day-use $5), three miles south of Seward. Parts of the trail follow the shoreline and can only be hiked at low tide; be sure to check the tide charts before heading out. Take a flashlight to explore the maze of underground passages and rooms at Fort McGilvray. Also here are ammunition magazines and firing platforms for the six-inch guns that guarded Seward. This area makes a fine overnight trip, and a walk-in campground complete with three-sided shelter is available at **Tonsina Point,** a mile in. Caines Head is very popular with sea kayakers, who paddle here from Seward to hang out with the sea otters and seals. Also within the park are often-booked hike-in **public-use cabins** ($80) at Derby Cove and Callisto Canyon.

Thumb Cove State Marine Park is on the east side of Resurrection Bay, seven miles from Seward, and accessible only by boat. The park includes a long sandy beach, forested uplands, and the waters of Thumb Cove. Porcupine Glacier towers behind. Thumb Cove is a favorite stop for recreational boaters, and camping is popular along its beaches. Two cozy cabins ($75) are in the park, each sleeping up to eight people.

Hiking

For an enjoyable one-mile walk on a winding trail through the forest and around the creatively named First Lake and Second Lake, look for the **Two Lakes Trail** behind the AVTEC Center (2nd Ave. and C St.). There's a picnic area at the trailhead.

The high bare slope hanging over Seward is **Mount Marathon,** featured attraction for the Fourth of July Mount Marathon Race. It generally takes nonrunners at least four hours to get up and back. Follow Jefferson Street due west up Lowell Canyon and look for the trailhead to the right just beyond a pair of large water tanks. You can run all the way back down the mountain on a steep gravel incline if your legs and nerves are good, but beware of slipping on the solid rock face near the bottom. The trail does not actually reach the summit of Mount Marathon (4,560 feet), but rather the broad east shoulder (3,022 feet), which offers a spectacular view of Seward and the entire surrounding country.

Looking for the easy way up? **Marathon Helicopters** (907/224-3616, www.marathonhelicopters, $75 pp 2-person min.) offers flights to the summit of Mt. Marathon, where you can hike downhill to town.

Kenai Backcountry Adventures (907/331-4912, www.kenaibackcountry adventures.com) leads day hikes to areas around Seward, along with multinight camping expeditions.

Biking

Rent mountain bikes, fat-tire bikes, hybrid bikes, and baby joggers from **Seward Bike Shop** (411 Port Ave., 907/224-2448, Apr.-Oct., $35 per half day) in the collection of "Train Wreck" Alaska railcars.

TOP EXPERIENCE

Fishing

Fishing is one of Seward's most popular activities, and in midsummer dozens of boats dot the waters while hundreds of anglers cast from the shore. Salmon are the main attraction, made all the more enticing by a summer-long fishing derby. Your odds of catching one increase if you can get away from the shore, and many charter boats are available. Halibut fishing is another favorite, but you'll need to get quite far out—sometimes all the way to Montague Island in Prince William Sound—to catch one.

Full-day halibut or salmon fishing typically cost around $285-350 pp. If you aren't fishing, drop by the harbor in the late afternoon when charter operators hang up the day's catch for photos. It's quite a sight.

Get a complete list of charter operators from the Seward Chamber of Commerce Visitor Center, or contact a booking agency. The oldest and largest, representing 30 or so boats, is **The Fish House** (across from the harbormaster's office, 907/224-3674 or 800/257-7760, www.thefishhouse.net). Other good charter operations include **ProFish-N-Sea Charters** (907/224-5122 or 888/385-1312, www.profish-n-sea.com), **J-Dock Sportfishing** (907/224-3300, www. jdockcompany.com), and **Crackerjack Sportfishing Charters** (907/224-2606 or 800/566-3912, www.crackerjackcharters. com). **Miller's Landing** (907/224-5739 or 866/541-5739, www.millerslandingak.com) has fishing charters and also rents boats ($500 per day) for do-it-yourselfers. In addition, they rent fishing equipment, from rods and reels to dry bags, waders, and VHF marine radios. Miller's Landing is on Lowell Point, 2.5 miles south of Seward. **Seward Alaska Boat Rental** (907/362-0019, www. sewardakboatrental.com, $400 per day) also rents sportfishing boats.

Sea Kayaking

Most Resurrection Bay sea kayaking originates from the scenic **Lowell Point** area, three miles south of Seward. Four companies—Adventure 60 North, Kayak Adventures, Liquid Adventures, and Sunny Cove Sea Kayaking—offer three-hour paddles to **Tonsina Point** ($75-85) in Resurrection Bay, all-day kayak-and-hike trips to **Caines Head** ($135-150), and grand day tours to

remote Aialik Bay. **Aialik Bay** day trips ($400-425, including lunch) begin with a small boat to the Aialik Glacier or Holgate Glacier, followed by a day of paddling in the berg-filled glacial waters and a return trip to Seward 11 hours later. Whales, otters, sea lions, and other animals are commonly sighted en route to Aialik Bay. These popular trips sell out early, so be sure to book ahead. In addition, all four companies offer multi-day trips to Northwestern Fjords and Aialik Bay within Kenai Fjords National Park. Kayak trips are typically available mid-May to mid-September.

In addition to these paddles, **Kayak Adventures** (328 3rd Ave., 907/224-3960, www.kayakak.com) has eight-hour trips with a water taxi to Humpy Cove for a day of Resurrection Bay paddling that ends at Fox Island, where a water taxi returns you to Seward. This trip costs $199 pp. The company specializes in personalized trips; any of their trips are available as a private family adventure (minimum 3 people) for the same price.

Sunny Cove Sea Kayaking (1304 4th Ave., 907/224-4426, www.sunnycove.com) has very popular kayak-and-cruise trips ($210) to Fox Island aboard a Kenai Fjords tour boat followed by a paddle, salmon bake, and wildlife cruise back to town. Their office is adjacent to the small boat harbor.

Located along the road to Exit Glacier, **Adventure 60 North** (31872 Herman Leirer Rd., 907/224-2600, www.adventure60.com) rents outdoor gear such as tents, fishing gear, bikes, sleeping pads, bear spray, and even rubber boots. Adventure 60's most unusual offering combines a scenic helicopter flight to Bear Glacier followed by sea kayaking on the lake ($600 pp for 5 hours, $660 pp for 8 hours). Overnight camping trips ($925 pp) to the glacier are also available.

Backcountry Safaris (907/205-5900, www.backcountrysafaris.com) operates a "glamping" base camp called Bear Glacier Wilderness Retreat. It's near spectacular Bear Glacier, 15 miles south of Seward. This is the largest glacier in Kenai Fjords National Park, and is only accessible by water taxi during twice-daily high tides or by helicopter. Prices depend on the number of people in your group. Day trips include round-trip transportation, kayaks, dry suits, and guides; rates for two people are $330 pp by water taxi or $545 pp by helicopter. Because of tide restrictions, trips via water taxi may depart at odd hours and typically last 12 hours or more, while helicopter trips can be of any length. Overnight and multiple-night trips are a better option to really take in this area. A one-night trip includes helicopter flights, kayak tours, lodging in a heated WeatherPort shelter, meals, and guide for $785 pp (2-person minimum). The same trip for two nights and three days is $950 pp.

Liquid Adventures (907/224-9225, www.liquid-adventures.com) is a great choice for day trips to Bear Glacier (five-hours, $299 pp). The company has a powerful and speedy jet boat that transports up to six people at a time into the glacial lake. There, you'll don dry suits and climb into kayaks for a paddle among towering icebergs in front of Bear Glacier (you won't actually get close to the glacier itself due to the size of the lake). After stopping for hot chocolate and a snack, you'll then paddle back for your jet boat return to Seward. Guests can choose to use stand-up paddleboards (SUPs) instead of kayaks on these Bear Glacier trips, but kayaks are better if you want to take photos or just don't feel comfortable on an SUP. A helicopter option ($600 pp) gets you there quicker, but the jet boat ride is half the fun. Liquid Adventures also leads 10-hour water taxi and kayak trips to Northwestern Fjords or Holgate Arm ($379 pp).

Miller's Landing (Lowell Point, 907/224-5739 or 866/541-5739, www.millerslandingak.com) rents kayaks for experienced do-it-yourselfers, and provides kayaking day trips and instruction, along with water-taxi service to transport kayaks into remote parts of Kenai Fjords. A double kayak rents for $55 per day.

Kayakers Cove (907/224-2662, www.kayakerscove.com) is a unique and well-run operation a dozen miles from Seward.

Reasonably priced hostel-type lodging and kayak rentals are available, with access by water taxi from Miller's Landing.

Canoeing and Stand-Up Paddleboarding

Liquid Adventures (907/224-9225, www.liquid-adventures.com) leads stand-up paddleboarding day trips to Bear Glacier ($299 pp by water taxi, $600 pp by helicopter). These trips include a water-taxi or helicopter flight from Seward and several hours on stable, inflatable paddleboards. Clients wear dry suits and are able to paddle around the lagoon and up to icebergs. Liquid Adventures also has easy three-hour SUP paddles ($85 pp) to Tonsina Creek, a good place to view spawning salmon.

Adventure 60 North (31872 Herman Leirer Rd., 907/224-2600, www.adventure60.com) leads 3.5-hour canoe and kayak trips ($74 pp) to Bear Lake, a salmon-filled pond a few miles north of Seward.

Surfing

Alaska Surf Guides (907/519-0407, www.alaskasurfguides.com) provides a totally unique service—surfing pristine beaches near Seward. Access is by helicopter or plane, and the beach in front of Bear Glacier is a favorite destination. A six-hour guided surf trip is $629 pp (minimum 2 people), including wetsuit and surfboard. The company also offers stand-up paddleboard trips.

Water Taxis

Local water taxis include **Miller's Landing** (907/224-5739 or 866/541-5739, www.millerslandingak.com), **Weather Permitting** (907/224-6595, www.watertaxiak.com), **Seward Ocean Excursions** (907/599-0499, www.sewardoceanexcursions.com), and **Seward Water Taxi** (907/362-4101, www.sewardwatertaxi.com). These water taxis go to Fox Island ($75 pp round-trip), Bear Glacier ($220 pp round-trip), Aialik Bay ($340 pp round-trip), and other destinations within Kenai Fjords National Park.

Sailing

Sailors say Resurrection Bay contains some of the finest sailing waters north of San Francisco Bay, with windy conditions almost every day. Because of this, there are two local yacht clubs, **Kenai Fjords Yacht Club** (www.kfyc.org) and **William H. Seward Yacht Club** (www.whsyc.org), plus dozens of sailboats berthed in the Small Boat Harbor. Two companies have lessons if you want to learn to sail on your Alaskan vacation.

In business since 1975, **Sailing, Inc.** (907/224-3160, www.sailinginc.com, May-mid-Sept.) provides American Sailing Association-certified classes for both novices and experts, starting with a four-day intensive learn-to-sail class ($985 pp). Their six-day basic-to-bareboat sailing package ($1,595 pp) is popular with travelers since it includes three days living aboard the boat. Sailing Inc. also has bareboat charters for experienced sailors.

Seven Seas Sailing (907/965-1900, www.sailwith7.com) has multiday sailing trips from Seward. These all-inclusive trips start at $5,560 (2-4 guests) for a three-day trip.

Dogsledding and Glacier Tours

Turning Heads Kennel (31722 Herman Leirer Rd., 907/362-4354, www.turningheadskennel.com, $69 adults, $34 children) operates the dog teams on Godwin Glacier, but their home base is on the way to Exit Glacier. Ninety-minute tours include cart rides and information about the dogs. Co-owners Travis Beals and Sarah Stokey are both veterans of the Iditarod.

Alaska Backcountry Access (907/783-3600, www.alaskabackcountryaccess.com) operates from the same Godwin Glacier base as the dogsled tours, with one-hour snowmobile tours on the glacier. During that time you'll cover a lot of terrain, with dramatic views in all directions. These cost $539 pp and last 2.5 hours including the helicopter flight from Seward.

Veteran musher—and 2017 Iditarod winner—Mitch Seavey operates **Seavey's IdidaRide Sled Dog Tours** (12820 Old Exit Glacier Rd., 907/224-8607, www.ididaride.com, $74 adults, $37 children) from his home north of town. Summertime visitors are pulled on a wheeled cart along a two-mile route. These 1.5-hour tours include an introduction to the Iditarod and a chance to play with adorable husky puppies. Winter visitors can mush their own five-dog team to Exit Glacier (3.5 hours, $249 adults, $199 children). The Seavey family has become an Iditarod dynasty, with Mitch Seavey winning in 2004, 2013, and 2017, while his son Dallas Seavey won in 2012, 2014, 2015, and 2016. You aren't likely to meet either of the mushers on this tour since they train elsewhere.

Exit Glacier Guides (405 4th Ave., 907/224-5569, www.exitglacierguides.com) leads six-hour excursions onto Exit Glacier ($130 pp), as well as more adventurous eight-hour ice-climbing trips ($195 pp). For more excitement, join a helicopter ice hike: a flight to Godwin Glacier followed by the chance to hike on the glacier with your guide before flying back over the mountains to Seward ($350 pp for 2 hours on the ice, $395 pp for 3 hours).

Flightseeing

The Seward Airport is just north of town. It lacks scheduled flights, but air charters are available from **Seward Air Tours** (907/362-6205, www.sewardair.com, May-Sept.). Charter the plane for $637 one-way to Anchorage; it holds two passengers for this price. A 30-minute scenic flight to spectacular Bear Glacier costs $129 pp with a minimum of two people.

Seward Helicopter Tours (907/362-4354 or 888/476-5589, www.sewardhelicopters.com, late May-early Sept.) has flightseeing trips and on-the-snow summertime dogsledding trips. The action begins from Seward Airport, where you climb aboard a helicopter for a 10-minute flight to a world of snow, ice, and rocky peaks on crevice-free Godwin

1: kayakers in Resurrection Bay near Seward; 2: Stoney Creek Canopy Adventures zipline; 3: Seward's busy boat harbor

Glacier. The base camp here has 30 dogs and their handlers, including experienced Iditarod mushers Travis Beals and Sarah Stokey. Guests are given a tour of the operation, an introduction to mushing, a fun ride behind a team of dogs, and the chance to pose with a bundle of cute puppies. The entire trip lasts 1.5 hours and costs $519 pp. A shorter option ($199 pp) is a helicopter ride to the glacier and 15 minutes on the ice, but no sled ride.

Marathon Helicopters (907/224-3616, www.marathonhelicopters.com) has a variety of glacier trips and flightseeing, starting at just $75 pp (2-person minimum) for flights to the top of Mount Marathon.

Horseback Riding

Bardy's Trail Rides (Old Nash Rd., 907/224-7863, www.sewardhorses.com, May-Sept., $129 pp) leads two-hour horseback rides twice daily throughout the summer. This is a fun way to explore the scenic country at the head of Resurrection Bay, with chances to see bald eagles, moose, and spawning salmon.

Zip-Lining

Adrenaline junkies will love **Stoney Creek Canopy Adventures** (1304 4th Ave., 907/224-3662, www.stoneycreekca.com, late May-late Sept., $149 adults, $119 ages 10-14). A van takes adventurers from their harbor-side office to a wooded location a few miles north of town. After gearing up, there's a short training session followed by a steep 4WD ride uphill to your first zip traverse. The course includes eight zip lines, three suspension bridges, and two rappels, but the best one is a 1,200-foot-long traverse that sails over a pond before landing you at a platform 75 feet up a Sitka spruce tree. The guides take photos along the way for a keepsake of your canopy adventure.

FOOD
Coffee

Housed within an old Lutheran church, **Resurrect Art Coffeehouse Gallery** (320 3rd Ave., 907/224-7161, www.resurrectart.

com, 7am-6pm daily summer, 7am-5pm daily winter, under $8) is a pleasant place to hang out over an espresso on a rainy day, play a game of chess, check your email (free Wi-Fi), or listen to frequent live music. It's also one of the best Seward spots to buy Alaskan art, pottery, and jewelry.

Brunch

Built in 1917, the old Alaska Railroad train depot sits along the downtown waterfront near the SeaLife Center. Trains now stop close to the harbor, but the lovingly restored historic depot building is home to **Zudy's Café** (501 Railway Ave., 907/224-4710, www.zudyscafe. com, 8am-7pm daily June-Aug., 11am-2pm daily Sept.-May, $8-14). There's a small choice of breakfast standards. Sandwiches, paninis, soups, and salads fill the lunchtime offerings; try the Hammy Grammy panini with black forest ham, gouda, and green apples.

Housed in a vintage Alaska Railroad car close to the harbor, **Smoke Shack** (411 Port Ave., 907/224-7427, 8am-3pm daily, $11-30) serves the best breakfasts in Seward, with snow crab eggs benedict, biscuits and gravy, carmelitas, and chicken-fried steak. Lunch fare veers to New Mexico-inspired dishes, including pork green chili and smothered burritos and tacos. There are a few tables inside, along with picnic tables on the deck. The kitchen is tiny, so expect a long wait on summer weekends.

Asian

A delightful surprise in all-American Seward, **Woody's Thai Kitchen** (800 4th Ave., 907/422-0338, www. woodysthaikitchenseward.com, noon-9pm Tues.-Sun., $16-26) serves authentic Bangkok-style dishes. Popular favorites include Panang curry, curry noodle soup, and holy basil (with chicken, garlic, Thai basil, chili, bamboo shoots, and fried egg). Check for the day's specials or avoid the crowds with a to-go order. Woody's also has a big selection of beers and sake.

Seafood

The food had better be good when the sign out front of ★ **Thorn's Showcase Lounge** (208 4th Ave., 907/224-3700, 10am-11pm Sun.-Thurs., 10am-midnight Fri.-Sat., $13-36) proclaims "Home of the Bucket of Butt," and the interior is filled with ancient velvet furniture and big TVs. The "butt" in question is, of course, halibut, and this old bar—probably not remodeled since its 1971 opening—really does serve the best fish-and-chips in town. Get a big bowl of deep-fried halibut chunks with fries for $32, or a basket for $22. Bacon cheeseburgers, chicken tenders, steamer clams, and other pub fare are also available, along with full dinners of steak or halibut. It's hard to miss the lounge's remarkable collection of 525 historic Jim Beam bottles covering the walls (with hundreds more in the basement); it's said to be one of the largest in existence. If you're into drinks, Thorn's White Russians are the best in town.

Ray's Waterfront (1316 4th Ave., 907/224-5606, 11am-9pm Thurs.-Tues. mid-Apr.-Sept., $29-48), at the small boat harbor, is especially convenient for grabbing a bite while you wait for your tour boat (or for a hot toddy when you get back). Picture windows look out over the harbor, and house specialties include seafood such as king crab cakes, cioppino, and macadamia-crusted halibut, but steaks are also popular. Ray's main problem is its popularity, so reservations are strongly recommended—especially on summer weekends.

A few doors up the street is **Chinooks Waterfront Grill** (1404 4th Ave., 907/224-2207, www.chinookswaterfront.com, 11:30am-10pm daily, $18-55), with two levels fronting the harbor and a menu of local seafood. This is the place to go for fresh-from-the-sea Alaskan fish. Halibut is always a good choice, whether it's ale-and-herb-battered fish-and-chips or linguine with salmon. Locals also love the scallop mac and cheese, handcrafted burgers, and steaks.

North of town on the way to the glacier, **Exit Glacier Salmon Bake** (31832 Herman Leirer Rd., 907/224-2204, www.sewardalaskacabins.com, 7am-10am and 5pm-10pm daily mid-May-mid-Sept., $13-24) is exceptionally popular with travelers, serving baked sockeye salmon dinners, along with fish tacos, halibut, steaks, king crab, and burgers in a wooded family-friendly setting. The restaurant's motto, not entirely correct, I hope, is "Cheap beer and lousy food."

A cozy downtown restaurant with a farm-to-table focus, ★ **The Cookery** (209 5th Ave., 907/422-7459, www.cookeryseward.com, 5pm-10pm daily mid-May-early Sept., reduced hours early Sept.-mid-May, $12-27) showcases the mastery of chef Kevin Lane. Start with fresh Kachemak Bay oysters followed by small plates of roasted brussels sprouts or delicious mushroom toast. Signature entrées include spicy fried chicken, smoked beef brisket, and a homemade super-veggie burger. Save room for an amazing cream cheese ice cream with fresh strawberries.

Brewpub

With its convenient downtown location, convivial brewpub atmosphere, and tasty food, ★ **Seward Brewing Company** (139 4th Ave., 907/422-0337, www.sewardbrewery.com, 11:30am-10pm daily mid-May-mid-Sept., $14-27) is a sure bet. Start with a plate of wings or fish tacos, and follow up with a killer burger or fish and fries. Burgers are served on homemade pretzel-bread buns with a big stack of fries. Save room for an ice cream sandwich like no other, with a triple chocolate cookie, vanilla ice cream, salted caramel, and a potato chip crust. Head upstairs to enjoy a separate pizza-and-salads menu and tall second-floor windows facing Resurrection Bay. A dozen brewery-made beers are available on tap or in to-go growlers. The food is a bit expensive—$17 for a burger—but worth it.

Sweets

Housed within the historic Brown & Hawkins Store, **Sweet Darlings** (205 4th Ave., 907/224-3011, www.sweetdarlings.com, 11am-9pm Mon.-Sat., 1pm-8pm Sun., $6-7) will be a hit with your sweet tooth, featuring wonderful homemade gelato, truffles, fudge, malts, shakes, and other treats.

ACCOMMODATIONS

Seward has plenty of indoor lodging options, but be sure to book ahead in the summer, especially around July 4 (for the Mount Marathon Race) and any weekend in August when the Silver Salmon Derby attracts throngs of visitors and fills every room for miles around. Lodging rates often double for the Mount Marathon Race. The city of Seward hits travelers with an 11 percent tax.

Hostels

Right downtown, **Moby Dick Hostel & Lodging** (432 3rd Ave., 907/224-7072, www.mobydickhostel.com, May-Sept., dorm rooms $27 pp, private rooms $75-85 d, larger units $95) has clean dorm-style units with kitchen facilities and showers. There are also three simple private rooms with queen beds, along with two nicer units containing kitchenettes.

Nauti Otter (13609 Seward Hwy., 907/491-2255, www.nautiotterinn.com, mid-May-early Sept., hostel $35 pp, rooms $124 d, cabins $55-124 d, trailers $99, yurt $129 d) is a bit difficult to explain. Owners Heather and Clint Davis operate two separate places: the original Nauti Otter (rooms, cabins, yurt, and hostel) and Nauti Otter Yurt Village (yurts), a mile away. The Nauti Otter location is six miles north of Seward and consists of three private rooms, six funky cabins, two vintage trailers, one yurt, and a cramped low-ceilinged six-bed hostel room. A bath and shower are indoors and the cabins share a separate flushable outhouse (toilet in an outhouse) and shower. A paved bike path provides access to town, and bike rentals are available. There's free Wi-Fi and guests can borrow fishing gear and boots. All guests have access to the kitchen, stocked with ingredients for a filling breakfast: eggs, cereal, milk, and waffles.

Adventurous travelers should check out **Kayakers Cove** (907/224-8662, www.kayakerscove.com, late May-early Sept., hostel $25 pp, cabin $75 for up to 3 people), on a small bay near Fox Island, 12 water miles from Seward. Rustic wilderness hostel-type lodging and a private cabin are available, with access to a full kitchen, a wood-fired sauna, and kayak rentals (doubles $25 pp per day). Kayakers Cove doesn't have showers, and you'll need to rent bedding ($5) or bring a sleeping bag. Access is by water taxi ($65 pp round-trip).

Hotels and Motels

Located in the center of town and decked out with stuffed critters, the **Hotel Seward** (221 5th Ave., 907/224-8001 or 800/440-2444, www.hotelsewardalaska.com, $145 d shared bath, $185 d private bath, $275-325 d deluxe rooms) has a variety of rooms for all budgets. The historic section (no elevator) contains economy guest rooms with two single beds and a bath down the hall. Standard guest rooms with private baths are in the older section. Deluxe rooms in the modern Alaska wing of the hotel are large and nicely appointed. A restaurant and lounge are on the premises.

Just two blocks from the boat harbor, **Murphy's Alaskan Inn** (909 4th Ave., 907/224-8090, www.murphysmotel.com, May-Sept., $159-199 d) provides a no-frills mix of older guest rooms and larger units with harbor views and balconies. All rooms contain fridges and microwaves.

Opened in 1916 and now on the National Register of Historic Places, the **Van Gilder Hotel** (308 Adams St., 907/224-3079, www.vangilderseward.com, late May-early Sept., $139 d shared bath, $169-189 d private bath, $259 suites) is a classic hotel just two blocks from the Alaska SeaLife Center. Small rooms feature brass beds and antiques, along with flat-screen TVs, Wi-Fi, and access to a kitchenette with a microwave and a refrigerator, but the lack of an elevator can be a challenge in this three-story structure. There are standard rooms with a queen bed and three budget "pension rooms" that share a bath down the hall. Families appreciate the four suites, each featuring a main room with a queen bed plus a connecting room with a queen bed and twin murphy bed; suites accommodate up to five guests. Guests occasionally report hearing or seeing the ghostly apparition of Fannie Guthry-Baehm; she died in room 209 after being shot by her husband in 1950.

Directly across the street from the Small Boat Harbor, clean and comfortable 100-room **Breeze Inn Hotel** (303 N. Harbor Dr., 907/224-5237 or 888/224-5237, www. breezeinn.com, $189 d, newer units $249-299 d) has two-double-bed standard rooms (no view) and newer units with limited harbor or mountain views. There are large flat-screen TVs and in-room fridges, plus a spacious lobby and summer-only shuttle service.

It's hard to beat the harbor-side location of **Harbor 360 Hotel** (1412 4th Ave., 907/865-6224, www.harbor360hotel.com, $349 d mountain-facing rooms, $394 d harbor-facing rooms, $444 d deluxe rooms), which also has a small indoor pool (the only one in town), a hot tub, a breakfast buffet, and a business center. This 91-unit hotel has modern guest rooms, each with two queens or one king bed; ask for a waterside room with a balcony. A summertime shuttle is available to the SeaLife Center. The hotel is owned by Major Marine Tours, and discount packages are available that combine lodging and a boat tour. Harbor 360 Hotel is especially popular with people getting ready to head out on (or getting off) a cruise vacation. It makes a fine place to overnight and explore the Seward area.

Fittingly located across from the railroad station, **Whistle Stop Lodging** (411 Port Ave., 907/224-2323, www.sewardak.net/ ws, mid-May-mid-Sept., $150 d) provides a fun opportunity to overnight in a vintage Alaska Railroad car from the World War II era. Originally used as a sleeping car, it was converted into a two-room lodging place with baths, microwaves, and fridges. Windows look out on the harbor. Also in the railroad cars is Smoke Shack, with the best local breakfast.

Popular with cruise ship travelers, **Seward Windsong Lodge** (Mile 0.5, Exit Glacier Rd., 800/808-8068, www.sewardwindsong.com,

$289-359) has a quiet location on the road to Exit Glacier. Hotel rooms are in 18 buildings set amid the trees behind the main lodge. The 216 units are comfortable and well kept, with premium rooms, queen beds, private decks, Wi-Fi, and TV. Resurrection Roadhouse Restaurant (three meals a day) is on the premises, or you can walk 0.25 miles down the road to Exit Glacier Salmon Bake. There's a free shuttle to Seward from the hotel.

Bed-and-Breakfasts

Seward has dozens of bed-and-breakfasts. The visitors information center has rack cards from most of these, and its website (www. seward.com) provides links, or give **Point of View Reservation Service** (907/224-2323, www.alaskasview.com) a call to book a good B&B.

Perhaps the finest B&B in Seward, ★ **Bell in the Woods** (13881 Bruno Rd., 907/491-0757, www.bellinthewoodsalaska.com, rooms $200-225 d, apartment suites $250-350) is a luxurious Scandinavian-style home on a quiet street just north of town. The B&B has three guest rooms and a suite upstairs, along with two apartment suites with kitchenettes below. The Mount Marathon king suite provides the most sumptuous accommodations. All rooms include private baths plus access to the expansive back deck, complete with a push-button gas fire pit. There are no TVs in the upstairs rooms, but a media room is available. Three-course gourmet breakfasts are included. Owners Brooke and Nick Degnan go out of their way to provide details on where to go and what to do in the area.

Blending Asian and Scandinavian sensibilities, **Soo's B&B** (810 2nd Ave., 907/224-3207 or 888/967-7667, www.soosbandb.com, $145 d) was designed by owner Soo Kang's architect son. Four bright guest rooms are available and include a full breakfast, private baths, TVs, and even freezer space for your fish.

Located at Lowell Point, 2.5 miles south of town, **Alaska Saltwater Lodge** (Lowell Point, 907/224-5271, www.alaskasaltwaterlodge.com, mid-May-mid-Sept., $359 d, $410 for 4 guests) is right on Resurrection Bay, with a sandy beach and striking vistas. This two-bedroom cottage features an upstairs turret, a deck overlooking the bay, a full kitchen, a bath, a living room, and a deck with a grill. The owners also operate a water taxi for customized small-group whale-watching tours.

Bear Lake Lodgings B&B (33820 Bear Lake Rd., 907/224-2288, www. bearlakelodgings.com, $195 d shared bath, $250-300 d suites) is six miles north of town along this quiet and pristine lake. Two guest rooms share a bath, while the two suites have private baths. A big breakfast is served in the 2nd-floor dining room, and the owners are famous for their hand-dipped ice cream bars, served each evening; they run the popular Original Gourmet Ice Cream Bar stand at the Alaska State Fair. Guests can borrow a canoe or kayak to explore the lake, or listen to the loons calling each evening. In the winter, the lake is groomed for cross-country skiing right out your door.

A modern home across from the beach at Lowell Point, ★ Alaska Paddle Inn (13745 Beach Dr., 907/362-2628, www. alaskapaddleinn.com, Mar.-Oct., rooms $199 d, house $289-364 d, additional guests $25 pp), has two very nice rooms with a good view of the bay. Owners Alan and Alison Heavirland are former kayaking guides with an affinity and strong knowledge of the outdoors. Alan's carpentry skills are exhibited in the artistically designed rooms, and Alison (a licensed massage therapist) offers massage services at the inn. Both units include kitchenettes stocked with breakfast ingredients, gas fireplaces, and private baths. The upstairs suite has a king bed, and the downstairs unit includes a separate bedroom with a queen bed, plus a futon couch. Families and groups will appreciate the Spruce House, a modern 1,500-square-foot custom home with two bedrooms, two baths, a full kitchen, a deck, a living room, and laundry. It sleeps eight comfortably and has its own private beach. There's a two-night minimum for both places.

Just a few blocks from the harbor, Bear's Den B&B (221 Bear Dr., 907/224-3788, www. bearsdenalaska.com, May-Oct., $195-215 d, additional guests $20 pp) has three lodging options, all with private baths, decks or patios, and TVs. The largest unit sleeps six and includes a full kitchen and a private entrance, but no breakfast. Breakfast ingredients are provided in the smaller units.

Sourdough Sunrise B&B (11837 Old Exit Glacier Rd., 907/224-3600, www. sourdoughsunrise.com, $200 d) is notable for the artistic woodwork both inside and outside this unique building. The custom home is three miles north of town on six acres of wooded land. Its three guest rooms include queen beds, TVs, and outdoor decks, plus a breakfast of sourdough pancakes; the sourdough starter has been in use for more than 110 years. Rates drop substantially for multiple-night stays.

Not far away is Steller B&B (11952 Old Exit Glacier Rd., 907/224-7294, www.stellerbandb. com, $109-149 d), with economical and immaculate rooms that share a bath and more luxurious ones with private baths and decks along a salmon stream. Continental breakfast ingredients are provided in each room.

Cabins and Suites

★ Alaska Creekside Cabins (11886 Old Exit Glacier Rd., 907/224-1996, www. welovealaska.com, mid-May-mid-Sept., cabins $125-260 d, additional guests $15 pp) consists of nine in-the-woods cabins north of town on the road to Exit Glacier. All contain fridges, microwaves, TVs, and a fire pit out front; the largest has space for five. The cabins share a modern bathhouse with showers. Clear Creek flows through the property, providing spawning habitat for chum salmon, and they in turn often attract brown bears. The cabins are rustic, but clean and authentically Alaskan, with a super friendly owner. Also available is a three-bedroom house that sleeps six ($395, 2-night minimum).

Situated up the hill behind Seward, the appropriately named A Cabin on the Cliff

(1104 Hulm Lane, 907/224-2411 or 800/440-2444, www.acabinonthecliff.com, $375 d) provides a unique perspective of Resurrection Bay. Originally a trapper's cabin, this adorable log cabin has an antique brass bed, a fireplace, a kitchenette, and a large private deck where a gazebo encloses the hot tub.

A quarter mile off Seward Highway, **Exit Glacier Lodge** (31832 Herman Leirer Rd., 907/224-6040, www.sewardalaskalodging.com, mid-May-mid-Sept., $169 d, suite $205 d, cabins $119-129, additional guests $15 pp) provides modern hotel rooms in a quaint Victorian-style false-front building that is also home to Exit Glacier Salmon Bake. Fifteen guest rooms have private baths, fridges, and TVs. The 2nd-floor suite has its own balcony, king and queen beds, and a leather sofa. Nearby are the four Salmon Bake Cabins, each with a queen and a bunk bed, a bath, a microwave, a fridge, and TV.

Located in a secluded forest setting a mile from Seward Highway, **Box Canyon Cabins** (31515 Lois Way, 907/224-5046, www.boxcanyoncabin.com, 1-bedroom $189 d, 2-bedroom $279-299, extra guests $15 pp) consists of six very nice log cabins, each with full kitchens (breakfast ingredients provided), private baths, and TVs. There are one-bedroom and two-bedroom cabins; the latter sleep four. Laundry facilities are on the premises.

Located on Fox Island and accessible only by boat, **Kenai Fjords Wilderness Lodge** (Fox Island, 907/224-8068 or 800/808-8068, www.alaskacollection.com, June-early Sept.) sits in the heart of Resurrection Bay. Guests stay in eight modern duplex or fourplex cabins facing the bay or a small lagoon and enjoy gourmet family-style meals at the lodge. There are no electrical outlets in the cabins and no Wi-Fi (it's nice to get away from the web occasionally), but the main lodge has electricity. Once the daily tour boats leave, this is a delightfully quiet place, with less than 20 guests at a time. The lodge is only available for two-night stays for two people ($2,680). The excursion includes lodging, gourmet meals, a special culinary program, guided kayaking, and an all-day boat tour into Northwestern Fjord. Due to its popularity and limited space, the lodge fills far in advance. Call a year ahead for July and August dates.

★ **Angel's Rest on Resurrection Bay** (13730 Beach Dr., 907/224-7378 or 866/713-7378, www.angelsrest.com, $240 d, suites $270 d, cabins $280-300 d) encompasses a variety of delightful lodging options in the Lowell Point area south of town. They include three modern waterfront cabins, two guest rooms, and two mini-suites, all with queen beds, private baths, kitchenettes, and barbecue grills.

Yurts

Yurts are a popular lodging option around Seward, with four vastly different offerings available. Yurts are comfortable and cozy, though it does take time to adjust to the curved walls.

Six miles north of town near Bear Lake, **Sourdough Sue's Bear Lake Lodging** (33910 Tressler Ave., 907/202-2117, www.sourdoughsue.com, May-Sept., smaller yurts $179 d, larger yurt $260 for 4 people, 2-night minimum) has three modern yurts, each with heat, a private bath, queen and futon beds, and a covered porch with a gas grill. Two sleep up to six and have kitchenettes, while a third larger yurt encloses two bedrooms and a full kitchen and sleeps up to eight. Banana bread, juices, and coffee are provided. There are no TVs, but Wi-Fi is available.

Seven miles north of Seward, ★ **Nauti Otter Yurt Village** (33395 Winterset Circle, 907/491-2255, www.nautiotterinn.com, mid-May-early Sept., yurts $135 d, cabin $204 d) consists of 11 Alaskan-made yurts in a quiet woodsy setting. Most yurts contain one queen bed, but three yurts have two bunk beds. There's also a separate cabin with a private restroom and a kitchen. The yurts are set beneath tall Sitka spruce trees and short paths link to a covered pavilion with baths, showers, a cooking area stocked with breakfast fixings (waffles, coffee, and more), a refrigerator, a barbecue grill, and picnic tables. The fire pit

is a fun place to chat with fellow travelers, pull out a musical instrument, tip back a beer, or roast marshmallows. Owners Heather and Clint Davis also operate the original Nauti Otter (rooms, cabins, and hostel), one mile closer to Seward, and can direct you to off-the-beaten-path sights in the area.

Close to the beach at Lowell Point is a large yurt at **Alaska Base Camp** (14000 Beach Dr., 907/224-4692, www.alaskabasecamp.com, mid-May-Sept., $200 d, additional guests $25). Inside are two queen beds, a kitchenette, a private bath, a deck with a barbecue grill, and Wi-Fi. Otters and bald eagles are commonly sighted from the deck.

Nine miles southeast of town in Humpy Cove, ★ **Orca Island Cabins** (Orca Island, 907/362-9014 or 888/494-5846, www.orcaislandcabins.com, mid-May-mid-Sept., $350 d) provides an incredible way to get in touch with your wild side; whales, otters, seals, and sea lions are often spotted from the cabins. Three surprisingly comfortable 20-foot yurts perch along the shore of this small island, connected to each other by elevated boardwalks. Four other yurts are on the mainland across a beautiful 80-foot arched footbridge. Each yurt has a waterside deck with Adirondack chairs, a queen bed and a futon, a kitchenette, a private bath, a heater, and a grill. Co-owner Susan Swiderski is an accomplished artist, and her works are on display in a separate gallery on the island. The owners emphasize an eco-friendly "glamping" experience, with on-demand hot showers, composting toilets, and other green features. The lodging cost includes round-trip water taxi from Seward. Rates drop if you stay extra days, and guests have access to kayaks, a rowing skiff, firewood, and fishing gear. Cell phone service is spotty, and don't come here expecting to surf the web. Kids under age 12 are not allowed for safety reasons. Highly recommended!

1: Kenai Fjords Wilderness Lodge on Fox Island; 2: Bell in the Woods B&B; 3: lunchtime sandwich at Zudy's Café; 4: RV camping at Waterfront Park

Camping

City officials provide a long stretch of crowded year-round camping at **Waterfront Park** (Ballaine Blvd., 907/224-4055, www.cityofseward.us, tents $10, RVs $20, with hookups $40) along the shore, with toilets, coin showers ($2), picnic shelters, beautiful views, free Wi-Fi, and lots of company—there are 450 sites. Two miles north of town, the city's **Forest Acres Campground,** (tents $10, RVs $20, with hookups $40) features large trees and some highway noise. Advance reservations are not required for city campgrounds; credit cards are accepted at registration kiosks.

Six miles north of town, **Stoney Creek RV Park** (off Stoney Creek Ave., 907/224-6465 or 877/437-6366, www.stoneycreekrvpark.com, late May-early Sept., $40-45) is a full-service RV campground (no tents) with Wi-Fi, satellite TV, showers, and laundry. The quiet setting includes 15 acres of well-maintained grounds.

Miller's Landing Campground (907/331-3113, www.millerslandingak.com, year-round, tents $27, RVs $37 with electricity) has RV and tent spaces in the Lowell Point area. This rough-around-the-edges campground contains oceanfront and wooded sites, laundry facilities, coin showers, Wi-Fi, a fish cleaning area, and a small store. The sites are a bit tight, and noise can be an issue if your neighbors are up late. Fishing charters, kayak rentals, and water-taxi services are available through Miller's Landing.

The National Park Service's **Exit Glacier Campground** (907/422-0500, www.nps.gov/kefj, free) has a dozen walk-in tent sites 11 miles from town, just a short distance from the glacier. There's also a bear-proof food locker and modern cooking shelter, but no cell phone coverage. The campground often fills by early evening in mid-summer.

INFORMATION AND SERVICES

Shower up at the **Harbormaster Building** (907/224-3138, $2) or the city campground

Side Trip into Chugach National Forest

Tern Lake

Much of the eastern Kenai Peninsula lies within Chugach National Forest, the second-largest national forest in the country after the Tongass. Covering 5.5 million acres—bigger than Massachusetts—the Chugach not only encompasses this part of the Kenai but also continues eastward across all of Prince William Sound and well beyond the Copper River. Developments and logging are relatively minor on the Chugach, but all this wild country provides incredible opportunities for recreation, with good fishing, hiking, mountain biking, river rafting, skiing, kayaking, wildlife-watching, glacier-gazing, and a host of other outdoor adventures. The **forest headquarters** (3301 C. St., 907/743-9500, www.fs.usda.gov/chugach) are in Anchorage, with district offices in Seward (907/224-3374), Girdwood (907/783-3242), and Cordova (907/424-7661).

CABINS AND CAMPING

The Kenai Peninsula has 18 U.S. Forest Service **public-use cabins** (518/885-3639 or 877/444-6777, www.recreation.gov, $75 plus $10 reservation fee). These are mostly Pan-Abode log structures that sleep four and have wood or oil stoves. Most of these are along hiking trails—including eight cabins on the Resurrection Pass Trail—but a few are accessible only by floatplane. The Chugach website has cabin details, or you can get brochures from the Alaska Public Lands Information Center in Anchorage. Because of their great popularity, it's wise to reserve cabins well ahead of your visit. Additional public cabins can be found within Kenai Fjords National Park and Kachemak Bay State Park.

Six U.S. Forest Service campgrounds are located along the Seward Highway south of Portage, with another four along the Sterling Highway and two more off the Hope Highway.

HIKING

A number of very popular hiking trails cover the eastern half of the Kenai Peninsula, and it's possible to hike (or mountain bike) all the way from the town of Hope to Exit Glacier near Seward, a distance of 74 miles. Contact the U.S. Forest Service for details on various hiking options within the Chugach.

at the foot of Madison Street. There's a **swimming pool** at the high school (2001 Swetmann Ave., 907/224-3900), where they throw in a free swim with your shower. Wash your clothes at the expensive **Suds-N-Swirl** (335 3rd Ave., 907/224-3111, 8am-10pm daily).

For medical emergencies, head to **Providence Seward Medical Center** (417 1st Ave., 907/224-5205, www.providence.org).

The **Seward Community Library** (6th Ave. and Adams St., 907/224-4082, www.cityofseward.net/library, 10am-6pm Mon. and Fri.-Sat., 10am-8pm Tues.-Thurs.) provides a welcome escape on a rainy day. Free computers and Wi-Fi are available.

Parking is often a challenge in Seward, particularly near the harbor. There's a two-hour maximum for parking next to the harbor if you can find a space, and many visitors have returned from Resurrection Bay trips to find an expensive parking ticket affixed to their windshield. Avoid this by parking a block away at the big lots where the cost is $10 per day. If you're heading out for the day, boat tour companies provide free lots with shuttle buses back to the harbor; ask for details when you make reservations.

Visitors Centers

For Seward maps and brochures, start out at the **Seward Chamber of Commerce Visitor Center** (907/224-8051, www.seward. com, 9am-5pm Mon.-Sat., 10am-4pm Sun. mid-May-Aug., 10am-4pm Mon.-Fri. Sept.-mid-May), located two miles north of town. It's one of the first places you pass as you're driving into Seward from Anchorage.

Adjacent to the harbor, **Kenai Fjords National Park Information Center** (1212 4th Ave., 907/422-0500, www.nps.gov/kefj, 8:30am-7pm daily late May-early Sept., 9am-5pm daily early May and Sept.) has videos of the park, along with maps and publications of local interest. Park rangers provide daily talks at the SeaLife Center downtown as well as daily hikes from the Exit Glacier Visitor Center, just north of town out Exit Glacier Road.

The staff at **Chugach National Forest Seward Ranger District** office (334 4th Ave., 907/224-3374, www.fs.usda.gov/chugach, 8am-5pm Mon.-Fri.) can tell you about all regional hikes, campgrounds, and cabins.

GETTING THERE

The Alaska Marine Highway ferry doesn't stop in Seward; the closest ports are Whittier and Homer.

Train

An **Alaska Railroad** *Coastal Classic* train (907/265-2494 or 800/544-0552, www.alaskarailroad.com, mid-May-mid-Sept., $172 adults, $86 children one-way) leaves Anchorage daily during summer at 6:45am and arrives in Seward at 11:05am. It departs Seward at 6pm, arriving in Anchorage at 10:15pm. For the deluxe version, **GoldStar** double-decker coaches ($351 adults, $203 children one-way) include second-level window seats, with meals and beer or wine included.

Bus

Seward Bus Lines (907/563-0800 or 888/420-7788, www.sewardbuslines.net) provides year-round bus service to Seward. The 9:30am departure to Seward ($65) includes a sightseeing tour; the 2pm departure ($50) doesn't stop en route. Buses stop in Anchorage (1130 West International Airport Way) and can take you directly to your hotel for an extra $5. In Seward, buses stop at the cruise ship dock.

The **Stage Line** (907/235-2252, www.stagelineinhomer.com, Mon.-Fri. May-early Sept.) runs vans connecting Seward with Homer ($100) and Soldotna ($70). Drivers can pick up or drop off passengers almost anywhere along the route.

Park Connection (907/245-0200 or 800/266-8625, www.alaskacoach.com, mid-May-mid-Sept.) has buses connecting Seward with Anchorage ($65), Talkeetna ($130), and Denali ($155); children under age 11 ride for half price. Park Connection buses only stop in Seward on days when cruise ships are in port.

GETTING AROUND

The city's **Seward Shuttle** (www.cityofseward.us, 10am-7pm daily mid-May-late Sept., free) runs from downtown to the harbor, cruise ship terminal, train station, and other locations. Buses circulate every half hour.

Rent a car from **Hertz** (907/224-4378 or 800/654-3131, www.sewardhertz.com), or catch a ride with **Resurrection Taxi** (907/224-5678, www.resurrectiontaxi.com) or

PJ's Taxi (907/224-5555, www.pjstaxi.com). It costs $5 around town or $15 from the harbor to Lowell Point (more if the road is in bad condition).

Exit Glacier Shuttle (907/224-5569, www.exitglaciershuttle.com, $15 pp round-trip) provides an hourly shuttle service from Seward to Exit Glacier throughout summer. It departs from both downtown and the small boat harbor.

Kenai Fjords National Park

Kenai Fjords National Park covers 580,000 acres of ice, rock, and rugged coastline on the southern end of the Kenai Peninsula. The centerpiece of this magnificent national park is the Harding Icefield, a massive expanse of ice and snow broken only by nunataks—the peaks of high rocky mountains. The icefield pushes out in all directions in the form of more than 30 named glaciers. Along the coast, eight of these glaciers reach the sea, creating a thundering display of calving icebergs. Kenai Fjords has only been a national park since 1980, but today it is one of the most popular attractions in Alaska. Many visitors come to ride the tour boats past teeming bird colonies or up to tidewater glaciers; many others hike to scenic Exit Glacier or up a steep path to the edge of Harding Icefield itself.

Next to the Seward harbor is **Kenai Fjords National Park Information Center** (907/422-0500, www.nps.gov/kefj, 9am-7pm daily late May-early Sept., closed early Sept.-late May). Inside are exhibits on Harding Icefield and little-known sights within the park.

The best way to see Kenai Fjords National Park is on board a tour boat. Departures are from the Seward harbor throughout summer.

TOP EXPERIENCE

★ EXIT GLACIER

One of Alaska's most accessible glaciers, Exit Glacier has a pretty setting, plus a mix of hiking trails, nearby campsites, and guided glacier hikes. This is the only part of the park that is accessible by road. Get to Exit Glacier by driving four miles north from Seward and turning left at the sign. The road ends nine miles later at a big parking lot. The glacier has been retreating rather shockingly in recent years—sometimes more than 180 feet in a single year—and areas that were under ice just a decade ago are now sprouting plants. President Obama used the Exit Glacier as a backdrop during his 2015 visit, to bring attention to dramatic changes as Alaska's climate warms.

Exit Glacier Nature Center (907/422-0500, www.nps.gov/kefj, 9am-5pm daily late May-early Sept.)—the only one in Alaska powered by fuel cells—houses interpretive displays and a natural history bookstore. Rangers offer programs and lead one-hour nature walks four times daily, along with half-day hikes to Marmot Meadows daily in July-August. Note that cell phones will not work in the Exit Glacier area.

Exit Glacier Guides (405 4th Ave., 907/224-5569, www.exitglacierguides.com) leads six-hour excursions onto Exit Glacier

($130 pp), as well as more adventurous eight-hour ice-climbing trips ($195 pp). For more excitement, join a helicopter ice hike: a flight to Godwin Glacier followed by the chance to hike on the glacier with your guide before flying back over the mountains to Seward (2 hours on the ice $350 pp, 3 hours $395 pp). The company also guides hikes to Exit Glacier and Harding Icefield.

Exit Glacier Shuttle (907/224-5569, www.exitglaciershuttle.com, $15 pp round-trip) provides an hourly shuttle service from Seward to Exit Glacier throughout summer.

Hiking

A one-mile round-trip **nature trail** provides an easy, quiet forest walk. Two paths break off from it: **Glacier's Edge Trail** climbs a steep 0.25 miles up to the 150-foot face of Exit Glacier; a second path, **Toe of the Glacier Trail,** crosses the rocky outwash plain where you'll probably need to wade an icy-cold creek or two (use caution) to reach the end of the glacier. Don't get too close, since the glacier can calve without warning.

Harding Icefield Trail, seven miles round-trip, forks off just after the bridge over the creek and climbs to 3,500 feet and to the icefield. Plan on at least six hours for this far more difficult hike, and check at the ranger station for current trail conditions since deep snow may block this route until midsummer. In the winter, the road into Exit Glacier is not plowed but is very popular with skiers and snowmobilers.

The 16-mile **Resurrection River Trail** starts at Mile 8 of the Exit Glacier Road. This is the southern end of the 74-mile three-trail system from Kenai's top to bottom. Resurrection River Trail leads to the 16-mile Russian Lakes Trail, which hooks up near Cooper Landing to the 38-mile Resurrection Pass Trail to Hope. The Forest Service's **Trout Lake cabin** (518/885-3639 or 877/444-6777, www.recreation.gov, $75 plus $10 reservation fee) is seven miles from the trailhead. Note that the Resurrection River Trail can become quite a quagmire when it rains, and it may be poorly maintained beyond the cabin; most folks simply hike to the cabin and then turn around. The trail is popular with cross-country skiers in wintertime because of its relatively low avalanche danger; it doesn't go into the alpine at all.

CAMPING AND CABINS

The excellent **Exit Glacier Campground** (907/422-0500, free) has a dozen walk-in

Exit Glacier has retreated rapidly in the last several decades.

tent sites just a short distance from the glacier. There's also a bear-proof food locker and modern cooking shelter. The campground often fills by early evening in July and August. There's no cell phone coverage here.

The Park Service (www.nps.gov/kefj) maintains two exceptionally popular public-use cabins within Kenai Fjords. **Aialik Bay Cabin** sits along a long cobblestone beach with direct views across to Aialik Glacier. It's a fine base for kayaking expeditions. **Holgate Arm Cabin** occupies a small bluff where you can watch the thunderous calving of Holgate Glacier or kayak to Pedersen Lagoon. Each cabin sleeps four, with a heating stove but no outhouse. You'll need to use "Wag Bags" for human waste; yes, *everything* has to be packed out! Access to the cabins is by water taxi from Seward.

The cost for each cabin is $75, with a three-night maximum stay, and they're available only mid-May-mid-September. Reserve far ahead for these extremely popular cabins (877/444-6777, www.recreation.gov). Bookings are available on January 1 for the summer season, and nearly all the spaces for the cabins fill up by the end of April.

During the winter, the National Park Service rents the **Willow Cabin** (near Exit Glacier, 907/422-0500, $50). To get to this cabin, ski the eight easy miles from the highway along unplowed Exit Glacier Road. There is also a second enclosed winter-use structure nearby that is used as a warming shelter.

Private Lodges

★ **Kenai Fjords Glacier Lodge** (907/783-2928 or 800/334-8730, www.kenaifjordsglacierlodge.com, late May-early Sept., 1 night and 2 days $850 pp, 2 nights and 3 days $1,650 pp) is tucked into a spectacular spot close to Pedersen Glacier along remote Aialik Bay. Located on an inholding of Native Alaskan land, this is the only lodge inside the park. There's a main lodge, 16 cabins (two double beds, private baths, heat, and a small porch), plus guided kayak trips and beach hikes. Guests are treated to striking views of Pedersen Glacier and Pedersen Lagoon from the cabins and the lodge deck. Family-style meals are served in the main lodge, and all meals are included, along with round-trip boat transport from Seward. Though shorter visits are possible, to really enjoy the remarkable setting, book a three-day, two-night visit (or longer). There is no cell phone coverage or Wi-Fi in this remote spot. This is an incredible place to splurge!

Backcountry Safaris (907/205-5900, www.backcountrysafaris.com) has a less ostentatious glamping operation called Bear Glacier Wilderness Retreat. It's on state land adjacent to Bear Glacier, 15 miles south of Seward. This is the largest glacier in Kenai Fjords National Park, with access by helicopter. A one-night trip ($785 pp, 2-person minimum) includes helicopter flights, kayak tours, lodging in a heated WeatherPort shelter, meals, and a guide. The same trip for two nights and three days is $950 pp. Day trips are also offered.

Northwestern Kenai Peninsula

The northwestern end of the Kenai Peninsula is accessible via the **Sterling Highway,** which joins the Seward Highway 37 miles north of Seward and 90 miles south of Anchorage. The mileposts along the Sterling also start counting at 37 from this point. The Sterling Highway heads west through Cooper Landing and Soldotna, then south all the way to Homer, a total of 142 miles from the junction.

Pretty **Tern Lake** sits at the junction of the Seward and Sterling Highways. Pull off to watch the arctic terns, trumpeter swans, beavers, muskrat, and other critters.

EAST TO COOPER LANDING
Recreation
Alaska Horsemen Trail Adventures (35090 Quartz Creek Rd., 907/595-1806, www.alaskahorsemen.com) leads trail rides into the scenic country around Resurrection Trail and Cooper Landing. Most popular are four-hour trips ($229 pp) into the Chugach National Forest backcountry, but shorter trips are available, including a two-hour ride ($149). For a real adventure, book a multiple-night wilderness pack trip. Alaska Horsemen also has three cute **cabins** ($90-95 d) and a wall-tent cabin ($100 d), and tent camping. All include access to a deck for relaxing, a barbecue grill, a fire pit, lawn games, free Wi-Fi, and a shared bathhouse with showers. They're located along the road to Quartz Creek Campground near Mile 45 of the Sterling Highway and close to Sunrise Inn.

Food and Accommodations
Sunrise Inn (8 miles west of the junction at Mile 45, Sterling Hwy., 907/595-1222, www.alaskasunriseinn.com) is a classic Alaskan roadhouse that's been here since 1952. The inn features hearty meals, lodging, and a small RV park (electricity only, no running water). A **restaurant** (7am-9pm daily summer, $17-29) serves hearty breakfasts along with flavorful burgers, seafood, steak, and other Alaskan fare. The bar stays open late, with a pub menu, pool tables, and live bands on summer weekends. Sunrise's 10-unit motel contains surprisingly comfy rooms ($129-179 d) with queen beds, microwaves, fridges, TV, and Wi-Fi.

Atop a hill just east of Sunrise Inn, **The Cozy Bear** (Mile 45, Sterling Hwy., 907/440-1923, www.vrbo.com/825270, $325 for up to 8 guests) is an immaculate 2,100-square-foot home with three guest rooms (each with a private entrance), tasteful common areas, a full kitchen, jetted tub, outdoor covered patio with fire bowl, porch swing, and views of the surrounding mountains.

The turnoff for Quartz Creek Road is adjacent to Sunrise Inn. A half mile down the road is **Quartz Creek Campground** (Quartz Creek Rd., 518/885-3639 or 877/444-6777, www.recreation.gov, tents $18, RVs $28, no electricity, $10 reservation fee). It's a beautiful setting right on Kenai Lake. **Crescent Creek Campground** (Quartz Creek Rd., $14) is three miles down Quartz Creek Road. The 6.5-mile **Crescent Creek Trail** climbs 1,000 feet from the parking lot here to Crescent Lake.

COOPER LANDING
A dozen miles west of the Seward Highway junction is **Cooper Landing** (www.cooperlandingchamber.com), with a scattering of businesses—lodges, river guides, restaurants, gas stations, and tackle shops—on both sides of the Sterling Highway. The speed limit is 35 mph, so slow down to avoid a ticket.

The little **Cooper Landing Historical Museum** (Mile 49, Sterling Hwy., 907/598-1042, www.cooperlandingmuseum.com, noon-5pm Wed.-Mon. mid-May-mid-Sept., free) houses the articulated skeleton of a

Northwestern Kenai Peninsula

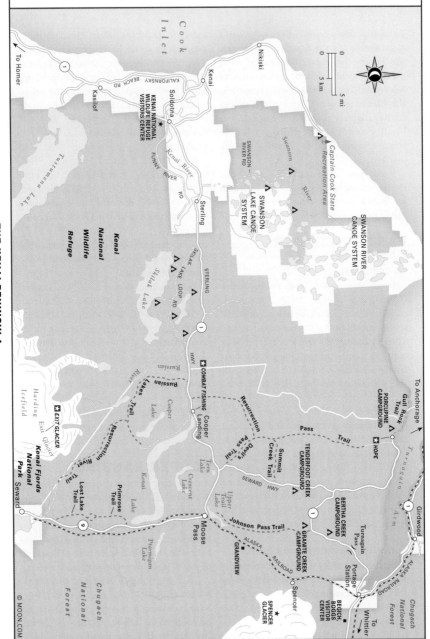

© MOON.COM

brown bear, historical items, and other items in two old cabins.

Managed by the Kenaitze Indian Tribe, **K'Beq' Cultural Site** (Mile 53, Sterling Hwy., 907/335-7290, www.kenaitze.org, 10am-4pm Thurs.-Sun. June-Aug., free) offers cultural tours to a prehistoric Dena'ina house site several times a day. A small gift shop sells local Native Alaskan crafts. It's directly across from the entrance to the Russian River Campground.

Recreation

Cooper Landing's main attractions are Kenai River fishing and float trips. The river flows out of Kenai Lake at Cooper Landing, heading 80 miles west to the town of Kenai, where it meets Cook Inlet. Many businesses provide guided fishing trips on the river; see the **Cooper Landing Chamber of Commerce** website (www.cooperlandingchamber.com), or find a multitude of guided fishing brochures in the Soldotna Visitors Information Center.

On the riverside just after the bridge, **Alaska Troutfitters Fly Shop** (Mile 49, Sterling Hwy., 907/595-1212, www.aktroutfitters.com) offers fly-fishing instruction and rents fishing gear and waders.

You can buy or rent fishing gear, including poles and hip waders and even rental bear spray, at **Gwin's Lodge** (Mile 52, Sterling Hwy., 907/595-1266, www.gwinslodge.com, 6am-11pm daily late May-Sept.). Drop off your catch to have them freeze it and process for shipping.

You can rent fishing gear from **Alaska Canoe & Campground** (Mile 84, Sterling Hwy., 907/262-2331, www.alaskacanoetrips.com).

RIVER RAFTING

The powerful Kenai River is one of the most popular rafting destinations in Alaska. Most river trips take place May-September on the upper section of the river between the outlet of Kenai Lake at the Cooper Landing bridge to where it flows into Skilak Lake—a distance

of 17 miles. The busy Sterling Highway parallels the river for much of the way, but the river becomes wilder and more challenging below Jim's Landing as it enters Kenai River Canyon and turns away from the road. The upper section of Kenai River is mostly easy Class II conditions, with a couple of Class II-III rapids at Fishermans Bend and Schooner Bend before Jim's Landing (11 miles downriver). Kenai River Canyon is more challenging Class III white water, and the river enters Skilak Lake nine miles from the nearest takeout point.

Upper Kenai River scenic float trips generally last 3-4 hours and cost $55-65 for adults, $30-45 for children. Some companies start at the bridge and others from private docks farther downriver. More exciting are all-day **Kenai Canyon raft trips** that include the gentle upper portion of the river, plus dramatic Kenai Canyon and a motorboat ride across the lake to the takeout at Upper Skilak Lake Campground. Canyon trips last seven hours and cost $155-175 for adults, $80-125 for children. Local rafting companies include **Alaska River Adventures** (Mile 48, Sterling Hwy., 907/595-2000, www.alaskariveradventures.com), **Alaska Rivers Company** (Mile 50, Sterling Hwy., 907/595-1226 or 888/595-1226, www.alaskariverscompany.com), **Alaska Wildland Adventures** (Mile 50, Sterling Hwy., 907/595-1279 or 800/478-4100, www.alaskarivertrips.com), and **Drifter's Lodge** (Mile 48, Sterling Hwy., 907/595-5555, www.drifterslodge.com). These companies also guide all-day fishing trips aboard drift boats ($250-300 pp, with lunch), and some have half-day fishing on the upper Kenai River ($150-175 pp).

TOP EXPERIENCE

★ COMBAT FISHING

Alaska's most famous salmon-fishing area is near the junction of the Russian and Kenai Rivers. The **Russian River Ferry** (Mile 55, Sterling Hwy., 907/522-8368, www.alaskaarm.com, $11 adults, $6 seniors and children) is a cable-guided current-powered ferry that shuttles anglers across the Kenai River to the sockeye-rich opposite bank. Come in July to learn the true meaning of "combat fishing" as hundreds of folks fight for space, hooking both sockeye salmon and fellow anglers in the process. You'll need hip waders, and you can only use flies, not lures. Local fishing shops have the correct flies and often rent out poles and boots. Nonfishers are bemused by the oddity of such crowds, but for anglers the salmon fishing is the attraction, since many folks get their limit despite the hordes. A real fly-fishing angler wouldn't be caught dead here, but this is all about catching fish, not enjoying a wilderness or purist experience. Limited roadside parking is available around the ferry, or you can park in the big lot ($12 per day).

Food

Popular with anglers, rafters, campers, and locals, **Sackett's Kenai Grill** (Mile 50, Sterling Hwy., 907/595-1827, www.sackettskenaigrill.com, noon-9pm Mon.-Thurs., noon-10pm Fri.-Sun., $15-24) is next to Cooper Creek Campgrounds. Owner Tre Sackett welcomes everyone with a hearty menu of pulled pork barbecue sandwiches, handmade 14-inch pizzas, and smoked prime rib—served in colorful plastic baskets. There's no Wi-Fi, so as the waitress says, "Just talk to each other." The bar has a good selection of Alaskan beers on tap.

★ **Kingfisher Roadhouse** (Mile 47, Sterling Hwy., 907/595-2861, www.kingfisheralaska.com, 5pm-10:30pm daily late May-mid-Oct., $16-36) serves Alaskan cuisine in a unique setting on the shore of Kenai Lake. Dining is rustic and relaxed, with friendly and efficient service, plank walls and wood burl tables, an outdoor beer garden, and big windows affording views across the lake. The enclosed veranda is a perfect spot on a rainy afternoon. House specialties include a tasty smoked salmon dip, curry chicken pot pie, the bleu burger (topped with gorgonzola, bacon, and green onion spread), and caribou sausage marsala. Owner Dominic Bauer emphasizes local seafood and uses organic produce and

burgers as much as possible. Beer and wine are available, and the bar comes alive with music several nights a week. No reservations.

Gwin's Lodge (Mile 52, Sterling Hwy., 907/595-1266, www.gwinslodge.com, 6am-11pm daily late May-late Oct., $13-40) is a classic Alaskan eatery. In business since 1952, this is a fun place to pick up tips from the anglers while enjoying down-home cooking, especially the smoked salmon chowder, burgers, halibut fish-and-chips, rib-eye steaks, and pies. The restaurant opens early for the fishing crowd and has Wi-Fi and a small bar with sports on the TV. The country store here rents outdoor gear and sells groceries, sodas, beer, gifts, ice, and fishing licenses.

Accommodations

Cooper Landing spreads out over a five-mile stretch that centers around Mile 50 of the Sterling Highway. Lodging options are listed from east to west.

Primarily for cruise passengers, **Kenai Princess Wilderness Lodge** (Mile 48, Sterling Hwy., 907/595-1425 or 800/426-0500, www.princesslodges.com, mid-May-mid-Sept., $230 d), near the Kenai River bridge, overlooks the roiling turquoise water of the river and features a restaurant and lounge, an exercise facility, a 0.5-mile nature trail, and a gift shop. Bungalow-style guest rooms include a sitting area, a wood-burning stove, a TV, a phone, limited Wi-Fi (only around the lodge), and a small private deck. There are no river views from the rooms, but the big deck is a fine spot for dinner with a view.

Alpine Motel (Mile 48, Sterling Hwy., 907/595-1557, www.alpinemotelak.com, late May-Sept., $125-155 d) has a dozen kitchenette units with dishes, TVs, private baths, and Wi-Fi.

Just up the road is **Drifter's Lodge** (Mile 48, Sterling Hwy., 907/595-5555, www.drifterslodge.com, year-round, $250 d rooms, $350 d cabins, additional guests $25 pp), with chalet-style cabins containing kitchenettes and private baths, along with shared-bath guest rooms with fridges and microwaves in the lodge. A continental breakfast, sauna access, and Wi-Fi are included in the rates. The lodge is right on the river and has nightly campfires. Guides lead rafting trips from the lodge. This is primarily a fishing lodge, and most guests choose all-inclusive multiday sportfishing packages.

Appropriately named ★ **Alaska Heavenly Lodge** (Mile 49, Sterling Hwy., 907/595-2012 or 866/595-2012, www. alaskaheavenly.com, rooms $196 d, cabin $700 for 7 people, lodge $1,000 for up to 10 people) has a fantastic hillside spot. Set on an 18-acre spread, this homey lodge overlooks the Kenai River and surrounding mountains, with a hiking trail into the forest. The Mount Cecil cabin contains three guest rooms, each with two beds, a bath, a kitchenette, and a grill. A historic homestead serves as the main lodge, with four bedrooms, three baths, a full kitchen, an open layout, a stone fireplace, and a big deck. A third cabin—open to all guests—houses a pool table, a hot-rock sauna, a flat-screen TV, and a seven-person hot tub on the deck. The location, lush grounds, friendly owners, and lovely accommodations make this a very popular spot for weddings, events, and family reunions. Wi-Fi is available.

A three-story hotel/B&B with wraparound porches, **The Hutch B&B** (Mile 49, Sterling Hwy., 907/595-1270, www.thehutchbandb. com, Apr.-mid-Oct., $105-129 d, additional guests $20 pp, $245 cabin for up to 6 people) has a dozen guest rooms with private baths, plus a two-bedroom cabin with a full kitchen and bath. A hearty continental breakfast is included, and The Hutch has Wi-Fi, a communal room with TV, and evening campfires. Some rooms have a two-night minimum; a three-night stay is required for the cabin.

Located on the western edge of "town," **Gwin's Lodge** (Mile 52, Sterling Hwy., 907/595-1266, www.gwinslodge.com, late May-late Oct., $80-220 d) has a wide variety of lodging choices, including 15 cabins (some basic dry cabins; others have private baths) and two full houses; the largest can accommodate eight guests. Rates vary widely throughout the season.

Alaska Wildland Adventures operates two Kenai Peninsula lodges. Located on the river in Cooper Landing, **Kenai Riverside Lodge** (907/595-1279 or 800/478-4100, www.alaskawildland.com) has a variety of all-inclusive fishing, food, and lodging packages, starting at $1,080 pp for a two-night stay. More unique is **Kenai Backcountry Lodge** (907/783-2928 or 800/334-8730, www.alaskawildland.com), hidden away on Skilak Lake and accessible only by boat. Accommodations are comfortably rustic tent cabins and log cabins, with a central bathhouse and a historic lodge. All-inclusive stays include lodging, food, kayaking, guides, and hiking; a three-night, four-day visit is $1,950 pp.

Camping

Just west of Cooper Landing is the Forest Service's **Cooper Creek North Campground** and **Cooper Creek South Campground** (Mile 50, Sterling Hwy., 518/885-3639 or 877/444-6777, www. recreation.gov, tents $18, RVs $28, no hookups, $10 reservation fee), with sites on both sides of the road. The campgrounds are just a short walk from Sackett's Kenai Grill.

The large **Russian River Campground** (Mile 52, Sterling Hwy., 518/885-3639 or 877/444-6777, www.recreation.gov, tents $18, RVs $28, no hookups, $10 reservation fee) is one of the best places in the state to catch sockeye salmon when they're running (generally mid-June and mid-July). The 83 campsites are strung along the two-mile paved road, and sites are large and well-spaced. Reservations are strongly advised for July visits to the Cooper Creek and Russian River Campgrounds.

Kenai Princess RV Park (Mile 48, Sterling Hwy., 907/595-1425, mid-May-mid-Sept., full hookups $45, no tents) is located close to Kenai Princess Wilderness Lodge at the Kenai River bridge. The facility includes Wi-Fi, cable

TV, and pay showers ($2) that are open to non-guests. No pull-through sites are available.

Kenai Riverside Campground and RV Park (Mile 50, Sterling Hwy., 888/536-2478, www.kenairv.com, late May-early Sept., tents $20, RVs $27-35, guest rooms $75 d) has RV sites and tent spaces, plus guest rooms with continental breakfast and shared baths. Showers are $5 if you aren't staying here. The campground is owned by Alaska Wildland Adventures, which also offers Kenai River fishing and float trips.

Additional campsites can be found at **Gwin's Lodge** (Mile 52, Sterling Hwy., 907/595-1266, www.gwinslodge.com, late May-late Oct., $20 tents, $35 RVs).

Information and Services
Cooper Landing Chamber of Commerce Visitor Center (Mile 49, Sterling Hwy., www.cooperlandingchamber.com, late May-Sept.) is next to Wildman's. It's not always staffed, but the doors are left open in the summer. Public restrooms are next to the boat launch on the south side of the Kenai River bridge.

A quarter mile before the bridge over the Kenai River, **Wildman's** (Mile 48, Sterling Hwy., 907/595-1456, www.wildmans.org, 6am-11pm daily late May-early Sept., 8am-9pm daily early Sept.-late May) is the local everything store. The convenience store sells basic supplies and gifts, and serves breakfast items, local pastries, deli sandwiches, hot dogs, espresso, liquor, and huge ice cream cones. Laundry and shower facilities are available; guests can check email using free Wi-Fi and get cash out of the ATM. Out back are a few RV spaces ($30 with hookups).

Getting There and Around
The Stage Line (907/235-2252, www.stagelineinhomer.com, Mon.-Fri. summer, once a week winter) has van service connecting Cooper Landing with Anchorage ($75 one-way), Homer ($70), and Seward (summer only, $75). Vans stop at Wildman's in Cooper Landing, and drivers will pick up or drop off passengers elsewhere with advance notice.

Wildman's (Mile 48, Sterling Hwy., 907/595-1456, www.wildmans.org) has a taxi to get you around, plus a convenient shuttle service for anglers, bikers, hikers, and boaters. They can move vehicles or deliver you to a trailhead.

KENAI NATIONAL WILDLIFE REFUGE
This large habitat (907/262-7021 or 877/285-5628, http://kenai.fws.gov) supports so many moose, bears, salmon, and other wildlife that it was designated a refuge by President Roosevelt in 1941. The Alaska National Interest Lands Conservation Act of 1980 changed the name from Kenai National Moose Range and expanded the refuge to its present 1.9 million acres, managed by the U.S. Fish and Wildlife Service. The **Kenai National Wildlife Refuge Visitors Center** (907/260-2820, http://kenai.fws.gov, 9am-5pm daily late May-early Sept., 10am-5pm Tues.-Sat. winter, free) is at the refuge headquarters along Ski Hill Road in Soldotna. This newly opened center has fascinating exhibits, trails, wildlife videos, and guided nature walks and talks. Stop here to pick up a copy of *Reflections,* the refuge's annual newspaper, with details on day hikes, wildlife viewing, fishing, canoeing, picnicking, and camping.

Hiking
The **Resurrection Pass Trail** crosses the Sterling Highway just west of Cooper Landing and is accessible from a trailhead at Mile 52. More challenging is the three-mile **Fuller Lakes Trail.** It takes off from a parking area at Mile 57 and climbs sharply to a pair of small lakes filled with small Dolly Varden (bring your pole).

Skilak Lake Loop Road
Located in the heart of Kenai National Wildlife Refuge, this very scenic—but dusty—17-mile gravel road meets the Sterling

1: winter at Upper Ohmer Lake cabin on Kenai National Wildlife Refuge; 2: fall colors along Kelly Lake in Kenai National Wildlife Refuge

Highway at two places: Mile 58 on the east end and Mile 75 on the west end. Five campgrounds, several trails, and two public-use cabins are located off this popular side road; it's a very popular recreation area throughout the summer.

Beginning at the east end (Mile 58, Sterling Hwy.), Skilak Lake Loop Road immediately passes Jim's Landing on the Kenai River, a busy picnic area and boat ramp for rafting and drift boats. Look for bald eagles in the trees and fly fishers along the shore. Hidden Lake Campground ($10) has 44 campsites, with campfire programs on summer weekends. It's the largest and most developed campground on the refuge.

A pair of overlooks near Mile 5 on Skilak Lake Loop Road provide a great view over Skilak Lake. The Skilak Lookout Trail at Mile 5.5 climbs to a high hillside above the lake, with good crops of berries in the fall. It's 2.5 miles each way. A short distance up the road at Mile 6 is the Bear Mountain Trail, a quick one-mile hike with a rocky promontory affording dramatic views across Skilak Lake.

At Mile 8, turn left and drive two miles to popular Upper Skilak Lake Campground (tents and RVs $10, walk-in tent sites $5), with 25 campsites for both tents and RVs (no hookups), and access to the three-mile Vista Trail. There's another campground at nearby Lower Ohmer Lake (Mile 8.5, Skilak Lake Loop Rd., free), and a couple more sites at Engineer Lake (Mile 9.4, free). The nearly level Seven Lakes Trail begins at Engineer Lake, connecting to three more lakes before ending at Kelly Lake Campground off the Sterling Highway. Lower Skilak Lake Campground (free) is on a side road at Mile 13.6 of Skilak Lake Loop Road.

Two popular public-use cabins are readily accessible off Skilak Lake Loop Road. Engineer Lake Cabin (518/885-3639 or 877/444-6777, www.recreation.gov, $45 plus $10 reservation fee) is on the north shore of this lake, a one-mile hike from the trailhead. The Upper Ohmer Cabin (518/885-3639 or 877/444-6777, www.recreation.gov, $45 plus

$10 reservation fee) is an easy 0.25-mile hike off Skilak Lake Loop Road at Mile 8. Fourteen more public cabins ($35-45) are scattered around the refuge, but most of these require boat or canoe access.

In addition to those along Skilak Lake, three other U.S. Fish and Wildlife Service campgrounds are on the Sterling Highway between Cooper Landing and Sterling.

Swanson River Area

Oil was discovered in 1957 in the northern wilderness near the Swanson River, and the 18-mile gravel Swanson River Road built to the oilfields also opened up this lake-studded lowlands. The road turns north off the Sterling Highway at Mile 84. Approximately 13 miles in is Dolly Varden Lake Campground (Swanson River Rd., free). It is not crowded, has nice views, is right on the lake, and has frequent moose visits.

CANOEING

Two canoe routes—the Swanson River Route and the Swan Lake Route—are accessible by Swanson River Road. Both offer a wonderful way to explore the refuge and to see wildlife up close. Pick up the U.S. Fish and Wildlife Service brochure Canoeing in the Kenai National Wildlife Refuge for detailed information, or find it at http://kenai.fws.gov. Kenai Canoe Trails by Daniel L. Quick is a useful guidebook for anyone heading out on the refuge's lakes.

Alaska Canoe & Campground (Mile 84, Sterling Hwy., 907/262-2331, www.alaskacanoetrips.com) has canoe ($55 per day), kayak ($45 per day), and drift boat rentals, along with a shuttle to nearby waterways. It's close to the turnoff for the Swan Lake Canoe Route.

Located on the northern Kenai Peninsula, the Swan Lake Canoe Route is the most popular canoeing area within Kenai National Wildlife Refuge. This 60-mile route encompasses 30 lakes that are connected by fairly short portages (the longest is under a mile). The entire 60-mile route can be traversed in less than a week. In addition, the route provides access to a 17-mile float down the gentle Moose River. Canoeing on this system offers not only scenic beauty but also excellent wildlife viewing and good rainbow trout fishing.

The **Swanson River Canoe Route** links 40 small lakes on the northern Kenai Peninsula, and also includes a 46-mile stretch of the Swanson River. The lakes are connected by portages of varying lengths and conditions, but they are more difficult than those on the nearby Swan Lake Canoe Route. Traveling from the Paddle Lake entrance (Mile 12, Swan Lake Rd.), trips can stretch from a long weekend to over a week. In remote lake areas of the Swanson River Route east of Pepper Lake, travel is difficult, and the routes and portages are often indistinct. This is true wilderness and can be challenging. Bring a compass, an accurate map, a pair of hip waders, and a lot of patience.

STERLING

The unincorporated and run-down settlement of Sterling (pop. 6,000)—spread over a wide area around Mile 83—is mainly notable for the four-lane highway that cuts across this part of the northern Kenai Peninsula; it seems totally out of place in such a quiet spot. The Sterling Highway crosses the Moose River in Sterling, where the Moose joins the widening Kenai River, and the fishhook frenzy pervades all your senses.

If kids are in your vehicle, pull into the **Cook's Corner Tesoro gas station** (Mile 82, Sterling Hwy., 907/262-6021) for a soft-serve ice cream cone or outsize cinnamon roll.

Recreation

The 13-mile stretch of highway from Sterling to Soldotna bristles with guides and outfitters, fish camps, bait and tackle shops, charters, fish smokehouses, boat and canoe rentals, boat engine sales and repairs, and so forth—essential infrastructure in the eternal struggle between sport anglers and salmon.

Ken Marlow, co-owner of Marlow's on the Kenai cabins, operates **Alaska Birding**

Tours (www.alaskabirdingtours.com), with personalized bird-watching trips throughout the Kenai. Pelagic birding out of Seward is a favorite, but he also leads trips to other parts of Alaska.

Accommodations

Marlow's on the Kenai (36370 Stephens Dr., 907/262-5218 or 800/725-3327, www.marlowsonthekenai.com, from $2,425 pp for a 6-night trip) consists of three spacious cabins (one has three bedrooms) just 50 feet from the Kenai River. The cabins include full kitchens, baths, Wi-Fi, TVs, outdoor grills, and decks. Most guests book for multiple-night fishing packages.

One of the most popular places in Sterling, **Alaska Red Fish Lodge** (32815 El Dorado Way, 907/262-7080 or 888/335-4490, www.alaskaredfishlodge.com, mid-May-mid-Sept., $199 d, additional guests $15 pp) has 15 modern cedar cabins with a main lodge and a dock right on the Kenai River. Each cabin contains space for four guests, a kitchenette, a private bath, a TV, a picnic table, and a patio with a gas grill. Nightly campfires are a highlight. The lodge is popular with anglers, but also caters to families, even offering a gated play area for children. The main lodge has a common area with couches, a guest computer, and Wi-Fi, plus a walk-in freezer. Access is from Mile 81 of the Sterling Highway.

Alaska Canoe & Campground (Mile 84, Sterling Hwy., 907/262-2331, www.alaskacanoetrips.com, tents $20, RVs $30-35 with full hookups, cabins $150 d, additional guests $10 pp) has a small RV park and campground with restrooms, showers ($5), laundry, Wi-Fi, and loaner mountain bikes. The shop rents canoes, kayaks, and drift boats, and provides shuttles to nearby waterways. You'll also find two cabins with private baths and full kitchens.

Camping

Bings Landing State Park (Mile 80, Sterling Hwy., 907/262-5581, www.dnr.alaska.gov, campsites $15, day-use $5) is located on the

Kenai River in Sterling, with 36 campsites, fishing on elevated boardwalks, and a picnic area.

Izaak Walton State Recreation Site (Mile 82, Sterling Hwy., 907/262-5581, www. dnr.alaska.gov, campsites $15, day-use $5) on the east side of the river is a pretty campground with toilets and water. Archaeological excavations conducted here indicate that Native Alaskans occupied this fish-rich confluence up to 2,000 years ago.

Services

A short distance up Swanson River Road, **Wash Out Laundry** (907/262-7666) has drop-off service, showers, a kids' play area, and even tanning beds.

SOLDOTNA

Soldotna was established in the late 1940s as World War II veterans filed for homestead lands along Soldotna Creek. Today this town of 4,000 is the seat of the Kenai Borough government and serves as a busy stopping point for travelers, anglers, and locals. "Slowdotna" has all the charm of Wasilla, another place disparaged by anyone not living there. Fast-food joints, strip malls, fishing supply stores, shopping centers, and a jumble of signs greet your arrival in this sprawling suburban burg with no real downtown—unless you count the big Fred Meyer store. The latter's parking lot also serves as a de facto free RV campground all summer.

Sights

The **Kenai National Wildlife Refuge Visitors Center** (907/260-2820, http:// kenai.fws.gov, 9am-5pm daily late May-early Sept., 10am-5pm Tues.-Sat. early Sept.-late May, free) is a mile south of town. Get here by turning onto Funny River Road at the light just after the bridge, then take an immediate right and go a mile up Ski Hill Road. Outside stand a life-size bronze moose sculpture and two historic cabins. Step inside for attractive exhibits about the animals and ecosystems of the refuge. You can buy books, watch wildlife videos, or stroll the nature trails down to Headquarters Lake or on a 2.2-mile forest loop. The staff leads hands-on nature walks and talks several times a week. While here, ask about renting one of the 14 public-use cabins that dot the refuge.

Follow the 0.25-mile **Kenai River Fish Walk** from the Soldotna Visitors Information Center to the **Soldotna Homestead Museum** (421 Centennial Park Rd., 907/262-3832, 10am-4pm Tues.-Sat., noon-4pm Sun. mid-May-mid-Sept., free), or drive there by turning up Kalifornsky Beach Road, followed by an immediate right onto Centennial Park Road. This collection of a half dozen log cabins contains the usual settlers' items, stuffed critters, and Native artifacts. The real treat is that this quiet spot is just a short distance from the bustling Sterling Highway.

Festivals and Events

Soldotna's biggest event, **Progress Days** (4th weekend in July), arrives with a parade, car races, arts and crafts booths, live music, and more. The **Kenai River Festival** (www. kenaiwatershed.org, early June) is another fun family celebration, with live bands, food and art vendors, a beer garden, and the Run for the River race. The **Peninsula Winter Games** (late Jan.) features ice carving, hockey, fireworks, and games.

Shopping

Far more down-home than the big Fred Meyer store, **Beemun's Variety Store** (35277 Kenai Spur Hwy., 907/262-1234, www.beemuns. com, 9am-6pm Mon.-Sat.) has an upstairs bike shop that becomes a ski and snowboard shop in winter, plus outdoor clothing, art supplies, sporting goods, and other gear downstairs. The shop rents mountain bikes and fat-tire bikes in summer.

If you're heading out on the water, be sure to stop at **Soldotna Hardware & Fishing** (44648 Sterling Hwy., 907/262-4655, www. soldotnahardware.com) for fishing gear. The store is packed with hardware oddities and animal mounts.

Soldotna

To Kenai and Nikiski

BEST WESTERN KING SALMON MOTEL

KNIGHT DR

KENAI SPUR HIGHWAY

MARYDALE DR

KOBUK ST

FIREWEED ST

BINKLEY ST

■ CENTRAL PENINSULA HOSPITAL

REDOUBT AVE

■ FRED MEYER

REDOUBT AVE

STERLING HIGHWAY

To Sweard and Anchorage

STERLING NEEDLE B&B

MACKEY LAKE RD

△ ▲ Soldotna Creek Park

Kenai River

CENTENNIAL PARK CAMPGROUND △

WILSON LANE

RIVERSIDE DR

△ ASPEN HOTEL

KENAI RIVER LODGE ■

SOLDOTNA SPORTS CENTER ■

SOLDOTNA VISITORS INFORMATION CENTER ■

KALIFORNSKY BEACH RD

FUNNY RIVER RD

△ KENAI RIVER FISHING AND RV CAMP

Soldotna Airport

← To Homer and Kasilof

△ KLONDIKE RV PARK

STERLING HIGHWAY

SKI HILL RD

■ KENAI NATIONAL WILDLIFE REFUGE VISITORS CENTER

Headquarters Lake

0   1 mi
0   1 km

SKYVIEW MIDDLE SCHOOL (POOL)/ TSALTESHI TRAILS ■

↓ To Homer and Kasilof

© MOON.COM

Dragonfly Gallery (183 S. Soldotna Ave., 907/260-4636, www.chellinelarsen.com, 11am-6pm Tues.-Sat.) displays silk scarves, quilted wall hangings, and prints by Chelline Larsen, plus the works of more than 20 other artists.

River City Books (43977 Sterling Hwy., 907/260-7722, 9am-5pm Mon.-Sat., 9am-7pm Sun.) has a decent collection of books. Also here is Fine Thyme Café, with espresso drinks, salads, sandwiches, quiche, and desserts.

For fresh veggies and fruits, food, arts, and live music, head to the **Central Kenai Peninsula Farmers Market** (193 E. Corral Ave., 907/262-5463, 10am-2pm Sat. June-mid-Sept.) at the corner of Kenai Spur Highway and Corral Avenue. The **Soldotna Wednesday Market** (907/262-7264, www.soldotnawednesdaymarket.com, 11am-6pm Wed. June-Aug.) at Soldotna Creek Park in downtown Soldotna has similar offerings, plus a beer garden. The food stands stay open till 9pm if you're just looking for cheap eats.

Recreation

Home to one of the best playgrounds on the peninsula, **Soldotna Creek Park** (States Ave., behind Don Jose's Mexican Restaurant) provides a break for the kids. It's a great place for running, jumping, and general mayhem. Just a short distance off busy Sterling Highway in the heart of town, this 13-acre park also has picnic tables, a pavilion, and 2,250 feet of elevated boardwalk along the Kenai River.

There are two nine-hole golf courses to choose from in Soldotna. **Birch Ridge Golf Course** (42223 Sterling Hwy., 907/262-5270, www.birchridgegolf.com, $20-30) is a private resort three miles east of town, and **Bird Homestead Golf Course** (37190 Funny River Rd., 907/260-4653, www.birdhomesteadgolf.com, $17) is 12 miles up Funny River Road.

Skyview Middle School (325 W. Marydale Ave., 907/262-7419, www.kpbsd.k12.ak.us) has an Olympic-size pool with open swim times. Adjacent to the high school are the **Tsalteshi Trails** with 10 miles of biking and running paths, plus a disc golf course. Come winter, these are some of the best cross-country ski trails in the area.

Food

BREAKFAST AND COFFEE

Moose is Loose (44278 Sterling Hwy., 907/260-3036, 6:30am-4:30pm Tues.-Sat., under $7) makes—without a doubt—the best doughnuts, pecan rolls, apple fritters, and maple bars on the Kenai Peninsula. Doughy, sweet, and fattening, these are the perfect match for a mug of coffee. Gargantuan six-inch doughnut rings are famous, and the back room is a locals' hangout. Make a stop here to stock up on calories before heading out for a day of fishing.

Hidden away on a side street near the Safeway store, **Kaladi Brothers Coffee** (315 S. Kobuk St., 907/262-5980, www.kaladi.com, 6am-7pm Mon.-Fri., 7am-7pm Sat., 8am-6pm Sun., $4-9) serves good espresso and features art on the walls as well as occasional live music. Be sure to check out the unique ceiling

tiles. There's a second Kaladi Brothers shop along the highway next to Subway.

Brew@602 (43540 Kleeb Loop, 907/398-2931, www.whistlehillsoldotna.com, 7am-5pm Mon.-Sat., 8am-5pm Sun., $5-10) is housed within a retired Alaska Railroad train car on the east end of Soldotna. It's a fun place with coffee, blended drinks, and ice cream, and delicious sweet or savory waffles in a playful setting. There's even a charging station if you're driving a Tesla.

LUNCH

Located at the Soldotna Y adjacent to River City Books, **Fine Thyme Café** (43965 Sterling Hwy., 907/262-6620, 9am-5pm Mon.-Sat., $9-13) provides an escape from the ubiquitous fast-food joints and large men in hip waders. This cute little café serves sandwiches, daily soups, quiche, salads, fresh-baked breads, cookies, homemade desserts, and espresso. Portions are on the small side.

Find the best sandwiches in Soldotna at **Odie's Deli** (44315 Sterling Hwy., 907/260-3255, www.odiesdeli.com, 8am-8pm Mon.-Fri., 9am-4pm Sat., $8-15), where the bread—including a jalapeño cheddar version—is baked on the premises. Fresh soups are made daily, and sandwiches are enormous—go for a half if you aren't really hungry. The chicken cashew salad is excellent, as are the hefty cookies. Odie's has live music on Friday evenings in summer and Wednesday-night trivia games. You'll probably recognize the Odie's building as an old Wendy's.

For an East Coast-style hoagie, **Jersey Subs** (44224 Sterling Hwy., 907/260-3343, 9am-7pm Mon.-Sat., $10-22) is the place to go. They're not cheap—a 10-inch Philly cheesesteak costs $14—but the bread is freshly baked and the staff knows their business. The shop is tiny and cramped, with slow service (call in your order if you're in a hurry) and tasteless bumper stickers straight out of the 1950s. Jersey Subs also has shops in Kenai and Kasilof.

Everything Bagels (35251 Kenai Spur Hwy., 907/252-8135, www.

everythingbagelsak.com, 6:30am-4pm Mon.-Fri., 7:30am-4pm Sat., $7-11) is a fine little bagelry. In addition to tasty toasted bagels, you can get something more substantial, including green eggs and ham bagel sandwiches, as well as good coffee.

INTERNATIONAL

Soldotna has several Mexican restaurants, but one really stands out: **Senor Pancho's** (44096 Sterling Hwy., 907/260-7777, 11am-9pm daily, $11-18). The small shop is in a strip mall next to Napa Auto Parts, but step inside to find great fresh food, big portions, and colorful furniture from Jalisco. Order at the counter and wait for it to be delivered to your table before heading over to the salsa bar for toppings and handfuls of tortilla chips. Halibut Baja fish tacos, carnita quesadillas, *sopes*, veggie fajitas, and Mexican ice drinks are popular, but save room for sopaipillas with chocolate, ice cream, and honey. There's not much space inside, and Pancho's is loved by locals too, so you may want to get your order to go.

Inside the Blazy Mall, **Pad Thai Café** (44539 Sterling Hwy., 907/690-6003, 11am-8pm Mon.-Fri., noon-8pm Sat., $14-15) is the best local spot for food from Southeast Asia. This bright café serves dependably good pad thai, massaman curry, and spring rolls. Colorful large Thai prints decorate the walls, and vegetarians will find plenty of options.

BREWPUB

It's easy to miss **St. Elias Brewing Co.** (434 Sharkathmi Ave., 907/260-7837, www.steliasbrewingco.com, 11am-10pm Sun.-Thurs., 11am-11pm Fri.-Sat. June-Aug., noon-9pm Sun.-Thurs., noon-10pm Fri.-Sat. Sept.-May, $12-15), located on a side road just east of the Fred Meyer store. The food is consistently flavorful, with small rustic pizzas emerging from the wood stone oven, plus salads and baked sandwiches. The Brewhouse pizza is a favorite, topped with bacon, sausage, pepperoni, marinated mushrooms, caramelized onions, and cheese. A central fireplace

adds to the allure, and local musicians show up for Thursday-night performances. Get a tasting sampler of the brewery's beers, or purchase a growler to go of Farmer's Friend Ale or Williwaw IPA. St. Elias also crafts tasty root beer and cream soda for teetotalers.

FINE DINING

In business for more than three decades, **Mykel's Restaurant & Lounge** (35041 Kenai Spur Hwy., 907/262-4305, www.mykels.com, 11:30am-9:30pm daily June-Aug., 11:30am-9pm Tues.-Thurs., 11am-10pm Fri.-Sat. Sept.-May, $25-60) is just up Kenai Spur Highway from the Sterling Highway and features fresh salads, pasta, seafood, steaks, and fine wines. Locals rave about Mykel's slow-roasted prime rib. The atmosphere is quiet and upscale, and the bar has live music Thursday evenings.

Accommodations

More than 100 lodging options crowd the Sterling-Soldotna-Kenai area, from rustic cabins to riverside wilderness lodges. Visitors center racks are crammed with descriptive flyers, and the chamber's website (www.soldotnachamber.com) has links to many lodging places. Many local lodges provide freezers for your freshly caught fish.

MOTELS

Aspen Hotel (326 Binkley Circle, 907/260-7736 or 888/308-7848, www.aspenhotelsak.com, $189 d, suites $209 d) is a large and modern place with an indoor pool and hot tub, exercise facility, and breakfast with waffles. All rooms include fridges and microwaves, and five suites provide room to spread out. The hotel is right on the river and across the street from fast-food places and a Safeway.

Not far away is the sprawling **Kenai River Lodge** (393 Riverside Dr., 907/262-4292 or 800/977-4292, www.kenairiverlodge.com, $210-230 d, suites $300-450) with motel rooms facing the river. The lodge has 300 feet of private shoreline for fishing, with cleaning tables, freezer space, and a barbecue grill once you pull one in. Rooms contain one or two queen beds, fridges, and microwaves. Suites are larger and can sleep up to six people for the same price.

Best Western King Salmon Motel (35545 Kenai Spur Hwy., 907/262-5857 or 888/262-5857, www.bestwestern.com, $189 d) has large rooms with two queen beds, fridges, and microwaves. Rates include vouchers for a full breakfast at the adjacent King Salmon Restaurant.

BED-AND-BREAKFASTS

The **Kenai Peninsula B&B Association** website (www.kpbba.net) provides links to Soldotna area B&Bs.

Sterling Needle B&B (355 Fairway Dr., 907/262-3506, www.sterlingneedle.com, $145 d) is a reasonably priced B&B containing three guest rooms, private baths, homemade quilts, and full breakfasts. The back deck and flower-filled garden are a plus, and the friendly owners know the area well. The B&B is on the east end of Soldotna just off the highway.

A 16-room European-style place along the river, **Soldotna B&B Lodge** (399 Lovers Lane, 907/262-4779 or 877/262-4779, www.soldotnalodge.com, $227-267 d shared bath) is a favorite of both anglers and families. A dozen of the rooms share four showers and five restrooms, while the other four have private baths. A filling breakfast is included, and the hosts are fluent in German and Japanese.

If you're looking for a romantic getaway, be sure to check out ★ **Escape for Two** (49300 Charlie Brown Dr., 907/262-1493, www.escapefortwo.com, $195 d), on a small pond five miles south of Soldotna. Two quaint and very private cabins are lovingly decorated, each with a forest setting, a king bed, a kitchenette, and a breakfast basket. One has a large jetted tub in the bath, along with its own dock with a central fire pit. The other cabin has heated floors, a hot tub on the outside deck, and a lovely gazebo with a fire pit. In addition to the cabins, there's a yurt (summer only) in the trees with a view of the pond from the deck. Two canoes and a paddleboat await for a tour around the pond. These cabins aren't for kids or anglers, just couples looking to escape.

CABINS

A Cabin by the Pond (Airport Heights Rd., 907/262-4728, www.acabinbythepond.com, cabins $199-249 d, log house $359, 2-night minimum) provides a relaxing setting just minutes from downtown Soldotna. Six cabins cluster around a tiny pond frequented by moose (hence their alternative name, Munch Moose Cabins). Each has a kitchenette, a private bath, and a porch; the largest has a gas fireplace and accommodates five people. Larger groups will love the classic 1970s-era Alaskan log house with two bedrooms, a full kitchen, a living room, and a bath. Also here is a picture-perfect log wedding chapel with space for up to 50 guests.

Halfway between Kenai and Soldotna, **Caribou Crossings Cabins** (48254 Prairie Ave., 907/262-7783, www.cariboux.com, June-early Sept., $225-250 d, extra guests $25 pp) consists of four log cabins, each with a kitchenette, a private bath, laundry, a barbecue, and space for 4-6 people, but no Wi-Fi. Befitting the name, caribou are often seen in the field out front each fall.

FISHING LODGES

Fishing is the main attraction for most Soldotna visitors, with many lodges catering to the hip-waders-and-tackle crowd. Each lodge has its own packages, but most include a minimum of four nights' lodging and three days of charter salmon and halibut fishing with river float trips and ocean charter boats.

Soldotna has an abundance of high-end fishing lodges where seven-night trips start around $2,500. A great one is **All Alaska Outdoors Lodge** (35905 Ryan Lane, 907/953-0186, www.allalaska.com), where the owner is also a pilot, providing floatplane trips to remote lakes and rivers. Also recommended are **Tower Rock Lodge** (38156 Woods Dr., 907/953-2669 or 800/284-3474, www.towerrocklodge.com) and **Alaska**

Fishing Lodge/Soldotna B&B Lodge (399 Lovers Lane, 907/262-4779 or 877/262-4779, www.soldotnalodge.com).

Other fishing lodges worth checking out include **Kenai Riverbend Resort** (45525 Porter Rd., 907/283-9489 or 800/625-2324, www.kenairiverbend.com), **Orca Lodge** (44250 Oehler Rd., 907/262-5649, www.orcalodge.com), and **King Salmondeaux Lodge** (33126 Johnson Dr., 907/260-3474, www.kingsalmondeauxlodge.com).

CAMPING

Two Soldotna city parks (907/262-5299, www.soldotna.org, first-come, first-served, $20-25) provide excellent camping close to town. Sites include picnic tables, water, fire pits, elevated riverbank boardwalks, and boat launches. Reach **Centennial Park Campground** by crossing the bridge on the Sterling Highway, taking a right at the light onto Kalifornsky Beach Road, then another immediate right into the campground. This big city park has 176 wooded sites (some right on the river) and boat-launching ramps. Equally attractive is **Swiftwater Park Campground** (States Ave., near the Soldotna Y), with 40 quiet campsites.

Find RV parking in the **Fred Meyer** parking lot (43843 Sterling Hwy., 907/260-2200, www.fredmeyer.com, 2-night limit, free).

Klondike RV Park & Cabins (48665 Funny River Rd., 907/262-6035 or 800/980-6035, www.klondikervpark.com, May-mid-Sept., RVs $50) has free Wi-Fi and showers, but no tent sites. You're just a short walk to fishing sites along the Kenai River.

Information and Services

The **Soldotna Visitors Information Center** (44790 Sterling Hwy., 907/262-9814, www.visitsoldotna.com, 9am-7pm daily late May-mid-Sept., 9am-5pm Mon.-Fri. mid-Sept.-late May) is on Sterling Highway just south of the bridge over the Kenai River. Stop by to sift through several hundred pamphlets describing B&Bs, fishing charters, RV parks, restaurants, and other businesses. There's free

Wi-Fi too. The walls are lined with photos, and be sure to see the 97-pound king salmon that was caught nearby in 1984; it's the largest ever caught by a sport angler. Just out the door, a path leads to a dock on the Kenai River, where you can try your luck at catching an even bigger one. The two-mile trail continues downriver to the Sports Complex.

The largest hospital on the Kenai Peninsula, **Central Peninsula Hospital** (250 Hospital Place, 907/714-4404, www.cpgh.org) is especially adept at removing fishhooks from all parts of the body; in a typical year they pull out 100 of them! Be sure to wear shatterproof eyewear to protect your eyes while rubbing shoulders with the Kenai River fishing crowds. The hospital has some of the most experienced surgeons in the state, able to even repair bilateral quadriceps tendon ruptures if you trip while carrying a canoe (speaking from personal experience here).

KDLL (91.9 FM, www.kdll.org) is the local public radio station.

The **Soldotna Public Library** (235 N. Binkley St., 907/262-4227, www.soldotna.org, 10am-6pm Mon., Wed., and Fri.-Sat., 10am-8pm Tues. and Thurs.) has Internet access and Wi-Fi, plus a free fishing pole loaner program for kids.

Take **showers** at **Soldotna Regional Sports Center** (538 Arena Ave., 907/262-3151, noon-4pm Tues.-Fri., $5), close to Centennial Park, or **Noble Car Wash** (355 Fairway Circle). Grab a shower or wash your duds at **Soldotna Wash-N-Dry** (121 Smiths Way, 907/262-8495, 7am-11pm daily); Wi-Fi is free while you wait.

Getting There

There are no scheduled commercial flights to Soldotna Airport. The nearby Kenai Airport has daily connections to Anchorage. Air taxis offering charters (as well as bear-viewing trips, fly-in fishing, and flightseeing) from the Soldotna Airport include **Talon Air Service** (907/262-8899, www.talonair.com), **Natron Air** (907/262-8440, www.natronair.com), and

High Adventure Air (907/262-5237, www.
highadventureair.com).

Get a ride from **Alaska Cab** (907/283-
6000, www.akcab.com). **Midway Auto
Rentals** (37452 Kenai Spur Hwy., 907/260-
3722, www.midwayautollc.com) has car
rentals.

The Stage Line (907/235-2252, www.
stagelineinhomer.com) runs vans connecting Soldotna with Anchorage ($75 one-way),
Homer ($55), and Seward (summer only,
$55). Service is Monday-Friday to Anchorage,
Seward, and Homer in the summer. Vans stop
at the Soldotna Visitors Information Center,
or other locations with advance notice.
Winter service runs once a week to Homer or
Anchorage, with no winter runs to Seward.

KENAI

The town of Kenai sits on a bluff above the
mouth of the Kenai River overlooking Cook
Inlet. With over 7,000 residents, it's the largest
town on the Kenai Peninsula. Across the inlet
to the southwest rise Redoubt and Iliamna,
active volcanoes at the head of the Aleutian
Range. The Alaska Range is visible to the
northwest.

History

Kenai is the second-oldest permanent settlement in Alaska, founded by Russian fur traders who built St. Nicholas Redoubt in 1791.
The U.S. Army built its own fort—Kenay—in
1869, two years after the Great Land changed
hands. Oil was discovered at the Swanson
River in 1957, followed by natural gas two
years later, and now Kenai is the largest and
most industrialized town on the peninsula.
Several of the 15 Cook Inlet platforms are visible from shore, but production has declined
in recent years, forcing the closure of a fertil-
izer plant and an LNG plant. A Tesoro refinery still operates in nearby Nikiski, along with
a power plant. The rich past has been buried
by Kenai's rather uneventful present in which
the town isn't much more than a series of in-
tersections, fast-food joints, and gas stations.

Sights

The **Kenai Visitors and Cultural Center
Museum** (11471 Kenai Spur Rd., 907/283-
1991, www.kenaichamber.org, 9am-6pm
Mon.-Fri., 10am-5pm Sat., noon-5pm Sun. late
May-early Sept., 10am-5pm Mon.-Fri., 10am-
4pm Sat. early Sept.-late May, free) houses cultural artifacts from Kenaitze Native peoples
and an amazing collection of walrus ivory,
local historical lore and natural history, and
art exhibits. The centerpiece is an enormous
scale model of a Cook Inlet oil production
platform.

From the museum, walk down toward
the bluff on Overland Avenue to the replica
of **Fort Kenay**, built in 1967 for the Alaska
Centennial. It isn't open to the public. Just up
the way is **Holy Assumption of the Virgin
Mary Orthodox Church** (1106 Mission Ave.,
907/283-4122), built in 1895 and the second-
oldest Russian Orthodox Church in the state
(the oldest is on Kodiak). It's a working church
with regular services; tours are available on
request, or peek through the windows at
the painted altar and brass chandelier. The
Chapel of Saint Nicholas (1906), across
the street, built atop the grave of Kenai's first
priest, also reflects the traditional Russian
Orthodox architectural style.

Entertainment and Events

In Old Town, **Kenai Fine Arts Center** (816
Cook Ave., 907/252-3661, www.kenaifineart.
com) provides gallery space for local artists and serves as home to regional art
organizations.

The **Kenai River Marathon** (www.
kenairivermarathon.org, late Sept.) is one of
the state's top marathon races.

The grounds of the Kenai Visitors and
Cultural Center are transformed into the
Kenai Saturday Market (11471 Kenai Spur
Rd., 907/283-1991, www.kenaichamber.org,
10am-5pm Sat. late May-early Sept.), with
arts, crafts, and fresh produce.

Recreation

My favorite Kenai destination is **Kenai Beach**

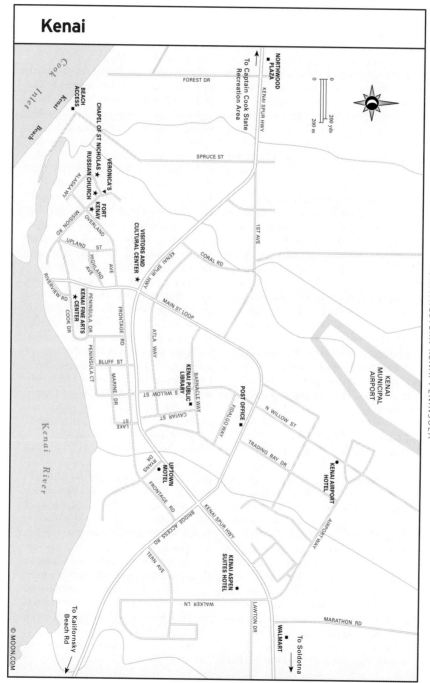

Kenai

Cook Inlet

Kenai Beach

To Captain Cook State Recreation Area

NORTHWOOD PLAZA

FOREST DR

BEACH ACCESS

CHAPEL OF ST NICHOLAS ★

VERONICA'S ★

RUSSIAN CHURCH ★

ALASKA HWY

MISSION RD

FORT KENAY ★

OVERLAND

UPLAND ST

HIGHLAND AVE

VISITORS AND CULTURAL CENTER ★

SPRUCE ST

1ST AVE

CORAL RD

KENAI SPUR HWY

KENAI SPUR HWY

MAIN ST LOOP

RIVERVIEW RD

PENINSULA DR

COOK DR

KENAI FINE ARTS CENTER ★

FRONTAGE RD

PENINSULA CT

ATLA WAY

BLUFF ST

MARINE DR

LAKE ST

CAVIAR ST

S WILLOW ST

KENAI PUBLIC LIBRARY

BARNACLE WAY

POST OFFICE

FIDALGO WAY

N WILLOW ST

TRADING BAY DR

KENAI MUNICIPAL AIRPORT

Kenai River

RYANS DR

UPTOWN MOTEL

FRONTAGE RD

BRIDGE ACCESS RD

KENAI SPUR HWY

KENAI AIRPORT HOTEL

AIRPORT WAY

TERN AVE

KENAI ASPEN SUITES HOTEL

WALKER LN

LAWTON DR

MARATHON RD

WALMART

To Soldotna

To Kalifornsky Beach Rd

0   200 yds
0   200 m

© MOON.COM

(end of Spruce St., north side of the river) near the mouth of the Kenai River and just a short distance from the Russian Orthodox Church; it's one of the best and most easily accessible beaches in Alaska. A line of low dunes backs the fine sand. However, the beach gets crowded with hundreds of **dipnetters** when salmon are running each July, and the carcasses can really stink up the place. Dipnetting is only open to Alaskan residents, but makes a great spectator sport for all. Special nets with 15-foot metal handles are used to catch fish as they head up the river to spawn.

The **Kenai Peninsula Oilers** (Cook Ave. and Main St., 907/283-7133, www. oilersbaseball.com) play semiprofessional baseball at Coral Seymour Memorial Park. Always fun to watch, the team has won several National Baseball Congress World Series championships over the years. It's one of six teams within the nation's top collegiate summer league, the Alaska Baseball League.

Kenai Golf Course (1420 Lawton Dr., 907/283-7500, www.kenaigolfcourse.com, daily May-Sept.) is an 18-hole public course. **Kenai Central High School** (9583 Kenai Spur Hwy., 907/283-2100, www.kpbsd.k12. ak.us) has an Olympic-size pool with open swim times.

Food

Hidden in a historic log cabin across the street from the Russian Orthodox Church in Old Town Kenai, **Veronica's Café** (604 Petersen Way, 907/283-2725, www. veronicascoffeehouse.com, 6am-8pm Mon.-Sat. May-Sept., 11am-4pm Tues.-Thurs., 11am-8pm Fri.-Sat. Oct.-Apr., $11-16) serves breakfast blintzes with reindeer sausage, polenta-crust quiche specials, Danish pancakes, soups, sandwiches (try the chicken cashew), espresso, and wonderful croissant bread pudding. Friday clam chowder is a locals' favorite, and this quirky café features open mike tunes on Friday evenings.

Inside the Uptown Motel near Bridge Access Road, **Louie's Steak & Seafood** (47 Spur View Dr., 907/283-3660, www. louiessteakandseafood.com, 5am-10pm daily, $24-45) is Kenai's surf-and-turf restaurant with rustic Alaskan decor accented by trophy animal mounts. The restaurant serves good steaks, king crab, beef stroganoff, and grilled king salmon—none of it for folks on a diet. Eggs benedict breakfasts are justifiably popular on weekends. The lounge attracts the sports crowd with 16 TVs and complimentary hors d'oeuvres.

The aptly named **Burger Bus** (912 Highland Ave., 907/283-9611, 11am-6pm Tues.-Sat., $6-11) is just up the street from the Kenai Visitors and Cultural Center. Try their Kenai killer burger, mushroom Swiss burger, green chili chicken, or fish-and-chips. It's all made while you wait and surprisingly tasty. These are easily the best burgers in the area.

Playa-Azul Mexican Restaurant (12498 Kenai Spur Hwy., 907/283-2010, 11am-9pm daily, $14-16) is *the* place for tacos, burritos, enchiladas, tostadas, and chiles rellenos. The guacamole is made fresh, and you can top things off at the salsa bar. Portions are ample and the food is authentic and flavorful. Playa-Azul is housed within a small strip mall (Northwood Plaza) just north of Kenai. The bar serves *horchatas* and margaritas. Colorful hand-painted chairs add to the festive atmosphere.

Kenai's fine dining restaurant, **The Flats Bistro** (39847 Kalifornsky Beach Rd., 907/335-1010, www.theflatsbistro.com, 11:30am-10pm Mon.-Sat.) has an out-of-the-way location overlooking the Kenai River flats. It's chic and modern with hardwood floors, high ceilings, an extensive wine list, and a back deck to enjoy the view. The limited dinner menu is divided into small bites ($8-12), including battered and fried pickles with lemon aioli, and more substantial entrées ($21-38) such as bacon-wrapped pork tenderloin, filet mignon, and codfish-and-chips. Lunch ($15-22) features build-your-own burgers, pulled pork tacos, and reuben sandwiches.

Accommodations

HOTELS

The Kenai Visitors and Cultural Center has a complete listing of local lodging places, along with their brochures. In the middle of Kenai town, **Uptown Motel** (47 Spur View Dr., 907/283-3660, www.uptownmotel.com, $139-189 d) has fridges and microwaves in all the guest rooms, plus Louie's Steak & Seafood and Back Door Lounge. There is free airport transportation and freezer space to store your catch. Check out the 100-year-old gold-plated cash register behind the front desk.

Kenai Airport Hotel (230 N. Willow St., 907/283-1577, www.kenaiairporthotels.com, $149-179 d) is a well-maintained, no-frills place adjacent to the airport. Rooms have two queens or a king bed, fridges, microwaves, laundry, and continental breakfast.

Kenai Aspen Suites Hotel (10431 Kenai Spur Hwy., 907/283-2272, www.aspenhotelsak.com, $199-209 d) has generously sized rooms, full kitchens, and an exercise room. It's right across the street from Safeway and fast-food places; Walmart is two blocks away.

BED-AND-BREAKFAST

On a 20-acre spread halfway between Soldotna and Kenai, **Red Cabin B&B** (44392 Carver Dr., 907/283-0836, www.redcabinbandb.com, mid-May-mid-Sept., $135-150 d) consists of two adorable and immaculate cabins. Each has a private bath, a queen bed, a pull-out futon, a TV, and a barbecue. The smaller cabin includes a kitchenette, while the larger contains a full kitchen. Red Cabin's owners provide everything you need for breakfast, and they have a barn with horses.

LODGES

Kenai is home to several fishing lodges, with packages to please anglers of all types. An excellent choice is **Jimmie Jack's Lodge** (36065 Reef Dr., 907/262-5561 or 866/553-4744, www.jimmiejackfishing.com, 7 days $2,700-3,000 pp), featuring a beachfront location, good food, boats, and pleasant

accommodations. Most guests stay for seven days, providing time to fish for kings, halibut, and silvers while also exploring the area.

Salmon Catcher Lodge (37911 Ralph Lane, 907/335-2001, www.salmoncatcherlodge.com, 7 days $4,000-5,000) is a luxurious modern fishing lodge—the largest on the Kenai Peninsula—with a variety of all-inclusive accommodations. Amenities include full kitchens, laundry, and Wi-Fi.

If you really want to get away, **Alaska Island Retreat** (907/598-9035, www.alaskaislandretreat.com, mid-May-mid-Sept.) is definitely the place. The 160-acre homestead sits on an island in the middle of Cook Inlet, 30 miles southwest of Kenai. A resident of the island for over 45 years, owner David Chessik knows this beautiful and very remote spot well. Alaska Island Retreat has three sleeper cabins, a main cooking cabin, outhouses, a sauna, and a smokehouse. Everything runs on solar power and batteries. Cell phones may or may not work, and the Wi-Fi is very limited, but this is a fine place to fish or just take in the quietude. There are no bears on the island, but moose, eagles, foxes, and other animals are seen, along with amazing runs of salmon. Guests stay on Kalgin Island for $300 pp per day (half price for children), including lodging and meals. Access is by air, and the closest airport is in Kenai. Expect to spend around $1,200 to fly up to five people to and from the island.

CAMPING

The nearest public camping places are in Soldotna. Twenty-five miles north of Kenai is quiet Captain Cook State Recreation Area, where **Discovery Campground** (39 Kenai Spur Hwy., 907/262-5581, www.alaskastateparks.org, mid-May-Sept., day-use $5, camping $15) has 53 campsites with water and pit toilets. The beach here is an outstanding place to find agates.

Five miles south of Kenai, **Diamond M Ranch** (48500 Diamond M Ranch Rd., 907/283-9424, www.diamondmranch.com, tents $65 d, RVs $70-95, rooms and cabins $85-209 d) is a full-service resort with laundry facilities, fish cleaning stations, freezer space, and Wi-Fi. The site overlooks the Kenai River estuary, a good place to watch for moose, caribou, and bald eagles. Paved walking and biking trails continue all the way to Soldotna. Located on an 80-acre spread, the RV park centers around a "Main Street" cluster of gold rush-style buildings that house suites with private baths, kitchens, and decks. Other lodging options include everything from B&B rooms to an authentic homestead cabin with a sod roof and outhouse. There's even a plastic "igloo" that sleeps one person.

Beluga Lookout Lodge & RV Park (929 Mission Ave., 907/283-5999, www.belugalookout.com, May-Sept., RVs $90-100 in July, $40-55 other summer months) has full hookups along Cook Inlet. It's near the Kenai River mouth, making it especially popular with anglers, and has a fish cleaning station, restrooms, showers, laundry, picnic tables, cable TV, a gift shop, and Wi-Fi.

Information and Services

For information, start at the **Kenai Visitors and Cultural Center** (11471 Kenai Spur Rd., 907/283-1991, www.kenaichamber.org, 9am-6pm Mon.-Fri., 10am-6pm Sat., 10am-5pm Sun. late May-early Sept., 9am-5pm Mon.-Fri., 10am-4pm Sat. early Sept.-late May), where you'll find a big rack of brochures about the area and a helpful staff.

Kenai Community Library (163 Main St. Loop, 907/283-4378, www.kenailibrary.org, 9am-7pm Mon.-Thurs., 9am-6pm Fri., 9am-5pm Sat.) has a large collection of Alaskan titles, plus computers and Wi-Fi.

Kenai Wash-N-Dry (500 Lake St., 907/283-8473, 7am-11pm daily) has laundry and showers. The Kenai **Walmart** (10096 Kenai Spur Hwy., 907/395-0971, www.walmart.com) is the largest store on the Kenai Peninsula.

Getting There and Around

The **Kenai Airport** (305 N. Willow St., www.kenaiairport.com) is close to the heart of Kenai. Both **Ravn Alaska** (907/266-8394 or 800/866-8394, www.flyravn.com) and **Grant Aviation** (907/290-3383 or 888/359-4726, www.flygrant.com) have multiple daily flights between Anchorage and Kenai. Flight time is 30 minutes.

Based on Arness Lake between Kenai and Nikiski, **Alaska West Air** (907/776-5147, www.alaskawestair.com) has flightseeing, bear-viewing trips, and sportfishing. They fly a fleet of floatplanes, including turbine otters and beavers. All-day bear-viewing trips to Brooks Camp in Katmai National Park ($795 pp) have a four-person minimum. Shorter bear-viewing trips ($350 pp) go to Wolverine Creek.

Great Alaska Adventures (907/262-4515 or 866/411-2327, www.greatalaska.com) has a comfortable glamping bear camp with Weather Ports, twin or king beds, showers, and composting toilets. The camp is surrounded by a bear-proof electric fence. All-inclusive stays start at $1,795 pp for a one-night, two-day stay.

Rent cars at the airport from **Avis** (907/283-7900, www.avis.com) or **Budget** (907/243-0150, www.budgetalaskaonline.com). Call **Alaska Cab** (907/283-6000, www.akcab.com) for rides around town.

NIKISKI

Approximately 15 miles north of Kenai is the settlement of Nikiski (ni-KISS-kee), home to around 4,000 people. There's no downtown, just a scattering of random businesses in varying stages of disrepair. The area has clearly seen better times. Cook Inlet's oil and gas platforms are visible from the shore, and onshore are more industrial facilities, including a Tesoro refinery and a gas-fired power plant.

Recreation

At the end of North Kenai Road, **Captain Cook State Recreation Area** (www.alaskastateparks.org, day-use $5, campsites $15) is 25 miles from Kenai and six miles north of Nikiski. This is a delightful place to camp, hike the rocky shoreline, look for colorful agates on the beach, enjoy the views across Cook Inlet, or simply relax. On summer weekends, locals come here to swim in the surprisingly warm waters of Stormy Lake.

Families will love spending an afternoon at the North Peninsula Recreation Area's dome-covered **Nikiski Pool** (Mile 23, Spur Hwy., 907/776-6410, www.northpenrec.com, $7), where the featured attractions are a corkscrew waterslide (1pm-9pm daily June-Aug., 7am-9pm Fri., 1pm-9pm Sat.-Sun. Sept.-May), a "rain umbrella," a hot tub, and a large pool for lap swimming.

Brewery

In the country a few miles south of Nikiski, ★ **Kassik's Brewery** (47160 Spruce Haven St., 907/776-4055, www.kassiksbrew.com, noon-7pm Mon.-Sat., noon-5pm Sun. late May-early Sept., noon-7pm Tues.-Sat., noon-5pm Sun. early Sept.-late May) is a small craft brewery with a strong regional reputation. Brewmaster Frank Kassik has 10 brews on tap, including Beaver Tail Blonde, Whaler's Wheat, Moose Point Porter, and the ever-popular Morning Wood IPA. Several of their beers have won gold medals in the World Beer Championship. The tasting room serves free tasting flights of their beers, or you can purchase a growler or half-growler to go. Kassik's beers are available in local stores as 22-ounce "bomber" bottles. The brewery is a bit hard to find, so call ahead for directions, or get out your GPS.

Accommodations

Numerous lakes dot the northern Kenai Peninsula, and one of the prettiest is two-mile-long Daniels Lake, located five miles east of Nikiski. It's a generally peaceful place where you'll hear the call of loons on a summer evening. Two B&Bs are located on the shore of the lake.

Daniels Lake Lodge B&B (Mile 30, Kenai Spur Hwy., 907/776-5578, www.danielslakelodge.com, $195-230 d, cabins $225-490, rates lower weekdays) includes three rooms in the main house and four log cabins that are perfect for families. This is a fine get-away-from-it-all place set on 10 acres of lakeshore. Amenities include a waterside hot tub, private baths, and self-serve breakfasts with fresh duck eggs and reindeer sausage. A canoe and small motorboat are available to explore the lake. Friendly owners Karen and Jim Burris have a well-behaved golden doodle dog and pet ducks. It's close to the Swanson River, a good place for fishing without the crowds. There's a two-night minimum in the cabins.

Grouchy Old Woman B&B (48570 N. Earl Dr., 907/776-8775, www.grouchyoldwoman.homestead.com, $110 d) should really have a "Not" at the end of the name. The owner really isn't that grouchy; she just appreciates the peace and quiet of Daniels Lake, where the B&B is located. Four rooms share two baths, and guests are served a big hot breakfast each morning. There's a large sitting room downstairs and a dock where you can borrow a canoe or rowboat.

SOUTH TO HOMER

South of Soldotna, the Sterling Highway hugs the coastline all the way to Homer, a distance of 75 miles. The view across the Cook Inlet is of the Aleutian volcanic crown, **Mount Redoubt** (10,197 feet) to the north and **Mount Iliamna** (10,016 feet) to the south—both within Lake Clark National Park. On a very clear day you can also see **Mount Augustine,** a solitary volcanic island with a well-defined cone at the bottom of the inlet. They're all very active; Augustine last erupted in 2006, followed by Redoubt in 2009. See www.avo.alaska.edu to check current activity.

KASILOF

Tiny Kasilof (ka-SEE-loff, pop. 600) is 15 miles south of Soldotna along the Kasilof River. Kalifornsky Beach (a.k.a. K-Beach) Road meets the Sterling Highway here. The road continues north to Kenai and Soldotna. Kasilof is home to four-time Iditarod champion Lance Mackey. There's a post office, but no visitors center; get details on local businesses at www.visitkasilofalaska.com.

The **Kasilof Historical Museum** (24117 Kalifornsky Beach Rd., 907/262-2999, 1pm-4pm Tues.-Sun. late May-early Sept.) has a collection of restored historic cabins from early-day fox farmers and trappers. Find it 0.5 miles out K-Beach Road off the Sterling Highway.

At Mile 5 of K-Beach Road, turn left on **Kasilof Beach Road** for access to the north side of the Kasilof River mouth. Access to the south side is via North Cohoe Loop Road, which turns off the Sterling Highway at Mile 110. During the height of the silver salmon run in July, hundreds of Alaskan dip netters descend upon this area, camping on the dunes and tramping down the muddy shore with giant nets as the incoming tide brings a rush of salmon up the river. Dipnetting is only open to Alaskan residents, but nonresidents can try their luck with a rod and reel.

At Mile 110, look for the big metal T and follow the road to pretty **Johnson Lake State Recreation Area** (day-use $5, campsites $15), where the lake is stocked with rainbow trout. The state recreation area has picnic shelters and campsites with water and toilets. Continue five miles out the road to a free boat launch that serves as an access point for **Tustumena Lake,** within Kenai National Wildlife Refuge. This huge lake is infamous for sudden weather changes that can swamp unprepared boaters.

Kasilof is the starting point for the **Tustumena 200 Sled Dog Race** (www.tustumena200.com, late Jan.). It's a qualifying race for the Iditarod, and a great place to meet mushers and dogs up close. Unfortunately, a warming climate has wreaked havoc on the race; it was cancelled in 2014, 2015, and 2016 due to a lack of snow.

Kasilof Mercantile (Mile 109, Sterling Hwy., 907/262-4809, www.thekasilofmercantile.com, 7am-10pm daily) has a café, groceries, video rentals, ice cream, and espresso.

Accommodations

Right on the banks of the Kasilof River, **Gallery Lodge** (Terrace Dr., 907/229-2999, www.alaskagallerylodge.com, house $250 for 4 guests, rooms and suites $130-250 d) has a two-bedroom house with a full kitchen and laundry, plus a variety of suites and rooms with private or shared baths. Fishing packages are also offered, and the lodge is popular for weddings and retreats.

Friendly and clean, **Kasilof River Lodge and Cabins** (Cohoe Loop Rd., 907/262-6348 or 888/262-7075, www.kasilofriverlodge.com, late May-early Sept., $75-125 d, yurt $75 d, cabins $95-175 d) has a variety of accommodations, including lodge rooms, a yurt, and cabins. Some units have private baths and kitchens, while others share a bathhouse and a cooking area. A hearty continental breakfast is included for all guests, and the owners have 20 acres of land with river access for fishing. Located near the mouth of the Kasilof River, the lodge is a good place to hang out with local commercial anglers and serves as the de facto community center for the settlement of Cohoe. RV hookups are also available.

Crooked Creek Retreat (59325 Sterling Hwy., 907/260-9014, www.crookedcreekretreat.com) is a good choice for multiple-night fishing packages based in Kasilof.

On a bluff overlooking Cook Inlet and Mount Redoubt, **Alaskan Sunset Cabins** (Mile 6, Kalifornsky Beach Rd., 907/283-9246 or 866/286-6946, www.alaskansunset.com, May-Sept., smaller units $79-139 d, larger units $189-499 d) consists of nine modern cabins that are popular with families and anglers. These range widely, from tiny two-person boxes to house-size units with three bedrooms and two baths. Most include full kitchens, private baths, decks, grills, and scenic vistas.

Alaska Riverview Lodge (24771 Amber Dr., 907/260-5432, www.alaskariverview.com, rooms $110 d, cabins $225 d, suite $140 d, house $325) has an array of lodging options: two cabins, an apartment suite, kitchenette rooms, a master suite, and even a four-bedroom house. Rates include breakfast in the main lodge. This is the only lodge with its own dock on the Kasilof River, and guests can borrow fishing or clamming gear. There's a fish cleaning station, picnic tables, and an observation deck. All rooms contain freezers to store your catch. The lodge is off K-Beach Road, a mile north of the junction with Sterling Highway.

Camping

At the confluence of Crooked Creek and the Kasilof River, **Crooked Creek RV Park** (23437 Trespass St., 907/262-1299, www.crookedcreekguides.com, RVs $50) is a good base for fishing. Access is from North Cohoe Loop Road at Mile 111 of the Sterling Highway. A variety of fishing and lodging packages are available.

CLAM GULCH

At a wide spot in the road sits Clam Gulch, which was for a long time Alaska's favorite clamming beach. Unfortunately, razor clam populations have crashed and the area has been closed since 2014. Contact the Alaska Department of Fish and Game (www.adfg.alaska.gov) for the current situation. If clamming does reopen, you'll need a sportfishing license, shovel, bucket, and gloves.

At Mile 117 is the turnoff for **Clam Gulch State Recreation Area** (day-use $5, campsites $15) and a two-mile gravel road down to the campground and former clamming grounds.

Clam Gulch Lodge B&B (Mile 119, Sterling Hwy., 907/260-3778 or 800/700-9555, www.clamgulch.com, $150 d, cabin $250) is a modern place with a hearty breakfast and shared baths. A spacious cabin has five bedrooms, a loft, a full kitchen, and a private bath. It sleeps up to six and has a three-night minimum. Located on a high bluff facing Cook Inlet, the lodge also offers a variety of fishing and adventure packages.

NINILCHIK

This small town of 700 is halfway between Soldotna and Homer. Located where the Ninilchik River empties into Cook Inlet, it was settled in the early 1800s by retired Russian-American Company workers who took Native Alaskan wives. You'll find classic water's-edge houses and weathered structures at the old village, down a short side road off Sterling Highway. Follow the road that parallels the Ninilchik River around toward the "spit"; you wind up on the other side of the river and village on the hardpan inlet beach.

Ninilchik's beloved **Transfiguration of Our Lord Russian Orthodox Church** was built on a hilltop in 1900. Access is via Orthodox Avenue (look for the sign at Mile 134, Sterling Hwy.), or by a footpath from Ninilchik Village. Fireweed fills the adjacent graveyard in midsummer, providing a colorful foreground for photos of the church with a backdrop of Cook Inlet and the volcanic summit of Mount Iliamna. The main town of Ninilchik is a mile south of the church, with a smattering of businesses along the highway.

A quaint old building in the center of old town, **Ninilchik Village Cache** (907/567-3228) is worth a visit for original jewelry and Native art pieces by Jim Lee. It's been here for more than 35 years.

Festivals and Events

Ninilchik hosts the **Kenai Peninsula Fair** (www.kenaipeninsulafair.com, 3rd weekend in Aug.) with a rodeo, rides, livestock, pig races, music, and food booths. It's decidedly small-town fun, and perfect if you have kids with you. The fairgrounds are right in the center of town.

Don't miss **Salmonfest** (www.salmonfestalaska.org, early Aug.)—three days of fish, fun, politics, and live music at the Kenai Peninsula Fairgrounds. Past festivals have included such bands as Michael Franti, Brandi Carlile, Rusted Root, Great American Taxi, Emmylou Harris, California Honeydrops, Indigo Girls, Young Dubliners, and Clinton Fearon, plus—of course—the jam

band Leftover Salmon. The festival is one of Alaska's biggest summertime concert venues, attracting several thousand people.

Fishing

Ninilchik is a very poplar starting point for Cook Inlet fishing trips. Many charter boats put in at Deep Creek State Recreation Area, where large **tractors** pull boat trailers down the beach and launch boats out beyond the waves. Don't miss this unique scene on a summer weekend morning, with the action generally taking place an hour or two before high tide. Local charter fishing operations include **Ninilchik Charters** (800/973-4742, www.ninilchik.com), **Gotta Fish Charters** (907/406-3474, www.gottafish-charters. com), **Afishunt Charters** (907/567-3393 or 800/347-4114, www.afishunt.com), and **Heavenly Sights Charters** (Mile 132, Sterling Hwy., 907/567-7371 or 800/479-7371, www.heavenlysights.com).

Food

On the north edge of town, **The Buzz Café** (15555 Sterling Hwy., 907/567-3307, 6am-4:30pm daily) serves Kaladi Brothers lattes and mochas; it's the best espresso buzz spot for 30 miles in either direction.

Rosco's Pizza (15915 Sterling Hwy., 907/567-1060, www.roscospizzaalaska.com, 11am-9pm Tues.-Thurs., 11am-10pm Fri.-Sat., 11am-9pm Sun., $12-30) serves tasty hand-tossed pizzas, lasagna, burgers, meatball subs, nachos, and salads to dine in or take out. Everything is made from scratch; be sure to check out the daily specials. Rosco's does not serve alcohol.

Across from the Ninilchik fairgrounds, **Keen Kow Thai Food** (66873 Robin Ave., 907/567-3211, noon-8pm Thurs.-Tues., $10-14) brings the authentic flavors of Thailand to small-town Alaska. The house special—Keen Kow—is a red curry with chicken or pork.

Also popular are shrimp pad Thai, cashew chicken, and Thai fresh rolls.

Accommodations

A completely unexpected find, ★ **Great House Lodge** (Mile 131, Sterling Hwy., 907/567-3599, www.aksupperclub.com, $200-350 d) crowns a high bluff three miles north of Ninilchik. The deck affords panoramic vistas of Cook Inlet and the summits of three volcanoes. The lodge has four luxuriously appointed guest rooms with private baths and a big deck, and sits on 12 acres of land. The lodge's restaurant, **aksupperclub** (five-course meal $65-85 pp, add $50 and up for wine pairings), is open nightly, with a single seating at 6pm. There's space for 12 guests around a large table, and the menu changes every day, reflecting the seasons. Fresh and local is the theme; the owners managed a local seafood company for years and use produce from their own garden. Don't miss the award-winning burgundy chocolate tart. Meals are a leisurely affair, so be ready for three or four relaxing hours to enjoy the food and intimate setting. Reservations are required at least 48 hours in advance.

One mile out Oilwell Road is **Drift-In B&B** (907/567-3448 or 800/567-0249, www.driftin. com, $115-125 d), where three rooms share two baths and a fourth room has its own bath. The house has a lounge and small kitchen with freezer space. Rates include a full breakfast, or a continental breakfast and sack lunch if you're leaving early on a fishing charter.

In the heart of historic Ninilchik village and just steps from the river, **Alaska Adventure Suites** (66710 Mission Ave., 907/277-1800, www.alaskaadventuresuites. com, $225-295 d, extra guests $35 pp, up to 7 people) has two nicely decorated apartment suites, each with a full kitchen, living room, and bath. The larger 1,200-square-foot unit has two bedrooms, panoramic views of Cook Inlet and three active volcanoes, hardwood floors, and a fireplace. Most guests stay several days to take advantage of local fishing charters. A two-night minimum is required.

1: Ninilchik village; 2: Transfiguration of Our Lord Russian Orthodox Church in Ninilchik

Camping

Three very popular state campgrounds (907/235-7024, www.alaskastateparks.org, day-use $5, campsites $15) are scattered around town: **Ninilchik River Campground** is big, woodsy, and uncrowded; **Ninilchik View Campground** is atop a high bluff; and **Ninilchik Beach Campground** has undeveloped sites. **Deep Creek State Recreation Area** is just two miles to the south at Mile 137 of the Sterling Highway.

Located on an eight-acre spread right in town, **Alaskan Angler RV Resort** (15640 Kingsley Rd., 907/567-3393, www.alaskabestrvpark.com, May-mid-Sept., tents $25, RVs $45-65, cabins $200-275) has showers, laundry, Wi-Fi, and cable TV service, as well as vacation cabins and mobile homes.

All Seasons Campground (Mile 3, Oilwell Rd., 907/567-3396, www.allseasonsalaska.com, tents $15 d, RVs $36-42 with full hookups, cabins $150 for 4 people) has a laundry, Wi-Fi, showers, and a few cabins.

Information and Services

Contact the **Ninilchik Chamber of Commerce** (907/567-3571, www.ninilchikchamber.com) for information on local places. Stock up at **Ninilchik General Store** (Mile 136, Sterling Hwy., 907/567-3378).

ANCHOR POINT

This no-frills town of 2,000 people is the most westerly highway point in North America (or, more precisely, the most westerly town on a road system connected with the Lower 48). The point of land was named by Captain James Cook after his ship lost an anchor here in 1787. It has never been found. Anchor Point has a handful of services, but the main attractions are fishing, camping, beachcombing, and its proximity to the far more interesting town of Homer.

Sights

Four miles south of Anchor Point is the easy-to-miss turnoff to **Norman Lowell Gallery**

(Mile 161, Sterling Hwy., 907/235-7344, www.normanlowellgallery.net, 9am-5pm Mon.-Sat. May-mid-Sept., free). It would be easy to just keep driving; after all, you're almost to Homer. However, this is one stop you really should make. Follow a winding gravel road steeply uphill to this stunning 10,000-square-foot gallery that exhibits more than 300 of Norman Lowell's paintings in a variety of media. Norman and Libby Lowell homesteaded here in 1958, and he built a reputation as a painter of traditional Alaskan landscapes. Many of his works are large, with one stretching 7 by 14 feet! The sales gallery has both prints (starting at $250) and originals (some for $85,000). Now in his 80s and blind, Norman is no longer able to paint, but his wife provides tours of their flower-bedecked family homestead. Even if you aren't a fan of traditional art, this is a must-stop for visitors.

Recreation

Anchor River is a premier fishing destination, attracting anglers in pursuit of king salmon, silver salmon, Dolly Varden, and steelhead. If you aren't into fishing, Anchor Point's most popular attraction is the long sandy beach at the mouth of the Anchor River. Get here by heading downhill from town on the Old Sterling Highway. Turn right after the old bridge and continue a mile down Anchor River Beach Road. Watch tractors launching fishing boats on the beach most summer mornings, or head up the beach in either direction for a long hike. This entire area is part of the **Anchor River State Recreation Area** (www.alaskastateparks.org).

Fireweed Meadows Golf Course (72749 Milo Fritz Ave., 907/226-2582, www.fireweedmeadowsgolf.com, $18) is a nine-hole course for golf enthusiasts.

For a good taste of the ruggedly wild country around Anchor Point, contact Ron Wilhoit of **Alaska Draft Horse** (907/299-2163, www.alaskadrafthorse.com). He leads 1.5-hour rides ($99 pp) on magnificent Percheron draft horses through the forests and hills in Chakok River Valley, with dramatic views along the way. These personalized tours are for one or two people.

Food

Anchor Point dining options are limited, and the dominant theme seems to be converted buses and Quonset huts. The best of these is **Ramiro's** (33840 Sterling Hwy., 907/235-9694, 11am-7pm Tues.-Sat., $10-13), an authentic family-run Mexican-American eatery housed in a little red bus. (This is not to be confused with The Blue Bus restaurant directly across the street.) There are a couple of picnic tables out front, or you can head down to the beach for a better vista. Get two enchiladas, rice, and beans; it's finger-licking good. Other menu items include a half-pound burger with fries, and shrimp fajitas. Breakfast items are served all day, and a kids' menu is available.

Accommodations

Bear Essentials Lodging (off Mile 150, Sterling Hwy., 907/350-2997, www. bearessentialslodging.com, $110-120 d, additional guests $20 pp) is a rustic and remote lodge with reasonable rates. Three large bedrooms are available, each with a private bath, handmade log beds, TV, and access to the kitchen and dining area. It's north of Anchor Point, three miles off the highway.

Just a short distance off the Sterling Highway, **Sleepy Bear Cabins** (34053 North Fork Rd., 907/235-5625 or 866/235-5625, www.sleepybearalaska.com, $125 d, add $10 pp for additional guests) consists of five well-maintained cabins, each with queen beds, a private bath, and access to a sauna.

Just off the highway, a mile north of Anchor Point, **Bear Paw Adventure** (72450 Camai Rd., 907/299-1650 or 866/286-0576, www.bearpawadventure.com, $230-285 d, additional guests $30 pp) has four unique log vacation homes of varying size on a 14-acre spread. The largest home sleeps 10; all contain kitchens, baths, laundry, and TVs.

Camping

Five very popular campgrounds ($15 d) are located along Anchor River Road within **Anchor River State Recreation Area** (www.alaskastateparks.org). They often fill during the peak of the king salmon run in July.

Four miles north of Anchor Point, **Stariski State Recreation Site** (Mile 152, Sterling Hwy., day-use $5, campsites $15) has one of the best views of any state campground. A steep road—not recommended for RVs—provides access off the highway.

Kyllonen's RV Park (74160 Anchor Point Rd., 907/235-7762, www.kyllonensrvpark. com, late May-early Sept., RVs $44-49) has view sites near the end of Beach Road and close to the Anchor River boat launch. Amenities include laundry, showers, Wi-Fi, and charter fishing. It's the most westerly RV park in North America, with views to match.

Information

Tiny **Anchor Point Chamber of Commerce Visitors Information Center** (34175 Sterling Hwy., 907/235-2600, www. anchorpointchamber.org, 10am-4pm daily late May-early Sept., hours limited in winter) has a few historical photos and memorabilia.

NIKOLAEVSK

The Russian Old Believer village of Nikolaevsk is nine miles east of Anchor Point via North Fork Road and Nikolaevsk Road. This isolated community of 300 is one of several on the Kenai Peninsula where these traditional people live; nearly all speak both Russian and English. Three other Russian villages (Kachemak Selo, Razdolna, and Voznesenka) are 25 miles east of Homer, and other Old Believer settlements are in Delta Junction, Kodiak Island, and Sterling. Many Old Believers fled from Russia following tsarist persecution and the Bolshevik Revolution, settling in such far-flung places as Brazil, Australia, Alberta, Minnesota, and Oregon.

There's a picturesque **church** in Nikolaevsk, and the women and girls wear scarves and ankle-length dresses, while men have beards and distinctive shirts. But they also have all the modern conveniences, including big pickup trucks, smartphones, and satellite TV. Many Old Believer men commercial fish for a living. As you might expect, villagers are not particularly welcoming to voyeurs, so don't go around pointing your camera at people.

Food

One ultra-friendly local is Nina Fefelov, the owner of the **Samovar Café** (907/235-6867, www.russiangiftsnina.com, Mon.-Sat. Apr.-mid-Oct., closed Russian holidays, cash only). The café serves such traditional dishes ($5-12) as borscht, *pelmeni, piroshki,* and Russian tea, along with Russian gifts. (Wait, did she just take those *piroshkis* out of a Costco bag?) Hours are a bit hit-or-miss, so call ahead to make sure she's open. Nina is quite the entrepreneur, and visitors will find themselves pushed into dressing in Old Believer garb to have their photo taken (for cash, of course).

Homer

TOP EXPERIENCE

Homer has a dazzling reputation for some of the finest scenery, the mildest climate, heaviest halibut, biggest bays, longest spits, coolest people, and best quality of life in the state. And the truth is, Homer is one of Alaska's peerless towns. It has an undeniably beautiful setting, with the unruly coastline, undulating fjords, and cavalcading Kenai Mountains across magnificent Kachemak Bay. The temperatures are generally mild—for Alaska. The halibut occasionally tip the scales at over 200 pounds, and you can try your luck at salmon fishing for the cost of a fishing license. An abundance of fine artists and craftspeople call Homer home, selling their wares at small galleries full of rare and tempting stuff. And some of the state's best fishing, boating, hiking, kayaking, natural history, wildlife, and photo ops are around Homer in Kachemak Bay. So the bottom line is: Homer distinctly deserves its reputation. Welcome to Homer, Cosmic Hamlet by the Sea.

HISTORY

The Russians knew of the limitless coal in this area in the early 1800s, and Americans were mining the seams only a decade after the Alaska Purchase. The gold rush began delivering people and supplies to the small port at the end of the sandy spit on their way to the gold fields at Hope and Sunrise up the Cook Inlet in the mid-1890s. One of the most flamboyant prospectors to pass through, Homer Pennock left his name on the settlement. Mining the hundreds of millions of tons of accessible bituminous fuel continued until 1907, when a combination of fire in Homer, federal policy, and falling prices burned out the market. Slowly and inevitably, the fishers and homesteaders began settling in during the 1920s, and they found a lifetime supply of home-heating fuel free for the taking right on the beach; it's still collected by some locals.

Homer remained a small fishing and canning port until the early 1950s, when the Sterling Highway finally connected the town with the rest of the continent. Since then, the population has grown, to over 4,000 today, with commercial fishing and tourism the primary economic pillars. Homer has an interesting mix of people. Drop by the docks and you'll encounter both the long-haired Rasta crowd and Russian Old Believers, whose women wear prim and proper long dresses while the men sport long beards.

SIGHTS
Overlook

Homer is the end of the line. After the five-hour drive south from Anchorage,

Homer

© MOON.COM

Kachemak Bay

To Kenai and Anchorage

KAREN HORNADAY PARK CAMPGROUND

KAREN HORNADAY PARK

FAIRVIEW AVE

SOUNDVIEW AVE

CAMPGROUND RD

SOUTH PENINSULA HOSPITAL

CRITENDEN DR

OCEAN SHORES RV PARK

OCEAN SHORES MOTEL

PRATT MUSEUM

BARTLETT AVE

HOPE ST

HOMER CHAMBER OF COMMERCE VISITOR CENTER

OLSON LN

JENNY LN

PIONEER INN

BAYVIEW

DRIFTWOOD INN/RV PARK

SAVE-U-MORE

HOMER THEATRE

MAIN ST

PAULA'S PLACE B&B

BUNNELL ST GALLERY

BUNNELL ST

PIONEER AVE

NOMAR

SPYGLASS INN

TWO SISTERS BAKERY

ISLANDS AND OCEAN VISITOR CENTER

STERLING HWY

SVEDUND ST

Bishop's Beach

Beluga Slough Trail

GRUBSTAKE

KLONDIKE

BONANZA

KACHEMAK WAY

Beluga Slough

LIBRARY

SAFEWAY

ALASKAN SUITES HOTEL

HEATH ST

PTARMIGAN ARTS

WHALESONG B&B

HIGH SCHOOL (SWIMMING POOL)

POST OFFICE

LAKE ST

CENTER FOR ALASKAN COASTAL STUDIES

ULMER'S

EAST END RD

EAST HILL RD

HOMER INN & SPA

OCEAN DR LOOP

OCEAN DR LOOP

OCEAN DR

LAKE ST

KREUTH WAY

OCEAN HOUSE INN

Beluga Lake

HOMER FARMERS MARKET

SEABREEZE CT

LAKESHORE DR

OCEAN DR

BAY AVE

DOUGLAS

A ST

HOMER BREWING COMPANY

GRACE RIDGE BREWING

BAY AVE B&B

AIRPORT TERMINAL

MARINER PARK

SPIT RD

KACHEMAK DR

AIRPORT

To End of Spit

THE HOMER SPIT

0   400 yds
0   400 m

travelers crest a high hill to a stunning view as they come into Homer. Pull off the Sterling Highway at Mile 170 where a **big overlook** looks over Kachemak Bay, the Homer Spit, and a line of snowy mountains, glaciers, and volcanoes. Don't arrive on a clear summer afternoon, or your next stop will be a real estate office in downtown Homer! But do stop for a photo or two to show you've made it to one of the prettiest places in Alaska.

TOP EXPERIENCE

★ Homer Spit

This four-mile finger of real estate jutting boldly into Kachemak Bay hosts the Small Boat Harbor, touristy boardwalks, a famous Fishing Hole, infamous Salty Dawg Saloon, Land's End Resort, public camping, charter halibut and salmon fishing, a ferry terminal, and lazy beachcombing with an incomparable view. It is Homer's main attraction, and a wonderfully busy place in midsummer. You could easily spend several days just exploring the shops, walking the beaches, flying kites, enjoying a seafood lunch, angling for salmon in the Fishing Hole, renting a stand-up paddleboard, soaking up the mountain-and-glacier vistas, and sitting around a campfire as the midsummer sun heads down around midnight. Day breezes kick up most afternoons, making for fine sailing and ideal conditions for kiteboarders. And when the wind really blows, the waves roll in, attracting surfers. No wonder so many folks fall in love with Homer!

The Pratt Museum's 1.5-hour **Historic Harbor Walking Tours** (907/235-8635, www.prattmuseum.org, 3pm Mon. and Thurs. June-early Sept., $10 pp) depart from Salty Dawg Saloon.

★ Islands and Ocean Visitor Center

Located on the edge of Homer, the extraordinary **Islands and Ocean Visitor Center** (95 Sterling Hwy., 907/235-6961, www.islandsandocean.org, 9am-5pm daily early May-early Sept., 10am-5pm Mon.-Sat. early

Sept.-late May, free) provides an introduction to the 4.9-million-acre **Alaska Maritime National Wildlife Refuge,** some 2,500 islands, spires, and coastal headlands scattered from Southeast Alaska to the Arctic. These remote islands provide the largest seabird refuge in the United States, with millions of them nesting on rugged cliffs. Inside the Alaska Islands and Ocean Visitor Center, a grand two-story glass lobby faces Kachemak Bay, and visitors can take a stunning voyage to the islands via a 14-minute award-winning video. After viewing the video, step into a room that recreates the sights, sounds, and smells of a bird rookery in the Pribilofs, and learn about the birds and marine mammals that inhabit these remote places, and the researchers that work there, through interactive exhibits.

Check the schedule for daily activities, including natural history and map talks and guided hikes and tide-pooling. Don't miss the hands-on **Discovery Labs** (1pm Wed. and Fri.). All of these free kid-friendly events are offered mid-June-mid-August. **Lake Clark National Park** (907/235-7903, www.nps.gov/lacl) also has an office in the building.

Bishops Beach

A short trail leads from the Islands and Ocean Visitor Center past Beluga Slough to Bishops Beach, which is also accessible by car from Bunnell Avenue; turn right on Beluga Avenue and follow it to the beach. This is a delightful spot for a low-tide walk, with extraordinary views of the mountains, volcanoes, and glaciers lining the bay. Pieces of coal wash ashore from nearby outcrops, and intrepid hikers can follow the beach north seven miles to the Diamond Creek Trail, which heads uphill to the Sterling Highway. Leave a car at the Diamond Creek Trailhead off the highway to make your return easier. You'll need to time this hike with the tides to avoid getting trapped against the cliffs.

Diamond Creek Trail is an easy and fun path, even if you don't do the long beach walk. The trailhead is directly across the Sterling Highway from Diamond Ridge Road. A narrow dirt road—small cars only—takes you a half mile in, or you can park along the highway and walk in. The trail drops down to the gorgeous, remote beach in a fun and scenic mile. The Homer Visitors Information Center has a very helpful free **Trails Map** that shows all the local hiking options.

For an in-town wildlife experience, check out the **bald eagle nest** near the stoplight on the Homer Bypass across from McDonald's. It generally has action all summer as the parent eagles raise their chicks. It's easy to find; just look for all the other folks with cell phones and big cameras. A second active eagle nest is at Bishops Beach, with access from the end of Crittenden Drive near Ocean Shores Motel. This one is in a tree leaning out over the beach.

★ Pratt Museum

Remodeled in 2019, the **Pratt Museum** (3779 Bartlett St., 907/235-8635, www. prattmuseum.org, 10am-6pm daily mid-May-mid-Sept., noon-5pm Tues.-Sat. mid-Sept.-Dec. and Feb.-mid-May, $10 adults, $8 seniors, $5 ages 6-18, free under age 6), just up from Pioneer Avenue. This is one of the finest small museums in Alaska, with interesting historical and cultural pieces, artwork, and wildlife displays. The beaked whale skeleton extends nearly the length of one room; follow the story of how it was shot and washed up onto a Homer beach, then was taken apart and put back together piece by piece. A gift shop sells Alaskan-made crafts. Help feed the sea critters (4pm Tues. and Fri.), or join a Homer Harbor tour ($10 pp) on Monday and Thursday in the summer.

Skyline Drive

Homer is famous for its dramatic mountains-and-bay vistas; some of the finest are from **Skyline Drive.** An enjoyable loop heads up West Hill Road, along Skyline Drive, and back down East Hill Road. Begin by heading 0.5 miles out the Sterling Highway from town. Take a right on West Hill Road, which winds steeply uphill to the junction with Diamond

Ridge Road. Turning left takes you along scenic Diamond Ridge and eventually back to Sterling Highway. Instead, continue straight onto **Skyline Drive.** You climb along a high ridge among expensive homes and B&Bs until you see the famous view of the Spit, the bay, and the march of mountains on the southern coast, all framed by fireweed late in summer.

Continue on Skyline Drive to the turn-off for **East Hill Road,** which takes you steeply downhill to Homer, or continue out East Skyline Drive 1.5 miles to **Carl E. Wynn Nature Center** (907/235-6667, www. akcoastalstudies.org, 10am-6pm daily mid-June-early Sept., $7 adults, $6 seniors, $5 youths, $20 families). Here you'll find 140 acres of forests and fields, miles of nature trails—many handicap accessible—and a learning center. Tour on your own, or join a guided walk at 10am or 2pm daily in the summer. Wynn Nature Center is maintained by the Center for Alaskan Coastal Studies, which also has harbor tours and day trips to Peterson Bay. Combine a visit to Wynn with a 1.5-hour Creatures of the Dock tour on the Spit for just $10. The Wynn Center also has special kid programs (ages 2-11, $10 pp) on Thursday and Friday in the summer.

Keep going out on East Skyline Drive and turn left on remote Ohlson Mountain Road until it ends at **Ohlson Peak** (1,513 feet) with good views of the volcanic summits of Augustine, Iliamna, and Redoubt. Return to town via East Hill Road, which meets East End Road on—you guessed it—the east side of town.

East End Road

Pioneer Avenue through town turns into **East End Road,** which has beautiful homes and great views of the Spit and Kachemak Bay. Nine miles along the road is the down-home Fritz Creek General Store (great lunches), along with increasingly jaw-dropping views of Kachemak Bay and the glaciers.

East End Road ends 20 miles from town, but you can walk down a steep dirt road from here to the shore and past the Russian Old Believer village of **Kachemak Selo** along the beach at the head of Kachemak Bay. (Stay on the beach and do not enter the village itself; you will not be welcome.) Not many folks get this far from Homer, but those who do are well rewarded for the effort. If you don't want to drive all the way, take a hard right onto Kachemak Drive three miles out of Homer and head back down to the Spit.

KILCHER HOMESTEAD

For a scenic blast from the past, visit the Kilcher Homestead, made famous thanks to the Discovery Channel's show *Alaska: The Last Frontier*. The program features a reality-show take on Atz, Otto, Charlotte, Eiven, Atz Lee, August, and other Kilcher family members. Singer Jewel Kilcher (daughter of Atz) is the best-known member of this talented family and makes occasional appearances. Charlotte and Otto operate a small seasonal shop called **Kilcher Country** (1392 Ocean Dr., Homer, noon-6pm Tues.-Sat. mid-May-Sept.).

The 600-acre perfect parcel of paradise is home to the **Kilcher Homestead Living Museum** (907/235-8713), which consists of several old farm buildings and a striking sod-roof homestead, built in the 1940s by Swiss emigrants Yule and Ruth Kilcher and their eight children. The Kilchers were some of the first people to homestead around Homer, and their descendants still live here. Highly informative one-hour **tours** (11am Mon.-Sat. summer, $20 adults, free under age 16) are offered of the homestead. Although the grounds are generally open in the summer, it's wise to call ahead to arrange a tour.

To get here, turn right onto Kilcher Road (10 miles out East End Rd.) and follow the narrow, potholed dirt road for three miles. Small signs mark the way to the homestead. The road gets muddy after rains, and don't even think of trying it in an RV. The drive ends at a gorgeous pasture that slopes to the bay.

Tours

The Pratt Museum (3779 Bartlett St., 907/235-8635, www.prattmuseum.org) leads informative 1.5-hour **Historic Harbor Walking Tours** (3pm Mon. and Thurs. June-early Sept., $10 pp), which include local history and lots of detail on commercial fishing and sport-fishing. Get tickets at the Pratt or in the little booth next to the Salty Dawg Saloon on the Spit.

GULL ISLAND

Most local water taxis have one-hour trips to Gull Island ($50 pp). These include **Bay Excursions** (907/235-7525, www.bayexcursions.com), **Bay Roamers Water Taxi** (907/399-6200, www.halibutcovealaska.com), **Coldwater Alaska** (907/299-2346, www.coldwaterak.com), **Mako's Water Taxi** (907/235-9055, www.makoswatertaxi.com), **Ashore Water Taxi** (907/399-2341, www.ashorewatertaxi.com), **Red Mountain Marine** (907/399-8230, www.redmountainmarine.com), and **Homer Ocean Charters** (907/235-6212 or 800/426-6212, www.homerocean.com).

COASTAL STUDIES

The nonprofit **Center for Alaskan Coastal Studies** (CACS, 708 Smokey Bay Way, 907/235-6667, www.akcoastalstudies.org) manages two environmental centers—Wynn Nature Center and the Peterson Bay Field Station—and leads a multitude of fun and educational nature tours. Coastal Studies has a seasonal office in a yurt near Ramp 2 on the Spit; stop there for details on all their trips. For an excellent introduction to the amazing invertebrate life of Kachemak Bay, join a 1.5-hour **Creatures of the Dock tour** (1:30pm and 4:30pm daily June-Aug., $8 pp, $25 family). Tours—great for all ages—depart from the CACS yurt. Coastal Studies also operates Wynn Nature Center on East Skyline Drive, and you can combine a visit to the nature

---

1: Bishops Beach; **2:** Homer Farmers Market; **3:** Kachemak Bay

1

2

3

center with a Creatures of the Dock tour for just $10. During their three-hour **Ocean Connection** tour ($109 adults, $50 kids), you'll get a naturalist-led boat tour to Gull Island, time at an oyster farm, and Peterson Bay.

The CACS's all-day tours to **Peterson Bay Field Station** (late May-mid-Sept., $175 adults, $155 seniors, $95 under age 12) starts with a boat trip to the Gull Island bird rookery, followed by a naturalist-led hike and tidepool exploration at Peterson Bay Field Station. Bring your own lunch, binoculars, and camera; rubber boots are provided. Combine this natural history tour with a two-hour guided sea kayak trip ($195 pp). Overnight stays ($35 pp in a yurt with kitchen access) are also available at the Peterson Bay Field Station; these are an amazing bargain if you want to relax in a delightful setting.

Coastal Studies has several options just for kids. These are a great way to drop youngsters off for a few hours so you can explore Homer in peace. **SPIT Kids** programs (9:30am-noon daily mid-June-mid-Aug., $10 pp) are perfect for ages 2-11, with all sorts of fun activities in the CAC yurt on the spit.

COOKING CLASSES

Kirsten Dixon, a Cordon Bleu-trained chef and nationally recognized cookbook author, operates **The Cooking School at Tutka Bay** (907/274-2710, www.withinthewild.com, mid-May-mid-Sept., $260 pp), where sessions include a round-trip water-taxi ride from Homer and three hours of training. These classes are offered Friday-Sunday throughout the summer, with an emphasis on local seafood and produce, recipes from Tutka Bay Lodge, and international cuisine. Classes take place on the *Widgeon II*, an old crabbing boat that has been moored to shore, with a two-story addition atop the deck. This now-landlocked boat provides a completely unique setting to learn the culinary arts.

ENTERTAINMENT AND EVENTS
Nightlife

Homer's grand old favorite, **Alice's Champagne Palace** (195 E. Pioneer Ave., 907/226-2739, www.alices.club, 11am-10pm Mon.-Thurs., 11am-1am Fri.-Sat., 4pm-10pm Sun.) is a great place with a family-friendly atmosphere. You'll find music and events on a regular basis, plus surprisingly good pub food.

A few blocks away is **The Alibi** (453 E. Pioneer Ave., 907/235-9199, www.alibi-homer. com, 4pm-midnight Mon.-Tues., 4pm-2am Wed., 4pm-1am Thurs., 4pm-3am Fri., 8am-3am Sat.), with pool tables, darts, frequent live music, and great bar menu of halibut tacos, burgers, burritos, wings, and salads.

Three miles east of town, **Down East Saloon** (3125 East End Rd., 907/235-6002, 10am-2am daily) has a large dance floor, colorful paintings on the walls, and bands most weekends. There's a big deck out back, with horseshoes and occasional barbecues.

The **Salty Dawg Saloon** (4380 Homer Spit Rd., 907/235-6718, www.saltydawgsaloon. com, 11am-closing daily), out near the end of the Spit, is Homer's most famous landmark. The original building dates from 1897, the second building from 1909, and the tower from the mid-1960s. Each building housed different companies in eight different locations before settling down here on the Spit. The bar was featured on episodes of *Deadliest Catch*. The Salty Dawg is open until the last patron staggers out the door; have a beer for the experience and leave your business card or signed bra with the thousands of others. And don't forget to buy one of their famous T-shirts to impress your friends back home. (By the way, the dollar bills are collected periodically and donated to local charities.)

Performing Arts

Homer has an extraordinary level of talent, and some of the performers have gotten together to do **Pier One Theatre** (3858 Homer Spit Rd., 907/226-2287, www.pieronetheatre. org, Thurs.-Sun. nights May-early Sept.) on the Spit. The frumpy red building next to the Fishing Hole houses a few dozen utilitarian seats, but whatever is playing, this is guaranteed to be one of the finest theater experiences in the state. You might see a youth musical, an old classic, or a controversial play that's definitely not for kids.

Cinema

Catch a flick at little **Homer Theatre** (106 W. Pioneer Ave., 907/235-6728, www.homertheatre.com), with a surprisingly high-tech sound and projection system. Get there early to snag one of the comfy couches up front. It's Alaska's longest-running movie house. Bring your own bowl for popcorn and get free refills. Every Thursday the theater screens something special—from documentaries to opera performances.

Festivals and Events

More than 100,000 shorebirds migrate through Kachemak Bay each spring, stopping to rest and feed at critical places, including the Homer Spit. Homer's biggest annual event is the **Kachemak Bay Shorebird Festival** (907/226-4631, www.kachemakshorebird.org, 1st weekend of May). More than 130 species have been recorded in a single day during the festival. Dozens of events await, including bird walks, bay tours, an arts fair, speakers, nature writing, and kids' activities, all in celebration of the great northward migration of shorebirds. The keynote speaker is usually an internationally renowned naturalist or birder.

The annual **Kachemak Bay Writers' Conference** (http://writersconference.homer.alaska.edu, early June) encompasses workshops, readings, manuscript reviews, agent consultations, and an array of other activities, including keynote speeches by such writers as Barry Lopez, Russell Banks, Amy Tan, Anne Lamott, Billy Collins, and Jane Smiley. It takes place at Land's End Resort on the end of the Spit.

If you're in town at the right time, don't miss the **Kachemak Bay Wooden Boat Festival** (907/235-2628, www.kbwbs.org, 2nd

weekend in Sept.), where it's practically illegal for men to not have a beard. Check out the classic wooden boats on display, watch old-time high-seas films, sing sea chanteys, and watch the kids building and painting their own wooden boats.

For an entirely different musical experience, Quiet Cove Lodge hosts **Halibut Cove Live** (907/235-0541, www.halibutcovelive.com) several times each summer. Guests are treated to round-trip transport from Homer to Halibut Cove, a gourmet meal, and a day of jazz. Guests sit beneath canopies on the deck, with a floating amphitheater for the musicians. Limited to just 60 people, this is an intimate way to enjoy an evening of jazz in a beautiful setting.

One of Homer's most creative events—**Burning Basket**—takes place in mid-September on the Mariner Park Beach. Every year artist Mavis Muller (www.mavismullerart.com) and friends build a 10-foot basket of wood, woven grass, and other natural materials. It takes six days to construct, and as the sun sets on the seventh day, the basket is ignited and erupts in a tower of fire. There are a few echoes of the Burning Man Festival in this, but the real focus is on remembering those who have died and emphasizing the release of emotion. It's surprisingly moving.

If you happen to be around in early December, do not miss performances of the **Nutcracker ballet** (Homer High School Mariner Theater, 600 E. Fairview Ave.). Not at all what you might expect from a small town, these productions have a cast of more than 100. The **Nutcracker Arts and Crafts Fair** takes place the last weekend of November.

SHOPPING

Gift shops, restaurants, art galleries, charter fishing shops, bear-viewing operations, and other businesses are located in several clusters near the end of the Spit. Nearly all of these are only open Memorial Day-Labor Day (late May-early Sept.), though a few places such as Coal Point Seafood and Land's End Resort stay open year-round.

Downtown near the movie theater, Nomar (104 E. Pioneer Ave., 907/235-8363 or 800/478-8364, www.nomaralaska.com, 9am-6pm Mon.-Fri., 9am-5pm Sat.) sells high-quality handmade clothing and outdoor gear. Some of its most popular items are specifically designed for commercial fishers, but Nomar also has warm and windproof outerwear, kids' garb, hats, rain gear, purses, duffel bags, and more. This is the real deal: tough, well-made Alaskan gear. It's also a great place for repairs of all types, from that broken zipper on your daypack to the torn stitching on your jacket.

Three miles out on East End Road is Kachemak Gear Shed (3625 East End Rd., 907/235-8612, www.ifsmarineoutdoor.com, 8am-7pm Mon.-Sat., 9am-5pm Sun.), selling quality clothing, rubber boots, and outerwear for anyone heading out on the water, not to mention freezer boxes if you're shipping fish home. It's a good place to check out the commercial fishing supplies too. The back wall has a rather unusual souvenir from the infamous *Exxon Valdez* oil spill.

Ulmer's (3858 Lake St., 907/235-8594, www.ulmersdrugandhardware.com, 8am-7pm Mon.-Fri., 9am-6pm Sat.-Sun.) is Homer's version of Walmart. You'll find everything from Xtratuf boots (all Alaskans must own at least one pair) and lawn mowers to T-shirts and toys.

Homer Bookstore (332 E. Pioneer Ave., 907/235-7496, www.homerbookstore.com, 10am-6pm Mon.-Sat., noon-5pm Sun. summer, 10am-6pm Mon.-Sat. winter) is a true book lover's shop, with works by local authors, a big Alaskana section, field guides, kids' books, and espresso in the back. You'll find humorous titles by Tom Bodett, known to most Americans as the folksy "We'll leave the light on for you" voice in the Motel 6 commercials. Like fellow celebrity Jewel, Bodett no longer lives in Homer. But another author, Dana Stabenow, still resides in the town. Many of her crime fiction novels starring Kate Shugak have landed on the *New York Times* best-seller list.

Old Inlet Bookshop (3487 Main St., 907/235-7984, www.oldinletbookshop.com, 10am-6pm daily) is a packed used bookstore with more than 20,000 titles. Owner Andy Wills really knows his books. This beautifully restored (and expanded) log cabin was originally part of a 1905 fox farm on Yukon Island.

The ever-popular Homer Farmers Market (Ocean Dr., 907/299-7540, www.homerfarmersmarket.org, 10am-3pm Sat. and 2pm-5pm Wed. late May-Sept.) takes place along Ocean Drive across from the Washboard. Booths carry fresh local produce, arts and crafts, jewelry, seafood, pastries, flowers, and more. A side tent has live music and games for kids; family activities take place at 11am Saturday. This is a fun way to find a sampling of work by local artists, gardeners, and chefs.

Art Galleries

Homer has a statewide reputation as an arts center, and local showcases are must-sees on any Homer itinerary. Pick up a map-brochure with descriptions of a dozen local galleries at the visitors center. The Homer Council on the Arts (355 W. Pioneer Ave., 907/235-4288, www.homerart.org) houses a small gallery and collaborates with local art events. If you're around on the first Friday of the month, don't miss the aptly named First Friday, when new exhibitions open at local galleries and the hors d'oeuvres come out.

Homer's most innovative gallery, the nonprofit Bunnell Street Arts Center (106 W. Bunnell Ave., 907/235-2662, www.bunnellarts.org), presents new exhibits monthly and has a choice selection of works for sale. You can't miss the enormous sculpture of buoys spilling off the front deck. It's in the old Inlet Trading Post, built in 1937, and just up from Bishops Beach. Although small, Bunnell attracts nationally known artists for residencies and presentations. Don't miss their First Friday openings, often with informative talks by the artists.

One of Alaska's oldest cooperative galleries, Ptarmigan Arts (471 E. Pioneer Ave., 907/235-5345, www.ptarmiganarts.com) has a diversity of artists, all of whom also work here one day a month. Here you'll find everything from handmade hats to ceramics, beaded jewelry, wildlife and landscape photos (including those of the author), and watercolors. Ptarmigan Arts has been here for more than 35 years.

Several other excellent galleries are within walking distance. Next door is **Fireweed Gallery** (475 E. Pioneer Ave., 907/235-3411, www.fireweedgallery.com), and it's just two blocks to **Art Shop Gallery** (202 W. Pioneer Ave., 907/235-7076 or 800/478-7076, www.artshopgallery.com). **Jars of Clay Pottery** (3975 Main St., 907/299-6118) is nearby.

Quality art galleries on the Spit include **High Tide Arts** (907/399-1563, www.hightidearts-ak.com), **Sea Lion Gallery** (907/235-3400, www.sealiongallery.com), **Brown Bear Products** (907/299-0762), and **Homer Clay Works** (907/235-6118, www.ahnairedale.com). In-town galleries generally stay open all year, but Spit galleries are only open mid-May to early September.

Beer and Wine

Spend any time in Homer and you'll encounter a bumper sticker that proclaims, "Homer: a quaint drinking town with a fishing problem." The town has its share of bars, and locals also craft a diversity of spirits. Find more than 1,500 different wines in a temperature-controlled room at **Grog Shop** (369 E. Pioneer Ave., 907/235-5101, 8am-midnight Sun.-Thurs., 8am-1am Fri.-Sat.).

A must-see for beer aficionados is **Homer Brewing Company** (1411 Lakeshore Dr., 907/235-3626, www.homerbrew.com, noon-6pm or later daily), where you can sample the China Poot Porter, Old Inlet Pale Ale, Red Knot Scottish, and other specialties—including seasonal brews—before buying a half-gallon growler to go. The brewery also crafts Zen Chai and Alaska Chai teas.

Near the base of the Homer Spit is friendly **Grace Ridge Brewing** (3388 B St., 907/435-0601, www.graceridgebrewing.com, noon-8pm daily). It's tiny inside, with barely enough space for a few tables, but the beer is good and you can sample five brews for $10.

Three miles east of town, **Bear Creek Winery** (60203 Bear Creek Dr., 907/235-8484, www.bearcreekwinery.com, 10am-6pm daily early May-mid-Sept., noon-6pm Mon.-Sat., noon-4pm Sun. winter) produces distinctive wines from local raspberries, rhubarb, blueberries, apples, and other fruits. The strawberry-rhubarb is the most popular, but if chocolate raspberry port is in stock, buy several bottles of this decadent dessert wine. Taste a few of the award-winning wines (no charge). The production building is just up the road, with **tours** on Saturday at noon.

RECREATION

Homer High School houses the public **swimming pool** (600 E. Fairview Ave., 907/235-7416, www.homerpool.org, $5), open daily for lap swimming.

For a beautiful view of Kachemak Bay while you work out, head to **The Bay Club** (2395 Kachemak Dr., 907/235-2582, www.homerbayclub.com, 5:30am-8pm Mon.-Fri., 9am-6pm Sat., 8am-1pm Sun.), a fine private facility with a pool, racquetball courts, workout equipment, yoga classes, saunas, and a climbing wall. A day pass ($18, no pool access) is available, but the seven-day pass ($50, includes the pool) is a better deal.

Seven miles out on East End Road, **Kachemak Bay Lynx Golf Course** (56910 East End Rd., 907/235-0606, daily mid-Apr.-mid-Oct.) is a par-3 course with fine views of the bay. The little clubhouse rents clubs.

If you have kids in tow, drive uphill on Bartlett Street, then left on Fairview Avenue to **Karen Hornaday Park** (629 Fairview Ave.), where the playground has all sorts of fun adventures, including forts, balancing beams, and a climbing rope maze. It will keep them happy and busy for at least an hour.

Biking

A paved four-mile **bike path** starts at the base of the Spit and continues all the way to the end; it's great for bikes and jogging, but the road traffic is constant and noisy. Come out early in the morning before the cars and wind pick up. A second paved bike path heads east from town for five miles along East End Road.

Located in the center of town, **Cycle Logical** (302 E. Pioneer Ave., 907/226-2925, www.cyclelogicalhomer.com, 10am-6pm Tues.-Sat., noon-6pm Sun.) is a full-service bike shop where owner Derek Reynolds sells and repairs bikes of all sorts. Rentals are a good way to get around, especially fat-tire bikes ($55 per half day), those bizarre balloon-tire bikes that are fun to ride on sandy beaches, dirt roads, and soft snow. Try one out for a low tide ride along the Spit, or transport the bike to beaches across the bay for a real adventure. (Water taxis don't charge extra to carry bikes.) Other bikes are also available: mountain bikes ($29 per half day), and cruiser bikes ($19 per half day). Guided **bike tours** are also offered. Homer's **Big Fat Bike Festival** (Mar.) is a great time to try out these bikes on snow and sand.

Horseback Riding

Mark Marette of **Trails End Horse Adventures** (907/235-6393) leads horseback rides (4 hours $110 pp, 2-person minimum, weight limit 250 pounds) in the very scenic Fox River area at the head of Kachemak Bay. It's a remote and fascinating place, with lots to see along the way. One of a handful of real-life cowboys in the Homer area, Mark spends a lot of time "off the grid," so he can be hard to reach, especially in the off-season.

TOP EXPERIENCE

Kayaking

Several local companies lead seasonal guided sea kayak trips within Kachemak Bay, or you can rent kayaks to do it on your own. Operating on protected Yukon Island near Kachemak Bay State Park, **True North Adventures** (907/235-0708, www.truenorthkayak.com, Apr.-Sept.) offers a range of guided trips, from half-day paddles ($125 pp) to multiple-night packages. The

all-day trip (includes lunch, $160 pp) is especially popular. All trips include a round-trip water-taxi ride to Yukon Island, sea kayaks, and a guide. Kayak rentals ($60 for a double) are available for experienced paddlers only; the kayaks are based on Yukon Island. True North also rents stand-up paddleboards and leads SUP trips across the bay.

St. Augustine's Kayak & Tours (907/299-1894, www.homerkayaking.com, late May-early Sept.) has a base in Peterson Bay, adjacent to the Center for Alaskan Coastal Studies field station, with half-day trips ($110 pp), full-day trips ($150 pp), and a combination version ($198 pp) that includes a morning with naturalists at CACS and an afternoon of paddling. For the everything-in-a-day adventure, book their paddle-hike-dine trip (not including dinner, $222 pp). This includes a water taxi from Homer, paddling at Peterson Bay, a water taxi and a hike to Grewingk Glacier Lake, dining at Saltry Restaurant in Halibut Cove, and transport on the *Danny J* back to the Spit. Several other options exist, all the way up to multiple-night adventures. All trips include round-trip water-taxi transportation from Homer.

A Seaside Adventure (907/235-6672, www.seasideadventure.com, May-mid-Sept., $150 pp) operates out of Little Tutka Bay, a lovely wooded spot surrounded by Kachemak Bay State Park. All-day tours include a water-taxi ride from the Spit, knowledgeable guides, a slow-paced natural history paddle in this protected cove (lots of eagles and otters), and a distinctive lunch that includes "beach soup" made from mussels and clams collected along the way. It's a real taste of Alaska, but call ahead, since group sizes are small and the tours fill quickly. German is spoken.

Mako's Water Taxi (907/235-9055, www.makoswatertaxi.com) rents kayaks (single $40 per day, double $50 per day). If you're booking a water taxi across the bay, Mako's and other companies will transport your kayak for no additional charge.

Stand-Up Paddleboarding

Two Homer Spit businesses rent the increasingly popular stand-up paddleboards (SUPs). The shop for **Ashore Water Taxi** (907/399-2341, www.homerwatertaxi.com, $35 per day with wetsuit) is directly across from the beach, so you can grab a SUP and head out for a paddle. Their office is at Harborview Boardwalk—the first one on the left as you drive out the Spit.

True North Adventures (907/235-0708, www.truenorthkayak.com) has an office near Ramp 2 on the Spit. In addition to all sorts of kayak trips, the company rents SUPs ($55 per day with wetsuit) and provides instruction for beginners (most folks figure it out on their own). True North's very popular **Ride the Tide SUP tour** (7 hours, $150 pp) starts with a water taxi to China Poot Bay, where you hop aboard a SUP for a fun paddle with the tide. More adventurous is the unique **Glacier Lake Hiking and SUPing trek** (all-day trip, $225 pp, maximum 6 people), which includes a round-trip water taxi to the trailhead, followed by a hike to Grewingk Lake. Paddle an SUP across the lake and among the icebergs to the towering face of Grewingk Glacier.

Surfing and Kiteboarding

In addition to more traditional sports, Homer has gained recognition for unique wind and water adventures. Surfing can be quite good during storms, particularly in the winter months. Day breezes kick up most afternoons, providing ideal conditions for kiteboarders. On a summer afternoon you'll see kiteboarders skimming waves along the base of the Spit. Check out **Kiting Alaska** (www.kitingalaska.com) for more info. Scott Dickerson of **Surf Alaska** (907/399-7873, www.surfalaska.net) rents surfboards and wetsuits, and has a good knowledge of local conditions. He is also captain of the *Milo* (907/398-7749, www.oceanswellventures.com), a 58-foot former fishing vessel that serves as a base for surfing safaris, cinematography, wildlife viewing, sea kayaking, and SUP trips.

Water Taxis

A small fleet of boats plies the waters of Kachemak Bay all summer, offering wildlife-viewing trips to Gull Island, whale-watching in the bay, beachcombing, tide-pooling, transport for kayakers and hikers heading into the state park, and access to lodges across the bay. The cost is $75 pp to most places in the bay, $50 pp for a one-hour Gull Island tour, or $50 pp for a ride-along. More distant locations, such as the head of Tutka Bay, cost $85 pp round-trip. The last is a fun way to check out the bay and join an existing trip. They're perfect if you're looking for a last-minute tour. Some water taxis also offer discounted rates for kids under 13 and families. A two-person minimum is required to hire a water taxi, but if you're flexible you can generally join another group heading in the same general direction. Water taxis transport kayaks and bikes at no extra charge. Most boats run May-September, but Mako's and Ashore are available year-round.

Mako's Water Taxi (907/235-9055, www.makoswatertaxi.com) is the largest and best-known Homer operator, with four boats, two of which are landing craft. He operates from a small building next to Ramp 2 on the Spit; look for the kayaks out front. In addition to trips across the bay, Mako's has boat in-fly back trips to Seldovia ($150 pp), fly-hike-boat trips to Leisure Lake ($225 pp), and kayak rentals (single $40 per day, double $50 per day). There's even a pile of mismatched rubber boots if you need to borrow a pair.

Dave Lyon's **Ashore Water Taxi** (907/399-2341, www.homerwatertaxi.com) is another busy company, with a small office on the left side of the Spit near Little Mermaid Café. Ashore also rents stand-up paddleboards ($35 pp per day with wetsuit), and even has inflatable ones. Ashore's prices tend to be a bit lower than Mako's.

Red Mountain Marine (907/399-8230, www.redmountainmarine.com) operates a beautiful custom-built wooden boat, the *Beowulf,* with space for 12 passengers; most other water taxis are six-passenger aluminum vessels.

Other recommended water taxis include **Bay Excursions** (907/235-7525, www.bayx. net), **Bay Roamers Water Taxi** (907/399-6200, www.halibutcovealaska.com), **True North Adventures** (907/235-0708, www. truenorthkayak.com), **Coldwater Alaska** (907/299-2346, www.coldwaterak.com), and **Homer Ocean Charters** (907/235-6212 or 800/426-6212, www.homerocean.com).

Fishing and Boating

Homer calls itself the **Halibut Fishing Capital of the World,** with commercial fishers often landing more halibut here than at any other port. Sportfishing attracts droves of enthusiasts every day of the summer, not only for halibut but also for king and silver salmon. Wear warm, layered clothing, and don't forget rain gear and soft-soled shoes. Binoculars are a definite plus, since seabirds, otters, and whales are often viewable. You can have your catch vacuum-packed, frozen, and shipped home for additional fees, but they add up quickly. Half-day fishing charters typically cost $175 pp, with all-day charters for $250 pp. Add $90 or so for a trip that combines halibut and salmon fishing. Rates are a bit lower on the larger boats that carry up to 18 people (versus 6 on most "six-pack" boats), and during the shoulder seasons. Lower rates are also available for seniors and kids.

CHARTER FISHING

Halibut populations have dropped throughout the Gulf Coast of Alaska and fish size has also decreased. At one time folks expected to pull in 50-pound halibut on a regular basis, with occasional fish over 150 pounds. Today, many charters return with a limit of what locals call "chickens"—fish weighing under 10 pounds. Due to these changes, regulations have tightened. As of 2018, the sport-caught quota is two halibut and one 28 inches or less, with a maximum of four charter-caught halibut per year. There is **no halibut charter fishing**

on **Wednesday** and **no halibut fishing on Tuesday mid-July to Mid-August,** but you can fish for salmon and rockfish those days.

Homer has dozens of fishing charter boats to help you go out and bag a halibut. Stop by the Homer Visitors Information Center in town to peruse racks filled with brochures from the various boats. An easy way to find one is through **Central Charters & Tours** (907/235-7847, www.centralcharter.com), **Homer Ocean Charters** (907/235-6212 or 800/426-6212, www.homerocean.com), **Inlet Charters** (907/235-6126 or 800/770-6126, www.halibutcharters.com), **North Country Charters** (907/235-7620 or 800/770-7620, www.northcountrycharters.com), or **Bob's Trophy Charters** (907/235-6544 or 800/770-6400, www.bobstrophycharters.com).

Do-it-yourselfers can rent 22-foot boats and fishing gear at the Homer harbor from **Homer Boat Rentals** (907/299-6065, www. homerboatrentals.com, $599 per day) and **Bayes Boat Rental** (907/235-6094, www. bayesboatrental.com, $625 per day).

Once you *do* catch a big halibut or salmon, how do you get it back home? **Coal Point Seafood** (4306 Homer Spit Rd., 907/235-3877 or 800/325-3877, www.welovefish.com) offers processing and flash-freezing, and will pack and FedEx the fish directly to your home. If you're going to be flying out and can take the fish with you, be sure to get the specially coated cardboard box (sold in grocery stores and at Gear Shed) and pack it with blue ice. Freezer space is available at the Anchorage airport, and many hotels provide freezer space for guests.

HALIBUT DERBY

Whatever you do, don't forget to enter the summer-long **Homer Jackpot Halibut Derby** (www.homerhalibutderby.com, $10) if you go fishing. In existence since 1986, this has long been the most lucrative halibut

1: Burning Basket is Homer's most unique event; **2:** Fishing Hole crowds on the Homer Spit; **3:** bike riding on a Homer beach; **4:** stand-up paddle boarders in Kachemak Bay

fishing derby in the state. Because of decreasing stocks of halibut, the derby was dramatically changed in 2012 to deemphasize keeping the largest halibut. Those giant 200-plus-pound halibuts are almost always females, and killing them negatively impacts the population. Today the first prize is $5,000 for the largest halibut of the season. Winners for tagged fish might also win up to $25,000, and released fish enters you in a drawing that could bring in $500. Everyone is entered in the $1,000 end-of-season drawing—even if you didn't catch anything. Sob stories abound of people who saved $10 by not entering, then caught potential prizewinners. In 2013, an angler caught a $59,000 tagged fish but lacked a derby ticket. Don't let this happen to you!

The Fishing Hole

If you simply want to drive into town and cast a line in the water, head out to the Fishing Hole on the Spit, across from Glacier Drive-In and Sportsman's Supply. The Alaska Department of Fish and Game stocks this little bight with king and silver salmon smolts. The returning adult salmon attract hordes of anglers in July and August, but they can be hard to catch.

Get fishing licenses or rent a pole from **Sport Shed** (3815 Homer Spit Rd., 907/235-5562) across from the Hole or **Sportsman's Supply** (1114 Freight Dock Rd., 907/235-2617) near the boat launch. Both places will also be happy to provide tips for catching salmon in the Fishing Hole.

Bear-Viewing and Flightseeing

Homer is a popular base for flightseeing trips and bear-viewing flights to both **Katmai National Park** and **Lake Clark National Park** (mid-May-mid-Sept., $625-800 pp for six-hour trips). These primarily head to the coastal stretch between Geographic Harbor and Swikshak Lagoon, or to Brooks Camp in Katmai or Chinitna Bay in Lake Clark. Call ahead for reservations during July and August; walk-ins may be available one day prior if you're lucky. Floatplane operations

are based at Beluga Lake next to the Homer airport.

Owned by Native Alaskan Jeanne Porter, **Bald Mountain Air Service** (907/235-7969 or 800/478-7969, www.baldmountainair.com) is a long-established company with a fine reputation. Bald Mountain flies fast turbine otters and spends more time in the park than most other operators.

Another company with highly experienced pilots, **Emerald Air Service** (907/235-4160 or 877/235-9600, www.emeraldairservice.com) has a seven-person Beaver on floats. They typically spend five hours on the ground in Katmai, and always have an experienced guide in addition to the pilot.

Jose de Creeft of **Northwind Aviation** (907/235-7482, www.northwindak.com)—one of the finest bush pilots around—offers flightseeing and bear-viewing trips to Brooks Camp or McNeil River. Other companies with floatplane bear-viewing trips from Beluga Lake include **Beluga Air** (907/235-8256, www.belugaair.com), **AK Adventures** (907/235-1805, www.goseebears.com), **Beryl Air** (907/299-5494, www.berylair.com), and **Steller Air** (907/299-0284, www.stellerair.com). Also based at Beluga Lake, **Alaska Ultimate Safaris** (888/696-2327, www.alaskaultimatesafaris.com) guides helicopter bear-viewing tours and flightseeing trips, including to the Harding Icefield and the stunning volcanic summit of Mount Augustine.

Smokey Bay Air (907/235-1511 or 888/482-1511, www.smokeybayair.com), **Adventure Airways** (907/299-7999, www.adventureairways.com), and **Alaska Bear Adventures/K Bay Air** (907/299-5229 or 877/522-9247, www.alaskabearviewing.com) provide flightseeing and air charters, along with bear-viewing trips to Katmai National Park or Lake Clark National Park. All three operate wheeled planes from the airport, landing on Katmai and Lake Clark beaches.

Pilot Zack Tappen of **Sasquatch Alaska Adventure Company** (907/299-7272, www.sasquatchalaska.com) provides fly-out bear-viewing day trips to Katmai, multiple-night

Side Trip to Katmai National Park

Katmai National Park occupies four million acres of wilderness on the west side of Cook Inlet, roughly 150 miles southwest of Homer. It's worth a visit for its volcanic landscape, outstanding salmon fishing, and the opportunity to see brown bears up close. Bears are the main attraction: they're big, bad, and ubiquitous, thanks to the salmon that run up the Naknek River from Bristol Bay each year.

brown bears at Brooks Falls in Katmai National Park

BROOKS CAMP

Bear activity centers on the Brooks River, which flows into Naknek Lake. Access is by air from Homer, Kenai, Soldotna, or Anchorage, with floatplanes landing on the lake near the **Brooks Camp Visitors Center** (907/246-3305, www.nps.gov/katm, daily June-mid-Sept.). Begin your visit with a park orientation and safety video. It's a short walk over a bridge to an elevated platform where you can watch bears catching salmon. An easy 1.2-mile hike beyond the bridge is **Brooks Falls,** where all those famous bears-with-jumping-salmon photos are taken. An elevated footbridge leads to a big covered area. Two footbridges continue beyond this, one to the lower riffles, and the second to a smaller viewing platform. You may need to wait to access the latter platform.

VALLEY OF TEN THOUSAND SMOKES

This fascinating and desolate area was created by the massive eruption of Mount Novarupta in 1912—heard in Ketchikan, 860 miles away! Hot ash and pumice piled up 700 feet deep over a 40-square-mile area. Four years later, the first visitors found a stunning valley where hot gases surfaced through thousands of cracks as the hot ash made contact with buried rivers and springs. Today—more than a century later—only a few fumaroles remain, but the land is still barren, with a lunar landscape cut by deep colorful canyons. **Tour buses** (907/243-5448 or 877/708-1391, www.katmailand.com, $96 pp with lunch) depart Brooks Lodge daily in the summer.

COASTAL BEAR-VIEWING

Along the remote rivers and the coast of Shelikof Strait, bears dig for clams and catch salmon. **Air-taxi operators** out of Homer, Kodiak, Soldotna, and Anchorage take clients on day trips to the park for $625-800 pp. Many of these fly-in trips have big groups; a number of planes can be in the area at once, reducing your wilderness experience. Book an early day trip: Bears are generally more active in the early morning or late in the day—after most bear-viewing flights have headed home.

WHERE TO STAY

Overnight stays are available at **Brooks Lodge** (907/243-5448 or 877/708-1391, www. katmailand.com, June-late Sept.). A one-night lodging-and-airfare package from Anchorage costs $2,366 for two people; two nights are $3,164 for two people. Meals (served buffet style) and natural history tours to the Valley of 10,000 Smokes cost extra. Reserve a full year ahead for summer stays. **Brooks Camp Campground** (877/444-6777, www.recreation.gov, June-mid-Sept., $12 pp plus $10 reservation fee) has potable water, a food cache, cooking shelters, vault toilets, and an electric fence to keep bears out. Reserve as early as possible. Reservations open in early January and often fill up for the month of July within a few hours. Campers can purchase meals and showers at Brooks Lodge.

stays in a tent camp, fly-out kayaking, and glacier landings.

Bird-Watching

Kachemak Bay provides an outstanding opportunity for birders, especially during the spring migration when thousands of sandpipers and other species crowd the tide flats. The **Kachemak Bay Shorebird Festival** (907/235-7740, www.homeralaska.org, early May) brings guest speakers and bird experts to town for one of Homer's most popular events. The **Kachemak Bay Birders** (www. kachemakbaybirders.org) is a very active local group of birders with birding trips and monthly meetings.

Sailing

Kachemak Bay is a great place for sailing, and the **Homer Yacht Club** (www. homeryachtclub.org) holds semi-competitive races on weekends all summer, with the Land's End Regatta the last weekend of June. Crewmembers are often needed; contact the club if you're interested in joining the fun—no experience necessary.

Winter Sports

Homer is just above sea level, and it might even rain in January, but surrounding hills often pile high with snow. **Kachemak Nordic Ski Club** (www.kachemaknordicskiclub.org) maintains more than 40 miles of groomed cross-country trails near McNeil Canyon (13 miles east of town), at Baycrest (just west of town, off Sterling Hwy.), and at Lookout Mountain (out on Ohlson Mountain Rd.). The last of these has the best snow and most adventurous trails. Check the website for current conditions and grooming status. Also popular in the winter are ice skating on Beluga Lake and snowmobiling in the Caribou Hills.

Located halfway out on the Spit, the **Kevin Bell Ice Arena** (907/235-2647, www. homerhockey.org) is open for skaters and hockey players throughout the fall and winter.

FOOD

Homer's dining-out options are surprisingly varied, with several excellent choices. Many of the town's second- or third-tier eateries would be standouts almost anywhere else in Alaska, and the town's best restaurants are truly memorable. Of the top 15 restaurants on the Kenai, at least a dozen are in Homer!

Coffee

Homer is a coffee drinker's paradise, with two roasters and several excellent coffee joints. There are literally dozens of espresso machines at businesses all over town, even in a local laundromat and the Radio Shack store.

In business since 1995, **Captain's Coffee Roasting Co.** (528 E. Pioneer Ave., 907/235-4970, www.captainscoffee.com, 6:30am-5:30pm Mon.-Sat., 6:30am-5pm Sun., $4-8) has a downtown location and a pleasant space to relax.

At ★ **K-Bay Caffé** (378 E. Pioneer Ave., 907/235-1551, www.kbaycoffee.com, 7am-9pm daily, under $10), right in the heart of town, owner Michael McGuire really knows his all-organic coffee—he once won top prize at a national barista contest—and is a connoisseur when it comes to creating the perfect roast. In addition to coffee, the café has organic baked goods, sandwiches, salads, and smoothies. Wander in most mornings and you're likely to hear piano music from a talented local musician.

Housed within an old homestead cabin, **Coal Town Coffee** (907/235-4771, www. coaltowncoffee.com, 5am-8pm daily early May-early Sept., $3-8) serves the best espresso on the Homer Spit, with K-Bay coffee, baked goods from Fritz Creek Store, and a fine selection of teas. Tables out front are set up for a fun game of checkers using painted rocks.

Bakeries

A Homer institution that should not be missed, ★ **Two Sisters Bakery** (233 E. Bunnell Ave., 907/235-2280, www. twosistersbakery.net, 7am-5pm Mon.-Tues., 7am-8:30pm Wed.-Sat., brunch under $10, dinner $20-28) is just a block from Bishops Beach. It's *the* place to go for a morning coffee-and-pastry fix. Two Sisters is always warm and fragrant with the scent of fresh-baked pastries, daily breads, roasted veggie focaccia sandwiches, sticky buns, and ham and cheese savories from the wood-fired brick oven. For brunch, try the quiche, biscuits and gravy, or house-made granola with a steaming espresso. Dinner (Wed.-Sat., reservations recommended) change seasonally, but always feature crispy rockfish with coconut rice, and an ultra-rich mac and gouda cheese, along with nightly specials. A covered deck wraps around the back side, and the backyard has a play area for families—or you can walk to nearby Bishops Beach.

★ **The Bagel Shop** (3745 East End Rd., 907/299-2099, www.thebagelshopalaska.com, 7am-4pm Tues.-Fri., 8am-4pm Sat.-Sun. Mar.-Aug. and Oct.-Jan., $3-14) is hands-down the finest bagel shop in Alaska, and even die-hard New Yorkers will appreciate the sesame, poppy, onion-garlic, salt, and everything bagels. Vivacious owner Mikela Aramburu sets the tone at this high-energy spot with a great choice of schmears and bagel sandwiches (try the chèvre-roasted garlic), plus K-Bay espresso. The Bagel Shop is near the Gear Shed store, four miles out East End Road at the junction with Kachemak Drive. It's a bit out of the way, but definitely worth the detour.

Breakfast

A longtime family favorite, **Duncan House Diner** (125 E. Pioneer Ave., 907/235-5344, www.duncanhousediner.com, 7am-2pm daily, $9-14) serves substantial all-American meals for breakfast and lunch; it's often crowded on weekend mornings, so get here early. The menu includes breakfast burritos, country-fried steak and eggs, blueberry flapjacks, and eggs Benedict served all day, along with lunchtime burgers, sandwiches, salads, and soups. Plenty of kids-only fare is offered too.

Wild Honey Crepery (106 W. Bunnell Ave., 907/435-7635, www.wildhoneybistro.com, 9am-2pm Fri.-Mon., $7-13) occupies

one of the oldest buildings in Homer, a lovely 1937 structure that also houses Bunnell Street Arts Center and Old Town B&B. Choose from sweet or savory crepes, including the Déjà vu, with house-made reindeer sausage, white cheddar, sautéed green apples, and maple syrup. It's not inexpensive, but is a wonderful treat.

Open since 1982 and a favorite of travelers, **Fresh Sourdough Express Bakery & Café** (1316 Ocean Dr., 907/235-7571, www.freshsourdoughexpress.com, 7am-5pm daily in summer, 8am-2pm Fri.-Mon. in winter, $10-19) is an earthy Homer spot serving sourdough hotcakes, scrambles, granola, muffins, and monster pastries for breakfast. Lunch includes sandwiches, buffalo burgers, homemade soups, and salads, while dinners cover the salmon, chicken, and steak terrain. The mostly organic menu includes vegetarian meals, but also plenty of carnivorous protein.

American

Mike's Alaskan Eatery (15 W. Pioneer Ave., 907/435-7800, 9am-4pm Wed.-Mon., $10-13) doesn't look like much from the outside—it's easy to drive by without seeing this little spot tucked away from the road, and that would be a mistake. Owner and chef Mike Hiller really knows his way around the kitchen, and though the lunch menu is limited to a handful of items, they're all amazingly good. Mike's Boom King sub (roast beef, pastrami, cream cheese, bacon, and jalapeño slaw) is a hit, and even a simple grilled cheese is perfectly prepared. Sunday brunch features classic breakfast favorites.

Homer has a McDonald's, but a much better option is **Boss Hogz Restaurant** (672 E. End Rd., 907/235-5555, 7am-7pm Mon.-Thurs., 7am-8pm Fri.-Sat., 8am-5pm Sun., $10-15), with 17 different burgers on the menu, from the Holy Guacamole burger to the more traditional Boss burger. Cheesesteaks, barbecue hoagies, and jumbo hot dogs add to the meat overload. Thick shakes and malts are made from big scoops of Alaska Supreme ice cream.

It's a few miles out of the way, but **Boatyard Café** (41935 Kachemak Dr., 907/235-5638, 8am-4pm Tues.-Sat. June-Feb., 8am-4pm Mon.-Sat. Mar.-May, $8-25) is the real deal, with down-home food in a simple setting. Located in a little blue and red building at the Northern Enterprises Boatyard along Kachemak Drive, this little gem serves 10 variations on the burger theme (including the Boatyard Special, with two patties, cheese, bacon, mushrooms, and onions), reubens, and the best halibut and chips in town. Breakfast is served till 11am.

On Bunnell Avenue in Homer's original downtown area, **AJ's Old Town Steakhouse & Tavern** (120 W. Bunnell Ave., 907/235-9949, 5pm-10pm daily, $16-59) specializes in mouth-watering steaks cooked to perfection, prime rib, halibut fish-and-chips, Philly cheesesteak sandwiches, and cheeseburgers. You can enjoy a $16 Reuben, or settle into a full pound of king crab for $59. The building has been used as a restaurant since 1941, though the name changed over the decades. AJ's is a pleasant place to sip a local microbrew while listening to mellow live music.

Far from the hubbub on the Homer Spit is ★ **Fritz Creek General Store** (55770 East End Rd., 907/235-6521, 7am-9pm Mon.-Sat., 10am-8pm Sun., $8-19), eight miles out on East End Road. The country store has a small selection of groceries (including goat cheese and coconut milk!), a little post office, booze, an eclectic video selection, funky tables made from old cable spools, and a fat black cat that craves attention. The real attraction at Fritz Creek is its deli, featuring daily breads, amazing hot sandwiches, tamales, pizza by the pie or slice, lemon bars, cakes, pies, and coffee. A 12-inch eggplant muffuletta sandwich is big enough to feed two, or just get a soup of the day with bread ($5). Check the coolers for baby back ribs, pork adobo, potato knish, or hoisin noodles with smoked duck. Fritz Creek is a delightful place to hang out in an old-time country setting.

Meals on the Spit

Often crowded **Boardwalk Fish and Chips** (4287 Homer Spit Rd., 907/235-7749, www.boardwalkfishandchips.com, 11am-9pm Sun.-Thurs., 11am-10pm Fri., 11am-11pm Sat. early May-early Sept., $14-22) is across from the harbormaster and Salty Dawg, with crunchy halibut fish-on-a-stick and chips that will have you smackin' your chops. Save a few bucks with cod and chips or a handmade salmon burger. Eat inside or—if the wind isn't too strong—on the deck.

A few doors down from Boardwalk is ★ **Finn's Pizza** (Homer Spit, 907/235-2878, noon-9pm daily early May-early Sept., pizzas $21-30, slices $5), with hot-from-the-oven wood-fired pizzas, daily soups, and local beers on tap. Be sure to try the blue pear version, made with D'Anjou pears, gorgonzola cheese, and roasted pine nuts. It's excellent, but you could spend $45 for a 15-inch pizza and two beers! Climb the side stairs for rustic solarium dining with a beach vista.

One of Homer's special-occasion places, ★ **Little Mermaid Café** (Homer Spit, 907/399-9900, www.littlemermaidhomer.com, 11:30am-9pm Thurs.-Tues. May-mid-Sept., $14-40) is cozy and friendly. There are just a few tables in the main café, with a few more in the adjacent room and a picnic table or two out front, so reservations are a must. Nightly specials are always a good bet, or try the stone bowl, Kodiak scallops, fresh rockfish, or brick-oven pizzas. The food is artful and fun, including a wonderfully fattening Montreal-inspired poutine with hand-cut fries, brown gravy, and white cheddar. Save money (and actually get a seat) by returning for lunch.

★ **La Baleine Café** (near the end of Homer Spit, 907/299-6672, www.labaleinecafe.com, 6am-3pm Wed.-Sun. late May-mid-Sept., $8-15) provides rustic fare with a twist. Chefs Kirsten Dixon and Mandy Dixon both attended Le Cordon Bleu, and the café's name, French for "The Whale," plays on a mix of Alaskan and French cuisine. (Kirsten Dixon is also co-owner of the acclaimed

Tutka Bay Lodge, where she teaches cooking classes.) La Baleine opens early for the fishing crowd, but the menu is anything but basic. No store-bought ketchup here; it's made on the premises. Breakfast is served all day, with an omelet of the day, eggs benedict, and biscuits and gravy. For lunch, the Alaska crab melt is rich and filling, and the veggie grain burger is easily the best you've ever tasted. Even meat lovers will like this one. All meals include coffee and tea. The café has a few tables inside, with picnic tables out front. Get a to-go boxed lunch ($14).

At the very tip of the Spit is **Land's End Resort,** where panoramic bay vistas and an expansive beachside deck are the main attractions. The **Chart Room Restaurant** (4786 Homer Spit Rd., 907/235-0406, www.lands-end-resort.com, 8am-10pm daily, $18-39) serves seafood, steaks, prime rib, and daily dinner specials. The food is nothing special, but the view makes it worthwhile.

At ★ **Carmen's Gelato** (4241 Homer Spit Rd., 907/235-4066, www.carmensgelato.com, 10am-11pm daily late May-early Sept., $5-7), owner Carmen Ricciardi makes authentic Italian gelato using organic fruit, milk, and sugars. This is a fantastic snack after dinner at a Spit restaurant, and you can mix and match gelato or sorbet flavors. For a sugar and coffee buzz, try the *affogato*: two flavors of gelato topped with a shot of hot K-Bay espresso.

International

Downtown's **Cosmic Kitchen** (510 E. Pioneer Ave., 907/235-6355, www.cosmickitchenalaska.com, 9am-8pm Mon.-Sat. late May-early Sept., 9am-6pm Mon.-Fri., 9am-3pm Sat. early Sept.-late May, $7-17) serves quick Mexican food such as Cosmic Burritos (with steak or chicken, rice, cheese, guacamole, and salsa), soft tacos, and steak enchiladas, plus avocado-bacon cheeseburgers, chicken tikka with chutney sandwiches, and dinner specials. With more than 150 items on the menu—including plenty of vegetarian and kid-friendly options—you're bound to find something to your taste. It's

all good and tasty, with homemade salsas to spice things up. Cosmic is popular for breakfast and lunch, when the front deck fills on a sunny day, but also serves dinner specials such as a fajita steak and shrimp platter and Greek gyros—*delicioso.* Beer, wine, smoothies, and even espresso (this is Homer, after all) are available.

Located five miles out East End Road, ★ **Wasabi's** (59217 East End Rd., 907/226-3663, www.wasabisrestaurant.com, 5pm-10pm Wed.-Sun. late May-early Sept., 5pm-9pm Wed.-Sat. early Sept.-late May, $28-48) provides a classy setting and Asian fusion fare; their motto is "Where East meets West, and ends up North." You'll discover a good choice of fresh sushi (try the Tutka Bay roll with shrimp, avocado, and masago), along with fresh halibut, Thai coconut curry rockfish, Muscovy duck, and tempura prawns. Get a window seat for bay vistas. Singles can sit at the wraparound bar for meals, and Wasabi's has a great selection of house-made infused rum and vodkas; they're in the big jars lining the bar.

You can't miss ★ **Café Cups** (162 W. Pioneer Ave., 907/235-8330, www.cafecupshomer.com, 5pm-10pm Tues.-Sat., $16-40)—four Alaska-size teacups hang from the front of this converted yellow house. You'll find a number of daily specials, and these are the real attraction, particularly the fresh seafood. The eclectic, from-scratch menu encompasses everything from steamer clams and Seoul city street skewers to Catalan seafood stew and king crab. Top the evening off with a slice of dark chocolate peanut-butter pie. Cups gets crowded and can be noisy at times; reservations are a must (the last reservation can be made for 9:30pm). Individuals without a reservation may find a seat at the bar. A small side patio is fun on warm afternoons.

A place that gets high marks is **Fat Olives Restaurant** (276 Olson Lane, 907/235-8488, www.fatoliveshomer.com, 11am-8pm Sun.-Thurs., 11am-9:30pm Fri.-Sat., $11-25). The setting evokes an Italian bistro, and the menu stars wood-fired pizzas, calzones, fresh salmon, Kachemak Bay oysters, seafood pasta, rib-eye steaks, and portabella manicotti. It's noisy and fun, perfect for kids and adults. Fat Olives is just off the Homer Bypass as you enter town. In a hurry? Get a giant thin-crust pizza slice to go ($5) or a gargantuan 28-inch cheese pizza—large enough to feed a hungry hockey team ($36). The box is so big you'll have trouble getting it through the door!

Vida's Thai Food (397 E. Pioneer Ave., 907/299-7913, www.vidasthaifood.com, 11am-8pm Wed.-Sat., $10-16) serves the best Thai meals in town. The menu includes such standards as fresh rolls, massaman curry, pork *pad see-ew,* cashew chicken, and Thai spicy basil.

Pub Fare

Sometimes called Homer's Living Room, **Alice's Champagne Palace** (195 E. Pioneer Ave., 907/226-2739, www.alices.club, 11am-10pm Mon.-Thurs., 11am-1am Fri.-Sat., 4pm-10pm Sun., $10-18) has been here since 1980. Alice's has a large back deck, live bands most weekends, TV sports at other times, and even a kids' room at this family-friendly bar owned by a local physician. It's a big woodsy timber-frame building with 16 beers on tap and a tasty pub menu. Favorites include any of the burgers, four-cheese mac, Caesar salads, and pub steak. Be sure to order a funnel cake, listed rather incongruously in the salads section of the menu. As the menu notes, "These are healthy choices because they are listed with the salads."

Groceries

On the Homer Bypass, **Safeway** (90 Sterling Hwy., 907/226-1000, www.safeway.com, 5am-midnight daily) is the main grocery store in town, with a pharmacy, a floral shop, liquor, and a deli. Seniors over 65 will appreciate the 10 percent discount every Tuesday.

Across from the Homer Visitors Information Center on the Homer Bypass, **Save-U-More** (3611 Greatland St., 907/235-8661, www.save-u-more.com, 8am-8pm Mon.-Sat., 9am-7pm Sun.) may be the most

bizarre store in Alaska, selling everything from freshly baked bread to wheelbarrows. Its concrete-floor industrial decor makes Costco look positively upscale, and half the products originated at Costco in Anchorage (with a Homer markup). The real surprise at Save-U-More is the diversity of items, with entire sections devoted to imported Irish, Greek, or Indian specialty products. The so-so deli has pizza by the slice and ice cream cones ($2).

Seafood Markets

In addition to its reputation as a halibut fishing center, Homer is famous for oysters, and you'll find acclaimed **Kachemak Bay oysters** in local restaurants and from the Kachemak Shellfish Growers Co-op building (across from the Fishing Hole on the Homer Spit, 907/235-1935, www.alaskaoyster.com, 9am-5pm daily mid-May-early Sept., 11am-5pm Tues.-Sat. early Sept.-mid May, $17-22 per dozen oysters). Also available are K-Bay mussels, king crab, Kodiak scallops, razor clams, spot prawns, and side stripe shrimp. The building also houses **Homer Spit Oyster Bar** (907/885-5340, $9-18), serving fresh oysters, oyster bisque, grilled cheese, and other finger fare in a bright waterside setting.

On a summer afternoon **Coal Point Seafood** (Homer Spit, 907/235-3877 or 800/325-3877, www.welovefish.com, 8am-8pm daily Apr.-Sept., 10am-6pm Mon.-Sat. Oct.-Mar.) is one of the busiest places on the Homer Spit, with a queue of folks waiting to have their catch processed, packaged, and flash frozen. They'll box and ship your catch via FedEx. Sidle up to the seasonal bar for seafood chowder, king crab, salmon burgers, and fresh K-Bay oysters on the half shell. Fresh salmon, halibut, and scallops are often available, and Coal Point always has frozen local seafood.

ACCOMMODATIONS

The Homer Chamber of Commerce website (www.homeralaska.org) has links to most local lodging places. Many people come to Homer to fish, and this typically means very early departures for the charter boats. Because of this, you may be subjected to noise at 5am as folks head out for the one day when you just wanted to sleep in.

Hostel

Homer's old-time favorite is ★ **Seaside Farm Hostel** (40904 Seaside Farm Rd., 907/399-7541, www.seasidealaska.com, late May-Sept., dorm $35 pp, $45 pp with bedding, guest rooms $80-90 d, cabins $90-100 d, additional guests $25 pp, tent spaces $15 d), five miles out on East End Road. It's a great rural location with horses in the pasture below, an organic garden (wonderful raspberries), beach access, campfire cookouts, and killer views across Kachemak Bay. There are accommodations in an eight-bed coed dorm that include cooking facilities and showers, private rooms in the lodge (with showers), and four simple cabins. The cabins have outhouses, but you'll need to walk to the lodge for a shower or to use the kitchen. Scenic tent spaces have access to a cooking pavilion if you bring a stove. Seaside Farm—a 40-acre spread—is owned by Mossy Kilcher, an avid birder and farmer. Her internationally known niece is the singer Jewel Kilcher, better known simply as Jewel. Homer's most famous former resident now lives in Texas.

Hotels

★ **Driftwood Inn** (135 W. Bunnell Ave., 907/235-8019, www.thedriftwoodinn.com, $119-155 d shared bath, $124-155 d tiny room with private bath, $169-199 d standard room with private bath, $199-245 with kitchen) is an unexpected gem in the rough. The historic main building has a common room with a stone fireplace, comfortable chairs for relaxing, a playground for kids, and inexpensive breakfast and snack items. Across the street is AJ's Old Town Steakhouse & Tavern (same owners) and Maura's Café. Several budget guest rooms—cute but basic—have shared baths, and a half-dozen "shipquarter rooms" provide only slightly more space than a ship's bunk but come with private

baths and a charming cedar-paneled nautical interior; they're not for anyone with claustrophobia. There are also more standard units with private baths; some contain full kitchens. Across the street are three places owned by Driftwood Inn, all with a two-night minimum. **Seaside Lodge** ($215-299 d), a modern home overlooking Bishops Beach and Kachemak Bay with five guest rooms, private baths, and a full kitchen, **Bluffview Lodge** ($215-265 d), with space for up to 17 people, and **Kachemak Cottage** ($300-399 for 4 people), a two-bedroom cottage that sleeps four. Together, these three places provide a very popular setup for summer weddings, with the big lawn and amazing vistas from Seaside Lodge, plus plenty of space for family and friends right next door.

Pioneer Inn (244 W. Pioneer Ave., 907/235-5670, www.pioneerinnhomerak.com, rooms $149 d, suites $169 d, additional guests $13 pp) is an unpretentious downtown motel with standard guest rooms and five large apartment-style units, each with a full kitchen. Rooms are very clean and the superfriendly owners make you feel at home. You'll be impressed with the colorful hanging baskets of flowers out front.

Popular with anglers are three units over the **Sport Shed** (3815 Homer Spit Rd., 907/235-5562, mid-May-mid-Sept., $159 d, extra guests $10 pp), a fishing shop on the Spit. These studio units come with full kitchens and water views.

Homer Ocean House Inn (1065 Krueth Way, 907/235-3294, www.homeroceanhouse.com, May-Sept., rooms and suites $199-269 d, condos $419-549 d) sits atop a low cliff facing the Homer Spit, with beach access, private entrances, two hot tubs, and a fire pit. Accommodations include rooms and suites with microwaves and fridges, along with condos containing full kitchens. Request a bayside room to really take advantage of the view.

Spread across four buildings on a gentle slope, **Ocean Shores Motel** (3500 Crittenden Dr., 907/235-7775 or 800/770-7775, www.akoceanshores.com, May-Sept.,

$179-229 d, additional guests $10 pp) has an old-fashioned plain-vanilla exterior, but the rooms are large and exceptionally well maintained. Each unit has two queen beds, a fridge, and a microwave. Rooms face Kachemak Bay, with prices matching your proximity to the water.

Advertised as Alaska's only beachfront hotel, **Land's End Resort** (4786 Homer Spit Rd., 907/235-0400 or 800/478-0400, www.lands-end-resort.com, $189-339 d) occupies the very tip of Homer Spit, with extraordinary bay-and-mountain views from some rooms, a waterside hot tub, and a tiny exercise pool (not for kids). The 84 rooms range greatly in price and quality, from economy units facing the parking lot to luxurious two-room suites in the new building. There's a spa on the premises, and the in-house restaurant and bar have a big back deck on the water and an upstairs reception hall that's popular for weddings. Also available are a number of totally luxurious condos known as **Land's End Lodges.** They're right on the beach and a short walk from dining and shopping on the Spit. These condos contain downstairs studio units ($575 d) with no kitchens, and far more impressive upstairs apartments ($625-675). The latter have two or three bedrooms, large kitchens and living rooms with enormous picture windows, and decks to take in the sunset vistas.

On the crest of the hill as you enter Homer, ★ **Alaskan Suites** (3255 Sterling Hwy., 907/235-1972, www.alaskansuites.com, $270 d, additional guests $10 pp) consists of five adorable cabins on the west side of town, each containing two queen beds, a Murphy single bed, a fridge, a microwave, a flat-screen TV, a private bath, a kitchenette, a grill, and an outdoor hot tub on the bluff. The panoramic views include Kachemak Bay and a parade of snowy mountains, glaciers, and volcanoes.

Aspen Suites Hotel Homer (91 Sterling Hwy., 907/235-2351, www.aspenhotelsak.com, $179-199 d) is directly across from the Safeway store and near the Islands and Ocean Visitor Center. Rooms are spacious with one or two queen beds and kitchenettes. The hotel was built a short distance from Homer's sewage plant (probably not an issue most of the time and trees screen the location).

Bed-and-Breakfasts

Homer probably has more B&Bs per capita than any town its size anywhere, with several dozen places—many with jaw-dropping vistas. A pair of bed-and-breakfast organizations provide one-stop shopping: **Homer B&B Association** (907/226-1114 or 877/296-1114, www.homerbedbreakfast.com), and the much smaller **Homer's Finest B&B Network** (www.homeraccommodations.com). You'll also find links to 30 or so B&Bs on the chamber's website (www.homeralaska.org).

★ **Old Town B&B** (106 W. Bunnell Ave., 907/235-7558, www.oldtownbedandbreakfast.com, $120 d shared bath, $130 d private bath) is owned by renowned artist Asia Freeman, who also manages Bunnell Street Arts Center downstairs. The three immaculate rooms have period pieces in this renovated 1937 building with a false-front exterior. Guests receive a voucher ($12 pp) for breakfast treats at Wild Honey Creperie downstairs. Asia's paintings hang in the rooms, and it's a deliciously old-fashioned place, but the walls are thin, the plumbing is original, and the 18 narrow stairs may prove a challenge for older travelers.

In business for nearly 30 years, **Halcyon Heights B&B** (1200 Mission Rd., 907/235-2148, www.homerbb.com, $179-249 d, additional adults $35 pp) has a beautiful East Hill location with panoramic views of Kachemak Bay from the deck. Amenities include an outdoor hot tub, private entrances and baths, excellent three-course breakfasts, and Wi-Fi. Three upstairs rooms open onto the deck, and families appreciate the two garden-level suites with a kitchen. Halcyon has a two-night minimum stay in summer, and discounts are available for extended stays. Co-owner Juxia is fluent in Mandarin.

Whalesong B&B (4002 Kachemak Way, 907/235-2564, www.thewhalesong.com, $195 d, additional guests $35 pp, 2-night minimum) is a block from the downtown galleries and restaurants. Two rooms have private entrances, and guests are served a continental breakfast. Only one group is allowed at a time, so you'll have the B&B to yourself.

On a quiet side street just two blocks up from Pioneer Avenue, **Paula's Place B&B** (4067 Calhoun St., 907/435-3983, www.paulasplacebandb.com, $85-150 d, extra guests $15 pp, up to 6) consists of a 900-square-foot two-bedroom lower level with a private entrance, queen beds, a bath, a flat-screen TV, a barbecue grill, a microwave, and a fridge. Owner Paula Riley cooks a delicious breakfast each morning, and her friendly corgi dog greets guests. The B&B is set up for just one couple or group at a time. Plan your stay early since Paula's fills quickly in the peak summer season.

A fine waterside option is **Bay Avenue B&B** (1393 Bay Ave., 907/235-3757, www.bayavebb.com, mid-May-mid-Sept., $169-210 d, additional guests $40 pp), with seven spacious rooms in the main house. Each unit has a private bath, kitchen access, and Wi-Fi, and a filling breakfast buffet is included. A private suite ($185 d) is also available, with a full kitchen and a private bath; breakfast is not included for the suite. The marsh below is a good place to spot shorebirds and bald eagles.

A Room with a View (840 Rosebud Court, 907/299-3542, www.aroomwithaviewhomer. com, $155 d) is a large hillside home off West Hill Road with two guest rooms, private baths, a big deck with dramatic views, and great breakfasts. Owner Manfred Gaedeke hails from Germany, and his decades as a florist shows in the lovingly landscaped grounds. No children under age eight.

Aptly named **Maria's Majestic View B&B** (1660 Race Rd., 907/235-6413, www.majesticviewbb.com, rooms $150-175 d, cabin suites $190 d, extra guests $15 pp) is a very comfortable three-story home with three guest rooms, all with private baths. The deluxe room includes a whirlpool tub, a private balcony, and tall windows. Two cabin suites offer more privacy, and each has a queen and twin beds, a kitchenette, and a bath. All guests

appreciate the big deck with unobstructed bay vistas, an outdoor deck with a gas grill, and homemade breakfasts served family-style.

Aloha B&B (62209 Glacier View Court, 907/299-0607 or 877/355-0607, www.alohabb. com, May-Oct., rooms $165 d, suite $215 d, additional guests $25 pp) has one of Homer's famous million-dollar views—a 180-degree panorama of bay, mountains, and glacier. The owners are natives of Hawaii, and a Hawaiian theme carries throughout the B&B. Two guest rooms share a bath and kitchen, while the apartment-style suite has a private entrance, two bedrooms, a bath, and a full kitchen. Breakfast ingredients are provided, and the B&B has flat-screen TVs.

A delightful log home six miles out on East End Road, **Good Karma Inn** (57480 Taku Ave., 907/299-6200, www.goodkarmainn. com, Apr.-Sept., $180 d, 2-night minimum) fits Homer to a T, mixing functionality and comfort with a fine bay and mountain view, plus distinctive local artwork on the walls. Kindly owner Michael LeMay will fill you in on local attractions, and he cooks a full hot breakfast. Three guest rooms with private baths are available; one is completely accessible for disabled travelers.

Three miles east of town, **Bear Creek Winery and Lodging** (60203 Bear Creek Dr., 907/235-8484, www.bearcreekwinery.com, cottages $200 d, house $375) has two lovely log cottages with kitchenettes and private baths. The main house has three bedrooms, a full kitchen, and a deck with bay views. Guests are provided a bottle of wine and can unwind in the cedar tub. A breakfast voucher ($15 pp) can be used at local restaurants. The winery here crafts distinctive fruit wines, and the immaculately landscaped grounds include a koi pond and flower gardens. A two-night minimum stay is required, and no children under age 12 are allowed.

A modern timber-frame home, **Timber Bay B&B** (51310 Timber Bay Court, 907/235-3785, www.timber-bay.com, rooms $160-190 d, apartment $220 d, 2-night minimum) sits atop a quiet ridge 15 miles east of Homer.

Inside are four guest rooms, along with a separate apartment over the garage. A filling breakfast is served, and other amenities include a seasonal outdoor hot tub, a sauna, private baths, and decks providing a view across Kachemak Bay.

Juneberry Lodge (40963 China Poot St., 907/234-4779, www.junberrylodge.com, $165-185 d) is a spacious log-and-rock home a few miles east of Homer. Three guest rooms feature handmade quilts, private baths, and Wi-Fi. The home is decorated with Alaskan artifacts, and co-owner Marcia's breakfast is always a treat. (Trivia note: co-owner Mannfried Funk is an award-winning cellist with the Seattle Symphony.)

A charming New England-style cottage in the heart of town, **Spyglass Inn** (385 W. Fairview Ave., 907/235-6075 or 866/535-6075, www.homerspyglassinn.com, $195-235 d) has three small guest rooms on two levels, private entrances and baths, fridges, and microwaves, along with king, queen, and handmade Murphy beds. Owner Pat Melone cooks a fabulous breakfast.

Vacation Rentals

Cabins and guesthouses provide the perfect option for families looking for a place to call their own, and Homer has a multitude of choices; find them on the chamber website (www.homeralaska.org) or visit **Homer Cabins & Cottages Network** (www.cabinsinhomer.com), with 10 or so rental cabins in the Homer area. Also check out several hundred (271 at last count) places listed on both **VRBO** (www.vrbo.com) and **Airbnb** (www.airbnb.com) for many other vacation rentals in the area. You'll find everything from a $30 room in a cottage to a $3,250 luxury lodge that sleeps 40.

High atop the bluff overlooking Kachemak Bay, ★ **Cozy Cove Inn** (205 Cozy Cove Dr., 907/399-6277, www.cozycoveinn.com, house $290 d, apartment $170 d, additional guests $15 pp) is one of Homer's premier vacation rentals. The main house contains two bedrooms (one with a king bed), a fireplace, a

full kitchen, and a large deck with a grill and Adirondack chairs. It's popular for families or four people traveling together. The studio apartment has its own entrance, with a queen bed, a pull-down Murphy queen bed, and a full kitchen. Breakfast ingredients are provided in the apartment. Cozy Cove is run by Marcella Suydam, who spent many years as a commercial fisher on the Alaska Peninsula. There's a three-night minimum in the main house or two nights for the apartment.

Sea Lion Cove (609/602-8509, www.sealiongallery.com, mid-Apr.-mid-Sept., $155 d) sits atop the gallery of the same name near the end of the Homer Spit. The two efficiency suites are right in the heart of the summertime action. Each has a kitchenette, a private bath, TV, and a shared deck, delivering full-on bay vistas.

Easily the most unique lodging in Homer, ★ **Kenai Peninsula Suites** (3685 Sterling Hwy., 907/235-1866, www.kenaipeninsulasuites.com, $260-300 for up to 4 guests) has five modern units, all with kitchenettes, private baths, large plasma TVs, and gas grills. There's a circular two-story log yurt, three cabins, a two-level loft house, and two dome-shaped subterranean units that are literally tucked into the hillside facing the bay. Access to these is via a spiral staircase from a circular tower. Most units have king beds, and guests can take in a panoramic view from the hot tub.

A fine waterfront place with an expansive deck, **Homer Inn & Spa** (895 Ocean Dr. Loop, 907/235-1000, www.homerinnandspa.com, rooms $279 d, villa $299 d, town homes $295 for 4 guests, 2-night minimum) has a beachside hot tub, a garden swing, day spa facilities (including side-by-side massage), plush king beds, fridges, microwaves, decks, and complimentary wine. There are three rooms as well as a separate villa, perfect for families. Also available are two modern townhouses in the center of Homer (no ocean view). Each has three bedrooms, two baths, full kitchens, and TVs.

Situated atop a high bluff on the west side

as the highway drops into Homer, **Alaska Adventure Cabins** (2525 Sterling Hwy., 907/223-6681, www.alaskaadventurecabins. com, $195-425 d, additional guests $35 pp) has a fun mélange of seven lodging places: gorgeous cabins, homes, and lodges, plus a restored Alaska Railroad caboose and a land-locked boat called the *Double Eagle* that began life as a Gulf Coast shrimper. Each unit contains a full kitchen, a private bath, and a large deck with all-encompassing views of volcanoes, glaciers, Kachemak Bay, and the Spit.

A dozen miles east of Homer, **Eagles Rest** (907/570-1027, www.vrbo.com/335518, $399, 2-night minimum) is a gorgeous log home with panoramic views across Kachemak Bay. The home was built by Atz Kilcher from the reality TV show *Alaska: The Last Frontier.* Eagles Rest has space for a large family or group, with four bedrooms and a loft, plus a full kitchen, a rock hearth, and access to 600 acres of the Kilcher family homestead country.

Camping

Camping on the Spit is what most budget travelers, RVers, and backpackers do, although it's no picnic. It's within spitting distance of the noisy road, and it's barren and often very windy. There are city-maintained **Homer Spit Campgrounds** (907/435-3199, www. cityofhomer-ak.gov, Apr.-Oct., tents $15, RVs $24) in four places: Mariner Park at the base of the Spit, and three more areas near the Fishing Hole. There are no hookups, but restrooms or portable toilets are close by. Self-register at the campsites or pay at the Camp Fee Office at Mariner Park. A few hardy folks try their luck in winter when the Spit is officially closed to camping.

Quieter and more protected from the wind (but less scenic) is **Karen Hornaday Park Campground** (629 Fairview Ave., tents $15, RVs $24), near the hospital on Fairview Avenue. The park has a wonderful playground that will keep your kids entertained, and downtown shops are a few blocks down the hill.

In addition to the city campsites, the Homer Spit is home to two RV parks with hookups. Close to the very tip of the Spit, the privately run **Homer Spit Campground** (907/235-8206, www.homerspitcampground. com, mid-May-early Sept., tents $40, RVs $45-55) has rustic and crowded sites—some right on the beach—with electricity, water, showers ($1), and Wi-Fi.

Heritage RV Park (3550 Homer Spit Rd., 907/226-4500, www.alaskaheritagervpark. com, mid-May-early Sept., RVs $75) commands top dollar with a prime spot next to the Fishing Hole. Sites include all the latest amenities—including satellite TV, Wi-Fi, showers, picnic tables, fire pits, a putting green, a gift shop, and espresso (this is Homer, after all). The beachfront spaces always go fast, and the park is often full much of the summer.

Driftwood Inn RV Park (907/235-8019, www.thedriftwoodinn.com, RVs $65) is in town close to Bishops Beach, with Wi-Fi, showers, laundry, and cable TV. Sites are jammed together in a small lot, but the location is very convenient and it's open year-round.

Ocean Shores RV Park (455 Sterling Hwy., 907/235-3951, www. homeralaskarvpark.com, May-Sept., tents $20, RVs $60) is a crowded RV lot on the west edge of town with Wi-Fi, cable TV, laundry, and showers. It's a short walk to Bishops Beach from the RV park.

At the crest of the hill before you roll into town, **Homer Baycrest KOA** (907/435-7995 or 800/562-9949, www.koa.com, mid-May-mid-Sept., tents $30, RVs $60) has full hookups and Wi-Fi, showers, and an adjacent gas station and convenience store. The location provides panoramic views of the bay, but is two miles from town. Small cabins and a yurt are also available.

If you're staying in the city campgrounds, **showers** are available at the Homer Spit Campground or local coin laundries. A good bet is **The Washboard** (1204 Ocean Dr., 907/235-6781), where you can even surf the Internet for free or get an espresso while watching the clothes spin. An even better deal is the **high school pool**, where they throw in a free swim for the cost of a shower.

INFORMATION AND SERVICES

Stop by the Homer Chamber of Commerce **Visitors Information Center** (201 Sterling Hwy., 907/235-7740, www.homeralaska.org, 9am-6pm Mon.-Sat., 10am-3pm Sun. late May-early Sept., 9am-5pm Mon.-Fri. early Sept.-late May) for local details and a plethora of brochures. The office is on the right side as you enter town, just past Fat Olives Restaurant.

The gorgeous **Homer Public Library** (500 Hazel Ave., 907/235-3180, www.cityofhomer-ak.gov/library, 10am-6pm Mon., Wed., and Fri.-Sat., 10am-8pm Tues. and Thurs.) has an atrium fireplace for relaxing, tall windows facing Kachemak Bay, a large kids' room, a fine choice of videos, and plenty of computers and free Wi-Fi for Internet users. The library is a block up Heath Street from the post office and near the Safeway store.

A number of businesses—even a laundry—provide free Wi-Fi hotspots, and one local company, **SPITwSPOTS** (www.spitwspots.com) has antennas on the Spit and around town providing free Wi-Fi for an hour; pop open your laptop for details.

Public radio station **KBBI** (www.kbbi.org) is one of Alaska's best and most eclectic radio stations; find it at 890 AM. (By the way, this is one of just a handful of NPR stations on the AM dial; the AM signal travels farther in the mountains.)

The **Homer Post Office** (Homer Bypass and Heath St., 907/235-6129) is a block beyond the Safeway store on the Homer Bypass.

South Peninsula Hospital (4300 Bartlett St., 907/235-8101, www.sphosp.org) is a modern, fully staffed facility. If you really need to spend a night in a hospital, at least this one offers the views for which Homer is so famous!

One of the few Alaskan towns with its own newspapers, Homer actually has two award-winning weekly papers: the *Homer News* (www.homernews.com) and the much smaller *Homer Tribune* (www.homertribune.com).

GETTING THERE

Air

Homer Airport (HOM, www.cityofhomer-ak.gov/airport) is 0.5 miles out East Kachemak Road, which forks off from the Spit Road. Inside the terminal are racks filled with brochures from local businesses, plus free Wi-Fi and local newspapers. **Ravn Alaska** (907/235-5205 or 800/866-8394, www.flyravn.com) flies between Homer and Anchorage ($160 one-way) several times a day; flights take around 45 minutes.

Smokey Bay Air (907/235-1511 or 888/482-1511, www.smokeybayair.com) has daily flights from the airport to Seldovia ($124 round-trip) as well as the Native Alaskan villages of Nanwalek and Port Graham. Neither of these villages is set up to handle tourism.

The Stage Line (907/235-2252, www.stagelineinhomer.com) runs vans between Homer and Anchorage ($97 one-way), Soldotna ($55), and Seward ($100). Drivers can stop almost anywhere along the route to pick up or drop off passengers, but you should call ahead. Service is Monday-Friday to Anchorage or Seward in the summer, but only to Anchorage in winter.

Ferry

The **Alaska Marine Highway ferry terminal** (907/235-8449 or 800/642-0066, www.ferryalaska.com) is out near the end of the Homer Spit. From here, you can catch the *Tustumena* or *Kennicott* to Seldovia three times a week and to Kodiak four times weekly. Once a month in the summer, the *Tustumena* runs all the way out to Dutch Harbor in the Aleutians.

Operated by the Seldovia Village Tribe, the **Seldovia Bay Ferry** (907/435-3299, www.seldoviabayferry.com, Thurs.-Mon. late May-June and Aug.-mid-Sept., daily July, round-trip $40 adults, $30 seniors, $25 children, free under age 2) is a high-speed catamaran ferry that makes a twice-daily

45-minute run between Homer and Seldovia. It departs Homer at 11am and 6:30pm, and leaves Seldovia at 9am and 4:30pm. This is not a tour, just a quick and inexpensive connection to Seldovia. The ferry office is on the back side of the Homer harbor at Ramp 7; get there via Freight Dock Road. The ferry overnights in Seldovia, making for easy overnight trips there. Add $15 to take a bike on board. Reservations aren't necessary; just walk on board.

GETTING AROUND
Car Rentals
Rent cars, vans, and SUVs at the airport from **Pioneer Car Rental** (907/235-0734, www. rentalcarhomeralaska.com). Just a few blocks away, **Adventure Alaska Car Rental** (1441 Ocean Dr., 907/235-4022 or 800/882-2808, www.adventurealaskacars.com) has used cars and will pick you up in town.

Taxis and Trolley
Call **Kachecab** (907/235-1950), **Nick's Taxi** (907/399-5553), or **Kostas Taxi** (907/399-8008) for a taxi ride from the airport to town ($7) or from the Spit to downtown ($15). All three companies operate 24 hours daily.

The **Homer Trolley** (907/299-6210, www. homertrolley.com, 11am-6pm daily mid-June-mid-Aug., $15 day pass adults) is a bright red-and-green trolley that circles through Homer and out the Spit hourly in the summer. It stops at 14 locations around town—including the Homer Spit, Pratt Museum, the Homer Chamber of Commerce Visitors Information Center, RV parks, and the Islands and Ocean Visitor Center—providing a good way to explore the area without a car. Drivers provide entertaining narration along the way.

Across Kachemak Bay

★ KACHEMAK BAY AND GULL ISLAND
If you have three days in Homer, spend at least one of them on beautiful Kachemak Bay. A great way to do this is through a tour to **Peterson Bay Field Station** (907/235-6667, www.akcoastalstudies.org, late May-mid-Sept., $175 adults, $155 seniors, $95 under age 12) with professional naturalists from the nonprofit **Center for Alaskan Coastal Studies.** You'll spend time at bird rookeries, tide pools, rainforest trails, and prehistoric sites, and will gain a lifetime appreciation for the marine world. These eight-hour experiences are a bargain and include a visit to Gull Island during your boat ride across to Peterson Bay. Bring your own lunch, binoculars, and camera; rubber boots are provided. Combine the natural history tour with a two-hour guided sea kayak trip for $195 pp. Overnight stays (just $35 pp in a yurt with kitchen access) are also available at the Peterson Bay Field Station. The Coastal Studies office is in a yurt near Ramp 2 on the Spit. At the nonprofit's headquarters (708 Smokey Bay Way), there are additional displays on local flora and fauna and snowshoes for rent during the winter. Coastal Studies offers many other day trips throughout the summer, from 1.5-hour Creatures of the Dock tours ($8) to four-hour Ocean Connection tours ($109) that include a visit to both Gull Island and Peterson Bay.

Water Taxis and Tours
A small fleet of boats plies the waters of Kachemak Bay all summer, offering wildlife-viewing trips to Gull Island, whale watching in the bay, transport for kayakers and hikers heading into the state park, and access to remote wilderness lodges. An hour-long visit to Gull Island costs $50 pp, and water taxis will drop you at remote beaches inside Kachemak

Bay State Park ($75 pp round-trip). The most popular of these hikes is from Glacier Spit Beach to Grewingk Glacier and then back over the Saddle Trail to Halibut Cove, where you can get a water taxi back to Homer. Just want to check out the scenery? A ride-along ($50) is a fun way to explore the bay and join an existing trip.

A two-person minimum is required, but if your time is flexible, water taxis can generally get singles on board with another group heading in the same general direction. Some water taxis have discounted rates for families and kids under 13. You'll find water-taxi kiosks on the Spit, though some just use their boat and cell phone as a floating office.

The following are all excellent operators: **Ashore Water Taxi** (907/399-2340, www.ashorewatertaxi.com), **Bay Excursions** (907/235-7525, www.bayx.net), **Bay Roamers Water Taxi** (907/399-6200, www.halibutcovealaska.com), **Mako's Water Taxi** (907/235-9055, www.makoswatertaxi.com), **Red Mountain Marine** (907/399-8230, www.redmountainmarine.com), and **Homer Ocean Charters** (907/235-6212 or 800/426-6212, www.homerocean.com). Most of these run May-September, but both Mako's and Ashore operate year-round. Kayak rentals and a variety of specialized tours are offered by Mako and other operators.

An avid naturalist and serious birder, Karl Stolzfus of **Bay Excursions** (907/235-7525, www.bayx.net, Apr.-Sept.) leads excellent two-hour Gull Island and Sixty Foot Rock trips ($65 pp). He also guides three-hour K-Bay birding trips ($75 pp).

Biologist Glenn Seaman operates **Seaman's Ecotour Adventures** (907/299-1748, www.seamansadventures.com, May-Sept., full-day custom trip $600 for 1-3 people, $450 half-day for 1-3 people), providing a variety of boat-based environmental tours around Kachemak Bay, covering the gamut from birding to cultural history. All-day custom trips are geared to your interests. This means having your own private guide and boat for seven hours. As the former head of Kachemak Bay Research Reserve, Glenn has a deep knowledge of the region.

Central Charters & Tours (907/235-7847, www.centralcharter.com, $69 adults, $59 seniors, $49 kids) has daily round-trip sailings to Seldovia, with a narrated wildlife tour that includes stops at Gull Island to watch nesting murres and gulls, and Sixty Foot Rock for sea otters.

Halibut Cove

HALIBUT COVE

The enchanting village of Halibut Cove (pop. 75, www.halibutcove.com) is across Kachemak Bay on Ismailof Island. At one time Halibut Cove was the center for a thriving herring fishery, with 36 salteries operating. The fishery collapsed in 1928, and today the town is a small center for artists and fishers. Its picturesque harbor is ringed by hills dotted with the summer homes of wealthy Alaskans. Halibut Cove consists of a long boardwalk that connects a couple of shorefront businesses and homes, so addresses have not been provided.

Sights

The ferry to Halibut Cove docks in front of the Saltry Restaurant. Follow the boardwalk through an old boat barn, past the horses, and on to **Halibut Cove Experience Gallery** (907/296-2215, www.halibutcoveexperience.com, 1pm-4pm and 6pm-9pm daily late May-early Sept.), an excellent cooperative with jewelry, pottery, photography, prints, and sculpture. A short distance down the boardwalk are stairs climbing steeply to **Cove Gallery** (1pm-9pm daily late May-early Sept.), the studio of the late Diana Tillion, known for her subtle octopus-ink watercolors. The boardwalk passes Clem Tillion's classic Alaskan home (now over 90 years old, Clem is jokingly called "the king of Halibut Cove") before ending at a sandy beach.

If you're looking for a little hike, walk along the boardwalk from the Saltry Restaurant till you see a gate on the left. Go through the gate and follow the trail up the hill for all-encompassing views of Halibut Cove, Kachemak Bay, eagles, and a rocky arch along the shore below. Be sure to check out the beautiful gazebo overlooking Kachemak Bay; it was built by Clem Tillion to honor his late wife Diana.

Food

Halibut Cove's acclaimed ★ **The Saltry Restaurant** (907/296-2424, www.thesaltry.com, 1pm-9pm daily late May-early Sept., $18-32) serves daily pasta specials, a wonderful seafood chowder ($12 with bread), Kachemak Bay oysters, black cod, salmon, and more. Everything is homemade, from the decorated plates to the fresh breads and celebrated Callebaut chocolate cheesecake. There's a waterfront deck for alfresco dining on a sunny afternoon, a full bar, a clamshell-shaped aquarium filled with tide-pool creatures (free talks are at 3:30pm), and a blazing fire in the outdoor pit. Dinner reservations are required. Access is via the *Danny J* ferry, so you will need to simultaneously book both the ferry and restaurant reservations. The office on the Homer Spit will help you with the details, or you can make online reservations.

Halibut Cove Coffee House (907/230-8949, www.halibutcoverentals.com, 9am-5pm daily late May-early Sept., $4-9) is on the boardwalk a short distance from the Saltry. It has free Wi-Fi, shakes, and snacks.

Accommodations

At **Cove Country Cabins** (907/296-2257 or 888/353-2683, www.halibutcovealaska.com, $200-250 d, additional people $25 pp), guests stay in three attractive timber-frame cabins, each with a kitchenette, running water, and an outhouse, plus a central shower house. Cabins range from a little unit to a two-story, six-person house with a fine view. The owners also operate Bay Roamers Water Taxi.

Alaska's Ridgewood Lodge (907/296-2217, www.ridgewoodlodge.com, mid-May-mid-Sept., $3,400 for 2 people for a 2-night stay) is a large and modern lodge with panoramic views of the Halibut Cove area. All-inclusive stays at this luxurious 8,400-square-foot lodge include gourmet meals, a water taxi from Homer, Glacier Lake kayaking, guided wildlife tours, and hiking. The owners take guests on a tour of their oyster farm.

Halibut Cove Rentals (907/230-8949, www.halibutcoverentals.com, late May-early Sept.) has five places in the Cove. A short walk from the Saltry Restaurant, the Boardwalk Cottage ($175, sleeps 4) is actually a beautiful 1,800-square-foot two-bedroom home with hardwood floors, a wraparound deck, a

Homer and Kachemak Bay

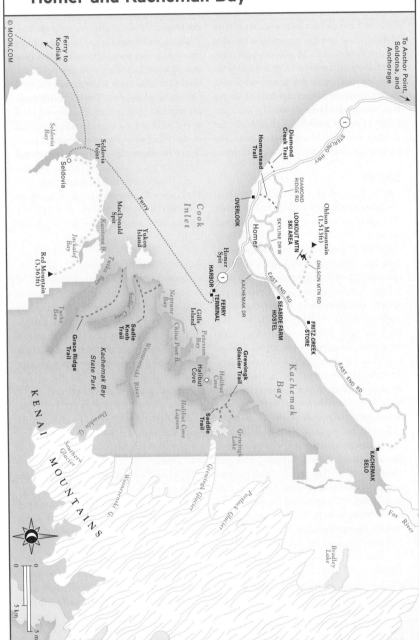

© MOON.COM

To Anchor Point,
Soldotna, and
Anchorage

STERLING HWY

Ferry to
Kodiak

Seldovia
Bay

Seldovia
Point

Seldovia

Diamond
Creek Trail

Homestead
Trail

DIAMOND
RIDGE RD

OVERLOOK

Homer

SKYLINE DR W

Ohlson Mountain
(1,513ft)

LOOKOUT MTN
SKI AREA

OHLSON MTN RD

MacDonald
Spit

Cook
Inlet

Yukon
Island

Kasitsna B.

Jackalof
Bay

Red Mountain
(3,365ft)

Tutka Bay

Tutka
Bay

Sadie
Cove

Homer
Spit

HOMER
HARBOR

FERRY
TERMINAL

KACHEMAK DR

EAST END RD

SEASIDE FARM
HOSTEL

FRITZ CREEK
STORE

EAST END RD

Neptune
Bay

China Poot B.

Gills
Island

Peterson
Bay

Grewingk
Glacier Trail

Kachemak
Bay

Sadie
Knob
Trail

Grace Ridge
Trail

Kachemak Bay
State Park

Wosnesenski River

Halibut
Cove

Halibut
Cove

Saddie
Trail

Grewingk
Lake

KACHEMAK
SELO

Halibut Cove
Lagoon

Ferry

Ferry

K E N A I

Dorotin G.

Southern
Glacier

M O U N T A I N S

Wosnesenski G.

Grewingk Glacier

Portlock Glacier

Fox River

Bradley
Lake

0   5 km

0   5 mi

kitchen, a bath, and Wi-Fi. The Green Cabin ($100 d) is a cozy budget option, including a king bed, a kitchenette, and an outhouse. The most unique place is the aptly named Lighthouse ($200 d). It's the quaint and very private white structure that stands out as you arrive in Halibut Cove. The Lighthouse is a 10-minute walk from the public boardwalk, and has an upstairs bedroom with a queen bed and bay vistas from the windows. A hand pump sink is downstairs, along with a nearby outhouse. Other options include a hilltop one-room log cabin ($200) and a lovely two-story cabin with surrounding boardwalk deck ($250, sleeps 4); these two are close to each other and can be combined for big groups.

Getting There

Most visitors arrive aboard the 34-passenger *Danny J* (907/296-2424, www.thesaltry.com, twice daily late May-early Sept.), a classic wooden boat that has been transporting passengers from Homer Spit to Halibut Cove for decades. The noon sailing ($66 pp round-trip) includes a tour of the Gull Island bird sanctuary. After three hours in Halibut Cove, the boat heads back to Homer, arriving at 4:45pm. Its second trip ($41 pp round-trip) leaves Homer at 5pm and gets back to the Spit by 9:45pm. This one is only for visitors with dinner reservations for The Saltry (or a Halibut Cove lodge), and it does not visit Gull Island. Make reservations online or phone, or by visiting the tiny *Danny J* office on the Spit. These trips often book up in midsummer, especially for dinner sailing; call at least a week ahead. Some people have been known to reserve a year in advance!

Homer water taxis can provide transport to Halibut Cove ($75 round-trip).

SELDOVIA

A sleepy fishing village (pop. 200), Seldovia (from the Russian for "herring") was once the bustling metropolis that Homer is now. The road, the earthquake, and fate exchanged their roles. On the same latitude as Oslo, Norway, Seldovia was first settled by Russians in the early 1800s and became an active fur-trading post. Through the years, Seldovia has had many ocean-oriented industries, from the short-lived herring boom to salmon, king crab, and tanner crab. The town has faced hard times in the last few years, but seems to be on the rebound, with a handful of newly opened shops.

Seldovia is a convenient place for really getting away from it all. Catch a ride over from Homer on the fast ferry, with its twice-daily service, or on a water taxi or tour boat. There's not much to do in the town itself, but dirt roads and trails provide outstanding mountain biking and hiking.

Note that cell phone service is limited; only Verizon is available in Seldovia. You might find service at Outside Beach and other locations away from town.

The **Seldovia Chamber of Commerce** has local info on their website (www.youotterbehere.com).

Sights

Start out by strolling along Main Street. Interpretive signs describe Alaska's Russian history, commercial fishing, the earthquake, and more. The picturesque **St. Nicholas Russian Orthodox Church** (built in 1891) sits atop a small hill overlooking the town like a proud parent.

The Seldovia Village Tribe's (SVT) **Museum and Visitors Center** (across from the boat harbor, 907/234-7898, www.svt.org, daily noon-5pm late May-early Sept., donation) has exhibits on Native Alaskan culture and the town. SVT is the largest local employer, operating the fast ferry and medical centers in Homer, Seldovia, and Anchor Point. Up the road is picturesque **Seldovia Slough,** where you can walk the last remaining section of original boardwalk—the rest was wiped out in the 1964 earthquake. There's a pocket-size park along the harbor at the start of the boardwalk, and it's a short stroll to **Thyme on the Boardwalk** (907/440-2213, www.thymeontheboardwalk.com), a fun

Seldovia

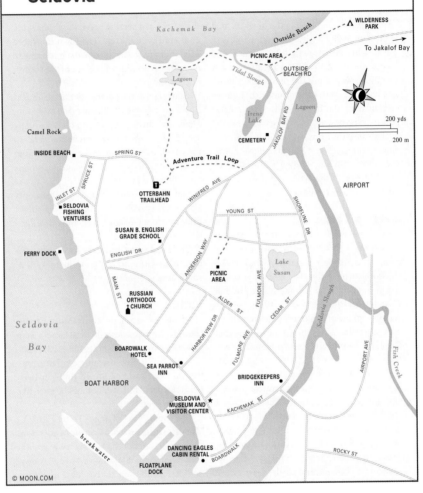

over-the-water shop with a plant nursery. A gift shop sells gourmet cheeses.

Festivals and Events

Head to Seldovia for the **Human Powered Fishing Derby** (Memorial Day weekend, May), where contestants compete with rowboats, kayaks, and even pedal-powered boats for the biggest fish. A community fish fry ends the event.

Held on the weekend closest to the solstice, the **Seldovia Summer Solstice Music Festival** (June) features live music, workshops, and jam sessions.

Seldovia's biggest party arrives on the **Fourth of July,** when this sleepy town kicks into action with a parade, canoe jousting, log rolling, an egg toss, a running race, and other events.

The **Craft Invitational Chainsaw Carving Competition** (Labor Day weekend, Sept.) attracts some of the top chainsaw artists (yes they really exist) in the nation. You'll see dozens of the resulting sculptures scattered around town.

Recreation

Well-marked **Otterbahn Trail** leads 1.5 miles from the school grounds though spruce forests to Outside Beach. The Seldovia area is famous for ripe **berries** in late summer. You'll find blueberries and raspberries in abundance, but make sure you aren't picking on private land.

Seldovia is perfect for mountain bikes, but there's nowhere in town to rent one. Pick up a bike in Homer and bring it over on the ferry. One of the most fun things to do in Seldovia is to pedal a bike out on the road to beautiful Outside Beach, where you can savor the great views across Kachemak Bay. The gravel road continues to MacDonald Spit and Kasitsna Bay (eight miles), and to the dock at **Jakolof Bay** (11 miles), before heading toward Red Mountain. The road-trail to **Red Mountain** is accessible for several miles, but upper stretches are challenging due to washouts.

For on-the-water fun, take a guided tour by Kirby Corwin of **Kayak'Atak** (907/234-7425, www.alaska.net/~kayaks, 3-hour tour $80 pp, 5-hour tour with lunch $120 pp). Kayak rentals are available for experienced kayakers.

Operating from Boardwalk Hotel, **KBay Kayaking** (239 Main St., 907/201-0599, www.kbaykayaking.com, late May-early Sept.) rents single kayaks ($20 per hour) and double kayaks ($35 per hour). Fun two-hour guided tours ($59 pp) include beachcombing and lunch. A variety of longer trips are also available, including half-day tours ($89 pp).

Thyme on the Boardwalk (907/440-2213, www.thymeontheboardwalk.com) rents stand-up paddleboards ($30 per hour) to play around the slough.

Food

Perry's Café (226 Main St., 907/234-7829, www.seaparrotinn.com, 7am-6pm daily late May-early Sept., $5-14) serves breakfast burritos and lunch sandwiches, but the main attractions are ice cream cones, smoothies, and milkshakes. Perry's is directly across from the harbor.

Housed within the Boardwalk Hotel, **Boardwalk Pub & Grill** (239 Main St., 907/234-7816, www.seldoviahotel.com, 8am-4pm Sun.-Mon., 8am-9pm Tues.-Thurs., 8am-10pm Fri.-Sat. mid-May-mid-Sept., $14-28) has a brunch menu of egg scrambles, paninis, seafood chowder, seared rockfish sandwiches, and espresso. Weekend dinners feature prime rib (Fri.) and baby back ribs (Sat.), along with small pizzas. There's a small pub with mixed drinks and beers on tap, plus a great outdoor deck with covered tents along the harbor and occasional live music.

Harbor Inn (273 Main St., 907/227-8466, 8am-4pm Mon.-Sat., 1pm-4pm Sun., $7-12) is a great spot for freshly baked sticky buns and scones, along with espresso, quiche, salads, and sandwiches—including a gourmet grilled cheese with bacon and apple on homemade sourdough bread.

Linwood Bar & Grill (253 Main St., 907/234-7674, www.linwoodbar.com, noon-2am daily late May-early Sept., noon-9pm Sun.-Mon., 5pm-9pm Tues.-Sat. early Sept.-late May) is the local bar, with a good selection of beers and live music most summer weekends. There's a pool table inside, the TV has sports most afternoons, and there's a big harbor-side deck. The pub fare ($12-20) is good: burgers, pizzas, fish-and-chips, clam chowder, and nightly specials. This is the only year-round restaurant in Seldovia; food service stops at 10pm.

Crabpot Grocery (266 Main St., 907/234-7435, 10am-6pm Mon.-Sat.) has basic groceries and produce.

Accommodations

Dancing Eagles Cabin Rental (907/360-6363, www.alaskadancingeagles.biz, mid-May-early Sept., $195 d, extra guests $40 pp, 2-night minimum) has perhaps the finest location in Seldovia, with a big deck perched on the water at the entrance to Seldovia Slough. The cabin sleeps six, with a kitchen, a bath,

and Wi-Fi. There's a queen bed downstairs and four single beds in the sleeping loft.

Sea Parrot Inn (226 Main St., 907/234-7829, www.seaparrotinn.com, late May-early Sept., $125 d) contains four nicely furnished guest rooms with a communal living room, a kitchen, a deck, Wi-Fi, and breakfast served in the downstairs café. The great room has a TV, but there are no TVs in the guest rooms.

Find three comfortable guest rooms, a big waterside porch, private baths, Wi-Fi, delicious full breakfasts, and ultra-friendly owners at **Seldovia Fishing Adventures** (227 Beach St., 907/234-7417, www.fishhalibut. com, $115 s, $180 d). Fishing charters are available on board their 30-foot cabin cruiser. They offer packages that include lodging, breakfast, dinner, and a day of fishing for halibut and salmon.

Boardwalk Hotel (239 Main St., 907/234-7816, www.seldoviahotel.com, $129-149 d) has a dozen comfortable rooms in a variety of layouts; be sure to request a harbor-side room. All have double or queen beds, private baths, flat-screen TVs, and Wi-Fi. There's a lovely deck for relaxing in the sun, cruiser bikes to borrow, plus a small restaurant and pub.

The Bridgekeepers Inn (223 Kachemak Dr., 907/234-7535, www.thebridgekeepersinn. com, May-early Sept., $150 d) is a two-bedroom B&B with private baths, queen beds, private balconies over the picturesque slough, and full hot breakfasts.

Camping

Pitch a tent at **Outside Beach Campground** ($10), one mile out on Jakalof Bay Road. The campground has a water pump, outhouses, a pavilion, and picnic tables, but no showers. Just up the hill is **Seldovia RV Park** ($15), with RV spaces and water hookups, but no electricity. A campground host is on-site, or call the town office (907/234-7643) for details. The dump station is in town.

1: harborside deck at Boardwalk Pub & Grill in Seldovia; **2:** Seldovia Slough

Information and Services

Find out more about Seldovia from the **Seldovia Chamber of Commerce** (907/234-7612, www.seldoviachamber.org) or the website for the **City of Seldovia** (www. cityofseldovia.com).

Showers and laundry facilities are in town at Sea Parrot Inn (226 Main St., 907/234-7829, www.seaparrotinn.com), across from the boat harbor. Seldovia's **Susan B English School** (907/234-7616) has a public pool where you can swim or shower ($4).

Getting There

The **state ferries** *Tustumena* and *Kennicott* (907/235-8449 or 800/642-0066, www.ferryalaska.com) sail to Seldovia from Homer four times a week. The trip takes 90 minutes, laying over for several hours before returning to Homer.

Operated by the Seldovia Village Tribe, the **Seldovia Bay Ferry** (907/435-3299, www. seldoviabayferry.com, Thurs.-Mon. late May-June and Aug.-mid-Sept., daily July, round-trip $40 adults, $30 seniors, $25 children, free under age 2) is a high-speed catamaran ferry that makes a twice-daily 45-minute run between Homer and Seldovia. It departs Homer at 11am and 6:30pm, and leaves Seldovia at 9am and 4:30pm. This is not a tour, just a quick and inexpensive connection to Seldovia. The ferry office is on the back side of the Homer harbor at Ramp 7; get there via Freight Dock Road. The ferry overnights in Seldovia, making for easy overnight trips there. Add $15 to take a bike on board. Reservations aren't necessary; just walk aboard.

Central Charters & Tours (907/235-7847, www.centralcharter.com, late May-early Sept., $69 adults, $59 seniors, $49 children) books for daily sailings to Seldovia on board either the 75-foot *Discovery* or the 65-foot *Rainbow Connection*. These narrated wildlife tours depart Homer at 10:30am, stopping to watch the gulls and murres at Gull Island and the sea otters near Sixty Foot Rock. They dock in Seldovia for three hours—perfect for lunch and a walk around town—before heading back across Kachemak Bay, arriving at 5:30pm. These are very informative tours. Both Central Charters and **Rainbow Tours** (907/235-7272, www.rainbowtours.net) have offices on the Spit where you can book these Seldovia tours.

Mako's Water Taxi (907/235-9055, www.makoswatertaxi.com) has combo trips that include a water taxi to Jakolof Bay, a taxi ride into Seldovia, and a return flight back to Homer for a total of $150 pp. This is a screaming deal, and they set up all the logistics. You can also do this as part of an overnight trip to Seldovia. Another option is to rent a bike from **Cycle Logical** (907/226-2925, www.cyclelogicalhomer.com) and take it by water taxi to the dock at Jakolof Bay. From there, it's a relatively easy 11-mile ride to Seldovia. Return the same way, or take the fast ferry back to Homer.

Smokey Bay Air (907/235-1511 or 888/482-1511, www.smokeybayair.com) has multiple flights daily from Homer. These 15-minute flights cost $62 each way. **Alaska Air Taxi** (907/243-3944 or 800/789-5232, www.alaskaairtaxi.com) flies between Anchorage and Seldovia for $180 one-way.

KACHEMAK BAY STATE PARK

One of the largest coastal parks in the nation, Kachemak Bay State Park spreads for 200 miles along the southwestern edge of the Kenai Peninsula. Within the park's 400,000 acres are glaciers, high mountains, lakes, islands, beaches, and a scenic rocky shoreline. Highlighted by constantly changing weather patterns, the park's outstanding scenery is a backdrop for high-quality recreation. Hiking and camping along the shoreline and in the surrounding forests and mountains are excellent. Above the tree line, skiers and hikers will find glaciers and snowfields stretching for miles.

Almost three-quarters of the land is wilderness; it's officially called Kachemak Bay Wilderness State Park. Land mammals include moose, black bears, mountain goats,

coyotes, and wolves. Kachemak Bay supports a rich diversity of marinelife and is famous for its halibut and salmon fishing, plus the chance to view sea otters, seals, porpoises, and whales. Five very popular public-use cabins are available ($75), along with over 80 miles of hiking trails. A major spruce bark beetle outbreak in the 1990s left massive stretches of dead trees within Kachemak Bay State Park, but new trees are gradually moving into these areas, and most of the dead trees have fallen.

Homer's **Kachemak Bay State Park office** (907/235-7024, www.alaskastateparks.org) is staffed intermittently, so you may need to contact the district office in Soldotna (907/262-5581). The **Kachemak Bay Water Trail** (www.kachemakbaywatertrail.org) is a 125-mile boat route connecting the bay's many sites; pick up a helpful map at the Homer Visitors Information Center or the Islands and Oceans Visitor Center.

Access

In addition to the daily summertime boat tours of Kachemak Bay, Homer-based water taxis provide hiker or sea kayaker drop-offs within park waters. The round-trip cost is typically $75 pp, but can be a bit higher for longer trips. Local operators include **Bay Excursions** (907/235-7525, www.bayx.net), **Bay Roamers Water Taxi** (907/399-6200, www.halibutcovealaska.com), **Mako's Water Taxi** (907/235-9055, www.makoswatertaxi.com), **Ashore Water Taxi** (907/399-2341, www.ashorewatertaxi.com), **Red Mountain Marine** (907/399-8230, www.redmountainmarine.com), and **Homer Ocean Charters** (907/235-6212 or 800/426-6212, www.homerocean.com). You'll find water-taxi offices on the Spit, though some do not have an office. There is no extra charge for kayaks or bicycles, but bikes are not allowed on state park trails. They are, however, okay on beaches outside the park boundary and places such as Jakolof Road. Rent mountain bikes or fat tire bikes from **Cycle Logical** (907/226-2925, www.cyclelogicalhomer.com).

Backcountry Yurts

For something different, **Alaskan Yurt Rentals** (907/299-6879, www.alaskanyurtrentals.com, May-Sept., $78) maintains eight cozy yurts located at trailheads and beaches around the park, including China Poot Bay, Tutka Bay I and II, Kayak Beach, Quarry Beach, Humpy Creek, Right Beach, and Haystack Beach. Each includes a woodstove, sleeping space for six, foam mattresses, and a camp stove. These can also be booked through local water taxis. The yurts are made in Homer, and you can visit the facility where they are manufactured—**Nomad Shelter** (907/235-0132, www.nomadshelter.com)—on Bear Creek Drive.

Grewingk Glacier

For an outstanding day or overnight hike, have the water taxi ($75 pp round-trip) drop you at the **Glacier Spit Trailhead,** where an easy and very scenic two-mile hike leads to a lake in front of picture-perfect Grewingk Glacier. You can camp nearby and return via the one-mile **Saddle Trail,** which takes you over a small ridge to Halibut Cove for the water taxi back to Homer. A multitude of side trips are available along this route, including ones that take you high into the alpine

area over the glacier, and a delightful beach walk. Contact the park for many other hiking options.

Guided sea kayak tours to Grewingk are available through **Three Moose Kayak Adventure** (907/299-1075 or 888/503-7160, www.threemoose.com, $199 pp). These all-day adventures include a guide, a water taxi from Homer, a hike to the lake, and inflatable kayaks to paddle up to the glacier. A variety of other trips are also available, from guided hikes to glacier ice trekking. The owners also operate Hideaway Cove Lodge, a fine base for exploring Kachemak Bay State Park.

True North Adventures (907/235-0708, www.truenorthkayak.com, $225 pp with snack) has an all-day Glacier Lake hike and stand-up paddleboard trek that includes a round-trip water taxi from the Homer Spit to the Saddle Trailhead, followed by a 45-minute hike to Grewingk Lake. Once there, you'll hop aboard a stand-up paddleboard to cross the lake and paddle among the icebergs at the towering face of Grewingk Glacier. Afterward you'll hike back and return to Homer by water taxi.

Grace Ridge

This challenging all-day hike begins at sea

hikers on Grace Ridge, Kachemak Bay State Park

level, climbs steeply into the alpine, and then drops down the opposite side to another bay. You can hike up and back the same way or over the top and down for more variety. Access is by water taxi ($75 pp round-trip) from Homer to trailheads at Kayak Beach or South Grace, with campsites and yurts at both trailheads. Starting from Kayak Beach at the mouth of Sadie Cove, the trail climbs steeply through old-growth Sitka spruce forests to an overlook at 2.3 miles, continuing into the alpine to the 3,100-foot summit of Grace Peak at approximately 4.5 miles. There are 360-degree views of Kachemak Bay, the Kenai Mountains, and a mix of coves, islands, glaciers, and forests. From the summit you can return the same way, or drop down to South Grace Trailhead along Tutka Bay, a total distance of nine miles. Grace Ridge Trail is equally fun from the other direction too. If you have more time, book one of the yurts (907/299-6879, www.alaskanyurtrentals.com, $78) at Quarry Beach, Kayak Beach, or Tutka Bay.

Halibut Cove Lagoon

This protected lagoon is one of the most popular destinations in Kachemak Bay State Park. Water taxis pull up to a big public dock that provides access to hiking trails, campsites, cabins, and a small visitors center. Two public-use cabins (www.dnr.alaska.gov, $75) are available within a short walk of the dock: Lagoon Overlook cabin and Lagoon East cabin. The Lagoon West cabin is 0.5 miles away, with access by boat. Miles of hiking trails crisscross the area around Halibut Cove Lagoon, leading to China Poot Lake and other destinations, making this a wonderful place to explore from your comfortable base in the cabins. (Note: Halibut Cove Lagoon is not accessible from the village of Halibut Cove on Ismailof Island.)

Private Cabins and Lodges

A number of delightful lodges fill coves surrounding Kachemak Bay State Park.

For a wonderful escape, Porter's Alaskan Adventures (Hesketh Island, 907/235-8060, www.portersak.com, May-mid-Sept., $150-165 for 4 people, add $80 pp round-trip water taxi from Homer) rents three modern cabins on the shore of Hesketh Island near the mouth of Tutka Bay, seven miles from Homer. All cabins contain full kitchens, decks, propane lights, barbecue grills, and waterfront views; there's no electricity. Bring sleeping bags, drinking water, a cooler for food, and towels. There's a wood-fired sauna on the beach for bathing, and outhouses behind each cabin. Sea kayak rentals are available through True North Adventures (907/235-0708, www.truenorthkayak.com).

Sadie Cove Wilderness Lodge (907/235-2350 or 888/283-7234, www.sadiecove.com, $650 pp per day, add $150 round-trip water taxi from Homer) is an off-the-grid wilderness retreat in the heart of Kachemak Bay State Park. Guests stay in quaint cabins built by Keith and Randi Iverson, who have lived here since the 1970s. This is a place to escape to a quieter time, so you won't find in-room phones or TVs, though they do have Wi-Fi, a sauna and creek-side bathhouse, a communal lounge, and a chef. Lodging, three meals, and kayaks are included in the cost. A two-night minimum is required, but most guests book for five nights.

Tutka Bay Wilderness Lodge (907/274-2710, www.withinthewild.com, mid-May-mid-Sept., $5,695 pp for 3 nights all-inclusive) occupies the south shore of Kachemak Bay between Halibut Cove and Seldovia, nine water miles from the Spit. The lodge caters to nature lovers, photographers, bird-watchers, and anglers with an appreciation for the finer things in life and a willingness to pay dearly. The cost includes round-trip transportation from Homer, gourmet family-style meals (the co-owner is a Cordon Bleu-trained chef), boat tours, sea kayaking, guided walks, beachcombing, clam digging, wildlife viewing, yoga classes, or just soaking in the hot tub. Each multiple-night stay also includes an all-day bear-viewing trip or halibut fishing charter. Accommodations are luxurious; there is no roughing it here, and it's where you might run into the likes of Jim Carrey and other celebrities. Tutka Bay is one of just two Alaskan lodges that are part of National Geographic's elite "Unique Lodges of the World."

Peterson Bay Lodge & Oyster Camp (907/235-7156, www.petersonbaylodge.com, June-mid-Aug., $195 pp, 2-night minimum, add $75 pp round-trip water taxi from Homer) occupies the head of this remote bay, where the owners raise famous Kachemak Bay oysters. Guests stay in four surprisingly comfortable canvas-walled cabins with screened porches, a sauna, showers, outhouse, and access to the lodge's communal kitchen to cook meals. Upon arrival, guests are given a tour of the oyster farm, along with the chance to sample fresh oysters and mussels. Borrow a kayak to explore this pretty bay.

A classic Alaskan lodge, gorgeous **Kachemak Bay Wilderness Lodge** (907/235-8910, www.alaskawildernesslodge. com, $2,100 pp for 2 nights all-inclusive, $4,500 pp for 5 nights all-inclusive) lies within China Poot Bay in the heart of the state park, with trails to nearby Peterson Bay. Guests stay in cozy artistic cabins, each with a cedar bath, a picture window, and homemade quilts, and are served gourmet organic meals. All-inclusive stays feature kayaking, halibut and salmon fishing, guided hikes, and other activities customized to your interests. Most guests stay for five nights, but shorter visits are available. This is the real deal—a great location, first-rate staff and chef, and cozy accommodations.

Located adjacent to a trailhead for Grewingk Glacier, **Hideaway Cove Wilderness Lodge** (907/299-1075 or 888/503-7160, www.hideawaycovelodge.com, mid-May-mid-Sept., from $399 pp all-inclusive for 1 night, $1,199 pp for 3 nights, $299 pp for 1 night unguided) has four waterside cabins that share a separate bathhouse and three hillside cabins with private baths. A variety of packages are offered, starting with a one-night stay that includes water taxi from Homer, lodging, Wi-Fi, and excellent meals in the central yurt, plus guided hiking and kayaking on Grewingk Lake. Cabins have propane stoves and limited power; everything runs on solar cells. You'll want to stay at least three nights to really appreciate the quiet beauty of this place. Their kayak company is called Three Moose Kayak Adventure (www.threemoose.com).

Between Beaches Alaska (907/290-6785, www.betweenbeachesalaska.com, $230 d, 2-night minimum) is on MacDonald Spit—a wooded peninsula near Seldovia—with access by water taxi from Homer (or a taxi ride from Seldovia followed by a 10-minute walk). Three gorgeous little cabins are just steps from this quiet beach (great for tidepooling), and each cabin has a private bath, a kitchenette, a full bed, and kayaks to explore the cove. You will need to bring your own food from Homer.

Background

The Landscape

South-central Alaska encompasses an extraordinary diversity of land, from deeply incised coastal fjords to 20,310-foot Mount Denali, North America's highest mountain. Four major mountain ranges dominate the region: the Alaska Range, the Talkeetna Mountains, the Chugach Mountains, and the Kenai Mountains.

Denali National Park lies near the center of the **Alaska Range,** comprising not just Mount Denali but many other high summits, including Mount Foraker (17,400 feet), Mount Hunter (14,573 feet), and Mount Huntington (12,240 feet). Large glaciers flow from both sides of

the mountains, feeding the Toklat, Teklanika, Denali, Kantishna, and Nenana Rivers that drain north into the Yukon River, and the Susitna, Yentna, Kahiltna, and Chulitna Rivers that drain south into Cook Inlet. Most visitors to Denali access it via the Park Road, a 92-mile gravel road along the north side of the Alaska Range. The southern side is only accessible by air or a very long hike.

The town of Talkeetna is south of Denali at the juncture of the Talkeetna, Chulitna, and Susitna Rivers. The **Talkeetna Mountains** rise east of here, with the Matanuska River just south of the Talkeetnas. Hatcher Pass (near Palmer) is a popular access point for the southern Talkeetna Mountains. The north side of the range is accessible from the Denali Highway that connects Cantwell with Paxson.

Cook Inlet reaches north into south-central Alaska, forming the region's western border. Two major rivers drain into Cook Inlet from the north, the Susitna River starting in the Alaska Range, and the Matanuska River, with headwaters in the Chugach Mountains. The valley they jointly form is known as the Matanuska-Susitna Valley, or more commonly, the **Mat-Su Valley.** It's home to the fastest-growing part of Alaska and the small cities of Wasilla and Palmer.

The city of **Anchorage** occupies a relatively flat area of coastal lowland jutting into upper Cook Inlet, with Knik Arm extending northward (it's fed by the Susitna and Matanuska Rivers) and Turnagain Arm separating the city from the Kenai Peninsula. The **Chugach Mountains** rise abruptly along the eastern side of Anchorage, with the lower areas dominated by upscale homes and the higher reaches within Chugach State Park.

The **Kenai Peninsula** has a rugged eastern half dominated by the **Kenai Mountains.** They extend across the peninsula from the southwestern tip to Turnagain Arm, encompassing Kachemak Bay State Park, Kenai Fjords National Park, Chugach National Forest, and Kenai National Wildlife Refuge. Glaciers cover extensive parts of the peninsula, with massive Harding Icefield taking in 300 square miles and feeding 40 glaciers. The Kenai River is famous as a fishing destination, flowing across the western side of the peninsula. The town of Seward sits at the head of Resurrection Bay and is bordered by mountains on all sides. The western portion of Kenai Peninsula has extensive areas where Minnesotans would feel at home, with relatively flat forested country pockmarked with thousands of small lakes and several large ones: Tustumena Lake, Kenai Lake, and Skilak Lake. The almost-twin small cities of Soldotna and Kenai are near the mouth of the Kenai River, and Homer lies at the end of the road—literally—along beautiful Kachemak Bay.

GEOLOGY
Plate Tectonics
Briefly, the huge Pacific plate (the ocean floor) is drifting slowly northeast. It collides with the North American plate, on which the continent rests, along an arc that stretches from the western Aleutians in the Gulf of Alaska to the Inside Passage—defining one section of the famous Pacific "Ring of Fire." This meeting of plates jams the ocean floor under the continental landmass and gives rise to violent geological forces: upthrust mountains, extensive and large earthquakes, volcanic rumblings and eruptions, and movement along fault lines.

Somewhere in the mists of early geological time, a particularly persistent and powerful collision between the two plates caused the Brooks Range to rise; erosion has whittled its highest peaks to 8,000 feet, half their original height. Later, a similar episode thrust the Alaska Range into shape. The Pacific plate even today continues to nose under the continental plate in the vicinity of Yakutat (near where southeast meets south-central Alaska). The force is pushing Mount Logan—Canada's highest peak—slowly upward. Learn more about the geological forces shaping Alaska at www.gi.alaska.edu.

Earthquakes

One of the world's most seismically active regions, Alaska has withstood some of the most violent earthquakes and largest tidal waves ever recorded. In the last century, more than 80 Alaskan earthquakes registered higher than magnitude 7. The most destructive occurred at 5:35pm on March 27, 1964, when the most powerful earthquake ever recorded in North America rocked south-central Alaska. This magnitude 9.2 quake (80 times bigger than the famous 1906 San Francisco earthquake, which is estimated at around 7.8) had a devastating impact on the region, flattening 75 homes and businesses in Anchorage, creating tsunamis that wiped out nearly every coastal village in south-central Alaska, and wreaking havoc all the way to California. The quake and its tsunamis killed 131 people. It was the second strongest in the 20th century; only a magnitude 9.5 quake in Chile in 1960 was larger.

Anyone who spends more than a few months in south-central Alaska will probably feel at least one earthquake. The **Alaska Earthquake Information Center** website (www.earthquake.alaska.edu) provides detailed information on Alaskan earthquakes, including today's activity. For additional background on earthquakes in Alaska, visit the **USGS Earthquake Hazards Program** website (http://earthquake.usgs.gov).

Tsunamis

An earthquake deep below the ocean floor in the Gulf of Alaska or the open Pacific is especially dangerous to the coasts of Alaska and Hawaii, along with the west coast of Canada and the United States. The activity creates enormous tidal waves (tsunamis), which, although they are only 3-5 feet high in the open ocean, can travel at speeds exceeding 500 mph. Contrary to popular fears, a tsunami does not slam into the coast with 20 or 30 feet of water, washing away everything in its path like a flash flood. Instead, the water slowly inundates the land to a depth of 4-5 feet. Then, after a brief and chilling calm, the wave is sucked back out to sea in one vast undertow. Most of the destruction caused by the great Good Friday earthquake was of this nature, attested to by hair-raising pictures that you'll see in places like Valdez, Seward, and Kodiak. If you hear a tsunami warning, get to higher ground immediately. The **U.S. Tsunami Warning Center** (www.tsunami.gov) is based in Palmer, and its website provides information on recent and historic tsunamis.

Volcanoes

Like its earthquakes, Alaska's major volcanoes are located along the Aleutian chain. In fact, 57 active volcanoes stretch along this arc, and most have been active in the last 300 years. The largest recorded eruption occurred when Novarupta blew its top in 1912, the most cataclysmic natural disaster since Krakatoa cracked 30 years earlier.

There's always an active volcano somewhere in the state, especially in the Aleutians and along the Alaska Peninsula. The University of Alaska Fairbanks **Alaska Volcano Observatory** (www.avo.alaska.edu) keeps track of volcanic activity, and its website has details on current and historic eruptions.

Several volcanoes get particular attention because of their recent activity and proximity to major population centers: **Mount Spurr** (78 miles west of Anchorage) erupted in 1992; **Mount Augustine** (171 miles southwest of Anchorage) in 2005; and **Mount Redoubt** (103 miles southwest of Anchorage) in 1989 and 2009. Each of these dumped ash in varying amounts on the region, closing schools and businesses, filling the air with ash (hazardous for people, electronics, and car engines), and creating havoc for air travel.

1: icebergs at Surprise Glacier in Prince William Sound; **2:** Denali National Park

The 1989 eruption of Mount Redoubt nearly brought down a KLM jet when it flew into the ash cloud, causing all four engines to shut down. The plane dove two miles before the pilots were able to restart the engines and land safely in Anchorage. That same year, Redoubt generated a massive debris flow down the Drift River, inundating an oil terminal and threatening to spill oil into Cook Inlet.

GLACIATION

A glacier forms in areas of high precipitation and elevation where the snow is allowed to pile up to great depths, compacting the bottom layers into solid ice. The great weight above the bottom ice (along with the force of gravity) pushes it slowly downward like a giant frozen river, scooping out huge valleys and shearing off entire mountainsides. When the rate of advance is balanced by melt-off, the face of the glacier remains more or less stationary. If the glacier flows more quickly than its face melts, it advances; if it melts faster than it flows, the glacier recedes. Air bubbles are squeezed out of the glacier by this tremendous pressure, which makes glacial ice extremely dense. It's so compact that the higher frequencies of light cannot escape or penetrate it, which explains the dark-blue tinge. And because of its density, it also melts at fantastically slow rates; a small chunk or two will keep beer in a cooler chilled for a day or two.

Signs of the Glaciers

As you travel up the coast or hike in the national parks of the interior, you'll soon start to recognize and identify glacial landforms. While rivers typically erode V-shaped valleys, glaciers gouge out distinctly U-shaped **glacial troughs.** Valleys and ridges branching from the main valley are sliced off to create **hanging valleys** and **truncated spurs.** A side valley that once carried a tributary glacier may be left as a **hanging trough;** waterfalls often tumble from these hanging valleys and troughs. Alpine glaciers scoop out the headwalls of their accumulation basins to

form **cirques.** Bare jagged ridges between cirques are known as **arêtes.**

As a glacier moves down a valley, it bulldozes a load of rock, sand, and gravel—known as **glacial till**—ahead of it, or carries it on top. Glacial till that has been dumped is called a **moraine. Lateral moraines** are pushed to the sides of glaciers, while a **terminal moraine** is deposited at the farthest point of the face's advance. A **medial moraine** is formed when two glaciers unite. These ribbonlike strips of rubble can be followed back to the point where the lateral moraines converge between the glaciers.

When looking at a glaciated landscape, watch for gouges and scrape marks on the bedrock, which indicate the direction of glacial flow. Watch too for **erratics,** huge boulders carried long distances and deposited by the glacier that often differ from the surrounding rock. Glacial runoff is often suffused with finely powdered till or **glacial flour,** which gives it a distinctive milky-white color; the abundance of this silt in glacial streams creates a twisting, braided course. With a little practice, you'll soon learn to recognize glacial features at a glance.

The vast majority of Alaska's glaciers, like those in many other parts of the world, are retreating as the global climate warms. In some cases, glaciers have drawn back many miles in the last few decades, exposing newly formed bays and producing massive outflows of icebergs. The 1989 *Exxon Valdez* oil spill was caused when the ship diverted to avoid ice from nearby Columbia Glacier; it didn't help, of course, that the captain was drunk.

Permafrost

To picture permafrost, imagine a veneer of mud atop a slab of ice. In the colder places of the Lower 48, soil ecologists measure how much surface soil freezes in winter. In Alaska, they measure how much surface soil thaws in summer. True permafrost is ground that has stayed frozen for more than two years. To create and maintain permafrost, the annual average temperature must remain below freezing.

Baked Alaska

Mention the word "Alaska" and many people will immediately think of deep snow, glaciers, and dogsleds. The state does indeed have all these things, but in recent years the warming climate is taking a major toll.

Virtually all national and international scientific organizations (including the National Academy of Science) are on the record saying that these changes are real, are caused by people, and will cause dramatic changes on a global scale. Studies by NASA and NOAA show a continuing rise in global temperatures. The world's 10 hottest years have all taken place since 1998; five of the hottest years have been in this decade, including 2016, the hottest year ever recorded.

What does this mean for Alaska? In northern climates, temperatures are increasing more quickly. The Arctic is warming twice as fast as the global rate. In the last 50 years, Alaska's temperatures have gone up an average of 3.4°F overall, and 6.3°F in winter. Cold, snowy winters are being replaced by mild, rainy winters. For the latest research, visit the University of Alaska Fairbanks **International Arctic Research Center** (www.iarc.uaf.edu) online.

Some of these changes are subtle, such as a northward-moving tree line or increasing carbon dioxide causing acidification of the oceans, but others are dramatic. Virtually all of Alaska's glaciers are retreating—some are moving back hundreds of feet in just a few years. At Exit Glacier near Seward, you will find plants growing where ice stood just a few years ago.

In the last decade, the Iditarod has been plagued with a lack of snow and warm temperatures. In the 2013-2014 and 2014-2015 winters, Alyeska Resort had to use expensive snowmaking equipment to stay open for skiing. Alaskan coastal towns such as Shishamaref are sliding into the sea. The loss of Arctic sea ice is forcing both polar bears and walruses onto land, and rising water temperatures are threatening the survival of juvenile salmon and seabirds. Fires are burning across wider reaches of the state every summer. Unfortunately, these changes are just the tip of the proverbial (melting) iceberg.

Alaskans face a daunting conundrum. They depend on oil tax revenues to run the state, but when that oil is burned, it causes a warming of the climate that endangers the land itself. Alaskan politicians are almost unanimous in support of the oil industry. U.S. Senators Lisa Murkowski and Dan Sullivan, along with Representative Don Young, all oppose any efforts to slow global warming. One glacier tour boat operator doesn't even want employees suggesting that human-caused changes are leading to glacial melting, even though you can literally watch the glaciers recede.

Whether we like it—and even if we don't believe it—Alaska's climate *is* warming rapidly. Only time will tell if we can act before the impacts are devastating for the entire planet.

The topsoil above the permafrost that thaws in the summer is known as the **active layer.** With the proper conditions, permafrost will penetrate downward until it meets heat from the earth's mantle. In the Arctic, permafrost begins a few feet below the surface and can extend 2,000-5,000 feet deep. This is known as **continuous permafrost,** which almost completely underlies the ground above the Arctic Circle. **Discontinuous permafrost,** with permafrost in scattered patches, covers extensive parts of Alaska, particularly boggy areas covered by black spruce forests.

The Arctic is warming twice as fast as the rest of the planet, and as Alaska's climate shifts due to global warming, the permafrost is also melting, creating all sorts of problems both within the state and potentially for the planet as a whole. Melting permafrost can severely damage buildings, roads, pipelines, and other structures. As it melts, organic matter trapped in the ice decays, causing the release of methane and carbon dioxide. These gases may in turn lead to catastrophic changes in the atmosphere and further warming of the planet; a 2015 study suggested dire global consequences if the permafrost melts.

CLIMATE

Granted, over the course of a year, in any given location, Alaska's weather can be extreme and unpredictable. Because of the harshness of the winters, comfortable travel to many popular destinations is difficult early October-late April. Contrary to popular perception, however, the weather can also be quite pleasant. South-central Alaska's spring, summer, and fall are not unlike these seasons in Minnesota. For the latest outdoor forecast, visit the **National Weather Service's** Alaska website (www.arh.noaa.gov).

It's possible to generalize about Alaskan weather and distinguish three climatic zones: coastal maritime, interior, and Arctic. The main factor affecting the southern coasts is the warm Japanese Current, which causes temperatures to be much milder than the norm at those latitudes. This current also brings continuous rain as humid Pacific air is forced up over the coastal mountains. For example, it rains in Juneau two out of three days. However, these mountains shield the interior plateaus from the maritime airstreams, so yearly precipitation there is low—a mere 15 inches. The interior experiences great temperature extremes, from biting cold in winter to summer heat waves. The mountains also protect the coastal areas from cold—and hot—interior air masses. The Arctic zone is characterized by cool, cloudy, and windy summers (averaging 50°F) and cold, windy winters—though not as cold as in the interior.

The **Alaska Climate Research Center** (http://climate.gi.alaska.edu) has detailed information on the state's climate, along with current weather conditions.

Northern Lights

One of the prime attractions for winter visitors to Alaska is the chance to view the aurora borealis—northern lights—in action. The finest viewing areas are in the northern part of the state, particularly around Fairbanks and Bettles, but when conditions are right, the sky lights up across Anchorage and the Kenai Peninsula. Denali National Park and Talkeetna are both far enough north to experience more aurora activity.

For detailed information on northern lights and predictions of upcoming aurora activity, visit the websites of the University of Alaska's **Geophysical Institute** (www.gi.alaska.edu/auroraforecast) and the extraordinarily detailed **Solarham** (www.solarham.net).

Plants

VEGETATION ZONES

South-central Alaskan forests are dominated by spruce, aspen, cottonwood, alder, birch, and willow. **Boreal forests** cover the western Kenai Peninsula. Much of the interior lowlands north of Talkeetna consist primarily of scattered open stands of white spruce, paper birch, alpine fir, lodgepole pine, and balsam poplar (cottonwood). **Taiga,** the transition zone between boreal forest and tundra, is characterized by sparse and stunted black spruce, dwarf shrubbery (mostly the ubiquitous willow), and swampy areas known as "muskegs."

The lower-elevation **tundra,** also known as the "moist tundra," starts at tree line, around 2,500 feet. There you find undergrowth similar to that of the taiga but without the trees. The higher-elevation alpine tundra consists of grasses, clinging mosses and lichens, and an abundance of tiny, psychedelically bright wildflowers, including the unforgettable forget-me-not (the state flower), with gaze-catching petals of light blue.

FLOWERS

While you're hiking, an excellent book to have along is *Field Guide to Alaskan Wildflowers* by Verna E. Pratt. The photographs are good, the descriptions are usable, and the flowers are conveniently arranged by color.

Fireweed is a wildflower you'll come to know intimately during your travels in the North. It enjoys sunlight and grows profusely in open areas along roads and rivers. Given proper conditions, tall fireweed can grow to seven feet high. Its long stalk of pink flowers blossoms from bottom to top; sourdoughs claim they can predict the arrival and severity of winter by the speed with which fireweed finishes blooming.

Three kinds of **primrose,** also a pinkish red, are another common sight on the tundra. Other red wildflowers of the tundra include **purple mountain saxifrage, moss campion,** and large bright-pink **poppies.**

White flowers include the **narcissus-flowered anemone,** similar to a **buttercup,** which also grows on the tundra. **Mountain avens** are easily recognizable—they look like white roses. A half-dozen kinds of white **saxifrage** are widespread throughout the state. Be careful of the local **water hemlock,** which is deadly poisonous. Similar is the **yarrow,** a medicinal herb with a disk of small white flowers and lacelike leaves. As soon as you identify **Labrador tea,** you'll notice it everywhere in the forest and taiga. **Cotton grass** looks exactly like its name. **Daisies** and **fleabane** complete this group of plants with white flowers.

Larkspur looks similar to fireweed, only it's a dark purple. It grows on a long stalk and a dwarf bush. **Monkshood** is a beautiful dark-blue flower of the buttercup family; **harebells** and **bluebells** are easily identified around Denali. Three kinds of **violets** grow in the boreal forest. Light-purple **lupine** flowers grow in 20-inch clusters. **Asters,** resembling purple daisies, bloom all over the interior.

BERRIES

Berries are the only fruits that grow naturally in Alaska, and luckily the many varieties are abundant, several are edible, a few even taste good, and only one is poisonous. If you're into berry collecting, get to know poisonous **baneberry** immediately. A member of the crowfoot family, it grows mostly in the southeast and the central interior. The white berries look like black-eyed peas; they ripen to a scarlet red. **Juniper berries** grow throughout Alaska, but the **bog blueberries, Alaska blueberries,** and **huckleberries** are much tastier. Blueberries also grow on poorly drained, shady alpine slopes and are generally the first to ripen. **Salmonberries** turn a dark salmon-red in late summer, and are quite similar to raspberries.

Bunchberries are good tasting but have been known to upset a stomach or two. **Bog cranberries** are best after the first frost, especially when they're a deep purple—deliciously tart. **High-bush cranberries** are common but are best just before they're completely ripe. **Wild strawberries** are even better, if you can get to them before the birds and rodents. The several kinds of **bearberries** (blue and red) are tasteless except to bears, and the **soapberry** will remind you of getting caught saying a dirty word as a kid. Pick up *Alaska Wild Berry Guide and Cookbook* for the complete lowdown on Alaska's berries.

FRANKENSTEIN CABBAGES

In 1941 the managers of the Alaska Railroad offered a $25 prize to the grower of the largest cabbage in the state, and since then cabbage growers have been competing. Usually the largest cabbages at the Alaska State Fair weigh in around 100 pounds, but a world record was set in 2012 when a Palmer man grew a 138-pound cabbage. Ten-pound celery, 3-pound beets, 2-pound turnips, and 1-pound carrots have also been blue-ribbon earners. Find them and more at the Alaska State Fair in Palmer in late August-early September.

Animals

If any aspect of Alaska embodies the image of the "last frontier," it's the state's animal kingdom. For millennia, Native Alaskan hunters, with their small-scale weapons and limited needs, had little impact on wildlife populations. Eskimo and Aleut villages subsisted comfortably on fish, small mammals, and one or two whales per year; the interior Athabascan bands did well on a handful of moose and caribou. This all changed in the mid-1700s with the coming of the Russians and Americans. Sea otters, fur seals, and gray whales were quickly hunted to the verge of extinction. By the 1850s the Alaskan musk ox had been annihilated. Wolves, in part because they preyed on the same game as humans, were ruthlessly hunted.

Conservation measures have nurtured their numbers, and today Alaska boasts one of the largest concentrations of animal populations remaining on earth. For example, there are nearly twice as many caribou in Alaska as there are people. There's a moose and a Sitka black-tailed deer for every three people. If 80,000 sheep strikes you as an impressive number, consider 40,000 grizzly bears. Bald and golden eagles are commonplace, and while the magnificent trumpeter swan was believed near extinction in the Lower 48, it was thriving in Alaska. Marine mammals, from orcas to the recovering otters, are common (though they have recently experienced major declines in the Aleutians and western Alaska), and Alaskan waters also contain fish and other sea creatures in unimaginable quantities.

WILDLIFE VIEWING

Alaska's wildlife is a major draw for both visitors and residents. The state's vast stretches of wilderness contain abundant mammals, birds, and fish, including some of the largest and most magnificent animals in the world. Land mammals such as brown (grizzly) and black

bears, caribou, moose, Dall sheep, wolves, and musk ox are the main attractions, but the state also has incomparable populations of birds, including such favorites as bald eagles, puffins, loons, and sandhill cranes. Marine mammals include seals, Steller sea lions, and sea otters, along with beluga whales, orca (killer) whales, humpback whales, gray whales, and others.

The *Alaska Wildlife Viewing Guide,* by Michelle Sydeman and Annabel Lund, is a useful introduction to finding wild animals. Visit the Alaska Department of Fish and Game's website (www.wildlifeviewing. alaska.gov) for details on dozens of species of Alaskan animals in their "Wildlife Notebook" series, and for descriptions of places to see wildlife. The state also produces regional wildlife-viewing guides, including *Anchorage Wildlife Viewing Hot Spots, Kenai Peninsula Wildlife Viewing Trail Guide,* and *Kachemak Bay Watchable Wildlife Guide.* Pick up copies in visitors centers around the state or find them on the website above.

In Alaska, wildlife may be encountered up close almost anywhere outdoors. Many animals are well prepared to defend their territories against intruders (you), and even the smallest can bite. Never attempt to feed or touch wildlife. It is seldom good for it, you, or those who follow. Any animal that appears unafraid or "tame" can be quite unpredictable, so keep your distance. One thing you don't have to worry about is snakes; there are none in Alaska. Surprisingly, however, there *are* frogs, even above the Arctic Circle.

LAND MAMMALS
Brown Bears

The brown bear, also called grizzly, is the symbol of the wild country and a measure of its wildness. Grizzlies once roamed all over North America. In 1800 there were over

100,000 of them; today, around 1,000 survive in the Lower 48. Ironically, the grizzly is the state animal of California, where it is now extinct. Things are very different in Alaska, where 40,000 of these magnificent creatures still inhabit the land.

Denali National Park offers some of the most accessible bear-viewing in the state. The estimated 200 Denali grizzlies are still wild, mostly in their natural state. This is especially important for the continued education of the cubs, who are taught how to dig roots, find berries, catch ground squirrels, and take moose calves. However, Denali grizzlies are not afraid of people, and they are extremely curious. One person was killed by a grizzly at Denali in 2012, but this is the only human fatality in the park's history. Maulings have occurred in Denali (and elsewhere in Alaska), usually because of the foolishness of novice hikers, runners, and photographers or as a result of improper food storage. Take care, but don't be afraid to go hiking.

The natural grizzly diet is 80 percent vegetarian. They eat berries, willows, and roots, and prey on anything they can take: from ground squirrels to caribou, from foxes to small black bears. And they're challenged by nothing, except humans with high-powered weapons. Grizzlies are racehorse-fast and have surprising endurance; they need about 50 square miles for home territory and travel several miles each night. During the day they like to eat, sleep in the sun—often on snow patches—and entertain tourists on the shuttle buses.

Grizzlies are solitary creatures. Full-grown boars and sows are seen together only during mating season, in early summer. The gestation period is a little over five months, and the sows give birth in December to 1-3 cubs. The cubs are hairless, weigh one pound each, and remain blind for a week. They stay with the mother for over 2.5 years—two full summers. They're then chased away sometime before July of the third summer, when the sow is ready to mate again.

Contrary to popular belief, bears do not hibernate. They do sleep deeply in dens during the winter, sometimes for weeks. But they often get hungry, lonely, or restless, and step outside to forage for frozen roots, berries, and meat. Sometimes a bear will stay out all winter; that's the one the Native Alaskans fear the most: the winter bear. Its fur tends to build up a thick layer of ice, rendering it nearly impenetrable, almost bulletproof. And of course, sows give birth in the deep winter, which they're certainly awake for.

Grizzlies and brown bears were once thought to be different species, but are now considered the same. The basic difference is in size, which is due to habitat. Grizzlies themselves are the world's largest land omnivore, growing to heights of 6-7 feet and weighing in at 500-600 pounds. However, they're the smaller of the two because they live in the interior and feed mostly on vegetation. Brown bears are coastal, and with a rich source of fish protein, they have achieved near mythical sizes. Kodiak brown bears retain a reputation for being the largest, reaching heights of over 10 feet and weights of up to 1,400 pounds.

Hiking in bear country requires special precautions. A number of areas offer outstanding brown bear viewing around Alaska; the most famous places are the McNeil River, Katmai National Park, and Denali National Park.

Black Bears

Black bears are found in most forested parts of Alaska. They are distinguished from grizzlies and brown bears by their size (much smaller), the shape of their face (much narrower), and the lack of a shoulder hump. Black bears can actually be more dangerous to people than grizzlies: There have been more attacks and maulings in Alaska by black bears than by brown. **Polar bears** are not found in southcentral or interior Alaska. You'll need to visit the North Slope around Barrow or Kaktovik to see these amazing animals.

Moose

The moose is the largest member of the deer

family, and Alaska has the largest moose. A bull moose in his prime gets to be about seven feet tall and weighs around 1,200 pounds, all from eating willow stems—about 30 pounds per day. They also eat aspen and birch, but willow is the staple of choice. The antlers, which are bone, are shed and renewed every year. Full-size antlers can weigh up to 70 pounds—that's mostly in September during the rut, or mating time. Bulls of near-equal rank and size butt their heads together to vie for dominance. You want to be really careful of bulls then; they're touchy. The cows have one or two calves, rarely three, in May, and that's when you want to be really careful of the cows too. The calves stay with the cow exactly one year; then she chases away the yearlings. Sometimes at the start of the summer season, you'll spot a huge pregnant cow with a frisky yearling on her heels, and you've never seen a more hassled-looking expression on an animal's face. But that's family life.

Moose don't cover too much territory—about 30 miles a year, mostly in the forest, which provides natural defense against predators. The word *moose* comes from the Massachusetts Algonquian dialect and means "muncher of little twigs." By the way, the little flap of hair under the moose's chin is known as the "moostache." (Just kidding, it's really called the "dewlap.")

Harsh winters are deadly to moose. Deep snow and bitter cold can cause one in three moose in central Alaska to perish. Annually, hundreds of moose make their last stand along the snowless railroad tracks between Seward and Fairbanks and are killed by trains that don't stop for them. Hundreds of others starve to death. Those hit by cars along roadways are butchered and distributed to local people.

If Alaska moose are the world's largest, Kenai Peninsula moose are Alaska's largest. A Kenai moose holds the Alaskan record: at 10-11 years old, his antlers were just under 75 inches wide, and he weighed 1,500-1,600 pounds.

Kenai National Wildlife Refuge was specifically established to protect moose, and these massive animals are a common sight along Kenai Peninsula roads at dusk, particularly in the winter. Other places to watch for moose are within the Anchorage Bowl and in the Matanuska-Susitna Valley northeast of Anchorage. Drive with care, since moose can suddenly step onto the road without warning, and their massive bulk means that a collision could be fatal to both the moose and people in the vehicle.

Moose can be very aggressive, particularly in the winter when food is scarce. A number of people have been killed by moose attacks, even in Anchorage. Always give moose a wide berth, especially if you're walking, on a bike or skis, or with a dog. If a moose appears ready to attack, quickly hide behind a tree, car, or other obstruction. Pepper spray may be effective if all else fails.

Caribou

Caribou are travelin' fools. They're extremely flighty animals—restless, tireless, fast, and graceful. Run and eat, run and eat is pretty much all they do—oh, yeah, and reproduce. Reindeer, although of the same species, are smaller and often domesticated. Caribou are peaceful critters, and they'll outrun and outdistance their predators, mostly wolves, rather than fight. They like to travel in groups, unlike moose, which are loners. And they cover 10 times as much territory. Their herding and migrating imperatives are similar to those of the plains bison; they gather in large numbers and think nothing of running 50 miles, almost on a lark.

Caribou are extremely well adapted to their winter environment. They have huge nasal passages and respiratory systems in order to breathe the bitterly cold winter air. Thick fur covers almost every inch of their bodies; the fur itself is protected by large, hollow, oily guard hairs. This tends to make caribou look

1: moose with calves; 2: bald eagles are common in coastal Alaska; 3: brown bears digging clams in Katmai National Park

much larger than they really are; a good-sized bull weighs 400-500 pounds, a cow about half that. Caribou have the richest milk in the animal kingdom: It's 20 percent fat. They've also got huge prancing hooves, immortalized in the Santa Claus myth, which are excellent for running, swimming, disco dancing, and pawing at the snow to uncover the moss and lichens on which they subsist all through the harsh Arctic winter. The word *caribou* comes from the Maine Algonquian dialect and means "scraping hooves."

The caribou is the only member of the deer family whose females grow antlers. Babies are on their feet and nursing within an hour of birth, and at one week they can run 20 miles. If they can't, they'll most likely die, since the herd won't wait. But this helps to keep the herd healthy, controls population growth, and provides food for the carnivores.

Native Alaskans are among the caribou's natural predators. Historically, Native Alaskans ate the meat raw, roasted, and stewed. They ate all the organs, even the half-digested greens from the stomach. The little gobs of fat from behind the eyes were considered a delicacy. They used almost exclusively caribou hide for clothes, rugs, blankets, and tents. The leg skins were used to make mukluks; the long strands of stringy sinew provided sewing thread.

Nearly one million caribou roam across Alaska, with the largest herds in the Arctic. They are also commonly seen within Denali National Park, along the Denali Highway, and in the Kenai area.

Dall Sheep

Named for William H. Dall, one of the first people to survey the lower Yukon (in 1866), Dall sheep are sometimes called Alaska bighorn sheep, because the Rocky Mountain bighorn is a closely related species. Distinguished by their brilliant white color, the rams grow large curved horns, formed from a specialized skin structure made up of a compacted mass of hair and oil. The horns aren't shed; instead the sheep add another ring to them

yearly, so the longer the horns, the older the ram, and the more dominant within the herd. The rams can weigh as much as 175 pounds; the ewes have small spiked horns and average 120 pounds.

Their habitat is the high alpine tundra, and they subsist on grasses, mosses, lichens, and flowers. Their bird's-eye view provides an excellent defense. They're also magnificent mountain climbers. Roughly 70,000 Dall sheep reside in the Chugach, Kenai, Alaska, and Wrangell mountain ranges. During summer, the rams migrate high into the ranges, leaving the prime lower grazing grounds for the ewes and lambs. It's natural that they migrate, the same way it's natural that they have predators. Their alpine tundra habitat is very fragile, and it can take decades to regenerate after overgrazing. Migration and predation thus keep the flock healthy, control population growth, and guarantee the survival of the habitat.

Dall sheep inhabit mountain hillsides throughout much of Alaska. They are frequently seen on rocky slopes in Denali National Park, near Cooper Landing on the Kenai Peninsula, and along Turnagain Arm, 20 miles south of Anchorage.

Wolves

Wolves have traditionally been one of the most misunderstood, misrepresented, and maligned mammals in both fact and fable. We've come a long way from the days when it was believed that wolves were innately evil, with the visage of the devil himself, eating their hapless prey—or little girls in red hoods—alive. But it wasn't until the mid-1940s, when wildlife biologist Adolph Murie began a long-term and systematic study of the wolves in Mount McKinley National Park, that all the misconceptions of the accepted lore about wolves began to change.

For three years Murie tramped mainly on the plains below Polychrome Pass and became extremely intimate with several wolf families. (His book, *The Wolves of Mount McKinley*, published in 1944, is still considered a classic natural history text.) Though Murie concluded that a delicate balance is established between predator and prey to their mutual advantage, declining Dall sheep populations, political pressure, and, indeed, tradition forced the Park Service to kill wolves, which were considered, against Murie's conclusions, to be the cause of the sheep decline. Typically, though, the wolf population was in just as dire straits as the sheep, and for several years no wolves were killed in the feds' traps because of their scarcity.

Since then, many researchers and writers have come to incisive conclusions about the wolf. It has been determined that their social systems—within the pack and with their prey—are amazingly complex and sophisticated. The alpha male and female are the central players in the pack, surrounded by 4-7 pups, yearlings, and other adults. The dominant female receives a long involved courtship from the dominant male (though he might not necessarily be the biological father of the pups). Territories can be as small as 200 square miles and as large as 800 square miles, depending on a host of influences.

With the advent of radio collaring and tracking, the movements of individual wolves and packs have continually surprised wildlife biologists. Wolves often travel 5-10 miles per hour for hours at a time. In a matter of days, an individual cut loose from a pack can wind up 500 miles away. Thus wolves are able to select and populate suitable habitats quickly.

Alaska's 7,500-10,000 wolves are thriving, even though roughly 15 percent of them are harvested yearly by trappers. They can be found on the Kenai Peninsula, in the Talkeetna Mountains, and in Chugach State Park near Anchorage. Denali National Park offers travelers the best chance to see a wolf from the road system.

Captive wolves can be seen at the **Alaska Zoo** (www.alaskazoo.com) in Anchorage. A highly controversial state-sponsored hunting program has targeted wolves in some parts of the state to increase the survival of caribou and moose. The program includes the aerial killing of wolves and is widely opposed by environmental groups but applauded by some hunting organizations.

Musk Oxen

The musk ox is a stocky, long-haired animal with a slight shoulder hump and a very short tail. Despite their name, musk oxen have no musk glands and are not oxen. The largest member of the sheep family, this shaggy prehistoric-looking creature was abundant in the north country until it was hunted into extinction by the mid-1800s. In the 1930s, several dozen musk oxen were transplanted from Greenland to Nunivak Island in the Bering Sea. The musk oxen thrived, and the resident Native Alaskans used the soft underwool to establish a small cottage industry knitting sweaters, scarves, and caps. And that's what it would have remained, a small cottage industry, if it hadn't been for Dr. John J. Teal Jr., a student of Arctic explorer Vilhjalmur Stefansson. Stefansson recognized the potential of musk ox wool and inspired Teal to experiment with domesticating them. After spending 10 years with musk oxen on his farm in Vermont, Teal concluded that they were amiable, hardy, and easy to domesticate. So in 1964 he started the Musk Ox Project at the University of Alaska in Fairbanks.

In 1984 the project moved to a farm in the Matanuska Valley, where musk oxen are bred to produce *qiviut* (KEE-vee-oot), the soft underwool, which is renowned in Alaska for its insulation (eight times warmer by weight than sheep wool) and tactile (softer than the finest cashmere) properties. The *qiviut* is collected from the animals in the spring. The raw wool is sent to a mill in Connecticut and then sold to **Oomingmak** (a Native Alaskan word for musk ox, meaning "bearded one"; www.qiviut.com), a co-op consisting of members in villages spread throughout western Alaska. Here the *qiviut* is knitted into garments, which are sold at retail outlets in Anchorage and at the farm near Palmer.

Today, wild musk oxen can be found on the Seward Peninsula near Nome, Nunivak and Nelson Islands, the Yukon-Kuskokwim Delta, the North Slope near Prudhoe Bay, and the Arctic National Wildlife Refuge. The best place to see them up close is the **Musk Ox Farm** in Palmer (www.muskoxfarm.org).

Lynx

Alaska's only native cat, the lynx is the northern version of the bobcat. Weighing around 20-30 pounds, these extremely secretive animals prey primarily on snowshoe hare, a species that undergoes an 8- to 11-year cycle of abundance. Lynx numbers fluctuate with those of hare but lag one or two years behind. When a hare population crashes, lynx numbers soon decline, and they sometimes travel up to 400 miles in search of food. Although snowshoe hare are an important prey for lynx, when they are scarce, lynx hunt grouse, ptarmigan, squirrels, and rodents, and may even take larger animals such as caribou or Dall sheep.

Lynx are sometimes seen during long periods of summer daylight, especially in years when they are abundant. Lynx have large broad feet that function as snowshoes for winter hunting and traveling.

Rodents

Ground squirrels and marmots are true hibernators: Unlike other mammals such as black, grizzly, and polar bears, they sleep for six months straight in a deep coma. This separation between life and death is one of the thinnest lines in the animal world. A ground squirrel's heart slows to about six beats a minute, and its body temperature lowers to just above freezing, around 38°F. (In fact, a zoologist at the University of Alaska Fairbanks has found that the core temperature of the arctic ground squirrel, the northernmost hibernator, can drop to as low as 26°F—six degrees below freezing! Of course, the squirrels don't freeze; they "supercool.")

The hibernating squirrel takes a breath every couple of minutes. It uses up half its body weight, since it isn't eating. If you stuck a needle in a hibernating ground squirrel's paw,

it would take the animal about 10 minutes to begin to feel it.

Ground squirrels provide a large part of the grizzly and wolf diet, and that of scavenger birds as well, since they're a common type of roadkill.

Marmots, similar to woodchucks, are sometimes mistaken for wolverines. They live in large rock outcroppings for protection and have a piercing whistle, which warns of approaching predators or other possible danger. Look for marmots around Polychrome Pass in Denali National Park.

Alaska has a number of other members of the rodent family: shrews, mice, voles, lemmings, and porcupines. Long-tailed and least weasels occupy a wide habitat in the taiga and tundra. Martens are another member of the weasel family, similar to, though much more aggressive than, mink; the pine marten is one of Alaska's most valuable furbearers. Wolverines are in attendance, though you'd be very lucky to see one. Red foxes are common in the interior and south-central Alaska, and you're likely to see one at Denali National Park; the white arctic fox is a gorgeous animal, though you'll only see one in pictures.

MARINE MAMMALS

Marine mammals are found all along the Alaskan coast. Sea otters are frequently found in harbors, bays, and inlets, particularly around kelp beds. Good places to look for whales, seals, sea otters, sea lions, porpoises, and other marine mammals are the Prince William Sound out of Whittier, Kachemak Bay near Homer, and Kenai Fjords National Park. Only Native Alaskans have the legal right to hunt marine mammals.

Sea Otters

A marine member of the weasel family, the sea otter had one characteristic that would seal its doom: a long, wide, beautiful pelt that's one of the warmest, most luxurious, and durable furs in existence. Otter fur catalyzed the Russian *promyshlenniki* to begin overrunning the Aleutians in the mid-late 18th century, sealing the doom of the Aleuts as well as the otters. In 1803, Alexander Baranov shipped 15,000 pelts back to eastern Russia. Up until the 1840s, otter hunting was the primary industry in the Pacific, and when the Americans bought Alaska in 1867, nearly one million otters had been killed in the northern Pacific.

During the extreme lawless period in the last quarter of the 19th century, the otters were annihilated. In 1906 schooners cruised the North Pacific for months without taking a single pelt. In 1910 a crack crew of 40 Aleut hunters managed to harvest 16 otters. In 1911 otters were added to the International Fur Seal Treaty, giving them complete protection from everybody. Small, isolated populations of otters had managed to survive in the western Aleutians, and their numbers have increased over the past century to roughly 100,000 today. Approximately 90 percent of the world's sea otter population can be found in coastal Alaska. For more on the current situation, visit the website of the U.S. Fish and Wildlife Service (http://alaska.fws.gov/fisheries/mmm).

Steller Sea Lions

George Wilhelm Steller was the naturalist aboard Vitus Bering's 1742 exploration of Alaska, and the first European to step on Alaskan soil. Two marine mammals ended up with his name: the Steller's sea cow, a coldwater relative of the manatee, and the Steller sea lion. The sea cow was driven to extinction just 26 years later, a casualty of not being afraid of humans and the tasty flavor of its flesh. Today, the sea lion in much of Alaska is equally endangered.

Steller sea lions are pinnipeds—marine mammals with flippers, not feet. Males can weigh up to 2,000 pounds; females peak at 600 pounds. Sea lions eat several kinds of fish, but mostly pollock. They range across the North Pacific from northern Japan and Siberia all the way to California. These playful but powerful animals were abundant in western Alaska waters until quite recently. In the 1960s, for example, an estimated 177,000 sea

lions lived in the Gulf of Alaska and along the Aleutians. Commercial hunting was halted in the mid-1970s, but the population continued to drop by more than 80 percent. By 2004, just 45,000 survived. The western Alaska population was officially listed as endangered in 1997, while sea lion populations in southeast Alaska and farther south to California are considered threatened.

Researchers are unsure why Steller sea lions are disappearing at such an alarming rate, and there are a multitude of possible causes—including overfishing, toxic chemicals, and predation by sharks and killer whales. Most likely it is some combination of factors, but if something isn't done, the southwest Alaska population could be headed for extinction. Learn more about these fascinating animals—including the latest research—at the National Marine Fisheries Service's website (www.fakr.noaa.gov/protectedresources).

Whales

The largest summer marine visitors to Alaska are the whales. Each spring **gray whales** are seen migrating north from along the coast off Seward; in the fall they return south. Also in the spring, **humpback whales** move north from Hawaii. The humpback is easily distinguished by its humplike dorsal fin, large flippers, and huge tail, which shows as it dives. These 50-foot-long creatures often breach (jump) or beat the surface of the water with their tails, as if trying to send messages. Smaller (30-foot) **minke whales** are also common.

The **killer whale** (orca), which is not actually a whale but the largest of the dolphins (up to 24 feet long), travels in groups hunting fish and marine mammals. Its six-foot-high triangular dorsal fin and its black-and-white piebald pattern make it easily identifiable.

Look for **beluga whales** in Turnagain Arm along the Seward Highway south of Anchorage. These small white whales are approximately 15 feet long, with a blunt head. Although belugas are doing well in other parts of the North Pacific, the distinctive

population within Cook Inlet is critically endangered, with just 300 individuals surviving; it had four times as many back in the 1970s.

Kenai Fjords National Park and Resurrection Bay—both accessible by boat tour from Seward—are popular places to spot killer whales and humbacks, along with sea otters, seals, sea lions, and colonies of puffins. The spring migration of gray whales is a big Resurrection Bay attraction in April each year. There's also a fair chance of seeing humpback and killer whales on the Kachemak Bay wildlife boat trips that depart from Homer.

For more information on whales in Alaska, visit the National Marine Fisheries Service's website (www.fakr.noaa.gov/protectedresources).

BIRDS

Nearly 500 species of birds have been seen within Alaska, from tiny rufous hummingbirds to the nation's emblem, the bald eagle. Because of Alaska's proximity to Siberia, many unusual species are sometimes seen, making the Aleutians and Bering Sea of great interest to serious birders.

The Alaska Department of Fish and Game produces a helpful **Wings Over Alaska** (www.birding.alaska.gov) checklist of birds. Also check out websites for the Anchorage Chapter of the **National Audubon Society** (www.anchorageaudubon.org) and for unusual sightings and rare bird alerts.

Eagles

As many eagles are found in Alaska as in the rest of the United States combined. **Bald eagles** are common sights along the coasts, but with their unmistakable white heads, seven-foot wingspans, and dive-bombing, salmon-snatching performances, the thrill of watching them is not quickly lost.

Golden eagles, found throughout the interior, come without the distinctive "baldness" but are no less magnificent for their size.

Plentiful around Denali National Park, golden eagles perched on the tundra, standing more than three feet tall, have been mistaken for everything from grizzly cubs to adolescent hikers.

Trumpeter Swans

The world's largest waterfowl, these swans boast wingspans as wide as eagles (seven feet) and can weigh up to 40 pounds. They're pure white and so have figured prominently over the centuries in legends, drama, music, and metaphor. They fly as fast as 60 miles per hour and as high as 10,000 feet on their migrations from Alaska to the Pacific Northwest for the winter (though a group of 500 overwinter in Alaska). They live to be 30 years old and have a hornlike call, which accounts for their common name.

Ptarmigan

The **willow ptarmigan** is the state bird, and one of the most popular targets of small-game hunters. Ptarmigan—willow, rock, and white-tailed—are similar to pheasant, quail, and partridge in the Lower 48. They reproduce in large quantities, molt from winter white to summer brown, and have a poor sense of self-preservation.

INSECTS
Mosquitoes

The mosquito—contrary to popular belief—is not Alaska's state bird. But skeeters are nearly as much a symbol of the Great North as glaciers, totem poles, and the aurora borealis. Mosquito eggs hatch in water, so the boggy, muskeg, marshy forests and tundra, plus all the ponds, lakes, creeks, sloughs, and braided rivers of Alaska, provide the ideal habitat for these bothersome creatures. Alaska hosts around three dozen varieties of mosquitoes.

Mosquitoes hibernate in the winter and emerge starting in March-April. Peak season is late June-early July. The males don't alight or bite, but they do buzz around people's eyes, noses, and ears, which can be as annoying, if not more so, than the bites. The males live

1: humpback whales; 2: sea lions hauled out on Prince William Sound

6-8 weeks, feeding on plant juices; their sole purpose in life is to fertilize the eggs the females produce. They also feed birds and larger insects.

The females live long lives producing batches of eggs, up to 500 at a time. To nourish the eggs, they feed on the blood of mammals, using a piercing and sucking mouth tube. The tube also injects an anticoagulant, which causes the itch and swelling from a bite. No Alaskan mosquitoes carry the diseases that tropical mosquitoes are known to, such as malaria, yellow fever, encephalitis, and elephantiasis.

Mosquitoes are most active at dawn and dusk. Windy conditions and low temperatures depress mosquito feeding and breeding. Mosquitoes are attracted to dark colors, carbon dioxide, warmth, and moisture. Mosquito repellent containing DEET (diethyl-meta-toluamide) is the most effective. A head net helps keep mosquitoes and other buggy critters away from your face and is a wise investment for anyone heading into remote parts of interior Alaska. If you wear light-colored heavy clothing (the stinger can pierce light materials), camp in high and dry places that are apt to be breezy, and rub repellent on all exposed skin, you should be able to weather mosquito season without too much difficulty.

FISH

Get someone going on fishing in Alaska and you won't be able to shut him or her up or get a word in edgewise for the whole afternoon, guaranteed. The fisheries program in Alaska is extensive because commercial, sport, and recreational fishing are important to almost every state resident. Commercial fishing is Alaska's second-largest industry, and Alaska accounts for more than half of the nation's total seafood production. Sportfishing has always been popular and is now playing a more important role in Alaska's economy as tourism increases.

Salmon

Five kinds of salmon—king, red, pink, silver, and chum—all return to the same bend in the same little creek where they hatched to spawn and die, ending one of the most remarkable life cycles and feats of migration and single-minded endurance of any living creature. You'll be steeped in salmon lore if only by osmosis by the end of your trip, and you'll get more than your fill of this most delicious and pretty fish.

The **kings** (also known as chinooks) are the world's largest salmon, and the world's largest kings spawn in Alaskan waters. The average size for a king is 40-50 pounds. The world sportfish record is 97 pounds, and a few 100-pounders have been caught in commercial nets. Kings generally spend 5-6 years in saltwater before returning to freshwater to spawn: The more years spent in the ocean, the larger the fish. They run mostly mid-May-mid-July.

Reds (sockeye) are the best-tasting salmon and the mainstay of the commercial fishing industry. They average 6-10 pounds and run in June-July.

Pinks (humpback) are the most plentiful, with massive runs of more than 150 million fish late June-early September. They're smallish, 3-4 pounds, with soft flesh and a mild taste; they're mostly canned (or caught by tourists).

Silvers (coho) seem to be the most legendary of the salmon for their speed, agility, and sixth sense. Their spawning growth rate is no less than fantastic, more than doubling their weight in the last 90 days of their lives. Silvers grow 7-10 pounds and run late, from late July all the way to November.

Chums (dog) are the least valued of the five Pacific salmon, even though they average 10-20 pounds, are extremely feisty, and are the most far-ranging, running way above the Arctic Circle. They're known as dog salmon because they've traditionally sustained working huskies, though chums remain popular with a hard-core group of sport anglers, who consider them terribly underrated. Surprisingly, they make some of the finest smoked fish.

Halibut

Halibut are Alaska's favorite monster fish and can grow so huge and strong that many anglers have an unsurpassed religious experience while catching one. "Chicken halibut" are the common 25-40 pounders, but 100- and 200-pounders are frequent sights in some ports; even 300-pounders are occasionally reeled in. The state-record halibut was a 464-pounder, more than 8 feet long, caught near Dutch Harbor in 1996. Even though halibut are huge and require 80-pound test line with 20-ounce lead sinkers, they're not the fiercest fighting fish, and just about anyone can catch one on a good day's charter from Homer, Seward, or Whittier. It has a very white flesh with a fine texture—many Alaskans regard it as the most flavorful (and least fishy-tasting) fish.

Hooligan

The fattiest fish in northern waters is the Pacific Coast eulachon, also known as hooligan, smelt, and candlefish (legend claims that the dried fish are so fatty they can be wicked and lit like candles). These silver and white fish are roughly as long and slender as pencils, and they run in monumental numbers for three weeks in early summer from Northern California to the Pribilofs. The mouth of the Portage River (just south of Girdwood) is a popular spot for dipnetting hooligan.

History

PREHISTORY

The Athabascan people of Canada have a legend that tells how, in the misty past, one of their ancestors helped a giant in Siberia slay a rival. The defeated giant fell into the sea, forming a bridge to North America. The forefathers of the Athabascans then crossed this bridge, bringing the caribou with them. Eventually the giant's body decomposed, but parts of his skeleton were left sticking above the ocean to form the Aleutian Islands.

In scientific terms, what probably happened was that low ocean levels—up to 450 feet below those at present—offered the nomadic peoples of northeastern Asia a 50-mile-long, 600-mile-wide land "bridge" over the Bering Sea. There is considerable controversy over exactly when humans crossed this isthmus, but it was certainly used at least 12,000 years ago, and perhaps considerably earlier.

One of the earliest records of humans in the Americas is a caribou bone with a serrated edge found at Old Crow in the northern Yukon. Almost certainly used as a tool, the bone has been placed at 27,000 years old by carbon dating. The interior lowlands of Alaska and the Yukon Valley, which were never glaciated, provided an ice-free migration route. As the climate warmed and the great ice sheets receded toward the Rocky Mountains and the Canadian Shield, a corridor opened down the middle of the Great Plains, allowing movement farther south. (Recent scientific evidence suggests that ancient peoples also sailed or paddled along the coast from Asia to North America.)

The Athabascans

The Athabascans and other Paleo-Indians were the first people to cross the Bering land bridge. Their language is spoken today from interior Alaska to the American Southwest (among Navajos and Apaches). Way back when (anywhere from 12,000 to 40,000 years ago), these people of the interior followed the mastodon, mammoth, and caribou herds that supplied them with most of their necessities. Agriculture was unknown to them, but they did fashion basic implements from the raw copper found in the region. Eventually, certain groups found their way to the coast.

The Aleut

Marine mammals and fish provided the

Eskimo-related Aleuts with food, clothing, and household materials. The Aleut were famous for their tightly woven baskets. Before the 1740s arrival of the Russians, 25,000 Aleuts inhabited almost all of the Aleutian Islands, but by 1800 only about 2,000 survived. The ruthless Russian fur traders murdered and kidnapped the men, enslaved or abandoned the women, and passed on their genes and diseases so successfully that today only 1,000 full-blooded Aleuts remain. The rest intermarried with the Russians, and scattered groups of their descendants are now found in the eastern Aleutians and the Pribilofs to the north.

EUROPEAN EXPLORATION
Vitus Bering

In the early 1700s, long before the New World colonists began manifesting their destiny by pushing the American frontier west to the Pacific coast, Russian *promyshlenniki* (explorers and traders) were already busy pushing their own frontier east to the Pacific. After these land conquerors had delineated Russia's inhospitable northeastern edges, they were followed by indomitable sea explorers who cast off from the coasts in search of answers to questions that had intrigued Europeans since Marco Polo's *Travels*—mainly, whether or not Asia was joined with America, the mysterious land to the east that was vaguely outlined on then-contemporary maps.

Danish-born Vitus Bering, a sailor in the Russian navy for nearly 20 years, set out in 1725 for Kamchatka Peninsula, Siberia, on orders from Peter the Great. It took him and his crew three years, dragging rigging, cable, and anchors 2,000 miles over trackless wilderness and suffering innumerable deprivations to reach the coast, where their real journey into the uncharted waters of the North Pacific would begin. Bering built his first boat, *Gabriel,* and sailed past St. Lawrence Island (south of present-day Nome) and the Diomedes, but fog prevented him from glimpsing North America. He returned and

wintered in Kamchatka, sailed again in the spring, and charted most of the Kamchatka coast, but foul weather and a shortage of provisions again precluded exploring farther east.

Over the next 10 years, Bering shuttled between Moscow and his beloved coast, submitting patiently to royal politics and ridicule from the leading scientists and cartographers while planning and outfitting (though not commanding) a series of expeditions that charted the rest of the Siberian coast and Japan.

Finally, in 1741, at the age of 60, Bering undertook his remarkable voyage to America. Commanding the *St. Peter,* he sailed southeast from Kamchatka, came up south of the Aleutians, passed Kodiak, and sighted Mount St. Elias on the mainland. By that time Bering, along with 31 members of his crew, was in the final throes of terminal scurvy. He died in December 1741 and was buried on what is now Bering Island, the westernmost of the Aleutians. Meanwhile, his lieutenant, Alexis Chirikov, commanding the *St. Paul,* had reached all the way to the site of Sitka. After much hardship, survivors from both ships made it back to Siberia—with a load of sea otter pelts. This bounty from the New World prompted a rush of Russian hunters and traders to Alaska.

Conflicting Claims

Reports of Russian advances alarmed the Spanish, who considered the entire west coast of North America theirs. Juan Pérez and Bruno de Heceta were ordered north from Mexico in 1774 and 1775. Spanish explorer Juan Francisco Quadra sailed as far north as Sitka in 1775 and 1779, but in the end, Spain failed to back up its claim with any permanent settlement north of San Francisco. It was Englishmen James Cook (in 1776-1780) and George Vancouver (in 1791-1792) who first carefully explored and charted

---

1: homesteader's cabin near Homer; 2: historic Chapel of St. Nicholas in Kenai; 3: Independence Mine State Park north of Palmer

this northern coast. In 1778, Cook landed on Vancouver Island, then sailed north all the way to what is now called Cook Inlet in south-central Alaska, in search of the Northwest Passage from the Atlantic. He continued to the Aleutians and entered the Bering Sea and the Arctic Ocean. A decade and a half later, Vancouver, aboard his ship HMS *Discovery,* charted the coast from California to southeast Alaska and claimed the region for Britain. His was the first extensive exploration of Puget Sound and circumnavigation of Vancouver Island; his maps and charts of this confounding coast were so accurate that they were used for another 100 years.

The Fur Trade

The excesses of the *promyshlenniki,* who had massacred and enslaved the Aleut, prompted the czar in 1789 to create the Russian-American Company, headed by Grigori Shelikhov, a fur trader and merchant who in 1784 had established the first permanent settlement in Alaska at Three Saints Bay on Kodiak Island. Alexander Baranov, a salesman in Siberia, was the first director of the company; he moved the settlement to present-day Kodiak town, and for the next 20 years Baranov *was* the law. One of the most powerful men in Alaskan history, he enslaved the remaining Aleuts, warred with the Panhandle Indians, initiated trade with the British, Spanish, and Americans, and sent his trading vessels as far away as Hawaii, Japan, and Mexico. Exhausting the resources of Kodiak and its neighborhood, he moved the company to Sitka, where, according to Merle Colby in his classic 1939 Works Progress Administration (WPA) *Guide to Alaska:*

> from his wooden "castle" on the hill surmounting the harbor he made Sitka the most brilliant capital in the new world. Yankee sailors, thrashing around the Horn, beating their way up the California coast, anchored at last in Sitka harbor and found the city an American Paris, its streets crowded with adventurers from half the world away, its nights gay with

balls illuminated by brilliant uniforms and the evening dresses of Russian ladies.

Except for the Tlingit people, who fought bitterly against Russian imperialism, Baranov's rule, extending from Bristol Bay in western Alaska to Fort Ross, California, was complete. His one last dream, of returning to Russia, was never fulfilled: On the voyage back to his homeland, Baranov died at the age of 72.

THE 19TH CENTURY
Political Units Form

In 1824 and 1825, Russia signed agreements with the United States and Britain, fixing the southern limit of Russian America at 54 degrees 40 minutes north latitude, near present-day Ketchikan. But the vast territory south of this line was left up for grabs. The American claim to the Oregon Territory around the Columbia River was based on its discovery by Robert Gray in 1792, and on the first overland exploration by Lewis and Clark. Britain based its claim to the region on its effective occupation of the land by the Northwest Company, which in 1821 merged with the Hudson's Bay Company. As American settlers began to inhabit the area, feelings ran high—President Polk was elected in 1846 on the slogan "Fifty-four Forty or Fight," referring to the proposed northern boundary between American and British territory in the Pacific Northwest. War between Britain and the United States was averted when both agreed to draw the boundary line to the Pacific along the 49th parallel, which remains to this day the Canada-U.S. border. Vancouver Island went to Britain, and the new Canadian nation purchased all the territorial holdings of the Hudson's Bay Company (Rupert's Land) in 1870. In 1871, British Columbia joined the Canadian Confederation on a promise from the leaders of the infant country of a railroad to extend there from the east.

The Russians Bail Out

The year 1863 was a difficult one for the Russian America Company. Back in the motherland, Russia's feudal society was breaking down, threatening the aristocracy's privileged status. In Alaska, competition from English and American whalers and traders was intensifying. Food was scarce, and supply ships from California were unreliable and infrequent. The worst, perhaps, was the dwindled numbers of fur seals and sea otters, hunted nearly to extinction over the past century. In addition, bad relations with Britain in the aftermath of the Crimean War (1853-1856) prompted Czar Alexander I to fear losing his far-flung Alaskan possessions to the British by force. Finally, the czar did not renew the company's charter, and the Russian America Company officially closed up shop.

Meanwhile, American technology was performing miracles. Western Union had laid two cables under the Atlantic Ocean from the United States to Europe, but neither had yet worked. So they figured, let's go the other way around the world: They proposed laying a cable overland through British Columbia, along the Yukon River, across the Bering Strait into Siberia, then east and south into Europe. In 1865, the Western Union Telegraph Expedition to Alaska, led by William Dall, surveyed the interior of Alaska for the first time, revealing its vast land and resources. This stimulated considerable interest in frontier-minded Washington DC. In addition, Czar Alexander's Alaska salesman, Baron Eduard de Stoeckl, was spending $200,000 of his own money to make a positive impression on influential politicians and journalists.

Secretary of State William H. Seward purchased Alaska on March 30, 1867, for the all-time bargain-basement price of $7.2 million—*two cents* per acre. The American flag was hoisted over Sitka on October 18, 1867. According to Ernest Gruening, first U.S. senator from Alaska:

> A year later when the House of Representatives was called upon to pay the bill, skeptical congressmen scornfully labeled Alaska "Icebergia," "Walrussia," "Seward's Icebox," and "[President] Johnson's Polar Bear Garden." If American forces had not already raised the

Stars and Stripes in Sitka, the House might have refused to pick up the tab.

Stoeckl, meanwhile, reimbursed himself the $200,000 he'd invested and sent the other $7 million home to Alexander. Subsequently, Alaska faded into official oblivion for the next 15 years—universally regarded as a frozen wasteland and a colossal waste of money.

Organic Act of 1884

This act organized Alaska for the first time, providing a territorial governor and law enforcement (though not a local legislature or representation in Washington). President Chester Arthur appointed federal district court judges, U.S. attorneys, and marshals. From 1884 to 1900, only one U.S. judge, attorney, and marshal managed the whole territory, all residing in the capital, Sitka. The first three appointees to the court in Sitka were removed in disgrace amid charges of "incompetence, wickedness, unfairness, and drunkenness." A succession of scandals dogged other federal appointees—and that was only in Sitka; the vast interior had no law at all until 1900, when Congress divided the territory into three legal districts, with courts at Sitka, Nome, and Eagle.

William H. Dall wrote of Alaska at that time as a place where "no man could make a legal will, own a homestead or transfer it, or so much as cut wood for his fire without defying a Congressional prohibition; where polygamy and slavery and the lynching of witches prevailed, with no legal authority to stay or punish criminals." Kipling's line, "There's never law of God or man runs north of 53," also refers to the young territory of Alaska. In contrast, Colby in his WPA guide commented that the gold-rush stampeders,

> although technically without civil authority, created their own form of self-government. The miners organized "miners meetings" to enforce order, settle boundary disputes, and administer rough and ready justice. Too often this form of government failed to cope with [serious problems], yet the profound instinct of the

American people for self-government and their tradition of democracy made local self-government effective until the creation of the Alaska Legislature in 1912.

Gold!

Alaska's gold rush changed everything. After the California stampede of 1849, the search moved north. In 1858 there was a rush up the Fraser River to the Cariboo gold fields. In 1872, gold was found in British Columbia's Cassiar region. Strikes in Alaska and the Yukon followed one another in quick succession: at Juneau (1880), Fortymile (1886), Circle (1893), Dawson City (1896), Nome (1899), Fairbanks (1902), and Iditarod (1908).

A mobile group of men and women followed these discoveries on riverboats, dogsleds, and foot, creating instant outposts of civilization near the gold strikes. Gold also caused the Canadian and American governments to take a serious look at their northernmost possessions for the first time; the beginnings of Alaska's administrative infrastructure date from those times. Still, in 1896, when Siwash George Carmack and his two Athabascan brothers-in-law discovered gold where Bonanza Creek flowed into the Klondike River in Yukon Territory, this vast northern wilderness could barely be called "settled." Only a handful of tiny nonnative villages existed along the Yukon River from Ogilvie and Fortymile in western Yukon to Circle and Fort Yukon in eastern Alaska, and a single unoccupied cabin sat on a beach at the mouth of the Skagway River at the terminus of the Inside Passage.

But by the end of 1897, perhaps 20,000 stampeders had skirted the lone cabin on their way to the headwaters of the Yukon and the sure fortunes in gold that awaited them on the Klondike. The two trails from Skagway over the coastal mountains and on to the interior rivers proved to be the most "civilized" and successful routes to Dawson. But the fortune-frenzied hordes proceeded north, uninformed, aiming at Dawson from every direction on the compass. They suffered every conceivable hardship and misery, from which death (often by suicide) was sometimes the only relief. And those who finally burst through the barrier and landed at the Klondike and Dawson were already two years too late to partake of the "ready" gold.

But the North had been conquered by whites. And by the time the gold rush had spread to Nome, Fairbanks, Kantishna, Hatcher Pass, and Hope, Alaska could finally be called settled (if not civilized).

The consequences of this Anglo invasion were devastating for the people who had lived in this harsh land for thousands of years. Epidemics of measles, influenza, and pneumonia swept through the Native Alaskan communities, particularly in 1900 and 1918, sometimes killing every person in a village. Rescuers found entire families who had frozen to death because they did not have enough strength to keep the fire going. The impact of these deaths, combined with the sudden arrival of whites who introduced alcohol, depleted game and other food sources, and then brought Christianity as a replacement for indigenous beliefs, was profound. The consequences still ripple across Alaska, most notably in the form of rampant alcoholism, which is a factor in the shocking rates of Native Alaskan accidents and suicides.

THE 20TH CENTURY

In the first decade of the 20th century, the sprawling wilderness was starting to be tamed. The military set up shop at Valdez and Eagle to maintain law and order, telegraph cables were laid across the interior, the Northwest Passage had been found, railroads were begun at several locations, vast copper deposits were being mined, and thousands of independent pioneer types were surviving on their own wits and the country's resources. Footpaths widened into wagon trails. Mail deliveries were regularized. Limited self-government was initiated: The capital moved to Juneau from Sitka in 1905; Alaska's first congressional delegate arrived in Washington in 1906; and a territorial legislature convened in 1912.

A year later, the first people stood atop the south peak of Mount McKinley (now Denali), and the surrounding area was set aside as a national park in 1917. At that time, Alaska's white and Native Alaskan populations had reached equivalency, at around 35,000 each. Judge James Wickersham introduced the first statehood bill to the U.S. Congress in 1916, but Alaska drifted along in federal obscurity until the Japanese bombed Pearl Harbor.

War

It has been said that war is good for one thing: the rapid expansion of communications and mobility technology. Alaska proves that rule. In the early 1940s, military bases were established at Anchorage, Whittier, Fairbanks, Nome, Sitka, Delta, Kodiak, Dutch Harbor, and the tip of the Aleutians, which brought an immediate influx of military and support personnel and services. In addition, in 1942 alone, thousands of miles of road were punched through the trackless wilderness, finally connecting Alaska to the rest of the world: the 1,440-mile Alaska Highway from Dawson Creek, British Columbia, to Delta, Alaska; the 50 miles of the Klondike Highway from Whitehorse to Carcross; the 151-mile Haines Highway; and the 328-mile Glenn Highway from Tok to Anchorage, among others. At the war's peak, 150,000 troops were stationed in the territory; all told, the U.S. government spent almost $1 billion there during the war. After the war, as after the gold rush, Alaska's population increased dramatically, with service members remaining or returning. The number of residents nearly doubled between 1940 and 1950.

Statehood

The 1950s brought a boom in construction, logging, fishing, and bureaucracy to Alaska. The decade also saw the discovery of a large oil reserve off the western Kenai Peninsula in the Cook Inlet. The population continued to grow, yet Alaskans still felt like residents of a second-class colony of the United States and repeatedly asked for statehood status through the decade. Finally, on July 7, 1958, Congress voted to admit Alaska into the Union as the 49th state. On January 3, 1959, President Dwight D. Eisenhower signed the official proclamation—43 years after Judge James Wickersham had first introduced the idea.

In the 92 years between Alaska becoming a U.S. territory and becoming a state, much of the land was split up into Navy petroleum reserves, Bureau of Land Management parcels, national wildlife refuges, power projects, and the like, to be administered by separate federal agencies, including national park, forest, and military services. By the time Alaska gained statehood in 1959, only 0.003 percent of the land was privately owned—mostly homesteads and mining operations—and just 0.01 percent had been set aside for Native Alaskan reservations, administered by the Bureau of Indian Affairs. The Statehood Act allowed Alaska to choose 104 million acres, but the issue of Native Alaskan land ownership was not considered, and it would take oil discoveries in the late 1960s to force redress for that injustice.

A little over five years after statehood, the Good Friday earthquake struck south-central Alaska; at magnitude 9.2, it remains the largest earthquake ever recorded in North America. But Alaskans quickly recovered and rebuilt with the plucky determination and optimism that still characterize the young state.

Oil Changes Everything

Alaska entered the big time, experiencing its most recent boom, in 1968 when Atlantic Richfield discovered a 10-billion-barrel oil reserve at Prudhoe Bay. The following year, Alaska auctioned off leases to almost 500,000 acres of oil-rich country on the North Slope. A consortium of oil company leaseholders immediately began planning the Trans-Alaska Pipeline to carry the crude from Prudhoe Bay to Valdez. But conservationists, worried about its environmental impact, and Native Alaskan groups, concerned about land-use compensation, filed suit, delaying construction for four years.

This impasse was resolved in 1971, when Congress passed the Alaska Native Claims Settlement Act (ANCSA), the most extensive compensation to any indigenous people in the history of the United States. It gave Alaska's aboriginal groups title to 44 million acres of traditional-use lands, plus $1 billion to be divided among all American citizens with at least 25 percent Athabascan, Eskimo, or Aleut blood. The act also created a dozen regional Native Alaskan corporations, a "13th Corporation" for Native Alaskans in the Lower 48, plus more than 200 village and urban Native Alaskan corporations.

The pipeline was built in 1974-1977. Again, after years of uncertainty, Alaska boomed, both in revenues and population. Since then, the state's economic fortunes have risen and fallen with the volatile price of oil.

Preserving the Wild Places

The Alaska Native Claims Settlement Act (ANCSA) of 1971 had designated 80 million acres to be withdrawn from the public domain and set aside as national parks, wildlife refuges, and other preserves by 1978. In the mid-late 1970s, in the wake of the completion of the pipeline, this was the raging land issue, generally divided between fiercely independent Alaskans who protested the further "locking up" of their lands by Washington bureaucrats, and conservationists who lobbied to preserve Alaska's wildlife and wilderness. When Congress failed to act, President Jimmy Carter took a bold move that forever changed the way Alaskan lands are managed: He withdrew 114 million acres of Alaskan lands as national monuments on December 1, 1978. The withdrawal still rankles the state's right-wing politicians, who regard it as a criminal act that should be prosecuted.

Two years later, with Ronald Reagan waiting to take over the reins of power, Carter signed into law one of the most significant pieces of environmental legislation ever enacted: the Alaska National Interest Lands Conservation Act (ANILCA). The act set aside 106 million acres of federal property as "public-interest lands," to be managed by the National Park and U.S. Forest Services, the U.S. Fish and Wildlife Service, and other agencies. These "d2 lands" (from section 17:d-2 of ANCSA) included the expansion of Mount McKinley National Park (renamed Denali); the expansion of Glacier Bay and Katmai National Monuments, which became national parks; and the creation of Gates of the Arctic, Kobuk Valley, Wrangell-St. Elias, Kenai Fjords, and Lake Clark National Parks, plus the designation of numerous national monuments and preserves, Wild and Scenic Rivers, and new wildlife refuges.

INTO A NEW CENTURY

The late 1990s were hard on Alaska, as oil prices dropped, pulp mills closed down, logging declined, and commercial fishing suffered from low prices and a market flooded with farmed salmon from Chile, Norway, and British Columbia. But the first several years of the 21st century brought a reversal, with sky-high oil and gold prices, a big push to develop a natural gas pipeline across the state (it's been in the works for decades with no signs of coming into existence), increased tourism, higher prices for Alaska's wild salmon, and major political upheavals as FBI investigations threatened the oil industry's stranglehold on state government.

In 2006, voters did the unthinkable by voting to tax and regulate the cruise ship industry while simultaneously throwing out an incumbent governor (and former U.S. senator), Frank Murkowski, and replacing him with an almost unknown politician named Sarah Palin. This was followed by a series of scandals that sent legislators to prison on corruption charges and eventually brought down Senator Ted Stevens. His conviction was later overturned, but not before voters had thrown him out of office in the 2008 election.

Even bigger news in 2008 was the sudden ascendancy of Sarah Palin, Alaska's then-governor. When John McCain brought her onto his ticket as the Republican vice presidential candidate, Palin garnered intense international attention—not all of it positive. She resigned in 2009 after less than three years in office, but remains a fringe figure on the national stage.

Alaskan's politics are schizophrenic. In 2014, voters elected very conservative state and national legislators while simultaneously electing a moderate independent as governor (Bill Walker) and voting for a higher minimum wage, restrictions on mining in Bristol Bay, and the legalization of marijuana. The hatred between Governor Walker and conservatives in the state legislature provides an endless source of amusement for Alaskans.

Today, both of Alaska's U.S. senators are Republican—the moderate (by Alaskan standards) Lisa Murkowski and right-wing Dan Sullivan. Even farther on the right is Representative Don Young, a bombastic man first elected in 1973; he's the longest-serving U.S. Representative. President Obama's 2015 visit to Alaska brought international attention to how a warming climate is impacting Alaska; at the same time, he ordered the nation's tallest peak be given its original name, Mount Denali. This move brought complaints from Ohio legislators (President McKinley's home state), but was greeted enthusiastically by most Alaskans.

The state of Alaska faces a challenging economic future, but by 2018 the economy was slowly improving after a recession of two years.

Government and Economy

GOVERNMENT

Like Delaware, Wyoming, Vermont, and North Dakota, Alaska has only one representative to the U.S. Congress, along with two senators. There are 20 state senators elected to four-year terms and 40 state representatives elected to two-year terms. They meet in the capitol in Juneau January-March. Local government is a mishmash of 16 first- and second-class boroughs, first- and second-class unincorporated villages, and tribal governments.

LAND USE AND MANAGEMENT

The vast majority of Alaska's 375 million acres is publicly owned, with less than 1 percent in private hands. Some 60 percent of this land is under federal management, with most of the rest in state or Native Alaskan corporation hands. Get details from Anchorage's **Alaska Public Lands Information Center** (907/644-3678 or 866/869-6887, www.alaskacenters.gov).

National Park Service

In the federal scheme of things, the National Park Service gets all the glory. National parks are the country's scenic showcases, and visitors come by the millions, usually to look, occasionally to experience. Denali National Park and Preserve—home to North America's highest mountain—is Alaska's most famous and overloved park, attracting well over 500,000 tourists each year. Kenai Fjords National Park is visited primarily by tour boat from Seward, and Katmai National Park and Preserve (on the Alaska Peninsula) is a popular bear-viewing destination by air from Anchorage, Homer, Soldotna, and Kenai. Another dozen national parks are found in other parts of Alaska, including the nation's largest, Wrangell-St. Elias National Park and Preserve. For details on national parks in Alaska, contact the **National Park Service** (907/271-2737, www.nps.gov/akso) in Anchorage.

U.S. Forest Service

In Alaska, the U.S. Forest Service manages the nation's two largest national forests:

Tongass National Forest in southeast Alaska and **Chugach National Forest** (907/271-3992, www.fs.fed.us/r10/chugach) in south-central Alaska. Covering 6.9 million acres on the Kenai Peninsula and around Cordova, Chugach is a popular recreation destination, with hundreds of miles of hiking trails and a number of campgrounds and visitors centers. Also here are 40 public-use cabins, accessible by road or trail. Reserve cabins and campgrounds through **Recreation.gov** (518/885-3639 or 877/444-6777, www.recreation.gov, $10 reservation fee).

U.S. Fish and Wildlife Service

The Fish and Wildlife Service manages 16 different refuges covering more than 75 million acres in Alaska. The most accessible of these is **Kenai National Wildlife Refuge** on the Kenai Peninsula, with a newly opened visitors center in Soldotna, hiking trails, canoe routes, public-use cabins, campgrounds, and world-famous fishing. The **Islands and Oceans Visitor Center** in Homer provides a fine introduction to the Alaska Maritime National Wildlife Refuge, which sprawls across 2,500 Alaskan islands. For details on Alaskan refuges, contact the **U.S. Fish and Wildlife Service** (907/786-3909, http://alaska.fws.gov).

State Lands

The State of Alaska owns 89 million acres—almost a quarter of the state—and manages this land for a variety of purposes, from mineral and oil development to state forests. The state manages more than 110 state parks and recreation areas spread over three million acres. Alaska's most popular state park, **Chugach State Park,** covers nearly 500,000 acres bordering Anchorage. **Denali State Park,** south of Denali National Park, is equally impressive, covering 325,000 acres of wilderness mountains and hills. **Kachemak Bay State Park,** accessible by water taxi from Homer, stretches across 400,000 acres of mountains, glaciers, forests, and bays. Other important state parks in south-central Alaska include **Independence Mine State Historical**

Park north of Palmer and **Caines Head State Recreation Area** near Seward.

Camping fees at Alaska state parks are typically $15 per night, with most parks charging a $5 day-use fee. Chugach State Park and Kachemak Bay State Park also have public-use cabins for $75 per night.

For additional state park information, call 907/269-8400 to request brochures and a statewide park map, or visit www.alaskastateparks.org. You can also use this website to check cabin availability and make reservations.

The Alaska Department of Fish and Game manages more than 30 state refuges, critical habitat areas, and wildlife sanctuaries, including the world-famous bear-viewing area at McNeil River. The agency issues sportfishing and hunting permits. For details on all its activities, contact the **Alaska Department of Fish and Game** (907/267-2253, www.adfg.alaska.gov).

Native Lands

Today, the 12 regional Native Alaskan corporations and more than 200 village and urban corporations created in 1971 by the ANCSA own some 37 million acres in Alaska. Much of this is closed to public access except with special permits; fees are commonly charged.

COST OF LIVING

No doubt about it—this place is expensive. Alaska ranks near the top in cost of living among all the states. Numerous factors conspire to keep prices high. Most consumer goods must be imported from the Lower 48, and transportation costs are tacked on along the way. In addition, the transportation and shipping rates within Alaska are similarly high, further inflating the cost of goods and services. In more remote regions especially, lack of competition coupled with steady demand ensures top-dollar prices. And let's not forget how long and cold and dark Alaskan winters are: The cost of heat and utilities is a hardship, and Alaska ranks first in per capita energy consumption in the United States.

Prices in the north are much higher, and are generally the worst in the most remote bush communities. Even in Homer—which is on the road system—food is 20 percent more expensive than in Anchorage.

MONEY FOR NOTHIN'

In 1976, with oil wealth about to come gushing out of the south end of the pipeline, voters approved a state constitutional amendment calling for a percentage of all oil and mineral revenues to be placed in a **Permanent Fund** (www.apfc.org). Money from this account can only be used for investment, not for state operating expenses, which explains why, during recent Alaskan recessions, when hundreds of state workers were laid off and state funds were severely cut back, billions of surplus dollars sat untouched in the fund. It's the only one of its kind in the country, the only state fund that pays dividends to residents, and the largest pool of public money in the country. In 2018 it totaled more than $65 billion.

A portion of the interest and capital gains income from these assets is distributed to all Alaska residents—even children—in a yearly Permanent Fund Dividend check sent out each October. In 1982, the first year of the dividend, each Alaskan received $1,000, but it didn't reach that level again until the stock market boom of the late 1990s. The payout most years is now around $1,500 per person, but varies with investment earnings. All this sudden cash doesn't go unnoticed by local businesses, especially car dealers, furniture stores, and airlines, which put out a plethora of special deals as soon as the money hits the banks.

MAKING A LIVING
Employment

Anyone thinking of moving to Alaska to get rich is in for a rude awakening. For a number of years after the oil boom, Alaskans earned the most per capita of any state. As of 2018, it was ranked seventh—but still has the fifth-highest cost of living. The state's unemployment figures are usually several percentage points above the national average, even during the peak summer season.

Despite this, you can still come to Alaska and make a decent living; after all, most Alaskans came from somewhere else (only a third of Alaskans were born in the state—the second-lowest such percentage in the country). But the opportunities, it should be stressed, are limited. For example, almost a third of the people collecting a paycheck in Alaska work for federal, state, or local government. And the industry that accounts for 87 percent of state revenues (oil and gas) accounts for just 3 percent of employment. The real growth of late has come at the bottom end, in service jobs and retail sales, where your income would probably leave you officially listed with poverty status. So if a job as a Walmart stocker is your dream, hop on the next flight to Anchorage. Fortunately, voters passed a ballot measure that raised the minimum wage to $9.75 per hour in 2016. (In reality, it would be very hard to actually live on that wage in Alaska, unless you're bunking with your parents or couch-surfing.)

For employment information, visit the Alaska Department of Labor's **Alaska Job Center** (www.jobs.state.ak.us), with an up-to-date listing of openings around the state. Here you'll find details on jobs in all sectors, including seasonal cannery work, state positions, and relocation information.

Fishing

Alaska's fisheries account for over half of the country's commercial fish production. Three-quarters of the value is in groundfish (pollock and cod) and salmon, the rest in shellfish, halibut, herring, and others. Alaska produces almost all of the U.S. canned-salmon stock (200 million pounds), and eight Alaskan ports are among the country's top 50 producers, with Dutch Harbor-Unalaska almost always in the top three, and Kodiak not far behind.

Alaska's fisheries are probably the most carefully managed in the country, with healthy stocks of wild salmon and halibut. Fish farming is illegal in Alaska, but farmed salmon from other areas flooded the market in the 1990s. Since then, there has been a resurgence in demand for high-quality Alaskan wild salmon as consumers see problems caused by the farm-raised version—not to mention the difference in taste.

Learn more about Alaska's seafood industry (and get some good salmon and halibut recipes) from the **Alaska Seafood Marketing Institute** (www.alaskaseafood.org).

Agriculture

The percentage of Alaska's land used for farming is as minuscule as the percentage of Alaska's total economy that is accounted for by agriculture. Of the state's 375 million acres (17 million of it suitable for farming), only 910,000 acres are considered cultivable; of those, only 31,000 acres are occupied by crops. The Matanuska Valley (Palmer and Wasilla) and the Tanana Valley (Fairbanks and Delta) contain almost 90 percent of Alaska's usable farmland. Hay, potatoes, barley, and oats are the state's top agricultural products. Despite this, there has been a remarkable growth in small farms across Alaska.

Peony flowers are one of Alaska's most unusual new crops. Because of vagaries of the market (brides love peonies for June weddings) and the timing of the growing season (Alaska peonies bloom in June), peony production is booming, particularly on the Kenai Peninsula and in the Mat-Su Valley. With peonies selling for $6 a stem, it's easy to see how this could be a profitable business! Check out the Alaska Peony Market Cooperative (www.alaskapeonymarket.com) for details.

Medical marijuana was approved by the voters in 1998, and a measure to legalize cannabis passed in 2014, making Alaska the third state in the nation to approve recreational marijuana. It is legal to grow and sell pot in Alaska, but rules strictly limit where and how it can be sold. A number of commercial growing operations are scattered across Alaska, along with several dozen cannabis shops, including more than 20 places in Anchorage alone.

Gold and Minerals

Thirty million ounces of gold were taken from Alaska between 1880 and 1980. Today, the Fort Knox Mine near Fairbanks is Alaska's biggest gold producer, extracting 1,000 ounces of gold per day.

Zinc is the state's most valuable mineral, mined at the enormous Red Dog Mine, 90 miles north of Kotzebue. The largest zinc mine in the world, it produces 575,000 tons of zinc and 100 million tons of lead per year. Coal is mined at Usibelli, near Denali National Park, and deposits of jade, molybdenum, chromite, nickel, platinum, and uranium are known, though the cost of mining in remote Alaska limits these ventures.

One highly controversial mine does not yet exist. Located in the upper reaches of the Bristol Bay watershed (home to the world's most productive red salmon fisheries) is an enormous gold, copper, and molybdenum deposit known as **Pebble Creek.** The mining company talks of valuations in the hundreds of billions of dollars, and a massive open pit mine has been proposed on the site. It is opposed, however, by an unlikely coalition that includes fishers, Native Alaskan corporations, environmentalists, and wealthy lodge owners.

Oil and Gas

Everything that moves in Alaska is lubricated with oil, primarily North Slope crude. Without oil, the Alaskan economy would stiffen, shatter, and disappear into thin air. Oil and gas revenues account for 87 percent of the state's tax revenue. Alaska is so addicted to oil revenue that when the price of a barrel of oil drops by $1, the budget must be adjusted by $150 million. Though the industry accounts for just 3 percent of the total workforce, the average annual salary for these workers is $100,000. Few elected officials would dare speak out against the oil companies; they all know who pays the tab when election bills come in, and they don't want that cash going to their opponents.

At more than 230 million barrels of oil per year, Alaska ranks third in the nation (after North Dakota and Texas). Peak production was in 1988, when 738 million barrels of Prudhoe crude flowed through the pipeline. The Prudhoe Bay oilfield, the largest in North America and 18th in the world, had produced 18 billion barrels by 2018, still producing around 180 million barrels annually.

Enormous quantities of natural gas lie beneath the North Slope, and proposals have been made to build a gas pipeline paralleling the existing oil line, or to develop a gas-to-liquids technology so that the gas can be sent down the existing oil pipeline. Higher gas prices and increased demand may finally lead to its development within the next decade. In addition to the North Slope, both oil and gas are produced from offshore wells in Cook Inlet. The natural gas is used in Anchorage and Kenai, but production has declined in recent years.

Tourism

Tourism is Alaska's third-largest industry, behind petroleum production and commercial fishing. It's also the second-largest employer, accounting for thousands of seasonal jobs. More than two million visitors travel to Alaska each year, with 90 percent of them arriving from the continental United States and Canada. The vast majority of visitors arrive May-September. Approximately half of all visitors (including business travelers) travel independently; the rest come up on cruise ships and package tours.

Native Corporations

Native corporations are major players in Alaska's economy, and they also have large investments (we're talking billions of dollars) spread all over the nation. The corporations include **Arctic Slope Regional Corporation** (www.asrc.com), **Cook Inlet Regional Corporation (CIRI)** (www.ciri.com), **Chugach Alaska Corporation** (www.chugach-ak.com), **Doyon Limited** (www.doyon.com), and **NANA Regional Corporation** (www.nana.com). Doyon, with more than 12 million acres, is the largest corporate landholder in the nation. All these companies are involved in tourism ventures around Alaska, but CIRI and NANA especially have major investments in tour companies, hotels, and other facilities. If you travel in the North, you'll probably spend time in a Native Alaskan-owned facility or on one of their tour boats or buses.

People and Culture

As of 2018, Alaska's population was 740,000. It ranks 48th in total population; only Wyoming and Vermont have fewer people. Of this, roughly 15 percent are of Native Alaskan descent. The non-Native population is predominantly white, with a small percentage of black, Hispanic, Asian, and Pacific Islanders. Anchorage has by far the most diverse population; more than one-third of its residents are Latino, Asian, black, or Native Alaskan. In fact, Anchorage's Mountain View neighborhood is rated the most diverse in the nation, including many immigrants from Sudan, Cuba, Iran, Bhutan, and the Dominican Republic.

ALASKAN NATIVES

Alaska Native people come from five cultural groupings: Athabascan; Aleutiq; Yup'ik and Cup'ik; Inupiaq and St. Lawrence Island Yupik; and Eyak, Tlingit, Haida, and Tsimshian. With intermarriage and migration, the cultural groupings have blurred somewhat, but Native Alaskans are very proud of their heritage. South-central Alaska Natives were historically from two groups:

Athabascan and Aleutiq. Athabascan peoples lived in interior parts of the region, while Aleutiq primarily occupied the coastline. On the Kenai Peninsula there are places where different groups were next to each other, with Kenaitze Dena'ina Athabascans in a village just a few miles from an Aleutiq settlement.

Athabascans

Nomadic hunters and migrants, the Athabascans are related to the Tlingit of southeast Alaska and the Navajo and Apache of the American Southwest. They subsisted on salmon and the interior's mammals, mostly caribou and moose. They passed the cruel winters in tiny villages of no more than six houses, with a *kashim,* or community center, as the focal point. They ice-fished and trapped in the dark, using dogsleds as transportation. Their arts were expressed primarily in beautifully embroidered clothing and beadwork. The men remained constantly occupied with survival tasks—finding food, building houses, and maintaining gear. When the first white explorers and traders arrived in the early 19th century, the Athabascans immediately began to trade with them, learning the new cultures and in turn educating the newcomers in local customs and skills, not the least of which was dogsledding.

Aleuts

As the Athabascans were almost entirely land-based people, the Aleuts (some prefer the terms Alutiiq or Sugpiaq) were almost entirely dependent on the sea. Clinging to the edge of tiny, treeless, windswept Aleutian Islands, they lived in small dwellings made of sealskin-covered frames, with fireplaces in the middle and steam baths attached on the sides. They made sea otter skins into clothing and processed walrus and seal intestines into parkas. Their kayaks (called *bidarka*) were made of marine mammal skins stretched over a wooden or whalebone frame. Basketry was their highest artistic achievement, and

their dances were distinctly martial, with masks, rattles, and knives.

When the Russians invaded the Aleutians in the mid-1700s like furies from hell, around 25,000 Aleuts inhabited almost all the Aleutian Islands and the southern portion of the Alaska Peninsula. Within 50 years, over half had died through violence, starvation, or disease. Most of the rest became slaves and were dispersed around the New World to hunt the sea otter and fight for the Russians. In fact, Aleuts traveled as far south as Catalina Island off the Southern California coast, wiping out the Gabrieliño Indians there, along with the entire otter population, in 1810. Many of the women served as concubines to the Russian overlords, further diluting the Aleut lineage. Today, most Aleuts carry only half or a quarter Aleut blood; only 1,000 are considered full-blooded.

NATIVE ARTS AND CRAFTS

Not unlike most other aboriginal cultures, Native Alaskan arts and crafts were intricately intertwined with animism, religious ceremony, and utility. Each group worked with its abundant natural resources to produce all the necessities of a lifestyle in which subsistence, religion, and artistic expression were inseparable.

Alaskan tourism and Native Alaskan crafts have gone hand in hand since the first Russian stepped ashore. When John Muir arrived in Wrangell by steamer in 1890, he wrote,

> There was a grand rush on shore to buy curiosities and see totem poles. The shops were jammed and mobbed, high prices paid for shabby stuff manufactured expressly for tourist trade. Silver bracelets hammered out of dollars and half dollars by Indian smiths are the most popular articles, then baskets, yellow cedar toy canoes, paddles, etc. Most people who travel look only at what they are di-

rected to look at. Great is the power of the guidebook-maker, however ignorant.

A similar observation holds today, especially in the shops selling made-in-China Alaskan trinkets or carved-in-Bali totem poles and masks. When buying Native Alaskan handicrafts from anyone other than the artist, always look for the **Silver Hand** logo that identifies the work as an authentic Native Alaskan piece. Get details from the **Alaska State Council on the Arts** (907/269-6610 or 888/278-7424, www.education.alaska.gov/aksca). Good places to buy Native Alaskan crafts are the various museum gift shops and the Alaska Native Heritage Center in Anchorage.

Ivory

The Inupiat Eskimo of northern coastal Alaska are renowned for their use of ivory, harvested only by Native Alaskans from the tusks and teeth of walrus, as well as ivory from woolly mammoths and giant mastodons uncovered by miners or erosion. The ivory is carved, also known as "scrimshawed," and made into various implements. Today you'll see ivory jewelry, *ulu* handles, cribbage boards, and the like. The use of ivory for handicrafts is severely restricted by federal regulations established to protect the walrus. Native carvers can carve on ivory obtained from walrus killed for subsistence food, and non-Natives can legally carve on fossilized ivory (darker-colored ivory that was buried in the ground). But don't make the mistake of buying an ivory piece and then taking it through Canada, unless you have a written permit from the Convention on Trade in Endangered Species (www.cites.org). Avoid border confiscations and other legal problems by mailing your pieces home. You won't have any problems carrying them on board an aircraft, unless your plane lands outside the United States.

Baskets

All Native Alaskan groups used available resources to fashion baskets for storage, carrying, and cooking. Birch-bark baskets, often lashed with spruce roots, were made by the forest Athabascans. The coastal Haida, Tlingit, and Tsimshian people used the bark of big cedar trees. They also made entire baskets of spruce roots, occasionally weaving in maidenhead ferns for decoration. The Yup'ik and Aleut indigenous people of western Alaska are known for small, delicate baskets fashioned from coastal rye grass. They also process baleen, the long strips of cartilage-like teeth that hang from the upper jaw of whales, and weave the strips into baskets.

The finest examples of the different baskets are displayed in the largest Alaskan museums; commercial baskets sell for anywhere from $40 for simple birch-bark trays to several thousand dollars for large baleen baskets.

Masks

Each Native Alaskan culture had its traditional mask-making technology and its complex ceremonial uses for masks. Eskimo mask art and ritual were among the most highly developed in the world. Masks, like totems, represented the individual animals and birds that were worshipped, and each mask was believed to embody the spirit, or *inua*, of the animal. The masks of the Athabascans were worn by dancers, accompanied by a tribal choir, to dramatize the tribe's relationship to animal spirits as well as to entertain guests at feasts. Some believe Aleut masks symbolized the faces of ancient inhabitants of the western Alaska archipelago, though these people were only distantly related to the Aleut, if at all.

The use of masks has declined in Native Alaskan cultures, and the art of mask-making isn't as prevalent today as it's said to have been before contact with the Western world. But you will see commercial masks in Native Alaskan galleries and gift shops around the north; these bear a close resemblance to those of long ago.

Other Pieces

Fur parkas are the quintessential Eskimo garment and are available in remote villages and at shops in Anchorage and Fairbanks. The finest of these are custom-made and cost a small fortune; ask locally for the best seamstresses. Beautifully crafted **dolls** are a hallmark of Eskimo artists, who typically use furs and other local materials. Other distinctively Alaskan items include **dance fans, beadwork,** and handcrafted silver or jade **jewelry.**

Essentials

Transportation

AIR

Ted Stevens Anchorage International Airport (ANC, 907/266-2525, www.anchorageairport.com) is the hub for air travel into Alaska. The state's flagship carrier, **Alaska Airlines** (800/426-0333, www.alaskaair.com), has jet service to all the larger cities and towns in Alaska, as well as throughout the United States (including Hawaii) and all the way to Mexico and Costa Rica, and the Alaska Air mileage plan is considered one of the best in the business.

Many other big domestic carriers fly into and out of Anchorage from

the Lower 48, including **American** (800/433-7300, www.aa.com), **Delta** (800/221-1212, www.delta.com), **JetBlue** (800/538-2583, www.jetblue.com), **Sun Country** (800/752-1218, www.suncountry.com), and **United** (800/241-6522, www.united.com).

The following companies offer nonstop international service to Anchorage: **Air Canada** (888/247-2262, www.aircanada.com) from Vancouver, **Condor** (800/524-6975, www.condor.com) from Frankfurt, **Iceland Air** (800/223-5500, www.icelandair.us) from Reykjavik, and **Yakutia Airlines** (www.yakutia.aero) from Petropavlovsk-Kamchatsky in Russia.

Regional Airlines

Alaska Airlines serves most large towns around the state, including Fairbanks, Barrow, Nome, Bethel, Yakutat, Kodiak, and Dillingham. **Ravn Alaska** (907/266-8394 or 800/866-8394, www.flyravn.com) has multiple flights daily connecting Anchorage with Homer and Kenai. **Grant Aviation** (907/290-3383 or 888/359-4726, www.flygrant.com) has daily service multiple times daily between Anchorage and Kenai.

Bush Planes

Flying in a real live Alaska bush plane is a spectacular way to see the state, and it's also the only practical way to access the vast majority of Alaska's roadless areas. You will never forget your first flight over Alaska, whether it's a floatplane heading to a lakeside lodge or a tiny Super Cub taking you to a remote wilderness camp. These airlines have regularly scheduled, though expensive, flights to towns and attractions that either have no public ground transportation or simply can't be reached overland—which accounts for more than three-quarters of the state. For many people who live in Alaska's bush, these planes provide a lifeline of mail, food, and supplies. The planes seat 2-12 passengers,

and they fly for the regular fare no matter how many passengers are aboard (if the weather is cooperating).

But if you're heading to a really remote cabin, fjord, river, glacier, or park, that's when you'll encounter the famous Alaskan bush pilots, with their equally famous charter rates, which can make Alaska Airlines' fares look like the bargain of the century. Still, you'll have quite a ride—landing on tiny lakes with pontoons, on snow or ice with skis, on gravel bars with big fat tires, loaded to the gills with people, equipment, extra fuel, tools, mail, supplies, and anything else under the sun. Make sure you agree on all the details beforehand—charges, drop-off and pickup times and locations, emergency and alternative procedures, and tidal considerations. Never be in much of a hurry; time is told differently up here, and many variables come into play, especially the weather. If you're well prepared for complications and have a flexible schedule and a loose attitude, one of these bush hops will no doubt be among your most memorable experiences in Alaska, worth every penny and minute that you spend.

As far as what you can expect to pay, most flightseeing operations have preset itineraries and prices. Some companies flying out of the larger towns also have set rates to some of the more popular destinations. However, for most drop-off trips, you pay for the ride according to engine hours, both coming and going. So if your destination is a spot that's an hour from the airstrip, you pay for four hours of engine time (an hour out and an hour back, twice).

Safety in the Air

Before you head out into the wild blue yonder, there are a few things you should know. Alaska has far more than its share of fatal airplane crashes every year, generally 3-4 times the national average for small planes. These have happened to even the best pilots flying for even the most conscientious companies, but certain operators cut corners in safety and allow their pilots to fly under risky weather conditions. You can't avoid all risks, of course, but you can improve your odds by taking a few precautions of your own.

First and foremost, you should choose your pilot and flight service with care. Just because someone has a pilot's license and is flying in Alaska doesn't mean that he or she is a seasoned bush pilot. You're well within your rights to ask about the pilot's qualifications, and about time spent flying *in Alaska*. The oft-repeated saying is, "There are old pilots and there are bold pilots, but there are no old bold pilots." Given a choice, you want an "old" one—not so much in chronological years, but one that has been flying in and out of the bush for a good long time. Ask locally about the air safety record of the various companies. Also ask which companies have the contracts with the U.S. Forest Service or other federal agencies, since they tend to be ones that aren't allowed to take chances. You can also search the Web for accident statistics for a specific company at the **National Transportation Safety Board's** website (www.ntsb.gov).

Even if you're just going on a 30-minute flightseeing tour, wear clothing appropriate for the ground conditions. Unplanned stops because of weather or mechanical problems aren't unusual. Warm comfortable hiking clothes, rain gear, and lightweight boots or sturdy shoes make reasonable bush plane apparel.

Weather is a major limiting factor in aviation. Small planes don't operate on airline-type schedules, with arrivals and departures down to the minute. Leave yourself plenty of leeway when scheduling trips, and don't pressure your pilot to get you back to the airstrip so you won't miss your bus, boat, train, dogsled ride, or salmon bake. More than one crash has been the result of subtle or not-so-subtle pressure by clients to fly when it was against the pilot's better judgment. Never pressure a pilot to fly, and always try to act as a second pair of eyes to look for any signs of danger, such as other aircraft in the vicinity.

Before taking off, your pilot should brief all passengers on the location of safety and survival equipment and airsickness bags, how to exit during an emergency landing (or crash), and the location and function of the Emergency Locator Transmitter (ELT) and survival kit. Ear protection may also be supplied, as most small planes are quite noisy. Just in case, buy a set of foam earplugs at a sporting-goods store before you go to the airport. They weigh nothing and are perfectly adequate for aircraft noise levels.

You'll probably be asked how much you weigh (don't be coy—lives are at stake) and told where you should sit. Weight and balance are critical in little planes, so don't whine about not getting to sit up front if you're told otherwise. Many companies place severe restrictions on how much gear they carry, charging excess baggage fees over a certain limit (sometimes less than 50 pounds).

Gear stowage can be a challenge in small planes, especially when transporting people who are heading out on long expeditions. Don't even think of showing up at the airfield with hard-sided luggage. Internal-frame backpacks, duffel bags, and other soft, easily compressed and stowed items are much easier to handle. Don't strap sleeping bags and other gear onto the outside of a pack. Lots of small items are much easier to arrange and find homes for than a few bulky things. Also, if you're carrying a canister of red pepper spray to deter bears, tell the pilot beforehand and follow directions for stowage. Pilots don't want the stuff inside the cabin (imagine what might happen if it went off in this enclosed space), but they'll store it in a float if the plane is so equipped, or you may be able to strap it to a strut with duct tape.

Whenever you fly, leave a flight route, destination, expected departure and arrival times, and a contact number for the flight service with a reliable friend. Then relax and enjoy the scenery. Flying in Alaska is a tremendous experience, one that relatively few people get to enjoy, and in spite of all the cautionary notes above, it is still a generally safe and reliable way to get to and see the wilderness.

Looking for the latest travel deals to, from, and around Alaska? Scott McMurren's **Alaska Travelgram** (www.alaskatravelgram. com) is an exceptional source for all sorts of travel info, including discounts on flights to or from Alaska.

FERRY SERVICE

The **Alaska Marine Highway** (907/465-3941 or 800/642-0066, www.ferryalaska.com) operates two primary state networks: one from Bellingham, Washington, and throughout southeast Alaska; the other through south-central Alaska from Cordova all the way to Dutch Harbor in the Aleutians. In addition, a ferry sails between Whittier and Juneau twice monthly in the summer, linking the two regions.

In south-central Alaska, Alaska Marine Highway ferries serve the communities of Whittier, Homer, and Seldovia. There is no ferry service to Anchorage or Seward. From Whittier, the ferries head east to Valdez and Cordova. From Homer, ferries head to Seldovia and on to Kodiak, with once-monthly summer sailings to the Aleutians.

The ferries have a relaxed and slow-paced atmosphere; it's impossible to be in a hurry here. Many travelers think of the ferry as a floating motel—a place to dry off, wash up, rest up, sleep, and meet other travelers while at the same time moving on to new sights and new adventures. Ferry food is reasonably priced and quite good, but many budget travelers stock up on groceries before they board. The hot water is free in the cafeteria if you're trying to save bucks by bringing along Cup-O-Noodles and instant oatmeal.

Staterooms or Solarium?

Alaska state ferries carry both passengers and vehicles, and offer food service, stateroom cabins, showers, storage lockers, gift shops, and cocktail lounges. Staterooms offer privacy, as well as a chance to get away from the hectic crowding of midsummer. These cabins have two or four bunk beds, and some also include private baths; other folks use the baths and showers down the hall.

If you don't mind hearing others snoring or talking nearby, you can save a bundle and make new friends with fellow voyagers. There's generally space to stretch out a sleeping bag in the recliner lounge (an inside area with airline-type seats), as well as in the solarium—a covered and heated area high atop the ship's rear deck. The solarium has several dozen deck chairs to sit and sleep on, and it can get so popular that at some embarkation points there's a mad dash to grab a place.

Getting Tickets

The ferries operate year-round. Get schedules and make reservations by calling or going online (907/465-3941 or 800/642-0066, www. ferryalaska.com). Reservations for the summer can be made as early as December, and travelers taking a vehicle should book as early as possible to be sure of a space. The ferry system charges an extra fee to carry bicycles, canoes, kayaks, and inflatable boats.

TRAIN

The **Alaska Railroad** (907/265-2494 or 800/544-0552, www.alaskarailroad.com) runs 470 miles between Seward and Fairbanks with a 7-mile spur between Portage and Whittier; it is the only state-owned railroad in the United States. The train—historic and a bit exotic—is also much roomier and slower than a tour bus but costs about the same. Dining service is available, and helpful tour guides are on board in the summer months. In addition, some of the trains will make flag stops to pick up hikers or people living in the Alaskan bush.

Two daily expresses (mid-May-mid-Sept.), one northbound and one southbound, run between Anchorage and Fairbanks ($244 adults, $122 children one-way). The train connects Anchorage to Denali ($171 adults, $86 children), Seward ($108 adults, $54 children), and Whittier ($100 adults, $50 children) daily in the summer.

The railroad has luxurious double-decker

GoldStar cars ($314 adults, $174 children for Anchorage to Denali); the price includes meals and alcoholic beverages. Also offered are various package tours that combine train rides with boat trips, glacier hikes, river rafting, and other activities. Princess Tours and Gray Line of Alaska hook their own double-decker superdome coaches to the end of trains in the summer.

BUSES

A number of companies provide bus or van service around south-central Alaska. **Alaska/Yukon Trails** (907/888-5659, www.alaskashuttle.com) has vans connecting Anchorage, Talkeetna, Denali, and Fairbanks. **Park Connection** (907/245-0200 or 800/266-8625, www.alaskacoach.com) operates buses connecting Anchorage, Seward, Whittier, Talkeetna, and Denali. **Seward Bus Lines** (907/563-0800 or 888/420-7788, www.sewardbuslines.net) has buses between Seward and Anchorage. **The Stage Line** (907/235-2252, www.stagelineinhomer.com) connects Anchorage, Homer, and Soldotna year-round, with seasonal service to Seward. **Interior Alaska Bus Line** (907/883-0207 or 800/770-6652, www.interioralaskabusline.com) serves Anchorage, Tok, and Fairbanks. It does not connect Anchorage with Denali, Talkeetna, or Seward.

Green Tortoise (415/956-7500 or 800/867-8647, www.greentortoise.com) is more than just a bus ride—it's a vacation and a cultural experience in itself. The buses have bunks that convert to seats and tables in the day, and passengers enjoy communal meals. Green Tortoise has multiple trips each summer to Alaska: Some trips leave from San Francisco and wind up in Anchorage; others start and end in Anchorage.

CARS

One essential for Alaskan drivers is *The Milepost,* a fat annual book that's packed with mile-by-mile descriptions for virtually every road within or to Alaska (including, of course, the Alcan). The book is sold everywhere in Alaska—even at Costco—and is easy to find in Lower 48 bookstores or online at www.themilepost.com. Warning: Don't believe everything you read in *The Milepost;* much of the text is paid ads for specific businesses—watch for the small notice.

For current road conditions, construction delays, and more, contact the **Alaska Department of Transportation** (dial 511 toll-free anywhere in Alaska or 907/465-8952, http://511.alaska.gov).

Winter Travel

During the winter months, travelers to Alaska need to take special precautions. Always call ahead for road and avalanche conditions before heading out. Studded snow tires and proper antifreeze levels are a necessity, but you should also have on hand a number of emergency supplies, including tire chains, a shovel and a bag of sand in case you get stuck, a first-aid kit, booster cables, signal flares, a flashlight, a lighter and a candle, a transistor radio, nonperishable foods (granola bars, canned nuts, or dried fruit), a jug of water, an ice scraper, winter clothes, blankets, and a sleeping bag. The most valuable tool may well be a cell phone to call for help—assuming you're in an area with reception.

If you become stranded in a blizzard, stay in your car. You're more likely to be found, and the vehicle provides shelter from the weather. Run the engine and heater sparingly, occasionally opening a downwind window for ventilation. Avoid carbon monoxide poisoning by not running the engine if the tailpipe is blocked by snow.

Car Rentals

One of the most popular ways to see Alaska is by flying into Anchorage and renting a car. Vehicles are available in all the larger towns, but they're cheapest out of Anchorage, where most of the major car rental companies have airport booths at the **Rental Car Center** (www.dot.state.ak.us/anc). For long rentals, it's usually best to get a car away from the airport, where the taxes and fees are higher. In

Cruising Alaska

Of the two million visitors to Alaska each year, half arrive aboard large cruise ships. For many people, these seven-day cruises act as a gateway drug to Alaska; after one trip they're hooked on the state. Cruises provide a comfortable, hassle-free way to see Alaska with minimal planning, but once you've had an overview this way, you'll want to return and explore at your own pace.

There are three types of Alaskan cruises: round-trip cruises, one-way cruises, and cruise tours. **Round-trip cruises** begin in Vancouver, British Columbia, or Seattle and head up through Alaska's Inside Passage to Ketchikan, Juneau, and Skagway (sometimes smaller ports as well) before returning to the home port. Although most cruises last seven days, Holland America has 14-day round-trip cruises that also dock in Anchorage, Homer, Kodiak, and Sitka.

One-way cruises generally begin in Vancouver and cover the same Inside Passage waters as round-trip cruises, but then cross the Gulf of Alaska, ending at Whittier or Seward. There, passengers continue on to Anchorage by bus or train before flying back home. These one-way cruises alternate directions, of course, so you may fly into Anchorage and end in Vancouver instead.

Many cruise passengers choose to spend several days on the ground in south-central and interior Alaska either before or after their cruise. These combination **cruise tours** usually last a total of 10-12 days. Cruise tours vary widely, but a typical 10-day trip might include seven days on the ship followed by overnights in Denali and Anchorage. On-the-ground travel is by bus or aboard the Alaska Railroad. All sorts of cruise-tour options exist, including many that end in Fairbanks instead of Anchorage.

Cruise tours are convenient if you're uncomfortable planning an Alaska trip, but can be frustrating if you don't want to feel like a cog in the machine. They're the McDonalds of travel; predictable but bland. By using this book and online resources, you can easily set up your own time in Alaska before or after a cruise. For many people, this combination provides the best of both worlds: the relaxing comfort of a cruise and the sense of adventure from exploring on your own. I recommend flying into Anchorage, renting a car, and traveling on your own to Denali and the Kenai Peninsula before your cruise. (Doing the cruise first is an equally fine way to do this.)

Prices for cruises are all over the map, with the best deals if you book well ahead, and for the less-crowded spring or fall shoulder seasons. There are, however, drawbacks to travel at these times, since much of Alaska doesn't turn green till late May and some businesses are only open in the peak of summer. You'll occasionally see 10-day cruise tours for $999 for travel in May; that's just $100 a day! Unless you plan to camp and hitchhike, it would be almost impossible to see Alaska for $100 a day on your own. These prices do not include shore excursions at the various ports of call, and they can add considerably to your cost.

the peak summer season, you should reserve up to two months in advance to get the best rates and to be assured of finding any car at all when you arrive.

If you plan to rent a car, it's worth your while to check travel websites such as www.expedia.com or www.priceline.com to see which company offers the best rates. When reserving a vehicle, be sure to mention if you have an AAA card or are a member of Costco; you can often save substantially on the rates. Also ask about driving restrictions, since most car rental companies prohibit their use on gravel roads such as the Denali Highway. Two exceptions are **Alaska 4x4 Rentals** (907/290-0173, www.alaska4x4rentals.com) and **GoNorth Car and RV Rentals** (907/479-7272 or 866/236-7272, www.gonorth-alaska.com). There are occasional reports of rental cars lacking spare tires or jacks. You don't want to discover this in the middle of nowhere, so it's always a good idea to check your vehicle before driving away from the car rental office.

cruise ship leaving Seward

In addition to the large ships—some of which hold over 2,000 passengers—several companies offer **expedition cruises** on ships with less than 100 guests. These are far more expensive and generally cater to more adventurous travelers looking to visit more remote areas. In addition, **Silversea** (www.silversea.com) operates the ultra-luxurious 382-passenger *Silver Shadow* in Alaska; think of it as a floating five-star hotel.

A good overall place to begin an exploration of cruise ship travel is the website of the **Cruise Lines International Association** (www.cruising.org). It has links to all the major players, plus general information. For a good overview of the pluses and minuses of different Alaskan cruises, head to **Cruise Critic** (www.cruisecritic.com). Scott McMurren's very helpful **Alaska Travelgram** (www.alaskatravelgram.com) has info on Alaskan cruise deals.

RV and Camper Rentals

Among Alaskans, recreational vehicles are infamous for cruising slowly down the Seward Highway south of Anchorage, wagging a tail of impatient cars for a mile or more behind. Many snowbirds drive up to Alaska for the summer in their RVs, fleeing to Arizona for the winters. Other folks fly into Anchorage and rent a land yacht. Recreational vehicles may be useful for larger groups, but consider their potentially disastrous environmental impact before renting them for fewer than six people—most RVs average just four miles to the gallon. At last count there were at least five RV rental companies in Anchorage, including two of the largest, **Clippership Motorhome Rentals** (907/562-7051 or 800/421-3456, www.clippershiprv.com) and **ABC Motorhome & Car Rentals** (907/279-2000 or 800/421-7456, www.abcmotorhome.com).

Recreation

FISHING

Alaska is world-famous for its fish and fishing. More than half of the country's commercial seafood production comes from the state, and sportfishing is a favorite activity of both Alaska residents and visitors. Fishing options are equally vast in Alaska, where undeveloped areas stretch for hundreds of miles and the population is clustered onto a tiny portion of the land. The state is speckled with more than one million lakes—including some of the largest in the nation—along with 34,000 miles of pristine coastline. The **Alaska Department of Fish and Game's** website (www.adfg.alaska.gov) has details on sportfishing, including descriptions of the various species, fishing regulations, news, and an abundance of other fish facts.

Popular Alaskan Fish

Salmon are the primary attraction for many sport anglers, and all five species of Pacific salmon are found in Alaska. Steelhead and rainbow trout, which are also salmonid, are famous for their beautiful coloration and fighting spirit. Rainbows are found in many streams and lakes around the state; the larger steelhead are the sea-run form.

Dolly Varden, also known as Arctic char, are a sea-run trout that flourish in many Alaska rivers. Arctic grayling occur in lakes and streams across the state, particularly in interior Alaska and the Alaska Peninsula. The fish have a large and distinctive sail-like dorsal fin, and they put up a big fight when hooked. Other important freshwater fish species include lake trout, brook trout (an introduced species), northern pike, sheefish, and whitefish.

Pacific halibut are a large flatfish that sometimes reach the proverbial barn-door size, and it isn't uncommon to see ones that weigh in excess of 100 pounds. Many Alaskans consider halibut the best-tasting fish in the state. In addition to salmon and halibut, other popular ocean-caught sport fish include rockfish and lingcod.

Fishing Regulations

Fishing licenses are required in Alaska. A one-day nonresident sportfishing license costs $25, 3-day $45, 7-day $70, and 14-day $105. If you plan to catch king salmon, these fees increase to $40, $60, $85, and $120, respectively. The Alaskan license is valid in Denali and other national parks.

Fishing licenses are sold in most outdoor stores, grocery stores, and by charter fishing operators. For all the details on open and closed seasons, bag limits, and the like—spelled out in minute bureaucratic detail—request a copy of the regulations booklet from the **Alaska Department of Fish and Game** (907/267-2218, www.adfg.alaska.gov).

Fishing Derbies

Many Alaskan towns have salmon or halibut fishing derbies in the summer. If one is going on when you visit, it may be worth your while to buy a derby ticket before heading out on the water. The prize money gets into the thousands of dollars for some of these events, and more than a few anglers tell of the big one that would have made them rich if they'd only bought a derby ticket first. Two of the biggest fishing derbies are in Seward and Homer.

Guided Fishing

Local knowledge is one of the best ways to be assured of a successful Alaska fishing trip. By using a charter or guide service, you're likely to have a more productive sportfishing excursion. Fishing guides can be found in most south-central Alaska communities, some offering float trips accessible by car and others going to more remote fly-in destinations. Charter fishing boats are available at coastal towns on the Kenai Peninsula, most notably

Birding

Alaska is an extraordinary place for birding enthusiasts. Nearly 500 species have been recorded in the state, and because of its immense size and diversity, Alaska has birds that are rarely seen anywhere else in North America.

INFORMATION

The Alaska Department of Fish and Game produces a helpful *Wings Over Alaska* (www.birding.alaska.gov) checklist of birds found in the state. The website also contains details on birding, bird identification, and hotspots to find unusual species.

Anchorage is home to a surprising diversity of bird species in the summer. The **Anchorage Audubon Society** (www.anchorageaudubon.org) offers bird-watching field trips, sells a helpful Anchorage birding map, and notes rare bird sightings.

Alaska eBird (www.ebird.org/ak) is an online place to record bird observations, find birding hotspots, and share sightings throughout the state. Maintained by the Cornell Laboratory of Ornithology and the Audubon Society, the site has a wealth of data on when and where to find birds, rare bird alerts, incredibly detailed range maps, and more.

One of the best local places to find birds is **Potter Marsh** on the south edge of Anchorage along Turnagain Arm. A quarter-mile wooden boardwalk provides a good vantage point through the marsh, and you may see Canada geese, Arctic terns, bald eagles, canvasback ducks, and even the occasional trumpeter swan.

TOURS

Based in Homer and run by hard-core birding expert Aaron Lang, **Wilderness Birding Adventures** (907/299-3937, www.wildernessbirding.com) leads trips to the Pribilofs, Adak, Gambel, Barrow, the Gulf of Alaska, and other remote places where you're likely to add new species to your life list. Ken Marlow of **Alaska Birding Tours** (907/262-5218 or 800/725-3327, www.alaskabirdingtours.com) is an expert on pelagic birds and has a boat based in Seward.

EVENTS

Kachemak Bay provides an outstanding opportunity for birders, especially during the spring migration when thousands of sandpipers and other species crowd the tide flats. On the first weekend of May, Homer's annual **Kachemak Bay Shorebird Festival** (www.kachemakshorebird.org) brings bird walks, bay tours, an arts fair, speakers, and other activities, all in celebration of this great northward migration.

The **Kachemak Bay Birders** (www.kachemakbaybirders.org) keeps track of Homer area observations year-round, and has monthly meetings and birding events.

In spring, visitors to Homer are often thrilled by the presence of **sandhill cranes** in fields and yards throughout the area. Approximately 200 cranes return to the area each spring to nest (they winter 2,400 miles south, in central California), and their arrival is a much-anticipated moment for locals. These loud and fascinating birds are always entertaining. Check with the Islands and Ocean Visitor Center for places to see them, and find more online at **Kachemak Crane Watch** (www.cranewatch.org).

Homer, Seward, and Ninilchik. Note that it's common to tip fishing guides, particularly if they're especially helpful or if you land a big one. There's no standard amount, but a 10 percent tip would certainly be appreciated.

INTO THE BACKCOUNTRY

South-central Alaska has an array of **hiking** options, whether you're looking for a waterside stroll along the Anchorage shoreline or a weeklong backpacking trip into Denali National Park. Some of the best hiking trails

Panning for Gold

Panning for gold is not only great fun, it's also a good way to get involved in the history of Alaska. Besides, there's the chance you'll find a nugget that will become a lifelong souvenir. You might even strike it rich! The amount of equipment required is minimal: an 18-inch plastic gravity-trap gold pan (buy one at any local surplus or sporting-goods store for a few dollars), tweezers and an eyedropper to pick out the gold flakes, and a small vial to hold them. Ordinary rubber gloves will protect your hands from icy creek water. An automobile oil dipstick bent at one end is handy for poking into crevices, and a small garden trowel helps dig out the dirt under rocks. Look for a gravel bar where the creek takes a turn, for larger rocks forming eddies during high water, for crevices in the bedrock, or for exposed tree roots growing near the waterline; these are places where gold will lodge. Try your luck on any of the old gold-rush creeks; tourist offices can often suggest likely areas. Stay away from commercial mining operations, and always ask permission if you're on someone's claim.

The principle behind panning is that gold, twice as heavy as lead, will settle to the bottom of your pan. Fill the pan half full of pay dirt you've scooped up from a likely spot and cover it with water. Hit the rim of the pan seven or eight times, or shake it back and forth. Break up lumps of dirt or clay with your hands and discard any rocks after rinsing them in the pan. Shake the pan again, moving it in a circular motion. Dip the front edge of the pan into the stream and carefully wash off excess sand and gravel until only a small amount of black sand remains. If you see gold specks too small to remove with tweezers, take the black sand out and let it dry. Later dump it on a clean sheet of paper and gently blow away the sand. The gold will remain. That's the basic procedure, though there are many ways to do it. It does take practice; ask a friendly sourdough for advice. Also, a number of spiked gold-panning facilities are found along the roads in Alaska—they are commercial, but good places to refine your technique. **Crow Creek Mine** (www.crowcreekmine.com) in Girdwood is the best place to learn gold panning techniques.

are in Chugach State Park near Anchorage and on the Kenai Peninsula in Chugach National Forest. Check out *50 Hikes in Alaska's Kenai Peninsula* and *50 Hikes in Alaska's Chugach State Park* for details, or talk with folks at the **Alaska Public Lands Information Center** (www.alaskacenters.gov) in Anchorage. Few trails exist within Denali National Park, but the country is open enough for cross-country hiking.

Public campgrounds are located throughout Chugach National Forest, Kenai National Wildlife Refuge, and Denali National Park, and in many smaller state and city parks. Most cost $18 and have potable water and vault toilets. Private RV parks can be found in nearly every town across southcentral Alaska.

Several dozen **public-use cabins and yurts** are located within Chugach National Forest, Kenai National Wildlife Refuge, Kenai Fjords National Park, Kachemak Bay State Park, Chugach State Park, and Denali State Park. These rent for $35-75 a night, but advance reservations are needed. Cabins (and some campgrounds) in Chugach National Forest and Kenai National Wildlife Refuge can be rented through Recreation.gov (518/885-3639 or 877/444-6777, www.recreation.gov) for a $10 reservation fee.

A number of prominent organizations guide **mountaineering expeditions** in Alaska, particularly climbs up Mount Denali within Denali National Park. Good wilderness guiding companies include **Alaska Mountaineering School** (907/733-1016, www.climbalaska.org), **Alaska Mountain Guides & Climbing School** (907/313-4422 or 800/766-3396, www.alaskamountainguides.com), **Alaska Alpine Adventures** (907/351-4193 or 877/525-2577, www.alaskaalpineadventures.com), and **NOLS** (907/745-4047, www.nols.edu).

BICYCLING

Bicycles are available for rent in Anchorage, Healy, Nenana Canyon (Denali National Park), Talkeetna, Homer, and Seward, providing an excellent way to see the local sights, especially in fair weather. Winter has not traditionally been a time for cycling, but the advent of **fat-tire bikes** (with balloon tires) has created a boom in snow and ice riding. Bike shops in Anchorage, Seward, and Homer all rent fat-tire bikes if you want to check out this fun winter sport.

The most popular mountain biking trails are in the Anchorage area and include many miles of paved and unpaved paths along the shore and within a couple of city parks. Paved biking paths can also be found paralleling portions of the Seward Highway south of Anchorage, and in Homer, Talkeetna, and other cities. Many Forest Service trails are open to mountain biking, but some of these are muddy and challenging to ride. Especially popular is the Resurrection Pass Trail on the Kenai Peninsula. The Denali Park Road is an excellent place to ride mountain bikes.

The Anchorage-based **Arctic Bicycle Club** (www.arcticbike.org) organizes road races, mountain bike races, and tours, and its website is an excellent source for anyone interested in cycling in Alaska. For bicycle tours, check out **Alaskabike** (907/245-2175, www.alaskabike.com) or **Backroads** (510/527-1555 or 800/462-2848, www.backroads.com).

ON THE WATER

River Rafting

White-water rafting trips are offered by numerous adventure-travel outfitters in south-central Alaska. Several of the more reasonable, short, and accessible trips include floats down Sixmile Creek near Hope, the Nenana River at Denali, the Kenai River at Sterling, the Susitna River near Talkeetna, and the Matanuska River east of Palmer.

Sea Kayaking

Sea kayaks are quiet and fairly stable, providing an outstanding way to explore hidden Alaskan coves or to watch wildlife. Because of this, kayaking has increased in popularity in recent years, both for independent travelers who rent a kayak and for those who choose a package trip with a professional guiding company. Companies offering sea kayak rentals and tours are in Homer, Seldovia, Seward, Whittier, and Eklutna Lake north of Anchorage.

Canoeing

Canoeing is a common activity on lakes and rivers in Alaska. Two canoe routes (Swanson River Route and Swan Lake Route) connect lakes within the Kenai National Wildlife Refuge; canoe rentals are available in the nearby town of Sterling. Canoe rentals are also available in Talkeetna and Matanuska Lakes near Palmer.

Sailing

Alaska has a small but active community of sailing enthusiasts. Resurrection Bay near Seward generally offers the state's top wind conditions, with day trips, sailing lessons, and bareboat charters. Kachemak Bay near Homer is another popular sailing area, with weekend races throughout the summer and day trips.

Surfing and SUPs

Surprisingly, surfing is growing in popularity in Alaska. It is never a particularly common sight, but Homer has a few hard-core souls who head out when conditions are right. Homer is also an increasingly popular destination for kite-surfers, with good winds most afternoons. Stand-up paddleboard (SUP) rentals or tours are available in Homer, Seward, Girdwood, Anchorage, and Wasilla.

WINTER SPORTS

Skiing and Snowboarding

Downhill ski and snowboard areas are near Anchorage (Alyeska Resort, Hilltop Ski Area, and Alpenglow). Alaska's largest ski area, **Alyeska Resort** (www.alyeskaresort.com), is south of Anchorage in the town of Girdwood, with 500 skiable acres, 60 trails, a

Festivals and Events

The biggest events in Alaska revolve around the sun and snow. A number of Alaskans, especially those who live in the interior and the north, believe that the purpose of summer solstice is to compress all the partying encouraged by the light and heat of summer into a single 24-hour period. There are fishing derbies in the waters off the coastal towns, and athletic competitions, such as triathlons and mountain races, everywhere.

The most famous winter festivals are Anchorage's Fur Rendezvous and the Iditarod. Every town has some sort of winter carnival that frequently includes dog mushing, a snow sports competition, and accompanying arts-and-crafts fairs.

Typically, the major public holidays are also a cause for celebration, including Memorial Day (last Mon. in May), Independence Day (July 4), Labor Day (1st Mon. in Sept.), Thanksgiving Day (last Thurs. in Nov.), Christmas, and New Year's Eve. The happiest days of the year, though, are in mid-October when the big Permanent Fund dividend checks show up in the mailboxes of state residents.

JANUARY
Anchorage—Anchorage Folk Festival; Seward—Polar Bear Jump Off

FEBRUARY
Anchorage—Fur Rendezvous

MARCH
Anchorage and Wasilla—Iditarod Trail Sled Dog Race

APRIL
Girdwood—Alyeska Spring Carnival

MAY
Homer—Kachemak Bay Shorebird Festival

JUNE
Anchorage—Anchorage Mayor's Midnight Sun Marathon and Half Marathon; Anchorage—Arctic Thunder Air Show (even-numbered years); Palmer—Colony Days

60-passenger aerial tram, eight chairlifts, and two pony lifts. Hilltop Ski Area and Arctic Valley are smaller areas near Anchorage, and Homer has a little community rope tow.

Cross-country skiing (both classic and skate) is very popular in Alaska, particularly in Anchorage, where many miles of lighted and groomed trails are available throughout the winter. Anchorage may well have the finest cross-country skiing of any American city, and a number of the nation's best Olympic skiers come from here—including 2018 Olympic gold medalist Kikkan Randall. The city's main cross-country ski areas are in Kincaid Park, Hillside Ski Area, and the Tony Knowles Coastal Trail. Additional groomed ski trails are around Homer, Talkeetna, Kenai, Palmer, Eagle River, Seward, and Soldotna. The **Nordic Skiing Association of Anchorage** (907/276-7609, www.anchoragenordicski. com) is Alaska's largest cross-country skiing association, and its website has links to the state's other Nordic skiing groups.

Tustumena 200 Sled Dog Race

JULY
Eagle River—Bear Paw Festival; Girdwood—Girdwood Forest Fair; Seward—Mount Marathon Race; Anchorage—Moose's Tooth Anniversary Party

AUGUST
Ninilchik—Salmonfest and Kenai Peninsula State Fair; Palmer—Alaska State Fair; Seward—Silver Salmon Derby

SEPTEMBER
Whittier—Silver Salmon Derby; Homer—Burning Basket

OCTOBER
Anchorage—Alaska Federation of Natives Convention

DECEMBER
Talkeetna—Winterfest

Dog Mushing
Dogsledding has a rich history in Alaska, and sled dog races are a major winter staple across much of the state. The most famous is the Iditarod Trail Sled Dog Race (www.iditarod.com) from Anchorage to Nome in March. A number of companies offer wintertime dogsled tours.

During the summer months, visitors can ride on wheeled sleds behind teams of dogs, providing a chance to get the feel of the real thing. These very popular rides—some led by Iditarod mushers—are offered in Seward, Wasilla, Willow, and Denali. In addition, summertime dogsled tours take place on glaciers near Seward, Girdwood, and Anchorage. Tourists are flown up to the glacier by helicopter and given a chance to ride along as the dogs head across the ice and snow. It's a unique—but very expensive—experience.

Snowmobiling
Snowmobiling—or snowmachining, as it's called in Alaska—is both a bush necessity in

the winter and a favorite of the motor-head crowd in urban centers. The **Alaska State Snowmobile Association** (www.ridealaska. com) has additional info on their website. Rentals and tours are available in Anchorage and Girdwood.

SPECTATOR SPORTS

Hockey is very big in Alaska, especially in Anchorage, where overachiever parents push their kids onto the ice by age four. The **University of Alaska Anchorage** (www. goseawolves.com) has a nationally competitive hockey team.

In bush Alaska, no sport is bigger than basketball, and any visitor who can play well stands a good chance of immediately being accepted by the locals. There's intense competition among high school teams at the state level, and the University of Alaska Anchorage has its own basketball squad.

The **Alaska Baseball League** (www. alaskabaseballleague.org) consists of six semi-professional teams: Mat-Su Miners, Peninsula Oilers, Anchorage Bucs, Anchorage Glacier Pilots, Alaska Goldpanners (Fairbanks), and Chugiak Chinooks. The teams include talented college players from throughout the country who come to Alaska to play during the season in June and July.

Alaska Baseball League teams play each other, along with Outside teams from the West Coast and Hawaii, with the top teams ending up at the National Baseball Congress World Series in Wichita, Kansas. Alaskan teams have won this World Series many times, and quite a few famous players have spent a summer on Alaska turf, including Mark McGwire, Tom Seaver, Graig Nettles, and Dave Winfield.

Travel Tips

ACCESSIBLE ALASKA

Because of the undeveloped character of Alaska, much of the state is not readily accessible to those with disabilities. This is particularly true in parts of bush Alaska, where even having a flush toilet may be a luxury, and entering small aircraft is a major challenge. Despite this, many towns and cities—particularly those that see an influx of seniors as cruise ship passengers each summer—have made great strides in recent years. Even in remote areas, some U.S. Forest Service and State of Alaska cabins have wheelchair ramps, outsized outhouses, and fishing platforms. In addition, quite a few trails around Alaska have been built for wheelchairs, including popular ones around Anchorage. Hotels, buses, trains, cruise ships, tour boats, and ferries throughout the state all have some sort of accommodation for travelers in wheelchairs or with limited mobility.

A good place for travelers with disabilities is **Access Alaska** (121 W. Fireweed Lane, 907/248-4777 or 800/770-4488, www. accessalaska.org), a nonprofit independent-living center in Anchorage that can assist travelers with specific needs, including wheelchair-accessible hotels and restaurants, along with accessible horseback rides and river trips. Satellite offices are in Soldotna and Wasilla.

In Anchorage, **Hertz** (800/654-3131, www. hertz.com) has rental cars with hand controls, and **Alaska Yellow Cab** (907/222-2222, www.alaskayellowdispatch.com) has wheelchair-accessible vans with lifts.

TRAVELING WITH CHILDREN

Long a destination for seniors and couples, Alaska is equally popular with families, and even the cruise lines have gotten into the act with all sorts of kid-friendly activities and child care aboard the larger vessels. Disney Cruise Line offers trips to Alaska, providing another option. The small adventure cruise ships are primarily the domain of couples, and children can get in the way or become bored. They're welcome on all state ferries, but parents need to keep a close watch due to the onboard hazards. Fortunately, the leisurely pace, engaging scenery, good food, naturalist talks, and free movies make the traveling easier.

It probably goes without saying, but anyone traveling with kids today should bring a tablet or smartphone with a stock of movies and games for those times when you need the kids to quiet down. Don't forget the headphones.

Most attractions and activities have lower rates for children, and some also offer one-size-fits-all family rates. Be sure to get your children into the great outdoors, since that's really what Alaska is all about. The long bus ride into Denali National Park can be challenging for little ones, but the chance to see bears, moose, and wolves makes the trip worthwhile for everyone. Of special interest is the National Park Service's **Junior Ranger Program,** in which children attend a nature program, hike a trail, or complete other activities. They're rewarded with an official Junior Ranger patch and are sworn in. It's always a big hit, but your kids may later try to arrest you if you get too close to a ground squirrel.

Be sure to set aside time for a special kid-friendly place such as the Anchorage Zoo, the Alaska SeaLife Center in Seward, the Islands and Ocean Visitor Center in Homer, or H2Oasis Indoor Waterpark in Anchorage.

Many tours are open to children, but the more hazardous ones (including helicopter flights, kayaking, white-water rafting, stand-up paddleboards, and zip lines) impose age restrictions. Children are accepted in most Alaskan lodging places, but they might not be allowed in certain wilderness lodges or bed-and-breakfasts.

TRAVELING WITH PETS

In general, travelers visiting Alaska should leave their pets at home. Dogs may be good hiking companions, but if not kept under control they could bring a bear charging in your direction. Most hotels do not allow pets, and those that do typically tack on an extra charge

for the privilege. Folks driving up the Alaska Highway—particularly RVers—frequently bring along a small dog or cat, but a current rabies certificate is required when crossing into Canada.

GAY AND LESBIAN TRAVELERS

Openly gay or lesbian individuals may feel uncomfortable in politically conservative Alaska, so discretion may be wise, especially in rural areas such as Glennallen, where Rush Limbaugh is regarded as a socialist. Anchorage, not surprisingly, is the primary center for gays and lesbians in the state. The nonprofit group Identity Inc. runs a **Gay and Lesbian Community Center** (336 E. 5th Ave., 907/258-4777 or 888/907-9876, www. identityinc.org) and operates a free help line. They also sponsor **PrideFest** (www. anchoragepride.org) each June, with more than 100 vendors and live entertainment on the Park Strip downtown.

Two Anchorage bars—**Mad Myrna's** (530 E. 5th Ave., 907/276-9762, www.madmyrnas. com) and **The Raven** (708 E. 4th Ave., 907/276-9672)—are favorite meeting places. **Out North Contemporary Art House** (333 W. 4th Ave., 907/279-8099, www.outnorth. org) sometimes presents plays with a gay and lesbian slant, and several Anchorage B&Bs promote themselves for LGBT travelers.

SENIOR TRAVELERS

Alaska is a very popular summer destination for seniors traveling by cruise ship or RV, and for a surprising number of retirees who move to the state. Alaska Marine Highway ferries offer half-price senior discounts on most wintertime sailings. Most museums and some tours have discounted rates for those over age 65, and visitors to national parks can purchase an **Interagency Senior Pass** (www.fs.fed. us/passespermits/senior.shtml) that allows entry to all national parks for $20 per year.

Travelers over age 55 should consider joining a **Road Scholar** (formerly Elderhostel, www.roadscholar.org) educational adventure,

Pack the Essentials

The following list assumes that your trip to Alaska takes place in the summer. If you're traveling before May or after September, additional winter supplies will certainly be needed. Whenever you visit, prepare for cool and wet weather.

Almost anything you need is available in Anchorage and larger towns. Prices are really not much higher than in the Lower 48. Larger towns have at least one place that rents outdoor gear.

A **cell phone** can be useful to stay connected, but be aware that coverage varies; check with your provider. And of course, don't forget your camera!

CLOTHING ESSENTIALS

- base layers
- hiking boots
- hiking socks
- light water-resistant coat (Gore-Tex works well)
- lightweight gloves
- liner socks
- rain pants
- sweater or wind-block jackett
- swimsuit
- sunglasses
- walking shoes
- warm cap

CAMPING ESSENTIALS

- 50 feet of line
- camp stove and fuel bottle
- compass
- cooking pot

- day pack
- first-aid kit
- fishing tackle (or get this in Alaska)
- insect repellent
- internal-frame backpack
- jackknife or Leatherman tool (a better option)
- plastic bags
- plates, cups, spoons, and forks
- swing kit
- sleeping bag
- small towel
- sunscreen
- tent and ground cloth
- day pack
- water bottle
- water filter
- waterproof matches and lighter

with dozens to choose from in Alaska. **AARP** (www.aarp.org) also has discounted Alaska trips and other benefits.

WILDERNESS SAFETY TIPS

The most important part of enjoying—and surviving—the backcountry is to be prepared. Know where you're going; get maps, camping information, weather, and trail conditions from a ranger before setting out. Don't hike alone. Two are better than one, and three are better than two; if one gets hurt, one person can stay with the injured person and one can go for help. Bring more than enough food so hunger won't cause you to continue when weather conditions say stop. Tell someone where you're going and when you'll be back.

Always carry the **essentials:** a map, a compass, a water bottle, a first-aid kit, a flashlight, matches or a lighter and fire starter (Vaseline and cotton balls work great), a knife, extra clothing (a full set, in case you fall in a stream), rain gear, extra food, and sunglasses—especially if you're hiking on snow. Many travelers also carry along a GPS unit to stay oriented. Cell phones are popular but often don't work in remote areas. Satellite phones are the ultimate safety toy, but they are a pricey addition to your trip.

Check your ego at the trailhead; stop for the night when the weather gets bad, even if it's 2pm, or head back, and don't press on when you're exhausted—tired hikers are sloppy hikers, and even a small injury can be disastrous in the woods.

Hypothermia

Anyone who spends much time in the outdoors will discover the dangers of exposure to cold, wet, and windy conditions. Even at temperatures well above freezing, hypothermia—the reduction of the body's inner core temperature—can prove fatal.

In the early stages, hypothermia causes uncontrollable shivering, followed by a loss of coordination, slurred speech, and then a rapid descent into unconsciousness and death. Always travel prepared for sudden changes in the weather. Wear clothing that insulates well and holds its heat when wet. Wool and polypropylene are far better than cotton, and clothes should be worn in layers to provide better heat trapping and a chance to adjust to conditions more easily. Always carry a wool hat, since your head loses more heat than any other part of your body. Bring a waterproof shell to cut the wind. Put on rain gear *before* it starts raining; head back or set up camp when the weather looks threatening; eat candy bars, keep active, or snuggle with a friend in a down bag to generate warmth.

If someone in your party begins to show signs of hypothermia, don't take any chances, even if the person denies needing help. Get the victim out of the wind, strip off his clothes, and put him in a dry sleeping bag on an insulating pad. Skin-to-skin contact is the best way to warm a hypothermic person, and that means you'll also need to strip and climb in the sleeping bag. If you weren't friends before, this should heat up the relationship! Do not give the victim alcohol or hot drinks, and do not try to warm the person too quickly, since it could lead to heart failure. Once the victim has recovered, get medical help as soon as possible. Actually, you're far better off keeping close tabs on everyone in the group and seeking shelter *before* exhaustion and hypothermia set in.

Frostbite

Frostbite is a less serious but quite painful problem for the cold-weather hiker; it is caused by direct exposure to cold or by heat loss because of wet socks and boots. Frostbitten areas will look white or gray and feel hard on the surface, softer underneath. The best way to warm the area is with other skin: Put your hand under your arm, your feet on your friend's belly. Don't rub the affected area with snow or warm it near a fire. In cases of severe frostbite, in which the skin is white, quite hard, and numb, immerse the frozen area in water warmed to 99-104°F until it's thawed. Avoid refreezing the frostbitten area. If you're a long way from medical assistance and the frostbite is extensive, it's better to keep the area frozen and get out of the woods for help; thawing is very painful, and it would be nearly impossible to walk on a thawed foot.

Beaver Fever

Although lakes and streams in Alaska may appear clean, you could be risking a debilitating sickness by drinking the water without treating it first. The protozoan *Giardia lamblia* is found throughout the state, spread by both humans and animals (including beavers). The disease is curable with drugs, but it's always best to carry safe drinking water on any trip, or to boil any water taken from creeks or lakes. Bringing water to a full boil for one minute is sufficient to kill *Giardia* and other harmful organisms. Another option—most folks choose this one—is to use a water filter (available in camping stores). Note, however, that these may not filter out other organisms such as *Campylobacter jejuni,* bacteria that are

Safety in Avalanche Country

Skiing and snowmobiling are becoming increasingly popular in Alaska's limitless backcountry. Unfortunately, many winter outdoor enthusiasts fail to take necessary precautions before heading out. Given the heavy snowfalls that occur, the steep slopes the snow piles up on, and the high winds that accompany many storms, it should come as no surprise that avalanches are a real danger in Alaska. Nearly all avalanches are triggered by the victims. This is particularly true for snowmobilers, who often attempt such dangerous practices as "high-marking"—riding as high as they can up steep slopes—and are killed in avalanches that result.

To avoid avalanches, ski only on groomed trails or "bombproof" slopes that, because of aspect, shape, and slope angle, never seem to slide. This isn't always possible, so backcountry skiers and snowmobilers need to understand the conditions that lead to avalanches. The best way to learn is from a class such as the avalanche safety programs taught by the **Alaska Avalanche School** (907/345-0878, www.alaskaavalanche.com) in Anchorage.

An avalanche safety course is extremely valuable, but you can also help protect yourself by following these precautions when you head into the backcountry:

Before leaving, get up-to-date avalanche information. The **Chugach National Forest Avalanche Information Center** (907/754-2369, www.cnfaic.org) has current snow conditions for the Kenai Peninsula; it's updated several times a week in the winter.

Be sure to carry extra warm clothes, as well as water, high-energy snacks, an avalanche transceiver, a lightweight snow shovel (for digging snow pits or excavating avalanche victims), an emergency snow shelter, a cell phone, first-aid supplies, a Swiss Army or Leatherman knife, a topographic map, an extra plastic ski tip, a flashlight, matches, and a compass or GPS unit. Many skiers also carry that cure-all, duct tape, wrapped around a ski pole. Let a responsible person know exactly where you are going and when you expect to return. It's also a good idea to carry special ski poles that extend into probes in case of an avalanche.

Avalanche airbags are the latest safety devices. They are designed to provide instantaneous flotation and head protection if you're caught in an avalanche. They're made by a number of companies but are expensive, starting around $350.

Check the angle of an area before you ski through it. Slopes of 30-45 degrees are the most dangerous, while lesser slopes do not slide as frequently.

Watch the weather. Winds over 15 mph can pile snow much more deeply on lee slopes, causing dangerous loading on the snowpack. Especially avoid skiing on or below cornices.

Avoid skiing on the leeward side (the side facing into the wind) of ridges, where snow loading can be greatest.

Be aware of gullies and bowls. They're more likely to slip than flat open slopes or ridgetops. Stay out of gullies at the bottom of wide bowls; these are natural avalanche chutes.

Look out for cracks in the snow. Additionally, listen for hollow snow underfoot. These are strong signs of dangerous conditions.

Look at the trees. Smaller trees may indicate that avalanches rip through an area frequently, knocking over the larger trees. Avalanches can also run through forested areas, however.

Know how much new snow has fallen recently. Heavy new snow over older, weak snow layers is a sure sign of extreme danger on potential avalanche slopes. Most avalanches slip during or immediately after a storm.

Learn how to dig a snow pit. Learn how to read the various snow layers. Particularly important are the very weak layers of depth hoar or surface hoar that have been buried under heavy new snow.

just 0.2 microns in size. Chlorine and iodine are not always reliable, taste foul, and can be unhealthy.

CRIME

Alaska has a surprisingly high violent-crime rate; the most recent figures put the state at the very top in the nation in terms of violent crimes, with 804 such crimes per 100,000 residents. Part of this is due to simple demographics, since Alaska has the second-highest percentage of young people in the nation, but it is also a reflection of the impact of alcohol abuse and the increasing use of heroin and other opioids. Alaska has a sexual-assault rate more than twice the national average, and the child sexual-assault rate is a shocking six times the national average.

In general you're quite safe traveling in Alaska, though you should take the standard precautions, such as not leaving belongings in an unlocked vehicle and not walking around certain Anchorage neighborhoods after dark. Also, it's wise to avoid situations where people have been drinking heavily, even in bush Alaska. To be honest, after 30 years in the North, my only experience with crime took place when gear was stolen from me in Prince Rupert, British Columbia, and (equally shocking) in my hometown of Homer. I'm not saying crime doesn't exist, but many Alaskan towns are so safe that folks leave their doors unlocked and their keys in the cars.

MONEY

Most consumer goods must be imported from the Lower 48, and transportation costs are tacked on along the way. In addition, the transportation and shipping rates within Alaska are similarly high, further inflating the cost of goods and services. In more remote regions especially, lack of competition coupled with steady demand ensures top-dollar prices.

Visitors to Anchorage will be pleased to find that prices are not totally out of line with the Lower 48, and large discount-chain stores help keep prices more reasonable. The big chains have also spread to Wasilla, Palmer,

Soldotna, and Kenai, driving down prices in those areas (and squeezing local businesses).

Beyond these exceptions, the prices in the north are much higher than elsewhere, and are generally the worst in the most remote bush communities. Food costs in places such as bush villages are more than twice those in Anchorage. Even in Homer, food is almost 20 percent more expensive than in Anchorage.

Debit cards and major **credit cards**—especially Visa and MasterCard—are accepted almost everywhere in Alaska. This is probably the easiest way to travel, especially if you can get airline mileage credit at the same time. You'll find **ATMs** in all the larger towns and increasingly even in the more remote settlements. For locations, head to www.mastercard.com and www.visa.com/atms.

Traveler's checks have become obsolete, and many businesses would probably reject them. The downtown Wells Fargo office in Anchorage will exchange Canadian dollars, Japanese yen, and euros for U.S. dollars, or you can exchange money at the airport's international terminal.

Tipping (usually 15 percent of the bill) is expected at most sit-down eating places fancier than snack bars or takeaway counters. Tourism employees, fishing guides, and others providing personal services often depend on tips for their real income.

SMOKE-FREE ALASKA

In 2018, Alaska enacted a state-wide measure banning smoking in all workplaces, restaurants, bars, taxis, and music venues. The ban includes not just cigarettes, pipes, and cigars, but also e-cigarettes and vape pens. Smokers must stay 20 feet away from entrances to places where people shop, eat, drink, or work. In addition to tobacco, the law also applies to marijuana consumption.

CANNABIS

When Alaskans legalized marijuana in 2014 it became the third state in the nation to allow the plant to be grown and sold commercially. Several dozen cannabis shops are located across the state, including more than 20 places in Anchorage and a half-dozen more in the Palmer-Wasilla area. Other towns with cannabis stores include Girdwood, Soldotna, Kenai, Homer, Sterling, and Talkeetna; there's even a shop near the entrance to Denali National Park. Visit Weed Maps (www.weedmaps.com) for locations of cannabis shops around Alaska and familiarize yourself with the state's marijuana laws before partaking. The State of Alaska's Division of Public Health (www.dhss.alaska.gov) has details; here are a few salient points:

- You must be 21 to possess or use marijuana.

- It's illegal to smoke pot in public places, including hotels and parks.

- Due to national laws, you cannot use pot on federal lands (including Denali National Park).

- It's illegal to operate a vehicle under the influence of cannabis.

- You cannot transport marijuana out of state, even if it was legally purchased in Alaska.

Information and Services

TOURIST INFORMATION

If you want to leave the trip planning to others, you may want to contact one of the many itinerary planners who specialize in Alaska. These could be as close as your local travel agent, or one of the online information sources such as www.alaskaone.com.

A great starting point when planning a trip to Alaska is the official Alaska State Vacation Planner, produced annually through a joint partnership between the state and private businesses. It's distributed by the Alaska Travel Industry Association (907/929-2200, www.travelalaska.com). Find chambers of commerce around the state at www.alaskachamber.com.

LAND MANAGEMENT AGENCIES

The following phone numbers and websites provide contact information for major public land-management agencies in south-central Alaska:

- Alaska Department of Fish and Game, 333 Raspberry Rd., Anchorage, 907/267-2253, www.adfg.alaska.gov

- Alaska Maritime National Wildlife Refuge, 95 Sterling Hwy., Homer, 907/235-6961, www.islandsandocean.org

- Alaska Public Lands Information Center, 605 W. 4th Ave., Anchorage, 907/644-3678 or 866/869-6887, www.alaskacenters.gov

- Bureau of Land Management, 4700 BLM Rd., Anchorage, 907/267-1246 or 800/478-1263, www.blm.gov/ak

- Chugach National Forest, 161 E. 1st Ave., Anchorage, 907/743-9500, www.fs.usda.gov/chugach

- Chugach State Park, 18620 Seward Hwy., Anchorage, 907/345-5014, www.alaskastateparks.org

- Denali National Park & Preserve, 907/683-9532, www.nps.gov/dena

- Denali State Park, 7278 E. Bogard Rd., Wasilla, 907/745-3975, www.alaskastateparks.org

- Department of Natural Resources, 550 W. 7th Ave., Anchorage, 907/269-8400, www.alaskastateparks.org

- Kachemak Bay State Park, Homer, 907/235-7024, www.alaskastateparks.org

- Kenai Fjords National Park, Seward, 907/422-0500, www.nps.gov/kefj

- Kenai National Wildlife Refuge, Ski Hill Road, Soldotna, 907/262-7021 or 877/285-5628, http://kenai.fws.gov

COMMUNICATIONS AND MEDIA

Newspapers

Alaska's unofficial state newspaper is the *Anchorage Daily News* (www.adn.com), and its website contains current stories, news blogs, classified ads, upcoming events, weather, and video. The company also produces a free *Alaska Visitors Guide* that can be found in the larger visitors centers.

The *Anchorage Press* (www.anchoragepress.com) is a free weekly newspaper available from racks all around Anchorage. Weekly newspapers also come out in Homer, Soldotna, Seward, and Wasilla.

Radio

Commercial radio stations are in all the larger towns, and the state is fortunate to have the **Alaska Public Radio Network** (www.aprn.org), one of the finest public radio networks in the country. Anchorage's **KSKA** (91.1 FM, www.kska.org) is the flagship station, but many Alaskan towns have their own versions. Anchorage's noncommercial **KNBA** (90.3 FM, www.knba.org) is one of the only Native Alaskan-owned radio stations in the nation, and it broadcasts some of the best music programming in Alaska. Two other notable stations are **KBBI** (890 AM, www.kbbi.org) in Homer and **KTNA** (88.5 FM, www.ktna.org) in Talkeetna.

Post Offices

Post offices are generally open 9am-5pm Monday-Friday, though a few open their doors noon-2pm on Saturday. Anchorage's airport post office is open 24 hours daily year-round. When post offices are closed, their outer doors usually remain open, so you can go in to buy stamps from the machines. Many grocery store checkout counters also sell books of stamps at no markup.

Phones and Internet

Cell phone coverage is variable in south-central Alaska, but generally quite good on the main highways. It's nonexistent in many backcountry areas, so don't expect to be able to pull out your phone and surf the internet at a remote campsite! Not all companies provide coverage even when services exist, so contact your carrier for a coverage map ahead of your trip.

If you're traveling into remote areas and are worried about keeping in touch, satellite phone rental kits are available from **Surveyors Exchange** (907/561-6501, www.satellitephonesak.com).

Alaska is surprisingly well wired, and even the most remote towns now have some sort of online connection. Nearly every library in the state has at least one computer where you can check your email or surf the internet for free. Wireless internet (Wi-Fi) is becoming the norm for many local businesses.

Resources

Suggested Reading

ART AND LITERATURE

Bodett, Tom. *As Far as You Can Go Without a Passport*. New York: Perseus, 1986. A collection of wry, bring-a-smile-to-your-face Alaska tales. Bodett's other books include *The End of the Road* and *Small Comforts*. This book is out of print.

Krakauer, Jon. *Into the Wild*. New York: Random House, 1997. Now a Hollywood movie, this is the tale of Chris McCandless, a young man whose 1992 death in the bush north of Denali does not merit the attention it received. The story is loved by many outsiders, but viewed with disdain by many Alaskans.

McGinniss, Joe. *Going to Extremes*. New York: Plume, 1989. One man's journey to Alaska leads him to a series of characters as diverse as the state itself. This reissue of a 1980 book, though quite dated, is still popular with travelers.

McPhee, John. *Coming into the Country*. New York: Noonday Press, 2003. Even though it was actually written in the 1970s, this remains perhaps the best portrayal of Alaskan bush lifestyles ever written. It's the book you'll still see folks reading on the long ferry ride north.

Schooler, Lynn. *Blue Bear: A True Story of Friendship, Tragedy and Survival in the Alaskan Wilderness*. New York: Harper-Collins, 2002. This beautifully crafted memoir chronicles Schooler's life and how it was changed by Michio Hoshino, the renowned wildlife photographer killed by a grizzly in 1996.

DESCRIPTION AND TRAVEL

Alaska Atlas & Gazetteer. Freeport, ME: DeLorme, 2004. This large book of up-to-date topographic maps is a wise investment if you plan to explore the more remote parts of Alaska. It's very easy to use.

Greiner, James. *Wager with the Wind: The Don Sheldon Story*. New York: St. Martin's Press, 1982. The true story of one of the state's most famous bush pilots.

Larson, Richard. *Mountain Bike Alaska—49 Trails in the 49th State*. Anchorage: Glacier House, 1991. An outdated but reasonably complete look at mountain biking in Alaska.

The Milepost. Augusta, GA: Morris Communications, published annually. For motorists, this publication—in existence for more than 60 years—is the best guidebook to Alaska. The highway maps and descriptions make it a must if you're driving north. Although the information is accurate and comprehensive, specific listings of hotels, bars, and restaurants are limited to advertisers, and the ads don't tell the whole story.

Moore, Terris. *Mt. McKinley: The Pioneer Climbs*. Seattle: The Mountaineers, 1981. An exciting history of the challenge to climb North America's highest mountain.

Quick, Daniel L. *Kenai Canoe Trails.* Anchorage: Todd Publications, 1997. A very helpful guide to canoe routes within Kenai National Wildlife Refuge.

Shepherd, Shane, and Owen Wozniak. *50 Hikes in Alaska's Chugach State Park.* Woodstock, VT: Countryman Press, 2008. An informative guide to hiking in the second-largest state park in the country.

Tally, Taz. *50 Hikes in Alaska's Kenai Peninsula.* Seattle: The Mountaineers, 2000. This is the authoritative guide to Kenai Peninsula trails.

Waits, Ike. *Denali National Park: Guide to Hiking, Photography and Camping.* Anchorage: Wild Rose Guidebooks, 2015. The complete guide to Denali, with detailed backpacking, day-hiking, and camping information.

NATURAL HISTORY

Hulten, Eric. *Flora of Alaska and Neighboring Territories.* Stanford, CA: Stanford University Press, 1968. A huge manual of vascular plants—highly technical, but easy to consult.

Murie, Adolph. *A Naturalist in Alaska.* Tucson: University of Arizona Press, 1990. This reprint of a 1961 classic still offers excellent insight into the fauna of Alaska.

Murie, Adolph. *The Wolves of Mount McKinley.* Seattle: University of Washington Press, 1985. Another Murie classic, originally published in 1944.

Sydeman, Michelle, and Annabel Lund. *Alaska Wildlife Viewing Guide.* Old Saybrook, CT: Globe Pequot Press, 1996. A small helpful guide to the state's animals.

Internet Resources

Alaska Climate Research Center
http://climate.gi.alaska.edu
This site includes climatic data, current weather conditions, and Alaskan forecasts.

Alaska.com
www.adn.com
Operated by the *Anchorage Daily News,* this site has current Alaska news, fishing info, and much more.

Alaska Department of Fish and Game
www.adfg.alaska.gov
The Fish and Game website is a good starting place for details on sportfishing and wildlife viewing around Alaska.

Alaska Marine Highway System
www.ferryalaska.com
Visit this website for current Alaska Marine Highway ferry schedules and fares.

Alaska State Parks
www.alaskastateparks.org
Find details on Alaska's state parks and recreation areas on this useful site.

Alaska Travel Industry Association
www.travelalaska.com
This organization distributes the official *Alaska State Vacation Planner.*

Alaska Travelgram
www.alaskatravelgram.com
Scott McMurren's website tips off the lowest airfares for flights to and around Alaska.

Don Pitcher
www.donpitcher.com
Author Don Pitcher's website provides details on all his books and photographic projects. Visit his Facebook page and become a fan!

511.Alaska.gov

http://511.alaska.gov

Especially useful for winter travel in Alaska, this site has details on road conditions, winter travel tips, highway construction updates, and more.

National Park Service

www.nps.gov/akso

The National Park Service's Alaska website has details on 15 national parks in Alaska, including Denali and Kenai Fjords.

Public Lands Information Centers

www.alaskacenters.gov

The Alaska Public Lands Information Center in Anchorage is an excellent resource, and their website offers an overview of federal lands in Alaska.

Recreation.gov

www.recreation.gov

Head here to reserve Chugach National Forest and Kenai National Wildlife Refuge cabins and campgrounds.

State of Alaska

www.state.ak.us

The State of Alaska website has links to state agencies and tourism sites.

U.S. Fish and Wildlife Service

http://alaska.fws.gov

Head here for details on the U.S. Fish and Wildlife Service, which manages 16 refuges across the state.

List of Maps

LIST OF MAPS

MAP SYMBOLS

═══ Expressway	○ City/Town	✈ Airport	⚲ Golf Course
┈┈┈ Primary Road	◉ State Capital	✗ Airfield	🅿 Parking Area
─── Secondary Road	⊛ National Capital	▲ Mountain	🛆 Archaeological Site
┄┄┄ Unpaved Road	★ Point of Interest	✛ Unique Natural Feature	⛪ Church
─── Feature Trail	● Accommodation	⚑ Waterfall	⛽ Gas Station
- - - Other Trail	▼ Restaurant/Bar	⚑ Park	Glacier
⋯⋯ Ferry	■ Other Location	⬟ Trailhead	Mangrove
═══ Pedestrian Walkway	Λ Campground	🎿 Skiing Area	Reef
▦▦▦ Stairs			Swamp

CONVERSION TABLES

°C = (°F − 32) / 1.8
°F = (°C x 1.8) + 32
1 inch = 2.54 centimeters (cm)
1 foot = 0.304 meters (m)
1 yard = 0.914 meters
1 mile = 1.6093 kilometers (km)
1 km = 0.6214 miles
1 fathom = 1.8288 m
1 chain = 20.1168 m
1 furlong = 201.168 m
1 acre = 0.4047 hectares
1 sq km = 100 hectares
1 sq mile = 2.59 square km
1 ounce = 28.35 grams
1 pound = 0.4536 kilograms
1 short ton = 0.90718 metric ton
1 short ton = 2,000 pounds
1 long ton = 1.016 metric tons
1 long ton = 2,240 pounds
1 metric ton = 1,000 kilograms
1 quart = 0.94635 liters
1 US gallon = 3.7854 liters
1 Imperial gallon = 4.5459 liters
1 nautical mile = 1.852 km

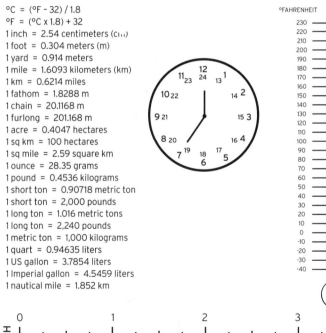

MOON ANCHORAGE, DENALI, & THE KENAI PENINSULA

Avalon Travel
Hachette Book Group
1700 Fourth Street
Berkeley, CA 94710, USA
www.moon.com

Editor: Sabrina Young
Series Manager: Kathryn Ettinger
Copy Editor: Christopher Church
Production and Graphics Coordinators:
  Suzanne Albertson and Rue Flaherty
Cover Design: Faceout Studios, Charles Brock
Interior Design: Domini Dragoone
Moon Logo: Tim McGrath
Map Editor: Mike Morgenfeld
Cartographers: Mike Morgenfled, Brian Shotwell
Proofreader: Alissa Cyphers
Indexer: Greg Jewett

ISBN-13: 978-1-64049-373-5
Printing History
1st Edition — 2013
3rd Edition — June 2019
5 4 3 2 1

Front cover photo: floatplane in flight with Mt. McKinley in the background © Design Pics Inc / Alamy Stock Photo
Back cover photo: Rafting on the Kenai River near Cooper Landing © Don Pitcher
All interior photos: © Don Pitcher except page: 57 © Roy Nesse (top), © Carrol Wade (bottom): page 61 © Tom Bol (top left), © Jody Overstreet (top right): page 67 © Cathryn Posey (top left): page 93 © Nichole Gells (top), ©Lisa Gill (middle left)

Printed in China by R.R. Donnelley